CALABRIA

TRAVELS IN THE TOE OF ITALY

CALABRIA

TRAVELS IN THE TOE OF ITALY

NIALL ALLSOP

© Niall Allsop 2016

All rights reserved.

No part of this book may be reproduced in any form or by any means, electronic or mechanical, including information storage and retrieval systems without prior permission in writing from the author.

The only exception being a reviewer who may quote extracts in a review.

ISBN-13: 978-1533514004

ISBN-10: 1533514003

Published by **In Scritto** *Italy in writing*
www.inscritto.com

Cover and book design by Niall Allsop – niallsop@mac.com

Text and captions set in Adobe Garamond Pro; headings set in Lithos Pro
Front cover test set in Lithos Pro

For Cara, Christopher and Rhys
... in the hope that one day they too will discover this place

Acknowledgements

As is often the case, this page is the most difficult to write for fear of leaving out someone's contribution, however small.

I'll start, as I always do, with grateful thanks to my wife Kay who accompanied me on many of my Calabrian excursions in the name of research.

As this book is based to a large extent on the journeys of thirteen English-speaking travellers (as opposed to tourists) who came to Calabria between 1777 and 1967, I would like to thank these pioneers for their curiosity, perseverance and their general good humour ... but most of all for their foresight in putting pen to paper afterwards: Henry Swinburne, Brian Hill, Richard Keppel-Craven, Craufurd Tait Ramage, Arthur John Strutt, Edward Lear, Emily Lowe, George Gissing, Norman Douglas, Edward Hutton, Eric Whelpton, Leslie Gardiner and Henry Morton.

And special thanks to these five contemporary writers who shared their expertise with me: Carmine Abate, Peter Chiarella, John Dickie, Charles Lister, Underico Nisticò and Páola Praticò.

Thanks also to those Calabrian friends who never tired of my questions or helped in other ways, even if they were not aware of it at the time: Luigi Apa, Salvatore Barone, Gino Bubba, Bruno Cortese, Anselmo Dattilo, Laura David, Stefan David, Francesco De Luca, Pino Fabiano, Giuseppe Fiorentino, Colette Fischer, Mario Gerardi, Silvana Gerardi, Renata Giordano, Maria Ierardi, Vicki Kelly, Leonardo Marzano, Denise Milone,

Cristina Olivo, Massimo Papini, Attilio Pugliese, Salvatore Ranieri, Raffaella Rizza, Maria Salerno, Franco Severini, Domenico Stumpo, Carlo Tigano, Francesco Tigano, Carolina Ventrella, Anastasia Verzino, Anna Maria Verzino, Vincenzo Verzino, Rafaelle Vizza and Enzo Ziparo.

Thanks too to those further afield, particularly those throughout Calabria, who put up with the questions of a complete stranger struggling to make himself understood: Antonio Accetta, Stefania Bondini, Vincenzo Davoli, Tommaso Perri, Francesco Pezziniti, Antonio Piserà, Francesco Praticò, Giuseppe Pungitori, Franco Musolino, Dino Ribuffo, Limardi Ruggero, Ugo Sergi, Ciccio Trimbóli, Franco Trimbóli.

I need also to acknowledge the debt I owe to a number of internet-based services and organisations:
For information ...
Wikipedia (www.en.wikipedia.org / www.it.wikipedia.org)
Encyclopedia Britannica (www.britannica.com)
For archived and out-of-print books ...
www.archive.org
www.babel.hathitrust.com
www.forgottenbooks.com
www.books.google.com

Finally, I would like to thank the proprietors and staff of all the bed and breakfasts and hotels I stayed at and in all the places I wined and dined throughout Calabria in the two years it took me to research this book. I remember you all fondly and, as some of you know, my first visit was not my last.

Contents

Notes on the text	11
Prologue ... writing about Calabria	13
Itineraries and context	27
The Grand Tour	43
Calabria ... who, when, what, where why?	57
Making connections	95
In search of *il Fondaco del Fico*	125
Lamezia Terme	135
Of skirmishes	149
Magna Græcia	181
When the earth moves	209
Outside the law	229
The Arbëreshë	263
Beyond belief	271
Northern gateways, then and now	283
The mountains	291
Pizzo ... a Calabrian contradiction	353
The provincial capitals	361
Seeing is believing	411
Travellers to tourists	417
Leaving Calabria	431
Coasting along	441
But apart from the *'ndrangheta* ...?	479
Matters of life and death	491
A climate of change	497
Calabrian women	505
Santa Severina	521
Changing Calabria	547
Travellers' Biographies	563
Selected Bibliography	567

Notes on the text

The place names of most of the important place in Calabria most often referred to in the text are on the map opposite; some chapters start with an additional map which reflects the contents of the chapter but also includes other locations such as those on the map opposite.

From time to time I have used Italian words and phrases which either have an obvious meaning or add flavour to a book about Calabria.

I have used International English throughout on the assumption that American readers (and others) will be conversant with the language of both cultures: autumn for fall, colour for color, centre for center, realise for realize, got for gotten ... and so on.

In extracts from other books I have used the punctuation, emphasis (usually italics) and spelling of the original. In some cases place names have changed slightly (Cortone/Cotrone, now Crotone), in other cases radically (Monteleone/Monte Leone, now Vibo Valéntia and Castel Vetere, now Caulónia). With slight changes I felt there was generally no need for additional explanation; more radical changes I have always noted (though when used repeatedly in the same chapter, only the first is noted). Text within square brackets is generally explanatory and has been added by me.

When I am referring to Calabria's Magna Græcia settlements, I will use the accepted Greek conventions as used by archæologists and historians; when I refer to the same sites in the modern age, I will use the current conventions. For example, modern Sibari was Greek Sybaris and modern Crotone was

Greek Kroton. Similarly with names of rivers: the ancient Crathis is today's Crati; the ancient Sybaris is today's Coscile. Quotes from travellers sometimes include other spelling variations but their intention is never lost.

Some of today's Calabrian towns appear to have two names ... the one on the map and the one it is generally known by; examples are Reggio (di) Calabria and Morano Calabro which would normally be known just as Reggio and Morano. The additional name is to distinguish it from other towns of the same name in other parts of Italy; in these cases Reggio Emilia (in Emilia Romagna) and Osteria di Morano (in Umbria). Also some towns have the suffix *Albanese*, to both highlight its Albanian heritage and to distinguish it from a town of the same name elsewhere in Calabria. Generally I will use the full name initially and thereafter the shorter version.

In captioning photographs, I have not generally annotated 'left' and 'right' on the assumption that the reader will realise that the first sentence or line of the caption refers to the photo on the left and the second to the photo on the right. In most cases the text itself makes it obvious.

Regarding dates, when I have needed to make a distinction between years or centuries before and after the beginning of the Christian era, I have used the acronyms BCE and CE ... for example, the Emperor Augustus was born in 63 BCE and died in 14 CE; he was seventy-seven.

Prologue ... writing about Calabria

"But where is Calabria exactly?" Amazing how many people have to ask. The word seems to belong more to gothic fiction than geographical fact.
Leslie Gardiner *South to Calabria*

It was while I was writing *Stumbling through Italy* I realised that we (my wife, Kay, and I) had passed through Calabria a few times before we first came to holiday here. The sprawling mass of the area know as Lamezia Terme was a destination airport for a budget airline flying from the UK but for us at the time it was no more than a springboard to Sicily via the eccentric A3 *autostrada*.

It wasn't until 2006 that we first saw Calabria as a destination in its own right and, when we did, we flew to Rome and drove down to Italy's remote toe.

Ten weeks after our third successive Calabrian holiday we were once again driving south, not as visitors, but as Calabria's two newest citizens. As I recounted in *Scratching the toe of Italy,* we had decided to move to the small hilltop town of Santa Severina in the Calabrian province of Crotone.

That was eight years ago and I have had time to reflect on what it is about this part of Italy that drew us, not just to come as visitors, but to decide that this was a place worthy of such a life-changing move.

But for many of our Calabrian friends the fact that we ended up in their *regione* was not at all surprising. Many were avid readers of the numerous travelogues, initially diaries of the so-called Grand Tour, going back well over two hundred years that were penned by foreign travellers, often British, who came this way and then felt impelled to write about their experiences.

The travels of some, like George Gissing and Norman Douglas, I had heard of, though at the time not yet read; others, such as Henry Swinburne, Craufurd Tait Ramage and Edward Lear, I had not. Nor at the time was I aware that the swashbuckling French writer Alexandre Dumas—he of *The Three Musketeers*, *The Count of Monte Cristo* and *The Man in the Iron Mask*—had also written an account of his Calabrian adventures.

Indeed some years ago one generous Calabrian friend even gave me a copy of Dumas' *Viaggio in Calabria* on the mistaken assumption that I would be able to read it in Italian. He added that, if I found it too difficult, I could always try the original French. Almost seven years on, and still no English translation available so, and necessity being the mother of invention, I have at last made inroads into the Italian text.

Some Calabrian friends were not only well-versed in the exploits of these travel writers, but also took immense pride in the fact that such 'gentlemen' (for it seemed at the time that they were generally men and all of the so-called 'gentleman' class of British society) came to their *regione* in the first place ... the fact that they then told their world about what they had seen and heard was a bonus.

In the province of Crotone, for example, where both Gissing and Douglas stayed, I was sometimes aware of polarised views on the merits of one as opposed to the other. Douglas was clearly the most well-known but in the Crotone area there is a bias in favour of the Gissing experience and his views on Crotone in particular. That said, to a man (and woman), they were just glad that both had come to Calabria and told the world about it; that both had, like a few others before them, chosen to extend the conventional boundaries of the what had once been the 'Grand Tour'.

I had encountered this we're-just-glad-they-came rationale elsewhere in Italy while researching *Keeping up with DH Lawrence*. DH Lawrence absolutely loathed his time in Sòrgono in Sardinia and pulled no punches when he wrote disparagingly about his overnight sojourn there in his travelogue, *Sea and Sardinia*. Nevertheless, despite his dislike for the town, he left his literary mark. Over ninety years on and many of the locals still talk in affectionate terms about his visit as if it were the day before yesterday. They are simply pleased that someone of Lawrence's stature came to Sòrgono in the first place ... that he hated their little town was irrelevant.

So I was not totally surprised when I discovered that this curiosity about which travellers visited Calabria and when, inspired one Catanzaro publisher to publish a book in 2001 with the title *Itinerari e viaggiatori inglesi nella*

Calabria del '700 e '800 (*English travellers and their itineraries in Calabria in the 18th and 19th centuries*) in which are detailed most of the accounts of travels in Calabria made and written by the English. Norman Douglas, whose book *Old Calabria* is probably the most widely read of all, happened to be the first traveller in the new century, the 20th century—which in Italy is generally written as '900—and therefore was not included.

But two other omissions initially puzzled me more. One of the most detailed and informative books on travelling in Calabria, Craufurd Tait Ramage's *The Nooks and by-ways of Italy: Wanderings in search of its ancient remains and modern superstitions*, was also conspicuous by its absence. Ramage travelled in 1828, though his account was not published for another four decades. The only explanation for his book's non-inclusion would seem to be that Ramage was a Scot; English-speaking British but not English. Would an English-language book on Italian scholars omit a learned philosopher who was born in Sicily?

The absence of Ramage is unfortunate and, if indeed it was because he was not actually English, it would seem to have been based on a narrow and inappropriate premise. It's a bit like excluding the likes of Samuel Becket, Maeve Binchy, Oliver Goldsmith, James Joyce, CS Lewis, Iris Murdoch, George Bernard Shaw, Bram Stoker, Jonathan Swift and Oscar Wilde from a list of fine 'English-language' writers solely because they were Irish.

And the irony is that, throughout his book, Ramage refers to himself as an Englishman; talking of Torchiara in Campania, he explained the rationale:

"I was, no doubt, regarded as a great curiosity as no Englishman had ever probably passed through their village before. I may tell you, that to declare yourself an Inglese [Englishman] secures respect wherever you go, and I am sorry to think that a Scozzese [Scotsman] would not sound so important in their ears."

And how was it, I wondered, that the only women to travel in the aforementioned book's designated time-frame, did not get a mention? Emily Lowe travelled with her mother Helen in early 1858 and an account of their unique mother-and-daughter road trip, *Unprotected Females in Sicily, Calabria and on the Top of Mount Aetna*, was originally published anonymously in 1859. The book is an illuminating and compelling read, not least in the descriptions of how two 'unprotected' women were fawned over and mollycoddled throughout their Calabrian travels. It is an important addition to the literature not only because Lowe was a woman but she was also the last British travel writer to observe and write about Calabria in pre-unification Italy.

I could not come up with any rational explanation for Lowe's omission and wondered if the fault lay on the British side of the literary establishment for not treating the book seriously? After all, weren't such travelogues very much part of a male-dominated society? Weren't women meant to stay in the home and not start gallivanting around the world? Perish the thought that they should actually write about it too.

I suspect the story of Emily and Helen Lowe only came to prominence after details of their travels (they had previously travelled together in Norway) were amplified in publications that focused on women travellers in the Victorian era. A Calabrian publishing house based in Vibo Valéntia did produce a translation in 2003 and in 2012 this was republished by the same Catanzaro publisher who had omitted Lowe's journey from its 2001 book about English travellers. Ironically the translation, *Donne Indifese in Calabria* begins with a quotation from that well-known 'Scottish' traveller to Calabria, Craufurd Tait Ramage.

Today, the publishers in question, Rubettino, have not only redeemed themselves but now produce an impressive, comprehensive and elegantly designed series of books and diaries by and about travellers to Calabria of all nationalities … including Scots and women.

It is important to note that, just because any one of these travellers put their experiences into print, does not guarantee that the picture they painted of Calabrian life and society was anything more than a mere glimpse. Above all else, their observations were the interplay between the expectations they brought with them and their nationality, background, experiences, prejudices and motives which do not, of themselves, necessarily guarantee either accuracy or reliability.

Not every Calabrian is a fan of what these foreign travellers wrote. In his *Controstoria delle Calabria*, the Calabrian writer, historian and raconteur, Ulderico Nisticò, tars them all with the same brush, deprecates their motives—which he sees as superficial—and suggests that such travellers generally came to Calabria expecting to experience just three things: brigands, hospitality and Magna Græcia (the historical remnants and legacy, largely along Calabria's Ionian coastline, which supported a Hellenic civilization from the 8th century BCE). And, mocks Nisticò, these 'fleeting tourists' invariably returned home satisfied …

"… after half a week in Calabria they go away convinced that they know more about it than the Italian king himself."

So, in deciding to tag my Irish (though English-speaking) pedigree on to the end of this austere list, in no sense am I trying to retrace the steps of Ramage, Lear or Lowe or anyone else but rather to intermingle some of my experiences and encounters with some of theirs in the hope that, collectively, we can shed some light on what brought us all to the toe of Italy.

In my case I was definitely not motivated to come to Calabria by either Magna Græcia or brigands (though I was aware of both in an historical sense) and the hospitality I assumed would be no different to what I had experienced in other parts of the Italian peninsula and islands. In this latter respect I was wrong as it exceeded anything I have ever experienced elsewhere.

That said, this was not strictly what Underico Nisticò meant when he spoke of 'hospitality'. Underico was referring to the network of hospitable accommodation that travellers generally set in place through letters of recommendation before embarking on their journey. They knew that the clergy and other local dignitaries—who of course had well-stocked larders and comfortable homes, devoid of the lower orders and sporting clean sheets—were generally curious about foreigners who passed through, added to which the kudos in entertaining such travellers was but a bonus. With the right connections, 'corporate Calabrian hospitality' could take the edge off any and all of the discomforts of 18th and 19th century travel.

But, as Richard Keppel-Craven discovered, it could all become too much:

"The aspect of this establishment was totally different from any other which had fallen under my observation in the course of my tour, and formed a grateful contrast with the profuse but embarrassed hospitality of some of the families I had visited."

When it was my turn, of course I had to pay for *my* hospitality. Nevertheless, and despite that 21st century convention, like the others I too came with the curiosity of the visitor but, unlike all but Swinburne and Douglas—both of whom visited Calabria more than once—I returned several times and eventually I stayed and made Calabria my home.

Some Calabrian friends tell me that I know and understand more about Calabria—its geography, its towns, its coastline, its countryside, its history in particular—than they do. And while in some cases that may be true, what is also true is that I can never know what is like to be a Calabrian ... I can never think, reason or talk like a Calabrian. The closest I will ever get is through my own late-in-life, Calabrian experiences and, second-hand, through those of my Calabrian friends.

Had I chosen to write this book in 2008, it would not, could not, be the same book. Nevertheless, the rider I added above about the reliability and accuracy of others also applies to my perceptions ... I too bring my own experiences and expectations to the table. I too am a foreigner in this land.

One of the first British travellers to write about his experiences in Calabria in 1777, Henry Swinburne, had this to say about people like me:
"The longer one man of candour resides in a foreign country, the greater difficulty he finds in giving a character to its inhabitants. He perceives so many nice varieties, so many exceptions to general rules, as almost destroy his hopes of drawing up one comprehensive description of them: he every day becomes conscious of the presumption of those who run and read; and, what is worse, write."

Calabria is therefore not a guide to Calabria but, rather a book *about* Calabria, today's Calabria and yesterday's Calabria, viewed through the eyes of a small group of English-speaking foreigners—myself included—who have not been able to resist penning observations and experiences from our travels. In addition, and fundamental to the book, is the notion of shedding light on Calabria as, through those same eyes, the reader is taken on divers excursions to almost every nook and cranny of a part of Italy that probably remains its least visited region.

But, unlike *their* travelogues, *Calabria* has neither chronological nor linear form but is rather a random journey—albeit one with some thematic and geographical undercurrents—a mix of both observations and experiences, of the physical and the emotional, of people and places.

Where I believe an account or observation to be inaccurate, exaggerated or unreliable, I will note my reservations; by the same token, should I not do so, it doesn't necessarily mean that there are not other misrepresentations.

And if I too can animate my friend Ulderico Nisticò, then that will be a bonus.

Initially my occasional travelling companions, my chronological sleeping partners, throughout this journey were to be Henry Swinburne (1777 & 1780), Brian Hill (1791), Richard Keppel-Craven (1818), Craufurd Tait Ramage (1828), Arthur John Strutt (1841), Edward Lear (1847), Emily Lowe (1858), George Gissing (1897)and Norman Douglas (1911).

Well, that was the plan until, that is, it occurred to me that, just like the book I have gently chastised for omitting a Scot on grounds of nationality, Norman Douglas on grounds of timing and a woman on grounds unknown, I was about to do the same and cast aside those who may have written about their Calabrian experiences *after* Douglas. Initially I was not sure there were any for I had willingly absorbed the prevalent notion that Norman Douglas was the last of such travellers and his travelogue, *Old Calabria,* the glorious finale of the genre.

Indeed when I discussed this possibility with Calabrian friends I knew to be knowledgeable about which travellers came to Calabria and when, they shook their collective heads as they too were certain that Douglas' iconic book was indeed the end of an era.

Nevertheless I returned to the drawing board where I recalled that I had read one such travelogue a dozen or more years earlier, long before all the others and at a time when I was more interested in the writer's thoughts on Apulia than Calabria. Henry Morton's book was literally staring me in the face on my bookshelf.

Subsequent research therefore added four more travellers and their books to the above list as I felt impelled to include the thoughts and observations of the following: Edward Hutton (1912), Eric & Barbara Whelpton (1957), Scotsman Leslie Gardiner (1966) and Henry Morton (1967).

Indeed Edward Hutton had travelled only a year after Douglas and on reading his lucid account of travelling in the south of Italy, I found it difficult to understand why it was that Douglas' book had become almost revered while Hutton's, published the very same year, had been consigned to near oblivion. Hutton was equally erudite about Magna Græcia and, like Douglas, was wont to going off at a classical tangent from time to time but, it seemed to me, in a more accessible way for the average reader. Simply put, Hutton was just more fun: less pomp, less gravitas, less Latin and less Greek *and* he was the first to make use of embryonic motorised transport.

The last three, the Whelptons, Gardiner and Morton, caused me some initial conflict in that, as all three were writing about travelling in post-war Calabria (the Whelptons in 1957, the other two in the 1960s), I wondered were they just too recent? Could they sit comfortably alongside the experiences of Henry Swinburne, Arthur Strutt or George Gissing?

Then again, as I was intending to include many of my own experiences and observations, were not the experiences of the Whelptons, Morton and Gardiner a convenient bridge between the Calabria of Douglas and Hutton and my own more recent experiences ... even if occasionally they were on the cusp of becoming a guide for would-be independent tourists? (But then isn't that what many so-called 'Grand Tour' books did too?)

And were not all three pioneers of a sort in that, just as Gissing and Douglas were embryonic travellers by rail, the Whelptons, Gardiner and Morton (some of whom also travelled by train) were the first to travel in Calabria by motorised public and private transport? It seems that, to varying degrees, the Whelptons and Gardiner were driven rather than sitting behind the wheel themselves but Morton was indeed a harbinger of things to come in that he was truly an independent motorist who, just as we had done in 2006, drove down from Rome … though I suspect the roads were much quieter.

Chronologically, the skeletal literary credentials of my thirteen fellow-travellers are as follows:

Henry Swinburne (1743–1803), *Travels in the Two Sicilies*; published 1783 and 1785. Henry Swinburne travelled in **1777** and **1780**.

Brian Hill (1756–1831), *Observations and Remarks in a Journey through Sicily and Calabria in the year 1791*; published 1792. Brian Hill travelled in **1791**.

Richard Keppel-Craven (1799–1851), *A Tour through the Southern Provinces of the Kingdom of Naples*; published 1821. Richard Keppel-Craven travelled in **1818**.

Craufurd Tait Ramage (1803–1878), *The Nooks and by-ways of Italy: Wanderings in search of its ancient remains and modern superstitions*; published 1868. Craufurd Tait Ramage travelled in **1828**.

Arthur John Strutt (1819–1888), *A pedestrian Tour in Calabria and Sicily*; published 1842. Arthur John Strutt travelled in **1841**.

Edward Lear (1812–1888), *Journals of a Landscape Painter in Southern Calabria*; published 1852. Edward Lear travelled in **1847**.

Emily Lowe (died 1882), *Unprotected Females in Sicily, Calabria, and on the Top of Mount Aetna*; published 1859. Emily Lowe travelled in **1858**.

George Gissing (1857–1903), *By the Ionian Sea*; published 1901. George Gissing travelled in **1897**.

Norman Douglas (1868–1952), *Old Calabria*; published 1915. Norman Douglas travelled in **1911**.

Edward Hutton (1875–1969), *Naples and Southern Italy*; published 1915. Edward Hutton travelled in **1912**.

Eric & Barbara Whelpton (EW: 1894–1981; BW 1910–?), *Calabria and the Aeolian Islands*; published 1957. Eric and Barbara Whelpton travelled in **1957**.

Leslie Gardiner (1921–1997), *South to Calabria*; published 1968. Leslie Gardiner travelled in **1966**.

Henry Morton (1892–1979), *A Traveller in Southern Italy*; published 1969. Henry Morton travelled in **1967**.

As there is generally no chronological element to what follows, when I quote from any of my fellow-travellers' works I will, in the interests of clarity, add in brackets the year they were travelling in Calabria. In the case of the Whelptons, I will acknowledge Eric Whelpton as the author; his wife Barbara was the photographer.

In addition, all such quotes retain the spelling and punctuation of the original text, though I will generally add a translation or explanation of any archaic or non-English words or phrases that might need clarification.

Delving into those who had written extensively about Calabria post-Douglas sent me scurrying back in time to see if the same was the case pre-Swinburne.

While Swinburne did indeed seem to the first to have published a detailed account of his travels, I discovered there were others, even as far back as the 16th century, who had not only come to Calabria but had left behind some sort of record of their travels.

One of these, Sir William Young, came to Apulia, Basilicata and Calabria but his travelogue, *A Journal of a Summer's Excursion by the Road of Montecasino to Naples. And from thence over all the Southern Parts of Italy, Sicily, and Malta in the year 1772*, has not generally become part of the literature as it was published privately and only ten copies were actually printed.

There were others (more of whom in a later chapter, *The Grand Tour*) who left a record of their journey, often as part of their, at the time unpublished, collected works or as an autobiography; thus William Young's book, it seems to me, falls into some literary no man's land—an interesting read but not widely read—and as such is deserving of special mention.

Of course over the years there were other British travellers and observers who found themselves in Calabria by accident or as part of a grander project and wrote about it, though not necessarily as their main focus or part of a travelogue.

In 1788 Thomas Watkins, on a voyage from Naples to Messina, was forced to land in Calabria because of inclement weather. Back on course, he again went ashore by choice to visit the interior. Watkins' brief, unplanned flirtation with Calabria is detailed in his *Travels Through Swisserland, Italy, Sicily, the Greek Islands, to Constantinople, Through Part of Greece, Ragusa and the Dalmatian Isles*.

Philip James Elmhirst was a Midshipman who saw service in the British Navy at the Battle of Trafalgar in 1805 but then, four years later, found himself a prisoner in Calabria having been shipwrecked off its southern coast before coming ashore at Bianco on the Ionian shore. He remained in custody for a little over six months and later wrote a short account of his experiences as *Occurrences during a six month's residence in the province of Calabria Ulteriore in 1809-10*.

Augustus Hare's *Cities of Southern Italy and Sicily* was published in 1891, not as a travelogue but more as an informative, albeit basic, guide to each region's major towns and cities with a description proportional to their perceived importance. There is no sense of Hare having travelled between one town and the next, to him being on the road and actually interacting with people en route.

Widely-read these may not have been but nevertheless the authors' observations are sometimes illuminating and ofttimes unique.

And of course I realise that the Calabrian travelogue was not solely the prerogative of a handful of English-speaking eccentric diarists in search of Magna Græcia, brigands and hospitality. Over the last three hundred years many other Europeans, predominantly French and German, travelled in Calabria and wrote full and colourful accounts of their experiences.

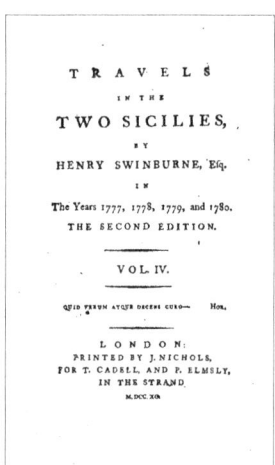  

Aesthetically the first travelogues to include Calabria were dreary tomes. The board covers were not illustrated and normally just bore the embossed title of the book on the spine. Title pages could be more elaborate, though still quite basic—Henry Swinburne's title page is a typical example of the time.
Arthur John Strutt's book was one of the first to add a touch of colour—the original image on his title page is one of the images reproduced on this book's front cover.
On the right is one of the many drab (and in this case, given the content, also completely meaningless) covers to adorn the several editions of Norman Douglas' *Old Calabria*.

Alexandre Dumas, who travelled in 1835, I have already mentioned though, as Ulderico Nisticò also records, some of Dumas' observations and experiences in his *Voyage en Calabre* are perhaps more imbued with the skill of the writer of fiction than other accounts.

Another traveller worthy of mention is Elpis Melena (the pseudonym of Marie Espérance von Schwartz), who was actually born in England of German parents and wrote about her travels in Calabria in her *Blicke auf Calabrien und die Liparischen Inseln im Jahre 1860*. However her observations at a time of political turmoil in the Italian peninsula can be one-sided as she was a close friend of Giuseppe Garibaldi ... indeed he had asked her to marry him a couple of years previously.

From time to time I will therefore dip into both the travels of Dumas and Melena; I shall also refer very occasionally to the observations of some of the other non-British travellers who wrote about their time in Calabria.

There was a time too when, for other northern 'Italians', to journey south of Naples was also considered to be an adventure worthy of record; after all, up until 1860, the Kingdom of the Two Sicilies—of which Calabria was a part—was a different country, albeit part of the same land mass.

I am also aware that in the last three decades there has been a surge of interest in writing about Calabria and other English-speaking writers have travelled here and written about their experiences. For me these contemporary travelogues were what brought me to Calabria in the first place and so from time to time I will acknowledge, with gratitude, the experiences and observations in Matthew Fort's *Eating up Italy*, Annie Hawes' *Journey to the South*, John Keahey's *A Sweet and Glorious Land*, Charles Lister's *Heel to Toe: Encounters in the South of Italy* and Mark Rotella's *Stolen Figs*.

Published in 2002, one other book is deserving of special mention: unlike the others, Peter Chiarella's *Calabrian Tales* is not a travelogue, at least not in the conventional sense. But it *is* about a journey, the journey of one particular family through the vicissitudes of poverty-ridden life, family intrigue and institutional inequality in late 19th century Calabria. It is an emotional, brutal and epic tale, it is the story of Peter Chiarella's own ancestors and the events that led to their desire to escape and their inevitable emigration to America.

Finally, I should also mention two American art historians, husband and wife Bernard and Mary Berenson, who wrote about Calabria separately.

Mary Berenson's brief account of a six-day visit in 1908 is included in her diaries but is not readily accessible in English. Bernard Berenson revisited

Calabria in 1955 and wrote a series of three articles in Italian for the Milan-based daily *Corriere della Sera*. These were collectively known as *Ritorno in Calabria: La Calabria di Ruggiero; Città e campagne; Fine dell'itinerario*. Though the Berensons were English-speaking, neither account is readily available in English, indeed Bernard's articles are available *only* in Italian. Calabrian publisher Rubbettino has published both in one small volume entitled *In Calabria*.

Thus, my selection criteria in respect of my thirteen fellow-travellers is straightforward in that it reflects the fact that all wrote in English and are thus more accessible to me; also their books themselves are generally more accessible.

The following chapter outlines the itinerary of each and there is a small accompanying map to illustrate the route they followed. In addition, at the end of the book there is a brief 'potted' biography of each which should put their travels into their personal, social, cultural, political and European context.

Often too I will include other maps, particularly to accompany chapters where a particular theme involves places in disparate corners of the *regione*. All maps will include the five regional capitals of Cosenza, Crotone, Catanzaro, Vibo Valéntia and Reggio Calabria as well as Santa Severina; in some cases space precludes including every place mentioned in the text that follows.

Of all my thirteen companions, only the last six—Gissing, Douglas, Hutton, the Whelptons, Gardiner and Morton—were travelling in what we now know as Italy; unification took place in 1860. The others were travelling either in one half of what was, pre-1806, known as the Two Sicilies (the peninsular part of which included Calabria, the insular part being Sicily) or what, from 1815 to 1860, was known as the Kingdom of the Two Sicilies.

The period between 1806 and 1815 was the Napoleonic era when the Bourbon regime was usurped, though King Ferdinand continued to rule Sicily from Palermo. No British travellers wrote about travelling in Calabria during this period, presumably because at the time Britain was at war with the Napoleonic regime that governed the Italian peninsula south of Naples which included Calabria. To have done so might have been construed as being either traitorous or dangerous; most likely both.

That said, it was during this period that Philip James Elmhirst was held prisoner for six months in various parts of southern Calabria so his forced 'Grand Tour' observations are both interesting and unique.

In making these political and historical distinctions I am highlighting the fact that throughout history the part of Italy that today we call Calabria has, like other parts of Italy, often been a pawn in the grander scheme of things. These days it is a defined geographical and administrative area, one of Italy's twenty *regioni*; over two hundred years ago when, for example, Henry Swinburne passed this way, Calabria's organization and boundaries were more fluid. Like the rest of Italy, today's Calabria incorporates many of the flaws, vicissitudes and randomness of history.

So my definition of Calabria is an arbitrary one, the one I know best, its current form.

Although, as I have already intimated, I have travelled in almost every nook and cranny of Calabria, I have not been everywhere, nor have I been everywhere my travelling companions visited. And of course, for obvious reasons, I have more direct experience of the people and places in central and eastern Calabria than other parts. Being aware of this, I have tried to resist any imbalance in what follows; nevertheless I accept that it probably exists.

That said, from time to time I have knowingly used my experiences in and around Santa Severina to illustrate certain aspects of Calabrian life and culture, though I have done so only when I am sure that such observations are not unique to Santa Severina and its environs.

And of course in some areas I have been selective; I have written about some places that I like or think are or were important; places like Castrovillari and Morano, Lamezia Terme, Pizzo, Tiriolo and, of course, Santa Severina.

Calabria is essentially thematic in structure but sometimes these themes cross-pollinate. While, for example, earthquakes, brigandage and the Calabrian mafia, the *'ndrangheta*, have dedicated chapters—*When the earth moves* and *Outside the la*w—all crop up in other guises in other chapters.

At the risk of repeating myself, *Calabria* is *not* a guide to Calabria; it is, in every sense, *about* Calabria and as such clearly does include some information that the independent traveller might find both useful and enlightening.

However, unlike the guide, *Calabria* does not include details of, for example, Calabrian castles or Calabrian churches; there are others who have made such things the focus of their words.

Of course I do sometimes refer to *specific* castles and churches (though more often the church as a body) when they are relevant to the story I am telling; that said, in such circumstances I am more likely to focus on a particular event relating to a castle (Joachim Murat and Pizzo Castle, for example) or the role of the church at a given time (Pope Francis and Oppido Mamertina, for example).

Travelogues are not generally seen as historical sources but sometimes travellers find themselves in the right place at, or close to, the right time. Innocently they are witness to and record observations and experiences that historians overlook at the time because they simply don't know they exist; they are written in another language, for another audience and published in another country. Generally too, travellers are unaware of the subsequent significance of what they may have seen or heard in a different culture.

In *Calabria* there are more than a few examples of this, particularly so in the accounts of those who travelled before Italian unification.

That said, when I started to write *Calabria*, I had no expectation that, from time to time, the first-hand experiences of many of my fellow travellers would throw new light on some of the accepted myths about Calabria and its history. The key to the accuracy, or otherwise, of some such tales—many of which already seemed to me to be either inaccurate, improbable or questionable—often lay dormant within the pages of these travelogues.

For me, investigating some of these 'cold cases', in the light of the new evidence lurking within the long-forgotten diaries of a few eccentric and pioneering British travellers, has been the most rewarding part of writing *Calabria: Travels in the toe of Italy*.

And finally, like many of my fellow travellers, I have allowed myself the luxury of expressing personal opinions, though I have generally not done so without the corroborative support of what they themselves observed and wrote about; for most, beating about the bush was neither their style nor their preoccupation.

Itineraries and context

> La Rotunda ... is the frontier of Calabria, and consequently the last place in the Province of Basilicate. Our hostess tells us that to-morrow we shall not be able to comprehend the language, so bad is the Calabrian dialect.
> **Arthur John Strutt** *A pedestrian Tour in Calabria and Sicily*

I have written elsewhere about how, like DH Lawrence, I feel that a travel book falls short in its goal if it does not include at least one map. In this respect Lawrence's *Sea and Sardinia* was well-served by his own hand-drawn efforts.

That said, not all of my fellow-travellers appended a map, fewer still a quick guide to their itineraries, so this short chapter redresses the balance.

Each accompanying map shows the same key places in Calabria and includes a linear representation of the route taken (a small, white triangular arrow in a black circle indicates the start point) and details of each itinerary with today's alternative names and spellings included in brackets. Also included are brief details of how and when each travelled and with whom ... with regard to companions some authors were vague and gave little information, except one or two initials.

There is no single route that is common to all *my* fellow-travellers though they generally came to and left Calabria via one of the following four entry and/or exit points: Reggio Calabria—by sea to or from Sicily; overland via the north-east corner (Rocca Imperiale); the central-north (Morano Calabro/Castrovillari); and the north-west corner (Scalea)—the last three are all to or from Basilicata.

There were of course those who opted for something different and arrived and departed by sea at points other than Reggio Calabria.

Henry Swinburne 1777 & 1780
Travels in the Two Sicilies

Henry Swinburne (1777) arrived overland from Basilicata and travelled south down the eastern seaboard to Monte Giordano, Roseto, Sibaris, Corigliano, Rossano, Cariati, Punta Alice, Stróngoli and Crotone; by sea to Catanzaro Marina, by land to Catanzaro, Squillace, Rocella, Gerace, Locri, Bianco, Brancaleone, Capo Spartivento, Bova, Amendolia (Amendolea), Pentedattolo (Pentedáttilo), Capo dell'Armi and Reggio ... thence by sea to Apulia.

Henry Swinburne (1780) landed at Tropea by sea from Sicily and travelled north to Monteleone (Vibo Valéntia), Nicastro, Páola, Cosenza, river Crati, Bisignano, Tarsia, Monte Pollino, Morano and Campo Tenese ... thence into Basilicata.

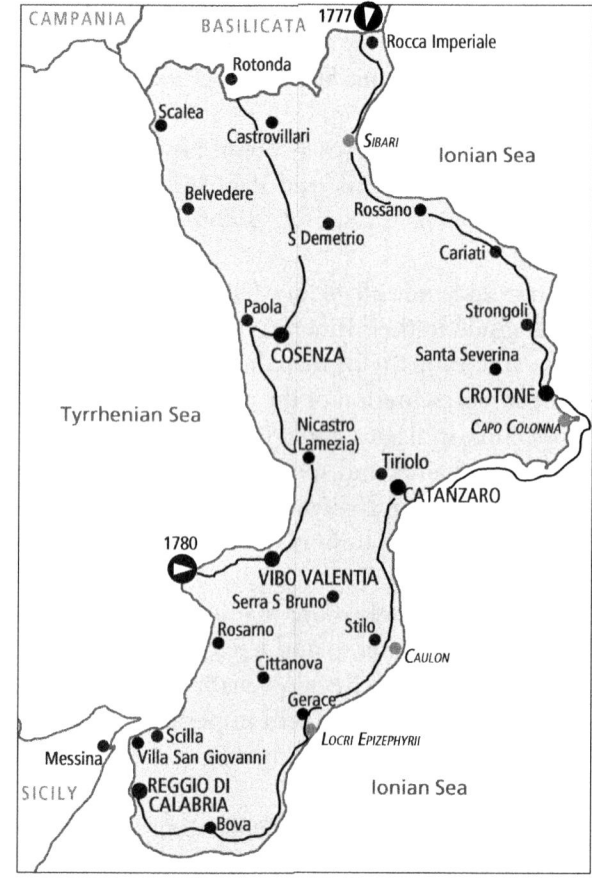

Swinburne was in Calabria in May 1877 and in February three years later. He travelled alone, generally by horse and usually with a guide.

CALABRIA

Brian Hill 1791
Observations and Remarks in a Journey through Sicily and Calabria in the year 1791

Brian Hill landed at Reggio Calabria from Sicily and travelled north to Scilla, Bagnara, Palmi, Monteleone (Vibo Valéntia) Nicastro, Cosenza and Morano ... thence into Basilicata.

Richard Hill who accompanied his half-brother Brian

Hill wasin Calabria in March, accompanied by his half-brother Richard Hill (above) and an unnamed nephew; they generally travelled by mule and often with guides.

Richard Keppel-Craven 1818
A Tour through the Southern Provinces of the Kingdom of Naples

Richard Keppel-Craven arrived from Basilicata on the eastern seaboard and travelled south to Rocca Imperiale, Monte Giordano, Roseto, Amendolara, Trebisacce, Cassano, Sibari, Corigliano, Rossano, Cariati, Fiumenica, Crocoli, Cirò, Stróngoli, Crotone, Cutro, Catanzaro Marina, Roccelleta, Squillace, Stallati, San Vito, Serra S. Bruno, Mongiana, Feroleto, Casalnuovo (Cittanova), Terranova, Gerace, Locri, Gerace, Casalnuovo, Palmi, Bagnara, Favazzina, Scilla, Porticello, Cannitello, Villa San Giovanni, Reggio (by sea via Messina), Gallico, Cantona, Fiumara, Melia, Solano, Palmi, Casalnuovo, Mileto, Monteleone (Vibo Valéntia), Pizzo, Angitola, Nicastro, Platania, Soveria, Carpanzano, Rogliano, Cosenza, Tarsia, Spezzano, Castrovillari and Morano ... thence into Basilicata.

Keppel-Craven was in Calabria between June and August and was accompanied by two servants and often a guide or local man; he travelled by horse with baggage on a mule.

CALABRIA

Craufurd Tait Ramage 1828
The Nooks and by-ways of Italy: Wanderings in search of its ancient remains and modern superstition

Craufurd Tait Ramage arrived overland from Basilicata on the western seaboard and travelled south to Madonna della Grotta and Scalea; by sea from Scalea to Páola then overland to San Fili, river Crati, Cosenza, Rogliano, Diano, San Mango, Nocera, S. Biagio (Sambiase), Nicastro, Máida, Vena, Pizzo, Monteleone (Vibo Valéntia), Bivona, San Fili (Melicucco), Casal Nuovo (Cittanova), Agnana, Gerace, Locri, Gerace, Roccella, Castel Vetere (Caulónia), Pazzano, Mongiana, Serra (Serra San Bruno), Spatola (Spádola), San Vito, Olivadi, Palermiti, Squillace, Rocccelleta, Catanzaro, Cutro, Cotrone (Crotone), Capo Colonna, Cotrone, Stróngoli, Cirò, Cariati, Rossano, river Crati, Cassano, Città Cassano, Francavilla, Trebisacce, Roseto ... thence into Basilicata.

Ramage was in Calabria between May and August; he generally travelled alone but on one occasion with a guard, and mostly on foot though occasionally by mule.

31

Arthur John Strutt 1841
A pedestrian Tour in Calabria and Sicily

Arthur John Strutt arrived overland from Basilicata near the western seaboard and travelled south to La Rotanda (Rotonda), Maroniano (Morano), Castrovillari, Spezzano, Társia, Cosenza, Córaci, Comerea (Soveria Mannelli), Terriolo (Tiriolo), Catanzaro, Caraffa, San Floro, Cortale, Conga (Curinga), Pizzo, Monteleone (Vibo Valéntia), San Pietro di Mileto, Rosarno, Palmi, Bagnara, Scylla, (Villa) San Giovanni, Reggio ... thence by sea to Sicily.

Strutt was accompanied by his friend William Jackson (J— throughout) though they later teamed up with three Frenchmen; he generally travelled on foot. He travelled in Calabria in May and June.

Edward Lear 1847
Journals of a Landscape Painter in Southern Calabria

Edward Lear landed at Reggio from Sicily and travelled south-east to Motta San Giovanni, Bagaládi, Condufori, Amendolea, Bova, Palizzi, Staìti, Pietrapennata, Bruzanno, Ferruzzano, Bianco, Carignano (Casignana), S. Agata di Bianco, San Luca, Bovalino, Locri, Gerace, Siderno, Rocella, Stignano, Stilo, Pazzano, Stilo, Placánica, Castel Vetere (Caulónia), Gioiosa, Agnano, Cánola, Gerace, Castelnuovo (Cittanova), San Giórgio, Polístena, Castelnuovo, Terranova, Oppido, Gioia (Gióia Tauro), Palmi, by sea to Bagnara, Scilla, Villa San Giovanni, Reggio, Gallico, Calanna, Basilicó, Reggio, Capo del Armi, Mélito, Pentedatelo (Pentedáttilo), Montebello, Fossati (Fossato), Reggio, Villa San Giovanni … thence by sea to Sicily.

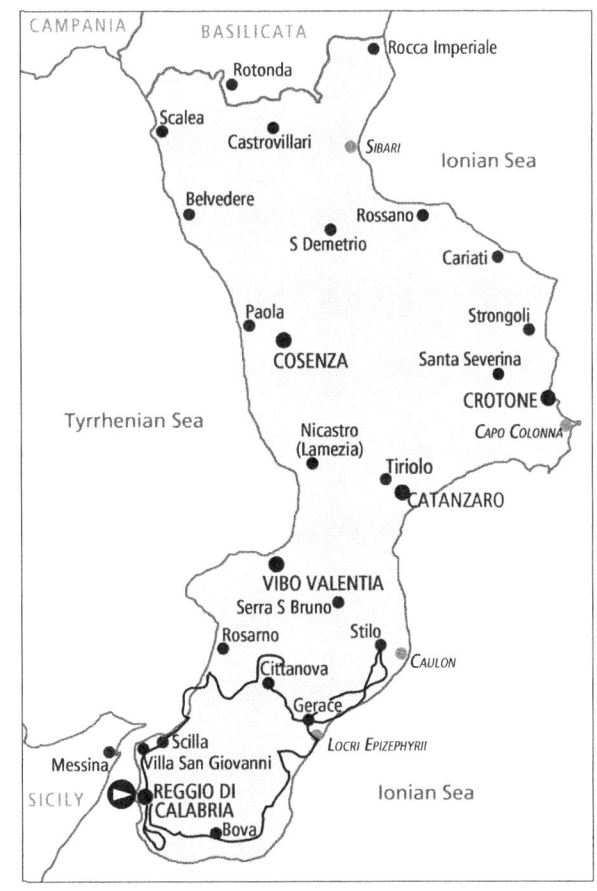

Lear was in Calabria between July and September and was accompanied by P—; he mostly travelled with a muleteer-cum-guide called Ciccio (and a mule, of course); he himself normally went on foot.

Emily Lowe 1858
Unprotected Females in Sicily, Calabria, and on the Top of Mount Aetna

Emily Lowe landed at Reggio from Sicily and travelled north on the *Diligenza Postale* (the postal service coach) to Villa San Giovanni, Scylla (Scilla), Bagnara, Palma (Palmi), Monte Leone (Vibo Valéntia), Pizzo, Tiriolo, Cosenza, Páola ... thence by sea to Naples

Lowe travelled with her mother Helen; they were in Calabria in early January, and travelled, sometimes day and night, as passengers on a horse-drawn carriage that carried both post and people.

CALABRIA

George Gissing 1897
By the Ionian Sea

George Gissing landed at Páola from Naples and travelled east to San Fili, Cosenza, by train to Sybaris *(and on to Taranto in Apulia and then back south along the Ionian coast into Calabria)*, all stations to Cotrone (Crotone), Capo Colonna, Cortone, Catanzaro, Marina di Catanzaro, Squillace, Coscia di Stalletti (Punto di Stalletti) ... thence all stations to Reggio ...

Gissing was in Calabria in November; he travelled alone by train and carriage.

Norman Douglas 1911
Old Calabria

Norman Douglas arrived overland from Basilicata on the eastern seaboard and travelled south to Rossano, north-east to Castrovillari, Morano, *(Terranova di Pollino and Madonna di Pollino in Basilicata)* Castrovillari, Cosenza, Castrovillari, Spezzano, Terranova di Sibari, Vaccarizza, San Demetrio, Macchia, San Demetrio, Acri, Verace (Ceraco?), Lungobucco, San Giovanni in Fiore, Taverna, Catanzaro, Tiriolo, Catanzaro, Reggio, Bagnara, Sant'Eufémia di Aspromonte, Sinópoli, Delianuova, Monte Montalto, Bova, Bova Marina, Locri, Caulónia, Ragona, Fabrìzia, Serra San Bruno, Soverato, Cortone (Crotone), Stróngoli, Capo Colonna ...

(Mapping Douglas' journey in Calabria is made more complicated because the text is clearly describing the fusion of at least three visits to Calabria.)

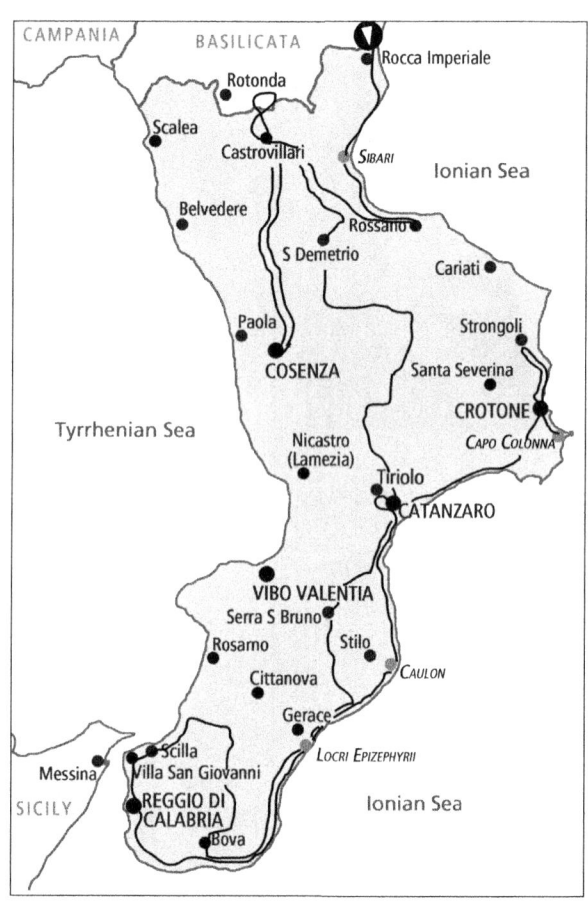

Generally Douglas travelled alone, though he often hired a guide; he travelled by train and carriage but largely on foot. The main chronology puts him in Calabria from May to July but he clearly also had been in Calabria at other times, certainly August and September.

CALABRIA

Edward Hutton 1912
Naples and Southern Italy

Edward Hutton arrived overland from Basilicata on the western seaboard and travelled south to Scalea, Belvedere Maritimo, Páola, San Fili, Cosenza, Rogliano, Carpanzano, Córace, Soveria Mannetti, Tiriolo, Catanzaro, Sant'Eufémia, Monteleone (Vibo Valéntia), Tropea, Capo Vaticano, Nicótera, Gioia (Gioia Tauro), Palmi, Scilla, Villa San Giovanni, Reggio, Mélito, Capo Sparivento, Marina di Gerace (Locri), Gerace, Roccella, Monasterace, Stilo, Monasterace, Catanzaro, Squillace, Roccelletta, Catanzaro, Cortone (Crotone), Capo Colonna, Cortone, Stróngoli, Punta dell'Alice, Crùcoli, Cariati, Rossano, Corigliano, 'Sybaris' (Sibari), Trebisacce, Amendolara, Roseto, Rocca Imperiale ... thence into Basilicata.

Hutton travelled with two companions, one of whom, Frank Crisp, was the book's illustrator; they were in Calabria from March to May and travelled by motorised public transport, train and on foot.

Eric Whelpton 1957
Calabria and the Aeolian Islands

Eric Whelpton arrived overland from Basilicata and travelled south to Campo Tenese, Castrovillari, Spezzano Albanese, Sibari, Thúrio, Corigliano, Rossano, Cariati, Stróngoli, Crotone, Catanzaro Lido, Catanzaro, Tiriolo, Taverna, Villaggio Mancuso, San Giovanni in Fiore, Caccuri, Santa Severina, Catanzaro, Nicastro, Pizzo, Tropea, Gioia Tauro, Palmi, Bagnara, Scilla, Reggio, Gallico, Gambarie, Bagaladi, Roccaforte del Greco, Reggio, Pentedattilo, Marina di Condofuri, Bianco, Bovalina Marina, Locri, Gerace, Monasterace, Stilo, Pazzano, Ferdinandea, Nardodipace, Mongiana ... back to Reggio *(broken line on map)*, Villa San Giovanni, Reggio (*via Lipari Islands*), Villa San Giovanni, Amantea, Fiumofreddo Bruzzo, Páola, Folcanara Albanese, Cosenza, Páola, Belvedere Maritimo, Diamante, Scalea, Praia a Mare ... thence into Basilicata.

Whelpton and his wife Barbara were in Calabria during the summer; they travelled by train and by car.

Leslie Gardiner 1966
South to Calabria

Leslie Gardiner arrived by train from Basilicata on the western seaboard and travelled south to Páola, then Spezzano Alabanese, San Giorgio Albanese, Vaccarizzo, San Cosmo Albanese, San Demetrio Corone, Santa Sofia d'Epiro, Acri, Spezzano Alabanese, Cosenza, Cerchiara di Calabria, Sibari, (CS), Celico, Camigliatello, (CS), Luzzi, Lungro, Luzzi, (CS), Bianchi, Soveria Manelli, Catanzaro, Crotone, Capo Colonna, Isola Capo Rizzuto, (CZ), Tiriolo, Soverato, Copanello, (CZ), Rocella Jónica, Gioisa Jónica, Gerace, Sant'Ilario, Benestare, San Luca, Sant'Agata, Motticello, Brancaleone, Palazzi, Sant'Elia, Pentedattilo, Mélito (di Porto Salvo), Reggio Calabria, Palmi, Bagnara, Scilla, (RC), Bianco, Bovalino, Locro, Siderno, Stilo, Pazzano, Mongiana, Serra San Bruno, Máida, Nicastro, (RC), Sant'Alessio, Santo Stefano, Gambarie, Vibo Valéntia, Amantea, Páola, thence by train to Naples.

Gardiner was in Calabria in April and May and travelled alone (though often with local guides), on foot, by public transport and in other people's cars. Unusually he used Cosenza (CS), Catanzaro (CZ), and to a lesser extent, Reggio Calabria (RC) as bases for visiting other places.

Henry Morton 1967
A Traveller in Southern Italy

Henry Morton arrived overland from Basilicata on the western seaboard and travelled south to Praia a Mare and along the Gulf of Policastro then Lungro, Castrovillari, Frascineto, 'Sybaris', Thurio, Coligliano Calabro, Rossano, Lake Cecita, Spezzano, Cosenza, Soveria Mannelli, Nicastro, Máida, Pizzo, Mileto, Gioia Tauro, Bagnara, Scilla, Reggio, Mélito di Porto Salvo, Bova, Bova Marina, Marina Palizzi, Marina di Brancalone, Ardore Marina, Locri, Gerace, Locri, Punto di Staletti, Copanello, Squillace, Girifalco, Catanzaro, Crotone, Capo Colonna, Coligliano Calabro, 'Sybaris'; then back to Crotone and Reggio *(not shown on map)*

Morton was in Calabria during the summer; he travelled alone and by car.

The journeys of these travellers span nearly two hundred years (from Swinburne in 1777 to Morton in 1967), during which period the southern Italian peninsula experienced some dramatic political and social upheavals. The following is a brief historical time-line to put their travels in their historical context.

At the time Henry Swinburne travelled in Calabria (1777 and 1780) the Two Sicilies (Naples and Sicily) were ruled by the historically French line of Bourbon monarchs. From 1759 the same monarch—a mere eight years old in 1759—ruled both territories and was known as Ferdinando III of the Kingdom of Sicily and Ferdinando IV of the Kingdom of Naples. As ruler of Naples he was deposed twice: once by the revolutionary (French) Parthenopean Republic for six months in 1799 and again for nine years by the Napoleonic regime from 1806.

This was the time of the Napoleonic Wars and because Ferdinand allied himself with Austria and Britain, Napoleon deemed that the Bourbon dynasty had effectively forfeited its crown. Napoleon's brother, Joseph Bonaparte, was then made King of the Two Sicilies, even though in reality he only reigned in the kingdom's peninsular half governed from Naples; King Ferdinand relocated in Sicily where he remained under British protection.

In 1808, Napoleon's brother-in-law, Joachim Murat—of whom we shall hear much more later—succeeded Joseph as King of the Two Sicilies and reigned until 1815 when, following Napoleon's defeat and the end of the Napoleonic Wars, he fled to Corsica.

Ferdinando returned to Naples and, in 1816, he became Ferdinand I of the re-united, and renamed, Kingdom of the Two Sicilies.

In 1825 Francesco I became king of the Kingdom of the Two Sicilies.

In 1830 Ferdinando II became king of the Kingdom of the Two Sicilies.

In 1859 Francesco II became king of the Kingdom of the Two Sicilies.

In 1860, following Giuseppe Garibaldi's successful expedition to unify the Italian peninsula, Francesco II was deposed and the Kingdom of the Two Sicilies ceased to exist; its territory was initially incorporated into the Kingdom of Sardinia which was soon renamed the Kingdom of Italy. This marked the end of the Bourbon dynasty in southern Italy.

In 1861, in post-unification Italy, Vittorio Emanuele II (of the House of Savoy-Carignano) became the first King of Italy.

In 1878 Umberto I became King of Italy.

In 1900 Vittorio Emanuele III became King of Italy.
In 1922 Benito Mussolini, the fascist dictator, came to power in Italy.
In 1946 Umberto II became King of Italy for one month.
In 1946 post-war Italy became a Republic.

The following is how all this political and monarchical background music fitted in with when my fellow British travellers were out and about in Calabria:

Henry Swinburne (1777 and 1779) and Brian Hill (1791) travelled during the reign of Ferdinand IV of Naples.

Richard Keppel-Craven (1818) travelled during the reign of Ferdinand I of the Kingdom of the Two Sicilies. (Ferdinand IV of Naples and Ferdinand I of the Kingdom of the Two Sicilies were one and the same.)

Craufurd Tait Ramage (1828) travelled during the reign of Francesco I of the Kingdom of the Two Sicilies.

Arthur John Strutt (1841), Edward Lear (1847) and Emily Lowe (1859) travelled during the reign of Ferdinand II of the Kingdom of the Two Sicilies.

George Gissing (1897) was the first to travel in post-unification Italy and during the reign of Umberto I, King of Italy.

Norman Douglas (1911) and Edward Hutton (1912) travelled during the reign of Vittorio Emanuele III, King of Italy.

Eric and Barbara Whelpton (1957), Leslie Gardiner (1966) and Henry Morton (1967) travelled in post-war Italy, by then a republic.

Though none of the above travelled in Calabria during the Napoleonic period, and specifically when it was under the rule of Joachim Murat (1808 to 1815), many refer back his reign as it clearly was a time when significant political, social and cultural changes took place.

The Grand Tour

> "Europe finishes at Naples and even there it finishes badly enough. Calabria, Sicily, all the rest is a part of Africa."
> **Creuze de Lesser** *Voyage en Italie e en Sicile*

Creuze de Lesser was not alone in his thinking when it came to what lay south of Naples in the early part of the 19th century. Those who travelled to Italy for pleasure and to inhale and revere the rich culture and extraordinary history of that ancient peninsula generally travelled no further south than Naples ... if indeed they came that far.

From the 16th century, the Grand Tour, as it came to be known, brought young British men—and a handful of women—to the tourist hot-spots of mainland Europe: France, Switzerland, Germany, Austria and Italy. The Grand Tour could appeal to the senses and sensibilities of every traveller: from the coffee-houses and brothels of Paris, to Voltaire's Swiss home at Ferney; from the Tiergarten of Berlin, to the theatres and fencing schools of Vienna; from the horse racing and 'football' of Florence, to the gaming-houses of Venice. All, and much more, could be a part of the young traveller's itinerary.

Although my focus will be on the British travellers who indulged in the Grand Tour, and especially those who ventured beyond Naples and into the south, De Lesser's observation above also serves to illustrate the point that it was not only the British who had a passion for exploring beyond their comfort zone.

Of course these were no ordinary young travellers, they were no more and no less than the well-educated offspring of Britain's wealthiest (and, by definition, best educated) classes for whom Europe between France and the Mediterranean was their Grand Tour finishing school. The European continent not only offered temporary respite from any unwanted pressures back home in Britain but was a recognised training ground for those who had aspirations to enter public service, perhaps as a diplomat, in the military or even the clergy.

Lest they might have to think for themselves, it was not uncommon for such travellers to be accompanied by a suitable companion who could act as guardian, guide and tutor on their European wanderings. And although all of Europe was theirs for the travelling, 'Italy' was frequently the main attraction and everywhere and everything in between, no more than a means to an end.

These were young people raised on a classical diet of 'Italian' customs, manners, music, art, architecture and history, people who were drawn to the Italian peninsula to feast on the real thing, to experience a unique and abundant blend of classical antiquity and the Renaissance.

All of this they could find north of Rome. There was no need to travel further south and few ever did though *if* they did venture south, then it was generally by sea to either Sicily and on to Malta.

J.H.W. Tischbein's 1787 portrait of Johann Wolfgang von Goethe reposing in the Roman Camgagna possibly in a 'state of intoxicated self-forgetfulness'.

Up to the 1860s, when the Italian peninsula became one identifiable political entity, to travel south of Rome meant venturing into what was in effect yet another 'foreign' country (first known as the Two Sicilies, later the Kingdom of the Two Sicilies) and one less associated with the more 'ordered' world further north.

But, for many, Naples had a special attraction. In Grand Tour terms it might have been off the beaten track but it was not only the largest city in 'Italy' *and* a capital city but also, after Paris and London, it was the third largest city in Europe.

In his guide book with the long-winded title of *The grand tour. Containing an exact description of most of the cities, towns, and remarkable places of Europe. Together with a distinct account of the post-roads and stages, with their respective distances ... Likewise directions relating to the manner and expence of travelling ...*, published in 1749, Thomas Nugent described Naples thus:

"'tis generally allowed that Naples is the pleasantest place in Europe. The air is pure, serene and healthful; it is scarce ever cold in winter, and in summer they have refreshing breezes both from the mountains and the sea, which is not subject to storms. The neighbouring country is the richest soil in Europe, abounding with corn, wine, and oil, which are excellent in their kind."

Personally I would take issue with the 'not subject to storms' part as I recall spending a night sleeping on the Naples-to-Palermo ferry for that very reason and when we did get underway nearly twelves hours later, it was not the most pleasant of crossings. But, apart from that, he had a point. Also, you will be pleased to note that all further references to Nugent's book will credit it with the simpler title, *The Grand Tour*.

In a later guide to touring Italy, Richard Colt Hoare's *Hints to Travellers in Italy* (1815), Hoare's concept of the Italian peninsula, like so many others, clearly finished at Naples:

"Having once more conducted the tourist to the shores of Naples, I shall there leave him to enjoy the luxuries and amusements of that gay city, to reflect on past scenes, and to form new plans and excursions for the ensuing spring."

Both Nugent and Hoare spoke of the delights of Naples in the language of the tour guide, nevertheless it was a viewpoint shared by others, albeit with more passion, who actually visited the city. In his *Italianische Reise* (first published in 1816, though he travelled some thirty years earlier), Johann Wolfgang von Goethe, the German writer and poet, was clearly smitten:

"Naples is a paradise; everyone lives in a state of intoxicated self-forgetfulness, myself included. I seem to be a completely different person whom I hardly recognise. Yesterday I thought to myself: Either you were mad before, or you are mad now."

Strange how even today's visitors to Naples frequently use the language of 'madness'—words like 'frenetic', 'chaotic' and 'manic'—to describe this compelling city.

People did not only come to Naples to be left in a 'state of intoxicated self-forgetfulness', there were other attractions, most notably Vesusius and the excavations at Herculanium and Pompeii as well as the nearby islands of Capri and Ischia.

But for most Grand Tour travellers Naples was the end of the line, as far south as they dared travel by land; some, like Creuze de Lesser, believed the ambience of the deep south to be closer to Africa than to Europe. For Goethe the next stop after Naples was Sicily but, like so many others, he chose to go there by boat and missed out on the delights of Calabria.

In Hoare's *Hints to Travellers in Italy*, it was as if the mainland south of Naples simply did not exist. According to Hoare, those travellers who had over-wintered in Naples—the notion of staying put for the winter months was something Grand Tour travellers were used to—and who, having enjoyed 'the luxuries and amusements of that gay city', and were ready for further adventures, had but two onward options:

"A good opportunity will now occur of visiting Sicily and Malta, which may be done with ease before the commencement of the summer heats. A commodious packet will convey the tourist to Palermo: and if times are not altered, the English name will procure him a good passport, and a friendly reception."

For Hoare it is unspoken, but the assumption has to be that, apart from reasons of comfort and expediency, the question of security was at the forefront of the traveller's mind when it came to considering continuing further south overland.

While staying at Naples, Henry Swinburne observed:

"At Naples there is nothing but a mere nominal police; yet burglaries are unknown, riots still more so, and the number of assassinations inconsiderable: it bears no proportion to that of the murders committed in the distant provinces [Apulia, Basilicata and Calabria], where, I am credibly informed, no less than four thousand persons are killed annually."

My guess is that his observations are somewhat exaggerated, both the burglaries and assassinations accredited to Naples and the four thousand murders in the south. Nevertheless it is an indication of how the 'distant provinces' south of Naples were viewed at the time and why it was that so few ever ventured there.

On the other hand, the Grand Tour was about experiencing the rich culture and history of the Italian peninsula and for some, albeit a minority, the draw of one unique aspect of this, the erstwhile Greek republics of Magna Græcia, was overwhelming. Thus, despite the perceived deprivations and dangers, a few realised there was only one way in which to truly experience Magna Græcia and that was to head further south, to venture into Apulia, Basilicata and Calabria.

Many too had high hopes of actually discovering the remains of these ancient Greek settlements, particularly Sibari, Locri and Caulon, all of which were located on Calabria's Ionian coast—then often referred to as the Adriatic Sea—and in doing so, aspired to become themselves part of the region's unique Magna Græcia legacy.

For some, the fact that Magna Græcia had all but disappeared was unimportant; with the innocence and determination of the pilgrim, it was enough to be in the same place, to stand on the Greek-Calabrian earth, to absorb its atmosphere, to be touched by the warm, gentle breezes of the Adriatic, and to imagine what it must have been like twenty-five centuries earlier as an ancient Greek civilization was laying down embryonic roots in the heel and toe of the Italian peninsula.

Despite Swinburne's unsettling statistics and talk of assassinations in the south, the draw of Magna Græcia was all-powerful and he himself was not put off by the perceived dangers and visited Calabria twice.

Although Henry Swinburne is credited with the first detailed and accessible Grand Tour travelogue or diary of a Briton travelling in Calabria *(Travels in the Two Sicilies)*, there were others who came to the south before Swinburne though, as I have already indicated, their writings are less well-known and generally do not constitute a full-blown travelogue.

Over two hundred years before Swinburne, the first of these, the true pioneer of the Grand Tour in respect of Calabria, was Thomas Hoby (1530-1566), who, at the tender age of twenty, travelled through Calabria to Sicily. An account of the journey is included in his autobiography, *The Travels and Life of Sir Thomas Hoby, Knight of Bisham Abbey, written by himself, 1547-1564*.

His motive for venturing into Calabria was, to say the least, unusual, albeit one I can sympathise with:

"... I took a journey upon me to go through the dukedom of Calabria by land into Sicily, both to have a sight of the country and also to absent myself for a while out of Englishmen's company for the tongue's sake."

(I have edited the spelling of the above as the original uses several archaic forms; similarly the quote below.)

This is Hoby's first impression as he entered Calabria from Basilicata via Laino before descending to the pass in the Pollino mountains that brought him into the elevated plain known as Campo Tenese:

"This [Laino] is a pretty town well compact about a round hill, and because the houses are on all sides joining together and stand bound on by another, therefore (I think) it is so named. After we have gone a good while from hence we come at length to descend from the hills through a straight, sharp, road and stony way which a man would judge to have been cut out of the rock by force of hand, for it is on both sides as if a man should enter into a gate. When we are down these hills we come into a fair plain, and on the right hand there is upon the hillside the town of Morano."

John Dryden Junior (1668-1701), the second son of the poet and playwright John Dryden, travelled by *felucca* along the coast of Calabria in 1700 en route to Sicily from Naples; he and his travelling companion, a Mr. Cecil, stopped off at both Scalea and Páola. An account of their journey,

Detail from Vilhelm Melbye's (1824-1882) *A Spanish Felucca, British Warships and Other Shipping in the Mediterranean off Gibraltar*. At one time the *felucca* was the Mediterranean's preferred coastal craft and these days it can still seen plying the river Nile.

credited to Dryden but seemingly with the help of several editors, was published posthumously in 1776 as *A Voyage to Sicily and Malta*.

Dryden was not impressed with what he saw when they made landfall in Calabria and preferred to sleep overnight in their *felucca*. This was his account of the 'odd treatment' they received at Scalea:

"We never lay ashore in any place, but always in our felucca, and, indeed, we found nothing but bare walls wherever we put in: and those people of Calabria are so barbarous as well as poor, that, when we only came into their bare rooms, where was not to be found so much as a chair to sit on, to sup there as well as we cou'd, they wou'd have exacted above a carlin [about 4.5 English pence] a head of us, besides the reck'ning, for our chambering, as they termed it, for they cou'd not give it the name of a night's lodging, for we went down to lye in our felucca."

John Dryden Junior died in Rome very soon after his Calabrian travels; he was thirty-three. I could find no record of the cause of death and wondered whether it was indeed Calabria and its endemic malaria that did for him at such a young age? He would not have been the first.

As the account of Dryden and Cecil's Grand Tour was not published until 1776, seventy-five years after the event, others who travelled pre-1776 were blissfully unaware that they were perhaps not the pioneers they thought they were ... and in particular Patrick Brydone (see below).

Delving into stories about those who defied the accepted limits of the Grand Tour, and particularly those who came to Calabria, I stumbled upon the name of George Berkeley (1685-1753) and allowed myself to wonder whether I had come across the first Irishman (he was actually of Anglo-Irish stock) to have come to Calabria.

Berkeley travelled in Italy between 1716 and 1720 as the tutor to another Angle-Irishman, George Ashe, the son of the then Vice Chancellor of Dublin University and, according to one commentator on his work and travels, 'his curiosity led him into several unfrequented places in Apulia and Calabria'. This was the summer of 1717.

However, because Berkeley was later Bishop of Cloyne near Cork in Ireland and subsequently became a household name in certain circles for his contribution to philosophy and mathematics, information was both scant and illusive regarding his travels in Italy.

Excited as I was by the idea of another person with Irish credentials having travelled in Calabria, when I eventually got to read his account of his journey, *Journals of Travels in Italy,* I realised it didn't seem likely after all. He and Ashe certainly came to Apulia and passed through the north-eastern corner of

Basilicata, notably Matera, but on that occasion never ventured any further south.

I wondered if the confusion about him having come to Calabria might have had its origins in Berkeley's fascination with the *tarantella*, the ritualistic dance accompanied by rhythmic, frenzied music that can go on for days and supposedly 'cures' those driven mad by the bite of tarantula spider? He encountered the *tarantella* phenomenon in several Apulian towns, including those in the heel of the Italian boot known as the Salento.

However, the *tarantella* was not confined to Apulia and was also endemic in Calabrian superstitions, folklore and music so there was the potential for confusion … particularly when, in a letter he wrote just after returning from the south, he himself mentions being in 'the old Calabria', referring to the antique name for the Salento.

Berkeley over-wintered on the island of Ischia and, in early 1718, he set off southwards again on a tour of Sicily and, as before, he kept a record of his travels. Academic and literary critic Joseph Warton (1722-1800), who later penned a biography of Berkeley's friend, the poet Alexander Pope, explained what happened to Berkeley's Sicilian journal:

"He went over Apulia and Calabria, and even travelled on foot through Sicily, and drew up an account of that very classical journey, which was lost on a voyage to Naples and cannot be sufficiently regretted."

Thus, assuming Warton's account of Berkeley's journey has credence—and there is certainly no reason to think otherwise—then George Berkeley did indeed travel through Calabria on his way to Sicily and did indeed write an account of his journey just as he had done the year before … only to mislay it!

Even if Berkeley did not make it to Calabria another Irishman of the cloth and part-time traveller, the flamboyant Richard Pococke, Bishop of Ossory (1756–65) and Meath (1765) did. In 1734 Pococke travelled through the region and kept a diary of his journey from Messina, via Scilla, to Naples. In his *A description of the East, and some other countries*, the Calabrian part of his journey, from Scilla to Castrovillari, lasted no more than six days and was recounted in just two pages. Herewith a synopsis:

"On the eighteenth of December we sailed from Messina ten miles to the north east to Scylla … From Scylla we set out by land for Naples, a journey which very few strangers have undertaken … On the twenty-fourth we went on into the valley of St Martin, [probably the Valle di Màuro between Campo Tenese and Rotonda] and travelled about thirty miles … We were now in the nether principality of the kingdom of Naples, and in the ancient Luciana [Basilicata]."

CALABRIA

A brief, but nonetheless unique, insight into Calabria at the time by a man who, it seems, was more interested in travelling and writing than he was in tending to his other ecclesiastical duties.

In the spring of 1770 a Scotsman, one Patrick Brydone (1741-1818), nearly found himself in Calabria for this was the original route he chose for his particular version of the Grand Tour.

On his travels he wrote a series of letters to his friend back in England, William Beckford—with whom I sense there was some rivalry in respect of travelling off the beaten track, of being a little more intrepid—and these eventually saw the light of day in 1813 as *A Tour through Sicily and Malta*.

It was almost as if Brydone was retracing John Dryden's footsteps though, at the time he travelled, he could not have known about Dryden's earlier journey. But by the time Brydone's book was actually published he was definitely aware of the Dryden edition ... and of the similarity in titles. Therefore in the introduction to his *A Tour through Sicily and Malta* Dryden's earlier journey is duly acknowledged with Brydone suggesting that his 'tour' and Dryden's 'Voyage' did not overlap significantly 'as many of the observations and descriptions have different objects'.

One major such difference was that at the last minute Brydone got cold feet and changed his mind about travelling overland through Calabria; he explained his reasoning thus:

"Our first plan was to go by land to Regium [Reggio Calabria], and from there cross over to Messina; but on making exact inquiry, we find that the danger from the banditti in Calabria and Apulia is so great, the accommodation so wretched, and inconvenience of every kind so numerous, without any consideration whatever to throw into the opposite scale, that we soon relinquished that scheme."

What a wuss!

Brydone's reluctance to set foot in Calabria did not stop him observing it from a close, but safe, distance and clearly with a modicum of regret as the sea journey had been particularly unpleasant:

"From hence we had the opportunity of observing a pretty large portion of Calabria, which formerly constituted a considerable part of that celebrated country by the name of Great Greece [Magna Græcia], and looked upon as one of the most fertile in the empire. These beautiful hills and mountains are covered with trees and brush-wood to the very summit ... Some of these forests are of a vast extent, and absolutely impenetrable; and no doubt conceal in their thickets many valuable monuments of its ancient magnificence."

How many travellers even thought about their travels in Grand Tour terms is difficult to gauge; certainly those who came to Europe after 1850 were less likely to have done so. Thereafter the Grand Tour was increasingly an anachronism; the railway age and the gradual breakdown of Britain's rigid class structure were but the writing on the wall.

There had been no rules to the Grand Tour, conventions aplenty but no order of play, no limits. For most who partook it was a unique experience, a time to cope with life outside their normal comfort zone, for some a pioneering adventure.

Richard Keppel-Craven did not intend to stray too far away from his comfort zone and, travelling with two servants, was clearly at the more prudent end of the travelling-in-Calabria spectrum.

At the other extreme—some might say at the more reckless side of the same spectrum—there was Craufurd Tait Ramage, the lone adventurer relying largely on his wits and his personality.

Somewhere between the two there was the Hill party who travelled as a family group of three males from different generations: Brian Hill (thirty-five), his older half-brother Richard (fifty-eight) and an unnamed nephew. Although it was Brian Hill who penned the story of their tour, *Observations and Remarks in a Journey through Sicily and Calabria in the year 1791*—which, he said, began as a diary 'with no other design than that of refreshing my own memory'—it was more likely that Richard Hill was the instigator of the expedition and the party leader.

Most who wrote about their travels did so to inform others rather than to credit themselves with any notions of pioneering bravado.

On the other hand, when, in 1772, some five years *before* Henry Swinburne, Sir William Young *(A Journal of a Summer's Excursion by the Road of Montecasino to Naples. And from thence over all the Southern Parts of Italy, Sicily, and Malta)* ventured further south than most of his contemporaries had ever done, he did realise he was something of a pioneer:

"Travelling through a Part of Italy, visited but by few, and described by none, I thought it incumbent on me to take such Notes as might thereafter give an adequate Idea of the State and Face of the Country, to the Curious of my Friends and Acquaintance. To render the Narrative less dry, I have interspersed several classical Remarks and Quotations; and for the Sake of my female Acquaintance, I have regularly and literally translated them."

Apart from the fact that only ten copies were ever printed—'a confined Publication' Young himself called his book—it is such a pity that it did not make it into the recognised travel literature of the period. It is not as detailed a day-by-day travelogue as some of the others but it is one of the first in English to give a flavour of Calabria, its towns, its countryside and its people. Young later became, along with William Wilberforce, a significant campaigner in the movement for the abolition of slavery.

Also, unlike many of those who followed, Young was clearly aware that there may be those *without* a classical education—mainly women—who might have wanted to read about his pioneering travels south of Naples. Young also acknowledged that there probably were others who travelled to the south before him but who did not put pen to paper and share their experiences. Later this was certainly the case as reported by Craufurd Tait Ramage (1828) who had been told that near Rosarno two of his fellow countrymen 'had been stripped here even of their clothes by a band of brigands'; from this hapless duo not a word in writing about their misadventures in Calabria.

When Young said that this part of Italy was 'visited but by few, and described by none', he was making the valid point that the Grand Tour was not about writing a book, it was about the experience itself. Only a few ever wrote about their travels but we are fortunate that these few did.

Had not William Young (as he was at the time) wanted to impress his friends and one female acquaintance in particular, then it is possible that this account too might never have seen the light of day.

I wonder how many others defied the scare-mongers and the anticipated privations and, undaunted and unfettered, came south to explore Calabria and to revel in its Magna Græcia legacy, its reputation for brigandage and its hospitality? And then, back home, shared their experiences and embellished their adventures with friends and family over a glass of port and a cigar in the library ... but never wrote a single word about where they had been and what they had seen? And were there others like George Berkeley whose precious words somehow were lost in transit?

Writing about the south, and Apulia in particular, Berkeley was more charitable than some others:

" ... in all [such places] we were stared at like men dropt from the sky, and sometimes followed by a numerous crowd of citizens, who out of curiosity attended us through the streets. The fear of bandits which hinders strangers from visiting these curiosities is a mere bugbear."

On the other hand, fifty years later, William Young was less generous in his description of Cosenza, though perhaps he had in mind his audience of impressionable friends and acquaintances (and that one special female) and was wont to embellish and exaggerate a little. He described what he termed the 'situation' at Cosenza thus:

"... terrible, from the Impositions and daring Villiany of the lower People; who in this Capital, and indeed throughout all *Calabria*, are, and look like the most cut-throat Devils I ever beheld."

Of course Young's view of the 'lower People' of Cosenza only has relevance as a comparison if he had similar experience of the same class of people in England ... though a cursory glance at his life and lifestyle would suggest this was probably not the case. Nevertheless, despite his obvious reservations and to give him his due, he persevered and continued on his Grand Tour and learned to cope with those 'cut-throat Devils'.

I wonder too ... were there other pioneers, like George Berkeley and William Young, who set off on their Grand Tour adventure to the south but never returned to tell the tale?

And, if some people never returned was it because they had a fatal encounter with bandits or brigands or with—and this is surely the more likely—malaria?

Or did they, like us, like the way of life enough just to stay?

The latter scenario is not beyond the realms of possibility for when, in 1788, Thomas Watkins and his crew were forced ashore because of the 'great violence' of the weather, he was told such a story by the monks at the convent near Scalea where they had taken refuge:

"On the summit of one of the neighbouring hills [the Pollino mountains] that commands an extensive sweep of prospect over the Mediterranean [Tyrrhenian], the Adriatic [Ionian], and the two Calabrias, stands an hermitage, whose lonely tenant (as our monks report) is an Englishman. He has resided there nine years, and subsisted on the alms of the country people, who are extremely partial to him from the happy supposition that he is a saint. Padre Vincenzo, the guardian of our little convent, tells me that he has often met him, and that once in a deep wood below the hermitage he found him weeping over a miniature [painting or drawing of someone], which, on being surprised, he put hastily into his bosom, and retired. He supposes him to be about forty years of age, and says his appearance is very noble and interesting."

I knew from my experience of the Pollino range that from within the main central arc of the *Massiccio del Pollino* (the Pollino Massif) around

Castrovillari and Morano, there was no place from which you could see both seas. In any case it is unlikely that anyone could have survived a winter atop any of the peaks there. I guessed this lone Englishman must have taken refuge atop one of the lesser peaks on the western edge of the Pollino nearer Scalea, from where the Tyrrhenian would be clearly visible and, possibly on a very clear day, also the Ionian.

Then, on re-reading Eric Whelpton's book, I discovered the following:

"At Campotenese the [railway] line is over three thousand feet above the level of the sea, and from the Rifugio Conte Orlando on one of the nearby hills, there is a view of the Ionian Sea to the south, and the Tyrrhenian to the west."

The *rifugio* referred to is a shelter or refuge for hunters, climbers, travellers or shepherds caught in the mountains and in need of a safe place to shelter from bad weather. This particular one, ten miles as the crow flies inland from Scalea, dates from 1907 and is clearly not where the lone Englishman lived. But, being in a sheltered spot close to the summit of Monte Palanuda, it might have been just the place to set up home and live off the local wild bounty. As far as the view of both seas is concerned then I suspect that this could only be possible from the summit of Monte Palanuda and in unique weather conditions.

Thomas Watkins, torn between his desire to visit 'this melancholy man' and the immediate prospect of better sailing weather, opted for the latter and continued on his journey south to Messina. In so doing he left behind the mystery of the Englishman who probably left home in the late 1770s on his Grand Tour adventure, never to return.

All we are left with is an imagined picture of this man's English family still mourning the son, brother, husband or father whom they will have supposed dead at the hands of brigands or the vagaries of malaria. They cannot have imagined that he had decided, for whatever reasons, to make the Pollino mountains his home.

Although Edward Lear (1847) used the word 'tour' frequently in his book, I don't think he saw his particular journey in Grand Tour terms. Emily Lowe never mentioned it at all; likewise all my fellow-travellers thereafter, not even a mention in the historical sense.

When he was visiting San Demetrio Carone in the Greek Sila, Norman Douglas (1911) was clearly referring to the Grand Tour when he made the following observations about earlier 'Grand Tour' adventurers:

"They tell me that within the memory of living man no Englishman has ever entered the town. This is quite possible; I have not yet encountered a single English traveller, during my frequent wanderings over South Italy. Gone are the days of Keppel-Craven and Swinburne, of Eustace [who never visited Calabria] and Brydone and Hoare! You will come across sporadic Germans immersed in Hohenstaufen records, or searching after Roman antiquities, butterflies, minerals, or landscapes to paint—you will meet them in the most unexpected places; but never an Englishman. The adventurous type of Anglo-Saxon probably thinks the country too tame; scholars, too trite; ordinary tourists, too dirty."

Thus John Strutt (1841) was the last of my fellow-travellers who may have seen his journey in such terms and even managed to slip it into his title, *A Pedestrian Tour in Calabria & Sicily*. That it was on his mind is certain for, on the book's title page, he quoted the following from Oliver Goldsmith:

"A man who is whirled through Europe in a post-chaise, and the Pilgrim who walks the grand tour on foot, will form very different conclusions."

In terms of the British travelling in Calabria, Arthur John Strutt was, I believe, the last great adventurer, the last to follow the conventions of the Grand Tour … except that he did it all on foot.

CALABRIA

Calabria … who, when, what, where, why?

"Ages of oppression and misrule have passed over their heads; sun and rain, with all their caprice, have been kinder friends to them than their earthly masters."
Norman Douglas *Old Calabria*

Calabria, Italy's most southern mainland *regione*, the toe of the Italian boot that seemingly kicks the 'ball' of Sicily, has had a colourful and unenviable history.

As befalls the story of many places, its geographic location has dictated and shaped the vicissitudes of its past, themselves inevitably essential to an appreciation of its present. The Calabrian landscape—its mountains, plains, seas, climate, fertility, geology and even maladies—have all played their part in moulding its people and their way of life. Their strengths and weaknesses, their abilities and capabilities, their power and impotence are the random embodiment of that unique Greek-Bruttian-Roman-Byzantine-Saracen-Norman-Swabian-French-Spanish-Italian inheritance they embraced and cultivated atop the twisted-arrowhead isthmus between the Ionian and Tyrrhenian Seas that came to be called Calabria.

The story of the toe of the Italian peninsula is complex; only in the recent past has Calabria ceased to be a battleground or springboard for other people's conflicts. This is the abridged, oft-times skeletal, version of that story, albeit with a little help from my travelling friends … most of whom knew it all, as they did the back of their hand.

That said, there are some aspects of Calabria's geographical and geological inheritance, its historical evolution and their ramifications that are too important to skim through and that are deserving of something more expansive. Thus, other chapters focus more on themes, people and places such as Magna Græcia and its sites, Cosenza and Alaric the Visigoth, the Albanian migration, Joachim Murat and French rule, earthquakes, the Pollino, Sila and Aspromonte mountains, malaria, brigandage, superstitions, unification, the mafia and emigration. Here, by contrast, they are intentionally sketchy *and* seen through the eyes of a non-Calabrian.

Originally settled by two tribes during the Iron Age (11th century BCE), the Oenotrians and the Itali, the area took on the name of first one, Oenotra, then the other to become, it is said, Italia, the first part of the Italian peninsula to have the name 'Italy'.

When the Greeks settled the area in the 8th and 7th centuries BCE, four 'Calabrian' settlements in particular became important cities in what is now called Magna Græcia: Rhegon (Reggio Calabria), Sybaris, Kroton (Crotone) and Locri. The indigenous tribes, it is believed, became subservient to the coastal Greek republics or took to the hills.

It was the remains of Magna Græcia, actual and imagined, that brought many travellers to Calabria between the 16th and 20th centuries. In his preface, Henry Swinburne (1777) summed up the thinking:

"Poetry and History have rendered this topography familiar to us, and every school-boy can point out the ruins of Magna Græcia and Sicily."

Two centuries on and the strength of the Greek republics was gradually weakened by fighting among themselves and by incursions from the north. The newcomers were a branch of the Samnites—who at the time inhabited what is now central-southern Italy, roughly corresponding to Molise and northern Campania—known as the Lucianians and later their offshoot, the Bruttii. According to Craufurd Tait Ramage (1828) the Greek republics ignored the writing on the wall:

"… it is said that Dionysius the elder proposed to erect a fortification across [the 'Calabrian' isthmus] to defend the southern part of Italy from the wild Bruttians; the Greek cities, however, were unwilling that this should be done …"

The 'wild Bruttians' founded many new cities, most notably Consentia (Cosenza), their capital, and gave the region its name, Bruttium, a name it retained for nigh on nine hundred years.

During the 3rd century BCE it was the turn of the Romans, now in the ascendency, who initially met fierce resistance from the Bruttians whom they then considered rebels and who were subsequently treated to the brutal subjection they supposedly deserved.

In the following century the continuing struggle between Rome's armies and, among others, the Carthaginians, resulted in another bloody campaign on 'Calabrian' soil. Although initially victorious against the Romans, the Carthaginian general Hannibal (he of the celebrated Alp-crossing elephants) didn't press his advantage and, after some years of stalemate, he retreated south from his capital at Capua, first to Thurii in north-east Bruttium, then Kroton (Crotone). He remained at Kroton until 203BCE when he escaped and returned to Carthage, close to modern Tripoli in north Africa.

Referring to the erstwhile (Magna Græcia) Greek Temple of Hera near Kroton, Richard Keppel-Craven (1818) suggested that Hannibal was perhaps indulging in a short vacation:

"Neither Pyrrhus nor Hannibal ventured to profane its treasures; while the last was so pleased with the situation of the temple, that he passed a whole summer near its precincts."

The subsequent Roman humiliation of Bruttium and its people was not helped when the rebel slave Spartacus, who had already defeated several Roman legions, moved south to over-winter (72-71BCE) at Thurii where he acquired bronze and iron to make weapons and trained his makeshift army.

Eric Whelpton's (1957) version of events was, I believe, based on a more romantic version of the Spartacus legend; I suspect that, like me, he had been exposed to Howard Fast's iconic novel, *Spartacus*, published a few year's earlier:

"... it was here that Spartacus ... established his capital. He held out for two years against the legionaries; with a little more skill and good fortune he might, indeed, have created a new state in southern Italy and changed the whole course of history."

In 71BCE Spartacus moved north to re-engage the Romans before heading south to Reggio where his intended crossing to Sicily was thwarted. Fleeing north again, some of his army crossed to Petelia, today's Stróngoli, while the main army turned and engaged the Romans in Bruttium where Spartacus and thousands of his men were slain. Eleven thousand others (6000 battle survivors and 5000 escapees) were subsequently crucified.

For a further four centuries the area remained a part of the Roman Empire. In 395CE, under threat itself, the erstwhile Roman Empire was split into an Eastern and Western Empire when Emperor Theodosius I bequeathed the imperial office jointly to his sons—Arcadius in the East and Honorius in the

West. Arcadius' seat of government was Constantinople (today's Istanbul) while Honorius ruled from Rome.

Today's historians see it as a major change, a definable schism in the Roman Empire, but at the time it was still ostensibly one large Empire, the extent of which necessitated two legal and administrative centres and separate emperors.

One of the series of events that precipitated the division was a self-inflicted problem with the Goths who had first entered the Empire in 376CE from the east (fleeing the Huns) as legal immigrants. But it was not long before they were in open conflict with their Roman hosts having been deceived and double-crossed by them.

The inevitable war lasted until 382CE and only affected 'Calabria' inasmuch as the area was a recruiting ground for the Roman army and its produce fed them.

Followed the split into Eastern and Western Empires, the latter began to disintegrate. The west was the more vulnerable and by 410CE the Visigoths (an offshoot of the Goths) under Alaric I had sacked Rome and overrun much of the Italian peninsula. While returning northwards later the same

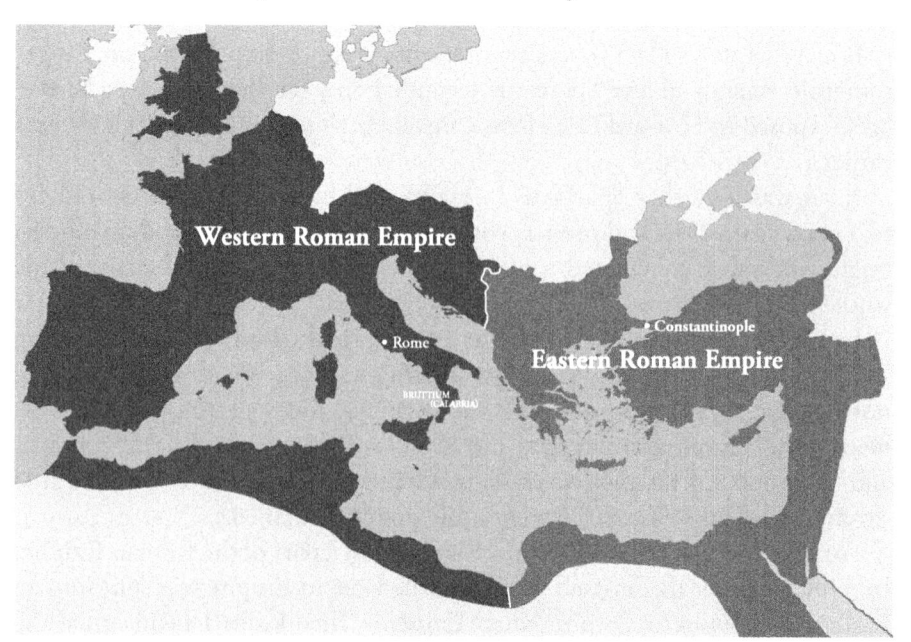

The 395CE division of the Roman Empire into East and West.

year, and having abandoned a planned occupation of Sicily and north Africa, Alaric died at Cosenza—probably of a malarial fever—and, as we shall see in a later chapter, later became the focus a dubious legend that has become an unconvincing part of that city's history. This extract from John Strutt (1841) is by way of a teaser; having described Cosenza as 'dirty and ill-built' he went on to say:

"The inn, however, is in a gay situation; commanding a view of the principal street, the ass-market, the river Vasento, the bed of which the grave of Alaric, king of the Goths, and the bridge over it."

For Alaric, traversing 'Calabria' had been a means to an end, namely north Africa; his untimely death on 'Calabrian' soil was no more than an unfortunate coincidence. His successor, Ataulf, was not interested in conquering the south, Sicily or Africa and turned his sights instead to Hispania (Spain and Portugal).

Bruttium and the south remained under the flaky rule of the Western Empire until it too succumbed to pressure from the Germanic nations to the north. In 480CE the Eastern Emperor, Zeno, decreed himself emperor of a reunited Empire. There followed a period of disruption and confusion as the erstwhile Eastern Empire, what later became known as the Byzantine Empire, re-established its authority over the southern Italian peninsula.

For the next few centuries the Byzantine Empire was continually under pressure from Vandals, Goths and, later, Lombards (Longobards, another Germanic tribe) continued to make incursions into the south, often *from* the south through Reggio Calabria. Nevertheless, somehow it clung on to its increasingly shrinking 'empire' in the toe of the boot where, from 620CE, Greek had become the official language.

Despite this plethora of short-lived incursions—when the indigenous people, the Greek-Bruttian-Roman-Byzantine 'Calabrians', did as they always did when under threat and took to the abundant mountains—as the new millennium approached, Calabria still remained part of the Byzantine Empire.

By the 9th century much of southern peninsula, except southern Apulia and Calabria, was under Lombard rule and still, despite staring the inevitable in the face, the Byzantine Empire hung on. Indeed it was after such a period of conflict between the still-pressing Lombards and the Byzantines that the area hitherto known as Bruttium was renamed Calabria.

Curiously, the part of Apulia which is geographically the heel of the Italian boot, and is known today as the Salento, was previously called Calabria.

According to Mark Rotella (*Stolen Figs*) the name is from the Greek *kalosbruo* which Denise, my friend and Greek-language expert, tells me means 'beautiful land' a description that could have applied equally well to the Salento but, I believe, sits more comfortably with the peninsula's toe, with today's Calabria.

The Lombards were a threat from the north but in the second half of the 9th century a new threat materialised from the south as the Saracens (Muslim Arabs) attempted to establish a similar foothold in Calabria as they already had in Apulia and Sicily. The most significant incursion took place in 918CE, when Reggio Calabria—strategically-important because of its proximity to Sicily, itself a springboard to Africa—succumbed to the Saracen leader Sultan Mofareg-ibn-Salem and most of the city's inhabitants were sold into slavery.

It was during this and subsequent Arab incursions along the Calabrian

An antique map of the south of the Italian peninsula when the Salento, the heel, was called Calabria and today's Calabria was called Bruttium.

coastline that much of the agricultural landscape was introduced that we associate with the area today, in particular citrus trees, and specifically the bergamot in the south, the mulberry tree, used to produce silk and the palm tree. Henry Swinburne (1777) noted the psychological impact of the latter in Reggio:

"Before the Saracens were driven back to their original habitations on the Arabian and African sands, the environs of the city were adorned with stately groves of palm trees, Many of these trees were felled by the Christians out of a whimsical hatred to the plant, as if it had been an appurtenance of Mahometism."

Though in the east the Byzantine Empire survived in one form or another until the 15th century (albeit with a brief interregnum in the 13th century), in Calabria Byzantine rule effectively ended in the 1060sCE ... not long after the Lombards had sought help from the Normans in their push south only to find that the Normans themselves were on a conquering spree.

Edward Hutton (1912) made the same point in a different way:

" ... the Normans seem to have wandered as a great band of freelances ready to sell their aid ... for any undertaking whatsoever."

Earlier in the 11th century Apulia had increasingly come under Norman influence, specifically the various members of the Hauteville family of Normandy (in today's France). One of these, a latecomer to the fray, Robert Guiscard, soon rose to prominence and distinguished himself in battle in Apulia before taking command of the armies that eventually conquered both Apulia and Calabria.

By 1044 the Hauteville's then leader, William Iron Arm, and his brother Drogo had already made several sorties into Calabria from their Apulian base and established a base at Squillace where they later constructed a castle.

In 1048, Robert Guiscard accompanied his older brother Drogo into Calabria, following the course of the river Crati south-west from Sibari towards Cozenza. The subsequent distribution of the conquered lands saw Robert custodian of a castle at Scribla—near today's Spezzano Albanese and the first of many Norman castles in Calabria—to protect their newly acquired territory. Such was their success that Guiscard later abandoned Scribla in favour of another castle further south at San Marco Argentano, nearer Cosenza itself.

In 1059, Guiscard took a break from laying siege to Cariati (on the eastern,

Ionian, coast between Crotone and Sibari) to attend the Council of Melfi (then the Norman capital in today's Apulia) where the then pope, Nicholas II, invested him as duke of Apulia, Calabria, and Sicily ... though at the time the Normans had no foothold in Sicily and the pope was merely indulging in a fairly fail-safe prediction.

Following the Melfi gathering, and brandishing his new title, Guiscard returned to Cariati which capitulated soon afterwards and by early 1060, when Rossano and Gerace also fell, he had almost completed the subjugation of Calabria; only Reggio Calabria remained in Byzantine hands. By the end of the year, Reggio too was under Norman rule. Next stop, Sicily.

It has to be remembered that, at this is time, the Papacy, the so-called Holy See and its succession of powerful popes, was a serious political mover and shaker and even had its own extensive lands and an army. Indeed time-lines of Italian history always include the names of the Popes as this was often as important a political factor at the time as, say, the name of a king.

It was Guiscard's understanding of this and his relationship with the Papacy that served him so well in many future political and military enterprises. From the Papacy's point of view, the entente with Robert Guiscard paid dividends ... his conquest of Calabria was instrumental in substituting the Greek Byzantine rite with Latin Christianity and, in so doing, further lining papal coffers.

In 1062 at Sant'Eufémia (today's town of the same name, now part of Lamezia Terme, is a more modern incarnation), as if to formally and symbolically consolidate the new order of things, Guiscard established Calabria's first Christian monastery, the Benedictine Abbey of Santa Maria. It was no accident that this Norman edifice sat atop an earlier Byzantine monastery.

Lest I fall into the trap of relating historical events only in terms of the main, more powerful, players, it has to be remembered that in all these political and military shenanigans, those who suffered most from each new upheaval were the people whose sole aim was to put bread on the table and lead a quiet life. That said, there were periods of calm between storms, time to get used to the new rules, or the new religion, before the next victor changed the rules—and the taxes—yet again.

When, for example, I say that Robert Guiscard was responsible for the construction of this or that castle, I realise it does not convey any real understanding or appreciation of the reality of events on the ground. To build a structure such as Squillace castle on top of a steep hill would, even with today's sophisticated machinery and technology not be an easy task.

Nor would it be done overnight. Nor without hardship and pain for many.

On the plus side, there was always work for stonemasons in Norman Calabria but Guiscard and his entourage were unlikely to have overseen their progress even from a distance. Their contribution (apart from funding) would have been no more than a pointing finger and an order to start building a castle.

Likewise, in the pages of history books, transitions from one regime to another may appear seamless but there is always an untold human cost that rarely makes it into the historical records and, of course, until recently, the accepted history is generally the victor's version of events. When you read about a town or village being 'sacked', apart from a few words of outrage, there is inevitably a paucity of information on the real humiliations and suffering that actually took place.

In the mediæval world, the real cost for those at the sharp end, whether they be building a castle or a church or fighting in a battle, vary only in degree. Life was about surviving to see another day and another year and not about the intrigues and rivalries that are the stuff of accepted history.

If today's Calabrians could trace their ancestry back across almost thirty generations to the Norman era, the only thing they would find in common with their ancestors would be fertility and tenacious sperm.

For the English (as opposed to the British on this occasion) the date in history that survives in the collective memory over all others is 1066. The date of the Battle of Hastings is learnt at school often without any real understanding of where Hastings is, why there was a battle there, who fought in the battle, who won, who lost … and why it was even worth remembering.

England's 1066 was Calabria's 1061, the date from which to accredit the beginning of the Norman era. In England it was a more decisive victory by William of Normandy (later King William I) over the Saxon King Harold and within a few years the Norman dynasty had not only become established but also most opposition (except in Scotland) had fallen into line.

Ten-sixty-six was the last time a 'foreign' army set foot on English soil. From 1066 to the present day Britain has experienced, give or take a few rebellions and the short-lived Civil War in the 17th century, a period of general and progressive stability; unlike any ordinary Calabrian, Britain's current monarch, Elizabeth II, can say with relative confidence that, give or take a few royal indiscretions here and there, she is the twenty-fifth great-granddaughter of William I.

In Calabria and southern Italy it was a different story. Here the

Normanisation was unplanned, unco-ordinated, dilatory and random. Nor did it bring in its wake similar seeds of stability ... Calabria's immutable geographic position saw to that.

Despite the fact that Norman castles were popping up in Calabria wherever the strategic randomness of the Norman barons took them, the struggle with the earlier Byzantine regime continued for a few years until, by 1071, the whole of the southern peninsula was under Norman rule.

In less than a decade Santa Severina too had its very own Norman castle which, as recent excavations have shown, sits atop an earlier Byzantine structure.

George Gissing (1897), a classicist to the core, had no time for these newcomers and their castles. He took not a little pleasure in describing the fate of Catanzaro's Norman castle which, having survived countless earthquakes, was 'pulled down, deliberately got rid of for the sake of widening a road'; he then continued:

"From my point of view, the interest of the place suffered because I could attach to it no classic memory. Robert Guiscard, to be sure, is a figure picturesque enough, and might give play to the imagination, but I care little for him after all; he does not belong to my world."

The story of castles such as that at Santa Severina is the story of the next seven centuries of life and power in Calabria.

The shell of Squillace's Norman castle as it is today.
Under Santa Severina's Norman castle are the remains of its Byzantine counterpart and a number of tombs—the remains of Santa Severina's Greek-speaking Byzantine citizens.

Built and governed by the Normans it passed into the hands of allies of the Normans, the Swabians (the German House of Hohenstaufen) in the late 12th century. Three members of the Hohenstaufen dynasty were also Holy Roman Emperors and carried much weight and prestige in middle-ages Europe.

In 1266, the Swabians gave way to the 'Italian' Angevins (founded by Charles I, the brother of the French king) who ruled the southern peninsula, the Kingdom of Naples, for nearly two hundred years.

In 1442, the Kingdom of Naples (and Sicily) became dependencies of the Spanish Aragon dynasty under Alfonso V. There followed a period of dispute between France and Spain that lasted over a hundred years though for much of that time the army on the ground in Calabria was Spanish. The French claim gradually receded and in 1559 it was finally abandoned.

Elsewhere in the Italian peninsula this was the time of the Italian Renaissance and though it did not generally have any associations with the south, the Naples-based king Alfonso V was, according to Edward Hutton (1912), not unaffected by what was happening up north:

"Although Alfonso broke his people with taxes, he was known as the Magnanimous, and his court was perhaps the most brilliant that Naples was to know. A great patron of the humanists, who flocked to him after the fall of [Byzantine] Constantinople, he was a true Prince of the Renaissance, thoroughly Italian, if not by birth by culture, a prodigal Mæcenas [a generous patron of the arts], a distinguished soldier and a fine scholar."

The Spanish Kingdom of Naples had its ups and downs, its fortunes—and therefore that of Calabria—largely dependent on the various treaties, alliances and marriage arrangements in the courts of Europe. In 1759, following a brief period in Austrian Hapsburg hands, Charles III of Spain, with antecedents back in the French Bourbon dynasty, left the Kingdom of Naples to his son Ferdinand.

Bourbon rule in southern Italy was established and, despite a couple of hiccups, continued until Italian unification in 1860/61.

The above is but a snapshot of how things changed for those who lived in what we call Calabria from Norman rule up to the establishment of the Bourbon dynasty in 1759. Of course the region was no more than a pawn in the grander scheme of things; for those who had the power at any given time—be they Norman, Swabian, French, Spanish or Austrian—it was all about what they could get from the land and their less fortunate subjects. For most of these conquering heroes the ultimate prize was the island of Sicily and in this respect control of the few miles of sea in-between, the Straits of

Messina, was the goal and Calabria but a constant springboard to that end.

Over the same period there were other significant events that directly pertained to Calabria but were not entirely specific to any one era or any one leader but nevertheless important landmarks that continue to impact on the story of Italy's toe.

The first of these dates from 1147 when the roots of today's organisational structure of the region were established. Initially there were two 'provinces', the names and concepts of which continued to be used for several hundred years: the northern Calabria Citeriore (Citra) and the southern Calabria Ulteriore (Ultra). In the 16th century, changes were made to the line of demarcation between the two and the lands north of the river Neto became Calabria Citra and to the south Calabria Ultra. In 1817 the latter was subdivided into two 'provinces', Calabria Ultra Prima and Calabria Ultra Seconda. Following Unification in 1860/61 these became the provinces of Cosenza (Calabria Citra), Catanzaro (Calabria Ultra Prima) and Reggio Calabria (Calabria Ultra Seconda), each of which retained its original capital of the same name. As we will see, this changed again following boundary changes made in the early 1970s.

During Spanish rule (after 1442) and over a period of several hundred years there occurred a significant migration of people from Albania to many parts of the Kingdom of Naples, but particularly Calabria. Over thirty towns were established in the region, many of which, in Italian, had the word 'Albanese' appended to their name. This was a relatively peaceful migration the first wave of which came about when the army of an inspirational leader,

Movers and shakers in the making of Calabria ... and not a local lad among them.
The Norman Robert Guiscard
The Angevin Charles I
The Aragonese Alfonso V
The Bourbon Ferdinand I

Skanderbeg, was given land in the south for services rendered to the then King of Naples, Alfonso V, and they never returned home. In the 18th century, a second migration took place when the then king, Carlo III, specifically wanted to repopulate parts of Calabria.

The Albanese brought with them their own language and religion and so, from time to time, they were the brunt of the same sorts of local prejudices that even today, in supposedly civilised countries, is directed towards those who don't appear to fit in.

Richard Keppel-Craven (1828) elaborated on how some Albanian communities were viewed by the indigenous population, whom he called the 'original natives of the soil':

"They represent them in the light of barbarians, equally jealous of their territory and their women, strongly united among themselves, but indifferent, if not hostile, to all intercourse with their neighbours. This unsocial disposition renders it difficult to gain any very satisfactory account of their customs and manners; but they are allowed to possess bravery, and a spirit of independence, which is exemplified by an obstinate resistance to all incroachments on their property, though unaccompanied by a disposition to interfere with that of others. Their industry and laborious habits are also admitted, as well as the comparative state of ease which these secure to them. Many retain the dress, and all have preserved the language, of their ancestors."

Since time immemorial the Italian peninsula, and specifically its toe, has been shaken to its core by catastrophic seismic events. Records date back to 91BCE when the Reggio Calabria area and it Sicilian neighbour Messina were reduced to rubble. Just over a hundred years later, the same area suffered again ... and yet again in the 4th century CE.

But the most devastating earthquakes to hit the region in the modern era were those of 1638, 1783, 1832 and 1908. The first three of these generally affected wider, more central, areas while the latter was once again centred on the Reggio/Messina area.

Of course there were many other earthquakes besides these and for those directly effected they were devastating events; nevertheless the two that seem to have become ingrained in the Calabrian psyche are those of 1638 and 1783.

It is almost impossible to imagine the extent to which these events have shaped the Calabrian landscape—geographic, social and political. Fortunately there is no shortage of observations and documentation for the years following the 1783 series of five earthquakes. Eight years later, Brian Hill (1791) observed some of the physical changes:

"The earth, for the space of two or three miles, seemed to be turned *topsy-turvy*, which indeed was literally the case, and we told that a man at work, with his oxen, was moved two miles without receiving any injury. Upon some parts of this hill the ground sounded hollow under our feet."

Hill also commented on one of the social repercussions:

"[travellers] have every real danger to encounter ... especially from the gangs of banditti, which have considerably increased, and become more desperate since the dreadful earthquake of 1783; inasmuch that even the barons of the soil dare not move half a mile from their own habitations without being accompanied with armed guards."

That said, Hill and his party never encountered any of these 'banditti'.

The political landscape changed too. The government ordered a state of emergency and funded relief in the short-term which it expected others to pay in the long-term. It did this by setting up the *Cassa Sacra* (literally the Sacred Fund) to facilitate reconstruction ... except that it didn't quite work out as planned.

The idea was that the government sequestered the assets of the ecclesiastical properties in the affected areas to create the fund. Many innovative landowners received money from the fund to put into practice some of the reforming ideas that they apparently expected would replace the feudal system and create a new class of hard-working peasant farmers.

When the church lands were put under the hammer, it cannot have been a big surprise that it was the wealthiest and not the 'hard-working peasant' that had the means to take advantage of the land on offer. Ultimately

Provinces.	Population in 1828.	Principal Town.	Districts (or Sott' Intendenze).
Calabria Citeriore (Northern Calabria, or Province of Cosenza)	406,359	Cosenza	Cosenza, Castrovillari, Paola, Rossano
Seconda Calabria Ulteriore (Central Calabria, or Province of Catanzaro)	298,239	Catanzaro	Catanzaro, Monteleone, Nicastro, Cotrone
Prima Calabria Ulteriore (Southern Calabria, or Province of Reggio)	260,633	Reggio	Reggio, Palmi, Gerace

Edward Lear (1847) appended a table to explain Calabria's organisation in 1847.

therefore nothing changed for the peasant class: they remained poor and the church land they might have once worked was now in new hands. They had been dealt a double-whammy: first their homes were destroyed, then the government did the much the same to their livelihoods.

The *Cassa Sacra* was dissolved amid controversy in 1796; it has been estimated that 740 thousand ducats was spent on reconstruction while some 448 thousand ducats was spent on administration.

In today's parlance *Cassa Sacra* could also mean 'sacred cash-register' or 'sacred check-out'.

With two notable breaks, it was the Bourbon regime of the Two Sicilies that was most associated with those whose Grand Tour took them south to Calabria during the 18th and 19th centuries.

The two 'breaks' came in 1799 and from 1806 to 1815 and were a direct result of the radical social and political movements that were abroad in Europe at the time, the first—and historically the most significant—being the French Revolution of 1789. Ultimately the Revolution brought Napoleon to power and its influence and his armies spread (the French Revolutionary Wars) throughout Europe until, in 1799, most of the southern Italian peninsula was part of the so-called Parthenopean Republic.

It is no accident that there were no British travellers who wrote about being in Calabria between Brian Hill in 1791 and Richard Keppel-Craven in 1818. What is curious is that Brian Hill failed to mention the monumental events that began only two years earlier in France.

The Parthenopean Republic was a short-lived period of less than six months when The Two Sicilies became a republic after King Ferdinand expeditiously took to his heels when he saw the writing on the wall in the shape of the advancing French troops. It was an anti-revolutionary ideal that caused Ferdinand himself to instigate hostilities against the French, aided and abetted by the British when Admiral Nelson visited Naples in 1798. But it all back-fired and by January 1799 the Kingdom was in republican hands and Ferdinand and his court safely reposing in Palermo. Referring to Ferdinand's unopposed foray into Rome the previous year, one contemporary satirist wrote of him: 'He came, he saw, he fled'.

Less than six months later it was all reversed following one of the bloodiest and most uncompromising periods in the history of the south and Calabria in particular.

The Calabrian element was personified by Cardinal Fabrizio Ruffo who, as a lieutenant of the exiled monarch, was sent to Calabria to organise a counter-revolution. Ruffo was not actually a member of the clergy at all and was born into a wealthy family from the small coastal community of San Lúcido, south of Páola. (Today there remain in Calabria many important buildings and castles the still bear the 'Ruffo' insignia.)

Nor was Ruffo a military leader, nevertheless he took his new job seriously and, once in Calabria, began recruiting for the so-called Christian Army of the Holy Faith. The accepted notion has been that he didn't seem to mind that his conscripts consisted mainly of unruly and undisciplined brigands, convicts, peasants and a smattering of ex-soldiers. Likewise the fact that the story of their 'liberating' march north involved terrible atrocities against people and places that appeared to support the new republic.

Norman Douglas (1911), the first British traveller to refer to Ruffo, did so over a hundred years later and didn't mince his words about events at Altamura in southern Apulia:

"Who would not like to spend a day at Altamura, if only in memory of its treatment by the ferocious Cardinal Ruffo and his army of cut-throats? After a heroic but vain resistance ... during which every available metal, and even money, was converted into bullets to repel the assailers, there followed a three days' slaughter of young and old; then the cardinal blessed his army and pronounced, in the blood-drenched streets, a general absolution. Even this man has discovered apologists. No cause so vile, that some human being will not be found to defend it."

This account is remarkably similar to the following from Eric Whelpton (1957):

"For over three days, the unfortunate inhabitants had to endure the wholesale plundering, raping and destruction that were the lot of a captured city in a barbarian age. Terror-stricken, they had to watch the peasants from the Sila carrying away all their household goods.

"At the end of it all, the Cardinal celebrated a *Te Deum* [a hymn of praise] in one of the principal squares of the city, after which he gave solemn absolution to his soldiers for any of the sins that they might have committed during the course of the siege."

But Whelpton was not speaking about Altamura in Apulia, he was referring to earlier events at Crotone in Calabria.

While there was clearly plunder and bloodshed at both locations, the very similarity of the descriptions has some of the hallmarks of collusion and propaganda directed specifically at Ruffo; it's almost as if in their original form they were both penned by the same hand and indeed they were ... the original scribe was Pietro Colletta, a judge in the Parthenopean Republic.

Ruffo undoubtedly had responsibility as the one in charge on the ground but his correspondence with his erstwhile colleague and first minister in the Naples government, the Englishman Sir John Acton, seems to suggest that he himself had little sympathy with the indiscipline of his followers, some elements of whom he had clearly lost control over.

But then Acton was Ruffo's commander, the power behind the throne and the lover of the Bourbon Queen Maria Carolina, herself the driving force against the French republic from Sicily, her place of exile. (Apparently her husband, King Ferdinand, was happy to go along with anything that didn't interrupt his hunting trips.) It was Queen Carolina and Acton who gave Ruffo the *carte blanche* to rampage through Calabria and the south so perhaps Ruffo's correspondence with Acton was perhaps no more than an attempt to be seen to distance himself from his army's outrages.

If he did hold a mass for his 'soldiers' at Altamura and/or Crotone, then he can scarcely complain about their excesses while at the same time absolving them of their sins. Nevertheless that is exactly what he did in a letter to Acton after he and this 'army of cut-throats' finally entered Naples:

"The responsibility of governing, although it would be more accurate to say trying to control, a people raised in total anarchy and of giving orders to twenty illiterate and insubordinate leaders of irregular troops, all of whom have no interest other than plunder, massacre, rape and violence, is something so horrible that it quite exceeds my strength!"

At Naples Ruffo's men joined forces with Frà Diavolo who had been directing his own version of anti-republican barbarity in the north.

Frà Diavolo, whose real name was Michele Pezza, hailed from Itri in today's province of Latina close to the Appian Way. During the Parthenopean Republic he made his headquarters nearby at Fortino di Sant'Andrea from where he orchestrated violent and vicious resistance to the republic, much of his venom revenge-fuelled by the earlier death of his father at the hands of the French.

That he and his men were adept at murder and torture is undisputed nor that they directed many atrocities against the French and their supporters. On one occasion Cardinal Ruffo even had him arrested for his alleged atrocities. The fact that he was subsequently released can perhaps be laid at the feet of the exiled queen, Ferdinand's wife Maria Carolina, who was a keen supporter of Frà Diavolo's barbaric endeavours and more than once didn't see eye to eye with Cardinal Ruffo.

I have dwelt over long on this short episode in Calabrian history—the Parthenopean Republic only lasted six months—for two related reasons.

Firstly, it is an example of how the accepted history of the period, as voiced by Norman Douglas, Eric Whelpton and others—that Ruffo was the archetypal 'baddie'—is, like Ruffo himself, flawed. His on-going correspondence with Sir John Acton suggests he was endeavouring to eliminate excesses and to encourage, rather than coerce, pro-republican people and places into changing sides.

If this stratagem was ever effective, it has become lost in the mists of time so that only the record of massacres and injustices remains in the collective psyche ... to the 'victor' often goes the honour of writing the history. His distaste for the actions of Frà Diavolo suggests there were limits to what, in a time of bitter and polarised conflict, he considered an acceptable level of behaviour. His over-riding crime seems to have been his inability to control his makeshift, feckless and disparate army coupled with gross political naivety. Publicly absolving the terrible excesses of his followers, in the name of the church and the crown, only gave them the freedom to act in the same way again elsewhere. And, of course, they did.

Nevertheless part of Ruffo's legacy is a recognition of the ease with which polarising events such as what happened in just six turbulent months came to dominate much of the subsequent political and social landscape of the southern peninsula.

Secondly, the Bourbon regime's official and brutal reaction to the

The two men most responsible for the overthrow of the Parthenopean Republic, Cardinal Fabrizio Ruffo (a Calabrian) and Michele Pezza known as 'Frà Diavolo'.

Parthenopean Republic, as personified by Cardinal Ruffo and Frà Diavolo, was the benchmark by which all future anti-Bourbon regimes were dealt with; political brigandage was here to stay and some Calabrians seemed particularly good at it.

As we shall see in a later chapter, during the second interruption to Bourbon rule, between 1806 and 1815 when the Napoleonic regime was in power, the same thing happened and anti-French, politically-inspired, brigandage was, in the early years at least, rampant and brutal. And Frà Diavolo put in another appearance too as the leader of an anti-French guerrilla group until, in 1806, he was caught, tried and executed in Naples. By 1811, aided and abetted by some pretty ruthless policing, such resistance had all but died out.

Later in the century, much the same thing happened when the Bourbon regime was once again overwhelmed as part of the unification process in 1860/61. The political brigands and other lawless individuals once more took to the hills in support of the Bourbons and the status quo.

But back to the second break in Bourbon rule when, in 1806, the Two Sicilies that was, became a Napoleonic state, though in reality Sicily was never annexed by the French and continued to be ruled by King Ferdinand from Palermo.

Despite the initial opposition and the excesses of both the brigands and those seeking to eliminate them, this was a time of profound change in the southern Italian peninsula, a time when many of the good things about post-revolutionary France became part of the southern Italian landscape.

Even the British travellers, brought up on anti-French diet before, during and after the Napoleonic Wars—including the 1806 Battle of Máida between the French and the British on Calabrian soil—saw the good points. Richard Keppel-Craven was the first traveller to experience life in Calabria after French rule; the following relates to the local police (gendarmes) in Apulia but applied equally to Calabria:

"This corps, which had been established by the French upon the same footing as in their own country, is certainly the most useful of any in time of peace, and although employed in offices which must necessarily be partially obnoxious to the lower orders, it is as universally respected as it is deserving."

He observed too that their were encouraging improvements to the road from Naples south:

"The carriage-road leading from the capital [Naples] towards Calabria had originally not been carried beyond Lago Negro [in north-west Basilicata], to which spot the diligences had consequently been limited. The French resumed the work, as I have before observed, and extended it somewhat beyond Cosenza; but still none of the public conveyances go further than Lago Negro, from whence it is necessary for the traveller to proceed with hired horses and vehicles.

"This may appear one of the strongest proofs of the attachment of the natives to their ancient habits, or show more unequivocally the little occasion existing for such facility of communication."

It might also be proof that some locals still were not happy to engage with something, even a good road, that had tenuous links to the French.

On the other hand, as Craufurd Tait Ramage (1828) noted, not all things French were considered unworkable:

"The French certainly conferred a great benefit on the country by reforming the legal code, which before their time, exhibited a strange incongruous mass. This part of Italy had been in the possession of Normans, Lombards, French, Spaniards Germans, and each in their turn had added to the laws already in force. The Code Napoleon now, however, supersedes these multifarious enactments, modified, indeed by the immemorial customs of the country, though it was not without a struggle that it maintained its ground on the return of the Bourbons, They made an attempt to re-establish the ancient order of things; the benefit of the change, however, had become so evident, that the most devoted friends of the Bourbons insisted that the organic law of Murat should be continued, and Ferdinand I was obliged to yield."

'Murat' was Joachim Murat, the brother-in-law of Napoleon and from 1808, King of Naples; between 1806 and 1808 Napoleon's brother Joseph Boneparte was king.

Ask any Calabrian to name a southern politician or leader before Garibaldi and the likely answer will be Joachim Murat. As we shall see in a later chapter, he was a charismatic leader who instigated many positive changes during his seven years in power, initiatives that frequently withstood the test of time. Even the British travellers seemed to have a fondness for him despite his familial connections. And no-one who visited Pizzo, near what was then Monte Leone, could resist retelling the story of the events that led to his untimely death there. But only one got the story right.

―∞―

Life in post-Napoleonic Calabria had returned to a degree of normality: the rich were still rich, the poor still poor and a few more Grand Tour travellers once again ventured south in search of brigandage, hospitality and Magna Græcia. The re-established Bourbon monarchy now presided over the Kingdom of the Two Sicilies, but their power was increasingly fragile as, throughout the European mainland, the winds of social and political change were wafting their way in and around the old order.

By the middle of the century the Grand Tour had all but run its course; the middle- and working-classes were on the ascendency and the privileged classes were increasingly under pressure and being made more aware of the injustices emanating from their very privilege.

This time too saw the burgeoning of the age of 'isms', particularly conservatism, socialism, liberalism and nationalism, that was to take Europe by storm in 1848 when their were revolutions right across the continent including France, Germany, Denmark, Hungary, Poland ... and Italy. At the time the inspirational 'ism' of choice throughout the Italian peninsula was generally nationalism.

Calabria got in on the act a little earlier than others with two false starts at Cosenza and Crotone in 1844 followed by something a little more full-blooded in 1847 in and around Reggio Calabria where Edward Lear happened to be at the time.

The Cosenza 'uprising' in March was both short-lived and fatal for the participants. Nevertheless it was one of the events that, three months later, inspired the failed Bandiera brothers' attempt at igniting a bid for Italian unity when they landed near Crotone. Nothing went according to plan, if indeed there was a plan, and those who weren't killed en route ended up in Cosenza as prisoners where they were tried and executed. On the plus side their martyrdom has since made them something of a *cause célèbre* in the Crotone area ... more of which later.

Three years later, towards the end of his travels in Calabria, Edward Lear had recrossed the Straits of Messina back to Reggio Calabria following a day-trip to Sicily; he immediately set off to explore the coast and countryside south and east of the city and spent the night at Mélito di Porto Salvo, Calabria's southernmost town. It was 1 September 1847.

Lear didn't much care for the 'ill-kept villa' of his host Don Pietro Tropæa: "... for albeit Don Pietro gave me a most friendly welcome, it is not to be disguised that his casino was one of the dirtiest; and when I contemplated the ten dogs and a very unpleasant huge tamed sheep, which animated his rooms, I congratulated myself that I was not to abide long with him."

But, over and above the noisome odours emanating from ten dogs and a lone sheep, there was something in the air of more concern to the well-off Tropæa family and their ilk ... you could almost touch the smell of revolution:

"Moreover, it appeared to me that some evil, general or particular, was brooding over the household, which consisted of a wife, haggard and dirty in appearance, and agitated in a very painful degree; an only son, wild and terrified in every look; and a brother and nephew from Montebello [a few miles inland], strange, gloomy, and mysterious in aspect and manner."

The Tropæa family, from the more privileged end of Calabria's social spectrum, was clearly ill at ease and when the sound of gunfire was heard Don Pietro's wife, Donna Lucia, burst into tears and left the room. The family's anxiety continued and, over dinner, Lear was quizzed about what he'd heard and seen when he passed through Reggio earlier that day. Insisting that he hadn't experienced anything untoward didn't seem to satisfy the edgy Tropæa family and so Lear decided that silence was the best policy:

"It was useless to protest [ignorance], and I perceived that a sullen ill-will was the only feeling prevalent towards me from persons who seemed positive that I would give no information on a subject they insisted in declaring I fully understood. So I remained silent, when another brother from Montebello was suddenly announced, and after a few whispers a scene of alarm and horror ensued."

Don Pietro's announcement that the revolution had already begun was followed by even more scenes of great distress which Lear described with the acumen of the writer of farce. More farce was to follow when, in bed at last, he found his slumbers interrupted by what he thought might have been a female intruder under his bed … his first forlorn hope was that he was 'to encounter some real Calabrian romance'. Alas it was but 'the large dirty tame sheep'; he opened the door and with a stick he unceremoniously ejected his 'domestic tormentor'.

The next morning, on 2 September 1847, the day Reggio's revolution officially started, none of the Tropæa household, not even the sheep, was around when Lear and his muleteer, Ciccio, set off again on their travels.

They lunched at Montebello at the home of Don Pietro Amazichi where once again Lear was quizzed about what he'd heard and seen in Reggio the day before. Again Lear protested his ignorance but nobody was convinced:

"It is impossible … you only left Reggio yesterday, it is true; but it is certain that the revolution broke out last night, and everyone has known for days past what would happen."

Don Pietro's wife started to wail about the imagined fate of her two sons (supposedly in Reggio) which touched a nerve in Lear, unable as he was to give them any further information.

After another afternoon and evening on the road Lear and Ciccio re-entered

CALABRIA

Reggio at one in the morning when, at long last, everything was revealed:

"How strange was the scene! All the quiet town was brilliantly lighted up, and every house illuminated; no women or children were visible, but troops of men, by twenties and thirties, all armed, and preceded by bands of music and banners ... were parading the high street from end to end."

Ciccio explained that the revolution had clearly started so, after a fruitless conversation with a drunk waiter at their hotel about love, liberty, friendship and the constitution, Lear decided to find out exactly what was going on and headed for the house of an acquaintance, Cavaliere da Nava:

"From him, whom with his family I found in serious distress, I heard that a concerted plot had broken out on the preceding day; that all the Government officials had been seized, and the Government suspended, he (da Nava), the Intendente [Land Agent], and others being confined to their houses. That the telegraph and the castle still held out, but would be attacked in a day or two; that the insurgents, consisting mostly of young men from the neighbouring towns and villages, had already marched into Reggio, and were hourly increasing in number, that on the opposite shore, Messina was also in full revolt; and that the future arrangements of the Government could only be known after time had been allowed for telegraphic communication between Reggio and Naples."

Led by Domenico Romeo and other members of his extended family, the September 2 revolution failed to achieve anything. The 'revolutionaries' were split into two factions, political agitators and a more hooligan element ... it was some of the latter who had tried to start the revolution the evening before. The tricolour flag flew on the castle for two days only and by 15 September it was all over and its leaders dead.

Although this particular revolution was short-lived, the political runes were not good for those in power in the Italian peninsula, particularly in the Kingdom of the Two Sicilies. The movement for unification of all the Italian states was gathering pace, fuelled as it was by the largely bankrupt northern states who saw their salvation in the wealth of the south.

I recall studying this period of Italian history at school where the impression given was that the overwhelming climate of opinion was that everything should and was progressing inevitably to the only credible logic—an Italian state that was synonymous with the peninsula. It just seemed to be such an obvious and rational outcome.

The only real political utterance from those who travelled in Calabria *after* the events of 1860/61 came from Edward Hutton (1912) who clearly had read the same version of Italian history that I did:

"The last years of the Kingdom were as wretched as it deserved and as we might expect. Then by God's grace, out of the north came Garibaldi, who, having conquered Sicily and taken Calabria too by violence, entered Naples on September 7, 1860. On October 1 the battle of Volturno was fought, and won by the Piedmontese; Frances of Bourbon retired to Gaeta, where after a fine resistance he capitulated on February 12, 1861. Piedmont had made a free gift of liberty to Naples, which became part of the Kingdom of United Italy upon November 7, 1860."

Put like that it all sounds pretty clear cut, inevitable even, but, as we shall see, as far as many southerners were concerned, it was not quite so straightforward.

The bones of Hutton's synopsis just need a little more clarification: Garibaldi and his thousand 'red-shirts' landed first in Sicily in May 1860 and, having 'liberated' the island, crossed to Calabria in July and made landfall at Mélito di Porto Salvo where Edward Lear had spend such an uncomfortable night in 1847.

Garibaldi burgeoning army headed north, 'liberating' the south as they went and reached Naples in September. The following month the nature of this 'revolution'—if, indeed, it were ever in doubt—became clear when, at Teano north of Naples, Garibaldi met the Piedmontese monarch, Vittorio Emanuele II and effectively handed him the south. The Bourbon king,

The popular caricature of Guiseppe Garibaldi and his red-shirted army on their way to glory and the unification of the Italian peninsula.

Francesco II, held out at Gaeta—on the coast between Naples and Rome—until February. The Papal States did not at this time become part of a united Italy, their independence having been guaranteed by the French Emperor, Napoleon III, who had a garrison stationed at Rome as security.

The Kingdom of Naples was no more and its lands part of a politically united Italy. Garibaldi departed temporarily from the scene and left it to the politicians to oversee the mopping up which effectively meant that, economically, the resources of the south was systematically moved north.

There then followed a period of instability in the south which in many quarters grew into out-and-out rebellion against the new regime which in turn created a new class of political brigand—agitators and guerillas who vehemently and violently opposed the new order. It was in this climate of disarray, disunity and lawlessness too that the mafia found its feet and found it all too easy to increasingly exploit and even control the situation.

The first capital of the new Italy was Turin (1861-1864), then Florence (1864-1871) before, in 1871, Rome became the country's permanent capital … well, almost … for seventeen months towards the end of the Second World War, Brindisi in Apulia was the temporary capital.

Though Garibaldi had left the scene when unification was assured, in 1862 he did briefly try to re-enact the glory days when, for the second time, he landed with two thousand followers at Mélito in Calabria. His aim on this occasion was to annex Rome; he believed it was time the Papal States were brought into line and into a united Italy. The logic of this enterprise seemed robustly clear and he assumed that he would encounter little resistance.

In this latter respect he was, with respect to the Calabrians, correct but the new nation's legitimate army didn't see it that way and had orders to stop him in his tracks. This they did in the Aspromonte mountains where Garibaldi was shot in the foot.

In the decades immediately following unification, the south, and Calabria in particular, became even more impoverished and marginalised than it had previously been and many people voted with their feet and left their homeland completely. Most went to North America though many also went to South America—and to Argentina in particular—and to Australia.

Generally there were two major waves of emigration from Calabria and the south: the late 19th and the early 20th centuries and again following the Second World War in the 1950s and 1960s. Specifically from within Calabria, there were many who left the Reggio Calabria region in the wake

1905 earthquake but many more following the more devastating 1908 quake.

In 1893, in the small town of Bisignano, near Acri in the province of Cosenza, was born Angelo Siciliano.

At the age of eleven Angelo and his parents, Angelo and Francesca, headed for Naples and boarded the steamship *Lahn* and two gruelling weeks later arrived at Ellis Island, New York. In February 1904 the Siciliano family set up home in Brooklyn where there was already a burgeoning Calabrian community including other family members.

As teenagers, both Angelo and I had something in common—we were both a bit on the weedy side. Angelo did something about it but all I did was wonder whether, if I subscribed to the special offer in my comic advertising the famous body-building programme of Charles Atlas, would I actually ever really look like him? If I pursued Atlas's 'dynamic Tension' programme, would I, as the adverts suggested, really become a new man in just a week?

I decided to hang on to my money and let nature take its course.

Angelo Siciliano, on the other hand, did do something about his weedy frame for Angelo Siciliano changed his name to Charles Atlas; Angelo Siciliano *was* Charles Atlas, the personification of the male American Dream, the man who had changed from a seven-stone weakling to become 'the world's most perfectly developed man'.

The jury is still out on whether or not *I* made the right decision.

In the first half century after unification, Italy was trying to establish itself as a late-arrival in the European scramble for empire; by this time France, Spain, Portugal, Britain and the Netherlands had already carved up most of the undeveloped world. Getting in late on the act was a major problem and many Calabrians found themselves in the horn of Africa (the Somali peninsula) as part of the armed forces who were trying to establish a foothold there in the 1890s. Early in the new century the war against the Ottoman Empire resulted in the annexation of parts of Libya in 1912.

Three years later, and despite an earlier pact with Germany, Italy entered the First World War on the side of the allies. The promises that secured Italy's support, as set out in the Treaty of London, never materialised. In common parlance, Italy was well and truly shafted which was certainly a contributory factor in the rise of Benito Mussolini in the early 1920s and the subsequent take-over of power by the fascists in October 1922.

Coincidentally this was just eight months after the election of a new pope, Pius XI, who called Mussolini 'the man of Providence' and who, recent research confirms, was initially happy to work alongside a dictator.

It is interesting how in the south one bigger, stronger group of thugs, the fascist government, tried to squeeze out another, the mafia. In 1925 Mussolini (known as *Il Duce*, the leader) effectively declared war on the mafia in all its incarnations—Sicilian, Neapolitan and Calabrian—when he proclaimed "Everything in the State, nothing outside the State, nothing against the State".

On the ground the leader of this crusade was Cesari Mori, who earlier had been nominated for a prefecture at Reggio Calabria but had wanted to remain Rome-based at the time. His subsequent nickname, *Il Prefetto di Ferro*, the iron prefect, succinctly explained his ethos and approach; in Calabria in 1932 ninety people were put on trial accused of being members of the mafia which, at the time, was known as *La Famiglia Montelbano*.

In 1939 Benito Mussolini made a whistle-stop tour of Calabria and held rallies at Crotone, Catanzaro, Vibo Valéntia, Reggio Calabria and Cosenza on March 30 and 31. People flocked to the main squares of the cities, not just locals but hundreds of villagers from the surrounding countryside. A visit from Mussolini had the draw of the modern rock star.

At Crotone the crowds, strictly and strategically arranged to display the various local fascist child and youth groups, waited for hours in the square which was closed off for the occasion; they were not allowed to leave either to eat or to the bathroom. Mussolini was supposed to arrive at ten in the morning but didn't make an appearance till the early afternoon and even then only reluctantly did he agree to say a few words to the assembled masses:

"Calabrians, Calabria has to stride forward, and it will do so."

At a massive rally for the faithful in Reggio Calabria the following day, he was only a little more loquacious:

"The impressions of my first day in Calabria are very deep. The Calabria region, for so long neglected, progressed during the initial seventeen years of fascism."

The smell of war in Europe was in the air—Mussolini's alliance with Hitler in May brought forward the inevitable—and, with the propaganda value of the recent completion of the new road along the Ionian coast from Apulia to Reggio Calabria fresh in people's minds, the timing was perfect to rally and inspire young Calabrians to the cause. When the hour approached they would be like lambs to the slaughter.

In his Calabrian speeches he failed to mention the inevitable outcome of his 1938 Manifesto of Race and that, like Hitler, he would need to plan for how and where to deal with 'undesirables' such as the Jews at whom the Manifest was aimed. By 1940 he had decided that the Calabrian province of Cosenza was just the place and in the summer of that year, a camp at Ferramonte close to Tarsia was hastily constructed and opened. This was no holiday camp but a new home for the country's Jews and political dissidents; it was a concentration camp.

Over 3800 were imprisoned here, only 141 of whom were actually Italian Jews … most of the remainder were from other European Jewish communities.

Ferramonte was never like Auschwitz or Buchenwald; there was no 'final solution' in Italy. Generally the Manifesto of Race was viewed as an unpopular piece of legislation that had been imported from Germany. Nevertheless for those families who were deprived of their liberty and livelihood, it was a terrible and terrifying experience.

The Ferramonte camp closed in September 1943 and today it is open to the public … a time to remember and a place to forget.

For us it is difficult to understand why it is that some of the elderly still hold on to fond memories of the Mussolini era though it seems much less of a taboo than having, say, the same feelings for Nazi Germany. It's nothing to do with the philosophy of fascism and all to do with stability and having a place in the order of things and a leader who, thanks to his propaganda machine, was seen by some to be a no-nonsense statesman and a fervent

Two faces of Italian Fascism. Six years before he was hung upside down in Milan, *Il Duce*, Benito Mussolini, gets a rapturous welcome from the citizens of Reggio Calabria in 1939. He also visited Cosenza, a few miles from which his regime later built the concentration camp at Ferramonte to incacerate Jews and other 'undesirables'.

Italian. The comparison is all too easy to make with some post-war Italian politicians, even in the recent past, who have been no more than crooks or a laughing stock and have not done justice to their country and its people.

Before it succumbed to the recession, we used to eat out regularly at a restaurant in the countryside a few miles from Santa Severina called Podere 22; in English 'Farm 22'. There are about twenty-five numbered farmhouses and adjoining land in the area between Altilia and Belvedere di Spinello, all built in the late-twenties by the Mussolini regime. From all accounts local peasant families in this part of the valley of the Neto, and elsewhere, were grateful for a government scheme that, unusually, recognised their needs.

Podere 22 had passed down through the generations and, by retaining its original designation, was a reminder that life was once so different in this pocket of Calabria.

Mussolini's fascist dictatorship came to an ignominious end, first at the hands of the Italians themselves and then at the hands of the allies: in July 1943 Mussolini was deposed and in September 1943 the Italian army surrendered and became part of the allied alliance the following month. Following a brief Hitler-assisted resurgence in parts of the peninsula, Mussolini was eventually captured and executed in April 1945. The war in Europe officially ended the following month with the unconditional surrender of Nazi Germany.

Despite the fact that in September 1943 Italy had, in effect, changed sides almost overnight, the period between then—when Mussolini and his allies were trying to refresh and regroup—and the end of the war in Europe was a period of uncompromising civil war in parts of Italy. On one side were the remnants of Mussolini's fascists and their cohorts, including German military still based in Italy, and on the other the Italian resistance or partisans, aided and abetted by the country's new allies, America, Britain and the Soviet Union.

In the south this was largely academic for units of the British Eighth Army crossed the Straits of Messina to Calabria the same month as part of a three-pronged, allied attack on the southern peninsula. The aim was to secure the ports of Reggio Calabria and Villa San Giovanni before taking the more strategic ports of Taranto in Apulia and Salerno in Campania.

There was little resistance in the south, neither German nor Italian, and as far as Calabria was concerned the war was soon over. Ironically much of the wartime damage that was inflicted on Calabria happened at this time when the retreating German army destroyed bridges and roads to thwart the allied advance. None of which could stop ordinary people from taking down the *Il Duce* banners and consigning them to the detritus of history.

Of course there were other Calabrians still in uniform in other parts of the country and Europe for whom the war remained very much a reality. One elderly man told me how, still dressed as a private in Mussolini's army, he was captured by the partisans and imprisoned near Genoa. But not for long for Mario Gerardi escaped and walked back home ... to Calabria. It took him a month and he survived by sleeping in abandoned outhouses or animal shelters and lived off whatever he could 'liberate' from the land.

Another local man, Leonardo Marzano, now in his mid-nineties and still with a razor-sharp mind, had the misfortune to be called up in late 1943 and, after training, was despatched to fight (for Italy's new allies) in Croatia where he was taken prisoner by the Germans. Eighteen days later, and after a horrendous journey cooped up with over fifty others in a railway wagon, he was a prisoner-of-war at Stalag VI-B near Meppen in Lower Saxony in north-west Germany where he saw out the remainder of the war. A month after being liberated by the Americans, Leonardo too was back in Calabria.

The experiences of both Mario and Leonardo were repeated all over Calabria in those troubled times.

The post-war period in Calabria was dominated by five things: agrarian reform, migration to northern Italy and southern Europe, emigration (particularly to the United States), the political success of the Christian

Mario Gerardi escaped from imprisonment near Genoa and walked back to Calabria. Leonardo Marzano was liberated from a German concentration camp in 1945; in 2015 he was presented with the *Medaglia d'Onore* in recognition of this and his extraordinary life.

Democrat (DC) party and the rise of mafia-related crime. All of which to varying degrees were interconnected.

Agrarian reform was long overdue and the sacrifices of the war years made it even more pressing in largely rural regions like Calabria where forty percent of the land was in the hands of fewer than two hundred landowners, most of whom added insult to injury by being absentee landowners.

In Calabria in 1949 things came to a head. The rural poor were not to be messed with and there were several incidents of dissent and led to outright revolt. One of these boiled over on 29 October that year when, according to an eye witness, things got out of hand at an estate at Melissa near Stróngoli:

"For months, bright and early, thousands of peasants, on foot and on their donkeys, flags and banners at the fore, had left towns such as Stróngoli, Cutro, Rocco di Neto, San Giovanni in Fiore, and headed for uncultivated properties, then divided up the land, fenced it off and started to turn over the soil. But on this ill-fated day, in the afternoon, around three hundred men, egged on in part by their extreme poverty and in part by those who wanted to take full advantage from the ensuing chaos, stormed the Fragalà estate."

The landowner, Baron Berlingiere, was not best pleased and there followed a skirmish between the protesters and the local police where shots were fired—who fired first remains in dispute—and two people were killed; a few hours later a young girl also died of her wounds. Subsequently these events became known as the Melissa Massacre.

(A less serious event involving the Baron may throw some light on who struck the first blow. It seems *he* did when, in Los Angeles on honeymoon in 1937, he struck his American wife because of her democratic attitude towards servants. She successfully sued for divorce on the grounds of cruelty.)

Incidents such as the events at the Fragalà estate sent the message to Rome that the south was on the cusp of open revolt. The DC government of Alcide de Gasperi was forced to respond quickly and positively which it did by embracing agrarian reform (the redistribution of land) and setting up the *Cassa per il Mezzogiorno*, a programme of state-funded initiatives to establish agrarian and industrial projects as well as improve the infrastructure of the southern regions with road and bridge-building projects and hydroelectric and irrigation schemes.

Already many had left the land and moved to the more industrialised north in search of work but migration was not for everyone and there were many tightly-knit Calabrian families and communities for whom it was not on the agenda. Thus agrarian reforms, and particularly the redistribution of land coupled with the *Cassa per il Mezzogiorno* brought hope. Of course the redistribution of land all depended on which land was going to be sequestered and where it was ... so it's not rocket science to guess what happened next.

Many landowners found ways round confiscation of their land; if they weren't able to divide their land between family members (smaller estates were exempt from confiscation) they found ways round the ambiguity intrinsic in the notion that only so-called 'unimproved' land was to be confiscated.

Yes, land was redistributed but generally it was not potentially the most productive and fertile land, nor was it necessarily where people wanted to live and work. For thousands of years Calabrians had lived in communities, often isolated communities but communities none the less. Leslie Gardiner (1966) observed the same on his train journey from Cosenza to Catanzaro:

"[From the train] you become aware of that other labour which the peasant adds to his daily toil: walking to work. Men, women and children, bent under their crude farming tools, tread the donkey-paths between the hamlets. Some of them put in a hundred miles a week, the engine-driver says. In the north of Italy it has always been the peasant's custom to live among his acres. In the south, he has always inhabited a citadel and commuted to his land."

Over many parts of the Calabrian landscape these farmhouses still exist, all in exactly the same mould, languishing in empty fields, their featureless forms overrun with ragged grasses; the land they guard no more fertile than it was three generations ago; and the next house along the abandoned track is just the same ... and the next ... and the next ... lonely reminders that noble ideas are not always discharged by noble men.

All such reforms, including the *Cassa per il Mezzogiorno (Casmez)*, were

A major agrarian *Cassa per il Mezzogiorno* project involved the reafforestation of parts of the Sila mountains in the 1950s.

An uninspiring tract of Calabrian land ... perfect, so it was thought, to construct small farmhouses to house rural families.

the brainchild of a government focussed on containing problems rather than solving them. The credit subsidies and tax advantages that they provided to encourage investment were embedded in cumbersome bureaucracies that had sufficient built-in loopholes to facilitate the squandering of funds meant to help ordinary Calabrian communities and the misappropriation of money and contracts into the hands of those who were more adept at political and financial manipulation ... into the hands of the mafia.

In Reggio Calabria, a city known to have a strong mafia presence, the Christian Democrats (DC) were in power without a break from 1946 to 1983; at various times it remained in power thanks to political alliances with the Italian Republican Party (PRI), the Italian Liberal Party (PLI) and the Italian Democratic Socialist Party (PSDI). The south was the DC's power base but nationally the party was in power throughout the same period except for a short break of eighteen months in 1981-82; in addition, from 1972 to 1992, the DC's Giulio Andreotti was Prime Minister seven times.

Andreotti was strongly suspected of having had links to the mafia and in the nineties was tried and acquitted of being a *mafioso* himself though the question of whether or not he had the sorts of indirect connections that gave succour to mafia bosses, remains a topic of discussion. Giulio Andreotti died in 2013.

That the mafia successfully infiltrated the Christian Democrats in Calabria is common knowledge and it all started back in post-war Calabria when the infrastructure was at it weakest and the money was there to help ... the word 'cassa' in the *Cassa per il Mezzogiorno* also means cash-register in Italian. For the mafia that is exactly what it became, the construction of the massive container port at Gioia Tauro being just one example.

Together the bureaucracy and the misappropriation of funds meant that for many southerners, particularly those in rural communities, nothing changed in the first decade after the war. So many people evolved an agrarian reform of their own and left the land and migrated to the north of Italy where there was always work and, in Calabrian terms, well-paid work. Those who were a little more adventurous went to Germany to work in the burgeoning manufacturing sector and in the car and construction industries in particular.

Following an agreement between Italian and German governments in 1955, many Calabrians headed for the expanding car industry in Germany and by 1960, 200,000 Italian workers, mostly from the south, were working for Volkswagen alone.

By the 1970s, these workers were so important to the Volkswagon company that a special train served Lamezia and went directly to the Volkswagon works in Wolfsburg. One of the many to take advantage of this service was a young Calabrian man who had been working previously as a *cantoniere*, a road worker. Once again, Mario Gerardi, the escapee who had walked from Genova to Calabria at the end of the war, was heading north—though this time by choice. Mario became a so-called 'guest' worker for Volkswagen.

But Volkswagen was not the only employer and Germany not the only destination for others went to Holland and France, indeed anywhere there was steady work and good money. In 1961 over 100,000 Italians were recruited to work in the construction sector in Germany alone.

Most of those who migrated did, of course, return to their communities but with cash in their pockets with which they were able to buy a good plot of land and a little three-wheeled, agrarian workhorse, the *Ape,* to get there and back; their version of agrarian reform eliminated all possibilities of weighty bureaucracy and mafia infiltration. And those, like Mario Gerardi, who went to Germany and only saw their growing families once or twice a year, came back too with the certainty of a pension in later life.

While at Luzzi near Cosenza, Leslie Gardiner (1966) was watching the Easter procession when there was a bit of a kerfuffle—a man had been shot. It turned out that he had just returned on the special train from Munich for the Easter celebrations and had unceremoniously been gunned down by his *fidanzata* (anything from girlfriend to betrothed). Apparently she had learnt that he had another *fidanzata* in Munich and now wanted nothing to do with her. Just one of the hazards of working abroad.

It would be wrong to be totally disparaging about the *Cassa per il*

For the mafia a licence to print money: one of the largest *Casmez* projects was the container port at Gioia Tauro and Rosarno in the 70s

Italian migrant workers arriving in Wolfsburg, home to Volkswagen, to do their bit for the regeneration of the German car industry and to earn more than they ever could have back in Calabria.

Mezzogiorno for there were many projects—dams, hydro-electric schemes, reafforestation, road-building—that were completed and did benefit the Calabrian community but, for some, it was too little too late and once again many decided to vote with their feet. In the 1960s there was another wave of emigration, particularly to north America where there was plenty of work and good prospects, albeit in a foreign language.

When I travelled to the States to research *Thank You Uncle Sam*, not one of the Calabrian families I visited who had emigrated during this period had any regrets. Yes, they missed their extended Calabrian families and for some the early years had been hard but they believed they made the right choice; some said the *only* choice. And these days with cheaper flights and the internet, families don't seem quite so far away.

When Eric Whelpton visited Calabria in 1957 the *Cassa per il Mezzogiorno* was in its infancy (it was finally wound up in 1984); this is what he wrote about the agrarian reforms:

"The peasants in their newly acquired farms are being taught modern methods of agriculture, and their production should increase sufficiently to provide work for people of all trades in the country districts.

"With greater prosperity, Calabria should offer a vast market for goods of all kinds, for the demand is there but the people are too poor to buy at the present moment."

Eric Whelpton was optimistic and certainly Calabria and Calabrians did eventually live up to some of his expectations but the prosperity he suggested was just around the corner was instead at the end of a very, very long curve.

And Henry Morton had this to say in 1967 through rose-tinted spectacles:

"The transformation of Calabria, if the word is not too strong, dates from 1950 when the Italian Government established the Southern Italy Development Fund — the *Cassa del Messogiorno* [sic]— which has poured millions into the south, and continues to do so, making roads, introducing industries, reclaiming land, draining, irrigating, even restoring ancient castles and cathedrals."

His observations were, to a point, justified; billions were indeed poured in, but the value of those billions never matched the real improvements on the ground nor the speed of change. One simple example (which I will elaborate on later) was the A3 *autostrada* project: started in 1966; finished in 1974; *upgrading* began almost immediately; at the time of writing it is still not complete. The reasons: sub-standard work and the mafia.

Together with Belgium, France, Luxembourg, the Netherlands and West

Germany, Italy was one of the founding members of the European Economic Community created in 1957 by the Treaty of Rome; since 1993 it has been known simply as the European Community and at present constitutes some twenty-eight countries including many from what was eastern Europe, former satellites of the Soviet Union.

As one of the poorer relations in both Italian and European terms, over the years Calabria has benefitted from European funding ... unfortunately some of this also started to go AWOL as soon as the mafia discovered how to work the system.

What is so frustrating about all of this is that, if all the money that was allocated to projects in Calabria and other parts of the south—whether from the *Cassa per il Mezzogiorno* or the European Union—had been used as intended, then today's Calabria would be quite different. Those corrupt politicians and *mafiosi* who have made the misappropriation and redirection of funds into an art-form, have done immeasurable damage to their own backyard; they are no more than callous, greedy, cynical and egotistical freebooters.

In 1970, as part of a state-initiated decentralisation of government, fifteen regions were created which would have their own administrative councils and a local parliament which would give them a degree of local autonomy. One of these was Calabria but the announcement of the region's new capital and administrative centre, Catanzaro, did not go down well in Reggio Calabria which in turn led to the so-called Reggio Riots.

The riots in Reggio initiated by the choice of Catanzaro as regional capital; 'representatives' of nearby Motta San Giovanni urge people to hang on in there and not to capitulate.

The initial riots were spontaneous, fuelled by anger at what the people of Reggio thought was a foregone conclusion and then saw as a snub. The riots soon escalated, led and fermented by those who had much to lose, a neo-fascist coalition called the Italian Social Movement (MSI) and the *'ndrangheta*, the Calabrian mafia which, since the mid-fifties, had acquired for itself a nice new name.

It goes without saying that the *'ndrangheta* had the most to lose for Reggio Calabria was its power base and with their political contacts and manipulative skills already in place—as well as many *confidente* in high places—they could have expected millions of lire to come their way in the wake of reorganisation. To say they were not best pleased is an understatement.

The riots went from local to national, to international news and lasted from July 1970 to February 1971 when a compromise was finally reached. Catanzaro would be the Calabria's regional capital and therefore the seat of the regional administration; Reggio Calabria would become the seat of the regional parliament.

(Further reorganisation in 1992 planned for the division of Calabria's largest province, Catanzaro, with the creation the two smaller provinces of Vibo Valéntia and Crotone; the former having been part of the south-west of Catanzaro, the latter the north-east. This came to fruition in 1995.)

The seventies was the decade that put Calabria on the international map for all the wrong reasons. First the riots in Reggio Calabria and the hints of mafia involvement. And then, in 1973, the kidnapping for ransom of John Paul Getty Jnr, the grandson of oil tycoon Jean Paul Getty ... and again the hints of mafia involvement. The media made sure that people knew where Calabria was and the impression given was that it was a lawless place, a notion confirmed when stories of past brigandage were aired to a wider audience.

But ironically it was the media, and specifically television, that probably did more to change Calabrian society and helped bring about many of the changes that we associate with the modern world. Even in 1967, Henry Morton, having stumbled upon a group of elderly men in a bar in the Sila mountains watching a mannequin parade from Milan, wondered whether television had 'done more than Garibaldi for the true unification of Italy'.

Just as these days most people expect to have a mobile phone, from the late sixties Calabrians felt the same about television; like their northern counterparts, they wanted to watch Italy win soccer's European Cup in 1968, witness the first man on the moon in 1969, cheer Italy on in the final of soccer's World Cup in 1970, see Angie Dickenson as the dubbed star of *Police Woman* and be in the front line when it was all in colour from the late 1970s.

And over the years television became the great leveller in two respects: with this new window on the world, Calabrians saw no reason why they shouldn't have the same choices in life as others and they therefore expected their politicians to work harder to make it happen; and, besides, weren't all those adverts for cookers, cars and cosmetics aimed at Calabrians too?

Also, on television everyone spoke Italian—even Americans, British and all other foreigners (Italians will dub anything and everything and are very good at it)—so gradually the hundreds of localised Calabrian dialects started to take second place to standardised Italian.

In 1971 Calabria did not have a university; yet before the turn of the new millennium it had three. In 1972 the University of Calabria was inaugurated at Cosenza; likewise in 1982 the University of Mediterranean Studies at Reggio Calabria; and in 1998 Catanzaro became the site for the University of Magna Græcia which boasts a well-respected medical school.

Nowadays all those born and bred in Calabria—in the mountains or on the coast; in a mafia town or a 'clean' town; near a tourist venue or in a quiet place; in a large city or a small community—increasingly have the same expectations for themselves, their children and grandchildren as other Italians and other Europeans. The young expect to study with the help of their computers and tablets; they expect the internet to be available and to be fast; they expect to call home on their smart-phones and Skype their friends; they expect the local bars to have wi-fi.

Things are changing fast, though the speed and quality of change can still depend on where in Calabria you are. What has not changed is the region's unique location, breathtaking landscape and colourful history which together make Calabria what it is and Calabrians what they are.

The main challenge that lies ahead is about finding the capacity to isolate and eradicate the influence of those few ruthless and rapacious people who for far too long have had the power to control the many *and* who have had effrontery to call themselves 'Calabrians'.

At long last there are signs that this is beginning to happen.

I shall end as I began, with the wise words of Norman Douglas (1911):
"Ages of oppression and misrule have passed over their heads; sun and rain, with all their caprice, have been kinder friends to them than their earthly masters."

Making connections

> "We crossed over to Regio [sic]... where we waited half an hour in the street, guarded like criminals, till the governor came from mass, and gave us permission to walk about the town."
>
> **Brian Hill** *Observations and Remarks in a journey through Sicily and Calabria in the year 1791*

A bit of a culture shock for Brian Hill, no doubt. But then travelling is all about shocking, stimulating and questioning ingrained senses of culture, history and reason.

Of course, at one time I too was one of those visitors, those travellers; albeit one who returned several times and eventually stayed. And, unlike my friends and fellow Calabrians who were born and brought up here, I have had to assimilate a sense of this place, to adapt to a different culture, to discriminate with a new language in my head, to understand how its past became its present, to master how it all works ... to make a million and one connections.

That process is on-going but there were some landmarks, things that I gleaned from the travels of others and my own travels and intuition that have facilitated my understanding and appreciation of today's Calabria; that helped me join the dots, to begin to complete a picture of Calabria, its people and places, past and present, and start to visualise it all in my mind's eye ... to make connections.

With more than a few diversions and tangents, and through many pairs of eyes, mine included, this chapter focuses on people and places that, in all sorts of different and intertwining ways, were key factors that enabled me to recognise and understand some of these connections. The likes of the

CAMPANIA
BASILICATA
Mormanno
Morano
Il Pollino
Castrovillari
Trebisacce
Il Mar Ionio
Sibari
Rossano
Belvedere
CALABRIA
Páola
COSENZA
La Sila
Stróngoli
Santa Severina
Roccabernarda
CROTONE
Il Mar Tirreno
Gizzeria
Gizzeria Lido
Nicastro
Sant'Eufémia
CATANZARO
Roccabernarda Station
Máida Marina
Máida
Squillace
'Fondaco del Fico'
Pizzo
VIBO VALÉNTIA
San Nicola da Crissa
Il Mar Ionio
Laureana di Borrello
Rosarno
Plaseano
Gióia Tauro
San Giorgio
Caulónia
Taurianova
Cittanova
Oppido
Gerace
Marina di Gioiosa Jonica
Lo Stretto di Messina
Scilla
L'Aspromonte
Locri
Villa San Giovanni
SICILIA
REGGIO DI CALABRIA

mafia, earthquakes and brigandage, I will engage with only briefly here and elaborate on later.

Many of today's visitors to Calabria, who don't arrive through Lamezia by train or plane, generally drive through Basilicata on either the east (Ionian) coast on the main highway, the SS106, or, most often, opt for the idiosyncrasies of the more central-west A3 *autostrada* route from some starting point to the north; there is also the A3's sea-hugging predecessor along the west coast, the SS18.

Others cross from Sicily to Villa San Giovanni or Reggio Calabria, just as Brian Hill did in 1791. Crotone and Reggio Calabria also have airports.

By rail, the west-coast route is the fastest and most accessible but there is also a slower, scenic option along the Ionian coast from Taranto in Apulia via Basilicata. Indeed, like the west-coast route, the east-coast railway's final destination is also Reggio Calabria, a seven-hour journey from Taranto via Crotone on the eastern side; less than half of that from Salerno (in Campania) via Lamezia on the west. Years ago there were some east-west rail connections but these were generally to accommodate local services; most are now defunct, the exception being the line from Catanzaro Lido to Nicastro and Lamezia.

Indeed, for those who live on the eastern side of the Pollino, Sila and Aspromonte mountains, collectively the Apennines, (people like us) there is a very real sense of having been omitted from the region's transport infrastructure. That said, it is the mountains themselves that are the historic root of the problem.

Two hundred years ago, it was infinitely worse. As Swinburne (1777) noted:

"Another cause of neglect lies in the excessive badness of the roads in this mountainous country, where mules, being much more hardy and enduring, are fitter for service, and consequently more marketable. They carry upwards of three cantara [one cantara is 47.6 kilograms / 105 pounds], through the most difficult, dangerous ways imaginable without stumbling ..."

Swinburne also included some useful pages for future travellers—weights, measures, money—in which he notes that carriages could travel no further south than Catanzaro and that 'litters are used from hence'.

Arthur John Strutt (1841) described his first encounter with a litter (*lettiga* or *litiga* in Italian):

"[it was] something like an immense sedan chair carried by two mules. The leader was a handsome grey fellow, ornamented with numberless bells and red tassels. Inside, two priests were enjoying the jogging swing peculiar to the *lettiga*, whilst a mounted muleteer rode in front, in the outrider fashion."

But then fifty years later, as Edward Lear (1847) observed, progress was being made on the 'coach-road, which skirts the western coast'.

It would not be unreasonable to have expected such progress to have continued and that today's Calabria would have a well-appointed, mature and modern road network. Indeed the first tentative steps in that direction were witnessed by Leslie Gardiner (1966) and he was understandably enthused by the 'mighty earth-shifting vehicles' he saw as the construction of the *Autostrada del Sole,* the motorway of the sun, got under way:

"Twenty miles of it is open already, north of Cosenza, and another twelve miles near Reggio. In 1970, they tell me, you will cover Calabria non-stop on that six-lane ribbon of non-skid, anti-glare tarmac (*autotsrada* completion dates are not far behind their forecasts as a rule), and soon afterwards perhaps, the dream of Italian engineers through the centuries will come true: they will bridge the Strait of Messina and a powerful car will drive on to the autostrada at Milan and drive off the same day at Palermo, a thousand miles away."

At least Gardiner's optimism was based on first-hand experience; Morton (1967), on the other hand, was given to believe that it was already a *fait accompli*:

"He [an Italian friend] described the *Autostrada del Sole*, which begins at Milan and now ends at the Straits of Messina, as the finest example of road

On the hillside above Scilla, one of the spans of the original A3 now goes nowhere ... its state-of-the-art replacement cuts through the hill behind. On the other hand, switching lanes on one of the last stretches of the A3 to be completed near Campo Tenese in the Pollino mountains was still in vogue in 2015.

engineering since the Via Appia and the military roads of ancient Rome."

Morton was writing almost two years after he visited Calabria and it seemingly never occurred to him that he never saw any evidence of construction work even though he passed along most of its route. There was an oblique reference to 'a fine new road' but nothing more specific.

Gardiner's optimism about completion dates may well have applied to the north of Italy where there was already a substantial *autostrada* network but in Calabria it didn't allow for the *'ndrangheta*, the Calabrian mafia. When, in 1974, the completion deadline was more or less met, the result was not a 'six-lane ribbon of non-skid, anti-glare tarmac' but a sub-standard, four-lane excuse for a motorway ... the optimism of its romantic name, *Autostrada del Sole*, already having given way to a more mundane designation, the A3.

So, a short diversion (pun intended) while I get the A3 off my chest.

Officially the *autostrada*, the A3, runs from Naples to Reggio Calabria in southern-most Calabria. It was first 'completed' in June 1974 but has been dogged with problems ever since. These problems were largely confined to the 290 kilometres of road *within* Calabria and the story is the sort of thing that gives the region a bad name.

When I first met Calabrians in their late thirties who maintained that throughout their life the A3 had always been a work-in-progress, I thought they were exaggerating. To me it was incredulous that they had *never* known a time when this important artery has not been a series of road works, diversions and lane changes, interspersed with short sections of 'normality'. But it was true.

At the time of writing it is almost sixteen years since *my* first experience of it and all that has changed is that the diversions and lane changes have just moved on to different stretches.

The problem is threefold.

Firstly, the quality of the original road was so poor that repair work and upgrading became endemic until the decision was eventually made to almost start from scratch and build a proper multi-lane *autostrada* along the same route.

Secondly, the route itself is an engineering nightmare, there are ways of skirting some parts of the Sila and Aspromonte mountains but the Pollino range straddles the region almost from coast to coast: it is no accident that the area between Mormanno and Campo Tenese will be one of the last to be completed.

And thirdly the *'ndrangheta*. Until recently, much of the monies allocated for the project found their way instead into the coffers of Calabria's mafia, the *'ndrangheta*. In June 2010, for example, there were fifty-two arrests in Reggio Calabria for corruption and extortion relating to the A3 *autostrada* ... the high-profile officer overseeing the arrests was Renato Cortese, a son of Santa Severina. Several more high-profile arrests later and with the original mooted date for completion, 2003, long since gone, the projected completion date has itself become a work-in-progress.

When I first started to write this book the latest official word was that the A3 *autostrada* would be completed by the end of 2014 ... more than 40 years since it was first 'completed'. When I mention this to Calabrian friends, the very notion that it would *ever* be finished invites a disparaging look and an accompanying hand gesture which says something akin to 'and pigs will fly'. Basically they have heard it all before.

The projected completion date has indeed shifted and the latest guesstimate

Dramatic, almost impregnable Gerace, on the road from Locri to Gioia Tauro.

Gerace's Casa Scaglione where Edward Lear stayed ... twice.

Almost inaccessible today, the ruins of Gerace's Norman castle.

was 'by 2018' ... until, that is, in March 2015 when part of a viaduct crossing the river Lau, north-west of Mormanno, fell into the valley with the loss of one life. At the time of writing, the ramifications of this tragedy have still to be accessed though Italy's young, dynamic Prime Minster, Matteo Renzi, publicly stated that completing the A3 was a priority and, in the same breath, bravely brought forward the date to December 2016.

When it is finished (and I'm optimistic enough to assume it eventually will be), I'm not sure how Calabrians would cope with uninterrupted driving from the north to Reggio Calabria ... the shock to the system could be immense. On the other hand the A3 has something in its favour in that it's Italy's only toll-free *autostrada* ... quite simply it would have been and would be a bloody cheek to expect anyone to pay to drive on it.

Today the two main east-west road routes are the SS280 from Catanzaro to Lamezia (not quite the shortest distance between the two seas, but by far the fastest) and the SS107 across the Sila linking Crotone with Cosenza and Páola on the west coast; our Santa Severina home is a few miles south of the SS107 at the Crotone end.

Further south there is the newish SS281 that connects the Ionian coast near Marina di Gioiosa Jònica with Rosarno close to the Tyrrhenian Sea. This latter is perhaps the shape of things to come as, either side of a two-mile tunnel through the mountains, it sits atop concrete columns as it follows the course of two rivers that gently fall to their respective seas.

These two are fairly direct routes that cross valleys on concrete columns and cut through mountains rather than follow the contours; the older roads that did follow the contours are still there doing what they did best and link the towns and villages along the way. In the past most travellers tended to avoid these tortuous mountainous routes (and of course their indigenous bandits and brigands), generally preferring to stick closer to the coast.

The other east-west routes which have not been upgraded are Sibari to Belvedere in the north and Locri to Gióia Tauro in the south. But because of the often serpentine and mountainous terrain, these latter no longer appeal to many of today's travellers ... except for the likes of me, that is. Two hundred, one hundred, years ago, *all* the east-west connections that crossed the Pollino, Sila and Aspromonte ranges were much the same: the same physical effort, the same remoteness, the same inhospitable terrain, the same perceived risks.

Nevertheless, some travellers defied the apparent dangers from bandits and brigands and went for it. And all survived to recall the unique and remote beauty of these places that few others had experienced.

Ramage (1828) recorded his descent to Gerace from the west thus:

"I can scarcely tell in what this eastern side of the Apennines differed from the western, for there was loneliness in both, but it was more striking here. The sides of the hills had no marks of cultivation, and even the footpath along which I was proceeding seemed seldom to be trodden, in fact, I could have imagined myself in the midst of an uninhabited country …"

And Lear (1847) approaching the small town of San Georgio in the foothills of the Aspromonte, right bang in the centre of southern Calabria:

"By long lanes, through the immensely extensive olive-grounds, and by descents into earthquake-marked ravines,—by crossing torrent-beds, and walking in irrigated gardens, we came in three hours to the foot of the hill of San Georgio, which is an isolated ridge, running out from the central range of hills, and crowned most magnificently with a town and castle."

So when I too set off to explore the Aspromonte interior for the first time, I felt like a pioneer of sorts for I knew that those who normally came this way did so for local and personal purposes. I knew that few of my Calabrian friends had ever ventured further west from the Ionian shore than Gerace; there are, after all, easier ways to cross from east to west than on the road connecting Locri with Gióia Tauro. Much later, I was to discover that there were harder ways too.

There are several things that put Calabrians off crossing the Aspromonte, here, the most obvious being the serpentine route, particularly between Gerace

Gerace as Edward Lear saw it in 1847.

and Cittanova; beyond Cittanova today's road passes round Taurianova as it drops in a more straightforward and leisurely fashion to the coastal plain and Gióia Tauro.

That said, the first six miles from Locri to Gerace are serpentine enough but nevertheless well-worn for many make the effort to come here, not least because, from afar, it is a stunning hilltop town. It is no less eye-catching close up, a tidy, well-appointed town that effortlessly attracts visitors to view its many edifices. Even in 1967 Morton, called it a 'fantastic site', and went on to make a very valid point when he noted that, had Gerace been anywhere else but Calabria, it would have been as popular with tourists as, say, San Gimignano in Tuscany has become.

Unusually, the community is not only aware but also immensely proud of the fact that one other British traveller came this way for Edward Lear made many sketches of the town, copies of which can be bought locally. And Lear (1847) also stopped off in Gerace twice, each time at the home of local Magna Græcia expert, Don Pasquale Scaglione.

But is was Henry Swinburne (1777) who first described the town and its approach, both of which he found more than a little disagreeable:

"Gerace is poorly built, on a hill of coarse granite rocks and stiff clay; the road to it is steep and difficult; the vale below is well cultivated, and yet does not produce corn enough to answer the demands of the Geracians ..."

Little wonder, then, that Swinburne did not leave his literary mark on the people of Gerace in the way that Lear did.

I suspect that Swinburne's disappointment derived in part from his belief that Gerace might have been the site of one of the most elusive and important Magna Græcia republics, Locri Epizefirii (now usually known as simply Locri and of which more in a later chapter). Sadly, Swinburne could find no evidence to substantiate this premise ... because there was none.

What seemed more credible to Richard Keppel-Craven (1820) was that Gerace is where the Greek-speaking population of Locri resettled *after* that town was sacked by the Saracens in the 9th century CE:

" ... it has by some been supposed to stand on the site of the ancient Locris; but it is more likely that it sprang from its decay."

Edward Lear (1847), wearing his landscape-painter hat, saw the good, the bad and the ugly:

"[Gerace] full of beautifully placed buildings, [is] situated on a very narrow ridge of rock, every part of which seems to have been dangerously afflicted by earthquakes—splits and cracks and chasms, horrible with abundant crookedness of steeples, and a general appearance of instability in walls and houses. Here are the dark and crumbling ruins of a massive Norman castle, from which, by a scrambling path, you may reach the valley below; but all other parts of the town are accessible only by two winding roads at the eastern and less precipitous approach."

Not only did Edward Lear stay with the Scaglione family twice, but he subsequently devoted some fifty pages of his book to his experiences in and around Gerace. Like a man besotted and besmitten, he waxed lyrical about it:

"In fact, Gerace is by far the grandest and proudest object in general position, and as a city, which we have yet seen in Calabria. A beautiful trait of Gerace is the admirable colour; its white or delicate fawn-hued cliffs, and gray or dove-coloured buildings coming beautifully off the purple mountains."

The lofty purple mountains are, of course, the northern slopes of the Aspromonte and beyond Gerace the road continues to twist and climb, onwards and upwards across the dark, wooded spine of the southern Apennines before dropping, in a more gentle fashion, first to Cittanova, then Taurianova.

Richard Keppel-Craven (1818) and Edward Lear (1847) were the only 19th century travellers to risk this trans-Aspromonte route but instead of being preoccupied with the potential dangers, their thoughts reflected largely on the physical and emotional aftermath of the devastating February 1783 earthquake, the epicentre of which was at nearby Oppido Mamertina.

Lear quoted extensively from Keppel-Craven's moving description for, travelling in 1818, Keppel-Craven met people for whom the events of that winter and spring still remained a terrible, lingering memory. He and Lear both realised that the landscape they were passing through was embryonic and evolving, the scars of what happened here were still raw, still healing, to slowly create a new, richer environment.

But Keppel-Craven, travelling west-east towards Gerace, also saw its intrinsic beauty:

"… nothing could be more beautiful than this ride, extending about sixteen miles, through the finest forests and amongst the most magnificent rocks I ever saw. The trees, especially the chestnuts, are of immense size; and some of the ravines are so narrow, that it would be no difficult matter to cross them on the upper boughs of the trees which grow out of them, so thickly are they interwoven."

There was one other British 'traveller' who came this way, after Swinburne and before all the others. The year was 1809 and at the time he was a prisoner-of-war and was being taken by his French captors from Bianco (on the Ionian coast) to Monte Leone (near the Tyrrhenian coast). Despite his difficult situation and the fact that he was a naval officer, Philip Elmhirst too experienced the 'remarkable convulsions' that created the range of 'abrupt and tremendous precipices', he also wrote eloquently about the moment he reached the highest point on the road between Gerace and Casal Nuova, today's Cittanova:

"… the beautiful and extensive view this elevated spot afforded, was of itself a sufficient requital for all the fatigue we had undergone. Few situations could have offered to the beholder objects more interesting, or more worthy of his attention; and the philosopher and the naturalist, the poet and the admirer of classic lore, would have found equal gratification."

Sadly, today's more serpentine road offers few such views …

The scars on the landscape that Elmhirst, Keppel-Craven and Lear experienced have finally healed; for today's traveller the tortuous, precarious road, the cavernous valleys and the rising wooded slopes are but the camouflage of nature.

Earthquakes aside, in Keppel-Craven and Lear's day this was, supposedly, dangerous territory for the traveller because of the perceived possibility of running into the infamous Calabrian brigand. Even today Calabrians avoid the same route beyond Gerace for a similar reason as many still consider the area to be 'bandit country'. But today's concerns have an altogether different connotation and 'connection' … they are referring to the Calabrian mafia, the *'ndrangheta*. Like many towns in and around the Aspromonte, both Cittanova and Taurianova have such a reputation, indeed the extremities of this road, Locri and Gióia Tauro—most notably the latter—are even more notorious for the same reason (see chapter *Outside the law*).

Nevertheless, like Keppel-Craven and Lear, I too emerged from the mountains unscathed. Feeling moderately pleased with myself, I carried on to the Tyrrhenian shore at Gióia Tauro and could not help but wonder what all the fuss was about. But then I knew too that this was how the mafia wanted me to think.

On a related, if slightly ironic, note, Ramage (1828) ruminated on the fate of brigands who were actually caught and convicted:

"They are condemned to the galleys, or, more correctly speaking, to be employed in the construction of public works. I have often seen fifty of them chained two and two, working at a new road under a boiling sun, with half a dozen soldiers standing over them with loaded muskets."

Thus the convicted brigand—felon would probably be more appropriate lest we assume everyone who stepped outside the law to have been a brigand—was forced to construct better roads which both enabled safer travelling and had a positive impact on Calabria's transport infrastructure such as it was.

Ramage's reference to 'galleys' recognises the fact that, pre-unification, the Kingdom of the Two Sicilies, including Calabria, prided itself on its maritime connections as opposed to its road network. Goods and services, including people, could the more easily be moved by water than over land, bearing in mind that Calabria not only boasts one of the peninsula's longest coastlines but some of its most impenetrable mountain ranges. In the south it was quicker and safer to go round the coast that to cross the Aspromonte.

Some travellers, like Swinburne, Keppel-Craven and Ramage—who all travelled by sea as well as land—chose to exploit extant fast and direct connections between coastal centres and, of course, saved themselves the experience of uneven roads, steep climbs, river crossings and, perhaps, brigands. On the other hand, they missed out on actually experiencing the places they only saw from afar.

By the early-19th century, the most efficient coastal services were operated by the Peirano Danovaro Company who ran both sailing vessels and steamers. Once a week, in the period just before unification, a steamer would leave Genoa and call at Naples on a return trip round the peninsula and up the western coast as far as Ancona, calling at all the main ports. By the mid-1870s this service, like so many others in the south, had ceased.

The *Pelero*, the ship in the foreground at the port of Naples, started life in 1842 as a coastal steamer; it was powered by two large (paddle) wheels, one on each side.
Initially the *Pelero* worked on behalf of the postal service of the Kingdom of the Two Sicilies and plied the ports between Naples and Sicily, including the east coast of Calabria. Following unification in 1861, it was, like so many of the steamers that served the south, reassigned as a military vessel and, as can be seen, thereafter flew the new Italian flag.

When, in 1787, the German poet and writer, Johann Wolfgang von Goethe, returned to Naples after his Sicilian adventures he did so by sea from Messina in a French merchant vessel, a journey that, with a favourable wind, would normally have taken no more than a couple of days. Unfortunately the wind was virtually non-existent and it was four days before he reached his destination; nevertheless still considerably faster than the same journey overland.

Though he mentions seeing the Calabrian coastline after leaving Messina—it would be hard to miss—there is no further comment on the land to starboard though he did do a drawing from the vessel's port side of the volcanic island of Strómboli, the most dominant and infamous of the Lipari Islands, west of Calabria and north of Sicily. And it is this drawing that leads some to believe that en route to Naples he may actually have ventured onto Calabrian soil for, it is argued, that particular view of Strómboli can only be seen from Tropea in Calabria. Why he might have failed to mention it in an otherwise detailed account of his travels, remains the inescapable problem with this theory.

Something that may have put Goethe off from landing at Tropea was the then equivalent of Passport Control for those arriving by sea. Then, as now, documents had to be checked at the port of entry and there was also a Customs (*Dogane*) check into what goods people brought with them over and above their personal belongings.

In 1835 Alexandre Dumas got himself into a bit of bother when he went by boat to Scilla from Villa San Giovanni (about four miles away). He went ashore and found a very agreeable place to relax and have lunch. As was customary, his host asked him for his passport and Dumas explained that he had left it back at Villa San Giovanni where he was staying.

After lunch, while relaxing with a cigarette in a room upstairs, his 'serene and fantastic dreams' were interrupted:

"I was in the middle of my Eldorado [golden moment, probably marijuana-induced as Dumas was known to have used it], when I heard three or four sabres banging against the steps on the stairway. I didn't pay much attention but given that the sabres seemed to be approaching my room, I started to take notice. Just as I turned round, the door opened and four *carabinieri* came in: it was the dessert that my host promised me."

Dumas repeated his passport story but it cut no ice and the *carabinieri* sergeant politely asked him to accompany them to the local Justice of the Peace.

He took the sergeant aside to have a private word in his ear and suggested his companions should step outside. He then put a proposition to the sergeant, whereby he would send for his passport, the sergeant's palm would be crossed with some silver and they would share some wine and cigars while they waited for the passport. The ship's cabin boy was delegated to take a letter to the captain of the ship who would return to San Giovanni and come back with the passport.

The sergeant went for it and Dumas was spared a visit to the Justice of the Peace ... perhaps just as well as he didn't actually have any authority to enter the Kingdom of the Two Sicilies at all for he was travelling on the documents of a friend, a Monsieur Guichard.

George Gissing (1897) arrived at Páola from Naples on a steamer and this was his first experience of Calabrian 'hospitality':

"I sprang into the midst of a clamorous conflict; half a dozen men were quarrelling for possession of me. No sooner was my luggage on shore than they flung themselves upon it. By what force of authority I know not, one of the fellows triumphed; he turned to me with a satisfied smile, and ... presented his wife ...

"Wondering, and trying to look pleased, I saw the woman seize the portmanteau (a frightful weight), fling it on her head, and march away at a good speed. The crowd and I followed to the *dogana*, close by, where as vigorous a search was made as I have ever had to undergo."

These days trade in goods by sea is generally confined to Gióia Tauro, and to a lesser extent Corigliano Calabro, and is international rather than local; like everywhere else, onward deliveries are by road and rail. The passage of people is no more, save for some local boat trips for tourists and a few cruise ships that put into Crotone for a day or two in the spring and summer. Day trip itineraries for their human cargo, generally English, American or Finnish, are predictable: the most accessible remnant of Magna Græcia in the area, Capa Colonna, and two local castles—Le Castella and Santa Severina.

Today's Calabria is well served by its two coast roads (see *Coasting along*). They are not the fastest of routes north-south but they offer breathtaking views of the sea on one side and, as you approach the toe of the boot, equally stunning mountain vistas on the other, as well as Sicily and Mount Etna.

On whichever side you travel it is impossible not to notice the countless river crossings as, every few miles, yet another natural drainage channel from the Apennines tumbles into the sea. Actually 'tumbles' is not really the right word ... 'trickles' would be more appropriate. In the winter these trickles do sometimes show more menace but generally they behave themselves and stay within their banks. Indeed, if the length of some of the bridges is anything to go by, some time in the distant past these rivers were fuller and faster at the point where they reached the sea.

I recall the first time I crossed the river Neto over its newly-constructed bridge near Santa Severina. It was June and I simply couldn't believe that good money had been spent on such a long structure when clearly there was hardly anything more down there than an almost-dry river bed. A few years later, in November, I watched in awe as a huge, meandering, turbulent torrent of water roared under the same bridge on its way to Stróngoli and the Ionian Sea.

I also recall how, during the construction of this new road bridge across the Neto, to connect Santa Severina more directly to the main road, remained tantalizingly unfinished for more than a year. This was particularly disheartening for local people as completion of the bridge would certainly have cut at least twenty minutes off journeys to either Crotone or Cosenza. So close, yet so frustratingly far.

Undaunted by the absence of that last span of steel and concrete, local people instinctively took matters into their own hands and gradually there evolved a steep earth ramp down from one side of the gap, across what remained of the river bed itself to the far bank and back up on to the main road. So close, yet so frustratingly far ... but no problem.

Documenting his journey north across the plain of Sant'Eufémia, from Pizzo to Lamezia, Richard Keppel-Craven (1818) observed:

"The road, though sandy, is quite good enough for a carriage, as is usually the case in all the large valleys; but the bridges necessary to render it practicable for carriages in the winter require a degree of expense which has probably hitherto proved the principal obstacle towards the completion of that branch of public accommodation, best calculated to promote the internal welfare of the country."

He went on to imply that work on the 'high road' (and therefore its bridges) had a stop-start character ... money had been set aside by government years previously but little work had been undertaken and what had been started was 'but partially carried on from year to year'. He had been told that things were set to improve, that the works 'were in a train to be forthwith carried into entire execution'.

This was some time before 1820 and at a time of political upheaval in the south in the wake of the re-establishment of the Bourbon monarchy following the Napoleonic period (1806–1815). Nonetheless, it's ironic that, nearly two centuries on, a similar story—in respect of the procrastinations in completing the bridge spanning the Neto—was being played out once again in Calabria.

The lack of such river crossings, particularly near the coast, was one thing that forced travellers in the past to travel via the nearest inland towns and the lack of river crossings also meant no continuous coastal road. When, for example, Swinburne (1777) bemoaned the 'excessive badness of the roads' when he was ostensibly following the coast, he was talking about the more elevated inland roads and tracks that followed the coastline with the purpose of linking towns and villages. It is only relatively recently that travellers actually travelled *along* the coast itself.

Of course travelling inland still meant that some rivers had to be crossed and in his 1780 journey, Swinburne describes crossing the river Amato in the plain of Sant'Eufémia:

"In bad weather this pass is esteemed very dangerous, as the waters are a muddy white colour, and the beds full of deep holes worn in the clay, which a stranger has no suspicion of; the river was white when I crossed it, though no rain had fallen for weeks, and no snow appeared on the mountains where it takes its rise: I therefore imagine this is the constant and natural hue of its streams. Our guides got up behind us to pass the river, and with extraordinary apprehension and vociferation pointed out to each horseman the precise direction he was to follow; and, by a due attention to their instructions, I and one of the servants traversed the plain without accident; the other, by his own awkwardness, or the indocility of his horse, missed the track, and plunged over-head in a deep but narrow pool, out of which he crawled, without any mischief but a thorough wetting."

This was Brian Hill's (1791) experience of negotiating the Crati north of Cosenza in March:

"We were twice obliged to ford the waters, which were so deep and rapid that a man walked on each side of the litiga [litter] to prevent us from being carried away. There are always a number of men waiting at the rivers, who transport foot travellers across on their shoulders; which, though a very dangerous operation, on account of the width and rapidity of those rivers, and the large loose stones which are in the water, yet these guides are so expert and careful that seldom any mischief ensues."

The resourcefulness displayed by the Santa Severinese in 2007-08 was clearly nothing new.

In his list of staging posts on the post-roads through Calabria in 1777, Swinburne mentions a place by the name of *Fondaco del Fico*. On his second visit to the region in 1880, he actually stopped there.

Other travellers mentioned it too and, though it featured on many maps of the area from the early 17th century up to the middle of the 19th century, it can't be found on any modern map.

When Edward Lear (1847) decried the lack of inns in Calabria 'except on the coach-road, which skirts the western coast', he was referring to, among others, places like the *Fondaco del Fico*. (He was also referring to the same 'high road' that Richard Keppel-Craven (1820) mentioned when he was bemoaning the lack of money being spent on the bridges.)

For travellers, both foreign and local, *Fondaco del Fico* was an important watering hole where they could take a break, have something to eat and change horses if necessary. Essentially a *fondaco* is an isolated building, often used as a local store-house as well as a place of lodging and a staging post; *fico* usually means fig. Swinburne (1780), it seems, was the first to drop by:

"... I drew up to the Fondaco del Fico where we baited [to stop for food and rest]. I dined at the door of this solitary inn, under the shade of a venerable cork-tree, and from my seat enjoyed a view of the whole gulf [of Sant'Eufémia].

Swinburne also wondered if this was the same place that the Roman philosopher, politician and consul, Cicero (106BCE–43BCE) stopped at and dated some of his letters, then known as Fundus Sicae. His argument seems plausible:

"The situation corresponds with his [Cicero's] route, and the present name bears a greater resemblance to the ancient one than those of many places fixed by topographers ..."

This notion is given further credence by an entry in Volume Three of Thomas Nugent's *The Grand Tour* published in 1847 where, listing an Italian itinerary, he refers to the same place as the *Fondico della Sica*. But given the similarity between an 'f' and an 's' in the typography of books at the time, this could simply have been a typographical error.

There is also a similar reference in the *Nuovo Dizionario Geografico Universale* published in 1828 but it is difficult to say whether this notion predated Swinburne or whether it became an accepted 'truth' *because* Swinburne had suggested it fifty years earlier. The same book also describes the *Fondaco del Fico* as an 'extensive building'.

In 1830 the Cicero story was repeated by the French traveller Charles Didier when he passed what he described as an 'awful inn' in 1830 ... the site was the *Fondaco el Fico* but its name had seemingly been changed to exploit the supposed connection with Cicero and was now the more illustrious-sounding *Osteria di Cicerone*, Cicero's Inn, despite it being, from all accounts, such a terrible place.

The name change seems to have taken place before 1807 when another Frenchman, army officer Duret de Tavel, called it 'a vast pile of building called *Fondaco-del-Fico* falling in ruins in every part, and converted into a wretched tavern, set off with the pompous designation of *Osteria di Cicerone*, (Cicero's Inn).'

I will call it the *Fondaco del Fico* for, as we shall see, there seem to be some inconsistencies around when and for how long this name change was in vogue.

Fondaco del Fico was on the north-south route near the west coast not far from where the river Angitola enters the sea a few miles north of Pizzo. This point is the western end of the narrowest part of the Italian boot (less than twenty miles across) though there is no direct or easily accessible road from coast to coast. During the reign of Carlo VII in the mid-18th century there was even a proposition to cut a canal between the two seas here, as the elevation was generally not excessive. This was around the same time as England's first major canal project, the Bridgwater Canal, was being planned.

Keppel-Craven (1818) described the river valley's 'desolate, wild, but beautiful aspect' as 'very striking' as he was taking 'an oblique direction towards Nicastro':

"The ruins of a few dilapidated cassinos, memorials of the earthquake, appear occasionally; but the only habitation I passed was a tavern, called *Fondaco del Fico*."

Traveling from Pizzo to Máida in 1835 Alexandre Dumas and his companion stopped around midday at 'a little place called *Fondaco del Fico*', a place where they could rest their horses and get something to eat. Other travellers too—Frenchmen Duret de Tavel, Vivant Denon, François Lenormant and Charles Didier; Germans Friederich Leopold von Stolbergand and Justus Tommasini; Italian Guiseppe Maria Galanti—came this way and referred to the *Fondaco del Fico* in their diaries and books.

Which takes me back to the name. It seems that the only inconsistent reference to the *Fondaco del Fico* as the *Osteria di Cicerone* is that of Charles Didier in 1830. While it might well have had a temporary incarnation as the *Osteria di Cicerone* in and around 1807 (Duret de Tavel), both Keppel-Craven (1818) and Alexandre Dumas (1835) called it the *Fondaco del Fico*.

I believe that the name *Osteria di Cicerone* was used only during the period of Napoleonic French rule between 1806 and 1815 and that thereafter it reverted to its original name of the *Fondaco del Fico*.

Didier's description, it seems to me, has many similarities to that of Tavel, in addition to which he incorrectly locates his '*Osteria di Cicerone*' a lot further south and next to Lake Angitola. I suspect therefore that Didier didn't actually recall the area well enough when he checked his notes and instead dipped into Tavel's description, married it to the wrong location and as such is essentially flawed. It is also possible that when he was in Calabria he was using an out-of-date French map which still carried the designation of *Osteria di Cicerone*.

In recent years the *Fondaco del Fico* name has cropped up in Italian literature, specifically in Carmine Abate's *Tra Due Mare* (*Between Two Seas*). This is the fictional story of a man's lifelong obsession with rebuilding the ruins of a long-abandoned and legendary family inn once visited by Alexandre Dumas. By middle age, Giorgio Bellusci is a fairly prosperous butcher and landowner who is imprisoned after he responds with uncharacteristic violence to the demands of the local mafia for protection money. Following his release he pursues his dream and begins the work of restoring the *Fondaco del Fico*. The mafia, meanwhile, still seek revenge …

I will reveal no more save to say that, should you ever get the chance, then read *Between Two Seas*. You will learn much about Calabria and its people.

Calabrian writer Vito Teti mentions the *Fondaco del Fico* too in his *Il senso dei luoghi: memoria e storia dei paesi abbandonati* (*A sense of place: memories and stories of abandoned towns*). He describes it as a place that is now overrun with brambles and figs that was once, 'a staging-post, a welcoming place, a place of refreshment and brawls'.

I was keen to locate this place, to get a sense of where it was and why it seemed so important to so many but did so in the knowledge that both Carmine Abate and Vito Teti had been there before me.

Over a couple of summers Carmine Abate had tried to locate it but became reconciled to the fact that not a single stone remained.

On the other hand, Vito Teti was brought up in nearby San Nicola da Crissa and, as a youngster, memories of *Fondaco del Fico* still lived on in the older generation. Teti believed its ruins lay below the A3 *autostrada* which runs parallel to the older inland road north of the river Angitola but closer to the sea.

But then Abate's searches were more than a dozen years ago and Teti's even further back and I wondered had they themselves sparked some interest in the place that might have borne fruit? Could I be the one to reveal the *Fondaco del Fico* to them?

Like Carmen Abate's fictional Giorgio Bellusci, was I too, I mused, becoming obsessed with the *Fondaco del Fico*? Having thus queried my own obsession, I decided to leave the details of my search for the *Fondaco del Fico* until the next chapter.

Besides the Ippolito, the Amato and the Angitola, there are countless smaller rivers and torrents that cross the plain of Sant'Eufémia to enter the gulf of Sant'Eufémia between Pizzo and Lamezia. It was these rivers themselves (and not solely the lack of bridges) that caused locals and travels alike an additional problem. Unlike others, Richard Keppel-Craven (1818) did not stop off at the *Fondaco del Fico*; he had good reason to be cautious:

"The faces of the inmates fully justified the reproach of malaria, which is attached to the whole valley …"

Even in the summer, when rivers were fordable closer to the coast, most travellers generally preferred to go via the nearest, more lofty, inland towns to avoid the coastal plain. In the summer months such areas were the province of the *zanzare*, mosquitoes, from which people caught malaria. Indeed the word malaria is the union of two Italian words, *mal* and *aria*, meaning 'bad air', born of a misconception regarding the cause of the disease.

Because it was generally picked up in low-lying, swampy areas, invariably close to rivers, the Romans and others made the wrong connection and thought it was caused by the air emanating from such places, the so-called miasma theory which prevailed well into the 19th century. This from the Roman writer Vitruvius in the 1st century CE:

"For when the morning breezes blow toward the town at sunrise, if they bring with them mist from marshes and, mingled with the mist, the poisonous breath of creatures of the marshes to be wafted into the bodies of the inhabitants, they will make the site unhealthy."

Describing the Cosenza area, Swinburne (1780) expounded a not dissimilar theory:

"The low grounds are fertile in an eminent degree; but from their situation and frequent waterings exhale vapours in summer that constitute a *Mal'Aria* very productive of fevers."

Ramage (1828) offered the following advice for travellers:

"Wherever we find a river in this country, we are sure to discover that it is a source of danger and not of profit; it desolates the lands through which it passes, leaving in its course a noxious deposit of mud, which spreads the seeds of disease over a wide district. Whoever can afford it, fly the low ground and take refuge in the mountains, where they find a pure and more temperate atmosphere."

At the time Ramage was in lofty Nicastro overlooking the same coastal plain of Sant'Eufémia, and its many rivers, across which Keppel-Craven had journeyed ten years earlier. Ramage's advice was sound enough even though, like Vitruvius and Swinburne, the science was completely wrong.

In his introduction to *Cities of Southern Italy and Sicily*, Augustus Hare lists some of the dangers associated with travelling in southern Italy as he saw them in 1891:

"... the torment of *zinzare* [mosquitoes], the terror of earthquakes, the insecurity of the roads from brigands, and the far more serious risk of malaria or typhoid fever from the bad water."

Even then the connection between the mosquito and malaria had not been made ... it was Ronald Ross who eventually did so in 1897 when he finally proved the hypothesis of Alphonse Laveran and Patrick Manson.

As I noted in *Thank you Uncle Sam*, by the time Norman Douglas (1911) was travelling in Calabria the problem was still rife and even those living in hilltop towns were not exempt when they sought work elsewhere. Douglas described how, in 1908, forty menfolk of one such town, Caulónia in what is now the province of Reggio Calabria, had no option but to seek work in Crotone and all returned infected save the two who had "made liberal use of quinine as a prophylactic".

Douglas concluded his malarial observations with a somewhat extreme view of Calabria:

"Malaria is the key to a correct understanding of the landscape, it explains the inhabitants, their mode of life, their habits, their history."

DH Lawrence, travelling in Sardinia in 1921, observed that where the tree-line began, there was no more malaria:

"For many miles the landscape is moorland and down-like, with no trees. But wait for the trees. Ah, the woods and the forests of Gennargentu [mountain range]: the woods and forest higher up! no malaria there!"

Thus, unlike today, travellers generally followed an inland route to avoid the low-lying land twixt the higher terrain and the sea. And even when the weather was cooler they were often forced inland to cross the many rivers.

The idea of populating the coast itself was not high on anyone's agenda as Ramage discovered when, en route to Castel Vetera (today's Caulónia), he described a brief flirtation with the coast thus:

"Proceeeding along the sea-coast I reached a few huts called Roccella."

Later, on the same trek north, he even ruminated on whether he should head for Squillace inland or via the coast and asked advice from miners at Pazzano near Stilo.

"The miners recommended that I should keep along the coast. I was so charmed, however, with the appearance of the mountains and the coolness of the air, that I resolved to face the brigands."

In this exchange Ramage's 'along the coast' did not mean literally by the sea but rather via the towns and villages that followed the coastline. Of course there were towns on the coast itself, towns such as Páola and Pizzo on the Tyrrhenian coast, that grew up where the higher land and the sea converged.

There is a hotel just outside Gizzeria Lido, not far from Lamezia Airport, on the SS18 coast road that runs along the edge of the once infamous malarial plain of Sant'Eufémia. As it happens its proprietor is immune to malaria and, because of this immunity, regularly gives blood. It was through medical advances and the fact that many people in and around these low-lying coastal areas gradually developed immunity to malaria that this and other coastal areas came to be peopled … that and the lure of the sea itself, not as a place to holiday, but initially as a food source and as a trading outlet.

The small hamlet of Gizzeria Lido is therefore no more than the coastal offshoot of another town called Gizzeria almost eight miles inland. These offshoots originated as a sort of port or landing point for loading and unloading people and local produce to and from the town whose name they bore. In an age of poor road communications and safer and more efficient maritime ones this was the most effective means of transporting goods and people.

This phenomenon can be found throughout Calabria and the south. It is almost impossible not to notice how many coastal towns, with the appendage Lido, Scala or Marina, have an inland equivalent, minus the appendage, of course. These namesakes—of which there are over fifty—are the original places of habitation and can sometimes be as much as six or seven miles away from the sea and of course to reach them always involves a climb (hence Scala, meaning incline).

Eventually people started to move to the sea and the original town sometimes became depopulated to the extent that, even today, locals would sometimes characterise the original place as being 'abandoned' or a 'ghost town'. While this may have been the case when the migration to the sea first started, it is no longer so.

That said, during the height of the summer there is often a temporary migration to the coast which does gives some towns the feeling of being empty. In July and August, for example, Santa Severina is vacated in two directions .... those with young families generally head to the sea while those who have had enough of the heat head to the hills and in particular the Sila mountains.

The prize for the furthest such coastal offshoot from its loftier and distant origins goes to Máida Marina on Calabria's west coast ... nearly nine miles from Máida as the crow flies, closer to twelve if the crow goes by road.

There is a similar phenomenon in respect of some railway stations and their names. In most places you would expect the name of a station to reflect the name of the nearest habitation and in Calabria that is generally the way of things too: Nicastro Station is at Nicastro and Crotone Station is at Crotone.

But with towns invariably on the higher ground and railway engineers having had a preference for winding their way round the lower slopes or running along the coast, there are some notable exceptions, particularly in the provinces of Catanzaro and Crotone.

George Gissing (1897-98) was wise to this when he was deciding how to get from Catanzaro to Squillace:

"I could have travelled from Catanzaro by railway to the sea-coast station called Squillace, but the town itself is perched upon a mountain some miles inland, and it was simpler to perform the whole journey by road, a drive of four hours, which, if the weather favoured me, would be thoroughly enjoyable."

Further up the Ionian coast, the station for Isola di Capo Rizzuto is seven miles from its name-giving town while, on the coastal stretch of the same line near Botricello on the SS106, is (the now defunct) Roccabernarda Station. However the town of Roccabernarda is almost twenty-seven miles away by road, though at least these days it's a reasonably direct road. The only obvious connection between town and station is that the river Tácina runs through Roccabernarda and enters the sea close to the station.

Leslie Gardiner (1966) also noted this strange anomaly and in doing so corrects Norman Douglas:

"In *Old Calabria*, Norman Douglas spoke of a village thirty-three kilometres from its station, but he was misinformed. Roccabernarda, on the way from Catanzaro to Crotone, is actually forty-three."

Gardiner goes on to paint a tongue-in-cheek picture of the unsuspecting Roccabernarda-bound traveller alighting from the only train of the day:

"The mountains are piled around you and so is your luggage. Taxi? They have not been seen in these parts. Bus? Once a week—it called yesterday. Mules? In short supply. Hard at work all day and needing to be brought from a great distance. Any kind of transport at all in the village? The station simpleton expressively indicates his wooden boots. And the village, then, how far is it? He shows you a signpost, just visible half a mile down the road. Someone mounts guard over the luggage while you shoulder a suitcase and tramp off to have a look. The signpost points up a track which would make a mountain goat's hair stand on end, and it says: Roccabernarda 43 km."

That was 1966; today it would be worse, there generally being no mules for hire these days. Sticking out an expectant thumb might just work instead.

The Calabrian penchant for improvisation when it comes to overcoming apparent obstacles to what, in other places, would likely result in a 'Road Closed' sign and a lengthy diversion, knows no bounds.

I suspect this is essentially an Italian trait in areas where there are fewer roads and limited access but it is my experience that Calabrians have made it into something akin to an art form. Why make a detour when the original road connection is probably passable or can be made so?

The disused Roccabernarda railway station and verdant platform ... over twenty miles from the town itself. The station may be redundant but trains still rattle along the track.

In addition to that missing span across the Neto, the Santa Severinese have experienced many landslides that have either ended up as a pile of rubble and mud blocking a road or part of the road itself has fallen away. *None* closed a single road for more than a few hours; if at all.

Even when, in 2009, half of the road approach to the new bridge over the Neto itself fell away, people just negotiated their way round it. 'Road Closed' signs did appear for a short time but were subtly moved aside to leave enough room for a car to pass; the next day the gap had miraculously become a little wider so that vans and trucks could also get through.

At the time of writing, for fifty yards the road to San Mauro on the outskirts of Santa Severina has been restricted to a single lane where part of the road fell down the hillside; that was in 2012 and four years on it bears all the hallmarks of a permanent fixture. Currently between Santa Severina and San Mauro there are a further three width restrictions caused by landslides but, this being Calabria, the road remains open.

What's more, as far as I am aware, everyone has negotiated these stretches successfully; no cars have collided or fallen down into the valley. Clearly everyone, locals and visitors alike, having the same interest in mutual survival, has observed some unwritten code ... and all without the aid of traffic controls or diversions.

Motoring in southern Calabria in July, I came across another such 'blockage'. I was heading north from the foothills of the Aspromonte, on the main road between Plasesano and Laureana di Borrello, and was looking forward to a break and a cup of coffee when I reached Laureana. I was enjoying being the only car on the road as it wound its way up the hillside ... at that point it had not occurred to me to question why it was that I was piloting the only moving vehicle.

I rounded a bend to find the road ahead 'closed' by large blocks of concrete though, to the left, there was a space just large enough for a car to sneak through. My instinct told me the locals had rearranged things and that the width of the gap was no coincidence. Nevertheless, I was not a local and did not know what lay up ahead so decided to return to Plasesano, seek out a bar and endeavour to find out whether or not it was possible to get through to Laureana. The burgeoning vegetation that had begun to take root around the 'blockage', suggested to me that, whatever damage the forces of nature had perpetrated up ahead, this was no recent event.

On my way back to Plasesano I double-checked that I had not inadvertently missed a 'Road Closed' sign. I had not or perhaps there was one lurking behind several years of tangled vegetation.

As I was downing my coffee and looking for an alternative route in my road atlas, I entered into conversation with some local men sitting at the next table. My question was simple ... I wanted to know if it was possible to get through to Laureana despite the apparent road closure. There followed an animated conversation the gist of which pointed towards a difference of opinion so that, by the time I left, I was really no better informed.

First of all, nobody could remember exactly when the road had been closed, though the cause, a *frana* (landslide) was in no doubt. Judging by the raised voices however, there seemed also to be a difference of opinion as to the details ... whether or not rocks and rubble had fallen *onto* the road or part of the road itself had broken away—or both—was clearly in dispute. The only person who seemed to know for certain where the landslide or landslides occurred, was me.

Similarly there were those who said it was passable and those who said it wasn't ... most of their information seemed second-hand for none had actually passed along the road themselves. It seemed to me that getting from Plasesano and Laureana was not a big issue locally as evidenced by the fact that one of these elderly citizens of Plaseano didn't seem to be aware that the road had even been closed. And besides, there was an alternative route, albeit a little longer, via Feroleto.

The ball was firmly back in my court, I was still none the wiser and, though the temptation to go boldly forth and find out for myself was immense, I

The Apple Maps view of the serpentine road from Plaseano (to the south) to Laureana di Borrello (to the north). All three circles highlight landslides.
The larger circle on the left shows how part of the road fell away and then blocked the same road further down on the other side of the hairpin bend.
In parts of Calabria this sort of occurrence is all too frequent.

CALABRIA

decided that it would be more prudent to head instead for Fereleto. Besides, there was a bonus in that I could see for myself if things had changed there since Richard Keppel-Craven (1818) passed through the town and observed that:

"... though surrounded by all that constitutes fertility, [Fereleto] scarcely afforded a small quantity of Indian corn for my horses, and a few ripe olives and bread for myself."

Still curious about what the problem was on the Plaseano to Laureana road, I later resorted to the internet. Conventional searches drew a blank so I took to the virtual skies and surveyed the area through the eyes of Google Earth, Google Maps and Apple's much-maligned Maps.

Google Earth was useless as I could scarcely see the road at all thanks to a canopy of trees; Google Maps 'street Level' function allowed me to travel up the road, in the virtual sense, as it was in 2010 but, as there was other traffic on the road, it was clearly shot before the blockage; only Apple Maps plainly showed a number of landslides, including one where the road had broken away and fallen down the hillside to cover a part of the same road lower down and round the hairpin bend.

Assuming nothing more serious had happened since the Apple images were taken, I could have probably made it unscathed to Laureana.

When Kay and I first came to Calabria as a holiday destination, we flew to Rome, stayed overnight between Rome and Naples and continued our journey south the following morning. At Salerno in Campania we joined the A3 *autostrada* which goes all the way down to Reggio Calabria.

We were driving along this stretch of the A3 for the first time, through that part of Basilicata that touches the Tyrrhenian Sea, when, responding to the tell-tale rumblings in our stomachs, we exited the *autostrada* in search of lunch.

Truth be told, we were glad to leave the *autostrada* for it was a welcome break from the then incessant roadworks and lane changes that epitomised that part of the A3 at the time. We know now that these works were not the result of the forces of unpredictable nature, or even good old-fashioned wear and tear, but rather, as I will expand on in the next chapter, of corruption and mismanagement on a massive scale.

(On a later occasion, and still ignorant as to what was really going on regarding the A3, we became so frustrated with it all that we decided to leave the *autostrada* at its intersection with the Belvedere to Sibari road and cut across country to the Ionian coast and thence south towards Crotone and our Santa Severina destination.)

However, on that first occasion, abandoning the *autostrada* at that particular point was no more than a spontaneous decision and, as it turned out, a fortuitous one.

At the time neither of us had any idea that, just a few miles earlier, and halfway through a tunnel, we had already crossed into Calabria.

Nor were we aware that we were traversing the same general area that travellers had used as a gateway to and from Calabria for hundreds of years.

Nor did we appreciate the fact that the glorious mountain scenery we were enjoying was the eastern edge of the Pollino National Park.

Nor did we realise that these mountains and their passes were once reputedly notorious for the activities of local bandits and brigands.

It was no more than hunger that drove us onwards and upwards, through a serpentine, richly-wooded landscape until we finally stumbled into the hilltop town of Mormanno.

Thereafter, a lunch break at Mormanno became part of our routine as we drove to and from Calabria. Not only were we attracted to the town itself, but we had also discovered the Chiarelli family—Lucio, his wife Maria, and their three children—who run a small restaurant in the town's *centro storico*. Apart from occasional snacks in and around Lamezia Airport en route elsewhere, dining courtesy of the Chiarelli family was our first real experience of Calabrian cuisine and Calabrian hospitality.

Almost immediately we knew that, quite by accident, we had stumbled upon a gem: a family that took enormous pride in preparing basic, authentic local fare with imagination and a touch of flare which they then presented to their customers with courtesy, pride and good humour. It was no accident that, even on a weekday lunchtime, in a small town with a population of just over three thousand people, this restaurant was always busy.

After we ate, just as we had done that first time, we always took a different route out of Mormanno and caught up with the *autostrada*—and its roadworks—a bit further south at Campo Tenese and close to neighbouring Morano Calabro.

The British travellers who came this way never climbed to the heights of Mormanno. Instead, those heading north out of Calabria usually passed through Castrovillari and/or Morano, crossed Campo Tenese, the plain south and east of Mormanno, before cutting through the Pass of Campo Tenese and between the mountains east of the town—'the most dangerous pass in all Calabria' according to Brian Hill (1791)—that took them on to Rotonda in Basilicata. Of course those entering Calabria *from* the north arrived via the same route in reverse, part of which corresponds roughly to the line taken by today's A3 *autostrada*.

The perceived danger that Hill cited came apparently from brigands and bandits though, when Swinburne (1780) mentioned the same pass, he did not accredit it with being dangerous at all. Likewise, Keppel-Craven (1818) travelling just thirty years after Hill and five years after the end of French Napoleonic rule, mentioned no such dangers. Strutt (1841) too, travelling in the opposite direction, did so seemingly oblivious to any such perils.

But then Brian Hill paid to be accompanied by an armed guard and seemed obsessed with the possible dangers; perhaps he would have been better off staying at home. He accredited the lack of any such encounter with Calabrian bandits to divine intervention rather than any monetary-inspired exaggeration on the part of his hosts:

"What *might* have happened, convinces me that the wise Disposer of *all* events has guarded our every step by his providential care, and has made us acquainted with the magnitude of our danger, that we may the more acknowledge his goodness in delivering us from it."

Likewise, I assume, the 'wise Disposer' was looking after his interests in respect of the good food and accommodation he enjoyed on his last night in Calabria at Morano Calabro:

"Our inn last night was, in comparison of our usual fare, capitally good. We had a fire-place adapted *to no other purpose*, and I lay in my clothes between sheets, without being disturbed by a single flea."

A few years ago the Apulia-born historian and writer Pino Aprile came to Mormanno to talk about his book *Terroni*, on the front cover of which there is an upside-down map of Italy. This is no printing error, but an attempt to illustrate that, before unification, the south of Italy was, economically, by far the wealthiest part of the Italian peninsula, just as the north is now. This was, of course, the reason the northern states and principalities were so keen on the idea of unification and the south was generally resistant to it.

During the Napoleonic period (1806–1815) Mormanno had a reputation for resistance and for a time a French detachment was stationed there. Fifty years on and the people of Mormanno were fighting a similar cause, the restoration of the Bourbon monarchy. In both cases those who resisted the new order of things were called brigands. Initially at least most were political brigands rather than roadside bandits—their cause during the Napoleonic period was anti-French, their cause in the 1860s was anti-unification.

Pino Aprile came to Mormanno to talk about the latter, about the time when politically-inspired brigands, opposed the forces—both political and armed—of Italian unification. In recent years, as we shall see, there has been a reassessment of what happened to the south in the years after unification, how the fortunes of Italy's north and south were turned on their heads.

In Mormanno, in the early 1860s, there were still those arguing and fighting for the return of the Naples-based Bourbon monarchy, for the 'good old days' of the Kingdom of the Two Sicilies. Their resistance was brutally repressed—as it was elsewhere in the south—until eventually the new *status quo* evolved into the accepted order of things. Like it or not, the unified nation of Italy, with its seat of government first in Turin then Florence and finally Rome, was here to stay ... of which some more later.

When, having lived in Calabria for several years, we returned to Mormanno to eat with the Chiarelli family, it was both a rewarding and humbling experience.

The little girl we used to say hello to us when she came home from school, weighed down by her satchel, was now a young woman, spoke very good English and at the time was just about to set off on a two-week adventure in England with her school. Her brothers too had shot up and, with courtesy beyond their years, abandoned their laptops and *cellulare* without being cajoled into doing so, and took time to engage in meaningful conversation.

Until that moment the Chiarelli family didn't know we now lived in Calabria, nor the part they played in our first tentative sorties into the toe of Italy. Nor, until then, did I realise the strategic importance of the area around this small community.

Perched high on the hillside on the northern edge of Calabria, for centuries Mormanno has stood, sentinel-like, overlooking one of the most important gateways to the *regione*. Nowadays it still does much the same as today's main artery to and from Calabria, the A3 *autostrada*, silently strides by on its concrete legs down in the valley on the other side of the town.

Mormanno was a place we had stumbled upon by accident and, had the lure of eating with the Chiarelli family not been so compelling, a place we might never have returned to. Later it became, for me, another important piece of the Calabrian jigsaw; at the same time the first and one of the last of many connections.

In search of *il Fondaco del Fico*

"... I drew up to the Fondaco del Fico where we baited. I dined at the door of this solitary inn, under the shade of a venerable cork-tree, and from my seat enjoyed a view of the whole gulf."
Henry Swinburne *Travels in the Two Sicilie.*

Having been bitten by the *Fondaco del Fico* bug it was time to run with my obsession and see if I could happen upon the whereabouts of the staging-post where Swinburne and others had stopped on their travels.

Having dropped Kay off at Lamezia Airport, I couldn't resist the challenge of driving south to see of I might happen upon the site of this elusive roadside inn. I knew it was, in Swinburne's estimation, 'some miles' from the northern bank of the river Angitola.

So, initially I drove south from Lamezia across the coastal plain of Sant'Eufémia and, with my head buzzing with the 'clues' I had gleaned from the writings of, among others, Carmine Abate, Vito Teti, Henry Swinburne, Richard Keppel-Craven and Alexandre Dumas, I turned back north onto the old road near the banks of the Angitola, where the river, railway, the coast road (the SS18), the A3 *autostrada* and the old road from Monte Leone (Vibo Valéntia) to Nicastro all converge. I also knew that this was the only road that took, in Keppel-Craven's words, 'an oblique direction towards Nicastro', albeit its modern, wider, tarmacked incarnation.

The road in question, today's SS19, was once an important Calabrian artery, the post-road from Reggio to Naples and the same route that Emily Lowe took in 1858 though she was fast asleep by the time the post reached

Fondaco del Fico. Leslie Gardiner (1966) explained the road's provenance:

"It was Murat [French ruler during most of the Napoleonic period, 1806-1815] who first opened up the province for the foreign tourist by extending a highway through Italy which had never gone further than Naples. In 1808 he continued it southward to Salerno and Lagonegro [in Campania], then into Calabria to Castrovillari, Cosenza, Catanzaro and Reggio."

As I set the car's odometer to zero, I reasoned that Swinburne's 'some miles' probably equated to between five and six kilometres, somewhere between three and four miles. Rightly or wrongly, my linguistic reasoning was this: had it been less than three miles, he would likely have said 'a couple'; had it been more than five, he would probably have said 'several'; to me, the fact that he used the word 'some', indicated a distance between three and four miles, definitely less than five.

That was the linguistic logic I carried in my head; I just hoped Swinburne and I were talking the same language. Also—and this too refers to the use of language—I definitely got the feeling from everything I'd read that the *Fondaco del Fico* was a little closer to Monte Leone than to Nicastro … any

Giacomo Cantelli's 1695 map, *L'Italia con le sue Poste e Strade Principali*, has *Fondaco del Fico* in the correct general location but no more than that. It's inclusion on such a map in the first place demonstrates its importance to the Two Sicilies' road network at the time. One of the several roadside contenders for being the site of the *Fondaco del Fico*; perhaps this derelict building did indeed once serve a similar purpose.

further north than five or six miles from the river Angitola and it would have been the other way round.

And I had some other pieces of documented geographical and statistical information in my armoury, though at the time I was not sure how accurate any of it might be.
As I mentioned in the last chapter, in Italian the word *fico* means fig but then I discovered—in Giovanni Fiore's *Della Calabria illustrata opera varia istorica, Volume 1*, published in 1691—that the river Angitola used to have another name, a name used by the lower classes ... l'Acqua della Fico. And, as Fiore quotes a source writing in Latin, it was clearly an ancient appellation. This of itself didn't tell me anything about the inn's precise location but it did confirm that the word *fico* had had local connotations for hundreds of years.

A little over a page into Irish cleric Richard Pococke's two-page/six-day dash through Calabria in 1733, his *A description of the East, and some other countries* was surprisingly precise about the location of what he called the 'Osteria Fondaclero':
"Under Monte Leone [Vibo Valéntia] we crossed a rivulet called Langeto, which, I suppose is the same as Angitola: We went in all twelve miles to Osteria Fondaclero, the first post from Monte Leone, and travelled four miles further to the large river Delamata, probably the ancient Lametus ..."
I reasoned that the shorter of Pococke's estimated distances, the four miles (six-and-a-half kilometres) to the 'Delamata', today's Lamato, was likely to have been the more accurate, particularly as the road down from Monte Leone was generally quite tortuous, making it more difficult to be as precise about the distance travelled.

In addition, in the *Nuovo dizionario geografico universale statistico-storico-commerciale*, published in 1828, over half of the entry for Filadelfia is about the *Fondaco del Fico*, also called the *Osteria di Cicerone*, and on the same site as the *Fundus Sicae*; but, most importantly, it puts its location as one league (three-and-a-half miles or five-and-a-half kilometres) north-west of Filadelfia.

And finally, in the *Corografia dell'Italia* published in 1833, there was a description of the *Fondaco del Fico* which indicated that it lay, as the crow flies, four miles from the mouth of the river Angitola. I assumed this had been worked out from maps of the area and that, given their level of accuracy at the time, that this could mean anywhere between three-and-a-half and four-and-a-half miles (five-and-a-half kilometres to just over seven).

When I plotted all this information onto a modern map of the area, I found that all the pointers converged at exactly the same spot that I had come up with using the linguistic reasoning described earlier.

Heading north-north-east from the Angitola river—in 'an oblique direction towards Nicastro'—I stopped more times than I care to remember to scrutinise possible sites on the inland side of the road to see if I could recreate Swinburne's 'view of the whole gulf' from my imaginary sitting position.

Where I came across a derelict building, there was no view; where there was a view the area seemed bereft of likely candidates for the site. I was clear too that the landscape had changed: fresh young trees blocked out some views and created new ones; the railway, the A3 *autostrada* and the new coast road, all running parallel to the Golfo di Sant'Eufémia, created a false perspective; newer homes, holiday apartments, small industrial sites and a veritable sea of greenhouses distorted the scene. I guessed I was on a hiding to nothing, nevertheless I persevered.

I accosted a few people working in the fields and tried to tap into their local knowledge but no-one had any idea what I was talking about. The initial, non-verbal response of one elderly man, unloading empty crates from an ancient, rust-ridden *Ape* (the three-wheeled, rural workhorse of southern

The fountains and adjacent house on the old road north of the Angitola.

Italy), did give me hope ... only to be dashed when he explained that he did recognise the name but only because someone else had once asked him the same question many years ago.

Could it have been Carmine Abate, I wondered? Or Vito Teti?

As the road continued to gently climb and the views of the gulf expanded and improved, I saw what appeared to be the outline of a red-brick building hidden a dozen yards above the road in a small overgrown copse and pulled over to take a closer look. The 'red-brick building' turned out to be no more than some rust-coloured netting strung up between the trees to form a protective canopy from under which I could hear the squawks of some excited chickens and could just about make out the form that was clearly feeding them. I called up and initially the only response was more audible squawking. A wary parting of leaves told me the 'shape' knew I had discovered his—or her—secret bosky chicken coup and was wondering whether to respond.

I called again and this time a young male "*Cosa?*" shrieked down to me from above; I could see a mop of long black hair but not any features that I would recognise again.

This voice is too young, I thought to myself, even as I explained my quest ... he'll not know anything.

"Maybe the fountains ... a few hundred yards up the road," was all he said before his head and his invisible body returned to the squawking task at hand.

It took me another ten minutes to get to the fountains as I was still stopping every now and then to take a closer look at this stone wall or that view of the not-too-distant sea. For a few moments, on one such pause, my gaze focused on the northern edge of the gulf as I watched a plane climb gently into the deep blue of the Calabrian sky before turning back across the Golfo di Sant'Eufémia to head northwards. A quick look at my watch confirmed what Kay had already messaged me; the flight to Rome was running late.

As I had expected it might, the chicken-fancier's 'few hundred yards up the road' turned out to be a few hundred Calabrian yards which I knew from experience could be up to five times longer than the thirty-six inches that I was once accustomed to.

I rounded a curve to see a long, low, stone wall with seven protruding spouts, each gushing water into a street-level trough below—this was a functional *fontana* and not a fountain in the ornamental sense, a source of clean, fresh spring water from the hillside above. The quality of the water was evident by the number of cars that drew in alongside with people filling their plastic water bottles. In Calabria the tap water is as good if not better than bottled water; Calabrian spring water from a fountain such as this is cool, crystal-clear and free; truly the nectar of waters.

Next to the fountains there was a two-storey building which seemed hemmed in on three sides by a tangle of trees and shrubs. Grasses fought for survival as they clung to the roof tiles, a flimsy white curtain fluttered out a first-floor window. Most recently a house it seemed, but who knows what before?

A young woman was coming down the stone steps at the side of the house. Her blonde hair tied back, she looked world-weary as she carried her overflowing laundry basket towards the fountains. For this young woman, the spark of youth already beginning to leave her body, it seemed that washing-day was as hard as it had been for her mother and grandmother ... a cold, labour-intensive, hands-on, repetitive chore.

I parked up just beyond the house and took a deep breath, drank the last of my 'bought' water and walked back to the fountains clutching my empty bottle in one hand and my camera in the other.

Is this, as the adjacent signpost suggests, the *Fondaco del Fico*? Or is it a more recent building occupying more or less the same site, midway between Monte Leone (as it was at the time) and Nicastro? The line of fountains goes off to the right from where the bottom of the original stone steps from the building meet the road.

To say I was feeling excited would be an understatement. A glance at the car's odometer had already told me that this building was exactly five and a half kilometres from the river, the equivalent of almost three and a half miles or, as Swinburne might have put it, 'some miles'.

I crossed the road to take a photo of the house and noticed a sign at the far end of the low wall of fountains, so re-crossed to have a closer look. It looked like a relatively new sign, erected by the local authority, and read as follows:

"The fountain of the *Fondaco del Fico*, a staging-post on the Royal Road of Calabria."

For a few moments I was speechless … not that I had anyone to talk to. But I soon rectified that and went over to have a few words with the young woman busy rinsing out her washing. I asked her if the house she was living in was the old *Fondaco del Fico*. She looked at me blankly and indicated, in broken Italian, that she did not speak Italian. I tried English; she shook her head. German, perhaps? Not a word. She was looking agitated.

Slowly the penny dropped … she did not *want* to speak to me. She was almost certainly East European and she was wary of me in case I represented some sort of officialdom for it was likely she and her family were 'squatting' in the house which may or may not have been the *Fondaco del Fico* itself.

A van pulled up and three men got out to fill their water bottles. I asked the oldest if he knew whether the house by the fountains was the old *Fondaco del Fico*. He said he wasn't sure but that he thought it was either this or the one across the road partially blocking the view of the sea. I was fairly certain that the other house was a much newer addition to the landscape and certainly wouldn't have been there in Swinburne's day and obstructed his 'view of the whole gulf'.

My new friend asked me if I was German; I told him I was Irish.

"You're fucking Irish?" he asked in perfect, socially-dodgy English.

Grinning broadly he repeating himself, "The fucking Irish in Calabria?"

I could see he was enjoying this as he explained that he had worked in England for many years in the seventies and eighties when the Irish 'troubles' were at their height and many of his English work-mates there used to speak of the Irish in such terms. It turned out I was the first fucking Irish person he'd actually met.

As the van drove off, another car pulled up and a couple got out to fill *their* bottles and so I tried once again to ascertain if this house was actually the *Fondaco del Fico*. I think I was expecting a ruin and not a building that, to all intents and purposes, remained habitable, though was almost certainly lacking in all essential services such as gas and electricity. Water, on the other hand, was clearly never going to be a problem.

This couple were incredibly helpful and though they were a little way from their home patch, they knew the area well enough and were fairly certain this was the place ... after all the sign more or less said so, didn't it?

I was still not sure; perhaps this was the site but not the original building? I think I was also sceptical because, if this were indeed the *Fondaco del Fico*, how was it I had found it so easily? I wondered if perhaps others had made the same mistake that I had nearly made myself and assumed that the coast road, the SS18, took the line of an older road? There may well have once been an older road there too but, in reality, the original road took a slightly more elevated and 'oblique' route ... and the line of that road still existed. I had just driven along it.

Everything pointed to this being the *Fondaco del Fico* but I couldn't be certain about what lay behind the rendered façade of the house and I knew I was unlikely to get an invitation to lunch. Certainly the only unrendered part of the building, the stone steps, looked as if they could have been a

On this aerial view, the *Fondaco del Fico* is indicated by a white dot; unfortunately the building itself is out of sight below some trees. The winding road (the SS19) runs diagonally across the right-lower corner. From the road the land drops away significantly towards the A3 *autostrada* and the adjacent railway, both of which are on the extreme left; from the *Fondaco del Fico* to the *autostrada* as the crow flies is half a mile. The silvery-white, angular shapes scattered between the SS19 and the *autostrada* are greenhouses.

couple of hundred years old or more. And to have the main entrance on the first floor would not have been unusual back then when the lower floors were generally used for storage and/or as stables.

Of one thing I was now fairly certain ... no ruins lay under the A3 *autostrada*; that was over half a mile away down in the valley from where Swinburne would only have had a 'view of the whole gulf' if he had climbed that cork-oak he talked about; and even then it would have been unlikely.

Nevertheless, I desperately wanted to plonk myself down, in imaginary sitting mode, at the front of the house to take in that view and compare it in my mind's eye with Swinburne's description. But, as I was already getting some strange looks from the young woman who couldn't possibly understand my interest in her temporary home and its environs, I knew it would not be appropriate. I had to accept that, at this particular time, I was a *persona non grata* and would have to make do with my imagination.

I decided it was time to visit the local authority, the *Comune di Francovilla Angitola*, to pick their local brains and see if I could finally draw a line under this particular Calabrian diversion. Everyone I met at the town hall was eager to help me with my quest and I spent some time there poring over old maps but, despite the knowledge and enthusiasm of the staff, I still came away with some unanswered questions.

I was given the impression that *Fondaco del Fico* may have been more of a general area than a specific place or building but every piece of evidence I had gleaned from both historical records and travellers' accounts suggested otherwise. It was put to me again that the actual inn might well be under the A3 *autostrada*, the theory of local writer Vito Teti. Quite simply if it had indeed been located there, then it would have been impossible for Swinburne to have seen the gulf from its roof, let alone the doorstep. And, besides, *everyone's* estimations of the distances involved would have had to have been wildly inaccurate.

Of course there may well have been a number of different buildings at more or less the same location over the centuries, all of which, at different times, fulfilled the needs of passing travellers. Nevertheless I am as certain as I can be that the building by the fountains, given the undoubted need for rebuilding, restoration and conversion with the passage of time, was indeed the site of the staging-post where so many travellers took a break or changed horses between Monte Leone and Nicastro. Also, for such a place to have been viable, the one essential would have been the availability of fresh water. In every respect this site was perfect and it even complied with Swinburne's description of being 'solitary' for, on that side of the road—and it had to be on the eastern edge to see the sea from the doorstep—there was not another building for many hundreds of yards.

Even though I was sure that this was the site of the *Fondaco del Fico*, it still felt a bit like Attila the Hun's axe being offered for sale on the internet ... definitely the original axe but over the years it had had two new heads and three new shafts.

Of course I had neither 'discovered' the *Fondaco de Fico*, nor put an end to the speculation and interest. All I had done was have a lot of fun trying to work out the location for myself from the available information. In that respect, perhaps I had a little more going for me in that some of the earlier texts were in English and I was the better able to understand the subtleties of the language than those relying on a translation.

Lamezia Terme

> ... as there are no inns in that province [Calabria] except on the coach-road, which skirts the western coast, the traveller depends entirely on introductions to some family in each town he visits.
> **Edward Lear** *Journals of a landscape painter ...*

My first footfall in Calabria was when I walked across the tarmac to the terminal at Lamezia Terme airport, en route to Sicily. On that occasion I was alone, though I had managed to 'pick up' a stray travelling companion who needed a lift to Reggio Calabria in my rental.

I didn't know I was in Calabria; I was at Lamezia Terme airport late at night, heading for Sicily via Reggio Calabria. Sicily was the goal, the 110 kilometres between airport and ferry no more than a means to an end. The notion of Italian regions simply not on my radar.

On my third such flight—and still heading for Sicily—I got talking to one of the in-flight attendants, an Irish lass who picked up on my accent. She asked me why on earth we were going to Lamezia Terme ... after all there's nothing there she said. She went on to recount how, on a previous flight there, one of the airport's ground staff somehow managed to poke a hole in part of the plane's fuselage and they had to stay put overnight instead of flying straight back to London.

This meant finding overnight accommodation locally for the flight crew who naturally assumed they were in for a great night out on the town.

She went on to explain that the Lamezia Terme flight was always one of their busiest, the people incredibly friendly—if a little boisterous—and always clapped vigorously when the plane landed. She had assumed therefore that Lamezia Terme was a largish city by the sea with lots of hotels and an exciting nightlife.

The only thing she got right was that it is relatively close to the sea ... not actually on the sea but close enough.

As it happened I was able to answer her question for, on an earlier trip to Sicily, again via Lamezia—by which time I had, like most others, dropped the 'Terme'—we had arrived back in the area a couple of hours before our flight with the intention of going into 'Lamezia' to eat before flying home. I told her how we kept going round in ever-decreasing circles, following road signs that didn't seem to lead anywhere until, in desperation, we gave up and headed instead for the airport in search of food.

As a consequence of that experience, back in England I had done some research on this curious place and was able to explain to the flight attendant that Lamezia was a relatively modern concept, a toponym which consists of three towns: the large, hillside sprawl of Nicastro, the smaller Sambiase and the location of the airport on the flat coastal plain, the very much smaller Sant'Eufémia Lamezia. In terms of population Lamezia is Calabria's third largest conurbation; in terms of a focal point it still remains a mystery.

If, on our search for food all those years ago, we had followed signs to either Sambiase or Nicastro, or even Sant'Eufémia, our appetites would have been sated.

Later, when we moved to Calabria to live, Lamezia, and in particular its airport, initially became the gateway for friends and family coming to visit. To collect and drop involved two round trips so gradually we got to know that corner of Calabria quite well, its restaurants, its large commercial centre or mall, *Due Mare*, its railway and its *autostrada*, the ubiquitous A3.

Over the years Lamezia Terme, or rather its name giver, the small town of Sant'Eufémia Lamezia, has become Calabria's most important communications hub. It boasts the region's largest airport, is an important station stop for trains between Rome, Naples and Sicily, is the western end of the region's shortest and fastest east-west artery linking the Tyrrhenian and Ionian coasts and is on Calabria's only *autostrada*, the aforementioned A3. It also, as it's full name suggests, has a *terme*, a spa area close to Sambiase in the hamlet known as Caronte.

Ironically one of the last parts of the A3 to be upgraded was arguably its most important junction at Lamezia Terme with both the airport and the station each less than two kilometres away. (The last to be completed was the stretch between Mormanno and Campo Tenese in the north.)

Like most such travel hubs Lamezia is a place from which people disperse; they arrive by plane or train en route to somewhere else. I was accustomed to doing the same until that fateful night en route back home from Chicago via London (where I was reunited with Kay) when our little Renault Clio blew up on the *superstrada*, the *SS280*, ten miles east of the airport and south-east of Nicastro.

When I say 'blew up' There was no explosion as such, the car just came to a grinding halt while, inside the engine, I later discovered there had been the equivalent of a minor explosion as pistons and push rods became mangled and distorted as the distribution belt snapped.

Luckily our insurance covered us for being towed off the road and to a mechanic in Nicastro though, it being eleven at night, no work could be done till the following morning and, in the meantime, we had to find somewhere to stay. Before taking the car to Nicastro the kindly mechanic drove us back Sant'Eufémia Lamezia where there was a cluster of hotels and of course an airport where we could rent a car should we need it.

The next morning when we found out the extent of the damage we knew we would be car-less for up to three days so we did indeed need to return to the airport to pick up a rental to get us home. Coincidentally, we were also able to pick up our missing luggage from the flight the night before which had just turned up on the first flight of the morning from Rome.

Three days later when we returned to the Lamezia area to exchange the rental for our rejuvenated Clio in Nicastro, I took the opportunity to try and piece together the curious hotch-potch of towns and communities that is Lamezia Terme.

Sant'Eufémia Lamezia is host to the area's latest link to the outside world, the airport—it is the nearby coastline that passengers look down on as their plane comes into land. The main street between the small town and the sea is where you'll find the area's first claim to fame as a travel hub, the railway station; the second, the A3 crawls north-south behind the railway. It's all very compact.

But even Henry Swinburne (1780) writing about his visit to the area recognised the position of 'Lamezia'—the focal point of the wide coastal plain, known as the *Piano Lamentina*, and the valley of the river Lamato (Amato that once was)—as a place of importance to the traveller:

"This is the narrowest part of Italy, and here the road from Naples by

Puglia and Catanzaro crosses from the shore of the Ionic sea to that of the Mediterranean."

The town of Sant'Eufémia Lamezia itself does not touch the other two parts of this jigsaw—Sambiase and Nicastro—in the way these two touch each other. The place that gives the area its modern name is off on a south-western limb, the custodian of the airport and the station. Sambiase is nearly five miles almost due north along a road that is, for the most part, dead straight (a rarity in Calabria); where this directness ends, and the road veers off to the right, the route ahead goes on to Caronte the site of the so-called Caronte thermal waters, the *terme* in the collective Lamezia Terme.

Accounts vary to the length of time the properties of Caronte's sulphurous waters have been recognised and exploited ... some say from antiquity, the 2nd century CE, while others point with more certainty to the 11th century and the Norman subjugation of Calabria. It is well-documented that, to recover from the rigours of battle, the Norman army of nobleman and adventurer Robert Guiscard camped near the area in 1056. There is no evidence that this was any more than coincidence as the area holds a commanding strategic position over the expansive coastal plain and the wide Gulf of Sant'Eufémia and is protected by mountains to the rear.

When Swinburne (1780) came this way, he recorded the following:

"Near that [town] of San Biaggio, are warm baths of great efficacy in many diseases; their sulphureous quality shews the volcanic composition of those hills, and the proximity of subterranean fires, which have contributed towards converting this delicious country into a scene of desolation."

The view from Caronte is truly breathtaking, as is the smell of sulphur. The public can take advantage of a small cascade of water into a shallow pond by the car park while those who favour a more private and expensive 'treatment' can cross over to the modern thermal complex which offers all sorts of claims for what these waters can do to the world-weary body—before, during and after battle.

In the modern parlance, wherein the language of science and evidence generally takes a back seat, it is seemingly an ideal place for 'prevention programmes, treatment and rehabilitation, in a climatically-favoured and ecologically-pristine environment, in which to regain health and well-being'. I arrived in the same rude health as I left and headed back down the hill to Sambiase or, as Henry Swinburne called it, San Biaggio.

When Sambiase turns up in the travels of Craufurd Tait Ramage (1828), he calls it S. Biagio and accredits it with also being host to '... sulphureous waters, considered a cure for many diseases'. But his main preoccupation is in finding somewhere to eat:

"Here I wished to dine, but there was no *locanda*. The shopkeeper, however, of the village undertook to furnish me with dinner, and I tried to get some rest by stretching myself on a hard bench. Meanwhile the inhabitants collected round the door, and jostled each other to get a peep at me. To think of sleep was useless unless I could eject a large body of the inhabitants, who showed much anxiety to question me on many points respecting England. The Thames Tunnel they had heard of, and that seemed to give them a higher idea of the power and riches of England than any fact in her history with which they were acquainted."

Mention of the Thames Tunnel sent me racing to the internet for I knew this to be a unique project involving the astonishing and innovative British engineer, Isambard Kingdom Brunel (about whom I have extolled elsewhere) and I seemed to recall that, when Ramage was travelling in Calabria, work could only just have begun on the tunnel. My instinct was correct, work had indeed started in 1825 but, because of many setbacks, both engineering and financial, it was not completed until 1841. I consider it more than a little strange that the inhabitants of a small town in deepest Calabria were so interested in a project so far from completion ... it was not until the 1840s that the American writer, William Allen Drew, gave the tunnel more international notoriety by dubbing it the 'eighth wonder of the world'. That said, Ramage's book was not published until 1868 and perhaps his recollections, were a little hazy and/or influenced by subsequent events.

Ironically Ramage was not the only one to be quizzed on the Thames Tunnel, on more than one occasion Edward Lear's (1847) hosts brought up the subject. One in particular, a priest no less, had a rather strange picture of England in his mind:

"England is a very small place, although thickly inhabited ... The whole place is divided into two equal parts by an arm of the sea, under which there is a great tunnel, so that it is all like one piece of dry land."

The Sambiase I visited had not only morphed its earlier names but had shed the 'sulphurous waters' that Ramage had erroneously bestowed on it and spread it wings across the hillside to touch its much larger neighbour— and Lamezia Terme partner—Nicastro. But what it has not yet completely shed is some of its very old buildings.

As you would expect, most Calabrian towns have a mix of modern and old, but the narrow streets and alleyways of Sambiase's *centro storico* are a cheek-by-jowl hotchpotch of what is, what was and what might have been. Surely some of these very houses, still relying on each other to keep upright, were part of the 'Sambiase' that both Swinburne and Ramage experienced, perhaps even the very *locanda* where Ramage caused such a fuss by just being a foreigner.

I was walking up one such street when I saw an elderly man sitting outside a featureless house on a rickety old chair which seemed much older than he was. His tanned and wrinkled face was taking the air, watching the same old, monotonous world go by ... until, that is, he spotted a new face crossing his domain.

I stopped to greet him, to shake hands and satisfy the unmistakable curiosity in his expression. But I was curious too and asked about the name of the town; I wanted to know when its name had changed from San Biagio (or Biaggio) to Sambiase.

Still holding on to my outstretched hand like a lifelong friend, he shook his head as he asserted defiantly that it had always been Sambiase, never been anything else, never heard of it ever being called anything else. When I asked if he'd lived here all his life, he confessed he was, like me, a relative newcomer to the town where he'd lived for more than fifty years but, nevertheless, he repeated his assertion that it had always been Sambiase.

Finally we disengaged and, as it was that time of day, I wished him *buon pranzo* (have a good lunch) before continuing uphill where I espied another elderly resident. This seventy-something had falteringly turned the corner out of a narrow alleyway and, using his stick to steady him on one side and the wall of a house on the other, slowly began to descend the uneven surface towards me. His shuffling progress was not helped by backless slippers that

Sambiase's *centro storico*, the old still clinging on to the new. Local poet Franco Costabile.

seemed to want to assert their independence from his feet.

I guessed he was probably en route to lunch at the home of one of his children, grandchildren even, and would be, I surmised, glad of the respite when I stopped to have a chat. He straightened up as if to deny any lack of mobility I might have witnessed seconds earlier; at the same time blaming it on a new hip that wasn't working properly yet.

"*Pian piano*", he said, trying to convince himself that there was no need to rush or perhaps entreating me to slow down. Maybe both.

Before I could get a word in edgeways he had already gleaned from my colouring and demeanour that I was indeed a foreigner. No, not German as he thought, but lived in Calabria in Santa Severina (of which he had heard) and, like others before him with a hearing problem, he flirted temporarily with the notion I might be *olandese* rather than *irlandese*. With my pedigree and nationality sorted, it was finally my turn to speak.

I started by confirming that he was indeed a local and had lived in Sambiase *all* his long life. He was and he had. He added, lest I might deem it relevant, that he had once been to Catanzaro. Again I tried San Biagio on him as a possible name he may have heard his parents or grandparents use and once again I drew a blank; Sambiase it had always been. Not in fact true, but any latent memory to the effect had long since evaporated.

He continued his faltering descent while I went onwards and upwards, reflecting on the vagaries of life and what my own life might have been had a been born here. I hoped I might have got further than Catanzaro.

On my descent ten minutes later, both men were gone, only the chair remained. The aromas wafting through the narrow streets told me that, behind closed doors, mothers, daughters, wives and sisters were bringing the pasta to the boil.

It was, I mused, in among these streets that the renowned Calabrian poet Franco Costabile (1924–1965) played and from where he must have drawn much of his inspiration. He was greatly effected by the separation of his parents who could not agree on where to live ... his father went to Tunisia and was adamant about staying there; his mother was equally adamant that they family should unite in Sambiase.

Brian Hill (1791) came this way too and in so doing remarked on its distance from his previous stop-over, Monte Leone (today's Vibo Valéntia), Nicastro was, he said, 'computed at twenty-five miles but I think they are very long ones'. Even then the Calabrian concept of distance, like that of time, appeared to have acquired a flexible quality. According to Hill, Nicastro was:

"… represented to us as a nest of robbers and plunderers; we mounted this long steep hill on foot, comforting ourselves by the way with the idea of reposing at ease in this Cassino, to the owner of which we had a letter from the naval priest of Monte Leone."

(In this context the word *cassino*, is the diminutive of *casa* and probably refers to a small house rather than a gambling house.)

I'll get back to the 'nest of robbers and plunderers' presently but first a diversion into the logistics of being a foreigner and travelling to places that were not exactly overrun with good inns. Even DH Lawrence discovered this as recently as 1921 in Sardinia even with his modern Baedecker guide.

Unlike Lawrence—whose Sardinian venture was spontaneous rather than planned—earlier travellers brought with them appropriate letters of introduction which generally guaranteed a reasonable night's sleep and adequate victuals for the length of their stay in a specific town or village.

It must be remembered that, unlike today, travellers who wrote about their travels were generally from the same class … the fact that they could write at all is a clue. They generally had the funds to satisfy their whimsy and with these letters of introduction they were indicating to their respective host that they came of good stock, were well-educated and were not going to trash the place.

Sometimes travellers had several letters of introduction in place before they set out, sometimes they picked them up along the way. Brian Hill (1791) had clearly been given such a letter in Monte Leone to guarantee him and his companion a comfortable overnight stop at Nicastro but, in this case, it didn't quite work out as planned …

"We had, however, the mortification of hearing, upon our arrival that the house, which consisted of two small rooms, was occupied but that an adjoining chapel was at our service, if we chose to make use of it."

Hill and company did indeed spend a comfortable night until their early morning call at half past three sent them on their way again—even in mid-March it was more comfortable to travel in the early morning. The next night they were at Cosenza, then the capital of Higher Calabria and fared much worse for, without any letter of introduction, they had to stay at an inn which he described as 'abominable'.

A worse fate befell Edward Lear (1847) when he arrived at one such stop-over and, clutching his letter of introduction, stood at the door of the house where he was expecting to be entertained:

"... but alas! Don Pasquale Zerbi, its owner, was away, and all his palazzo shut up for repairs! Our only hope and help, therefore, was in a most wretched locanda—a very horrid den: at its door we sat, and prolonged our supper of eggs till late: but the numbers of formidable vermin were so great and distressing in the sleeping apartments, that we could not contemplate the animated beds without a shudder; whereon we sat up and waited till daybreak, as best we might."

Norman Douglas (1911), on the other hand, did not like this passion for letters of introduction:
"In olden days I used to visit south Italy armed with introductions to merchants, noblemen and landed proprietors. I have quite abandoned that system, as these people, bless their hearts, have such cordial notions of hospitality that from morning to night the traveller has not a moment he can call his own. Letters to persons in authority, such as syndics [mayors] or police officers, are useless and worse than useless. Like Chinese mandarins, these officials are so puffed up with their own importance that it is sheer waste of time to call upon them. If wanted, they can always be found; if not, they are best left alone."

The only time that we arrived somewhere without the modern equivalent of the letter of introduction—an internet booking—was, as it happens, the night our car was taken ill and despatched to Nicastro and we were left stranded in Sant'Eufémia. It was around half-eleven at night when we straggled into the Grand Hotel just opposite the station; I had, if you recall, just flown from Chicago and had already gone thirty-five hours without proper sleep. The receptionist threw up his hands in horror that anyone should arrive at such an hour *and* without a letter of introduction. After much animated key-punching and several negative hand gestures to an accompanying shaking of the head, he gloomily confirmed there was not a single room available; the Grand Hotel was full to bursting.

I bent down and lifted my bag and said, "Don't worry, we'll try the Piccolo Hotel, down the road"; fortunately I'd noticed the sign for the Piccolo when the breakdown truck dropped us off.

"*Aspetta, aspetta*", was his not unexpected entreaty to wait a moment as, once again, his keyboard fingers swung into action and, having thus hastily rechecked his computer, miraculously—and accompanied by a flurry of conciliatory hand gestures—he found us a room after all.

Ironically, according to Leslie Gardiner (1966), it was at Nicastro that Gaetano Marzotto located his first Jolly Hotel in southern Italy:

"Nicastro is by no means an international tourist's paradise ... but it was there that Count Marzotto of Vicenza saw his vision of a chain of luxury hotels stretching across the south, and there that he built his first Jolly Hotel. It still functions – Category One, rather expensive, ignored by Nicastrians."

Gardiner's description of Nicastrian night life is not dissimilar to the experience of the air crew I described earlier though of course they were not actually in Nicastro but in and around the airport and the much smaller Sant'Eufémia Lamezia out of season:

"Arrive there after dark ... and you find the shroud of apathy, boredom and somnolence spread over the town. The citizens have withdrawn, each inside his own four wall, and the few who remain about the ill-lit streets wear characteristic expressions of resignation to a life without hope or purpose. The hotel lounge is a morgue. The clerk mentions, apologetically, two cinemas—both closed."

Half a century on and things have changed ... though not necessarily for the better. Today's Nicastro is a sprawling mass of all the things that these days personify urban living; it exudes the impression of being no more than the usual mish-mash of twenty-first century housing and shopping.

The chain stores have found their way here and generally occupy the lower, out-of-town hillside. Onwards and upwards, in the heart of the town

The Jolly Hotel at Nicastro in the mid sixties as it would have been when Leslie Gardiner was in the town.

above the railway station, there are a couple of long, older, prouder streets, a reminder of what this city was before its rebirth in 1968 as the largest part (and administrative centre) of Lamezia Terme. Ironically it's the two much smaller satellites, Sambiase and Sant'Eufémia Lamezia, each receive infinitely more coverage on their respective *Wikipedia* pages.

Overseeing all of this, there is a reminder of past glories in the ruins of the city's castle; the town's name, Nicastro, means 'new castle'.

As scholars in such matters, Swinburne (1780), Keppel-Craven (1818) and Ramage (1828) all refer to the castle's main claim to fame as the place where the Emperor Frederick II (1194–1250) imprisoned his rebellious and incautious son, Henry.

Young Henry had ambitions beyond his station and, when it came to forging and maintaining appropriate political alliances, was wont to disregard the wishes of his father Frederick, a powerful and astute man who was Emperor of the Holy Roman Empire that stretched from Sicily to Germany and east to Jerusalem. Nicastro was Henry's second place of incarceration. He was in Apulia for a time, then Nicastro and in 1242 was moved to Martirano, a short distance north-west of Nicastro, where he died.

This is Swinburne's account of what happened:

"[He] was afterwards transferred, for greater security, to Nicastro, and then to the neighbouring city of Martorano, where despair put an end to his existence; Bocaccio says that in a fit of frenzy he forced his horse to leap over a bridge, and was drowned in the river Savuto."

Recent examination of Henry's skeleton suggests that, at the time of his death, he was suffering from advanced leprosy.

The observations of both Swinburne and Ramage paint pictures of a place which is both bounteous in its natural beauty and in its commanding vistas.

Swinburne: "Its neighbourhood is replete with beauties of landscape.— High, woody mountains seem to block up all communication with any country further north, while an easy passage opens towards the gulf of Squillace: the plain that lies to the south is diversified in the most luxuriant manner with corn fields, plantations of fruit trees, and ever-green groves."

Ramage: "The hills around Nicastro ... are covered with immense groves of olive-trees, and the balsamic odours which were exhaled from the orange and lemon trees in this neighbourhood might have led me to believe that I had come upon 'Araby the blest'"

Ramage's homage in the last line to a romantic notion of Arabia is a typical reference that permeates his writing and that of all other travellers of the time. Their classical education seeps from their very pores; they cannot help themselves. Talking about antiquity (and in particular Magna Græcia) and the classics was second nature and in this respect being in Calabria was a particularly fertile source of potential conversation, elucidation, embroidery and of course for brandishing and sharing one's knowledge. They were writing for an audience they knew intimately, it being more than likely that the only people ever to read their accounts were those with a similar background and education.

Back in the real world, I recall stopping, opposite a Chinese restaurant, to look back up at Nicastro and couldn't resist a wry smile as I recalled Swinburne's reference to the high, woody mountains that appeared to 'block up all communication with any country further north' for things have truly gone full circle. It is those very high, woody mountains behind the city and their attendant telecommunications masts that these days are the conduits for 'all communication' north, south, east and west.

Back at Sant'Eufémia Lamezia I once again bump into Henry Swinburne who is in contemplative mood as he looks down on the small hamlet that is the gateway to the nearby Gulf of Sant'Eufémia. (Ramage never came this way, preferring instead to take a more direct route to Sambiase from his previous port of call, Nocera.)

Swinburne is the only of my fellow-travellers to have visited Calabria *before* 1783, in the winter and spring of which year five earthquakes struck the region.

So Swinburne was blissfully unaware what was just around the corner when he wrote about an earlier cataclysmic event which hit Sant'Eufémia in March 1638. As it happened there was an eye-witness, the German scholar, polymath and lateral thinker, Athanasius Kircher, who wrote about what he saw in his *Mundus subterraneus, quo universae denique naturae divitiae* from which Swinburne quotes extensively. I make no apology for doing the same:

"We landed beyond Lo Pizzo: but there our situation appeared more shocking than ever: on one side the sea ran mountains high; on the other, nothing was to be heard or seen but the destruction of towns and villages. I now cast an anxious eye back upon Strómboli, and found that it burnt with uncommon fury; one sheet of fire covered its whole extent; a more dreadful conflagration could no be seen.

"And now a dead kind of noise, like distant thunder, crept along the bowels of the earth, growing gradually stronger and stronger, till it reached the spot beneath our feet; then indeed its quakings and noises were terrible beyond conception; and each man finding his feet no longer able to maintain his equilibrium, caught at the shrubs and twigs on the shore, lest, as he expected, his very limbs should be disjointed by the various and contrary motions of the basis he stood upon.

"When nature had recovered from this convulsion: and we rose again as from the grave to look once more up to the light of heaven, we cast our eyes towards the town of Saint Eufémia, whither we were bound; but in the place where we expected to find it, a dark cloud covered every object; as it dispersed, instead of houses and churches, nothing appeared but a fetid lake!

"Though most petrified with amazement, we hastened to seek some survivor who might explain to us the phenomenon we beheld; not one was to be met with, till at last we found a youth sitting on the shore, stupefied with terror; of him we enquired the fate of St. Eufémia, but obtained no answer; for fear, grief, and despair, had bound up his powers of speech, and frozen his soul!—No kind offers, no soothing terms we could employ, were able to extort a word from him. Overpowered by sorrow, he rejected with loathing the victuals we tendered; but just had courage to extend his arm, and point to the place where St. Eufémia stood.

"Thus dead to consolation, with down-cast looks, and the countenance of a man distracted with sorrow, he walked from us, and hid himself in the neighbouring thicket. We pursued our route through many places amidst scenes of desolation; and , during the course of two hundred miles, saw nothing but ruined towns, inhabitants wandering about the open fields; and persons almost senseless through dismay."

What Athanasius Kircher witnessed were emissions of smoke and ash from two volcanoes, Etna and Strómboli, and on the same day (March 27) a devastating earthquake struck the region, centred just north-west of Nicastro; in June there followed another earthquake, centreed close to Savelli in the Sila massif. Later the same year Kircher was also a witness as Vesuvius, the erstwhile destroyer of Pompeii, erupted.

1638 was the year the southern Italian peninsula was literally on fire.

The area around Sant'Eufémia Lamezia has recovered from both 1638 and the lesser ravages of the 1783 earthquakes, but the original town itself never did. Ramage, en route to Nicastro from Nocero, never ventured this way as there was little to see. The town of Sant'Eufémia had been all but wiped off the face of the earth by the final blow, the massive tidal wave that destroyed anything and everything that the earthquake left standing. Today, between the coast road, the SS18, and the sea there are some lakes—often visible on the left just before touchdown at Lamezia Airport. These are half salt and half fresh water and were formed when, in 1638, the land imploded and the sea rushed in.

When Richard Keppel-Craven (1818) passed this way he described what was left of Sant'Eufémia thus:

"… now a wretched village of 200 inhabitants, is the representative of one of the most respected towns in the province, swallowed up in the earthquake of 1638 …"

This 'wretched village' was not on the same site as the original Sant'Eufémia but rather on the present site of Sant'Eufémia Vetere, ('Vetere' is a derivation of the Latin for 'old') a small hamlet founded after the 1638 earthquake north and east of today's Sant'Eufémia Lamezia and of course also now a part of the larger Lamezia Terme.

In today's incarnation of Sant'Eufémia Lamezia you will find no old buildings such as those in Sambiase or Nicastro for Sant'Eufémia Lamezia as we now know it was born again during the Mussolini era and became a town, a *comune*, in it's own right in 1935.

A modern booklet that gives information on the thirty-three historical buildings in the Lamezia Terme area only has one that relates to Sant'Eufémia Lamezia and even this, a church, is a relatively modern structure.

Nevertheless, today Sant'Eufémia is a small, thriving Calabrian community with an international airport which, if the ever-increasing number of hotels in the area is anything to go by, is getting used to being the centre of attention, if not attraction, for many visitors to Calabria.

In the conurbation that is Lamezia Terme, I retain a deep affection for this place that was my first Calabrian experience … even if I was not aware of it at the time.

For a couple of years, between 2010 and 2012, Crotone became our airport of choice mainly because it was a much easier, thirty-five-minute drive compared to the one hour, thirty-five minutes to Lamezia. But the Crotone flights were discontinued for a couple of years and, once again, we had to travel to and from Lamezia—it was only then I realised how much I missed that corner of Calabria.

Since then things have changed again and the low-cost airline Ryanair has now discovered the potential of the south and has inaugurated new domestic routes to and from Crotone.

Of skirmishes

> ... I confess I was prepared to brave every danger, that I might wander over these scenes that had witnessed the noblest exhibition of human prowess. With these feelings, I threw myself unarmed and fearlessly on the protection of the Italian people ...
> **Craufurd Tait Ramage** *The Nooks and by-ways of Italy: Wanderings in search of its ancient remains and modern superstitions*

The road that links Catanzaro and Lamezia Terme is the fast and modern SS280, the aforementioned shortest and fastest east-west artery linking the Ionian and Tyrrhenian coasts; earlier travellers often called the former the Adriatic and the latter the Mediterranean. Lamezia Terme is situated to the north of the western end, the Tyrrhenian end, near to where it joins the A3 *autostrada*. Although there are mountains to cross it has always been an important east-west artery ... though of course today's SS280 now goes *through* the high ground rather than *over* and *round* it.

Driving to and from Lamezia airport it soon became our custom to stop off at what was—and possibly still is—Calabria's largest retail park known as the *Centro Commerciale Due Mare*. A brief stop-over at *Due Mare* was, and continues to be, an essential part of every trip to and from Lamezia Terme.

The *Due Mare* exit off the SS280 is sign-posted to Máida, a name not unfamiliar to those who know London well for the area known as Máida Vale, north of Paddington in west London, takes its name from a battle in Calabria.

It was between the town of Máida and the Lamezia end of the SS280 that the Battle of Máida was fought between the French and the British ... though,

CAMPANIA
BASILICATA
Il Pollino
Il Mar Ionio
CALABRIA
St Giovanni
in Fiore
Stragola
Stróngoli
COSENZA
Il Mar Tirreno
Belvedere
di Spinello
'Bandiera'
monument
La Sila
Santa Severina
CROTONE
LAMEZIA TERME
Isola di Capo Rissuto
Sambiase
Nicastro
Sant'Eufémia
CATANZARO
Máida
Caraffa
Cortale
Il Mar Ionio
VIBO VALÉNTIA
Messina
L'Aspromonte
Lo Stretto di Messina
Scilla
Cippo di Garibaldi
SICILIA
REGGIO
DI CALABRIA
Mélito di Porto Salvo

truth be told, it was more of an exaggerated skirmish. I first became aware of this, not from the town of Máida itself, but from the name of a restaurant in Crotone, The Máida; it was the fact that the 'The' was in English that caught my eye. Outside the restaurant there was a brief explanation (now gone) of how the name came about and it was this that first sparked my curiosity for it seemed odd, to say the least, that a British army should have found itself taking on the French somewhere between Lamezia and Máida.

As a student of history in my rebellious years, it never ceased to amaze me how the British had never ever lost a battle or a war ... in this respect, you understand, the American War of Independence doesn't count. So when I started to get interested in why it was that the French and the British clashed in Calabria I admit to having had a fervent desire for this to prove to be the exception by secretly willing a French victory. It wasn't to be.

I eventually found a plan of the battle site but, sadly, apart from the river Amato, it was devoid of any helpful markers as to where it might actually have taken place. It was only when I discovered that the French called it *Il Combat de Santa Eufémia*, and not after Máida, that things finally began to fall into place. Also Richard Keppel-Craven (1818), when talking of the town of Máida, stated that:

"The battle to which it gave a name was fought at some distance; but it was the first to receive the victorious troops."

Thus it appears that the site of the battle site was between the rivers Amato and Ippolito but not, as I first thought, a little to the west of *Due Mare,* almost exactly equidistant from both Máida and Sant'Eufémia. I then discovered that I was not the only person interested in this skirmish and following a short correspondence with Andrea Di Bernardo from Locri we were in accord that the battle site was not to the west of the *Due Mare* complex but rather *under* it and therefore just south of what is now the SS280. As Andrea put it ... "only in Italy such a thing ..."

And now for the hard part ... to try and explain why, in 1806, the French and the British were actually trying to kill each other on Calabrian soil.

As you might guess, it was all part of a much larger European picture and at a time when it was not unusual for two powers to appear to be skirmishing on the soil of a third to justify or settle some other grander scenario. In this context I use the word 'appear' because, from the French viewpoint at the time, Calabria was French territory.

That grander scenario was the Napoleonic Wars (1803-1815) and the principal combatants, France and Great Britain, and their coalition allies. One of these coalitions united Great Britain with, among others, the Bourbon Kingdom of Naples (the southern part of the Italian peninsula and Sicily) of which Calabria was clearly a part.

For years this part of Italy had been governed by the House of Bourbon but in post-revolutionary France this soon became a tussle between the House of Bourbon and Napoleon which resulted in Napoleon's brother Joseph Bonaparte becoming King of Naples in March 1806. The incumbent Bourbon king, known as Ferdinand III of the Kingdom of Sicily and also Ferdinand IV of the Kingdom of Naples, fled to the other part of his 'Two Sicilies' kingdom, to Sicily itself.

The position of Calabria, in respect of its proximity to Sicily, was crucial to what happened next. The British, fearing a French (Napoleonic) invasion of Sicily, either exploited the discontent of some Calabrians with their new rulers or helped instigate a revolt to justify sending a small army there. Unfortunately at the time there were no British travellers in the vicinity so information on this apparent Calabrian uprising is scant though increasingly the latter scenario seems the more likely.

All we know for certain is that the two armies—each just over 5000 men—crossed swords, guns and bayonets on 4 July 2006 on the plain of Sant'Eufémia. At the time the French army was already in residence in Calabria and the British forces had just arrived from Sicily at the beginning of the month. The ensuing battle lasted just fifteen minutes and the result was a British victory; Major-General John Stuart had effectively thwarted any immediate invasion of Sicily and completed his short stay in Calabria

An artist's eye-view of the Battle of Máida with the British fleet offshore and the river Amato flowing into the Gulf of Sant'Euphemia. The Maida restaurant at Crotone.

by picking off other French garrisons between Sant'Eufémia and Reggio Calabria.

In 1841 John Arthur Strutt and *his* fellow-travellers, some of whom at the time were French, were forced by events to spend over a week at nearby Cortale (I will elaborate on this story later in this chapter) and, one evening, he took a stroll with the Captain of the local constabulary and their host's son. Their goal was a commanding elevation from which they enjoyed a superb panorama of the entire countryside. Looking into the setting sun they could see the Gulf of Sant'Eufémia and between them and the sea, the broad coastal plain; to the east they could also see the Ionian coastline of the Gulf of Squillace.

The Captain told them the local version of events that led to the Battle of Máida and, while the outcome is not in dispute, the story, passed down by eye-witnesses, has the local Calabrians generally siding with the French and giving them advice as how they might defeat the English.

The advice was simple ... all the French had to do was stay where they were, control the higher ground and force the English to camp in the lower marshy ground close to the rivers Amato and Ippolito. Nature would do the rest without a shot being fired for this was an area which, it being July and the beginning of the long, hot Calabrian summer, was the perfect breeding ground for malaria-carrying mosquito (though at the time nobody knew it was the mosquito that was to blame). The impatient French commander, Jean Regnier, ignored this sound advice and lost the ensuing skirmish.

Perhaps the Battle of Máida did generate some pro-British sentiments in the area for, when Ramage (1828) passed through Nicastro some twenty-two years later, he happened upon an inn with an unusual name but one which appealed to him:

"Observing the sign of La Gran Bretagna, I thought that I could not do less than honour it with my company, and I found it really a very respectable inn."

―∞―

It was a strange day in Mormanno, the small hilltop town close to the A3 *autostrada* where Basilicata becomes Calabria. Not because it was our wedding anniversary but because it was just one of those days when everything seemed to go wrong.

After breakfast, and despite the intermittent slight drizzle, we went for a walk round the town and climbed the hillsides either side of the main street to take in the views. Later, just off the main street, we discovered a small market—always a magnet for us, even if we rarely buy anything—from where I noticed a good photo opportunity looking down over the hills into the tunnel-mouth of the *autostrada* partially covered in low cloud. I had my back turned to Kay when it happened and neither saw nor heard a thing.

Kay too had been snapping away when she stepped on a manhole cover, wet and slippery from the rain, and went flying. She stuck out her right arm and hand to break her fall and by the time I realised something had happened she was back on her feet, shaken but otherwise unscathed.

The same couldn't be said for her camera which, zoom lens extended, had taken the full impact of the fall right on the lens and was, to all extends and purposes, an ex-camera. This was confirmed later when we spend a frustrating half-hour with the kindly man from the local camera shop who finally conceded defeat and, with due solemnity, pronounced the last rites.

The weather cleared up after lunch and so, undaunted, we decided to take a leisurely stroll out of town and along the wooded road that overlooks the lake. We were over a mile from habitation when it suddenly got dark, as quickly as switching off a light, and the heavens opened to deposit an avalanche of rain right on top of us; even the roadside trees offered little protection. It was definitely not a good day.

Soaked to the skin, we decided to cut our losses and squelch our sodden way back to Mormanno, to seek the succour of our homely bed & breakfast and stay put for the rest of the day. On the bright side it was an opportunity to check out our hosts' extensive library.

It was here I first stumbled across books by two Frenchmen, Duret de Tavel and Charles Didier, both of whom were in the Mormanno area in the early 19th century. De Tavel was a soldier in Calabria during the Napoleonic period from 1807 to 1810, and Charles Didier came to Calabria in 1830 as a traveller more in the 'Grand Tour' mould.

The first decade of the 19th century was a time when British travellers—except for the prisoner Philip Elmhirst—were generally not abroad in Calabria and therefore de Tavel's memoir in particular is an intriguing insight into what, from the French point of view, life was like in the region during that period.

Especially interesting to me at the time was the fact that de Tavel devoted several pages to a little-known skirmish between the French army and the local insurgents which started in and around Mormanno:

"After resting some days we marched out for Mormano ... We entered it without encountering any difficulty; but at night, three soldiers having imprudently gone out from a church, where they were quartered, fell under the poniards [daggers] of some wretches, and this was quite sufficient to convince us of the bad dispositions of the inhabitants towards our countrymen."

The mayor and four of his colleagues were arrested but could or would not throw any light on who was responsible. These five were kept under house arrest (in the convent), guarded by a detachment of soldiers, while the rest of the battalion set out to scour the countryside for the perpetrators or others with malice aforethought. After a while, 'two ferocious-looking beings employed in tending flocks' told them that an 'assemblage of several thousand men waited [their] approach in a defile' to ambush them.

The French battalion therefore surprised the sleeping 'multitude of peasants' and pursued them south-west to Orsomarso where a significant skirmish ensued, a much more ferocious and touch-and-go affair than that near Máida in 1806. De Tavel's description is breathtakingly lucid and fast-paced and seems generally fair to the strengths and weaknesses of both sides. The French ultimately defeated the 'insurgents ... the most determined of any [they] had yet encountered in Calabria' and marched through the night back to Mormanno.

The inhabitants were shocked to hear the French drum enter the town for they had been led to believe that the French had been routed by the peasants. So, fearing any reprisals, they seamlessly changed sides and 'had the boldness and insolent hypocrisy to congratulate [the French] upon [their] safe return'.

Charles Didier too recorded a story from the same era that he was told when he was passing through the region; it was the story of the aftermath of a skirmish involving French soldiers and some local people which, conceivably, could have been a sub-plot to the events de Tavel described:

"A French soldier was injured in a skirmish with some local Calabrian insurgents but managed to get himself into the woods and hide. He would have died there of his injuries and lack of food had it not been for a young Calabrian girl, out collecting wood, who found him and promised to help and keep him safe. She tended to his wounds and made him a shelter with some leaves and branches and brought him food every day. Later when a French detachment passed through the area she led the soldiers to their comrade: she said goodbye to the injured soldier and reminded him that she had kept her promise."

Apocryphal or not, both stories seem to confirm that even four years and more into the Napoleonic era there was still a degree of resistance to it from local people. But all is perhaps not what it seems for there appears to have been external influence and collusion at work with insurgents armed and supplied by those outside Calabria in whose interests it was to maintain instability in the south.

But, as the main fomenters of this 'instability' were based a short hop across the water in Sicily, the area of the south most affected by the agitation and unrest they instigated was clearly going to be Calabria, it being not only the easiest to supply from Sicily but was also the furthest region from the seat of government in Naples. Not by chance were the two main beneficiaries of any successful revolt in Calabria—the exiled court of the Bourbon King Ferdinand and the British fleet and attendant forces—sitting on its very doorstep.

There is much evidence that the British were funding the insurgents from Sicily (and had been doing so at the time of the Battle of Máida) and even that some of these 'insurgents' were actually Sicilians shipped across to Calabria and paid to sow dissent. Frenchman de Tavel records how, in 1809, he and his battalion came across some 'Calabrian' brigands who were no more than paid Sicilian agitators and mercenaries:

"Harassed by our troops, who killed a good many of them, they fought with timidity and distrust, in a country with which they were unacquainted; and have offered to surrender, on condition of being allowed to retain their arms, and furnished with means of returning to their island.

"Can the English deny their acts, now that this brigand leader, incensed at being abandoned by them, gives such details with regard to their plots and schemes, as must overwhelm them with confusion?"

This French version of events is corroborated by the *English* mariner Philip Elmhirst, a prisoner of the French that same year, who noted that English ships were supplying local brigands who …

"… frequently with impunity made plundering excursions into the villages and cultivated territory, where their extortions and the devastation they committed, attended sometimes with the most shocking cruelty and outrage, made them equally dreaded with the most savage hordes of barbarians."

It it likely therefore that the many skirmishes between the French and the 'Calabrians' during the period of French rule were not always what they seemed. But never let it be said that the truth should get in the way of a good story and as far as many British travellers were concerned the words 'Calabrian' and 'brigand' became almost synonymous.

Try as I might I can recall only one Calabrian being either unkind or rude to me. Actually in this one case the word 'obnoxious' would be a more appropriate, I even called him Mr. Obnoxious when I wrote about him elsewhere. I recall another being short-tempered with a fellow 'foreigner' who was trying to help me—but my foreign friend himself had adopted a verbally aggressive tone and so the response was warranted.

I mention this because all of those who wrote about their travels in Calabria extolled the genuine and uncomplicated kindness of people and, almost in the same breath, discussed the question of brigands—though surprisingly few ever seems to have encountered one.

The accepted story was that the Calabrian brigand was lurking behind almost every rock and tree just waiting to rob and murder the unsuspecting, well-off, north-European traveller. And yet these same travellers crossed remote mountain ranges, strayed off the beaten track and passed through isolated villages and generally remained unscathed by the experience.

Many recount how they were warned about going from here to there without an escort or guide; some did indeed opt for the guided tour or armed escort and paid for the privilege; others took their chances.

Brian Hill (1791), you will recall, was told that Nicastro was a 'nest of robbers and plunderers' and of course found it not to be so ... at least on the day he was there. In his introduction to his book he elaborates on his fears in this respect and explains that travellers to Calabria had:

"... every real danger and misery to encounter ... especially from the gangs of bandits, which have considerably increased and become more desperate since the dreadful earthquake of 1783; insomuch that even the barons of the soil dare not move half a mile from their own habitations without being accompanied with armed guards."

He goes on to talk about his good fortune:

"When therefore I reflect that we have been mercifully preserved from these depredators and murderers ... I feel myself not a little thankful for the return of myself and friends to a land of peace, plenty and comfort."

For not one moment did Brian Hill appear to doubt that things were as bad as was being made out, even when he hadn't actually encountered any of these 'depredators and murderers'. Not one.

It's almost as if he wanted to encounter brigands in order to justify having made the trip ... he even wrote more about fear of encountering them than he did about the fact that they never crossed his path.

And it was this notion that brought me back to the thoughts of writer Ulderico Nisticò whom I mentioned in the Prologue and who remarked about travellers coming to Calabria in search of brigands, hospitality and

Magna Græcia. He illustrates his point with the following tongue-in-cheek consideration:

"If they [travellers) met a person who, was going hunting and was carrying a shoulder bag and rifle they would duly say, that's a brigand; if he greeted them and were to offer them a glass of wine, that's hospitality; if the person they met had a dignified nose, that's a Greek. Millions of people across the planet go hunting, offer wine and have normal noses, but back at home the foreign traveller talked about hospitality, Magna Græcia and brigands, publishing through their journals what they had already written before they left and what they would have also written had their whole life been spent in a cloistered monastery in a wheelchair. Such were the legendary foreigner travellers, with Calabrians listening to their voices as if they came from the infallible Oracle of Delphi."

The quote from Ramage (1828) at the beginning of this chapter includes allusions to antiquity and to brigandage; it concludes thus:

"... and I am delighted to acknowledge that from almost all I received unvarying kindness."

Ramage went for Nisticò's full set ... hospitality, Magna Græcia and brigandage in one sentence in his Preface.

Of course Ulderico Nisticò is not denying that there were indeed Calabrian brigands just as I wouldn't suggest that there are no pickpockets in London ... just that the chances of being the victim of one was generally slim.

Throughout the period that my travelling friends were abroad with their notebooks, every country had its elements who lived outside the law and, depending on either the extant socio-political climate or the severity of their 'crimes', or both, they could either be seen as no more than outlaws (of the traditional Robin Hood genre) or villains, bandits, cut-throats and brigands.

That there were such people in Calabria is a matter of record but how many were just socio-political agitators (and therefore labelled 'brigands' by being anti-government) and how many just simple thieves and ne'er-do-wells remains a subject of fierce debate in today's Calabria.

I wonder to what extent the 18th and 19th century travellers who ignored local advice were being foolhardy or just suspicious that talk of brigands was exaggerated as a way of making money as guides or escorts?

That said, it seems that some local dignitaries never travelled without an escort though, of course, being a local dignitary does not necessarily correlate with being a good and kindly person and without local enemies.

So relentless and graphic was the talk of these brigands and other ne'er-do-wells that travellers would often see danger when there wasn't any.

Ramage (1828) for example was heading towards Nicastro and his guide suggested a place where he could partake of some refreshments:

"… as we entered its massive gateway I was surprised to find it occupied by a party of men deeply engaged in conversation. They started up hastily, and waited in silence to hear an explanation of my intrusion. Their glances towards me were fierce and forbidding, and, had I known that the house was honoured with such company, I should have been willing to endure my thirst a little longer."

Ramage, in search of no more than a glass of wine to quench his thirst, was told by his guide that they were cut-throats and brigands and downed a quick glass before beating a hasty retreat:

"… and I confess that I threw behind me many a fearful glance as I hurried along, but I saw no more of them."

Whether or not Ramage had any reason to fear these people, we'll never know, but if they were of nefarious intent they clearly had an opportunity they chose *not* to exploit. Having mulled over the encounter Ramage finally gave them the benefit of the doubt … as if they had not already done so themselves:

"I believe that they were a good specimen of the Calabrian peasant; they were of the middle size, well proportioned, and very muscular. Their complexion was swarthy, their features strongly marked, and their eyes full of fire and expression. They were fully armed, and might easily have made me their prey."

But they didn't.

Perhaps Ramage was also aware of a remarkably similar experience that befell Swinburne (1780) in the same area:

"Being overcome with thirst, I went down to the river [Savuto], and was about to drink, when a hoarse voice called to me with great vehemence; on turning round I perceived near me half a dozen ill-looking fellows, and two women sitting under a rock round a kettle; this appearance was rather alarming, but I soon recollected myself sufficiently to know, that if there was any danger, I had no means of escaping from it. I therefore put the best face I could upon the matter, and walked up to them to ask the reason for them calling me; one of the men immediately jumped up, and presenting a skin of wine, desired me to drink of it … I accepted the proffered draught, and after a little conversation about himself and company … tendered him some money for the wine, but he refused to take any, and bringing me my horse, wished me a good journey."

In the end, Ramage became somewhat sceptical about the whole issue of brigands when, on his way to Pizzo, he noted:

"No brigands, however, made their appearance, and I cannot help feeling somewhat callous to the alarming reports with which the inhabitants are constantly assailing me."

The nearest I have come to being accosted in Calabria was when we stopped in a small town to have a cooling beer in the searing heat of summer. One of the elderly men sitting outside the bar we were walking towards mistakenly thought we were tourists in the traditional mould and, despite our protests, frogmarched us (in a kindly manner) to the town's famous church which he assumed was the reason we were there. We were actually there for the cooling beer and didn't know anything about the 'famous' church.

So, that being the worst-case scenario, when I drive off the beaten track in search of something new which, from time to time, I am wont to do, I am pretty confident that nothing untoward will befall me, nor will I encounter today's equivalent (in the sense of their lawlessness) of the brigands of the past, the *'ndrangheta*, Calabria's very own mafia.

Actually comparing the *'ndrangheta* with brigands gives brigandage a bad name for the *'ndrangheta* is arguably worse and is no more than a highly-organised criminal organization peopled by those prepared to incapacitate the infrastructure and destroy the reputation of their *own* homeland. That is the contradiction in all of this ... in order to line their own pockets, they allow the place of their birth, Calabria, to suffer. In addition to their drug trafficking, it is the 'softer' projects like the aforementioned A3 *autostrada* scandal that do so much harm to Calabria itself.

On one such off-the-beaten-track detour, I was curious to find out what lay south of the SS280, the road from Lamezia to Catanzaro, and in particular I was interested in visiting two small towns east of Máida, Cortale and Caraffa. I knew there was a fascinating story hidden amongst those hills and I wanted to get a sense of the place. I knew that in doing so I would be entering an area that I would soon find irksome; it's what I call the windmill belt.

In recent years wind turbines have become a feature of the drive from Catanzaro to Lamezia but when you leave the main road towards Máida, Caraffa or Cortale they loom larger than life and generally seem to be doing more than some others I've seen; nevertheless they are scarcely decorative.

Those 'others' are in and around the Isola di Capo Rizzuto area near the airport south of Crotone. Here wind turbines similarly dominate much of the landscape but, unlike those around Cortale, very few ever seem to be

CALABRIA

turning. And how can one be turning when its neighbour hangs motionless in the same breeze?

I used to weary of explaining to others *my* theory that they were actually *powered by* electricity on a rotation basis ... a few turning, the rest awaiting their turn. So, imagine my feigned surprise when, in 2013, news broke that all indeed was not what it seemed.

The *'ndrangheta* had got in on the act and was involved in laundering money accumulated through the more-than-generous grants that such projects attract just because they can be labelled 'green'; Italian police confiscated €350 million. No, not a misprint, €350 million! The *'ndrangheta* had cleverly cashed in on a 'green' energy scam and converted it to a money-laundering scam. Once again, they demonstrated a blatant disregard for their own landscape, their own backyard, their own fellow Calabrians.

In April 2014 the *'ndrangheta* was described by Europol, the EU's security agency, as one of the world's most powerful crime syndicates. According to a study published the previous month, the Calabrian mafia had a turnover of €53 billion in 2013, equal to 3.5 percent of Italy's GDP.

In terms of the mafia and wind farms, there is no current evidence that the same corruption is happening elsewhere in Calabria but the same aesthetic impact for minimum energy gain applies to all such projects. I have a personal rule of thumb in this regard: if you can count the wind turbines, then there are not enough to be doing anything worthwhile; if there are too many to count, then they are an eyesore; to which I have now added ... if only a few of them ever seem to rotate, they're a mafia scam.

So, having braved the wind turbine onslaught, I ascended to Cortale, a high place but not a typical hilltop town—along a hill rather than atop a hill like Santa Severina. I found it to be a tidy place with a long main street; the air of a place which people pass through on their way somewhere else.

I stopped opposite an unusual five-alcove, red-brick fountain which, at the time, was being cleaned by powerful water-jets. I paused to watch, standing next to a group of elderly men who politely acknowledged the stranger in their midst. I toyed with the idea of conducting a straw poll about the local wind farm but thought better of it ... the last time I did something similar I started a heated argument between friends and they became so animated that they talked too fast for me to keep up. So instead I wandered down towards another building that had caught my eye, a long building set back from the main street yet dominating it too.

It was far from its prime. These days nobody sleeps in the many rooms that the mind's eye can imagine behind that proud stone façade; nobody dines or laughs here any more. It remains a noble residence in every sense but that day it looked in a state of, slow, depressing decay, with each day a little further away from some glorious heyday.

I took a photo and read the plaque on the wall which told me that this house had once been the country seat of the Cefaly family ... the name rang a bell and, I wondered, was that the same family that ...?

I needed to re-read the story of one of my fellow travellers, the story of how it came about that Arthur John Strutt (1841) was the only traveller who *did* actually have a serious *contretemps* with his Calabrian hosts though even he wasn't sure to what extent his assailants were brigands or opportunists ... or, worse still, Albanians. Only one thing was certain ... they weren't from Cortale.

This all happened twixt Catanzaro and Máida when Strutt and his companions—five in total, two of whom were French—were headed across the valley from Catanzaro to Caraffa on their way to the Tyrrhenian shore but took a wrong turn and realised they were lost.

Then, as now, you can see Caraffa from Catanzaro, the latter being a lofty

A much better photo of the extensive fountain at Cortale than the one I took; c1930.

place with commanding views in every direction but, as you descend towards the south-west, so Caraffa becomes hidden from view in the undulating landscape. For today's traveller on foot it would be so much easier to pick out Caraffa for there's that forest of wind turbines to focus on and use as pointers ... if there had been wind farms in Strutt's day, perhaps he would not have lost his way.

So Strutt (1841) and his companions found themselves literally off the beaten track; they had just crossed a stream and found that there was no obvious path on the other side. Nevertheless they persisted in their chosen direction until it became clear that they hadn't a clue where they were. What follows and its aftermath takes up some eighty pages of the 368-page book. Mind you, it is a rollicking good yarn but I will try to be more brief.

Some shepherds confirmed they were not on the right track to Caraffa and pointed to a ridge that they were to aim for and follow. They climbed the ridge and saw two women in a nearby field and two of the company approached them for further directions when the women ran off:

"... and when we called to them not to be afraid, they only replied by a shrill whistle, that might be heard far around; this sound, so famed in all annals of brigandage and robbing, might have awakened some alarm in us, but our moment of apprehension was not yet arrived."

Three of the group, including Strutt, headed down towards a cottage-like building and were forty metres away when a group of men, some armed with guns, appeared from behind a wall. At first they thought nothing of it but when they noticed the leader cocking his gun and raising it to the firing position their suspicions were aroused; nevertheless one of the party (whom Strutt called De W—) persisted in asking them the way to Caraffa. He repeated the question just as the men raised their guns, roaring "Ah, aspetta brigante!" (Ah, look brigands) as they rushed forward. Everyone ran.

"We had no sooner turned to the right about, than we heard a discharge behind us, which, fortunately not wounding any of us, only gave fresh impetus to our speed, and we rapidly gained the ridge from which we had just descended. Our pursuers, in the meantime, following with shouts, and seeming to increase in number at every step, fired again, still without effect, as we mounted the slope; De W—) then, beginning to flag from the up hill work and the great weight of his knapsack, slipped the straps from his shoulders, and, letting all his treasures fall to the ground, continued, more unincumbered, his speedy retreat."

At least one shot and several whistles later, they were being pursued by more men who appeared from all sides and they were soon surrounded but not before they managed to hide their money and their own pistol in a bush. The 'villains' were brandishing their weapons and telling them to lie down.

"At this moment a great scuffle took place amongst our aggressors themselves; we were pulled up by one party, dragged down by another, whilst each struggled to get absolute possession of our persons."

But help was at hand ... the cavalry had arrived ...

"At last we managed to get to our legs, and perceived some better dressed men, with guns and cartouche [ammunition] belts, approaching rather to the dissatisfaction of the robbers, who were ordered to set us free immediately, and to give an account of the fray."

Their saviours were the local Urban Guard, an innovation for which the erstwhile King of Naples, Joachim Murat, had been responsible. The man travelling with the Guard was a local magnate, Don Domenico Cefaly of Cortale, and thereafter it was through his offices that the matter was investigated and, in the interim and apart from the first night, Strutt and his companions were his guests at Cortale.

The house I had photographed in Cortale was the Cefaly family residence, the same building where Strutt and his companions passed much of the next week while the law took its course.

The erstwhile residence of Don Domenico Cefaly di Cortale.

The 'villains' who attacked Strutt's group were Albanian villagers from Caraffa. These Caraffoti maintained that they were only doing their duty as they believed the five strangers were themselves bandits. The fact that they were quickly labelled as 'Albanese' or 'Arbëreshë' was, I suspect, a way of pointing the finger at 'foreigners', not uncommon today in many parts of the so-called civilised world.

There were many villages and towns in Calabria with large Albanian populations and often the name of the place includes the suffix 'Albanese'. Many, Strutt included, linked the Albanese with the Greeks mainly based on the fact that they were originally spoke a language related to both their local Albanian dialect and late-mediæval Greek (see later chapters on *Magna Græcia* and *The Arbërshë)*. Nor were these 'Greek' speakers, as suggested by Swinburne, the same as those who also lived in parts of southern Calabria at the time the Hellenised-Byzantine Greek-speakers whose language survived until relatively recently as greco-calabro, still less descendents of the much earlier Greek communities, of Magna Græcia.

Most of the Caraffoti involved were rounded up and taken to Cortale; and nearly all the possessions of Strutt's party were recovered but among the few missing items that weren't, was the sum of fifty-nine ducats which became the focus of events over subsequent days.

After a rest and something to eat, the group, still nursing their aching and stiff limbs, were taken to the house of a friend of Don Domenico at nearby San Florio where their wounds were attended to and where they later enjoyed a great feast where water was a scarcity and 'whilst plenty of excellent wine went merrily round'.

The following day they moved on to Cortale, the home town of Don Domenico Cefaly, and there they stayed while an investigation into the incident was conducted. En route they went via the site of the previous day's rout and some of their attackers were brought there too and were duly charged by Don Domenico; they denied everything even though some of the missing items were recovered but not the money.

It was late when they arrived at Cortale which Strutt describes as having clearly suffered some earthquake damage—presumably the 1783 quakes—and how the replacement buildings were built with fewer storeys:

"… and even the Palazzo, before which we are now halted, was fain to make up in length and breadth for what it wanted in elevation. We entered … The great hall soon filled with the *beau monde* [fashionable elite] of the village, alike attracted by the desire of paying their respects to Don Domenico, and by their curiosity as to his guests."

Strutt's depiction of the prison at Cortale where those accused of attacking his group were brought following a nocturnal raid by the Urban Guard on nearby Caraffa.
The building in the left background is, I believe, the town's church which would put the prison on the corner of today's main street and just opposite the decaying Cefaly *palazzo*. Even today a feature of many buildings in Cortale is the short flight of steps up to the entrance on the floor above ... exactly as illustrated and described by Strutt.

There follows a description of how the other half lived in Calabria ... as they were summoned to supper a little after midnight:

"Water is still less in vogue at Cortale that at San Floro, for one beaker sufficed for all the company; perhaps on account of the absence of the ladies; for Donna Carolina and her daughters do not sit down to table with us, but are content with superintending the general arrangements, and the safe arrival of various caravans of dishes, which emerge in savoury solemnity from a vast kitchen, whose oft open door allows us to catch glimpse of a fire, blazing on a stone hearth raised in the centre, and surrounded by toiling servitors, have concealed in steam and smoke; whilst supported on rafters of strong reeds, hams, bacons, *salama*, and salted meats innumerable, enjoy obscurity and fumigation in the upper regions of this scene of hospitable turmoil."

For the local dignitaries and their political master, the authorities of both Nicastro and Catanzaro, this incident involving both English and French citizens was one they wished to contain; a diplomatic incident was to be avoided. It was even mooted that nobody should involve their respective Ambassadors as such a step 'would be productive of much uneasiness to the authorities ...'

Everyone was being proactive and a nocturnal expedition was directed against Caraffa:

"The returning party, as it would slowly up the steep street, was picturesque, and, to us, novel. At the head rode the Capo Urbano [Don Domenico's nephew], with a great cavalry sabre buckled round him; next came the *élite* of his band, with the prisoners bound, and accompanied by their unhappy wives, in splendid though somewhat faded costumes; whilst in the rear followed the sombre train of Urbans, looking really quite as desperate as the brigands themselves, with their black dresses, peaked hats and long guns. They marched at once to the prison and ascended the exterior wooden staircase, which led to the apartments of the gaoler, who resides, *al primo*, as it were, over his charges. That functionary received the prisoners, and having shown them down an interior flight of stairs, or dropped them through a hole, *à l'ancienne mode*, for we did not observe their method of transit, they soon made their appearance at the bars below."

Strutt then drew the scene which was later reproduced in his book.

The next day a local judge and his clerk oversaw a visit back to the 'field of battle':

"A few miles brought us into more verdant regions, and presently, from a well-known ridge, we surveyed the scene, which, now so tranquil, had lately rung with shouts, and echoed to the firing of our pursuers.

"The Judge, a real Dogberry [a blundering, incompetent official], tormented us by the minute-ness of his enquiries, and his indefatigable repetitions. We had to shew the old oak under which J— and I had endured such a disgraceful bastinadoing [beating with a stick], the bush in which the money had been concealed, the hedge De W— jumped through, the ditch in which he was beaten and pillaged, the cattle sheds whence came our aggressors, the exact situation and relative distances of all parties, where the different shots were fired; whilst the clerk, at each halt, wrote a copious description, dictated in due form by our worthy investigator, who even went as far as to institute a rigorous search after the bullets on the side of the hill, and told his clerk to write down they had examined the ground but found no trace of balls. At last the law was satisfied, and we set out upon our return."

For its time, this was indeed a very thorough investigation and shows how, under the Naples regime, the capacity was there within which to administer justice fairly and openly. It is to be hoped all other such crimes against less fortunate local people were investigated with the same assiduousness though the evidence in Peter Chiarella's *Calabrian Tales* might suggest otherwise.

The whole saga ended with almost everything being recovered except, initially, the golden ducats. Thus the Governor of Catanzaro decreed that the travellers be reimbursed from parish funds and, just as this transaction was about to take place, a message from the priest at Caraffa confirmed that the missing money had been handed over in the confessional box.

Face was saved all round and, after Strutt and his friends signed a paper to the effect that all their property had been restored and acknowledged that the affray had been the result of 'mistaken zeal' on the part of the Caraffoti and recommended leniency, the matter was duly concluded.

At long last Arthur John Strutt bade farewell to his friends at Cortale and continued his journey to Monteleone and the Tyrrhenian shore.

In *Old Calabria*, Norman Douglas (1911) wrote a chapter on brigandage, focusing not on any such encounters he had himself but rather on the few famous brigands, the many infamous (some of whom we shall meet later), their predilection for violence and the often brutal measures taken to deal with them. He concludes thus:

"Calabrian brigandage, as a whole, has always worn a political character."

To emphasise the point Douglas quotes an unnamed British officer who, around the same time as the Battle of Máida, viewed these same brigands as Britain's 'chivalrous brigand-allies.'

It is clear that Strutt's attackers were not cut from the same cloth as these politically-motivated brigands; the 'brigands' of Caraffa were no more than a handful of opportunists who expected that they could get away with it.

And they very nearly did; had not Don Domenico Cefaly been in the area at the time, this story may have had a very different ending.

For a number of years now we have bought our wine in a small cantina in Marina di Stróngoli. In the autumn, winter and spring we usually buy forty to fifty litres at a time of a fine Merlot and in the summer their cool, fresh Chardonnay is simply exquisite.

Our cross-country journey to the Cantina Mauro takes us past a huge, unedifying, concrete structure which is clearly an important memorial of some sort and, for a while, that was as much as I wanted to know and I was not inclined to climb the unnecessary wide steps to learn more. The view from the road was enough and basically told me that whoever thought up this monstrosity as a memorial must not really have had any profound feelings for those being remembered. Its architect had clearly been seduced by the notion, prevalent in the sixties, that concrete was the new marble.

Even when I found out who exactly the Bandiera brothers (the Fratelli Bandiera in Italian) and their friends were and that the memorial was acknowledging their ill-fated insurrection back in 1844, I was still not inspired to stop and take a closer look.

Then one morning I happened to be in a house in Santa Severina in the company of a genial elderly pillar of the local community who wanted me to translate something that had been written in English about his son.

On the living-room wall I couldn't help but notice that inside a large wooden and glass cabinet, there was a flag which I assumed was as an early version of the Italian tricolour that incorporated the insignia of the House of Savoy and therefore dated from sometime in the 19th century. I was curious ... I wondered what it was that made this flag so important that warranted its display in such a grand cabinet. I asked Luigi Apa for an explanation.

First of all, the cabinet had literally been on the wall for only a matter of days; the flag inside was apparently one of those carried by the Fratelli Bandiera on their brief and fatal time in Calabria in 1844 and seemingly had been passed down through the Apa family for several generations. The story that unfolded was one I was partially familiar with but what I was about to learn was something *not* in the history books or in any of the many versions of the Fratelli Bandiera story that I had already heard. How it was, for example, that Santa Severina's Apa family had come to be associated with the Fratelli Bandiera and what part they played in the events of 1844.

In Italian the story is made even more confusing as *bandiera* means 'flag'.

You will recall that the mid-19th century in Europe was a time of revolution, a time when young men such as Attilio and Enrico Bandiera had idealistic aspirations for which they were not afraid to die. In 1841 these two Venetian noblemen—and supporters of iconic, pro-unification politician Giuseppe Mazzini—had formed a secret society which they called Esperia, from the Greek meaning the land to the west which, in this case, was Italy and which, for the Fratelli Bandiera, represented Italian unity. Their failed attempt at inspiring and igniting such fervour in Calabria began in Corfu where they had based themselves having beat a hasty retreat there following other revolutionary misdeeds elsewhere on the Italian mainland.

In Corfu, the brothers and their confidants had picked up information that, in the wake of an earlier small uprising at Cosenza in March, Calabria was rife with revolutionary fervour and they believed that all they had to do was turn up armed and dressed in military-style uniforms and brandishing the tricolour and the locals would drop everything and flock to their cause. Unfortunately their information about the apparent revolutionary sentiments

The hideous concrete memorial to the Bandiera 'patriots' which has all the ambience and charm of an abandoned petrol station. Something more intimate and more subtle, might have been a more concrete (pun intended) celebration of their achievements.

extant in Calabria came in part from reporting of the events at Cosenza in March which, according to historian Christopher Duggan, had been deliberately exaggerated abroad through persistent pressure on the foreign press from Italian exiles.

Hardly surprisingly therefore that when the Fratelli Bandiera and their eighteen companions landed in Calabria, somewhere between Crotone and Stróngoli, they were not welcomed with open arms as revolutionary saviours but rather with general indifference and some suspicion.

The next evening the party set out on foot to cross Calabria to Cosenza, perhaps believing that, given what had happened there in March, they would be met with a more positive response in the provincial capital. It was then that one of their number went AWOL and turned up later in Crotone where, so the story goes, he apparently spilled some of the beans but not all.

In the many re-tellings of the Bandiera story this absentee, a Corsican called Pietro Boccheciampe, is suspected of having been a traitor and thus the reason the group was eventually caught. But there is also a body of opinion that rejects this theory suggesting instead that this is just another 'there-was-a-traitor-in-our-midst' story that frequently accompanies such heroic tales that didn't go according to plan.

So, by daybreak on the second day, the remaining nineteen revolutionaries and their Calabrian guide were following the valley of the river Neto westwards towards Cosenza and passed, on the southern bank of the river, the hilltop town of Santa Severina, some fifteen miles from the coast.

In Santa Severina there resided the two Apa brothers who, unlike the Fratelli Bandiera, did not always see eye-to-eye; politically the brothers were miles apart. One, Giuseppe, was a royalist, a fierce supporter of the Bourbon regime and the Kingdom of the Two Sicilies, of which Calabria was then a part. His younger brother, Nicola, on the other hand, was inspired by the ideal of a united Italy and was inclined to side with those involved in the odd skirmish here and there in support of unity.

Don Giuseppe Apa's trusty herdsman, Giuseppe Cordua, was tending his animals somewhere between Santa Severina and the river Neto when he spied a short column of 'soldiers' in an unknown uniform heading west, following the valley of the Neto. Cordua was suspicious and immediately reported what he'd seen to his employer. It will be less confusing if I call Giuseppe Apa 'Don Giuseppe' and Giuseppe Cordua just 'Cordua'.

(I should clarify the appendage 'Don' used above. It is Spanish in origin and harks back to the time when Spanish monarchs controlled Calabria; it is an archaic term of respect that was used to address members of the community who were deemed to have been from a nobler background. Normally it was used with a Christian name such as 'Don Giuseppe'. Some Calabrians continue to use it today and would argue they do so as a mark of respect. Personally, in the modern world, I feel that those who do so demean themselves by appearing to be in servitude, particularly so when the 'recipient' himself does not feel it either necessary or important. In addition, and thanks to the movie industry, it is an appendage that also has mafia-related overtones. In the case of Don Giuseppe, I use the term only because it was how he was addressed at the time.)

What made Don Giuseppe suspicious was that Cordua told him he recognised the group's Calabrian guide, an individual with a colourful reputation locally. So, sensing that there was something untoward afoot, Don Giuseppe despatched his herdsman at once to Crotone to tell the authorities what he'd seen. His brother Nicola, who probably guessed what was happening, was less than happy with his older brother's precipitous action.

This part of the Bandiera story has not been common knowledge and only came to light recently when, Luigi Apa, discovered among the family's papers, letters from the authorities at Catanzaro and Crotone thanking his ancestor for the information he supplied that resulted in the apprehension of the revolutionaries.

The first of these, from the Intendenza at Catanzaro (the Office responsible for the economic administration and logistics of the forces of law and order), is dated 19 June 1844 (the day after) and thanks Don Giuseppe for having passed on the information about the twenty individuals that his herdsman Cordua had seen, including being able to recognise among them a local man from San Giovanni in Fiore. This was the group's guide, Giuseppe Meluso, known as Il Nivaro, and was well-known locally as a brigand who, like the Bandiera brothers themselves, had earlier fled to Corfu to escape the law.

The second letter, dated 28 July, thanked Don Giuseppe once again for his vigilance (and that of his herdsman) and outlined how both would be rewarded for the part they played in the apprehension of the revolutionaries. Don Giuseppe was to receive some sort of official recognition and the sharp-eyed Cordua was given a one-off payment of fifty ducats, at the time a tidy sum.

This version of events, as confirmed by both letters that Luigi shared with me, would seem to suggest that Boccheciampe may not have been a traitor at all and was therefore not directly responsible for what happened next. After all, why would the authorities reward both Don Giuseppe and Giuseppe

Cordua for information they already had from Boccheciampe?

The Fratelli Bandiera did eventually make it to Cosenza but as prisoners rather than leaders of a revolutionary army. They were involved in one or two skirmishes along the way, including one a little to the west of Santa Severina at the small hamlet of Pietralonga when the Urban Guard from Belvedere Spinello, a hilltop town on the other side of the Neto, challenged them and lost two of their number for their trouble. In the end the authorities—in the form of a posse of the able-bodied from San Giovanni in Fiore—caught up with them at Stragola in the Sila mountains and those who were not killed in the subsequent skirmish, surrendered and were tried in Cosenza, then executed.

In the Crotone area, the whole Fratelli Bandiera affair has become something of a *cause célèbre*. At a spot near where the brothers and their followers landed, there is the aforementioned extensive, and ugly, concrete memorial to the group which acknowledges their revolutionary intentions and zeal, gives them the appendage 'patriots' and recounts the story of their ignominious end in Cosenza. Like me, Luigi Apa has strong reservations about the monument itself—'brutto' was the onomatopoetic word he used—for me it had all the ambience and charm of a long-abandoned and derelict petrol station.

Nevertheless, for many this remains a place of pilgrimage which, until now, I have never quite understood for, it seemed to me, the Fratelli Bandiera expedition to Calabria was quite naive, foolish even. That said, their subsequent status as martyrs cannot be ignored or denied and at the time their bold stand in support of Italian unification became an important focus and rallying call for those who were striving, with political argument and on the streets, to achieve this end.

Causes célèbres are not always what they seem.

One thing still puzzled me about the whole affair and that was the flag itself, the one I'd seen and photographed in Luigi Apa's living room. So I returned to take another look and to try and check the provenance.

Luigi couldn't be precise about the circumstances through which it had come into the possession of Don Giuseppe, other than through the connection his family had clearly had with events as they unfolded on the ground in 1844 and his great-great-grandfather's decisive action. That said, he was assured by accounts that had been passed down through subsequent generations of the Apa family that it was indeed one of the flags being brandished by the Bandiera band when they were passed by Santa Severina.

The Italian tricolour had an important symbolic status in the various revolutionary movements whose ultimate aim was Italian unification. Often is was embellished with the insignia of the House of Savoy—a white cross on a red shield—the monarchy of choice for revolutionaries who weren't also of the republican persuasion. Thus the flag in Luigi's cabinet pushed all the right buttons. Except one: the Italian tricolour was normally rectangular and not square.

Resorting to the internet, I found only one square 'Italian' tricolour and that dated back to the so-called Cisalpine Republic in northern Italy which ceased to exist in 1805. Indeed the first tricolour—equal bands of green white and red— was the *square* Cisalpine Republic flag and as such it would have had imbued with strong symbolism for the Fratelli Bandiera. I could find no square flag that included the Savoy insignia until post-unification.

Ten of the Fratelli Bandiera group were from the area of northern 'Italy' (the territory south and east from Milan as far as and beyond San Marino) which had once been part of the Cisalpine Republic and therefore the square tricolour would have been something with which they may well have been familiar and possibly have had access to.

Republics like the Cisalpine were where the seeds of unification first

Luigi Apa is the great, great, grandson of Don Guiseppe Apa who, in 1844, helped thwart the Fratelli Bandiera revolutionary march through Calabria ... and somehow the Apa family ended up with one of the group's 'hybrid' square flags.

Attilio and Emilio Bandiera, Venetian revolutionaries who made their last stand in Calabria; here they are depicted in idealistic, 'patriot' mode, an image also used at the memorial constructed to their memory on the outskirts of Crotone.

flourished and in the early part of the 19th century the tricolour, in its present rectangular form was seen as a revolutionary standard and its use therefore generally stifled. Whether or not the flag as shown in the various artistic representations of revolutionary events pre-1844 are accurate is difficult to assess but in all cases the tricolour is clearly rectangular and usually incorporating the insignia of the House of Savoy.

So the square Fratelli Bandiera flag appears to be a hybrid, their own interpretation of what the Cisalpine Republic and the insignia of the House of Savoy meant to them, perhaps even the standard of the Esperia society. Whatever its origins, the composite Bandiera *bandiera* was ready to be brandished in the face of all things Bourbon; their own unique revolutionary flag held aloft in the name of unification.

Perhaps too there is a sense in which the hybrid flag reflects the whole Bandiera enterprise and the flaws endemic to it. It was an endeavour that had little chance of achieving anything in a region historically generally pro-Bourbon.

Why would the people they encountered at Crotone rally to a flag they almost certainly didn't recognise, a flag being brandished by armed people they didn't know, people dressed in uniforms which had no known association or status?

In retrospect the Fratelli Bandiera and their eighteen revolutionary friends, and one brigand-guide, were fortunate their endeavours didn't end there and then on the Ionian shore in a more decisive skirmish at the hands of the local peasants.

Nevertheless, their story was one of unfettered idealism and had all the ingredients of a daring and fearless personal crusade, including even the later intrigue surrounding a perceived traitor in their midst. Despite the flaws in the execution of their revolution, the story of the Fratelli Bandiera continues to represent the ideal of a united Italy and as such they will be forever seen as uncompromising and unflinching 'patriots'.

Another thing about this whole affair, this fruitless skirmish, has continued to unsettle me. Many of the Calabrians I know who speak about the Fratelli Bandiera and their idealism in glowing terms, also talk about the legacy of unification as something negative, iniquitous even. Yet the Fratelli Bandiera died in pursuit of unification.

Try as I might, I can get no coherent answer to this contradiction other than acknowledgement that it is indeed a contradiction. Perhaps Calabrians, even those who recognise and accept both the injustices of unification (as they have been seen to effect Calabria and the south) and the folly of the Bandiera 'rebellion', need heroes. And the Fratelli Bandiera satisfy that criteria … naive and disorganised they may have been but cowards they certainly weren't.

Nor, it has to be said, were they Calabrians.

Whether these noble brothers and their followers would have approved of what happened to the south following unification, is another matter. They were, after all, from the north of the peninsula and therefore I suspect that, had they survived their Calabrian misadventure and experienced the reality of unification, they would have slept well in the new Italy.

Despite the *cause célèbre* status that the Fratelli Bandiera have posthumously enjoyed in the provinces of Crotone, Cosenza and Catanzaro in particular, not one of the British travellers who subsequently passed this way ever mentioned this episode. I might not have done so myself at such length had it not been for the unusual flag I discovered hanging on a wall in Santa Severina.

That morning, Luigi Apa also showed me another document which related to how Don Giuseppe was subsequently rewarded for his diligence and allegiance. The Bourbon government offered him a prestigious post in Caserta (north-east of Naples) which he respectfully declined but asked instead that one of his sons be given a place at the Royal Medical College of Cosenza as he was particularly interested in and suited to that particular discipline.

Sixteen years later, Don Giuseppe's brother, the young Nicola Apa—he who would probably have turned a blind eye to the Fratelli Bandiera as they passed by Santa Severina—had *his* dream fulfilled when unification became a reality.

Finally, and once again in pursuit of that excellent Merlot at Marina di Stróngoli, I thought it incumbent upon me to make just one more visit to the abandoned-petrol-station memorial to the Fratelli Bandiera to check out some of the detail on the interpretation boards and in particular to see if there was any obvious link between the story they told and the one that had emerged in the Apa family archive.

One of the boards details the route taken by the insurgents from the mouth of the river Neto where they landed though, according to the accompanying map of their route, their overland journey began at the memorial itself. Poetic licence I would suggest. Then, at the crucial point of the story on 18 June, there are two conflicting accounts of where exactly the group were, only one of which—the minority version—fits in with the evidence of the letters subsequently sent to Don Giuseppe in June and July 1844.

I was not surprised to discover that there is no mention of the Fratelli Bandiera having been rumbled by a local herdsman nor of the authorities having been alerted as a result. Blame for that is, of course, firmly directed towards the 'traitor' Pietro Boccheciampe.

Perhaps the most famous skirmish in Calabrian history involved Italy's most famous historical citizen, Guiseppe Garibaldi.

Following the initial flush of success with the unification project, Garibaldi retired to the island of Caprera off Sardinia's north coast. But two years later, having been frustrated that the Papal States and Rome were still not part of a unified Italy, he decided to re-enact his previous successes and take matters into his own hands. He assuredly believed this venture would be a walk in the park compared with events in 1860.

Once again he landed with a small army of two thousand men in Sicily and then crossed to Mélito in Calabria from where he proceeded north through the Aspromonte mountains, deliberately avoiding towns and villages where he might have come into conflict with the Italian army.

What happened next is a cross between an anti-climax and a farce. Perhaps this explains the reticence among the British travellers, post-1860, to talk about the exploits of Garibaldi, except in terms of places and roads called after him—Via Garibaldi, Corso Garibaldi, Teatro Garibaldi, Albergo Garibaldi and the like. Not a word from George Gissing (1897); Norman Douglas (1913) was tight-lipped:

"Aspromonte, the wild region behind Reggio, was famous, not long ago, for Garibaldi's battle."

Edward Hutton (1912) mentions it in passing:

"... one passes over the barren rocks and sandhills about Mélito, the most southern town in Italy, famous for the landing and surrender of Garibaldi."

Only Eric Whelpton (1957) saw the story as worthy of record:

"So when Garibaldi landed at Mélito with three thousand volunteers, he [the Italian king] gave orders that the advance of the Redshirts should be stopped at once, before their movement could gather force and collect supporters.

"The Dictator [Garibaldi] wished to avoid conflict with regular troops of the Italian Army, and it was for this reason that he had led his men through the dense forests of the Aspromonte and as far away as possible from villages and roads.

"In spite of these precautions, his force was suddenly attacked by a detachment of infantry and Bersaglieri [light-infantry unit who jogged rather than marched] ... Though Garibaldi ordered his volunteers not to return the fire of the Italian troops, the latter continued to shoot, and only stopped when it was seen that the Dictator had been hit.

"Fortunately his wound was a slight one, and so, spending a night in the mountains, he was carried down to Scilla on a stretcher where he was embarked on a warship."

When Henry Morton (1967) stopped off at Mélito, the Garibaldi connection was the last thing on people's minds:

"[Mélito is] famous as the place where Garibaldi landed twice from Sicily during the Risorgimento ... Garibaldi had been temporarily forgotten in Mélito when I was there and everyone was obsessed by a witch."

The 'warship' referred to by Eric Whelpton was the *Duca di Genova*—commissioned pre-unification, launched post-unification—and more of an armed government steamer. Garibaldi was taken almost as far away from Calabria as was possible, to a prison fort near La Spezia in Liguria where his wound was treated. (In fact he was hit three times but only one of his injuries was considered to be serious.)

The wound—he was shot in the foot—healed eventually but only after

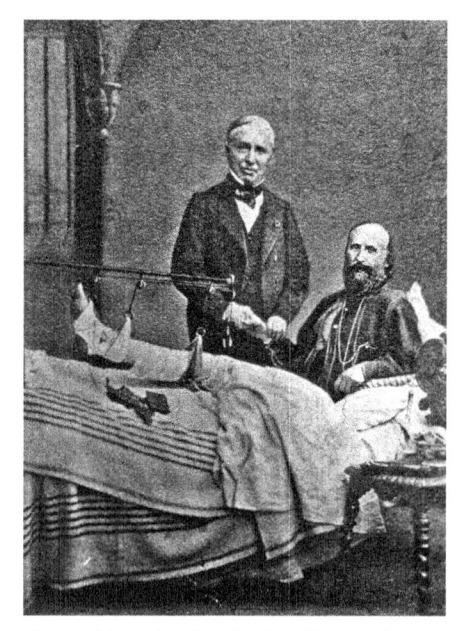

Garibaldi shakes hands with French doctor Nélaton who, despite the scepticism of many, confirmed that there was a bullet in his foot. It was removed by Italian doctors.

The tree in the Aspromonte where the wounded Garibaldi was brought and where, supposedly with cigar in hand, he surrendered to the Italian forces.

several doctors, from several countries, prodded, poked and postured in search of the elusive bullet and all except one came to the conclusion that there was no bullet.

It was the French doctor, Auguste Nélaton, who eventually devised a tool for distinguishing between bullet and bone and the offending article was found and removed. Back on his feet, Garibaldi was excused from his undemanding imprisonment and returned to Caprera. He later went on a speaking tour around Europe, including Britain, before once again rallying to the Italian cause in 1866.

Early one summer I visited the spot in the foothills of the Aspromonte where this unfortunate skirmish put an end to Garibaldi's second foray into Calabria in pursuance of his unification dream, to the place where he was shot in the foot both literally and figuratively: the *Cippo di Garibaldi*.

The *Cippo* (meaning memorial) lies north of Gambarie and consists of a dead-end clearing in the forest with one tree fenced off and a small mausoleum nearby which commemorates his exploits. The tree itself, with its large central recess, is where Garibaldi was apparently taken to rest after being shot.

At first it was not easy to picture the events here in August 1862, particularly when the only other people there were a family with three disinterested kids and a young starry-eyed couple who clearly had other things on their mind. It seemed to me they were more interested in finding the right tree against which to cement their union ... in the short time I was there they had tried, and seemingly rejected, two or three. Not that I was watching, you understand.

Of course they might well have been looking for the sunniest spot as the shafts of light penetrating the clearing were indeed spectacular. Then again perhaps they had their sights on that special tree, the one behind the low fence, and were just waiting for everyone else to leave them to it. Perhaps they were thinking that being conceived in such an iconic spot would give their firstborn, little Guiseppe or Guiseppina, the perfect start in life.

With difficulty I tried to refocus on my reason for being here, to picture instead in my mind's eye this charismatic, popular and usually victorious Italian hero propped up against that same tree, smoking a cigar, having just been shot in the foot by the army he helped create. Then having to surrender to a detachment of the same army with hundreds of bewildered and red-shirted volunteers swarming over the hillside and jostling for the best view of this historic moment from beside, behind and up trees. And all this following a skirmish that lasted no more than ten minutes with a total of fifteen casualties on both sides.

It was then I became aware that the young man waiting his turn by the tree was sporting a red tee-shirt which set me wondering whether he had a greater sense for the drama and irony of history than I imagined. Perhaps I had got it all wrong and in their own way they were trying to bond with events here in 1862.

When, to everyone's relief, the family of five finally departed, the couple looked unashamedly happy so I decided to make them suffer a little longer and made a couple of nonchalant visits to and from the car for nothing in particular before finally leaving them to their tree and their unusual sense of history. I knew enough about Garibaldi's private life to feel sure that whatever they got up to in my absence, he would undoubtedly have approved.

When I finally turned the key in the ignition and headed back down into the present, a backward glance told me that I was making two young people very happy. I suspect too that, like me, they were not unaware that it was lunchtime and that few Italians would be out and about at this time.

Guiseppe Garibaldi was not a fan of the power of the Church and resented the fact that the Papal States, centred on the Vatican and Rome, were not yet part of his ultimate goal of a united, secular Italy. And, like many others, he believed that Rome was the natural choice as the country's capital city.

Though this short-lived skirmish in the forests of the Aspromonte was, for Garibaldi, an ignominious and painful affair, his goal was eventually realised in 1870, albeit not directly by means of the sort of military action he had envisaged.

It was the outbreak of the Franco-Prussian War that year that lost the Papal States the insurance policy of having French troop loyal to the Papacy stationed there. Now the French troops were needed elsewhere and their withdrawal enabled the Italian army to take on the Pope and his less intimidating home-grown forces *and* have a real chance of winning. Another ten-day token skirmish later and Garibaldi's dream was realised and Rome, unfettered by foreign troops, subsequently became the capital of Italy.

Garibaldi himself was not involved in this skirmish for, a fortnight earlier, he himself had joined the Franco-Prussian War and, ironically, he did so to fight for the French, the very army he had been trying to oust from Rome eight years earlier.

Magna Græcia

"I am now at last in that part of Italy which I have long wished to visit."
Craufurd Tait Ramage *The Nooks and by-ways of Italy: Wanderings in search of its ancient remains and modern superstitions*

It was a gloriously warm Sunday in late spring and we were heading south aboard a packed *pullman*, a coach, alongside the beautiful Ionian coast. Our destination was the Bova area of Reggio Calabria, almost as far south as you can go on the Italian mainland.

Once we passed through Lido di Catanzaro it was, for Kay and me, uncharted territory. I was familiar with the names of the many coastal towns, as well as several of those perched high inland like Squillace, Stilo and Gerace. I knew too that, over the last two hundred years, most of my fellow-travellers, and many others besides, had been this way in search of Magna Græcia, the Calabrian legacy of which is most prolific on the eastern seaboard.

We were on a *gita*, an outing, organised by the ex-Mayor of Santa Severina and my fellow-passengers that day, many of whom were good friends, thought it strange that I followed our route every step of the way in my trusty Touring Club Italiano road atlas. Some soon took to teasing me by asking me where we were and, even though I realised they already knew, I played along with them by responding with authority, clarity and precision. Occasionally somebody would ask to borrow the atlas and I recall feeling almost naked for those few moments without it.

Our immediate destination was *Il Bergamotto* an *agriturismo* (farm accommodation and restaurant) at Amendolea west of the area's linguistic and cultural centre, Bova, which we visited later in the day. But this was no

CAMPANIA
BASILICATA
La Pollino
Il Mar Ionio
Copia / Thurii
Sibari
Belvedere
CALABRIA
Páola
COSENZA
La Sila
Stróngoli
Santa Severina
CROTONE
Capo Colonna
Il Mar Tirreno
Terina
Lamezia
Terme
CATANZARO
Roccelletta / Scyllacium
Hipponium
VIBO VALÉNTIA
Il Mar Ionio
Medma
Caulon
Caulónia
Gerace
L'Aspromonte
Locri Epizefri
Lo Stretto di Messina
SICILIA
REGGIO
DI CALABRIA
Rhegium
Bova
Amendolea

ordinary farm for it specialised in the cultivation of the bergamot.

Before we got down to the main business of the day—lunch—our guide, Ugo Sergi, took us on a walk round his plantation and told us all there is to know about the humble bergamot, a small citrus fruit peculiar to southern Calabria where more than 80% of the world's production originates. Earl Grey tea would not be Earl Grey tea without Calabrian bergamot plantations such as this.

Our group was standing in a small clearing in the middle of a bergamot orchard. Signor Sergi cautioned us not to touch the bergamots hanging on the inner fringe of trees as these were his visual aid—normally they would have been harvested in February but every year they left a few on the tree otherwise many visitors would never actually see a bergamot.

He went on tell us about the history of the Amendolea area and how it was one of several communities in this part of southern Calabria that had retained its Greek language heritage until very recently. Indeed, he told us that the last man to have been raised to speak the local Greek dialect from birth, generally known as *Greco-Calabro*, had died just two weeks previously.

As Signor Sergi continued to wax lyrical about the bergamot, my mind had wandered off elsewhere. I was thinking of that little boy who had been brought up speaking such an old language, not ancient Greek as such but a residue of its ancient and mediæval counterparts. He was not just the last of his generation he was the last person to have a direct linguistic link back over hundreds of years.

A Calabrian *gita* is all about the lunch, an extended lunch that can last up to four hours. Now that we knew all there was to know about the bergamot, people's attention was waning and we were itching to walk back to the farm itself and get our legs under that long table being prepared when we arrived.

As we lunched by the river below the long-abandoned town of Amendolea, its ragged castle still clinging on high up on the craggy hillside, I recalled that Henry Swinburne (1777) had breakfasted up there in the town itself. He had not fared as well as we did and called Amendolea a 'poor, but well situated' town before going on to talk about its Greek origins. But Swinburne make a mistake that is not uncommon, even among Calabrians, in that he accredited the area's 'Greekness' to the wrong 'Greeks'.

It so happens that our Santa Severina home is on Via Grecia, the narrow road on the eastern side of *lo scoglio* … the pet-name many locals use for their town which literally means a lump of rock. The name Via Grecia acknowledges that this was once the Greek quarter of the town and as such

183

the oldest quarter. That said, today it is the most modern part of *lo scoglio* as much of the eastern side was destroyed by an earthquake in 1832.

Like many places in Calabria, the 'Greekness' that people refer to is the historically relatively recent era (from around the 5th century CE) associated with the time when the erstwhile Eastern Roman Empire, later known as the Byzantine Empire, started to re-establish its authority over the southern Italian peninsula. In 620CE Greek became the official language of the Byzantine Empire so linguistically and culturally the south and Calabria became essentially Greek-speaking.

It was the remnants of this culture that prevailed in and around Amendolea and Calabria's deep south; a time, a place and a language a thousand years or more removed from the much earlier culture of Magna Græcia.

The reason that so many travellers got excited about Magna Græcia (literally Greater Greece) was that this was a much earlier period of Hellenic Greek migration and colonisation that went back to the 7th and 8th centuries BCE, to a time when the words 'Greek' and 'civilization' were difficult to separate. Furthermore, the area we now know as Calabria was an important focus of this civilization and hosted many of Magna Græcia's most important institutions and cities.

To save further linguist confusion, there are two words that are used by

Finally abandoned in 1956, the 'Greek' community of Amendolea sat atop a narrow hill overlooking the river of the same name (background left). The Amendolea, which enters the sea between Mélito di Porto Salvo and Bova Marina, is Calabria's broadest river and has a reputation for its uncompromising ferocity during the winter months.

At Bova, the area's cultural centre, many of the signs are in three languages: Ancient Greek, Greco-Calabro and Italian.

classicists and historians when they refer to Greek civilization, 'Hellenic' and 'Hellenistic' ... and I have already used the former without explanation. My fellow travellers frequently used both on the assumption that their readers would understand the difference; I will not make that assumption.

'Hellenic' refers to a Greek culture or geographic area people by ethnic Greeks; thus the early cities of Magna Græcia, such as Sybaris and Kroton, would have been Hellenic. 'Hellenistic' refers to the cultural and linguistic development of an area, originally peopled by Greeks, but where the culture and language has been absorbed by non-ethnic Greeks.

Obviously these distinctions represent a gradual, undefined process, nevertheless some prefer to append a more precise date to such things, a time after which everything Greek-related can be described as 'Hellenistic'. In this respect the date that many adhere to is 323 BCE, the year Alexander the Great died, by which time traditional Greek civilization had started to meld with other influences and cultures.

People sometimes use words incautiously and in relation to Calabria the word 'Greek', in respect of the language and culture, has three distinct interpretations that sometimes become confused.

The ancient Greeks of Magna Græcia spoke ancient or Hellenic Greek; the Byzantine Greeks spoke mediæval Greek (a cross between Hellenistic and more modern Greek); while the Albanese or Arbëreshë communities (who migrated from their native Albania to Calabria between the 15th and 18th centuries CE) spoke a language related to both their local Albanian dialect and late-mediæval Greek.

The confusion arises from the fact that many people refer to the Arbëreshë as 'Greek-speakers' which up to a point they were, but they were not the Hellenised-Byzantine Greek-speakers whose language survived until relatively recently as *Greco-Calabro* in some parts of Calabria, most notably in certain parts of southern Reggio Calabria. Until the 15th and 16th centuries *Greco-Calabro* was the dominant language in the south but thereafter it was increasingly overtaken by the Italian dialect.

When Henry Swinburne (1777) was in this same area, and talking specifically of nearby Bova, he recognised it as a Greek-speaking town but wrongly attributed their Greek language to the Albanese migration:

"Most of the inhabitants are of Greek origin and rite, I do not mean that they can trace their pedigree up to the old republicans of Magna Græcia, for all such filiations have been cut off, and confounded in the darkness of many revolving ages. These people are of a much later importation, having emigrated from Albania only a few centuries ago."

Edward Lear (1847) gently castigates Swinburne for this error from which it is clear that others have made the same mistake:

"The Bovani are particularly anxious to impress on the minds of strangers that they have no connection with the modern emigrants from Albania …"

Neither Bova nor its surrounding area have any Arbëreshë connections; indeed there are Arbëreshë settlements throughout Calabria *except* in the two most southerly provinces of Vibo Valéntia and Reggio Calabria.

In the preface to *Travels in the Two Sicilies*, Swinburne wrote the following:

"Our earliest history has made us acquainted with those classic regions; Poetry and History have rendered their topography familiar to us, and every school-boy can point out the ruins of Magna Græcia and Sicily. No country, Latium alone excepted, has so frequently employed the pen of the antiquary."

Of course the school-boys that Swinburne was referring to were those who belonged to a particular class of British society—those enjoying a classical education, those likely to read his book, and those who might anticipate embarking on a 'Grand Tour' of their own some day.

The parts of Calabria closely associated with Magna Græcia were, as Swinburne noted, well-known to his peers so, as is evident from their itineraries. Despite what Ulderico Nisticò maintains, there were some travellers—Strutt, Hill and Lowe for example—for whom Magna Græcia was not at the top of their agenda.

For Craufurd Tait Ramage (1828), on the other hand, it was definitely at the top of *his* list … you can almost touch his school-boy anticipation when he finally realised his dream:

"I am now at last in that part of Italy which I have long wished to visit."

He went on to help his readers by succinctly defining Magna Græcia and its important places:

"It has been sometimes asked why it should have been called Magna Græcia, and various ingenious reasons have been suggested, but the one which is most obvious is probably nearest to the truth—that it was from the importance and power of the Greek colonies, which had at a very early period extended over the whole of this part of the country. The name, indeed, does not seem to have had any very definite application, including sometimes even the island of Sicily, yet it was more usual to restrict it to the portion of Italy lying between Locri and Tarentum. It thus contained eight republics, which were generally independent of each other—Locri, Caulónia, Scyllacium, Kroton, Sybaris, Heracleia, Metapontum, and Tarentum. Many other smaller cities might be enumerated, which were included under the appellation of Magna Græcia; these, however, were the most important."

In today's Calabria these were assumed to be: Locri, Caulónia, Squillace, Crotone and Sibari. Eraclea (Policoro) and Metaponto are in Basilicata and Taranto is in Apulia. All were on the side of the Italian boot that faces Greece.

Ramage's list included Scyllacium—originally believed to be today's Squillace—which now appears to have had less importance than he attached to it and was probably no more than a dependency of nearby Kroton. Furthermore, its site by the sea at Roccelletta (and not Squillace) has been superseded by a larger Roman site, Scolacium, still in the process of excavation.

(Incidentally, Ramage referred above to 'Italy' for, even though he travelled in what was called the Kingdom of the Two Sicilies, the account of his travels was not published until eight years after unification.)

The 'other smaller cities' in Calabria that Ramage refers to are likely to be Regium (Reggio Calabria), Scyllaeum (Scilla), Medma (Rosarno), Terina (Sant'Eufenia Vetere) and Thurii (Thúrio). The first three of these were on the Sicily-facing south-western coast; Terina, also on the west coast, was situated opposite Crotone and Squillace on Calabria's narrow 'waistline'; Thurii was close to Sybaris.

That said, many would have placed Regium (Reggio Calabria) in the list of important republics instead of Scyllacium (Squillace).

Travellers from Keppel-Craven (1818) to Douglas (1911) to Whelpton (1957), Gardiner (1966) and Morton (1967) knew every single detail about the history of these places, especially those on Ramage's list of republics. That said, all but the last three were at a distinct disadvantage in that, as far as the republics within Calabria were concerned, the actual sites were often unknown. It is clear that some of the earlier travellers visited Calabria in the hope that they might actually be the one to make that great discovery.

By the time Morton was driving round Calabria, most had been revealed.

I have to confess that at the time I first became aware of Magna Græcia (through Morton's book) I found it all a bit confusing; when I read Gissing (1897) and Douglas (1911), it became even more so. All of these, it seemed to me, made the basic assumption that it was a subject on everyone's radar. Even Morton's first mention of Magna Græcia (in relation to Apulia) did not attempt any sort of explanation or clarification ... just an assumption that I and other readers would know what he was talking about:

"The sea plain ... and the tall promontory to which I was now journeying struck me as a country haunted by the ghosts of Greek adventurers and merchants who centuries before the Christian age had settled among the sheltered bays and established the colonies of Magna Grecia ..."

At least Ramage had attempted to pass on some basic information, even if it was sometimes limited by a lack of archæological evidence.

So now it is my turn to offer a crash course on Magna Græcia in relation to today's Calabria, though first I will attempt to explain why I believe it remains, for different reasons, such an important part of Calabria's historical landscape. I will try to make it simple.

It will not have gone unnoticed to people interested in all things Italian that Southerners, and probably Calabrians in particular, have been viewed as *Terroni* ... both the title of Pino Aprile's excellent book and a derogatory word for the lowest of the low, the sort of word that makes calling someone an 'asshole' sound like a compliment.

I will examine this phenomenon in greater detail in a later chapter but suffice to say that, before unification, the state known as the Kingdom of the Two Sicilies (which included Calabria) was the richest of all the states that later became part of the unified Italy.

Within a generation it was the poorest. The wealth of the new nation had mysteriously migrated northwards and those 'dissatisfied' people who lived in the south became Southerners and, for some, *Terroni*. It was no coincidence that Turin, the capital of Piedmont, was also the first capital of the unified Italy.

Now that the story of what really happened in and to the South after unification is becoming clearer through the research and writings of, among others, Pino Aprile and Lino Patruno, Southerners have started to take more pride in who they are and in their cultural inheritance, for they too were not impervious to the notion that they inhabited an inferior place inhabited by inferior people—themselves.

Today's perceptions of Magna Græcia are therefore more relevant and are no longer just the flights of fancy that once satisfied the whims of a handful of foreign travellers and academics. For a region of Italy eager to re-establish its rightful place in the Italian diaspora, the story of the area's Magna Græcia civilization is a potent weapon. And these days Calabrians can actually do what Ramage and Douglas and others would have given their eye-teeth to do ... they can visit many of the sites, including what was once the most elusive of all, Sybaris.

The absorption of history should not be a chore, so herewith my attempt at what all the fuss was about regarding these important Magna Græcia republics in Calabria.

When we first came to holiday in Calabria one of the places we were told we 'must' visit was Capo Colonna, a headland jutting into the Ionian Sea just south of Crotone. We went … and were singularly unimpressed by the lone column despite its spectacular setting and the glorious Ionian backdrop.

With a nod of his head, an elderly sun-bronzed man, as solitary as the column itself, acknowledged our presence fifty metres away behind the perimeter fence. He appeared to be tending the nearby grass where once were tended goats and cattle. Like us, he seemed indifferent to the column itself.

When, a few years later, one of our visitors from England actually asked to be taken there we tried unsuccessfully to change his mind. Nevertheless, I thought it prudent that I do some research in the hope that I might see this lonely column in a new light.

It is strange how observing a single column—just as we had once done—can be a completely different experience when you know what you are looking at. Edward Hutton (1912) knew what *he* was looking at and not surprisingly his first impressions were light years away from mine:

"It is perhaps impossible to convey to the reader the impression of noble and tragic which this lonely column, standing upon that far headland in the midst of that classic sea, makes upon the traveller. Beyond anywhere else in Magna Græcia it recalls that fair and ancient world that is irrevocably lost; and if only for this reason it is better worth the trouble and fatigue of a visit than any other fragment left to us upon all this coast."

That lone Doric column is the last remaining of forty-eight that supported the roof of the largest and grandest Greek temple in Magna Græcia, the Temple of Hera.

Over the years its riches were plundered by Carthaginians, Romans, Goths and Byzantines but the structure itself remained largely intact. When Swinburne (1777) came to see the Temple there were only two columns left and one of those had fallen over. When Richard Keppel-Craven (1820) was there he assumed he knew what had happened to the others, including the fallen one which had now also disappeared:

"I was informed, that other fragments of the columns were to be discerned in the sea; if so, I presume the destruction of the temple may be attributed to earthquake. I could not see them."

But Keppel-Craven had been told the abridged version of the story and by the time George Gissing (1897) visited the same site the story was less of a mystery. Unfortunately he found that the predisposition of the antiquarian for preservation took a back seat when it came to the apparent recycling instincts of the Crotonese themselves.

I say 'apparent' as the first project for which stone from the temple was recycled took place in the early 16th century and was for something that Gissing did not regard as a 'legitimate pillage'. I am inclined to agree:

"Then it [the Temple of Hera] was assailed, cast down, ravaged by a Bishop of Cotrone [sic], one Antonio Lucifero, to build his episcopal palace."

What a pity the aptly-named bishop and his extended family weren't prepared to share the humbler lifestyle of their parishioners.

The second project later the same century that required a convenient source of stone was more pressing, the restoration of the crumbling walls of Crotone itself. This from Eric Whelpton (1957):

"Practically the whole of the citadel and ramparts was made from the plundered stone, and the fact is still evident in the present day: Both the castle and the bastions of the city wall are coated with a layer of brownish dust, but even so, it is possible to distinguish the outlines of a column or of a cornice embedded in the solid masonry which doubtless conceals all sorts of hidden treasure."

The lone column at Capo Colonna, all that remains of the erstwhile Temple of Hera at Kroton on the Ionian coast-south east of today's Crotone.
The depiction of Hera is a Roman-Greek representation from the 5th century BCE.

Whelpton was clearly despairing when he described the third project and how the stones from the temple's basement were used:

"This act of vandalism was repeated after the disastrous earthquake of 1783, when the harbour works were partially destroyed. This time the moles and piers were rebuilt out of the walls and foundations of the Temple of Hera …"

After chastising the bishop, Gissing said something similar:

" Nearly three hundred years later, after the terrible earthquake of 1783, Cotrone strengthened her harbour with the great stones of the temple basement. It was a more legitimate pillage."

Unlike Whelpton, Gissing did not say that the harbour was strengthened *because of* the 1783 earthquake—though perhaps it was implied—which, as we shall see, may not have had much impact on Crotone.

Gardiner (1966) had a real sense of loss, imbued with melancholy, when he visited Capo Colonna:

"When the Sybarites flourished, when Pythagoras lectured esoteric and exoteric on either side of the curtain in Crotone's academy, when Milo astonished the world with his feats of strength and agility, there were forty-eight such columns on the headland, forty-eight pillars dazzlingly painted in blue and gold, each of them nine yards high. Inside the priestesses and attendant virgins kept watch over the artistic treasures of Hellenic culture, brought over from the homelands or commissioned on the spot. Zeuxis employed ten Crotone girls as models for his 'Helen of Sparta', the Mona Lisa of the ancient world. (no one has ever discovered what happened to that picture: did some Calabrian official take it home 'for safe keeping'?)

Almost certainly, from the moment the Bishop of Crotone sanctioned, by default, the use of the temple's stone, other more random and localised 'recycling' has taken place. Apparently it is still taking place for, in January 2014, it was reported that a man was arrested while trying to leave what is now called the Capo Colonna Archaeological Park with stolen artefacts. His hidden 'artefacts' were picked up by a metal detector and he was subsequently charged with illicitly acquiring cultural assets and damaging public property.

Of the Magna Græcia republics along the Ionian coast, Kroton (as it was called at the time) was the most powerful and, despite the above tale of woe regarding the Temple of Hera, in modern times its physical remains have always been the most recognizable and accessible. Of the others, the two most important and elusive were Locri and Sybaris and it was these two that continually occupied the minds of travellers.

Swinburne (1777) did not discover the site of Locri as he had hoped:

"Locri had no doubt some safe retreat for gallies and rowboats, though nothing now appears but an open road. Without a few remarkable monuments to guide us, it is not easy to discover the true position of any ancient town on this coast."

By the time Keppel-Craven (1818) had joined in the hunt, things were a little better:

"… several piles of masonry are scattered over the flat on which the lower portion of the city stood; and an immense quantity of tiles, bricks, and pottery is visible among the Indian wheat …"

Eight years on and Ramage (1828) is foraging around the same site with more success:

"Its ancient walls can be traced nearly round its whole circumference. A portion of them to the south are in a tolerable state of preservation …"

Lear (1847) didn't get too enthusiastic and just noted that there were the foundations of antique buildings in the local vineyards and that those working the land had found lots of coins. By the time Lear actually got to view the site, it is likely that he had lost all enthusiasm for all things Locrian as his host in nearby Gerace was Don Pasquale Scaglione, a local expert on Locri:

"… our good host victimised us fearfully by reading aloud chapter after chapter of a work he is writing on Locris—a, "opus magnum" which, however learned, was vastly dull."

(Don Pasquale's book, *History of Locri and Gerace*, was finally published in 1856 though I suspect Edward Lear never availed himself of a copy.)

In 1889 the renowned Italian archæologist, Paolo Orsi, began his work on the site and explored and exposed the town's walls in many places. But other major projects, such as the excavations at Siracusa in Sicily, diverted his attention from Locri for over a decade. When he returned in 1902 after a short stint as commissioner of the *Museo Nazionale di Napoli* he found that much of what had been achieved had been undone; in several places the town walls had been destroyed and other material had been removed thanks to a number of unauthorised, clandestine excavations.

Thus by the time Hutton (1912) was on the case, things were a little more defined … but not a lot:

"There is not much to be seen: the foundations of a Temple of the Ionic order of the fifth century B.C., a part of the old walls, a smaller Temple, and a shrine, little beside … "

Eric Whelpton (1957) had a different and better experience:

" … the ruins of Locri which are without any doubt the most complete and the most interesting in Calabria. The excavations at Locri are spread over a very wide area in a delightful setting of trees and flowers."

A decade later Morton (1967) was decidedly less impressed:
"There was nothing much for the untrained eye to see but mighty blocks of grey stone from which weeds and grass were sprouting ... I found the ruins confusing, but was glad to have seen the sight of so many happenings."

Morton was also told that excavations had been discontinued because of a land dispute.

Morton probably never knew it at the time but being the site of an ancient city of Magna Græcia was not Locri's only claim to fame, nor its preoccupation, for Locri was a modern town dominated by the Calabrian mafia, the *'ndrangheta*.

In the June of the year Morton was there, a 'massacre' took place in the local market where three people died and two were seriously injured. This was all about inter-clan mafia rivalry between the Cataldo and Cordí families and in this case the assassination of Domenico Cordí.

Mafia towns are noted for, among other things, the way in which money designated for one purpose can so easily vanish and end up lining other people's pockets. There is, as far as I am aware, no direct evidence that this was happening at Locri in respect of the archæological research being carried out at the time ... suffice to say that when Morton drove by the townsfolk had other things on their mind and the ancient ruins of Locri Epizefirii, to give it its full name, was not one of them.

Nevertheless it was two years later, in 1969, that serious excavations and research began when an agreement was reached between Calabria's Archæological Department and the University of Turin was implemented. Today the impressive LocriAntica website certainly gives the impression that work at Locri is ongoing ... but then seeing is believing. With a little scepticism, I added it to my list.

But my scepticism was unfounded, in part at least.

It was blistering hot July day when I finally visited the Locri site, first the museum then the excavated sites close to the museum and finally the theatre, a drive of almost a mile inland.

Between the two lies much of ancient Locri under land that remains in use ... I couldn't get a definitive answer as to whether this is still part of the land dispute referred to by Morton but what is clear that there are still parts of Locri Epizefiri to see the light of day. Land dispute or not, it is probably better that it remains safely underground for the immediate future rather than for its integrity to be put at risk.

While I applaud the fact that the Italians have a penchant for making ancients ruins accessible for modern-day events—for example, there is no theatrical experience that can compare with watching a Greek tragedy in the Greek theatre at Siracusa in Sicily—it defeats the object if the integrity of the site is not maintained in the aftermath of such occasions.

The day I visited the theatre at Locri it was clear there had recently been such an event and that I was not the only one to notice the incongruity of what had been left behind. The scattered remains of stalls or platforms were bad enough but it was the tall, unstable-looking Coca-Cola refrigerator that stole the show and almost certainly features in the photographic memories of many who visited this ancient Greek-Roman site that day.

I feel it is important to highlight this as it is exactly the sort of sloppiness that gets Italy, and Calabria in particular, a bad name in some quarters. I wonder how many saw the fridge and took it as a sign that the Museum was

The theatre at Locri Epizeferi, complete with the detritus of the day, looking towards the sea nearly a mile away.
Though the theatre's origins are Greek, in reality its remains represent a Greek-Roman theatre.
The complete site extends as far as the sea with its roadside museum and the excavated areas between the Centocamere quarter and the Temple of Marasà.

probably not worth a visit? If they did, it would have been a big mistake for the Museum at Locri is a gem—well-organised, well-lit, uncluttered, clearly labelled and even a corner that engages with children who are getting bored. My only criticism is that, though much of the labelling was in two languages, not all was and, like it or not, for many non-Italian speakers their second language is probably English.

All was not sweetness and light when it came to relations between the Magna Græcia republics, large and small, and the frequent skirmishes that broke out generally seemed to involve Kroton. Swinburne (1777) described their relationships thus:

"We crossed numerous streams, the banks of which were no doubt marked, in ancient times ... between the different Greek states, who were continually undermining their common fabric by intestine dissentions."

Two were particularly noteworthy conflicts that stirred the imaginations of those travelling scholars interested in Magna Græcia. The first was the rivalry between Locri and Kroton for, though both were Greek republics, the Krotons and all the other settlements on the Ionian coast were Arcæan Greeks, one of the four major tribes into which the Greeks were divided, while the Locrians were North-West Greeks, a linguistic offshoot of the Doric Greeks.

You can probably already tell where this is going ...

The background involved almost every permutation of alliances and rivalries between the republics but the outcome was a major dispute surrounding the founding of Caulon which Kroton supported but Locri didn't. The result was a battle between Kroton and Locri, the Battle of the Sagra, named after the nearby river. And though there is no doubt the battle took place, the exact date is unknown with most recent research suggesting that it was around the middle of the 6th century BCE.

There is, however an even greater mystery, the exact location of the Sagra, a puzzle that has niggled away at the inquisitive genes of successive travellers to the area, though that did not stop some inspired speculation from, for example, Richard Keppel-Craven (1820):

"On the banks of the Sagra, now the Alaro, which runs near that town [Caulónia], the Crotoniates were defeated by the Locrians, and the extraordinary disproportion of numbers between the conquerors and vanquished gave no less celebrity to that event than the marvellous communication of its intelligence at the Olympic games, on the same day that it occurred."

Swinburne (1777) had been of the same opinion as was Douglas (1911). Even today scholars are not in total agreement about whether it was the today's Allaro or the nearby Torbido, though the consensus seems to be for the former.

As ever, Ramage the Scot (1828) is the only one to try and put some meat on the bones of his speculation:

"Beneath it [a hill called Foca] stretches a plain nearly two miles in breadth, through which flows the small stream Alaro, which there is little doubt is the ancient Sagras. It was on the banks of this river that the inhabitants of Croton sustained a memorable defeat from the Locrians ... In talking to the inhabitants of the country, I could hear of no other level piece of ground within twenty miles where two large armies could be drawn up. There is a spot in the plain called "Sanguinaro," which may be considered a corruption of "sanguinarius," the Latin word for "bloody.""

I have stood there, relishing the heady scent of *agrumi* (citrus fruit) that pervades that Calabria plain stretching between hilltop Focà and the Allaro; Ramage was right, it would indeed be the perfect place for such a battle and, by coincidence, the narrow road that runs along the northern edge and parallel to the river is called Via delle Zagare. Looks and sounds like Sagra ... but the *zagara* is the name for citrus fruit flowers.

Not surprisingly, the local name of 'Sanguinaro' that was passed on to Ramage in 1828, elicited nothing but blank stare from all those I asked.

Two other things are worth recording ...

Regarding the Battle of Sagra, Keppel-Craven (1818) mentioned the 'extraordinary disproportion of numbers' while Ramage talked of a 'memorable defeat'.

The battle is an event, as I have already suggested, that has been shrouded in a degree of mystery but the biggest mystery of all was how on earth the Kroton army, numbering some 120,000 men, was defeated by the Locrian army of just 15,000? (The numbers vary in the ancient sources so I have used the lowest for the Crotonites and the highest figure for the Locrians.)

Of course, as the story of the battle spread—as far as the Olympic games 'on the same day that it occurred' according to Keppel-Craven (1818)—it is likely that the numbers became exaggerated, as did the time it took for the news to get to Greece. That the Krotonites vastly outnumbered the Locrians is undisputed though the exact numbers will probably never be known.

Because at the time they were the only source, travellers generally took as gospel the writings of ancient scholars such as the Greeks Strabo (c64BCE– c24CE) and Diodorus (1st century BCE) and the Roman Justin (3rd century

CE). And as these sources were detailing events long after they happened there has to be a question of reliability. Nowadays the picture is even more complicated as other sources and other types of sources confirm or contradict the previously accepted order of things.

As new information emerges and is interpreted we generally come a little closer to the truth; the ancient Caulon (Caulónia) is a case in point ...

Many of my fellow-travellers visited the town of Castel Vetere believing it to be the ancient site of Caulon. Indeed the local community itself was so convinced of this that they renamed the town Caulónia in 1862.

Keppel-Craven (1820) agreed with this premise:

"... Castel Vetere, a place of much greater renown under the name of Kaul, or Caulon, and capital of a district which separated the Crotoniate from the Locrian territories."

Ramage (1828), still questioning the sources, was not of like mind and substantiated his argument by pointing out that 'no ancient remains, cameos, or coins' had ever been discovered at Castel Vetere. Furthermore Ramage was convinced that it would be found much nearer the sea and possibly near the hill he called Foca when referring to the Battle of the Sagra.

Lear (1847) went with the consensus and could see Caulon clearly in his minds's eye as, having just crossed the river Alaro, he glanced up at the 'high hills and walls of the then Castel Vetere':

" ... ancient Caulon ... a town built on one of those isolated hills which, to antiquarians, at once proclaim an ancient site."

All got it wrong, including the local community who were so adamant about changing the name of their town. In the 1890s the Magna Græcia settlement of Caulon was discovered by archæologist, Paolo Orsi, over ten miles away from today's Caulónia at Punto Stilo on the coast close to Monasterace. Ramage got it right when he said it was located by the sea.

Ironically it was by Punto Stilo that Swinburne (1777) was standing when he looked up at Castel Vetere:

"Castelvetere, in a lofty situation, three miles from the sea, occupies the site of Caulon, of which some vestiges are said to exist. I saw none that have any claim to such antiquity."

Had he but known it at the time, if he'd scraped around in the undergrowth on his left, he could well have been the one to find ancient Caulon.

Douglas (1911) was the first to acknowledge that Caulónia/Castel Vetere was probably not the site of Caulon:

"The site of the original Caulónia is quite uncertain. Excavations now going on at Monasterace, some ten miles further on, may decide that the town lay there."

On the other hand, word hadn't yet got through to Hutton (1912) who was still stuck in the mind-set that hillside Caulónia was indeed ancient Caulon. Having just crossed the Allaro, 'the Sagras that once flowed with Crotoniat blood', he observed:

"Here, beside the river-bed to the north was set the city of Caulónia ..."

Ramage got it more or less right ... Caulon *was* on the coast. This photo, looking towards the sea from the coast road, shows how modern developments such as the road and railway narrowly missed Caulon's Doric temple.

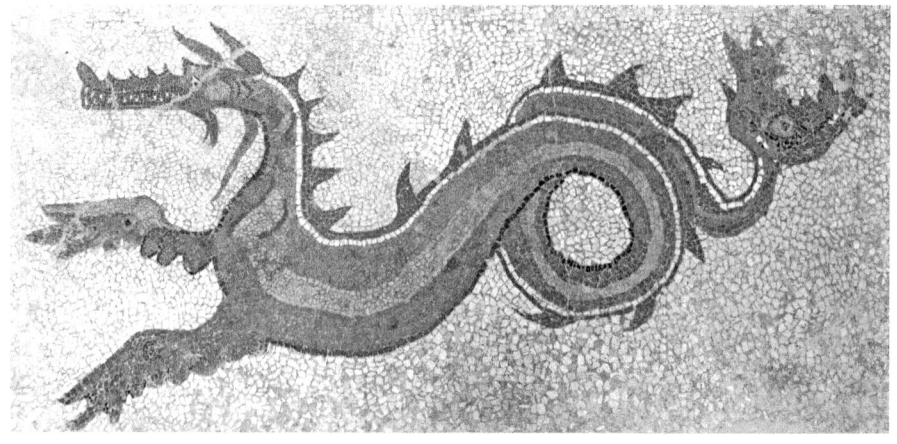

What would Keppel-Craven, Ramage, Lear *et al* have given to cast their eyes upon the Caulon dragon mosaic?

For many Magna Græcia seekers, the city of Caulon did not have the same draw as either Sybaris or Locri. Neither Whelpton (1957) nor Morton (1967) even mention Caulon but both wrote extensively about both Locri and Sybaris.

The irony is that today's Caulon site and its on-going excavations are more than a little impressive. As the remains are generally unadulterated by later Roman buildings and add-ons they are almost entirely Hellenic and Hellenistic. (The Romans did leave their mark but only by destroying the city for having sided with Hannibal during the Punic Wars.)

Among its gems the site boasts one of the largest (25 square metres) mosaic floors of the period ever found and in the nearby *Museo Archeologico di Monasterace* there is a smaller more delicate and distinctive mosiac of a dragon from the 3rd century BCE. Like that at Locri Epizefiri, this modern, well-planned museum is an important and impressive addition to the story of Magna Græcia.

The second conflict that became more than a mere passion for so many travellers who were students of Magna Græcia focused on the history of Sybaris and its relationship with Kroton, a story of brutal, inventive retribution ... apparently. Many visitors to Calabria hoped they might stumble upon this ancient site, might locate a city that had been effectively and purposefully wiped off the face of the earth. Furthermore, geographically and historically, there appeared to be more clues to identifying its general location.

Sybaris was founded in 720BCE on the fertile land between two rivers, the Crathis (today's Crati) and the Sybaris (today's Coscile); it was also an important and busy port. It soon became the wealthiest and most opulent of the Greek republics and, it is said, was known for the pleasure-seeking excesses of its inhabitants, a characteristic that spawned the word 'sybarite' still used today to describe those with hedonistic tendencies.

It was the destruction of Sybaris at the hands of the Crotoniates that fed the imagination of many and made the task of finding the site especially difficult.

No traveller interested in Magna Græcia could resist telling his version of the tale and how it was that Sybaris vanished. This from Keppel-Craven (1818):

"... the Crathis derived its brightest fame from the town of Sybaris, which rose between its stream and that of the river to which that city gave, or from which it took, its name.

"The power, opulence, and celebrity of this place, were put an end to in a short war with the Crotoniates, who, after vanquishing the inhabitants, destroyed their capital in the most effectual manner, by directing upon its magnificent edifices the waters of the very river which had so long contributed to enrich and embellish them, and which now render all research after their vestiges impracticable. The broad bed of the Crathis probably embosoms all of Sybaris that is not returned to its primitive elements."

Day and night, week in, week out, the pumps at Sibari draw out water from the remains of Copia, Thurii and Sibari.

Access to the Greek worlds of Thurii and Sibari is via the Roman world of Copia.

And this from George Gissing (1897):

"Of Sybaris no stone remains above ground; five hundred years before Christ it was destroyed by the people of Kroton, who turned the course of the river Crathis so as to whelm the city's ruins ... he [archæologist François Lenormant] held it certain that here, beneath some fifteen feet of alluvial mud, lay the temples and the streets of Sybaris, as on the day when Crathis first flowed over them."

The veracity of the story about how the Krotonites redirected the course of the river Crathis to obliterate Sybaris has been called into question, nevertheless the main tenet of the story, the disappearance of the city, holds true. As you might have come to expect, Ramage (1828) went the extra mile to locate Sybaris.

He spend a day ferreting around the countryside near the confluence of the two rivers and drew a blank though he did rule out that particular area:

"I persevered till I reached the confluence, notwithstanding there was a great deal of marshy ground ... nor can I imagine that Sybaris was placed here, unless nature has completely changed the ground on which I was standing."

Ramage went on to wonder whether the small lake that 'communicated with the sea', some miles distant and known as Laghetto, might be the remains of Sybaris' port.

Though he left for Rossano empty-handed, he may have right about the port and if he were to have drawn a line from the confluence of the two rivers and Laghetto and stood dead centre, he would have found himself standing on top of Sybaris, just north of the Crati. So close, yet so far.

The problem for amateur travellers and archæologists alike searching for Sybaris was the fact that its ruins had been built over twice and now lay well below groundwater level. The first city to overlap in part was Thurii, another Greek settlement founded in 446BCE. Thurii in turn succumbed to the influence of Rome, first as an ally, which led to its downfall at the hands of Hannibal. Thurii later became a Roman colony and was given the name Copia (though many still continued to use the appellation Thurii) and remained an important 'overlapping' Roman city until, that is, it too finally succumbed to the alluvial sediment emanating from the nearby river Crati.

In Calabria the winter and spring of 2013 was wetter than usual ... but some felt it more than others. In the north-east the swollen river Crati overflowed its banks and a wall of water engulfed the archæological remains of Copia, Thurii and Sibari, the site known collectively by its oldest and least accessible component, Sibari.

The water brought with it alluvial mud, the solid residue of which covered the site when the water was pumped out. Once again Sibari had succumbed to the vicissitudes of the Crati, the very river which, as the Crathis (and along with its then neighbour, the Sybaris), made the area fertile and created and sustained the wealth of a unique Greek republic ... and eventually brought about its demise.

Since 2013 there have been other alluvial incursions and pumps are in use twenty-four-seven to extract water from the depths of the site and sometimes access to the site is therefore restricted. It is hoped that with financial assistance from the European Union, the site can be successfully re-excavated and

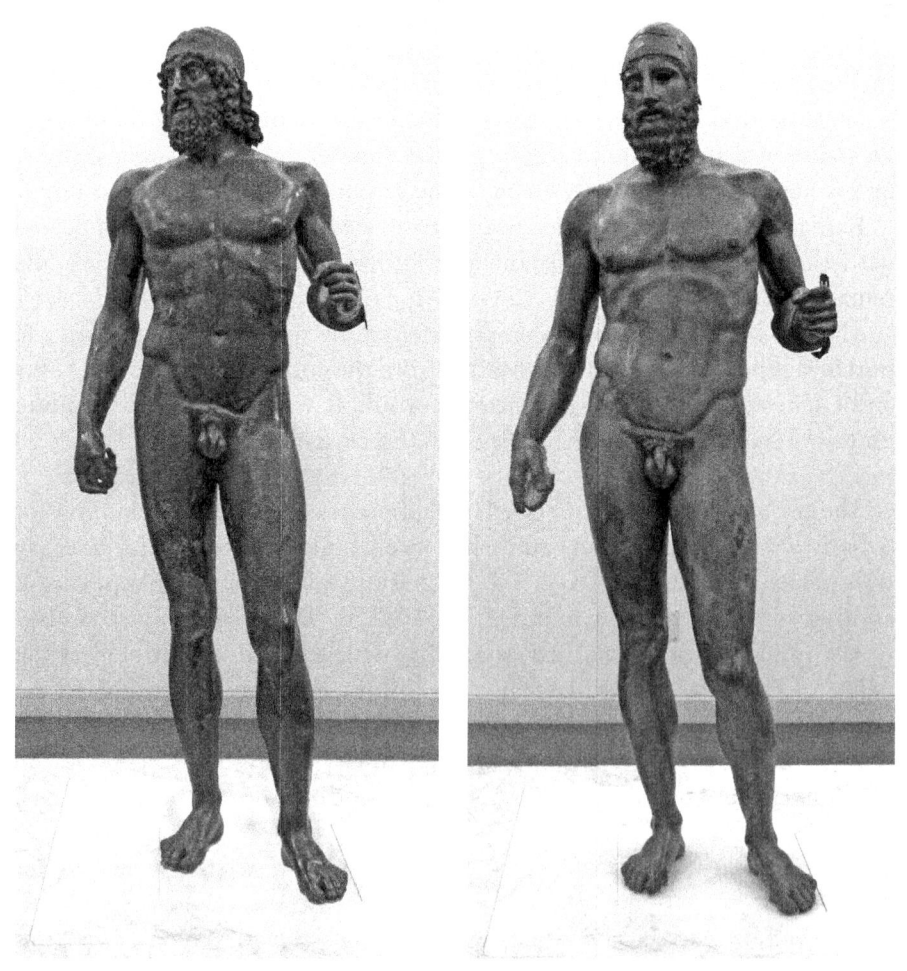

The Riace Bronzes, inspirationally named as Statue A and Statue B, atop their earthquake-proof plinths at Reggio Calabria's Museo Nazionale della Magna Græcia.

measures put in place to control future incursions from the capricious Crati.

At the site there is a floor mosaic, one of several that are part of a large 1st century BCE Roman villa. Here a neat, rectangular hole in the floor is the gateway to another world ... first Thurii and then Sibari itself.

Unlike Ramage and Gissing and all the other travellers who sought the illusive Sibari, today's travellers can, the river Crati permitting, at least catch a glimpse of what remains. For much more than a mere glimpse there is an excellent museum close by which has a separate room dedicated to each level and each city—Sibari, Thurii and Copia—all of which , to varying degrees, claimed this site, this area, as their homeland before falling to the vagaries of politics and nature.

In addition, the first room is dedicated to the pre-Greek period with displays and artefacts from the bronze and iron ages that serve to put the site in its archæological context.

I realise that, in concentrating on Kroton, Locri, Sybaris and Caulon, I have made sparse mention of the other Magna Græcia sites in Calabria that, for the people who settled there, were just as important. What a transformation there might have been in Rosarno if it had become known for being the site of the Magna Græcia city of Medma, rather than as a mafia stronghold?

There are however two artefacts that are, for many, probably the most famous and recognizable relics of Magna Græcia in Calabria.

In the summer of 1972, Rome chemist, Stefano Mariottini, was snorkeling off the Calabrian coast in water six to eight metres deep, two hundred metres offshore from Riace, when he spotted an arm sticking up from the sand. He had discovered the first of what came to be known as the Riace Bronzes. Since then the statues have been carefully restored and given the highly original appellations of Statue A and Statue B.

The precise provenance of the two naked bronze warriors is unknown but it is believed that Statue A dates from between 460 and 450 BCE while Statue B dates from between 430 and 420 BCE; in other words Statue A is possibly older by some thirty years.

Coastal Riace itself (there is also an older town inland) is situated south of what was Caulon and north of Locri Epizefirii, though is closer to the former. It is assumed that the bronzes were aboard some sort of vessel when it floundered though no remains of a wreck has been found in the vicinity. No-one knows where the bronzes were travelling to or from though it is considered possible they were part of booty en route to Rome when the Romans had free rein to plunder the Magna Græcia republics.

The Bronzes are now on display at the *Museo Nazionale della Magna Græcia* in Reggio Calabria where they stand on special plinths that are designed to absorb the shock of an earthquake which, bearing in mind Reggio's history, is not an unreasonable precaution (see the next chapter *When the earth moves*).

Be assured that to gaze upon the Riace Bronzes in the flesh, so to speak, is a singularly moving experience. Perhaps more than any other artefacts, the Bronzes personify the ancient Magna Græcia civilization that became a passion for so many, not least my fellow travellers.

I have often found it puzzling how historical time-lines appear to change so effortlessly between one regime and another without any real explanation of what actually happened. Nor is there often any sense of how these changes might have effected real people whose lives and livelihoods were at stake.

Almost seamlessly, it seemed, did Magna Græcia appear to become part of the Roman Empire and the city republics were gone forever, awaiting only the passage of time and the growing of grass.

In the case of Magna Græcia, the writing had been on the wall for some time with the ever-increasing power and influence of Rome. It all started in 281BCE with a dispute between the Romans and Greek Tarentum (Taranto in Apulia) which led to open conflict between the two; the leader of the 'Greek' side was a formidable Egyptian, Pyrrhus of Epirus, who was repaying a favour to Tarentum.

The convoluted campaign lasted three years by which time Locri had made the mistake of accepting a Roman garrison whereupon, Pyrrhius sacked the city in 278BCE, Effectively Locri was no longer a part of the already fragile Magnia Græcia.

For the previous two hundred and fifty years the influence of the foundling Roman Empire had been expanding to the north and to the south. By the end of the 3rd century BCE its mission was complete and the city republics of Magna Græcia became little more than communities on the fringes of the new, dominant civilization directed from Rome.

New cities and towns were established, sometimes, like Roman Copia and Scolacium (Greek Scyllacium), on the same sites, and much of what has been Magna Græcia succumbed to the ascendency and edifices of a new regime, to the elements, to nature and to recycling ... and all but vanished.

Their disappearance was a physical phenomenon only, for countless scholars and travellers never forgot these places and their extraordinary histories. And though they never lived to see it, they knew that one day others would walk in these ancient cities and marvel at the architecture and artefacts left by the Magna Græcia civilization.

—✄—

On a warm Saturday in February, Kay and I set off from Crotone with our friend Denise for a weekend excursion south along the Ionian coast to Locri, Gerace and Stilo; we had booked bed & breakfast overnight at Locri, our first stop. I should have known things would not go exactly as planned … this is Calabria, after all.

Denise was at the wheel when she unexpectedly took an off-road detour just south of Lido di Catanzaro.

"Thought you might like to see this place," she offered by way of explanation, "it's called Roccelletta. I'm going to call Marco, he doesn't live too far away, so he might turn up if he's not still in his pyjamas."

Knowing Marco, an ex-colleague of Denise and occasional acquaintance of ours, I knew that the pyjama scenario was a distinct possibility. Now I was even more certain that, only an hour into our journey south, this day was definitely not going to turn out as expected.

Dishevelled, but otherwise fully dressed, Marco did indeed turn up just as we finished our walk round the ruins of Roman Scolacium at Roccelletta. Marco convinced us that it would be impertinent to be so close to Squillace and not visit the place where the great Roman statesman, writer and inventor, Cassiodorus was born and to gaze upon the town's impressive Norman castle. He offered to accompany us.

To cut a long, convoluted story short, shielding our eyes from the light, we eventually staggered out of the restaurant next to the closed Squillace Castle a little before five in the afternoon; we were all, except driver Denise, very much the worse for wear; some more so than others. Somewhere between Roccelletta and Squillace Castle our group had swollen in number to eight, all male friends of Marco. Essentially this band of modern-day Calabrian brigands had hijacked us, forced unsolicited hospitality upon us and for over three hours we ate, drank and were merry in the only restaurant we could find that was open.

For George Gissing (1897) too, his time in this same area did not go according to plan. He too had just arrived at Squillace and, having survived an horrendous downpour, was looking forward to finding somewhere to eat and a place to stay so that he could spend some time relaxing in the home town of Cassiodorus, a 'delightful pedant ... liberal statesman and patriot' whom he admired greatly. He had even carried two of Cassiodorus' books with him the whole way to Calabria:

"I jumped out. We were at the entrance to an unpaved street of squalid hovels, a street which the rain had converted into a muddy river, so that, on quitting the vehicle, I stepped into running water up to my ankles. Before me was a long low cabin, with a row of four or five windows and no upper storey; a miserable hut of rubble and plaster, stained with ancient dirt and, at this moment, looking soaked with moisture. Above the doorway I read "Osteria Centrale"; on the bare end of the house was the prouder inscription, "Albergo Nazionale"—the National Hotel. I am sorry to say that at the time this touch of humour made no appeal to me; my position was no laughing matter. Faint with hunger, I saw at once that I should have to browse on fearsome food. I saw, too, that there was scarce a possibility of passing the night in this place."

As far as we can recall, Kay, Denise and I definitely fared much better in Squillace than dear young George but, like Gissing, we were forced to change our plans for, after more than six hours on the road, we were still closer to our

Looking east towards the sea, the amphitheatre at Roccelletta part of the Roman city of Scolacium below which lies the Magna Græcia world of Scyllacium.

point of departure, Crotone, than we were to our destination, Locri. That afternoon's planned visit to the Magna Græcia remains of Locri Epizefiri and its museum was not going to happen.

It was already dark when, exhausted from our indulgences, we finally arrived at Locri.

But Locri Epizefiri's loss was Scyllacium's gain for at Roccelletta we had inadvertently visited the site of Roman Scolacium which sits atop Magna Græcia's Scyllacium. The amphitheatre we walked round that morning was Roman but its orientation and position on the hillside was essentially Greek in nature. As with Sybaris and Copia, what might remain of Greek Scyllacium, one of the earliest Magna Græcia republics, lies beneath Roman Scolacium.

I mention this particular adventure, not only because, tongue-in-cheek, it happened to involve all three of Ulderico Nisticò's reasons for visiting Calabria—modern-day 'brigands', hospitality and Magna Græcia—but also because Denise, who had visited the Roccelletta site a number of times previously, was clearly disappointed in what she saw that day.

It seemed to her that the amphitheatre in particular was in a worse state than it had been when she had last visited. It appeared that no additional excavations had been initiated and the site had not been well maintained with the result that the forces of nature had started to encroach once again. That said, the interpretation boards were excellent and thus far the grass hadn't grown tall enough to cover them.

In Italy this is, and will be, an on-going problem for the Italian peninsula is bursting at the seams with the legacies of many civilizations. In times of economic crisis and restraint, finding the cash to fund excavations and museums has always been a question of how and what to prioritise … even finding the money to maintain and prop up the iconic Pompeii has not been easy.

In the case of that part of Magna Græcia that lies within Calabria, the excavations continue and, despite financial constraints, the archæological community is endeavouring to make these sites, and their attendant museums, accessible.

The problem will not be just to make them physically accessible on the ground but also to encourage enough people to come and visit … people, like me, who didn't have a 19th or 20th century classical education.

CALABRIA

Il Pollino

Il Mar Ionio

Mormanno

Rossano

Il Mar Tirreno

San Giovanni in Fiori • Acerenthia
● **COSENZA** *La Sila* Cerenzia Stróngoli
Santa Severina ●
CROTONE
Cutro

1783 Earthquakes Epicentres
February 5: Oppido Mamerti
February 6: North-east of Messina
February 7: Soriano Calabro
March 1: Filadelfia
March 28: Valleflorita

Nicastro
Sant'Eufémia **CATANZARO**
Filadelfia
Valleflorita

Il Mar Ionio

● **VIBO VALÉNTIA**
● Soriano Calabro

Messina
Oppido Mamerti
●
L'Aspromonte
SICILIA Villa San Giovanni
● **REGGIO DI CALABRIA**
Pentedattilo

CAMPANIA BASILICATA

When the earth moves

"Sir W Hamilton thinks that the centre of the earthquake [5 February 1783] may be placed at Oppido ... and that a radius of two and twenty miles from this point would inscribe a circle including within its boundary all the cities and villages subjected to entire overthrow ..."
Richard Keppel-Craven *A Tour through the Southern Provinces of the Kingdom of Naples*

It was a quiet Monday morning in January 2011.

Kay and I slept on a little longer than usual and, after a late breakfast, took up our usual positions at our computers.

Our 'office' is next to the front door and looks out on the narrow street that runs straight up to Via Grecia, itself a narrow road running along the eastern edge of Santa Severina's *centro storico*. At the back, our apartment is one house away from the steep precipice that is the natural eastern 'wall' of this hilltop town.

The name of the road, Via Grecia, acknowledges that this was once the town's oldest 'Greek-Byzantine' quarter, La Grecia. But all that changed after an earthquake, generally accredited to March 1783, caused some of this quarter to break away and tumble down the hillside.

Damaged buildings were never replaced which explains why houses and apartments in and around today's Via Grecia are more modern than those less than five minutes walk away on the western side of the town though here too the quarter known as San Domenica suffered earthquake damage.

Back to that Monday morning ...

Kay, whose desk faces the window, asked me who I thought the guys in orange were. Walking down towards our apartment were three men dressed in orange jumpsuits and sporting what looked like serious climbing gear. Had it not been for the hard hats and their innocent, almost jovial, gait, they could have been taken for escapees from the nearest penitentiary.

At our front door they turned to the right and instinctively both Kay and I walked through to the back of our apartment to see if the reemerged at the other side. They did not. Whatever they were up to, it was definitely something off in the other direction.

Soon it was time for our daily constitutional, a walk up to the square for a cup of coffee and to catch up on the news. We stepped outside and immediately were aware that there seemed to be more of our neighbours out and about than was usual. One asked if we had heard it ...

"Heard what?", we asked puzzled.

"*La frana, la frana*", was the animated response. "Didn't it wake you up?"

Our lack of language kicked in and the blank look on our faces was a clear indication that we did not know what *la frana* was and, even if we did, we clearly hadn't seen, heard or felt it.

Gradually the tale unfolded. A *frana* is a landslide and the night before, just after midnight, a large chunk of Santa Severina, no more than sixty yards from our door, had broken off and fallen down the hillside. We, enjoying our beauty sleep, had heard and felt nothing.

Part of the north face of Santa Severina that broke off in January 2011; at the top are the houses affected and below lie some of the large rocks that tumbled down into the valley. The approach ramp to the bridge over the river Neto gave way following torrential rain in September 2009; the road was fairly new so, apart from the weather, poor workmanship may have contributed.

Later our neighbour, Raffaele Vizza, whose house is the one in front of ours and right on the edge, told us the full story.

Like us, the Vizza family were all tucked up in bed when, unlike us, Raffaele heard the noise and felt the earth move. His instinctive reaction was 'earthquake' and he quickly woke up his wife, Silvana, and their two children, Francesco and Alessia, told them to wrap up and go outside while he checked for news on the television. The fact that the television was still working, he recognised as a good sign.

With Italy being prone to devastating earthquakes, news of one gets picked up by the media very quickly and so Raffaele flicked through the channels until he was satisfied that there was no immediate danger. What he and others had heard was a sizeable piece of rock breaking away from the top of the hill and what they felt was it rolling and tumbling a thousand feet down the hillside into the valley below.

It was no more than a *frana*, a landslide, and Kay and I had slept through the whole thing.

No more than a *frana* for us sixty yards away, but for those who were living closer to the edge it was a more traumatic experience—one family actually lost part of its garden.

The men in the orange jump-suits had come to inspect the damage and assess if there was any potential danger to people and property living close to the edge. Following their deliberations they felt pretty sure that the *frana* had only affected the wetter, northern face of the hill and that people like us, those just around the corner on the drier eastern side, had nothing to worry about. Nevertheless, several families were advised to relocate.

Like Raffaele and his family, almost all our neighbours had gathered in the streets the night before in anticipation of something worse. By the time they noticed our absence, the danger was past and they all drifted back to their beds.

Eighteen months later there was another similar event a little further round the northern edge of the hill; once again, though the whole town seems to have heard and felt it, we did not. It made me wonder whether people here were tuned into expecting such events in a way that we clearly weren't? Perhaps I should have taken the warning of Norman Douglas (1911) more seriously:

"In one year alone (1903), and in the sole province of Cosenza … there were 156 landslides."

Almost two hundred years earlier Craufurd Tait Ramage (1828) had an almost identical experience while staying in Rossano:

"This morning I was surprised to find that I had been unconsciously exposed to another danger during the night which had never occurred to me. A severe shock of an earthquake had taken place, and the whole inhabitants of the village had been so much alarmed that they had spent the greater part of the night in the public square, afraid of being buried in the ruins of their houses. Of course no one felt any particular interest in my safety, and I was allowed to sleep undisturbed amidst all their alarm. I have no doubt I was entirely forgot, and as there was no disastrous result, I am not sorry that I was allowed to remain quietly in bed."

For Kay and I—and Craufurd Tait Ramage—the earth had definitely moved, even if we didn't know it at the time. But our experiences were no more than hiccups in the grand scheme of things for Calabrians have long endured greater and more devastating shocks.

Calabria is in an earthquake zone and throughout its recent history has been plagued by these natural disasters.

We have already seen how, in March 1638, Sant'Eufémia was obliterated first by a terrible earthquake and then engulfed by nature's double whammy, the tidal wave. That year there were three major earthquakes, all in the same western side of the *regione* and many towns and villages were destroyed and thousands of lives lost.

But the most devastating series of earthquakes took place in the winter of 1783. There were five in total and only the northern half of Calabria escaped serious damage.

Although Brian Hill (1791) was the first of my fellow-travellers to visit Calabria after 1783, Thomas Watkins, on his way to Messina by sea in March 1788, took a short detour inland to visit Oppido, the epicentre of the most destructive of the five earthquakes.

From his *speronara* (a small Mediterranean sailing vessel that could also be rowed), Watkins had already noticed the many ruined buildings along the shore and so decided to land at Gioia Taura and see for himself:

"What a scene of sorrow is there [in Oppido], what a glut of desolation! I remember to have shuddered at our newspaper recital of the destructive earthquake, but how faint a picture was that of the reality! I know not indeed how to describe it, as it resembles nothing in nature. Could you however bring your fancy to form an idea of the field of battle, on which Jupiter and the giants hurled rocks and mountains at each other, when they disputed the government of heaven, you may conceive the appearance of Oppido and its neighbourhood. The ground on which the ground stood is a continued heap of stones, and on the northern side near its castle is a deep winding valley, where the earth has gaped most tremendously. at the bottom of which are two large lakes."

Reading Brian Hill's description of the same area only three years later you could be forgiven for assuming that life had got back to some sort of normality:

"The ravages of the earthquake appeared on all sides, every town and village having been laid level with the ground, though they are now rebuilding in a superior style to what they were before."

But, as Richard Keppel-Craven (1818) discovered, even thirty-five years on, these events and their terrible aftermath were still relatively fresh in the memory, He wrote both sensitively and eloquently about what he heard and saw:

"Three particular days, the 5th and 7th of February, and the 28th of March, of the year 1783, are recorded as the periods of the most severe efforts of the convulsion; but six successive weeks, from the first of these dates, would perhaps be more correctly assigned to the continued internal fever, marked, during that period, by not less than a thousand distinct shocks: these were neither periodical, or attended by any particular symptoms in the state of the temperature.

"It is difficult to imagine a more extraordinary picture than the appearance of this portion of Italy, during the first few months which followed this awful visitation, by which an extent of territory, exceeding 140 miles, was more or less laid to waste, and which can only be assimilated to the dissolution of the human energies and frame under the activity of operation of a violent poison. Here the finest works of nature, and the improvements they have received from the industry of man, were swept away by the same terrible agency which hurled mountains from their bases, and checked rivers in their speed. The convulsion extended from sea to sea, and the wreck through out was universal. The wretched survivors fled from the few buildings which might have afforded shelter, while they only threatened destruction; and either wandered round the ruins which had overwhelmed the bodies of their friends and relatives, or, mutilated and disabled, lay in hopeless apathy among their vineyards and fields, now affording neither fruit or vegetation. These, as well as the necessities of life, which the fertility of soil and benignity of climate render so abundant in these provinces, were involved in the great destruction; mills and magazines [small warehouses] were annihilated; the wine and oil which could be saved had suffered such singular and offensive alterations as to render them useless, and even the waters were not drinkable. All domestic animals seemed struck with an instinct of terror, which suspended their faculties, while even the wilder species appeared deprived of their native shyness and ferocity. The stillness of the air was remarkable, and contributed to render more appalling the deep-seated thunder which rumbled in the recesses of the earth, and every fresh throe was responded by the apprehensive lamentations of the human, or the howls and screams of the brute creation.

"An epidemical disorder, produced by the stagnation of water, the want or bad quality of food, and the exposure to night air, filled the measure of misery up to the very brim, and left unfortunate victims of such accumulated calamities no hope but that of a speedy termination of their woes in the apprehended dissolution of the world itself, which they looked upon as awfully impending, nor is it surprising that such an opinion should take possession by minds weakened by continued suspense, and terrified by appearances so supernatural, that they might be looked upon as the last convulsive agonies of expiring nature.

"Thirty-five years have elapsed since the occurrence of this dire calamity, and, during the ten first which succeeded it, the paternal solicitude of the sovereign, and the attention of the government, had united in beneficent efforts to restore prosperity to this afflicted province; but the political vicissitudes to which it afterwards was exposed, have probably retarded the improvements which should have been the result of those measures."

Keppel-Craven went to describe how timber-framed buildings, *barrache*, no more than makeshift shacks or huts, replaced earlier stone structures and how there now seemed to be many more streams and rivers running in to the sea on the west as opposed to the Ionian side, the east.

He was writing about the conditions he found in the western Aspromonte close to the epicentre of the first, devastating tremors at Oppido but, as he noted, the earthquakes effected an area extending at least 140 miles, as far south as Reggio Calabria and as far north as Cosenza.

Eight years later Craufurd Tait Ramage (1828) was also travelling through the same area and also found that memories of 1783 remained fresh in people's minds:

"I was now on the central spot where the earthquake of 1783 had been felt most severely, when the greater part of the village had been swallowed up. The houses are now built principally of wood [*barrache*], as few months pass without a shock more or less severe being felt, and yet they speak of the insecurity of their situation with the utmost nonchalance. About a week ago they had felt a severer shock than had taken place for many years before, and they had thought it prudent to spend the night in the open air. Several of the inhabitants were old enough to have a very vivid recollection of what had taken place in 1783, and shuddered at the thought of what they had witnessed. They said that the appearance of the sky gave warning of some fearful catastrophe impending; close, dark mists hung heavily over the surface of the plain; the atmosphere appeared in some places so red hot that they would not have been surprised to see it burst into flames; even the waters of the river had a turbid colour, and a strong sulphureous smell was diffused around.

"I was anxious to see some of the more striking effects of the convulsions, and I was conducted a few miles to a deep glen, which they said had been formed by the earthquake. They pointed to a forest which had been hurried down to the bottom of a deep ravine, without having been in the least separated by the shock. In other parts, rivers had been arrested in their course by the fall of mountains, and had become large lakes, but of this I saw nothing."

At the extremities were towns like Santa Severina where the damage was believed to be significant but nothing like that experienced further south. It had been assumed that this was when the old Byzantine-Greek quarter, on the eastern side of the town, broke away and what was left was abandoned. There is no record of casualties.

Over the years, nature overran this abandoned eastern quarter and it became just like any other part of the countryside. Soon there were olive trees and vines, cattle, sheep, goats and mules and all on the summit of a hilltop town. It was not until after the Second World War that the first house was built on this land and gradually all vestiges of that lofty, transitory countryside disappeared.

The last house was built here in 2008; it is the home of our neighbours and friends, the Vizza family. I remember well the day they moved in for the next day *we* moved in to the apartment that had been their home for fourteen years.

Often the communities that become the victims of earthquakes have to be abandoned, sometimes later rather than sooner. Italians call such places *paesi fantasma*, ghosts towns, and there are many scattered throughout the country with Calabria having its fair share. Some are abandoned and forgotten, places to stumble upon rather than visit. Others, like Amendolea, Pentedattilo and Roghudi near Reggio Calabria and Acerenthia near San Giovanni in Fiore are accessible to the public as permanent memorials to the way in which the unpredictability of nature has directly affected communities and literally shaped the landscape.

The first *paesi fantasma* we ever visited was Gibellina in southern Sicily. The people had moved on and what remained of their homes had been transformed into Alberto Burri's controversial, white, concrete artwork. Curiously, we found it to be stunningly beautiful and compelling, a silent memorial to those whose lives changed irrevocably following the earthquake of January 1968. Perhaps, given its current concrete coat, it now no longer qualifies as a *paesi fantasma*.

Both Amendolea and Pentedattilo suffered in the earthquakes of 1783 and became severely depopulated as a result though it was not completely abandoned until the 1960s. Today it remains essentially a *paesi fantasma*

Edward Lear's sketch of Pentedattilo in 1847.
Today the town is a cluster of mainly abandoned houses centred on the church (the spire of which can be seen below the pointed rock on the left); clustered around the church there are a number of small craft shops and a museum ... and Giorgio.

despite ongoing efforts to repopulate it as a sort of base for local arts and crafts and a tourist attraction. It will always be the latter because of its striking position in the shadow of the dominant, name-giving, 'five-fingered' escarpment and the breathtaking views therefrom; whether it can ever be repopulated remains to be seen though it won't be for want of trying on the part of the town's ebullient, live-in 'curator', Giorgio Vasta.

As it happened Henry Swinburne (1777) came to Pentedattilo before 1783 and described what seemed an idyllic place:

"At Pentedattolo, a pretty village, I found the state of agriculture much better than what I had hitherto seen in the province. The ground is managed with more skill and neatness and consequently productive of greater crops. Its hemp is the best in Calabria."

Seventy years later, when Edward Lear (1847) was here, the earthquakes had done their worst and initiated some changes. Having described the 'perfectly magical' setting, he goes on …

"… [here] the houses of Pentedatilo are wedged while darkness and terror brood over all the abyss around this, the strangest of human abodes … the habitations on its surface now consist of little more than a small village, though the remains of a large castle and extensive ruins of buildings are marks of Pentedatilo having once seen better days."

As Lear set about drawing the scene, he was initially startled when …

"… the whole population bristled on wall and window, and the few women who passed me on their way to the hanging vineyards, which fringe the cliffs low down by the edge of the river."

Viewing the town from afar sixty years later, Norman Douglas (1911) saw it all quite differently:

"… Pentedattilo, a most singular landmark which looks exactly like a molar tooth turned upside down, with fangs in air."

When Leslie Gardiner (1966) passed this way the distinctive rock formation was still there even if the people were not:

"… the clutching hand of Pentedattilo, a grotesque five-finger exercise in stone … It is one of Nature's jokes: the five grey fingers of a granite hand thrust out of the mountainside, rigid from wrist to nail-tip, two hundred feet high."

As if to lay more intrigue and mystery at the hand of Pentedattilo, both Lear and Gardiner retell the same story about the place and the rivalry between the two ruling families at Pentedattilo and nearby Montebello … though clearly Gardiner is just repeating Lear's account. It is a sordid tale of local intrigue and revenge that had its roots in events that were infinitely more dramatic than those surrounding Romeo and Juliet. But like the tale of Romeo and Juliet their story was fiction, albeit with a few nuggets of truth in that the rival families in the story did exist, that were sworn enemies and of course that unrequited love did playa part.

Lear and Gardiner both finish with the assertion that it was the 1783 earthquake that put paid to the main protagonists. Lear's version is straight to the point, albeit an erroneous point:

"Finally, as if it was ordered that the actors is such a wholesale domestic tragedy were unfit to remain on earth, the castle of Pentedattilo fell by the shock of an earthquake, crushing ... every other agent in this Calabrian horror."

It's an intriguing story with that a wonderful twist of irony at the end which has the 1783 earthquake bring everything to a tidy end. But even those few nuggets of reality in the Lear-Gardiner version predate the 1783 earthquakes by almost a century.

Sadly Gardiner had not read Eric Whelpton's 1957 account of the same events, the so-called 'Massacre of the Alberti' (the family name of the Marquis of Pentadattilo). Whelpton not only placed the story in the right century, but he didn't even connect the earthquakes with its denouement.

What the earthquakes of 1783 did contribute to the 'Massacre of the Alberti' story was to wipe the slate clean, to focus the minds of all those who lived in both Pentedattilo and Montebello on the here and now, on the reality of what was happening to their communities, on surviving, perhaps rebuilding, maybe moving on.

Eric Whelpton might have got his facts right but, it seems, he was not blessed with the adventurous gene, and so never actually made it up to Pentedattilo itself:

"I was not able to visit the village, for even now, it is not accessible by road, and I could not face up to the rough and tortuous mule track which provides the only means of communication with the outside world."

Today he would have the option of being whisked quietly up to the town in Giorgio's small electric car. Perhaps 'quietly' is the wrong word for there is no escaping Giorgio's exuberant and fascinating retelling of every known fact about his beloved Pentadattilo. His enthusiasm is infectious and if he can't entice people back to 'the strangest of human abodes', then nobody can.

For Acerenthia, hitherto a small, unassuming Calabrian hill-top town between Santa Severina and San Giovanni in Fiore, the earthquakes of 1783 was said to be almost the last straw. Almost, but not quite.

Acerenthia had once been a thriving town of some several thousand inhabitants. As if the plague that struck the town in 1528 and the earthquakes of 1638 were not enough, the population was apparently further depleted by the last of the 1783 season of five earthquakes.

Even before 1783, Acerenthia's population had already dwindled to no more than a few hundred and, according to some modern accounts, the 1783 destruction was so great that many decided not to rebuild on the same site and headed instead for the higher ground closer to San Giovanni in Fiore. Here they established a new settlement, Cerenzia.

It is said too that in the wake of the earthquake, when malaria became endemic in the lower-lying area around Acerenthia, that *was* almost the last straw. Little is said about the other two earthquakes in 1832 and 1836, and particularly the former, which must surely have brought back memories for those who still recalled the stories of what happened in 1783.

The evidence is clear, Acerenthia was finally and completely abandoned just a few years after the two quakes in the 1830s. It was in 1844 that the last families voted with their feet and moved to Cerenzia or elsewhere.

For the people of Pentedattilo the decision to abandon their town was a slow process that spanned close on two centuries; for those in Gibellina it was one propelled by a single cataclysmic event. Following the earthquakes of the 1830s, the inhabitants of Acerenthia did not hang about … after all, most already knew where they were going.

What they left behind still sits atop a broad, oval-shaped hill that itself occupies the valley of the river Lese, almost completely surrounded by the lesser foothills of the Sila.

It was mid-April when we walked around what was left of this small Calabrian community and tried to picture in the mind's eye what life might have been like up here. Bracing, most definitely: bracing with quite extraordinary views in every direction and, clinging to the hills on three sides, many more fortunate communities, including Cerencia.

From the north-east, the Lese meanders lazily down from Lake Cecita and soon augments the much wider valley of the Neto as it snakes past a far-off Santa Severina, swings round Rocca di Neto before falling into a distant shimmering sea near Stróngoli.

From a distance the top looked flat but like most towns it has its highs and lows and here the higher ground to the south-east is dominated by the grey, almost white, stone ruins of the cathedral.

Mostly what remains are the same white-grey roofless walls of ordinary people's houses and outhouses—generally undefined and inaccessible, structures that surely are what any community is really about. It is no accident that the three buildings that lay claim to their own interpretation boards are the Cathedral, the church of San Teodora and, in between, what is called the *casa del principe*, the big house, the provenance of which remains uncertain though it has all the hallmarks of having once being a convent or monastery.

Of course these were, and still are, Acerenthia's largest structures but I would have also liked to have had a better sense of what it would have been like to live here rather than just worship here. I would have liked to have walked along a street where ordinary people lived and got a sense of what life might have been like here every day of the week and not just on Sunday. In that respect, perhaps I am just eccentric.

The hilltop site of Acerenthia.
The *casa del principe* and an outhouse probably for animals.

While describing the earthquakes of 1783 in relation to Santa Severina and Acerenthia, I have deliberately used words and phrases that suggest a degree of doubt in my mind regarding the generally accepted notion that it was the events of 1783 that were responsible for the damage inflicted on either town. The main evidence seemed to be that of hearsay based on the fact that, in the areas they are known to have affected, the 1783 earthquakes were truly destructive and received massive publicity throughout Europe.

It is, I believe, much more likely that it was the devastating earthquake of 1832 that brought so much physical and emotional hardship to the area west of Crotone and led to the final abandonment of Acerenthia and also destroyed the so-called Greek quarter in Santa Severina.

The earthquake of 1832 (and to a lesser extent that of 1836) did considerable damage to the area known as the Marchesato which more or less corresponds to the southern part of today's province of Crotone. In a letter sent by local dignitary and landowner, Baron Barracco, to Cavaliere Monticelli, professor of Ethics and Secretary of the Royal Academy of Sciences in Naples, he described the aftermath:

"Cotrone [sic] is deserted; its people are hospitalised in the warehouses outside of the city ...

"Cutro and the villages of Steccato and St. Leonard are completely destroyed with the death of more than 200 individuals ... A similar fate befell Roccabernarda, Rocca di Neto, Santa Severina and Altilia with the loss of many people. Places such as Policastro, Cotrone, Mesuraca, Caccuri, Scandale, Marcedusa, Sellia, Stróngoli, Ciro and Crucoli are extremely badly damaged, some more than others, and many of their inhabitants have lost their lives. Every house and factory scattered over the vast rural plains of the Marchesato is either collapsed or uninhabitable ... The inhabitants of all these destroyed and damaged places are forced to wander the countryside; and without any means of subsistence they are in the throes of squalor and despair."

It was when I came across this letter it rekindled lingering doubts I'd always had around the prevailing story that it was the 1783 earthquakes that wreaked so much havoc on Santa Severina and the surrounding area. The problem for me was that only the last two of the five quakes in the late winter of 1783 could possibly have had an effect as far north and east as Santa Severina. These were the earthquakes centred on Filadelfia (March 1) and that centred on Vallefiorita (March 28).

Also, I noted that in a letter to Sir William Hamilton, dated July 1783,

Count Francesco Ippolito's account of the damage done by the 28 March Vallefiorita quake (the closest to Santa Severina) did not mention any towns being affected any further north than Tiriolo, some twenty-six miles away.

Subsequently, in May 1783, Sir William Hamilton (who resided in Naples at the time) had an essay published in the *British Magazine and Review* in which he focussed on the damage throughout Calabria. Hamilton's account is quite detailed and is based on first-hand experience for, earlier in the same month, he came to Calabria to see for himself the damage caused by the five earthquakes. This is what he wrote about the damage specifically between Cosenza and Crotone:

"… its greatest violence has been exerted, and still continues to be so, on the western side of the Apennines, precisely the celebrated Sila of the ancient Brutii, and that all those countries situated to the eastward of the Sila had felt the shocks of the earthquake, but without having received any damage from them."

With regard to Santa Severina specifically, in his 1982 book on the Calabrian earthquakes (*L'iliade funesta. Storia del terremoto calabro-messinese del 1783*), Augusto Placanica appears to confirm Hamilton's assessment with the following observation on the 28 March earthquake:

"The inhabitants of Santa Severina, 1100 in number, and those of San Maura, 739, remained uninjured but some of the buildings were shaken violently none of which had to be demolished."

For me that put the final nail in the coffin of the accepted story that some of Santa Severina's original 'Greek quarter', the place where I live, fell away as a direct result of the 1783 earthquakes.

Wasn't it just more likely, I reasoned, that the 1832 earthquake was the culprit given that it was centred on the area that roughly corresponds to today's province of Crotone?

I therefore made a point of collaring Santa Severina's resident historian, Francesco de Luca, whose local knowledge and expertise is second to none. I showed him a copy of Baron Barracco's letter, from which I had removed all references to the date and I could see he was puzzled. He knew right away that it didn't refer to 1783 for which he knew all the sources and asked me when it had been written. He was aware of the 1832 earthquake but now realised that, in respect of Santa Severina, it was this earthquake that had probably done all the damage to the Greek quarter and another part of the town known as San Domenica.

In Cutro in 2013, local Cacurri historian Giuseppe Marino, presented his book, *Il terremoto del 1832 nel Marchesato Crotonese* (*The Crotone earthquake of 1832*) and began by telling his audience how information on the 1832 earthquake seemed to have dropped off the radar. He too had always understood that it was the 1783 quake that had done all the damage locally ... but his researches told a different story.

For example, in the vast swathe of land known as 'Calabria Centrale', there were eighteen sites affected by the earthquake of March 1, 1873; by contrast, in the Crotone area alone in 1832 there were seventy-eight sites affected.

This 1783 quake was recorded as IX on the then standard, the Mercalli Scale; the 1832 quake was IX-X on the same scale. The epicentre of the former was over forty miles from Santa Severina; we can see the epicentre of the latter (between San Mauro and Cutro) from our balcony. In 1832 in Cutro sixty people died; in Santa Severina, eight.

Napoleon Boneparte said 'What is history but a fable agreed upon?' by which he meant that often we come to believe in a version of what happened in the past because it's what most people have come to believe. It is the apparent consensus. Napoleon's words imply too that there remains the possibility that, in time, our understanding of the past can be refined and perhaps redefined.

In Calabria there has been, I believe, just such a consensus around the destructive earthquakes of 1783 to such an extent that, in the areas that were *least* affected, a more recent and more destructive seismic event has somehow been drawn under the 'umbrella' of the collective memory of 1783. Even the people of Acerenthia didn't give up their town after 1783; it was within a dozen years of the 1832 earthquake that they finally threw in the towel.

Though every British traveller wrote about earthquakes in Calabria—some at great length and with great passion—they always refer to the earthquakes of 1783. That said, clearly Swinburne (1777 & 1780) could not have done so.

Neither John Strutt (1840) nor Edward Lear (1847), the two travellers who were in Calabria not long after the 1832 quake, made mention of it though they did refer to the 1783 quakes.

In 1897 George Gissing was the first to travel through the Crotone area after the 1832 earthquake; typically Gissing only made references to the events of 1783. Likewise Douglas, Hutton, Whelpton and Morton.

Actually it was a French traveller who was the first to travel in Calabria just after the 1832 earthquake. Alexander Dumas travelled in 1835 and devoted a complete chapter to the region's earthquakes. But, like the others, Dumas never mentioned 1832 but then he was clearly preoccupied with the aftermath of the October 1835 earthquake which affected Cosenza and the surrounding area. Dumas was in the city just a few days later and described the scene when he arrived at his lodgings where, thinking initially the building had been abandoned, he finally found life in the cellar:

"The scene which we beheld was one of the strangest which we had ever seen; three distinct groups of people occupied the space. The first was a church canon who, since the earthquake began eight days ago, did not want to get up. He was in a great bed pushed into the far corner of the room. Next to him four men armed with muskets, who had worked as guards in the countryside, became his guards day in and day out. Opposite the bed there was a table where cattle merchants played cards. Finally, close to the door, a third group ate and drank; provisions of bread and wine were piled up in a corner so that, if the house were to collapse, the inhabitants wouldn't die of hunger or thirst while they waited for help."

And of course the stay-in-bed canon was much more use to this small group of fortunates than he would have been had he decided instead to get up off his backside and tend to the needs of his distressed, homeless and starving flock around the city ... wasn't he? Perhaps he simply wasn't up to answering those awkward philosophical questions that come to the minds of many when their homes, families and livelihoods have just been destroyed?

Clearly the five earthquakes of 1783 were devastating seismic events that destroyed much of the infrastructure of southern Calabria and killed thousands of people ... some estimates are as high as 50,000. Perhaps the five earthquakes of 1783 remained at the forefront of the collective psyche simply because they did so much damage to some of the region's major cities that nobody could ever begin to imagine anything worse?

But, just as clearly, it is unlikely they did extensive damage in central and eastern Calabria, the one major city that came off lightly was Crotone. For whatever reasons, the devastating earthquake of 1832 in the Crotone area has been all but wiped from the collective memory ... perhaps it's just easier to remember a single date.

Few people in southern Calabria were spared the devastation meted out by the earthquakes of, among many others, 1528, 1638, 1783, 1832 and 1835 but, by the time the next such events struck, memories of the most recent had begun to fade.

But, according to Emily Lowe (1858), it was not so in Reggio Calabria where things still had not got back to normal after seventy-five years ... and she was not impressed:

"The town of Reggio, which by an extraordinary hallucination once called itself 'le petit Paris', totters on its legs like a baby; two thirds of the buildings were levelled at once by a grand earthquake [1783], and little shocks are constantly adding to the heaps of rubbish; the painted houses, frittering their stories away, look like rows of sugared cakes that have been nibbled."

Unfortunately worse was to come for yet again southern Calabria bore the brunt of two earthquakes, the second of which centred on Reggio Calabria and its Sicilian neighbour, Messina.

The first, in September 1905, was centred at Nicastro near Lamezia but nevertheless did extensive damage between Cosenza and Reggio Calabria but an even more catastrophic quake occurred three years later, at dawn on 28 December 1908, when Reggio and Messina and their immediate vicinity were laid waste by the most destructive earthquake ever recorded in Europe. It is believed that the 1908 earthquake and subsequent tsunami killed up to 100,000 people. Estimates vary on the exact number of fatalities though there is no doubt that the suffering was greater on the Messina side with perhaps four times as many dead as on the mainland.

Although Messina came off worst, Reggio and southern Calabria also suffered terrible damage and loss of life and many Calabrians voted with their feet, crossed the Straits of Messina one last time with such worldly goods as they could muster and headed for Palermo and a one-way passage to the United States.

In *Thank You Uncle Sam* I told the story of a family, all but wiped out by the 1908 quake ... only 15 year-old Maria Cavallero and her father survived. Like many others he departed for America to start afresh and left his daughter in the care of other family members. But Maria got restless and in 1910 she too arrived in America ... but as a stowaway. Her story was subsequently published in the *New York Times* in an attempt to reunite father and daughter.

Norman Douglas (1911) visited Reggio a few years later when memories were still fresh and people still desperate. Here he reflects on the *barrache*, the hastily-built timber shacks that, just as in the aftermath of 1783, became the temporary homes of many survivors:

"If, as seems likely, those rudely improvised sheds are to be inhabited indefinitely, we may look forward to an interesting phenomenon, a reversion to a corresponding type of man. The lack of the most ordinary appliances of civilization, such as linen, washing-basins and cooking utensils, will reduce them to the condition of savages who view these things with indifference or simple curiosity; they will forget that they ever had any use for them. And life in these huts where human beings are herded together after the manner of beasts—one might almost say *fitted in*, like the fragments of a mosaic pavement—cannot but be harmful to the development of growing children."

Douglas goes on to enlighten his readers on the seamier side of such natural disasters, when desperation dehumanises some people whose subsequent actions then verge on the barbaric:

"The Calabrians, I was told, distinguished themselves by unearthly ferocity; Reggio was given over to a legion of fiends that descended from the heights during the week of confusion. "They tore the rings and brooches off the dead," said a young official to me. "They strangled the wounded and dying, in order to despoil them more comfortably.""

Reggio Calabria 1905: the homeless children of *le barrache*.

Reggio Calabria 1908: *i superstiti*, the survivors.

Edward Hutton (1912) painted a slightly more optimistic picture of Reggio, albeit one with a sting in the tail:

"It is now a mass of ruins scattered with mere shelters, but is slowly being rebuilt, certainly to be destroyed again in time to come, since it lies upon the direct line of volcanic disturbance between Etna and Vesuvius."

That parts of other Calabrian towns and roads will fall away is a given; in Santa Severina since the *frana* of 2011 there have been others, one of which was worse. That said, efforts are ongoing to stabilise the town's most vulnerable north-facing edge and those families that had to relocate back in 2011 have all returned home.

Back in 1973, in a *frazione* (district) of Santa Severina called Armirò—a scattered community about four miles north-west of the town—there was a more significant *frana* that changed people's lives. This small community of seventeen homes, a school and a church was tucked away in the lee of a modest hill, part of which, in April that year, was overcome by several days of incessant and torrential rain and tumbled downwards and through Armirò. Though nobody was seriously injured, almost every building was damaged, some beyond repair, and the road that linked the hamlet with the outside world was completely swamped. The havoc wreaked was so devastating that it was decided to relocate the entire community and most moved to Santa Severina itself.

Today those who once worked the land around Armirò still do so; en route to their olive groves, orchards and vines, on a bend on the old road to Cosenza, they pass the gaunt ruins of Armirò's church and school, stark reminders of what the untamed forces of nature can do to Calabrian communities.

At the time of writing the most recent seismic events of note in Calabria were the tremors in the Pollino mountains four miles south-east of Mormanno in October 2012. The maximum strength of 5.3 on the Richter Scale was enough to cause significant cracks on many roads and buildings. Nor were the town's square and church spared. There being just one fatality, in historical Calabrian terms this was a minor event.

That there will be other more dramatic landslides and seismic catastrophes in Calabria is a certainty … but what is just as certain is that nobody knows with any certainty when or where they will occur.

This is something all Calabrians live with.

CAMPANIA
BASILICATA
La Pollino
Il Mar Ionio
Sibari
Belvedere
CALABRIA
Páola
Camigliatello
Stróngoli
COSENZA
La Sila
Santa Severina
Petilia Policastro
Parenti
Scigliano
CROTONE
Cutro
Isola di Capo Rissuto
Il Mar Tirreno
Lamezia Terme
CATANZARO
Máida
Il Mar Ionio
VIBO VALÉNTIA
Mongiana
Rosarno
Gióia Tauro
Monasterace
Cittanova
Taurianova
Gerace
Oppido Mamertina
Lo Stretto di Messina
Platí
Locri
Santo Stéfano
San Luca
Bovalino
SICILIA
L'Aspromonte
Africo
REGGIO
DI CALABRIA

Outside the law

Not so long ago it [the Sila] was a haunt of brigands; now there is no risk for the rare traveller who penetrates that wilderness ...
George Gissing *By the Ionian Sea*

In December 1973 the world's press was full of the story of how John Paul Getty Jnr, the kidnapped grandson of oil tycoon Jean Paul Getty, was found wandering around somewhere in 'southern Italy', minus an ear, having just been released by his captors following payment of a ransom.

I recall the story well but at the time had no real understanding of exactly where these events were taking place nor who was involved. The only information that survived the passage of time was 'southern Italy' and 'mafia'.

At one level it was a well-organised crime for the kidnappers clearly knew that the young Getty would be out and about in Rome on the evening he was taken. And while they may have done their homework into the Getty millions, they failed to pick up on the Getty family dynamics which meant that within the family itself, some thought it was an elaborate subterfuge engineered by Paul Getty himself to acquire money from his family and particularly his thrifty grandfather. The fact that he had earlier joked about staging such a scenario, did not help his cause.

Thus the family did not respond positively to the first ransom demand for $18 million and grandfather Getty refused to help. As the days became weeks, and the weeks months, the confusion escalated and a second demand, sent to a newspaper, gave the family fifteen days to cough up or they would receive an ear and a lock of hair in the post.

More confusion and distrust between Paul's mother, Gail, and her son's kidnappers ensued and on October 21 the kidnappers finally carried out their threat, cut off his right ear, parcelled it up with a lock of hair and posted it to the Rome daily newspaper, *Il Messaggero*.

But they overlooked one important factor ... the ongoing postal strike in Italy and it was almost a month before the package arrived with young Getty's partially decomposed ear. Still more confusion gripped the dysfunctional Getty family until finally grandfather Getty agreed to pay $2.7 million for the release of his grandson. Paul was subsequently unceremoniously dumped from a car somewhere between Rome and Naples ... as far north from their home turf as the kidnappers could safely go and be certain of being back home to Calabria before the police got their act together.

The subsequent hunt for the kidnappers—after the police had got over the shock that it wasn't a hoax after all—focused on the Calabrian *'ndrangheta* and it wasn't long before arrests were made.

These days, the 'friends-in-high-places' syndrome that once seemed to ensure that few such mafia trials rarely led to a conviction is less of a problem—the 1992 mafia assassinations of Sicilian judges Falcone and Borsellino in Sicily precipitated a backlash against the mafia that resulted in investigative and judicial environments more likely to prosecute and to convict.

But back in 1974 the Getty kidnapping and its aftermath was played out in a less rigorous and accountable legal regime and, though arrests were made, only two convictions ensued.

At the time what attracted the attention of the world's press was that there seemed to be a part of Italy that was almost primitive 'bandit country', a place where the rule of law was abused or ignored. Calabria, it seemed, was a place where you could hide someone in a cave for five months in a remote mountain location and, by implication, with the complicity and even approval of the local population.

This was the picture the media painted of Calabria and to back it up there was of course the area's colourful history of banditry and brigandage—people outside the law who had their bases in remote mountain locations. All of which took no account of the political and social context at the time nor that the only obvious connection between the *'ndrangheta* and distant brigandage was their choice of hideout.

Nor were these bandits and brigands cut from the same cloth as the Albanians from Caraffa who accosted Arthur Strutt and his friends in 1841, these were the bandits and brigands who generally had a cause, definitely had a name and notoriety and often came to an ignominious end.

In the Mongiano area, west of Stilo, Craufurd Tait Ramage (1828) was told the following story:
"A short time ago when the government ordered all the arms in the country to be collected in the capital of each province, a band of twelve brigands had marched through some village in the vicinity, and proceeding to the house of the curate had carried him off to their fastnesses [strongholds], regardless of the excommunications of the Church. They fixed on a large sum for his ransom, and despatched a shepherd to convey the information to the village. As the curate was beloved by his parishioners the money was collected, and the poor clergyman released from his unpleasant thraldom [bondage]."
Though this brigand band was nameless, it had all the hallmarks of some of the later brigand bands that roamed Calabria: they were organised, they had a safe base (probably in the mountains as they used a shepherd as a go-between), they had discovered the crime of kidnapping, an indifferent attitude to the Church and finally—and this is conjecture—they probably had a leader who was revered by some, feared by others. Given the year, it is unlikely they had a political agenda.

While at Cosenza and hobnobbing with local dignitaries, Ramage challenged his host, 'his excellency', regarding stories he had heard:
"Though his excellency was unwilling to allow it, I have heard from others that the only way they are able to secure their safety is to pay *black mail* [sic] to the heads of some bands of brigands, who secure them from all others."
Though this 'blackmail' was the chosen money-making scam of these particular brigands, it has all the hallmarks of 'protection', *il pizzo*, which, in less than forty years, was to come into its own as the trademark of the so-called 'men of honour', the mafia, in Sicily and southern Italy.

I should clarify my use of the term 'mafia'.
Geographically there are four such organizations in Italy: Sicily's *cosa nostra*, Calabria's *'ndrangheta*, Naples' *camorra* and Puglia's lesser known and less active, *sacra corona unita*. All are no more than criminal gangs whose main aims appear to be to accrue as much money, control and power as possible at the expense of their fellow citizens, both locally and nationally, by defrauding, abusing, threatening and murdering them.

The word 'mafia' is a shorthand for all these gangs and groups ... indeed it was not until the mid-1950s that the use of the word *'ndrangheta*, referring specifically to the Calabrian mafia, came into use. In today's mafia league table the *'ndrangheta* is believed to be the wealthiest, most prevalent, most powerful and most ruthless of all. These days its most lucrative criminality is the trade in cocaine, much of which is conducted outside Calabria itself.

As I have already suggested, the extant political runes played a part in whether those who took to the hills in the 19th century were common or garden robbers, felt a degree of political persecution or were political agitators. Establishing whether or not there is a direct link between these political outcasts and the evolvement of the mafia is difficult, if not impossible, to judge though generally it seems unlikely given the provenance of each group.

In his award-winning book, *Cosa Nostra*, recognised authority on the mafia, its origins and its history, John Dickie, links the burgeoning of Sicilian organised crime with the years immediately following the unification of Italy in 1860/61. This was a time of confusion, lawlessness, the ruthless settling of old scores and establishing, protecting and developing power bases. (Naples' *camorra* has a longer history than the Sicilian *cosa nostra* and dates back to a similar time of political and social confusion during and following the ousting of the Bourbons by the French in 1799 and 1806.)

At this time too there were definitely a lot of so-called brigands at large, many of whom were labelled as 'brigands' and hunted down precisely because of their political opposition to the unification of the Italian peninsula. Today unification is a *fait accompli* but at the time the subjugation of The Kingdom of the Two Sicilies was not the obvious way forward for many southerners.

Therefore many such 'brigands' would have argued that they were motivated (initially at least) by perceived injustices rather than criminal intent. For the mafia on the other hand criminal intent, and particularly protection, was their *raison d'être*; they exploited and abused perceived injustices. That said, the mafia has always had a political agenda too—to control and manipulate the political establishment to further its own ends. In this respect, over the years they have been particularly successful though there are signs that this is beginning to change.

That somewhere, sometime, there was an element of crossover between individual brigands and individual 'men of honour' is possible but probably uncommon. For different motives both were taking advantage of the confusion that followed in the wake of unification and in this respect the mafia was the new kid on the block and, unlike brigandage, with an agenda that was timeless.

The only obvious link between the two groups is the church, an organization that, theoretically at least, should have had no links with either, but has had involvement with both at an individual and local level.

Though his excellency Cavaliere di Caria, the royal governor of the province of Cosenza, denied to Craufurd Tait Ramage that he was paying 'protection' to local brigands, such a notion is so familiar that it is almost certainly true. The year was 1828 and his excellency's unknown blackmailers were clearly an organised gang as opposed to opportunists.

Looking back at these times is always complicated by a shifting political, social and cultural scene, particularly in the south of the mainland peninsula—to illustrate this, the short historical synopsis at the conclusion of the chapter 'Itineraries and Context' is worth refining and repeating.

When Swinburne (1777) was in Calabria the Two Sicilies (Naples and Sicily) was ruled by a French Bourbon monarch. From 1759 the same king—eight years old in 1759—ruled both territories and was known both as Ferdinand III of the Kingdom of Sicily and Ferdinand IV of the Kingdom of Naples. As ruler of Naples he was deposed twice: once by the revolutionary Parthenopean Republic for six months in 1799 and again by Napoleon Bonaparte from 1806.

This was the time of the Napoleonic Wars and because Ferdinand allied himself with Austria and Britain, Napoleon deemed that the Bourbon dynasty had effectively forfeited the crown. His brother Joseph Bonaparte was then made King of the Two Sicilies, even though in reality he only reigned in the peninsular half governed from Naples; Ferdinand fled to Sicily where he remained under British protection.

In 1808, Napoleon's brother-in-law, Joachim Murat (of whom more later) succeeded Joseph as King of the Two Sicilies and reigned until 1815 when, following Napoleon's defeat and the end of the Napoleonic Wars, he fled to Corsica.

Ferdinand returned to Naples and, in 1816, he became Ferdinand I of the Kingdom of the Two Sicilies. His descendents continued the Bourbon line in Naples for another forty-four years.

In 1860 Ferdinand I's great-grandson, Francesco II, was deposed and the Kingdom of the Two Sicilies ceased to exist. Its territory was eventually incorporated into what became the Kingdom of Italy. This marked the beginning of a united Italy and end of the Bourbon dynasty.

In 1861, in post-unification Italy, Vittorio Emanuele II (of the House of Savoy-Carignano) became the first King of Italy.

It was when the Bourbons were *not* in power—for six months in 1799, between 1806 and 1815, and after unification in 1860/61—that political brigandage was rife and at its worst. In between, when the Bourbons kings ruled from Naples and when most of the British travellers and diarists were abroad, was when brigandage was generally non-political—sometimes organised, sometimes opportunist.

When, for example, Craufurd Tait Ramage (1828) commented almost daily on his concerns about brigands (until, that is, he decided that he couldn't help feeling 'somewhat callous to the alarming reports with which the inhabitants [were] constantly assailing [him]') he was talking about local highway robbers rather than political brigands.

The worst excesses of political brigandage were almost always pro-Bourbon—even, as we have seen, Bourbon-inspired and funded—and, by the same token, the worst excesses in dealing with these brigands occurred during the Napoleonic era and post-unification. One round of brutal excess often begot another.

Norman Douglas (1911) did not mince his words:
"The men who gave the French so much trouble were political brigands, allies of Bourbonism. They were commanded by creatures like Mammone, an anthropophagous monster whose boast it was that he had personally killed 455 persons with the greatest refinements of cruelty ... This was the man whom King Ferdinand and his spouse [Queen Carolina] loaded with gifts and decorations, and addressed as 'Our good Friend and General – the

Parco Old Calabria today; one of Don Alfonso Barracco's estates in the early 1800s.

faithful Support of the Throne.' The numbers of these savages were increased by shiploads of professional cut-throats sent over from Sicily by the English to help their Bourbon friends."

I wonder were these 'professional cut-throats' the same instigators of the Calabrian revolt which the British apparently came to support just before the Battle of Máida?

Douglas, clearly not a fan of the anti-French brigands, said this of one of the most notorious, Giacomo Pisani, a native of Parenti near Cosenza, the 'perfidious', brigand known as Francatripa:

"... under pretence of hospitality, [Francatripa] enticed a French company into his clutches and murdered its three officers and all the men, save seven."

The political nature of brigandage at the time meant that some brigands were unofficially 'sponsored' by members of the land-owning class who saw it in their interests to do so during the Napoleonic era. The innovations of the new regime included the abolition of feudalism and the division of the common lands.

In 1810 Murat's government had appointed General Manhès to seek out and destroy all vestiges of brigandage, a commission for which he had already demonstrated a penchant elsewhere in the kingdom.

According to John Davis in his *Naples and Napoleon: Southern Italy and the European Revolutions, 1780-1860*, in December 1810 Manhès was hunting the *capo-brigante*, brigand leader, Benincasa, when he left his assistant Colonel Ianelli in charge while he took care of some other, more pressing, business. Manhès felt it incumbent on him to visit Don Alfonso Barracco, a wealthy landowner who had acquired large swathes of land in the Sila mountains during the short-lived revolutionary French occupation in 1799. Barracco's property had been attacked in 1806 but later he was well compensated for supporting the French.

But in 1809 a regional administrator suspected Barracco of double-dealing and passed on to Manhès his suspicions that Barracco was taking the French coin and at the same time was almost certainly the leading protector of the many anti-French brigands operating in the area. In December 1810 therefore Manhès turned up unannounced at the Barracco estate and told him straight that he was suspected of being an enemy of the state and that his previous good services would count for nothing unless he could demonstrate his loyalty.

Coincidentally, within two months all the remaining brigands in the area had been either rounded up or killed. Barracco received safe-conduct and a large sum in compensation and, as a token of his respect he presented

Manhès with two white stallions. Everybody was happy ... except for the brigands, that is.

Barracco clearly got something from supporting his local brigand bands but he got more from knowing what side his bread was buttered on. Manhès was a shrewd judge of character and knew that people like Barracco would fall into line rather than forfeit their land and lifestyle.

As a footnote to this story, in late 2013 I shared a platform in Santa Severina with one Mirella Stampa Barracco and she invited me to visit her at the *Parco Old Calabria* near Camigliatello Silano. *Parco Old Calabria* is a park inspired by Norman Douglas's *Old Calabria*, with exhibits inspired by and dedicated to those, like Douglas, who extended the accepted boundaries of the Grand Tour and came to Calabria.

As I was shown round what had once been a grand stately home (and was again, thanks to its recent and elegant restoration) and paused to look at the many family portraits, I realised I was traversing the same ground as General Manhès had done over two hundred years earlier. I was in Don Alfonso Barracco's erstwhile home where my welcome was, I feel sure, more generous than the one Manhès probably received when he too dropped by unexpectedly

---

Brigandage, as opposed to banditry, went on the back burner following the re-establishment of the Bourbon monarchy until after unification in 1860. Garibaldi's friend Elpis Malena was actually travelling in Calabria که October while her friend and would-be suitor, Garibaldi himself, was still embroiled in the cause of unification around Naples.

Heading south—and out of harm's way—alongside the Calabria coast by steamer, Malena made the following observation about banditry in Calabria:

"The graceful form of the hills, the fresh green of the plains, the balmy warmth of the air, all combined to furnish a classic banquet to the eye: and yet this was the robber's nest, the widely abused Calabria, which lay before me, whose very mention conjures up the well-known bandit, the cone-shaped hat, the embroidered jacket, the pistols, the dagger, and the long flint-lock, with which he plays his half-knightly, half rascally part in opera and ballet."

Little did she know at the time that, in the wake of Garibaldi's military and political successes, banditry would once again morph into politically-inspired brigandage.

In 1865, two Englishmen, W.J.C. Moens and Rev. J.C. Murray Aynsley, were captured by brigands Pepino Cerino and Gaetano Manzi, near Battipaglia in Campania. Moens subsequently published a diary (based on letters to his wife and hers contemporaneously to him) in which he gave a unique, contemporary, eye-witness account of brigand-life on the run.

These events took place five years after unification and, though Cerino and Manzi may well have embarked upon their brigand careers as a protest against the new regime and in support of the Bourbon *status quo*, they had now outlived such political considerations and moved instead into the kidnapping-for-ransom business. Both were clearly in it for the money. Seemingly too, their on-the-run lifestyle, though basic, did not stop either from acquiring and displaying some ostentatious mementoes of their misdemeanours. Moens described it thus:

"The smaller band had four women with them, attired like the men and all these displayed a greater love of jewellery than the members of Manzi's band. They were decked out to do me honor, and one of them wore no less than twenty-four gold rings, of various sizes and stones, on her hands at the same moment; others twenty, sixteen, ten, according to their wealth. To have but one gold chain attached to a watch was considered paltry and mean. Cerino and Manzi had bunches as thick as an arm suspended across the breasts of their waistcoats, with gorgeous brooches at each fastening. These were sewed on for security; little bunches of charms were also attached in conspicuous positions."

An Australian newspaper article from January 1866 details the later trial of some of Manzi's men, all of whom received long jail sentences. Another victim of their kidnapping tactics wrote:

"I have little hope of seeing this state of things cease, even if Cicillo [deposed King Francesco II] quits Rome. Manzi is by no means a politician, but a pure brigand."

Other kidnapped victims of the same band lost ears as a way of ensuring that a ransom was paid. Sound familiar? Manzi was subsequently caught, tried and executed in 1868.

Clearly these were not your average rob-the-rich-and-give-to-the-poor brigands. Is it little wonder that, when brigand leaders were caught or killed, the first thing the soldiers did was to strip them to see what riches lay hidden beneath?

That said, for many of those who stood against the overthrow and subjugation of the Kingdom of the Two Sicilies, political protest and even guerrilla tactics were all they had left. Whether they liked it or not, they were seen by the new regime as troublemakers and in many cases brutally dealt with. Some had no option but to head for the hills and survive as best they could; for opposing the new order they were cast aside, brutalised, labelled brigands and hunted down.

In recent years historians and writers have given this aspect of Italy's unification greater prominence as the scale of the persecution and retribution meted out has become better documented. Pino Aprile's *Terroni* paints a harrowing picture of the atrocities perpetrated in those early years and, as more evidence comes to light, it seems the full story has yet to be told and acknowledged. John A. Davis's *Naples and Napoleon: Southern Italy and the European Revolutions, 1780-1860* is a less emotional, but nonetheless authoritative, reassessment of the same period.

Both point out that the soldiers who wreaked most havoc in the south and represented the new order, the new Italian state, were mostly from Piedmont. Further proof, if proof were needed, that unification was as much about the north annexing and subjugating the south and less about the ideology of unification.

In post-unification Italy there were brigands ... and there were brigands. And it was in such turbulent times that the mafia blossomed and flourished, ready and able to take full advantage of the endemic chaos of the time—and

Four of Giacomo Ciccone's band of brigands from Benevento in Campania surrounded by some of the soldiers who captured them in the late 1860s. As was the custom, they photographed themselves with them, executed them ... and then photographed them again.

the preoccupation of those whose job it was to protect lives and property and maintain order.

In the forty-plus years between the two eras that spawned the political brigand there were brigands of a different complexion, those who robbed and ransomed for financial gain. These were the brigands—probably bandits is a better word—that preoccupied the minds of travellers, the bandits they constantly imagined (because they were told it was so) were lurking in every dark corner of Calabria.

Richard Keppel-Craven (1818) was told this story in Cutro about a gang of *banditti* under the leadership of Vito Caligiuri:

"The richest inhabitant of Cotrone and his eldest son had been carried off by them the preceding year: they had allowed the former to go home, securely relying on the workings of paternal affection for the payment of his son's ransom, which was bargained for at 17,000 ducats [nearly 3000 British sovereigns at the time], and punctually discharged. This young man accompanied me on this day's journey, but he seemed unwilling to enter into any details respecting an event which, however interesting to the curiosity of a stranger, could only bring painful recollections to himself. At present the band was dispersed, and its leader wandering in the Sila; but his mistress, *la sua donna*, a very pretty girl, had been taken and confined in the citadel of Cotrone, where I had the curiosity to visit her. A few days after my passage, Vito, with only three companions, contrived to seize an agent of government employed in superintending the felling of timber in the mountains, and demanded as the price of his release the sum of 1200 ducats, and the liberty of his beloved; but my departure from the province prevented my learning the final result of the negotiation."

Douglas (1911) reflected on the bandit Gaetano Ricca, whom he called the 'last genuine bandit of the Sila':

"On account of some trivial misunderstanding with the authorities, this man was compelled in the early eighties to take to the woods, where he lived a wild life (*alla campagna; alla macchia*) [in the country side in hiding] for some three years. A price was set on his head, but his daring and knowledge of the country intimidated every one. I should be sorry to believe in the number of *carbineers* [police] he is supposed to have killed during that period; no doubt the truth came out during his subsequent trial. On one occasion he was surrounded, and while the officer in command of his pursuers, who had taken refuge behind a tree, ordered him to yield, Ricca waited patiently till the point of his enemy's foot became visible, when he pierced his ankle-bone with his last bullet and escaped. He afterwards surrendered and was imprisoned for twenty years or so; then returned to the Sila, where up to a short time ago he was enjoying a green old age in his home at Parenti."

Douglas wrote about the Ricca style of banditry with a greater degree of sympathy. Ricca was not a political brigand but rather a local bandit who apparently took to the hills 'on account of a trivial misunderstanding'. Douglas even went on to reflect on how he wished he'd known about the activities of the retired, Sila-based ex-bandit during an earlier visit to Calabria:

"I would certainly have paid my respects to Ricca had I been aware of his existence when, some years back, I passed through Parenti on my way—a long day's march!—from Rogliano to San Giovanni. He has died in the interval."

For Douglas brigands such as Manzi and Ricca were an anachronism; time had moved on and the Calabrian brigand and bandit phenomenon had passed into local folklore.

Likewise Gissing (1897/98) had this to say about travelling in the Sila:

"Sila—locally the Black Mountain, because dark with climbing forests—held my gaze through a long afternoon. Not so long ago it was a haunt of brigands; now there is no risk for the rare traveller who penetrates that wilderness; but he must needs depend upon the hospitality of labourers and shepherds."

But it was, according to Leslie Gardiner (1966), in the Pollino mountains in 1928 that Calabria's last (unnamed) brigand, 'the last deterrent to the solitary traveller' gave himself up and, like the wolf, stepped into the 'extinct' section of the Calabria history books. The wife of a local farmer told him the story:

"My mother often spoke of him ... He came to her vegetable-patch one day and requisitioned all the green stuff. While his men filled the sacks and took them away, he came and thanked her and handed back one cauliflower. When she cut it up that night she found a piece of gold in the stalk, payment for all the brigands had helped themselves to."

Even in 1967, the notion of the romantic, essentially heroic and misjudged, brigand persisted.

For hundreds of years, Calabria's remote forests and mountains have provided the perfect environment for living outside the law, whether as a brigand or as a *mafioso*. But when the press made this same connection in the aftermath of the John Paul Getty kidnapping, they inadvertently—or carelessly—linked the two as if one was the natural precursor of the other, as if brigandage begot the mafia.

Puglia too has a history of brigandage, indeed some of the south's most notorious nineteenth-century political brigands operated in that region; some of the worst excesses of the embryonic Italy were perpetrated in Puglia too.

On the other hand, Puglia's mafia, *sacra corona unita*, only dates from the late 1970s—perhaps its inception was a considered response to the publicity given to the *'ndrangheta* in wake of the Getty kidnapping.

Nor does it help clarify the situation when the 'official word' from within the Italian school history syllabus is that brigandage was the natural precursor of the mafia, as if they were one and the same group of people.

For the record, John Paul Getty returned seamlessly into the high life; he married the year after his release and had a son, the actor Balthazar Getty. In 1977 he had his ear rebuilt. By 1981 a drug and alcohol cocktail caused liver failure and a stroke which left him a quadriplegic and almost blind. He was cared for by his mother until he died in 2011, aged fifty-four

---

There are towns in Calabria where stories of brigands and their exploits do get told in a way that does not highlight the excesses on both sides. This view of brigandage can be somewhat selective in how it plays down the violence of the brigands themselves and focuses on that of their pursuers.

For those who take pride in their brigands, they have become folk-heroes; these are generally those who became notorious for their exploits and defiance post-unification, their place in local folklore embroidered by the injustice they endured and the manner of their capture and/or their death

There are restaurants and hotels called *I Briganti* or a variation; there are dishes with names like *pasta dei briganti*, there are even wines called *Briganti*. And although towns and villages that were the birthplaces and/or the strongholds of brigands don't usually advertise the fact officially, there are a few that do. This from the official website of Scigliano in the province of Cosenza in its list of famous sons ... sandwiched between a literary linguist and a professor of law:

"The famous 'brigand Parafante' who managed to pass himself off as dead by lying still even though he had burning embers on his naked chest."

At the time of writing, and unlike most official town websites, the website for the small town of Santo Stefano in Aspromonte does not contain any historical information at all and therefore there is no mention of perhaps its most famous—or infamous—son, the legendary Calabrian brigand Giuseppe Musolino. Within Calabria—even Italy itself—Musolino, the 'King of the Aspromonte' is the region's most well-known brigand, not least because in the fifties a film, *Il Brigante Musolino*, was made that romanticised his apparent exploits.

Norman Douglas (1911) devotes a whole chapter to Musolino whom he described as a man who:

"... infested the country up to a few years ago, defying the soldiery and police of all Italy. He would still be safe and unharmed had he remained in these fastnesses [strongholds]. But he wandered away, wishful to leave Italy for good and all, and was captured far from his home by some policemen who were looking for another man, and who nearly fainted when he pronounced his name."

His reign as a brigand was short-lived; it began in 1898 and ended three years later when he was tried and convicted. According to the December 1901 edition of Australia's *West Gippsland Gazette*, it all started following a minor quarrel with one Vincenzo Zoccali, the aftermath of which was:

"... Musolino was repeatedly stabbed by Zoccolli [sic] in the arms and hands, and carried home. Two days later Zoccolli was shot from an ambush, and Musolino was arrested, and charged with the murder. He declared that he never left his bed, and that he was the victim of an infamous plot, while his sympathisers continue to assert that he was not given fair play at his trial. Witnesses came forward who swore that they had seen him commit the murder, and he was convicted, and sentenced to twenty-two years' hard labour ..."

And so the account goes on in like vein as the story of Musolino is embellished, embroidered and romanticised with the notion of an innocent man, wrongly accused and convicted.

As far as is possible to get to the truth from the multitude of conflicting accounts, these seem to be sober facts that precipitated Musolino on his road to brigandage notoriety.

It all started with an argument and fight in a local bar. The following day someone attempted to shoot Vincenzo Zoccali and Musolino's cap was apparently found at the scene. Musolino then fled Santo Stefano but was picked up several months later and taken to Reggio Calabria to stand trial for *attempted* murder. Throughout the trial he protested his innocence and vowed to seek out and take revenge on all those who had spoken against him; he was sentenced to twenty-two years and sent to prison in Locri. Two years later, in a dream, St. John apparently showed him where exactly to dig to expedite his escape. Musolino was once again a fugitive.

On the surface, Musolino was not a political brigand, he had no obvious political axe to grind, though that did not stop him adjoining pseudo-political reasoning to the pursuance of his case. Thus in the popular idiom he became more akin to a folk-hero, a Robin Hood of sorts, an innocent, misunderstood fugitive from blind justice who only wanted to do good by his fellow citizens.

But this story had always puzzled me ... little of it rang true, or those parts that did, seemed to be contradicted by other events. Take the story of Musolino's supposed prison dream ... apart from the fact that it's clearly unadulterated rubbish, why did he need to invent such far-fetched nonsense in the first place? He would have known that a good religion-based yarn would be the perfect diversion tactic in a region where many set store by such tales. Few would have questioned how he came to escape so easily in the first place as soon as they heard that the hand of St. John was behind it ... and, by implication, said St. John was clearly on Musolino's side.

The end of the Musolino fable is no less bizarre.

Having escaped, Musolino set about try to eliminate all those who had apparently wronged him ... and managed to see off seven of those on his hit list and injured others. Apparently, while he was embroiled in murderous mayhem on the one hand, his other persona was cementing his name in brigandage mythology by helping the needy with his generosity. One part of the Musolino story was contradicted by another and little could be authenticated; the fusion of myth and reality seemed difficult to disentangle.

In October 1901 Musolino was eventually captured near Urbino, in today's Marche region, while seemingly on his way to seek pardon from Rome-based monarch, King Victor Emmanuel III. If this was indeed his intent, his sense of Italian geography seems to have been a little awry.

This time he was imprisoned for life, initially in the north, and a dozen years later declared insane. He died in a mental home in Reggio Calabria in 1956 at the age of 79.

It was not until I read another book by John Dickie, *Mafia Republic*, that all became clearer and my niggling reservations around the Musolino myth were finally laid to rest. Dickie has the knack of separating fact from fiction.

It seems that, in 1933—a decade before Musolino was moved back south to take up permanent residence in a Reggio mental institution—Giuseppe

Travia, a Calabrian-born Italian-American, confessed on his death-bed that it was he and not Musolino who had tried to kill Vincenzo Zoccali back in 1898. In so doing he inadvertently gave further credence to the 'wronged man' myth that Musolino liked to perpetuate ... though this failed to explain how being wronged gave Musolino a licence to kill seven people.

Back in Reggio, and now seemingly a misunderstood man, the ageing, demented Musolino found himself the centre of attraction for a few visiting Calabro-Americans. One in particular visited frequently and even took him out on day-release for a jaunt around old haunts.

Dickie gets to the crux of the matter and explains just who the 'King of the Aspromonte' really was; the clue is in his other nickname, 'Don Peppino' and the fact that certain Calabro-Americans deemed him worthy of the odd visit.

Musolino was not the 'wronged' bandit that he liked to portray but nothing more than a member of the Calabrian mafia. Dickie's research has shown that the local Santo Stefano branch of the mafia was founded by Musolino's father and uncle in the 1890. Musolino was no more and no less than a thug going about mafia business, a mafia killer answering to the collective will of his mafia bosses,

Dickie backs up his assertion with a tranche of corroborating evidence much of which was available at the time these events took place but which was either inadvertently overlooked or deliberately ignored. At a time when

The cinema poster speaks for itself. An image of the young 'King of the Aspromonte', Guiseppe Musolino, embellished many Italian postcards; this one, onto which his image seems to have been glued, was sent from Naples to Mézières in northern France in November 1901. Written in French, and pleasantries aside, it reads as follows:
"'This is not to pay homage to brigands but nevertheless I know that there is always a certain curiosity to know about these good fellows. In this case I want to pass on to you this photo of the celebrated brigand Musolino who has fallen into the hands of the police."

many denied the existence of the mafia, the notion and image of the romantic bandit made better press. It was an image that Musolino revelled in till his dying day, an image that, despite evidence to the contrary, still persists.

Musolino was not a bandit who became a *mafioso*, he was a *mafioso* who took on the persona of a bandit.

What's more, within his lifetime, he got away with it ... as testified by the poster for the 1950 film.

Recently I was passing through Santo Stefano in Aspromonte and stopped off to have a snack at a local bar. I was half expecting to see the occasional reference to the town's most famous son and was quite surprised when I could find none. I dared to wonder if perhaps the Musolino image had at long last lost it's tarnish? I mean, if he were indeed such a 'Robin Hood' character wouldn't there at least be a bar or a hotel, maybe even an airport, bearing his name?

I was genuinely—and pleasantly—surprised but then, on the way up the hill to Gambarie, I passed a road-side sign indicating the turning up to the B&B Musolino. Naturally I metaphorically patted myself on the back for having been right all along, I knew that somebody would have to use the infamy of the Musolino name to attract clients. My curiosity got the better of me and, there and then, I decided to stay another night in the area and discovered the B&B Musolino was so-called (it has since changed its name) because the proprietor, Franco Musolino, was a descendent of *the* Musolino. Franco's grandfather and Musolino were cousins and, though there are family photos on the wall (including a 'Wanted' poster), there was no sense that Musolino was being glorified; quite the opposite in fact.

Despite mounting evidence to the contrary, there are many who still view Guiseppe Musolino as a some sort of folk-hero. On a second visit to see the Riace Bronzes on their new, permanent, earthquake-resistant plinths of residence at the *Museo Nationale Archeologio* at Reggio Calabria, I noticed that the museum's bookshop carried an extensive range of titles on Musolino's exploits, nearly all of which basically made him out to be a victim of circumstances or a variation of the 'wronged man' syndrome he so carefully cultivated.

What hope is there for some sort of re-interpretation of his story when such a prestigious museum flaunts what is little more than absurd popular fiction alongside more thoughtful works on, for example, Magna Græcia and the Bronzes themselves?

On that same journey south, I was staying in Scilla-by-the-sea when my Bed & Breakfast host, Francesco Praticò—who also runs a wine bar in the Chianalea, the old fishing quarter of Scilla—introduced me to one of his father's books *Malandrini,* tucked away in the bar's small library of titles with Calabrian themes.

Paolo Praticò writes novels but has also written a book of short stories about *malandrini*, people who were, to all intents and purposes, Calabria's embryonic mafia, *picciotti*, *malandrini*, members of the *'ndrangheta* before it had the name.

That evening my electronic Italian dictionary and I worked overtime as I launched into Paolo's book … I was enjoying myself but had so many questions for him. Next morning when I went down to the wine bar for breakfast I found the man himself there chatting to his son. An hour and a half later two oldies were still talking and drinking coffee, still exploring the world of the embryonic *'ndrangheta*.

A physicist and lecturer at the Univerity of Reggio Calabria, Paolo was fascinated by the stories of these *malandrini* that never made it into the history books, the stories of how ordinary people fell foul of their thuggery, how they themselves had little respect or consideration for their local community, of how they became involved in such things in the first place. Some of his stories did not have an exact location in time or place and it was these that interested me; I wanted to know where and when but I could see that Paolo wanted to remain imprecise. These were stories for which he had sound provenance but for which he felt naming names and places was not always appropriate … his aim was to focus on the Calabrian mentality at work that allowed such things to happen.

But one story did have a date … it was right at the end, it was 9 January, 1899, the day that Guiseppe Musolino escaped from the prison in Locri, with Musolino's version of events citing St John as his helpful accomplice.

Paulo's story is about two young friends, 'Ntoni and Melo, and how it was they who became two of the earliest *malandrini* foot soldiers, young men at the beck and call of those higher up the mafia food chain. The story ends with how 'Ntoni and another friend assisted in the escape of one Peppe Musolino from his incarceration at Locri. Before the grateful Musolino finally made off to become 'a wolf in the woods ready to take his revenge', he apparently found time to thank 'Ntoni for arranging everything.

All of which points to two things: the St John story was—as was already obvious—a total fabrication and Musolino's real 'saviour' in this regard was in fact 'Ntoni the Fixer; secondly, and more importantly, the story establishes yet another link between the mafia and Musolino and ought to be yet another reason for clearing the shelves of all those 'Musolino the folk-hero' books and exposing him for what he really was, a *'ndrangheta* thug, a *'ndrangheta* assassin.

Paolo and I went on to talk about non-Calabrians, like myself and John Dickie, who have chosen to write about such things and agreed how impossible it was for us to appreciate the nuances of such stories that only the Calabrian psyche can truly understand. *Malandrini* has an extensive glossary at the back to help other Italians with some of the dialect as well as language and words used here in a different context. A few simple examples: *vuoto* normally means empty but in *malandrini* terms it means 'unarmed'; *pungere* means to sting or wound but here it means 'injured by a bullet'; *la maschera* means a mask or a façade but here it refers to an identity card.

But, I ventured to suggest, there is also the other side of the same coin … we *stranieri* are not clouded by the intrinsic Calabrian element, we have the ability to stand back, to view things unburdened by centuries of history, of social and political manipulation. Both are valid positions, perhaps both together get closer to a true understanding of what was and is actually happening.

When it comes to towns with mafia connections, the story is somewhat different to those with connections to brigands. Mention the names of particular Calabrian towns and Calabrians will often run the back of their right thumb down their left cheek … the Italian hand-gesture for 'mafia'. How they know the town is a mafia stronghold used to be a mystery to me and I would just accept it as such. Now I know most of them too.

In the area where we live, the two towns that, rightly or wrongly, instantly solicit that hand-gesture response are Cutro (which we can see from our balcony) and Isola di Capo Rizzuto where we sometimes shop. Apart from the fact that both towns have a run-down, unkempt ambience, the only other obvious similarities I have observed are that both are surrounded by wind farms (that at Isola di Capo Rizzuto being the one I mentioned in an earlier chapter as a mafia scam); coincidentally, they both have railway stations some distance away from the town itself.

Like me, Richard Keppel-Craven (1818) was not overly impressed with Cutro:

"This town … contains 2000 inhabitants; its streets are tolerably wide, but present no good houses, and the principal church is mean: the whole conveys an incorrect impression of depopulation and poverty, as it has a good market for cattle, grain, and pulse of all kinds, but little wine."

Though he did go on to concede that his bed at Cutro was one of the cleanest he'd slept in since leaving Naples.

Likewise Craufurd Tait Ramage (1828) was not over enthusiastic about the ambience but his experience of the local wine was more favourable:

"I was obliged to take refuge in the miserable *locanda*, and felt so thoroughly knocked up that I resolved to give up my intention of proceeding forward to Cotrone [sic]. A pretty fair modicum of wine, however, revived my spirits, and, after resting a couple of hours, I again proceeded on my journey."

There are other towns in the area that also have a mafia presence, notably Petilia Policastro and even the provincial capital, Crotone, though neither seems to consistently warrant the same hand gesture as the other two ... it's like some local unspoken mafia rating system.

That said, on an evening when we had arranged to meet some friends at a restaurant in Petilia Policastro, we found our way blocked by a flurry of police vehicles responding to a killing in the town which we naturally assumed was mafia-related. It was, and it turned out to be a revenge killing involving two local 'ndrangheta clans. Later we discovered that in this particular town it is not the control of drugs that is the big issue between rival gangs but rather the control of the market in grapes and chestnuts.

Such incidents, though disturbing at the time, are not common but they do have an effect on local people. I recall when, a week or so later, we did finally get to eat at that restaurant, the streets of Petilia Policastro were deserted, it was like driving through a ghost town.

The further south you go in Calabria, the more such 'mafia' towns seem to exist: Rosarno, Oppido Mamertina, Monasterace, Locri, Africo, San Luca, Platì and of course, the apparent hub of it all, in and around Reggio Calabria itself.

In late 2013 one of these towns even made it on to the international stage when British celebrity chef Nigella Lawson took two Italian-born employees, sisters, Elisabetta and Francesca Grillo, to court for fraudulent use of credit cards. In reporting the case the press generally referred to the sisters as 'Italians' or 'Italian-born'; a few dug a little deeper and came up with 'Calabria'.

When the dust had settled, and with the sisters acquitted, their lives came under closer scrutiny. It turned out that they came from Platì, a town in the eastern foothills of the Aspromonte, and that their father, Michele Grillo, had once been a well-known member of the local *'ndrangheta*. Indeed he had spent much of his daughters' youth locked up ... convicted, among other things, for kidnapping Tulia Kauten, the sister of an Italian fashion designer.

With characteristic and unstinting thoroughness, the British tabloid press located and interviewed Michele Grillo. They wrote about a man running a respectable haulage business near Milan, a man who had put behind him the sins of his past and was now leading a respectable and honest life away from his native Calabria. A veritable saint, no less.

That was December 2013. Three weeks later, in January 2014, truck driver Michele Grillo was arrested and accused of conspiracy to sell cocaine and hash and using threats of violence to extort €85,000 from the owner of a gas station. It is also claimed that he helped suppress evidence needed in criminal trials involving men allegedly tied to the mafia. The police also believe Grillo to be the right-hand man of Agostino Catanzariti, who was also arrested, reckoned to be a high-ranking mafia commander. Both men had been under police surveillance since 2011.

Of course he may be completely innocent of all charges ... time will tell.

In recent years John Dickie, the author of *Cosa Nostra* and *Mafia Republic*, has turned his attention to the Calabrian 'ndrangheta and in 2013 he visited Platì and reported on his findings. This was more than six months *before* the trial of the Grillo sisters so it is more than a little ironic that the same tabloid press, who also reported on Dickie's Platì visit, never seemed to have made the connection. Then again, making meaningful and relevant connections is not what the tabloid press is good at.

What John Dickie was looking at was the 'ndrangheta's astonishing network of tunnels underneath the town that had been their secret means of escape when the police came a-knocking. In recent years the 'ndrangheta has had to get used to the reality that they are being hunted with renewed efficiency and resolve.

Since the setting up of an elite arm of the Police (the *Servizio Centrale Operativo*) in 2005, and particularly since this was under the leadership of Renato Cortese based in Reggio Calabria, much progress has been made in arresting 'ndrangheta criminals. More importantly these arrests have resulted in successful prosecutions. Since his successes in Reggio, Renato Cortese—a native of Santa Severina—has moved on to head the *Squadra Mobile* (the Flying Squad) in Rome where one journal gave him the nickname of 'the fugitive catcher'.

The network of tunnels in Prati that John Dickie spent several hours exploring was discovered by the police following the arrest of prominent members of the local 'ndrangheta clan. The tunnels run under the town and have several elaborate 'hidden' access points in different parts of the town—

through concealed trapdoors, sliding staircases, even a pizza oven—all of which eventually link together before finally emerging in the bushes by a dry river bed outside the town.

At Rosarno, on the other side of the Aspromonte, the police also found a network of underground bunkers but these were altogether a more sophisticated affair: they were constructed by welding together empty shipping containers furnishing the inside and then burying them. These were 'acquired' from nearby gargantuan container port and mafia stronghold Gioia Tauro; indeed the entrance to the port is actually much closer to Rosarno than its name-giver, Gioia Tauro.

To dig a hole big enough to inter such a structure can scarcely have gone unnoticed and to get something like that out of the Gioia Tauro port complex would undoubtedly involve the connivance of those who job it was to keep the site secure. On the surface, security is tight and documentation examined thoroughly ... which I discovered at first hand when I tried to get in to take a few pictures. But then, perhaps my timing was bad, it *was* the week after the chemical weapons from Syria passed through the port. I was told in no

Even before its opening in the early 1990s, the gargantuan port of Gioia Tauro was regarded as being under *'ndrangheta* control.
This photo was taken from the northern, Rosarno, end of the port, near its entrance; the outskirts of Gioia Tauro itself are just visible at the top left.

uncertain terms that it wasn't going to happen and was allowed to go through the barrier only on condition that I exited immediately on the other side.

It is said that the money from the Getty kidnapping was used to buy the trucks needed to establish a transport monopoly for the construction of the port in which the two main suspects, Girolamo Piromalli and Saverio Mammoliti, were involved. Neither was convicted but Mammoliti subsequently (2003) decided to cooperate with the justice system by becoming a *pentito*, a penitent—one who 'repents' and spills the beans on past misdemeanours, usually to ensure a more lenient sentence and to incriminate others; a grass.

I heard a slightly different story from a teacher in Bovalino on the opposite coast, the Ionian. On the outskirts of Bovalino there is a small row of roadside apartments, known locally as the Paul Getty apartments. The nickname dates back to when they were built in the seventies, apparently with money 'earned' from the Getty kidnapping. It is likely the Getty money funded both the trucks at Gioia Tauro *and* the apartments at Bovalino for in the heart of the Aspromonte between the two lies the *'ndrangheta* stronghold of Platì.

These days the sense is that the Gioia Tauro port is one huge, complex hotch-potch of political and criminal activity that is almost beyond dismembering into what could and should be a massive asset to the nation and the region rather than lining the pockets of the *'ndrangheta*.

In 2008 the Antimafia Commission concluded that the mafia controlled or influenced 'a large part of the economic activity around the port and uses the facility as a base for illegal trafficking' and that 'the entire gamma of internal or sub-contracted activities is mafia-influenced, from the management of distribution and forwarding to customs control and container storage.'

The Commission also acknowledged that there was extortion in the form of a kickback scheme that guaranteed the security of each container and that those behind this 'security tax', which grew with the port, also control 'activities tied to the port, the hiring of workers, and relations with port unions and local institutions'.

Their report went on:

"It effectively eliminated legitimate competition from companies not influenced or controlled by the mafia in providing goods and services, performing construction work and hiring personnel. And it threw a shadow over the behaviour of local government and other public bodies."

Clearly Calabria's mafia are inventive but at the same time they are not having it all their own way. Ordinary people are beginning to stand up to them and in some essentially mafia towns the locals have elected mayors on an anti-mafia ticket. This is what happened in Monasterace, a small town close to the Ionian coast.

Pharmacist Maria Carmela Lanzetta was elected mayor of the town and made no bones about her anti-mafia stance—her objective was straightforward, to endow Monasterace with the sense of normality.

Her efforts were continually thwarted by the local mafia and in 2012, after months of intimidation, they fire-bombed her pharmacy and then took shots at her car. Despite local support, including that of other local mayors, Maria decided to resign and in doing so made her stand a national talking point.

She agreed to withdraw her resignation on condition that the then government made the necessary changes for her to govern normally within three months.

Finally, in 2013, Maria Carmela Lanzetta had had her fill of ineffectual leadership and commitment from the state and countless broken promises. She told a BBC correspondent:

"I'm tired and I've had enough. I want my life back.

"I had no political experience. The only thing I knew was that I wanted to bring legality to Monasterace – I did not want any connections with the mob, and I have managed to keep all our contracts clean, but I don't have the resources to continue.

"Mayors get a small salary but I don't draw mine, I do this as voluntary work. I'm paying others to do my job while I'm working for free."

(From February 2014 to Fanuary 2015, Maria Carmela Lanzetta was the Minister for Regional Affair and Autonomy in the cabinet of Prime Minister, Matteo Renzi.)

Around the same time, Elisabetta Tripodi was the Mayor of Rosarno and, like Maria Carmela Lanzetta, she took on the *'ndrangheta*. She too lived

Standing up to the *'ndrangheta* on a national stage: Elisabetta Tripodi, Maria Carmela Lanzetta and Renato Cortese. Standing up to the *'ndrangheta* at a local level: the plaque outside Santa Severina's town hall asserting that the town is a *'ndrangheta*-free zone. The plaque was unveiled by Renato Cortese in 2012.

under 24-hour police protection because she dared to stand up to the local *'ndrangheta* Pesce clan boss. Her administration sued the clan and won a settlement of €50 million for Rosarno ... money which had to be paid out of confiscated mafia funds.

On the other hand, in 2015 the small Calabrian town of Nardodipace and its *sindaco* have found themselves the centre of attention for all the wrong reasons.

Nardodispace is situated between the Serra mountains and the Aspromonte and is officially Italy's poorest community; the town's 1200 residents have the country's lowest per capita income. You would think the *sindaco* of such a place would be striving to make the town a better place to live for his constituents? After all, that is presumably why they elected him ... assuming, of course, they did so without any form of intimidation.

Apparently not so (and I stress that the *sindaco*'s side of the following story is yet to be heard in court) for in February 2015 he and his wife were placed under house arrest, along with others with known *'ndrangheta* connections, and charged with the alleged misappropriation of €100,000 of European Union, State and Regional funds intended for training courses in the community.

At the time of writing this case still has to go through the legal process, but the point I am making in mentioning it at all is that this sort of activity is known to be commonplace and has resulted in several communities, with known mafia connections, having their local councils suspended and to be administered instead under so-called 'Extraordinary Measures'. In Nardodispace this had already happened once in 2010.

Nevertheless, in Calabria some things seem to be changing and it is women who seem to be on the front line. Many mothers are beginning to take a stand against their sons becoming drawn into the *'ndrangheta's* sphere of influence. They know from personal experience that this can lead to no more than a life on the run ... or worse.

Unfortunately some of these women have paid with their lives for taking such a stand. All Maria Concetta Cacciola from Rosarno and Lea Garofalo from Petilia Policastro and Tita Buccafusca from Polistena wanted to do was lead a normal existence but the *'ndrangheta* men in their lives had other ideas. Their attempts to defy the inflexible claustrophobia of living the *'ndrangheta* way, ultimately led to their deaths at the hands of their respective 'families'.

Such practices are more what we have come to expect from certain parts of the Indian sub-continent.

I mentioned earlier that the only common factor between brigandage and the mafia was the Church ... at different times and for different reasons it and its servants often turned a blind eye to both, much as they did during the fascist era, a period and a role it still has to come to terms with.

It has to be remembered that one of the other losers in the unification process was the Catholic Church when, in 1870, Rome and the Papal States were forced to join the burgeoning Italian nation. It is not surprising therefore that, moral and ethical considerations notwithstanding, at a local level it sometimes found itself allied with both brigands and *mafiosi*. Increasingly, the mafia exploited the church to pursue their own ends, and particularly so when they used—and continue to use—saints' days as a show of strength.

In July 2014 I happened to be in Oppido Mamertina at the western edge of the Aspromonte mountains and a town I was curious to visit because it was the epicentre of the first of the 1783 series of devastating earthquakes which killed many and did extensive damage to the town and the surrounding area.

Also, I knew I could kill two birds with one stone for it was in this area that the unnamed village which was the focus of Annie Hawes' *Journey to the South* was located and I was curious to get a sense of the locality.

I stopped off to have a cooling drink outside a local bar and, as is my way, started to eavesdrop on a group of senior citizens, all male as is normal, who were vociferously discussing the ways of the world, their conversation as ever punctuated with an abundance of hand gestures. Briefly they acknowledged my presence before continuing with their discussion which seemed to focus on something that had happened in the recent past.

They assumed—up to a point, rightly so—that, as they were talking fast and partly in the local dialect, I would understand little or nothing. But I did pick up on some keys words, the most frequent of which were 'procession' and 'bishop' though some of the hand gestures and voice-lowering indicated that there was another unspoken word lurking in the background ... 'mafia'.

Occasionally someone would throw me a glance as if to make sure I was disinterested in their business. I feigned indifference as I made a mental note to check Oppido on the internet as soon as possible. Then I had a better idea.

Having paid and before leaving, I called my friend Denise in Crotone and, though we normally speak in English, this time I spoke to her in Italian about nothing in particular, except that I did mention where I was. I just wanted to see the heads turn as my 'companions' realised I understood more Italian than it took to order and pay for a cold drink. I was not disappointed; their voices came down an octave or two as their conspiratorial heads moved closer.

But Denise had already given me the bare bones of the Oppido 'story' and later I was able to fill in the blanks.

I had known that Oppido was a town with *'ndrangheta* connections but, on my radar at the time, it was not in the same league as places like, say, Rosarno, San Luca or Platì.

On 22 June 2014 Pope Francis was in northern Calabria where he denounced the *'ndrangheta*, saying they had an 'adoration of evil and contempt for the common good' and that those who had chosen 'this path of evil' were 'excommunicated'.

Unfortunately his words of wisdom did not seem to have filtered through to some of those involved in a religious procession which carried a statue of the Madonna through the town of Oppido just ten days later.

My experience of such processions here in Santa Severina, apart from finding the concept of adults revering a man-made effigy slightly questionable, is that they follow a proscribed route that never changes.

That was almost certainly the case in Oppido until that Tuesday when the rules were blatantly broken and those carrying the effigy stopped momentarily and caused the statue to 'bow' by bending down. The problem was that this just happened to be outside the home of a convicted and ageing *mafioso*, Giuseppe Mazzagatti, who was serving the remainder of his life sentence under house arrest for reasons of ill health.

In other words the Church, and the Madonna in particular, was openly seen to pay its respects to one of the most notorious *'ndrangheta* bosses. Was it possible, I wondered, that this was a deliberate act of defiance against the Pope's speech just a few days earlier?

The hierarchy of the local Church was, of course, duly outraged by the incident and the Bishop of Oppido-Palmi immediately banned all such religious processions indefinitely ... the Church's equivalent of closing the stable door just after the horse has bolted.

Hasn't the same Church had a repeated history of paedophilia among its clergy which it has frequently acknowledged as unacceptable but, until very recently and under the tutelage of Pope Francis, has never been seen to be pro-active in putting a stop to it and naming names?

I mean, how difficult would it have been to look at video footage of the procession and name every single person who was responsible for ingratiating themselves, and the procession, outside the home of Giuseppe Mazzagatti? It's not exactly rocket science, is it?

If there had truly really been a will, excommunications could have started the next day.

Instead, in less than a fortnight, the pope's 'excommunication' speech, however well-intentioned, had withered on the vine; I'm afraid Pope Francis may as well have tried to climb Mount Everest backwards. In 1993 John Paul II tried something similar to no obvious effect ... no mafia organization has ever listened to the Church and of course the majority of members of these criminal organizations would consider themselves to be 'believers'.

Indeed, according to Italian writer and mafia expert Roberto Saviano, the 'ndrangheta even has its own patron saint, Saint Michael the Archangel, to whom new conscripts apparently swear allegiance. Saint Michael the Archangel is a busy person for he is also the patron saint of sickness, grocers, mariners, paratroopers ... and police.

One further twist to the Oppido story is that the Mazzagatti clan had also been in the news just a few months earlier when a *pentito* maintained that they orchestrated the murder of Francesco Raccosta, a member of a rival 'ndrangheta clan at nearby Castellace. Raccosta was allegedly beaten with iron bars before being fed, still alive, to the Mazzagatti pigs.

Saint Michael the Archangel was not available for comment.

Three victims of the 'ndrangheta:
In 2005 Gianluca Congiusta, who owned three small shops in the Locri area selling mobile phones, refused to pay protection money, *il pizzo*, and one of his shops was firebombed and when he continued to defy the 'ndrangheta, he was gunned down in Siderno.
Later the same year a local politician from Locri, Francesco Fortugno, was assassinated at a polling station in the town. Fortugno was Vice President of the Regional Assembly of Calabria and was noted for encouraging young people to reject and fight the 'ndrangheta.
In 2002, a 'ndrangheta wife from Petilia Policastro, Lea Garofolo broke ranks and became a *pentito*, an informer; her ex-husband eventually caught up with her near Milan in 2009 where she was tortured and shot and her body dissolved in acid.

Although six of my fellow travellers—Gissing, Douglas, Hutton, Whelpton, Gardiner and Morton—were travelling in Calabria when the mafia was an active force, none made direct mention of such an organization or of any kind of organised crime.

That said, I have long wondered about something Norman Douglas wrote when bemoaning the small-minded 'feudal animosity' of inter-community rivalries that resulted in the then unfinished road between San Demetrio and Acri. Was his ambiguity, I wondered, in reality pointing a finger at the mafia?

"You will find in the smallest places intelligent and broad-minded men, tradespeople or professionals or landed proprietors, but they are seldom members of the *municipio* [town council]; the municipal career is also a money-making business, yes; but of another kind, and requiring other qualifications."

Speaking of emigration to America insofar as it related to towns in the Sila mountains, Douglas also wrote the following:

"There has also been—in these parts, at all events—a marked diminution of crime. No wonder, seeing that three-quarters of the most energetic and turbulent elements are at present in America, where they recruit the Black Hand."

Douglas was obviously aware that the 'Black Hand' was an extortion racket, the recognised *modus operandi* of mafia organisations—though the word 'mafia' was little used at the time. Certainly more than a mere oblique reference and a clear indication that he was aware of Calabrian involvement in organised crime stateside. He goes on to relate such activity to the Calabrian character and specifically 'Arab domination of much of his territory' which may have 'infused fiercer strains into his character and helped to deserve for him that epithet of *sanguinario* [bloodthirsty] by which he is proud to be known.

Speaking of his visit to Cosenza, Leslie Gardiner (1966) may have been alluding to the mafia when he made the following observation:

"... between the dilapidated fronts of the old-town slums and the glossy *art-nouveau* of the new the scent of corruption drifts down from City Hall."

In the *Magna Græcia* chapter I noted that Henry Morton (1967) had actually been in Locri the very month of the so-called *Piazza Mercato* massacre but seemingly only had eyes and ears for the town's Magna Græcia excavations. Or perhaps he just chose not to embarrass his hosts and decided not to report on such events.

And this is the reality of such towns today; apart from that down-at-heel and 'closed' ambience I mentioned in relation to Cutro and Isola di Capo Rizzuto, for the outsider it is sometimes difficult to know if a town has mafia connections or not.

How many visitors to the Magna Græcia site at Locri Epizephyrii will have realised that, for many Calabrians, the local mafia connections are more on the collective radar than the part it played in Calabrian history and Greek civilisation? How many will make the connection between the historical Locri and the tragic events that, for example, befell the local Locride (the greater Locri area) Congiusta family in May 2005 when their law-abiding and entrepreneurial son, Gianluca, refused to pay *pizzo* (protection money) to the local *'ndrangheta* thugs and paid instead with his life?

Also, of course, most towns, large or small, have *had* mafia connections in the past. Even here, in Santa Severina, there are certain families known to have inherited a mafia past just because of their surname ... about which they can do little. Any influence their antecedents may once have had—or might have wanted—has all but evaporated. Common sense, local pride and strong leadership have won the day.

Shortly after we came to live in Calabria, one demented soul in his mid-forties, perhaps under the misapprehension that we were conducting some sort of confessional in all the local towns, spilled the beans about his past. In truth, he was not the sharpest pencil in the box and assumed that we, being *stranieri*, wouldn't know anything about the mafia and its activities.

Continuing the allusion of unspoken intrigue, I told him that his secrets were safe with us as he unburdened himself and explained how he had once been a very bad young man and had done some terrible things that Jesus wouldn't have approved of. He did not want to go into any detail but, he assured us, he had turned over a new leaf and those days were in the past. He had found Jesus and Jesus had forgiven him for all his past transgressions.

Momentarily I wondered if John Paul II's speech back in the early 1990s threatening the mafia with 'excommunication' had indeed filtered down to this particular town and saved one young man—our dim confessor would have been in his early twenties at the time? Then again, I thought, it seemed more likely that his ne'er-do-well friends had 'excommunicated' *him* for being a potential liability.

As if to confirm my suspicions, and his 'confession' over, our new best friend asked us (both at the time in our mid- to late-sixties) if we had any children. My reply of "Not yet" did not kindle the disbelieving laughter I might have anticipated.

Off the beaten track, Edward Lear (1847) waxed lyrical about a small community in the foothills of the Aspromonte where he stayed overnight. If he was in Calabria to experience hospitality then it was here that he found it in abundance. He effused about the wine, the food (heaps of macaroni, marrow and tomatoes and roast hare), and the company of Don Giacomo Stranges:

"The worthy man pressed us much to stay, to see all the hills. "Since you *are* come to this out-of-the-way place, what difference *can* a week or two make? Stay and hunt—stay and make this your home.""

Ask any Calabrian which mafia town they would find the most intimidating and many, if not most, would say San Luca. On the other hand, as we have seen, Edward Lear had a great time there with his host Don Giacomo Stranges. How times have changed ... or have they?

One of the leading mafia clans in today's San Luca? The clan Strangio.

Finally, I feel the urge to put an additional spin on the mafia and its apparent influence at a local level. In my opinion it is all too easy to blame the mafia for all the ills that befall Calabrian society. Ordinary people and politicians must shoulder some of the responsibility for allowing it to happen.

I am not denying that the influence of the mafia, past and present, is a major factor in that, among some communities, there has evolved a kind of collective lethargy to dealing with problems generally and the mafia in particular. The ongoing legacy of the mafia is that many people expect nothing to happen and recall nothing but previous failures. Thus new initiatives are watered down by lack of support for those who are trying to bring about change. Sometimes the status quo is easier to cope with than change; change can be challenging. And challenging the mafia and its almost soporific power cannot be easy.

I was speaking to a teacher about a trip I had made in and around the Aspromonte and mentioned some of the towns I had visited. She looked physically ill when I rattled off my list and picked up on one in particular ... Rosarno. As far as she was concerned, this was 'bandit country' and therefore I was lucky to make it out in one piece. When I told her about how the mayor of Rosarno was taking a stand against the local mafia and had actually successfully sued them for €50 million, she was shocked almost to the point of disbelieving. And did it change her view of Rosarno? Absolutely not.

The saddest thing about this encounter is that my acquaintance's conditioning appeared unshakable ... and, worse still, he is a teacher.

Another problem is that tired, disinterested, unquestioning conversations like the following are not uncommon ...
'The rubbish bins haven't been emptied ... it must be the mafia ... well then we can't do anything about it, can we?'
Or ...
'I've heard there are many people with tumours in that part of town ... must be where the mafia dumped the toxic waste.'
Both would be followed by that but-what-can-we-do-about-it shrug of the shoulders which is no more than an unquestioning question.

Let me make it clear, if I haven't already done so ... I am deeply anti-mafia in all its forms and shades, in Calabria and elsewhere. On the other hand, I am pro-evidence ... if, say, a factory owner, not connected to the mafia, dumps toxic waste, the business should be brought to book irrespective of any mafia affiliations. It sometimes appears that to assume or suggest mafia connections can be a way of *not* doing anything about an issue.

The other side of the same coin is when people get all hot and bothered by events such as the ship that apparently was deliberately scuppered off the Calabrian coast with toxic waste and a few bodies aboard *before* actually investigating the matter. In this case, after many protest marches and rallies, it turned out not to be true. No toxic waste, no bodies.

When people indulge is such pre-emptive action without collaborative evidence and based only on hearsay—in this case an ex-member of the 'ndrangheta, Francesco Fonti, and therefore not necessarily the most reliable source in the world—they dilute their cause and when it happens again and just might be true, fewer will believe.

It's called shooting yourself in the foot and is the sort of thing that eventually leads people to credit all perceived wrongs to the mafia and not to the politicians except insofar as they are perceived to be one and the same. It also breeds the expectation that nothing can be done ... which of course suits the mafia.

Of course I realise that Calabrians are not the only people to have to put up with being drip-fed information blurred and confused by a mix of unsubstantiated hearsay and shoddy reporting. When it comes to separating fact from fiction, generally the tabloid press (and its television equivalents) in every country focus on the sensational and are less than thorough when it comes to first recognising, and then separating, fact from fiction.

But not every country has the mafia and unfortunately all mafias are past masters at intimidating communities and manipulating the political process and when people fail to question hearsay, they play straight into their hands.

Calabrians have a right to expect that the unselfish, uncompromising stand taken by the likes of Elisabetta Tripodi at Rosarno, is better publicised and recognised, particularly in Calabria itself, in the hope that, not only will ordinary people themselves become more pro-active, but also that other local politicians will start to follow her example and try to shift the balance of power and influence within their communities away from the mafia.

It is to be hoped too that other places will elect people like Maria Carmela Lanzetta and Elisabetta Tripodi and that their towns will emerge from the blight of the mafia. It is a sad fact that many mafia strongholds do not have a single place for visitors to stay or even a restaurant. The lack of such normal amenities is yet another characteristic of the 'mafia' town and serves to perpetuate the feeling that they are 'closed' to the outside world.

The leaders of mafia clans like it that way. Many of their 'subjects' have never experienced life in the normality of a town which is clean (in all senses) and organised, has roads that are pothole-free, is a place that welcomes, and is welcoming to, outsiders.

These days Edward Lear would not be able to find a single place to stay in San Luca nor, according to TripAdvisor, are there any recommendations as to where to eat out.

And lest you should leave these pages with the notion that all crime is mafia-related, Leslie Gardiner (1966) found that the small town of Luzzi with 9,500 or so inhabitants, was used to crime of a more passionate nature:

"A young woman in the [Easter} procession had shot a bystander and escaped into an empty house. She had barricaded herself in, threatening the *carabiniere* with her pistol through the window, but it was only a matter of time before they dislodged her. Caterina Mele, said Franco, was her name—he knew her well."

When the full story emerged it pointed to a crime of passion. Caterina's *fidanzata* (betrothed) worked in Germany and, with others, had returned for Easter; unfortunately one of these 'others' told her about the *fidanzata* in Munich. In the same town a man couldn't accept that his wife would go to confession without having something to confess. So he stabbed the tight-lipped priest and shot his wife who clearly had so many dark secrets.

CAMPANIA
BASILICATA
Il Pollino
Civitá
Castrovillari
Trebisacce
Il Mar Ionio
Sibari
Spezzano Albanese
San Cosmo
Macchia
Vaccarizza
San Demetrio Corone
San Giorgio
Santa Sofia d'Epiro
CALABRIA
Páola
COSENZA
La Sila
Pallagorio
Carfizzi
San Nicola dell'Alto
Stróngoli
Santa Severina
CROTONE
Il Mar Tirreno
Nicastro
CATANZARO
Vena di Máida
Caraffa
Cortale
Pizzo
VIBO VALÉNTIA
Il Mar Ionio
Rosarno
Gióia Tauro
Gerace
L'Aspromonte
Locri
Lo Stretto di Messina
Scilla
Villa San Giovanni
SICILIA
REGGIO
DI CALABRIA

The Arbëreshë

> Their [the villagers of Spezzano] dialect seemed to us very peculiar, and we soon learnt that they were of Albanian origin, and consequently still preserve the Greek language. Many villages are to be found in Calabria, inhabited entirely by these *Albanesi* and, at one called Santa Sophia, after the name of their patroness, scarcely a man can speak Italian.
> **John Arthur Strutt** *A Pedestrian Tour in Calabria & Sicily*, 1841

Following on from Strutt's experience in Caraffe, it would seem timely to touch on the Albanian or 'Arbëreshë' tradition in southern Italy, much of which is concentrated in Calabria.

In English we use the word 'Albanian' to describe the Arbëreshë people. In Italian they use the word *Albanese* and some towns have this as an appendage to distinguish them from others with a similar name; for example, Spezzano Albanese and San Giorgio Albanese. The Arbëreshë themselves prefer the word Arbëreshë as it is in their own original language. I will therefore use Arbëreshë throughout except when I quote from others who have written something different.

Calabrians seem to know instinctively whether or not a particular town is Arbëreshë. There is, as far as I can discern, no racial or ethnic point being made, it's no more than suggesting that their traditions may be different and that the town's name may be recorded in two languages as well as some the more important signs and notices close to and within the town ... much as the Irish, Germans and Italians brought many of their traditions to America and still celebrate them today.

Across the valley of the river Neto from Santa Severina lies the hilltop town of San Nicola dell'Alto. For the people in Santa Severina the town's elevated position is very important for it is from here than everyone's television signal emanates. And, as Santa Severina remained an ADSL-free zone until recently, for many their internet connection was also relayed from San Nicola dell'Alto.

San Nicola dell'Alto happens also to be an Arbëreshë town though you would be hard-pressed to recognise it as being in any way different from other small Calabrian communities. Apart from its Arbëreshë name, Shën Kolli, the town's website, makes little mention of its Arbëreshë heritage; similarly the website of nearby Pallagorio (Puhëriu), also largely ignores its Arbëreshë origins. Of the three Arbëreshë towns in the Province of Crotone only Carfizzi (Karfici), the home town of writer Carmine Abate, makes more than a passing reference to the town's Arbëreshë inheritance online.

For the record, the town of Santa Sofia d'Epiro (Shën Sofia), a small town close to Acri in the province of Cosenza, mentioned above by Strutt (1841) is, if the *comune*'s website is anything to go by, now fully integrated linguistically. And, of course, as many travellers also recorded, almost every Calabrian community has its own distinctive 'Italian' dialect, a tradition that continues today, even here in Santa Severina.

The Arbëreshë migration to the southern Italian peninsula and Sicily began in the 15th century and continued into the 17th century.

While at Caraffa (Garafa) and Cortale, Arthur Strutt (1841) was told the accepted history of the Arbëreshë migrations which he managed to pass on to his reader (initially his mother, his letters to who form the basis of his book) in layman's language:

" ... and we learned that they are in part the descendents of an army of Albanians, sent by Scanderberg to the succour of Alphonso, King of Arragon and Naples [1442–1458], which never returned to its native land; and in part of a much more recent colony, invited over by Carlos [Carlo VII, 1734–1759], the third great grandfather of the reigning king [Ferdinand II]; who, in order to increase the populations of the Calabrians, gave to every Albanian family, willing to come and settle therein, a pair of oxen, a house and small portion of land, with five-and-twenty ducats for *les frais du ménage* [household expenses]. These conditions were sufficiently alluring to procure for the country the advantage of some thousands of settlers, who were dispersed about, and formed villages of three or four hundred souls; not being allowed, for political reasons, to congregate in any one place in great numbers."

The misspelled 'Scanderberg' that Strutt referred to was George Kastrioti Skanderbeg, was an extraordinarily successful Albanian military leader who had once served the Ottoman Empire. However in 1444, at the age of thirty-nine, he deserted the Ottomans and organised resistance to Ottoman rule in Albania.

Albania was strategically important as its position made it the first line of European (and therefore Christian) defence against the Ottoman (or Turkish) Empire. Over a period of twenty-five years Skanderbeg and his armies effectively delayed Ottoman expansion into western Europe. In so doing he enabled those areas most vulnerable, the Italian principalities and the western seaboard in particular, to be the better prepared.

The reward for his services was that he and his followers could remain in the south and establish communities, twelve of which were established in the hills around Catanzaro, one of which was Caraffa to where Strutt (1841) was heading when he and his party were ambushed.

In today's Italy there are seven regions with Arbëreshë communities but by far the greatest number are in Calabria where there are thirty-one towns or *frazioni* (distinct districts within towns).

As demonstrated by Strutt (1841), for 19th century travellers there was sometimes a degree of reserve surrounding the Arbëreshë communities on their route. Again with Strutt as an example, this was generally picked up from their native Calabrian hosts who themselves often displayed a reticence that came from sharing their homeland with people whose customs, language, dress and religion were different.

Richard Keppel-Craven (1818) described Spezzano Albanese (Spixana) as 'a clean-looking Albanian village' as if surprised that it should be so.

On the other hand Craufurd Tait Ramage (1828), seemed genuinely interested in what he saw in Vena di Máida (Vina), a few miles from Caraffa:

"We did not meet a single individual till we approached the village. The inhabitants were attending evening mass, so that I had a good opportunity of examining the costumes of the peasantry, and their external appearance. The chapel was small and crowded principally by women, so devoutly engaged in prayer that even the presence of a stranger did not distract their attention. Their features were more distinctly oval than those of Italian women, and they had high cheek-bones, so as to remind me forcibly of my own countrywomen. I observed none striking for their personal charms, but there was a modesty and simplicity particularly pleasing. Their gowns were richly embroidered, the colours being generally bright blue or purple. Their hair was fantastically arranged, so as to tower above their heads like an ancient helmet.

"They had a perfect a perfect acquaintance with the Italian language, though they employed the Albanian in conversation with each other."

Ramage enquired about marriage customs and was told of a dance that takes place when the womenfolk convey the bride to her husband's house:

"It is a dance called the Valle [Vallje in Arbëreshë], which must precede the ceremony. The women unite in a ring, clasping the hands of each other, and, with a flag carried in front, proceed dancing and singing the war-songs of their country, when they were fighting the Turks."

Ramage clearly enjoyed his time in Vena and in his writing there is no sense that he was ill at ease or felt under threat:

"I regretted that the day was now drawing to a close, as it prevented me from any further intercourse with the inhabitants of Vena."

Norman Douglas also wrote about the colourful Arbëreshë costumes. He had taken a detour into Basilicata, 'by devious woodland paths', to go to the area's largest annual festival at the Madonna del Pollino, always the first Saturday and Sunday in July. He was, he was told, one of the very few foreigners who had ever been there:

"One is struck with the feast of costumes here, by far the brightest being

The bust of the Arbëreshë warrior and hero Skanderbeg at San Demetrio Corone (Shën Mitër).

The traditional Vallje performed at Cività (Çifti); the same dance was described to Craufurd Tait Ramage when he visited Vena di Máida (Vina).

those of the women who have come up from the seven or eight Albanian villages that surround these hills. In their variegated array of chocolate-brown and white, of emerald-green and gold and flashing violet, these dames move about the sward like animated tropical flowers. But the Albanian girls of Cività stand out for aristocratic elegance—pleated black silk gowns, discreetly trimmed with gold and white lace, and open at the breast."

Douglas also devotes a chapter to all things Arbëreshë and another to one place in particular, San Demetrio Corone, one of six Arbëreshë towns on the northern slopes of the Greek Sila—the others being San Giorgio (Mbuzati), Vaccarizza (Vakarici), San Cosmo (Strihàri), Macchia (Maqi) and the aforementioned Santa Sofia d'Epiro. The reason he singled out San Demetrio Corone was because of its importance to Arbëreshë history and culture in Calabria and beyond:

"San Demetrio, famous for its Italo-Albanian College, lies on a fertile incline sprinkled with olives and mulberries and chestnuts, fifteen hundred feet above sea-level. They tell me that within the memory of living man no Englishman has ever entered the town."

(Ramage (1828) wrongly attributes nearby Bisignano with being the site of the college; Bisignano is not even an Arbëreshë town—though it did spawn bodybuilder Charles Atlas. The confusion probably arose because the daughter of Skanderbeg, who was the wife of the Prince of Bisignano.)

Having described with great affection and impertinent humour, an Arbëreshë wedding which he stumbled upon at San Demetrio, Douglas re-positioned his serious hat to rattle through the College's history and explain its importance to the Arbëreshë community:

"The pride of San Demetrio is its college. Founded under the auspices of Pope Clement XII in 1733 (or 1735) at San Benedetto Ullano, it was moved hither in 1794, and between that time and now has passed through fierce vicissitudes. Its president, Bishop Bugliari, was murdered by the brigands in 1806; much of its lands and revenues have been dissipated by maladministration; it was persecuted for its Liberalism by the Bourbons, who called it a "workshop of the devil." It distinguished itself during the anti-dynastic revolts of 1799 and 1848 and, in 1860, was presented with twelve thousand ducats by Garibaldi, "in consideration of the signal services rendered to the national cause by the brave and generous Albanians."

"But only since 1900 has it been placed on a really sound and prosperous footing. An agricultural school has lately been added, under the supervision of a trained expert. They who are qualified to judge speak of the college as a beacon of learning—an institution whose aims and results are alike deserving of high respect. And certainly it can boast of a fine list of prominent men who have issued from its walls."

Douglas' synopsis is the story of integration, of a community seen as outsiders when they first founded their settlements in Calabria but who became Italians while retaining their Arbëreshë customs and language.

That said, the place itself did not overly impress Douglas:
"The accommodation and food in San Demetrio leave much to be desired; its streets are irregular lanes, ill-paved with cobbles of gneiss and smothered under dust and refuse. None the less, what noble names have been given to these alleys—names calculated to fire the ardent imagination of young Albanian students, and prompt them to valorous and patriotic deeds!"

But the traveller who really got his feet on the ground of the Arbëreshë Greek Sila was Leslie Gardiner. Over half a decade after Douglas, Gardiner (1966) walked around all the towns centred on San Demetrio and described

San Demetrio Corone (Shën Mitër) is the capital of the Greek Sila's Arbëreshë community and home to the College that has been so important to it. In the College grounds is an impressive bust of Giuseppe Garibaldi in recognition of his generous donation to it.

For the record, the town appears to have got over the refuse disposal problems experienced by both Norman Douglas in 1911 and Leslie Gardiner in 1966. Today San Demetrio Corone is a tidy Calabrian town and, apart from the bilingual road signs and street names, almost indistinguishable from other such communities.

people and places that were still having difficulty integrating into Calabrian society ... at least it seemed that way to him. At San Demetrio he echoed much of Douglas' sentiment:

"Strangers are likely to be welcomed with a bucket of potato peelings from an upstairs window. The alleyways, deep in rubbish which disgusted early travellers to San Demetrio still await the refuse collector."

Gardiner does not make this point because the town is Arbëreshë for he goes on to acknowledge that there were other places in Calabria with the same issues when it came to the disposal of rubbish. Indeed, even today there are Calabrian towns and cities that sporadically seem to have such problems, albeit of a different nature and for a different reason. This arises when the local mafia gets in on the act and when there is a stalemate between the needs of the community and the political machinations vis-a-vis some local mafia clique and its predilection for blackmail.

For the record, the rubbish problem at San Demetrio Corone is most certainly a thing of the past.

Cività (Çifti) is the Arbëreshë community I know the best. It is a compact, hilltop town set against a spectacular Pollino backdrop of soft pinks, yellows, greys and greens on one side and a stunning panorama towards the Ionian Sea on the other. It is famous for, among other things, its intricate chimney stacks and the nearby *Gole del Raganello*, a deep and spectacular ravine that funnels the Raganello river on its way to the sea close to Sibari.

Craufurd Tait Ramage (1828), ever on the look-out for traces of antiquity, was convinced by his host's assertion that Cività and the ancient city of Cossa, mentioned by Caesar, were one and the same:

"... accompanied by Signor Cafasi, [I] started for the site of the ancient Cossa, which was said to be situated at a spot called Cività, three miles distant from Cassano."

When he got there Ramage was clearly clutching at straws:

"... the foundations of some buildings are scattered here and there on the summit of a rising ground. What remains is very little, and shows that it had at no time been of great size. I looked around for inscriptions, but nothing of the kind could be seen."

There were no inscriptions for, whatever remains he found near Cività, this was not ancient Cossa. That has since been located about thirty miles to the south-east at Castiglione di Paludi near Rossano.

The people of Cività are bilingual but the relationship between the languages is subtly changing. As at Santa Sofia d'Epiro, on the façade of the town hall the word *Municipio* is inscribed and underneath, slightly smaller, the word *Bashkia*, the same word in Arbëreshë. A hundred years ago, it would have been the other way round with *Bashkia* being the more prominent.

I have two friends there, Stefania and Antonella, both have young daughters; both suspect that their daughters' generation will be the last to speak Arbëreshë, if indeed they ever do embrace both languages with the same fluency as their mothers. Antonella confessed that she thought, spoke and dreamt in Italian and only spoke Arbëreshë when she was with the older generation.

Cività is also where a quarterly magazine for the Calabrian Arbëreshë community is produced. Stefania's father is the editor of *Katundi Ynë* which carries features and news in both Arbëreshë and Italian though, increasingly, it is the Italian that dominates.

Cultural events at Cività continue to display with pride the Arbëreshë dress and custom and are, just as in other Arbëreshë communities, both a link with the past and a modern colourful spectacle for locals and visitors alike.

I was in Cività on a fine, warm Thursday evening in June. I ate outside on the verandah of a restaurant overlooking the square which was teeming with people, all there to enjoy an evening of dance on the small stage in front of the *Municipio*. But there was not a single traditional costume in sight; that evening children from five to eighteen were strutting their stuff to the more modern rhythms of the local dance school. And very good they were too.

I thought back to exactly a week earlier; another warm June evening and I was sitting in the square of Santa Severina watching a similar display by the local children. The only difference was that at Cività there were almost as many boys as girls performing.

Calabrians, both Arbëreshë and Italian, love to dance.

Santa Sofia d'Epiro's Town Hall proclaims itself in two languages ... as do local road signs.

Beyond belief

> "The Calabrians have some very capricious notions deeply rooted in their minds".
> **Henry Swinburne** *Travels in the Two Sicilies*

Southern Italians are a superstitious people; some would say that the Calabrians are the worst.

Many towns will have the equivalent of their own practitioner of *stregoneria*, of a sort of witchcraft or sorcery that in the past was identified with doing people harm but today, like so much else, claims to be more on the 'healing' end of the spectrum. These days people generally visit the *stregone* when they've had some minor ailment for too long; the *stregone*, having reluctantly accepted a generous donation or a six-pack of beer, then incants a few unintelligible oaths to chase said ailment away.

These days too it is on the internet (and to some extent also in the High Street) where people worldwide find the modern *stregone*, the man or woman who peddles innumerable, untested 'cures' that claim to alleviate those irritating, short-lived ailments.

All *stregoni* are, of course, frauds. They rely on the fact that people sometimes get exasperated with minor ailments and, just when its about to get better of its own accord, they finally succumb to something 'alternative'.

And so they pay good money for the touch of the blessed hand or the magic, holistic potion or the secrets of the newly-discovered Amazonian cura-all berry or the book of infinite wisdom and, lo and behold, a couple of days later the ailment that was driving them crazy enough to listen to such nonsense has been 'cured' or—and this is what really happens—they just got better as is the natural way of things, as they would have anyway.

Sadly, what has also happened is that a new convert to the world of hocus-pocus and psycho-babble has been signed up ... they have fallen for the oldest trick in the book, they have erroneously assumed that their apparent 'cure' was in some way connected with the most recent so-called 'treatment'. Which, of course, in one sense it was ... but only in the mind.

Henceforth they will visit the man or woman who draws an anti-clockwise, imaginary circle with his or her right thumb on the back of their head when they're not feeling too good. Until, that is, they find it doesn't work for cancer.

Most Calabrian communities had such a person. In the early 1860s the Italian writer and criminologist, Cesare Lombroso, described how a typical *stregone* shared his unique gift when it came to couples who wanted to part:

"When two lovers want to separate for good, or when an ill-omened husband failed at the first hurdle, they would head for the stregone ... who, after uttering many spells and magic words, burnt the clothes of both the man and the woman."

A criminologist of some standing at the time, Lombroso was on to the 'hocus-pocus' factor and clearly realised it was all a scam and that the *stregone* was observing his clients and coming up with a solution to their problems that fitted in with these observations:

"Thus the stregone interprets people's aspirations and sells them certain black ribbons that he says are favoured to protect the herd from being seduced."

And even in today's Calabria many communities still have a *stregone* in their midst. There is one in Santa Severina ... an elderly man who, so some people will swear, can make you feel as right as rain, with a few hand movements and unintelligible utterances in some archaic dialect.

Between bouts of uncontrollable laughter—some of which may also have been embarrassment—Alessandro told me about a visit to the *stregone* when he was young. He did admit to feeling better afterwards but only because he found the whole experience incredibly funny and people usually feel good when they laugh.

He remembers sitting in a chair that was too big for him while the *stregone* sat on the floor, on his knees, in front of him, looking ferociously serious and uttering incomprehensible words to try to help him sleep better at night. The *stregone* then left the room and from another part of the house continued with his verbal, remedial onslaught before telling Alessandro he could leave ... he was now cured of his tendency to wake every couple of hours.

Alessandro sleeps soundly now and possibly the *stregone* contributed but only in the sense that the experience took his mind off it and provided some light relief as a diversion. Innocent it might seem, but how many are there who, unlike Alessandro, convince themselves that there is a more direct connection between their ailment and the *stregone*'s apparent powers?

For a time, this particular *stregone* was a neighbour and a very genial and courteous person who never tried to peddle his extra-terrestrial skills in our direction. Indeed I don't think he ever peddles his so-called powers, you won't find him in the Yellow Pages, local people just know that he's the person to see when all else apparently fails.

The reason he was, for a time, a neighbour was that he had to relocate following a landslide literally a few metres from his door … an event which, despite his incredible powers, he clearly didn't see coming. *And*, believe it or not, the other day I saw him popping in to see the local doctor … which left me wondering whether he had gone *for* some medical advice, or *to give* some?

I spoke to a lapsed Catholic about the Calabrian predilection for superstitions and she told me that the things the church believed in, any church, not just the Catholic church, generally necessitated a leap of faith into the implausible and the improbable so that it was little wonder that people were superstitious … such questionable notions and rituals were already built-in to their psyche and their everyday lives. This marriage of religion and superstition was observed by Brian Hill (1791) when he was describing the *litiga*, a sort of windowless sedan chair:

"The sides are painted with superstitious devices, to secure you from dangers: among these, the virgin and child, and the souls in purgatory, are seldom omitted."

Hill's unfortunate use of language does not make it clear whether the 'virgin and child' and the 'souls in purgatory' are the superstitions or the dangers.

When Henry Swinburne (1777) observed that 'the Calabrians have some very capricious notions deeply rooted in their minds', he went on to elaborate on some of the stories he had heard. One such Calabrian notion could scar a family for life …

"… every child, whose mother had been true in her marriage vow, must necessarily resemble the father … if [the father] were to become thoroughly convinced that no such resemblance existed, he would never be persuaded to pardon his wife, or look the child in any other light than that of a bastard."

Now I wonder who made that one up? And did it just apply to the peasantry or to landowners too? And what happened when the child bore a striking resemblance to the lord of the manor?

Swinburne came across another superstition even worse:
"If a person dies in the fields by a violent or accidental death, it is believed that his spirit will appear in the same place in white robes, and that the only way of laying it, is to send out young boys to approach silently, and cover it with a volley of stones."

He went on to recount the story of how some youths spotted a white-garmented priest sitting on a hill near Tropea at a place where an elderly woman had died. No prizes for guessing what happened next though apparently the unlucky friar was eventually able to convince the boys that he was alive and well but would not remain so if they persisted in hurling stones at him.

Irrational it may seem, but I wonder to what extent Swinburne would have been *au fait* with some of the customs and superstitious beliefs of the English peasantry at the time? Is it not likely that in Calabria he was having a more direct experience of the 'uneducated' classes than, given his background, he would have encountered at home

---

Norman Douglas (1911) coined an interesting phrase (and possibly a new word) to describe such goings on ... 'lack of sweet reasonableness'. He was recounting the story of two doctors who had been asked to report on the conditions in San Giovanni in Fiore in the Sila mountains. These two well-meaning doctors were 'horrified at the filth, mud and garbage' in the streets which enveloped the town in a 'pestilent odour'. But they were more horrified by the response of the town's mayor:

"*My people cannot live without their pigs wallowing in the streets. San Giovanni in Fiori is exempt from earthquakes and epidemics because it is under the protection of Saint John the Baptist, and because it provincial councillor is a saintly man.*"

This was of course the same John the Baptist who apparently facilitated the escape from his prison of the murderer Musolino.

Craufurd Tait Ramage (1828) even included the word 'superstitions' in his subtitle: *The Nooks and by-ways of Italy: Wanderings in search of its ancient remains and modern superstitions.* One of his observation remains perhaps the one story that is still prevalent even in today's more rational Calabrian culture—*il malocchio*, the evil eye:

"We passed also a few mulberry-trees, which supply food for the silkworm, and ... I expressed a wish to see the cocoons ... but I observed from their answer that they were averse to the proposal, and I afterwards found the cause of the refusal to be not particularly flattering to me. They were afraid to expose the silkworm to the gaze of a stranger lest an ill-omened look should destroy them."

In its crudest form, *il malocchio* is the fear of a gaze, particularly from a stranger; worse still are the calamities that will befall one if the stranger has a squint and appears to cast the evil-eye. Of course there are all sorts of things that can be done to thwart the effects of the evil-eye but it seems that if the recipient is not already wearing one of the various anti-evil-eye amulets that give protection, then neutralising measures must be undertaken immediately. One of these is to insert the thumb under the forefinger and point it at the offender. Of course, it's just tough luck (so to speak) if you didn't see the evil-eye being given in the first place ... best always to keep the thumb under the forefinger and point it at everybody. I find that works.

But it is not always strangers who are capable of casting *il malocchio*. An American woman, originally from Fossato Serralto near Catanzaro, told me how, when she and her husband were preparing to leave their home town for a new life in America in the sixties, he bought his first ever suit. However the purchase was kept secret from those the family thought capable of ill-will, of casting *il malocchio*. The reasoning was both convoluted and simplistic: if such people were kept in the dark about the suits existence, they would not know why he had bought it. And if nobody knew they planned to emigrate, then their new life in America would not be compromised.

In contemporary western society there remain those who, on their wedding day cannot resist indulging in the superstition game and insist that about their person there should be something old, something new, something borrowed, something blue; and I'm not talking about the groom. At least two of these—something old and something blue—are also about thwarting the influence of the equivalent of the evil eye. So, if some of the Calabrian predilections for superstition seem a little archaic, maybe we should look closer to home.

The Calabrian wedding is, of course, generally no different to others when it comes to superstitions. Today the 'something old, something new ...' one, which has its origins in late 19th century England, has been translated literally into Italian as if it had always been so. It seems that there is no copyright when it comes to superstitions.

But there is a uniquely Calabrian superstition that my friend Teresa told me about which was part of her own wedding ritual in the mid-1990s to Vincenzo.

Salt, she told me, was considered one of the things that would keep at bay the effects of *il malocchio*, the evil eye, and on the day Teresa was married, she was given a huge block of salt from her closest neighbours which she had to keep in a secluded corner of her apartment as a sort of gargantuan, on-going insurance policy to sustain their marriage against *il malocchio*.

Teresa, aware that I knew that she and Vincenzo had recently become legally separated, concluded with a typically wry comment:

"Of course, it goes without saying that, in my case, it didn't work. I was seventeen at the time and am much wiser now."

I recall the same sort of cynicism at a *Capodanno* (New Year's Eve) dinner when lentils are always on the menu. This is not because anyone actually wants to eat lentils but because to serve them at *Capodanno* supposedly brings financial fortune for the following year. But recently I have noticed how people are starting to openly question the role of lentils in shaping their fiscal future. It might be obvious to the rational mind that there is no connection between the two, but it is a big step forward in communities, used to believing such things with religious fervour, when they finally start to doubt such superstitions. The real breakthrough will be when the collective will of those who don't actually want to eat lentils on *Capodanno*—even if they do resemble small coins—overturns the superstition and lentils are not on the menu.

There is another aspect to this that Douglas (1911) hints at and that is the part superstitions play in the control, in social terms, of women. Referring to the perceived 'superior strength and utility of boys over girls', he notes that:

"… in South Italy [it] is universally proclaimed by the fact that everything large and fine is laughingly described as 'maschio' (male), and by some odd superstitions in disparagement of the female sex, such as these: that in giving presents to women, uneven numbers should be selected, lest even ones 'do them more good than they deserve'; that to touch the hump of a female hunchback brings no luck whatever; that if a woman be the first to drink out of a new earthenware pitcher, the vessel may as well be thrown away at once—it is tainted for ever."

All of these, it seems to me, were subtle (and perhaps not-so-subtle) ways of keeping Calabrian women in their perceived place.

Douglas also makes one other observation, this time regarding the church and superstitions:

"The attitude of the clergy in regard to popular superstitions is the same here as elsewhere. They are too wise to believe them, and too shrewd to discourage the belief in others; these things can be turned to account for keeping the people at a conveniently low level of intelligence."

Gardiner (1966) discovered something similar, with the Church actively exploiting people's superstitious nature to encourage belief in apparently 'historical' miracles as well as less extraordinary contemporary versions:

"At Luzzi, as devoutly as in Paola, they believe in miracles. Franco could recite stories which for him were just as much a part of history as the campaigns of Garibaldi and the sir raids on Cosenza. They told of saints who flew, who walked on water, resurrected dead cattle, transported shrines from one village to another, made dry paths through the torrents of spring. There were modern tales of saints turned falling olive branches aside from the heads of peasants still alive, who threw labourers clear of falling rock on the *autostrada* works and who kept trains waiting at the platform until they were ready to climb aboard, for all the engine-driver could do to get them under way."

Henry Morton (1967) seemed to have the knack of stumbling upon stories that illustrate the Calabrian penchant for investing in superstition.

When he was at Catanzaro the town was preoccupied with the story of a missing person, Antonio Agostino, who was unheard of for eighteen years. Then a local newspaper had a tip-off regarding his possible whereabouts and his remains were found at a place called the 'sacred rock'. The rock was so-called because, if it were to be doused in sufficient blood, it would part to reveal a huge fortune in the form of gold.

The tip-off came from a local octogenarian who, years earlier, claimed to have witnessed what happened to Antonio Agostino which was no more nor no less than his murder:

"The old man said that he saw the three murderers cut their victim's throat and hold him down over the rock so that his blood poured over it. The men waited for hours but the rock did not move; but the men did."

The old man confirmed that, after the incident, all three men had emigrated, empty-handed of course, and never returned to Calabria.

Of course there may been other motives for the murder of Antonio Agostino and his assailants merely thought they'd kill two birds with one stone and give the old superstition a chance to prove its worth. The story does of course beg the question as to how many other dastardly deeds were inflicted on the innocent to prove (in reality disprove) some superstition. How many other 'sacred rocks' were there in Calabria and elsewhere? How many other old men—and women—took their secrets to the grave?

While at Mélito di Porto Salvo, the southernmost town in Calabria,

Morton (1967) came across another strange story, in this case a tawdry mix of religion and irrational superstition.

It being just over a century since unification, he was expecting that Giuseppe Garibaldi would be the main topic of conversation at Mélito as it was here that Garibaldi landed from Sicily on both his sorties (1860 and 1862) into Calabria. Instead the locals was obsessed by a so-called witch, not of the 'old hag', Macbethian vintage, but a nine-year old girl called Nicolina.

According to Morton's source, it all started, apparently, the moment young Nicolina set foot in the home of her uncle and aunt:

"Tables and chairs were overturned, jugs shot across the room and a barrel of grain, which was too heavy for a strong man to move, was easily transported through the air."

I don't think so ...

Naturally too, immediately after young Nicolina's presence had destroyed all the furniture, the hens stopped laying and the rabbits started killing each other. There clearly being a poltergeist at work, the priest was summoned to sort things out but sadly his embryonic exorcism technique failed.

Now there's a surprise ... the priest was unable to successfully emulate something that doesn't exist except in the movies, (an exorcism) to something that doesn't exist (a poltergeist). Already a little local difficulty for Nicolina's aunt and uncle was becoming a major local problem. Morton continued:

"The villagers then called in a wizard from the mountains who was familiar

Corso Giuseppe Garibaldi in Mélito di Porto Salvo runs down from the old town to the sea ... and could that be Nicolina struggling up the road with her shopping?

with werewolves and all forms of black magic, and he, after having sealed the house, called upon the evil spirit to depart: but his charms also failed."

This story was full of surprises … all those who claimed to have special powers had failed (though how they measured this failure is even a greater mystery) but, instead of turning on *them* and suggesting they might be incompetent charlatans, the villagers turned on little Nicolina herself. Morton again:

"The villagers chased the poor child across the fields with pitchforks, while her counterparts stoned her. I asked if I could see her, but she had since returned home when peace had descended immediately upon Mélito and life had become normal again."

Funny how, nearly two hundred years after Henry Swinburne was in Calabria, the irrational and unquestioning hurling of stones at people was something that Morton also came across. To put it in historical perspective, Morton was travelling in Calabria at the same time as The Beatles' *Sgt Pepper's Lonely Hearts Club Band* was the number one album in America.

I strongly suspect that Nicolina was the innocent in all this … isn't it terrible the lengths wicked aunts and uncles will go to just to get rid of unwanted visitors?

When I travelled to Mélito, I did so the old-fashioned way, by train from Reggio Calabria. Like Morton, I was attracted by the Garibaldi connection but I also wanted to experience the glorious Mount Etna from just across the water. Also, at the back of my mind, was the possibility that I might do one better than Morton and actually find Nicolina, whom I guessed would have been in her early sixties … that was, of course, assuming she was still alive and hadn't been stoned to death by god-fearing neighbours.

Etna did not disappoint though, in the bright mid-winter light, it was hard to distinguish between snow, cloud and smoke swirling around the summit. On the other hand, the spot where Garibaldi landed in both 1860 and 1862 was no more than a deserted beach not far from the station and close to the museum which now bears his name.

Strange how one of the main architects of Italian unification is less revered in Calabria than he used to be. The evening before, I mention to a Calabrian couple that I was going to Mélito and made the mistake of linking the place to Garibaldi. They pointedly reminded me that not everybody was a fan of Garibaldi and that he had done little for Calabria. I was inclined to agree.

Etna and Garibaldi notwithstanding, I turned my attention to Morton's 'Nicolina' story, to see if, and to what extent, her story remained in the local memory; I drew a complete blank. Perhaps I asked the wrong people or perhaps, as Nicolina was staying with relatives at the time, was not local at all.

When Morton was there, Mélito's population was around 7,700 ... I would have thought that somebody might have remembered events less than fifty years ago? I certainly do. On the other hand perhaps this episode was deemed to be embarrassing to the community and one worthy of being expunged from the collective memory, particularly so in a town that was trying to establish itself as a tourist attraction and a holiday destination. And perhaps too the collective memory is easier to expunge when the town also has a history of mafia connections.

In addition, at the time I was there, the local council had been dissolved because of its 'connections' and the town was, like nearby Reggio Calabria itself and several other local mafia towns, being administered under so-called 'Extraordinary Measures'. Perhaps a short, bearded—albeit genial—Irishman asking awkward questions was the last straw and succeeded in closing the collective ranks.

Nearly a decade and a half earlier, Craufurd Tait Ramage (1828) encountered a story at Scalea where he stayed longer than expected while waiting for a break in the weather to continue his journey to Páola by boat. Ramage displayed the same healthy scepticism as I do when it came to such things but was aware too of the potential for irrational violence when superstitions are challenged such as that which later befell Nicolina.

Ramage was told about a statue of Christ in the nearby town of Aieta (which he called Ajeta) that had started to exude manna though, it seemed, the statue favoured only at one particular location in the town. The clergy had already laid claim to it and removed it from a private chapel and placed it in the local church where its manna-exuding activities seemingly ceased; on its return to its original location, the manna 'miracle' recommenced.

Patiently Ramage listened to the whole tale and successfully hid his incredulity from the teller, the judge from Páola whose task it was to verify the story. But Ramage was not buying it and, given a taste of the wondrous liquid itself, believed that it 'had exactly the taste of sugar and water':

"I then stated, in a way least likely to hurt his feelings, that, as I was what he would regard as a heretic, I was very sceptical in all such matters, and could not doubt that he must have been in some way deceived, and that if he would only take proper measures to discover it, I had no doubt he would find it so. I pointed out the various ways in which it might be accomplished, and proved by his statement to me, that he had allowed his feelings to get the better of his judgement ..."

This 'delightful old gentleman' was surprisingly open to Ramage's viewpoint and tried to persuade him to return to Aieta with him to conduct some more science-based research into the matter but Ramage declined. Ramage knew that, just as young Nicolina was to discover, the heady and unpredictable mix of irrational superstition and religious fervour could so easily turn nasty. In his mind's eye, I'm sure he could already see the headline in the *The Times* ... 'Doubting Scotsman beaten to death by angry Calabrian mob':

"I told him that I knew too well the superstitious character of his countrymen, and their excitable temperament, to venture on any such Quixotic enterprise. I was satisfied that he would protect me as far as was in his power, but an unreasoning mob was the last danger I should wish to face, and I did not believe that the few police he could muster would be any protection in case of a commotion."

Perhaps the judge did indeed take Ramage's advice to heart and displayed a more sceptical head when he returned to Aieta to reassess his initial findings. Today's history of the town does not seem to include any extant record of the manna-exuding statue.

In *Calabrian Tales*, Peter Chiarella describes the superstitious tendencies of those who were acquainted with his unnamed great-grandfather, the father of one of the book's main protagonists, the unfortunate Angelo Chiarella, here reflecting on the family he was born into in Gimigliano:

"Some say that he [my father] was part animal and that he had mystical power over other creatures. He could tame wolves and direct their course by an animal sound that emanated from his throat. He was able to keep them from attacking certain villages in the dead of winter when the hunt for food was most difficult. Or, he could send then coursing in packs through an errant town seeking any bit of food they could find in refuse piles and, often, in homes whose doors had not been secured."

As with most superstitious tenets, few will have truly questioned such notions (or motives for not refuting them) nor challenged their veracity even when this 'part animal' was 'killed by a pack of wolves that attacked him while he was sleeping under the stars'. The few who did consider the irony of his demise, were generally content to stick with and expand on the 'mystical power' hypothesis, reasoning that either the wolves were 'tired of his mastery' or that they were 'taking revenge for all the animals he had trapped and killed'.

Implausible as it might seem, my own theory is that they were just hungry.

When I re-read the stories of Antonio Agostino in Catanzaro, Nicolina in Mélito, the statue at Aeita and the wolf-man of Gimigliano, I think how lucky I am to live in a Calabria where such things don't happen to the same extent ... though that doesn't stop them from still being repeated with an authority that implies fact rather than fiction.

What seems to have happened instead is that such folderol has been imported from places where the people should know better and has become the stuff and nonsense of countless television programmes and series that feed the fears and fragility of the insecure, the feeble-minded and the susceptible.

You will have gathered that I am not a fan of superstition and anything that remotely whiffs of it. Nor do I prescribe to the notion that it's all good, clean fun and no harm is meant; to spread such notions is, in my opinion, equally reprehensible. Nor am I a fan of anything that belittles and/or subverts the human experience, that tries to cloud the achievements of science and medicine by, for example, shrouding them in meaningless jargon and uncorroborated doublespeak that some people fall for almost without drawing breath.

If Apple's Steve Jobs hadn't done precisely this, he might well still be alive today. According to his biographer, Walter Isaacson, Jobs died regretting that he had spent so long attempting to treat his cancer with alternative medicine before agreeing, too late, to undergo surgery. (Initially his cancer was treatable by a well-proven and relatively straightforward procedure which had a very high degree of success and without recurrence.)

What leaves a bitter taste in my mouth as far as Steve Jobs is concerned is that I don't recall ever having heard that any of the people who directly or indirectly advised or influenced him, actually stood up and acknowledged their culpability, apologised for it, stopped giving others the same useless advice and then wound up their disreputable businesses. My guess is that they just moved on to their next victim and, inevitably, their next corpse.

Over the last fifty years many Calabrians had started to distance themselves from the iniquitous pointlessness of superstition in all its forms. Unfortunately however there is evidence that many are already succumbing instead to the modern-day equivalents. In recent years I have noticed how, increasingly, many Calabrians (and of course not just Calabrians) will automatically relate a person's date of birth to a star-sign, their fortune to tarot cards and anything not immediately interpretable to the paranormal.

Worse still, these days people are becoming more and more prepared to register, subscribe and pay in advance for their superstitious fix; the modern-day *stregone* is more organised and, above all, internet-savvy.

All very worrying.

Northern gateways, then and now

"... a flatter road ... brought us at Castro Villari, where we have actually had the fortune to find five beds."
John Arthur Strutt *A pedestrian Tour in Calabria and Sicily*

Unlike John Strutt (1841), on my first visit to Castrovillari I did not have need of accommodation; I was, like so many travellers before me, just passing through.

Today's Castrovillari is the main centre in the Pollino National Park; if the Park has a capital, then this is it. But for many others who came to Calabria, from Richard Pococke in 1733 to Eric Whelpton in 1957, the town was no more than their first, sometimes their final, overnight stop.

Castrovillari, the largest town to the south-east of the pass in the Pollino mountains and the elevated plain of Campo Tenese, used to be an important staging-post for travellers to and from Basilicata and the north. Today the region's major north-south artery, the A3 *autostrada*, makes a brief east-west detour to cross Campo Tenese and wrap itself round both Castrovillari and nearby Morano Calabro.

On my first 'passing through' visit I felt especially pleased with myself for having found the only space in a small car-park close to the centre. However, my euphoria was short-lived for, having studied the signs indicating the hourly parking costs, I could not find the ticket-machine to pay. And, brandishing my ingrained north-European scruples, I could not possibly leave the car park without paying. In desperation, I accosted a replete shopper returning to her car and asked her what I should do ... she shrugged her shoulders:

"They tried that but nobody paid so now they've taken away the ticket-machines. It's free again; like it was before." And then, as an afterthought, and with a shrug of the shoulders, "This is Calabria, you know."

This was not the first time I'd come across a similar story … generally Calabrians do not expect to pay to park and sometimes will go to extremes just to save a euro, or less.

Cheaply parked, I went in search of my mid-morning coffee fix and, no sooner had my bottom hit the seat, shaded from the heat of the late-morning sun by a kerb-side tree, than I was joined by a well-meaning local, sporting his loud, 'I'm-a-lumberjack', checked shirt.

As he proffered me an outstretched hand, he uttered just two words, "Barack Obama".

I couldn't quite make sense of whether he was introducing himself as Barack Obama or was wondering if I was called Barack Obama; or perhaps it was just something he liked saying to people? I finally opted for the latter reasoning as the name was never mentioned again.

My new best friend was one of Castrovillari's finest fifty-somethings and seemed like a man who might be described as not being 'the sharpest pencil in the box'. This often happens to me … I'm not sure how it works exactly but sometimes I feel as if there is a large neon sign above my head which invites those of questionable mental agility to come and talk to me.

He asked me if I might be able to help with lighting his hand-rolled cigarette. I couldn't. Undeterred, he left the table momentarily, found a light elsewhere and then returned to engage me in meaningless conversation.

He told me how, the minute he saw me, he knew that I was German and, before I could put him straight, dug an even deeper hole for himself by explaining how he used to live in America, in Brooklyn to be specific, and therefore spoke some English but, sadly, not German. When I was finally allowed to explain that I was Irish (and therefore English-speaking) *and* went through that whole rigmarole that always plagues me of explaining the difference been Irlandese (Irish) and Olandese (Dutch), his ability to speak English somehow seemed to have evaporated … except for the name of the (then) president of the United States.

He went on to explain how he'd had to return to Calabria because of a mysterious illness contracted in Brooklyn which had effected his memory which was why he was having difficulty with his English on this particular occasion. He also confessed to feeling homesick for 'la bella Castrovillari'.

Until he opened his mouth, his unshaven look could conceivably have been taken for the latest in designer stubble but the open mouth, the smoky haze *and* the stubble together soon put paid to such a notion. I looked at my watch and explained that I needed to go to the post office and that there had been a queue there 'earlier' and it was important I get there before it shut. This, I knew, was the perfect Calabrian excuse to get out of such situations for, wherever you might be, it will always be true.

Despite having implied that I had already been there once, he offered to accompany me, to show me where it was. A generous gesture which generated a modicum of guilt even as I said I was fine and knew where it was—which was actually true as I'd already noticed the road-sign to it. I allowed my conscience this small concession as I reasoned that my little white lie cancelled out his bigger one about his ability to speak some English. We were well matched.

I walked past the post office not only to confirm that the queue was indeed lengthy and to feel a little less guilty, but also because I knew it was on the way to one the older parts of town, one which I wanted to explore.

Six months later I was back in Castrovillari, not 'passing through' this time but staying instead at a very pleasant Bed & Breakfast. Here I discovered that things have changed somewhat since the Irish cleric, Richard Pococke, and his companion found themselves in Castrovillari at the end of their six-day race through Calabria in 1733:

"[We] ascended the hills to a poor town called Castra Villari, where we had no accommodations but an old empty house …"

Settled into my more salubrious quarters, I went for a walk in the early evening drizzle just to get my bearings. Imagine my surprise therefore when, passing a small bar, I was unexpectedly pounced on and unceremoniously embraced with a bear hug of joyous recognition and the two words I was least expecting, 'Barack Obama'?

Yes, my new old friend not only recognised me but he even remembered the password.

Later I did some discrete local research and found that 'Carlo' was a man to whom not being 'the sharpest pencil in the box' was *not* an appropriate epithet. Seemingly he has two university degrees which belies his apparent mindless behaviour, itself seemingly the result of being thwarted by the one and only love of his life. Basically, my source told me, he never got over her.

Apart from 'Carlo', today's Castrovillari is dominated by a broad, tree-lined thoroughfare, Corso Giuseppe Garibaldi, both sides of which strut their stuff with elegant façades. By contrast, at one end is the old town with its Aragonese castle sitting atop its Norman predecessor.

Around and beyond the castle, sprawls the town's oldest quarter, known as Civita (not to be mistaken for the nearby accented Arbëreshë town of Cività), which still clings on with robust character to the arrowhead escarpment and almost certainly the quarter where, in 1733, Richard Pococke, stumbled upon that 'old empty house'.

By the time Richard Keppel-Craven (1828) passed through things had changed and he too found that there were two quite different aspects to the town which I suspect corresponded more or less to the old and new town as they are today:

"[I] proceeded to Castrovillari, a town consisting of two distinct portions; the first dirty, ill paved, and irregular, and the second composed of large houses, built in straight rows, along wide streets or spacious squares. I dined at this place ... and afterwards resumed my route."

Like the older quarters in many towns, Castrovillari's Civita is having a facelift and many of its oldest buildings have been or are being renovated.

As we have seen, when John Strutt and his French friends were here they had no trouble in finding accommodation and beds ... though no prizes for guessing on which side of the town they probably found them.

Having drawn some of the local women in their 'picturesque costumes' Strutt and his four companions received word that some of the local *Galant'uomini* were going to visit them. Strutt explained who these *Galant'uomini* were:

The older Civita quarter of Castrovillari looking back towards the more modern facades of the town with the Pollino mountains in the background. On the edge of the escarpment (the left above) is the *Chiesa di San Giuliano* with its distinctive cupola.

"[They are] that class of men who are not absolutely obliged to work for a living; but having, perhaps, a *carlino* a day, of independent property are enabled to exist in idleness, to lord it about the village, and to be, in fact *Galant'uomini*."

Perhaps my loquacious friend 'Carlo' was a modern-day *Galant'uomini*? Perhaps not.

Both Strutt and I enjoyed our time at Castrovillari, we both slept well and ate well. On the TripAdvisor website I later waxed lyrical about both, particularly the restaurant where I ate the best *tagliata*—strips of beef in a balsamic sauce, with lots of rocket and topped with flakes of cheese and my favourite Calabrian dish—I have ever eaten. This is Strutt's equivalent:

"Our repast was at last ready, and we all supped together very gaily. My friends are already giving audible tokens of their sound repose, and I am now going myself to prove the good qualities of the fifth bed.—Good-night."

Strutt's familiar 'Good-night' was directed at a specific reader, his book being a compilation of letters he sent to his mother detailing his adventures.

Castrovillari is 'on' the river Coscile in much the same way as Stansted Airport is 'in' London. The river skirts the east and south of the old town on its way from the Pollino mountains to the sea and had, for classicists like Norman Douglas (1911), a very special claim to fame:

"The houses ... overlook the Coscile river, the Sybaris of old, and from a spot in the quarter a steep path descends to its banks. Here you will find yourself in another climate, cool and moist. The livid waters tumble gleefully towards the plain, amid penurious plots of beans and tomatoes, and a fierce tangle of vegetation wherever the hand of man has not made clearings."

When Eric Whepton was here in 1956 the Coscile merited only a line:

" ... the muddy green waters of the Coscile flow slowly past the old town of Castrovillari ..."

In less than fifty years Douglas's tumbling 'livid waters' had become Whepton's slow 'muddy green waters'; a decade later Henry Morton (1967) made no mention of the Coscile at all. The reason is simple, these days you would be hard-pressed to find any evidence of it in or around Castrovillari. Nearer the coast, it hooks up with the Crati and it was the supposed tampering with the confluence of the Sybaris and the Crati by the Krotons that is said to have finally destroyed the Greek city of Sybaris.

My first attempt to find the Coscile, be they 'livid' or 'muddy green' waters, was thwarted by incessant rain and the fact that I was on foot, despite ignoring some disbelieving, you-must-be-mad looks when I said I intended to walk. I was determined, even in this small way, to emulate the capacity of Douglas (and others) for walking long distances but, on this occasion, I knew that the elements had beaten me. I also knew that Douglas's 'steep path'—a more direct route down from Civita—was probably only negotiable in the summer if, indeed, it could still be found at all.

The next morning, from a point beyond Civita, I drove down into the valley of the Coscile on a narrow, serpentine, metalled track until I arrived at two small pools in a setting that was indeed almost other-worldly ... a rich green, moist micro-climate, the silence broken only by the nearby babbling of water over stone and the occasional complaining of some fenced-off and curious geese.

Beyond the pools I could see a small, basic bridge, itself 'fenced off' by red and white plastic tape which normally means 'thou shalt not pass' but in Calabria is generally translated as 'to pass, duck under the tape'. The bridge spanned what Calabrians call a torrent and this particular torrent, gurgling below my feet, was indeed the 'livid waters' of the Coscile, the Sybaris that was, on their way to the sea and a greater union with the Crati.

I continued through the trees and dank vegetation until I could get a clear view back up the hill to Civita and the distinctive cupola of *La Chiesa di San Giuliano*. I pictured Douglas carefully picking his way down some overgrown path from somewhere near the church, just to glimpse the ancient Sybaris in

The elusive Coscile trickles through a hard-to-find vale below Civita, the oldest part of Castrovillari. The distinctive cupola of Civita's *Chiesa di San Giuliano* looks down on the tangled vegetation which purportedly hides an old path from the town.

its infancy. I didn't envy him his climb back up, I knew mine would be more straightforward; nevertheless we did share the elusive sight and sounds of the 'livid waters' of the Coscile in its secret bosky vale.

The less intrepid Whelpton and Morton both likened the ambience of Castrovillari itself to some Irish provincial towns (albeit without the summer heat), a comparison I could go along with despite today's lack of dowdy and discouraging window displays which to Morton seemed as if 'a careless hand had tossed a selection of the goods to be obtained therein'. Today's Castrovillari has all the charm of times past but all the sophistication of the modern world with its outlets for expensive children's clothes and all the electronic gadgets you could ever want.

I could understand why anyone might feel homesick for such a place.

But Castrovillari was not the only staging-post for travellers who crossed the Pollino mountains into and out of Calabria; for some the smaller, more northerly, town of Morano Calabro fulfilled the same purpose.

Brian Hill (1791) described how he and his group stumbled upon Morano and, later, how surprised he was by the accommodation he found there:

"… we passed between two rocky hills into a sweet little vale enclosed by snowy mountain. In this delightful situation we found Morano, a curious town upon the side of a steep round hill … Our inn last night was, in comparison of our usual fare, capitally good. We had a fire-place adapted *to no other purpose,* and I lay in my clothes between sheets, without being disrupted by a single flea."

For other reasons Richard Keppel-Craven (1818) also took a fancy to Morano:

"Morano … has scarcely undergone any change. It is beautifully situated in a dell, which is sheltered by frequent trees of a large size, casting their broad shadows over an undulated surface of verdure, kept constantly fresh by the various rills [small streams] which tumble in little cascades from the lower ridge of Mount Pollino, and form the Coscitello"

It was while heading for Morano, where the elevated flatness of Campo Tenese gives way to the more undulating landscape on the approach to the town, that Arthur John Strutt (1841) and his companion William Jackson joined forces with the three Frenchmen they were still travelling with when later got involved in that skirmish near Catanzaro.

Here Strutt describes how Morano and its surroundings blended in with its mountainous backdrop:

"… placed as usual on the rock eminence which has furnished materials for the construction of all its buildings; so that the colour being exactly the same, and the architectural forms not very striking, it is rather difficult at a distance, to determine whether you behold a town or a bare rock."

Perhaps the Norman castle that dominated the crest of the hill, then as now, blended in too well for neither Hill nor Strutt mentioned it. Keppel-Craven, on the other hand, did so at length:

"[Morano is] crowned by a fine Gothic castle. We are accustomed to look upon these kind of edifices as more particularly appropriate to the northern portion of Europe; but I had soon perceived that Calabria contains a much greater number of ruins of this description than any other province of the same extent; as there is scarcely a village that does not present some vestige of these baronial mansions, which, however, had ceased to serve as residences for their possessors long before the abolition of feudal institutions."

The 'Coscitello' mentioned above by Keppel-Craven is, of course the diminutive name for the younger Coscile which, still in its infancy, skirts Morano Calabro with even greater anonymity than it exhibits at Castrovillari.

Today's Morano Calabro is probably seen by many as the area's most picturesque town though, for me, nearby Mormanno is also in the running. Whatever the season, the castle-topped town, set against the backdrop of the majestic Pollino mountains, ensures that it is a photogenic place, a place that offers the right balance of delightful setting, olde worlde charm and knick-knacks for travellers.

Morano as it is today ... described by Brian Hill in 1791 as 'a curious town upon the side of a steep round hill', though neither he nor Strutt seem to have noticed the castle *(right)*.

The mountains

Ask any Calabrian to compare the scenic merits of the region's three mountain ranges and their associated National Parks—the Pollino, the Sila and the Aspromonte—and to choose their favourite and the answer will always be the same ... the one closest to where they live. They say it with such certainty, as if there can be no doubt about it, and they will assume you agree.

Sneakily, I asked the same question of someone I knew lived equidistant from both the Sila and the Pollino in the hope I might force an actual opinion. I should have known it would get me nowhere:

"In the summer I prefer the Pollino and in the winter the Sila", was the noncommittal response.

On the other hand, some of those who live between the Sila and the Aspromonte ranges will mention another area of high land, the Serra Regional Natural Park, with two sites over twenty miles apart: one centred on Serra San Bruno and the other by Lake Angitola. Though smaller and less dramatic than the others, the Park's tallest mountain Monte Pecoraro (at almost 4700 feet) is taller than Ben Nevis, the UK's highest mountain, so I think it qualifies for inclusion.

Collectively all are part of the Apennines, the mountains that run the length of the Italian peninsula and form the backbone of Italy, and of course the mountains themselves and their lesser outriders extend far beyond the areas designated as National Parks.

And yes, *I* definitely do have a favourite but, in the interests of not offending anyone, I will try to be equally fair to all four. I will start at the top, the north ...

San Lorenzo Belizzi
Mormanno
Il Pollino
Morano
Castrovillari
Acri
Lungobucco
La Sila Greca
Camigliatello
San Giovanni in Fiore
COSENZA
La Sila Grande
Santa Severina
La Sila
La Sila Piccola
CROTONE
Villaggio Mancuso
Sersale
CATANZARO
VIBO VALÉNTIA
Serra San Bruno
La Serra
Mongiana
Stilo
Gerace
Delianuova
Platí
Gambarie
San Luca
L'Aspromonte
REGGIO
DI CALABRIA

Il Pollino

To enter or leave Calabria in the north via the A3 *autostrada* is to experience the cosy, verdant face of the Pollino mountains but it is an aspect of these mountains that belies their essentially rugged, uncompromising beauty. When you leave behind the area around magnificent Mormanno (about which I have already written) and head either west towards the Tyrrhenian Sea at Scalea or east into the vastness of the mountains, as they stride towards Trebisacce on the opposite coast, the Pollino range is full of surprises and contrasts.

Like the Sila and the Aspromonte, the Pollino range forms part of the spine of Calabria but in striding east and west, almost coast to coast, there is a sense in which these mountains are like a border in themselves, a border that separates Calabria from the rest of Italy.

Of course mountain ranges do not recognise regional boundaries so much of the Pollino range is in Basilicata. Mount Pollino itself straddles the border while the highest point on the Serra Dolcedorme (2267m), is just on the Calabrian side and the highest peak in Calabria. It is these mountains that form the backdrop to Mormanno, Morano Calabro and Castrovillari and, ironically, it is from the much-maligned A3 *autostrada* that some of the most dramatic panoramas can be experienced.

For many other travellers entering and leaving the region inland, the Pollino mountains left their mark for, from whichever direction they were travelling (heading to or from Rotonda in Basilicata), they always had to cross Campo Tenese which Swinburne (1780) described as 'a large circular plain encompassed by mountains'.

Today the A3 *autostrada* dissects Campo Tenese and takes a slightly more westerly route in and out of Calabria; nevertheless between Mormanno and Morano there are spectacular views of the mountains in all directions, particularly to the north towards Mount Pollino. But Campo Tenese is itself an elevated plain and thus, as Swinburne noted, is prone to the same extremes of climate as the nearby mountains:

"In a corner of this amphitheatre is a convent of capuchins, who succour and harbour travellers that happen to be surprised by a fall of snow, or are benighted [overtaken by darkness] in this high and lonely region."

At first I thought this convent was *Il Convento di Collerato*, the ruins of which are well-known in the area. Norman Douglas (1911) described its position in the shadow of Mount Pollino:

"On a shady eminence at the foot of these mountains, in a most picturesque site, there stands a large castellated building, a monastery. It is called Colorito, and is now a ruin."

I wonder what he would think of its current position sitting on the top of a short *autostrada* tunnel, a *galleria*?

When I first saw the ruins of the convent, seconds before I drove under them, I realised it could not be Swinburne's 'convent of capuchins' after all. *Il Convento di Collerato* was clearly on higher ground above Campo Tenese and in any case these were the ruins of an Augustinian establishment and not Capuchin, the sort of mistake that Swinburne would surely not have made.

Like many such institutions *Il Convento di Collerato* was closed down during French rule (1806–1815) as part of the Murat regime's policy of cutting back on the power, land and wealth of the church and its clerics. This was not a simple anti-church measure but an efficient means to a financial end, to try to cancel out the Two Sicilies' estimated inherited debt of 105,000,000 ducats; by 1815 that debt was less than 1,000,000 ducats.

But money was not the only reason for closing such institutions for they also had a reputation for harbouring the anti-French brigand-allies of the exiled Bourbon monarchy. Norman Douglas went on to elaborate on this apparent contradiction:

"Nearly all convents in the south, and even in Naples, were at one time or another refuges of bandits, and this association of monks and robbers used to give much trouble to conscientious politicians."

Snow-topped Mount Pollino in December.

As you might imagine, I continued to wonder about in which 'corner of this amphitheatre' I might find evidence of the convent mentioned by Swinburne until, that is, I was stopped in my tracks by a herd of goats and sheep. I was on a cross between a road and a track, south of the *autostrada* between Mormanno and Morano, in the south-eastern corner of Campo Tenese and took a photo of the animals as they bounded off to explore—and devour—their new pastures. It was later that I noticed that there was a densely wooded hillock in the background of the photo and, still later, I discovered that this small blip in the landscape was called Convent Hill.

Strutt (1841), on his way south to Morano, had to cross Campo Tenese and was also aware of its climatic extremes:

"... a dreary flat, surrounded on every side by towering heights, was to be traversed before we could gain the ascent, and see, what one is always so impatient to do in travelling, the other side ... Tall columns are places at short distances, all along the road, and serve in winter to mark out its direction, when the snow is deep; and about half-way a solitary station of soldiers graces the scene, not misplaced in such a lonely and otherwise unprotected spot."

Travelling in the summer, Richard Keppel-Craven (1818) still found Campo Tenese to be both bleak and uninviting:

"Some corn, but much more fern, grows over the flat, which is totally unfurnished with trees or shrubs, though the flanks of Mount Pollino ... famed for simples [plants believed to have medicinal properties] and pasturage, show a scanty covering of sickly beech, scantily intermixed with holly. The snow, which generally falls early, lies during the whole of the winter on this plain, exposed, by the wide opening terminating the opposite extremity from that by which I had entered, to the sweeping impetuosity of the north wind, in its whole extent."

These days this gateway to and from Calabria via Campo Tenese is not as obvious as it once was ... new highways such as the A3 *autostrada* and its predecessors, the road that links Mormanno and Morano and its more serpentine neighbour between Morano and Rotonda, have seen to that. Nevertheless, on a bright and sharp December day, with the first falls of snow already settled on Mount Pollino itself, I took to the hills to get a flavour of where Campo Tenese and Hill's 'the most dangerous pass in all Calabria' met.

I abandoned the car on the roadside and wandered on foot round several hairpin bends looking for an easy way into what I knew was the north-west corner of Campo Tenese. As I picked my way across a field, looking for dry footholds after the previous day's heavy rain, I could see the valley open up before me as the land fell away through the gap in the mountains and into Basilicata. Momentarily I glimpsed Rotonda before the low, swirling cloud snatched it away and left only its memory and the pictures others drew of this place.

For Strutt (1841), coming up from Rotonda, this was where he entered Calabria, where perhaps he turned and looked back before striding off across Campo Tenese:

"We have at last entered Calabria in good earnest, and hitherto the prospect has been wild and sometimes grand ... A long, long ascent brought us at last to an eminence ... before us the view was far less interesting ..."

Swinburne (1780), Hill (1791) and Keppel-Craven (1828) left Calabria by the same route. This view was there last memory of Calabria and, for Hill and Keppel-Craven, a time to reflect.

For Hill, the eternal pessimist, this view of Rotonda in the distance came as a blessed relief; he was just glad to have made it this far and in one piece:

"Upon leaving this plain, we entered the terrific pass. It is a deep chasm between towering mountains, darkened by the thickest shade, so that a small party of robbers, by securing a good position on the higher parts, may begin an attack upon a large company without the least fear of being overcome, as they might easily escape among the thickets, should the travellers attempt to

Descending from Campo Tenese, this is the view of the erstwhile gateway to and from Calabria which, on account of its reputation for brigandage, Hill (1828) described as 'the most dangerous pass in all Calabria'.
Behind the cloud to the right of the trees lies the town of Rotonda in Basilicata.

climb the rocks, and make them prisoners. We descended by a very rugged path, which led us out of the chasm to a forest of oaks, and then entering a fine new road, soon arrived at Rotunda …"

And this despite the fact that nothing untoward happened to him or his party.

On the other hand, Keppel-Craven (1818) saw the greater picture:

"The valley contracts suddenly beyond Morano, and at last ends in a narrow defile called Rocca Prerupata, along the sides of which the modern road is conducted in zigzag lines, with so much judgment, as never to render the ascent too abrupt. This pass is tedious, and leads to the opening of an upland plain of some miles in length, but not very broad, called Campo Temese, or Tenese, and looked upon as one of the most bleak exposed tracts of country in the whole kingdom."

East and west of Monte Pollino itself, the mountain landscape is quite different. That to the west and south towards the Tyrrhenian Sea is a blend of both the dramatic and the mellow, an accessible landscape punctuated with less daunting mountains and spectacular river valleys such as the Lao and the Argentino. It was in this part of the Pollino that, according to a story related to Thomas Watkins in 1788, there lived an Englishman, a man who, at the time, had 'resided there nine years, and subsisted on the alms of the country people'.

Such an existence would have been more difficult, if not impossible, on the eastern side of the Pollino range towards the Ionian Sea; here there is drama and beauty too but the landscape is more rugged and uncompromising, a wild terrain that blows the cobwebs away.

Some would say that the Lao and Argentino valleys are among the most beautiful in Italy. The former gives its name to the *Riserva Naturale Statale Valle del Fiume Lao*, a protected area with the river itself and the small town of Papasidero at its heart. The latter, the Argentino, runs through Orsomarso, the town near which French writer and soldier, Duret de Tavel, finally defeated the insurgents his battalion had chased from Mormanno.

The last few miles of the tortuous road between Scalea and Papasidero follows the Lao, sometimes at extreme elevations. Sheer walls of peach-coloured rock, punctuated with random green outcrops, are kept in their place with almost invisible wire netting lest they break off and devour the road below. It is one of the most beautiful mountains drives in Calabria but I assume its serpentine nature around Papasidero puts people off; on the two occasions I came this way I scarcely saw another vehicle.

Papasidero is one of those places in the Pollino, like Morano, Città and San Lorenzo Belizzi, where in some lights it can be difficult to distinguish between some of the buildings and the natural rock backdrop. Strutt (1841) wrote about this phenomenon too in relation to Morano:

"... placed as usual on the rock eminence which has furnished materials for the construction of all its buildings; so that the colour being exactly the same, and the architectural forms not very striking, it is rather difficult at a distance, to determine whether you behold a town or a bare rock."

Papasidero has another claim to fame as it is here that some of the oldest and most significant examples of prehistoric art can be found at *La Grotta del Romito*. Prehistory has time zones and for the record this is an Upper Paleolithic site which means it dates from between c23,000 and c10,000 BCE which makes it one of the oldest sites in Europe. The art is simplistic but surprisingly detailed, that of a bull being particularly so. An interesting, unique and well organised historical site that suffers, at the time of writing, from a Calabrian/Italian problem that I have written about before ... signage or, more accurately, the inconsistency of appropriate signage to get you to your goal without having to turn round or ask for directions locally.

Sometimes it seems to me that, deep down in the Calabrian psyche there

Clinging to the small triangular piece of land in the centre of the photo is the town of Papasidero. On the road between Scalea and Mormanno not far from Papasidero.

exists an obscure and ancient logic which decrees that, to give someone that last piece of information to facilitate their arrival at their destination, is a sign of weakness. It frequently happens that the directions to any given destination are all straightforward until that last T-junction when the seeker has to decide whether to turn left or right without the benefit of a clue.

It is/was/used to be like that at Papasidero ... maybe there is/was/used to be someone in charge of signage who doesn't/didn't want anyone to visit *La Grotta del Romito*. It just remains a mystery to me why it should be like this ... but so often it is.

I feel so much better for having got that off my chest ... yet again.

East from Castrovillari the Pollino becomes more rugged, more remote more impregnable. One of the routes into the heart of the mountains leaves the main road between Castrovillari and the sea at Francavilla Marittima and twists and turns as it climbs to Cerchiara di Calabria from where there are dramatic views, across a deep impenetrable chasm and over the distant curves of the Ionian coastline.

Leslie Gardiner (1966) came here and was captivated by the same vista:

"The village sits on a saddle between gaunt conical hills and seems to be gazing in consternation at the almost vertical limestone ladders at its doorstep where, by the look of the land, a mountain split and half collapsed onto the plain."

But on the other side of Cerchiara there is more climbing to do, more hairpin bends to negotiate, as the rugged, treeless mountains seem to loom larger—bare, sheer faces that dare you to keep climbing towards the last outpost in Calabria on this rim of the Pollino, San Lorenzo Bellizzi.

Even in summer, San Lorenzo feels remote and isolated because it *is* remote and isolated, a place where few other than locals come because there is nowhere beyond to go. It is like being abandoned on a small, remote island adrift in a sea of primordial rock formations.

There is a road that continues to climb north to cross the mountains to Terranova del Pollino in Basilicata but even locals will shake their heads and hands at the very notion and wonder why, these days, anyone would want to take on such a journey.

Norman Douglas (1911) found the same reaction when he considered crossing the mountains from Morano to Terranova. He knew he was embarking on an unusual, and perhaps hazardous, journey, a journey that few, if any, locals would ever consider:

"As a matter of fact, although I spoke to numbers of the population of

Morano, I only met two men who had ever been to Terranova, one of them being my muleteer; the majority had not so much as heard its name. They dislike mountains and torrents and forests, not only as an offence to the eye, but as hindrances to agriculture and enemies of man and his ordered ways."

Considerations of overnight comfort led him to opt for leaving instead from Castrovillari:

"Marching comfortably, it will take you nearly twelve hours to go from Morano to the village of Terranova di Pollino, which I selected as my first night-quarter. This includes a scramble up the peak of Pollino, locally termed "telegrafo," from a pile of stones—an old signal-station—erected on the summit. But since decent accommodation can only be obtained at Castrovillari, a start should be made from there, and this adds another hour to the trip. Moreover, as the peak of Pollino lies below that of Dolcedorme, which shuts off a good deal of its view seaward, this second mountain ought rather to be ascended, and that will probably add yet another hour—fourteen altogether. The natives, ever ready to say what they think will please you, call it a six hours' excursion."

Though his interim goal was Terranova, Douglas' ultimate destination appears to have been the annual fair at Madonna di Pollino which makes his description of his excursion into Basilicata seem somewhat curious.

He describes in detail the trek from Castrovillari across the mountains to Terranova and then his onward journey the following day, north towards

The formidable remoteness and stark beauty of the Pollino mountains just inside Calabria ... the view from the road on the approach to San Lorenzo Belizzi.

Noepoli and another overnight stop with some shepherds. There doesn't seem any logic to this journey and, if his ultimate destination was indeed the fair at Madonna di Pollino, then he was travelling in the wrong direction; even going to Terranova seemed pointless:

"A dirty little place; the male inhabitants are nearly all in America; the old women nearly all afflicted with goitre ... The sights of Terranova are soon exhausted."

Then, after several pages of detail on his two-day journey thus far, he arrives at Madonna di Pollino as if by magic in a single sentence:

"Leaving the hospitable shepherds in the morning, we arrived after midday, by devious woodland paths, at the Madonna di Pollino."

Later Gardiner (1966) described the same fair as 'a grand picnic in the name of the Virgin [where] boy meets girl in circumstances sometimes discreet and sometimes not so discreet'.

Douglas had been in the Pollino before and sometimes it appears as if his *Old Calabria* is not a travelogue in the conventional sense but a fusion of at least two different journeys. Douglas's account of crossing the Pollino mountains into Basilicata and returning via the fair, seems to make no sense if taken at face value. Indeed in the 'several pages of detail' already alluded to, he does mention that this was not his first time walking in the Pollino mountains. Similarly, when he was at Crotone some weeks later, he stayed at the Hotel Concordia because it 'has twice already sheltered me within its walls'.

Whatever the chronology, it was a brave venture and even the intrepid Douglas had his moments of weakness:

"I thought with regret of the tepid nights of Taranto and Castrovillari, and cursed my folly for climbing into these Arctic regions; wondering, as I have often done, what demon of restlessness or perversity drives one to undertake such insane excursions."

And to think ... when I was talking about crossing the same mountains from San Lorenzo Bellizzi to Terranova, I meant by car and still got looks of disbelief.

Not unnaturally the population of San Lorenzo is dwindling but, despite the remoteness, there are those who have chosen to stay and as a community these few hundred are trying entice others to come and live here. The incentive is cheap-to-buy housing, albeit houses that need to be restored and modernised. It is hoped that these will become more than mere summer holiday homes in the mountains, but rather homes where people will live and contribute something to their adopted community.

In 2014-15 there was a further incentive for those thinking of moving to San Lorenzo: residents did not have to pay the tax known as TASI (*Tassa sui Servizi Indivisibili*), a tax that covers local expenditure on services such as road maintenance, street lighting and public safety. Thereafter, those living

San Lorenzo Belizzi is a work in progress with efforts to revitalize the town on-going.

The summer tranquility of *Le Gole di Raganello* at Cività's Devil's Bridge.

The *loricato* pine's trunk and branches appear dead but, despite appearances, it is thriving.

in the *centro storico* who opted to renovate their homes wouldn't have to pay the tax for a total of five years. The reason that little San Lorenzo can afford this is that, through its town council, the community invested in generating solar energy on land it bought near Corigliano Calabro.

Thus San Lorenzo has, and will continue to have, the ambience of a work in progress; for such a small and remote place there is a little more scaffolding in evidence than you might expect, a few more cement-mixers churning out their fluent bounty, the intermittent pulsation of some distant drill as men and women go about the business of regeneration.

San Lorenzo and the Arbëreshë town of Civita have a more or less direct link … unfortunately however, it is not a road but the river Raganello. By river it would be less than five miles, by road nearly five times that. Both towns have, as a natural attraction, *Le Gole di Raganello*, steep-sided canyons that funnel the fast-moving water on its way to the sea near Roseto.

The river Raganello rises in Basilicata and, as it forces it way down through narrow, self-made gorges, it creates rapid torrents that those who like getting wet seem to enjoy exploring, particularly at the San Lorenzo end. At Civita the river is, arguably, more controlled and certainly more accessible for those whose passion in life is *not* to bounce about in foaming pools of water. People like me who just want to look.

From the town there is a steep, serpentine path that goes the whole way down, accessible on foot as long as you remember that what goes down must come up. There are also excursions down into the *la gola* in Jeep-like vehicles when the weather conditions are suitable and there are enough people who want to share the costs. The reward is a unique and breathtaking experience, for my money every bit as spectacular as the Grand Canyon in Arizona, simply because you can almost touch the towering walls of rock, hear the effervescent waters and feel the spray. It is a mystery to me how it is that the Raganello experience at Civita is not better known and appreciated, even within Italy.

For Calabria, the Pollino mountains, and their modern incarnation as the Pollino National Park, are the region's natural northern border. To travel coast to coast from Scalea to Amendolara with occasional sorties into the heart of the mountains is, these days, more problematic for those married to the car. Earlier travellers had no option but to take the direct route across, through and over the mountains with or on shank's pony … and their reward was to experience the area's remote communities, the raw and natural beauty of such places and the abundant and unique flora and fauna.

With respect to the latter, the golden eagle, the wolf, the boar and the livid red *poenia peregrina* have always alluded me but I have encountered many a hare bounding across fields, the grazing grey-white *podolica* cow and the strange, dead-looking, *loricato* pine.

La Sila

Many early travellers experienced the Pollino out of necessity; however, when it came to the Sila, they had a choice and so it was not a part of Calabria that many explored. The Sila mountains had no connection with their preoccupation with Magna Græcia and it was a formidable barrier between east and west, between Crotone and Cosenza. And, whatever the prevailing political climate, there was another reason for not entering this inhospitable terrain, the perceived threat from brigands.

Henry Swinburne (1780), Arthur Strutt (1841) and Emily Lowe (1858) all skirted the western perimeter. Swinburne, journeying between Nicastro and Cosenza in February, was impressed with what he saw:

"The highest parts of this wild mountainous country has a slight covering of snow, which grows thicker towards the north-east, where the mountains

Gracefully the new Sila-Mare road to and from Longobucco meanders through the valley of the river Trionto. High on the hill to the left is the line of the of the old serpentine road is just visibile as it clings to the edge of the escarpment.

rise that are called La Sila, known in antiquity by the name of the Brutian forest. This forest covers a surface of two hundred miles in circumference: from hence Hiero, King of Syracuse, and after him, the Romans drew their masts for shipping."

Lowe, on the other hand, reflected not on their bounty but on their reputation:

"The mountains above [Páola] seem exactly formed for the use made of them—a favourite retreat of robbers."

But it was not until Norman Douglas (1911) that any British traveller wrote about the heart of these mountains.

Douglas, travelling from the north, traversed all three areas of the Sila: *La Sila Greca*, that runs east of the spine towards the Ionian Sea and takes its 'Greekness' from the concentration of Arbëreshë towns that centre on San Demetrio Corone; *La Sila Grande* (the Great Sila) which straddles the central land-mass of the east-west route between San Giovanni in Fiore and Cosenza; and *La Sila Piccola* the most southerly area that almost touches Catanzaro.

These are Douglas' brief impressions of each:

La Sila Greca: "The streamlet Trionto, my companion to Longobucco, glides along between stretches of flowery meadow-land—fit emblem of placid rural contentment. But soon this lyric mood is spent. It enters a winding gorge that shuts out the sunlight and the landscape abruptly assumes an epic note; the water tumbles wildly downward, hemmed in by mountains whose slopes are shrouded in dusky pines wherever a particle of soil affords them foothold. The scenery in this valley is as romantic as any in the Sila. Affluents descend on either side, while the swollen rivulet writhes and screeches in its narrow bed, churning the boulders with hideous din."

La Sila Grande: "This is the typical landscape ... There is not a human habitation in sight; forests all around, with views down many-folded vales into the sea and towards the distant and fairy-like Apennines, a serrated edge, whose limestone precipices gleam like crystals of amethyst between the blue sky and the dusky woodlands of the foreground."

La Sila Piccola: "By keeping to the left of [the river] Circilla, I might have skirted the forest of Gariglione. This tract lies at about four and a half hours' distance from San Giovanni; I found it, some years ago, to be a region of real "Urwald" or primary jungle; there was nothing like it, to my knowledge, on this side of the Alps, nor yet in the Alps themselves; nothing of the kind nearer than Russia."

Douglas, the only traveller to explore *La Sila Greca,* approached Longobucco from the north-west from the semi-circle of Arbëreshë towns north of Acri. On the other hand, on my first visit to the town I approached it from the other side, from the Ionian coast. I picked up the valley of the Trionto just beyond Cropalati. It was 5 July 2014.

The date is important for, unknown to me at the time, earlier that same week the area had been celebrating the inauguration of a major road construction ... and I missed the turning; the road might have been finished but the road-signs directing the uninitiated to it were still not in place. That said, as compensation *I* had the best views.

Mention of driving to Longobucco had always generated the same response—raised eyebrows of disbelief—as if anyone who wanted to go there without good reason was clearly bonkers. The combination of the mountainous terrain and endless hairpin bends were enough to put off even the most adventurous Calabrian.

But all that changed, at least from the seaward side, when the new road, known as the *Sila-Mare*, opened running alongside and above the Trionto, a road, much of it on concrete stilts, following the more gentle wanderings of the river south of Cropalati and Longobucco. I could see the road down in the valley as I tried to concentrate on negotiating the serpentine and

Somewhere down in among the roofs of Lungobucco lies the site of the erstwhile Hotel Vittoria where Norman Douglas was so warmly welcomed.

precipitous edge of the same steep valley until, at Longobucco itself, both roads finally met. I couldn't believe I had added at least twenty minutes onto my journey by missing that turning.

Not long afterwards on a flight to Rome I found myself sitting next to a young woman from South America who now worked in Longobucco but lived in Rome. I told her how I had 'by-passed' the new-road experience and went on to extol its graceful meanderings and how impressive it looked from above. She, on the other hand, didn't seem overly impressed with this new addition to her local landscape and I momentarily assumed that, unlike me, she saw it as some sort of blot on the landscape. No, that wasn't the case, it was the time it took to construct that she was taking issue with ... thirty years, she said.

Bearing in mind what I knew to have occurred with the A3 *autostrada,* this was not beyond the realms of possibility but it did seem rather excessive for a relatively short distance, about five miles. Later, therefore, I tried to find out for myself and discovered that, even though it might have felt like thirty years, it was actually nearer twenty. The aim—in an unspecified timescale of course—is for it to continue northwards to the sea which will finally make its name, *Sila-Mare,* a reality. Sometimes, in my idle moments, I wonder which will be finished first ... the A3 *autostrade,* the *Sila-Mare* or this book?

When Douglas arrived in Longobucco it was at the end of a momentous walk from Acri via a little-known track ... as the crow flies fourteen miles across mountainous terrain.

These days this 'little know track' from Acri to Lungobucco appears to be a little known road. A look at the map shows three main roads emanating from Acri, one each to San Demetrio Corone, to Bisignano (the birthplace of Charles Atlas) and to Lungobucco. Nowhere in Acri could I find a sign indicating the way to Lungobucco and it was with great difficulty that I eventually found the right road. At least when I finally got to Lungobucco, almost thirty miles later, I was certainly in better shape than Douglas:

"Soon enough, be sure, I was enquiring as to supper. But the manageress [of the Hotel Vittorio] met my suggestions about eatables with a look of blank astonishment.

"Was there nothing in the house, then? No cheese, or meat, or maccheroni, or eggs—no wine to drink?

""Nothing!" she replied. "Why should you eat things at this hour? You must find them yourself, if you really want them. I might perhaps procure you some bread."

"Undaunted, I went forth and threw myself upon the mercy of a citizen of promising exterior, who listened attentively to my case. Though far too polite to contradict, I could see that nothing in the world would induce him to credit the tale of my walking from San Demetrio that day—it was tacitly relegated to the regions of fable … He became convinced, however, that for some reason or other I was hungry, and thereupon good-naturedly conducted me to various places where wine and other necessities of life were procured.

"The landlady watched me devouring this fare, more astonished than ever—indeed, astonishment seemed to be her chronic condition so long as I was under her roof. But the promised bread was not forthcoming, for the simple reason that there was none in the house. She had said that she could procure it for me, not that she possessed it; now, since I had given no orders to that effect, she had not troubled about it."

On my first visit to the town, I too was tired and hungry and in need of something to eat and, like Douglas, could find no obvious eatery in the town centre. I too collared several citizens 'of promising exterior' but much scratching of their collective heads later was no nearer sating my appetite. As a last resort I entered a shop and finally found someone who had not only eaten out before but who also remembered where it was he'd been. I was given directions to a not-too-far-out-of-town restaurant … conveniently situated, it appeared, right on the very road I was taking on my way cross-country to San Giovanni in Fiore. I was assured I couldn't miss it.

But miss it I did and it was another two hours before I arrived home and tucked into a hastily heated bowl of soup.

On the assumption that it did actually exist, I put the restaurant's apparent 'non-existence' down to one of two quirks of Calabrian direction-giving that I had fallen foul of many times previously.

On more times that I care to remember I have been given directions from where the direction-giver either lives or most often approaches the said goal. The fact that I might happen to want directions from where I am actually standing is not always be taken into consideration. This happens more often with directions given on the telephone … I want directions from where I am, but all too often have been given directions from where the other person is.

The other lapse in directional communication in Calabria occurs when people give directions to the general area of the restaurant or shop on the assumption that the last turning is so obvious that you can't miss it. *They* probably know it well enough, so well in fact that they don't realise that that last turning, that last change in direction, in all probability has no accompanying sign to help the uninitiated.

Thus, in trying to help me find this particular restaurant, Longobucco-man may have meant well but was either mentally directing me there from his home or some other place or making too many assumptions. So naturally, as I was tucking into my bowl of soup, I was also checking out TripAdvisor for places to eat in Longobucco. There is indeed a restaurant close to the road out of town but, sadly, to get there I would have had to make at least two additional turns that were not part of the directions I was given ... and there had been no roadside clues to help me.

I have mentioned these quirks to a number of Calabrians, all of whom recognise them as idiosyncrasies they have either experienced or, more likely, been party to themselves.

Douglas too headed for San Giovanni in Fiore, the capital of *La Sila Grande* and the unofficial capital of the Sila itself and, in my opinion, a place that does not live up to its enchanting name, literally San Giovanni in flower or blossoming. Douglas painted a more extreme picture and described its streets as 'populous and dirty' and even called it the 'Siberia of Calabria'.

That said, he enjoyed his walk which for him was fairly routine:

"It is an easy march of eight hours or less, through pleasing scenery and by a good track, from Longobucco to San Giovanni in Fiore ... The path leaves Longobucco at the rear of the town and, climbing upward, enters a valley which it follows to its head. The peasants have cultivated patches of ground along the stream; the slopes are covered, first with chestnuts and then with hoary firs—a rare growth, in these parts—from whose branches hangs the golden bough of the mistletoe ... At the summit the vegetation changes once more, and you find yourself among magnificent stretches of pines that continue as far as the governmental domain of Galoppano, a forestal station, two hours' walk from Longobucco."

Somewhere on that two-hour trek from Longobucco to Galoppano the *Sila Greco* became the *Sila Grande* ... perhaps what distinguishes one from the other is the *pino della Sila*, the familiar and increasingly dominant tall pine trees that are particular to the *Sila Grande* and described by Douglas:

"... it is found over this whole country, and grows to a height of forty metres with a silvery-grey trunk, exhaling a delicious aromatic fragrance."

His route took him close to Savelli and he picked up what he called the 'driving road' connecting Savelli with San Giovanni, a road that twists and turns round the valleys of the Neto and Lese rivers. It is also a road that, depending on the season, yields some of the bounty that characterises this part of the Sila. We discovered it by accident when we revisited San Giovanni just to check whether there was anything we had missed on earlier visits and then took to the hills north from the town. It was late October.

We were exploring the road that takes in the three Arbëreshë towns in the Province of Crotone—Pallagorio, Carfizzi and San Nicola dell'Alto—dotted round the hills north of the valley of the Neto, a road that would bring us back to the Ionian Sea near Stróngoli. Savelli was therefore no more than one of the towns we would pass through to complete the large circular *giro* that would eventually bring us back to Santa Severina.

As our route climbed and twisted towards Savelli, we became increasingly aware of the number of cars that had pulled onto the side of the road; experience told us that this wasn't people being caught short but rather that there was something worth collecting in among the trees. It did not initially register that it was the trees themselves that were casting their bounty to the ground ... they were chestnut trees, *la castagna*, and it was the chestnut harvesting season.

The poster for the 31st incarnation of Savelli's 2014 *Sacra della Castagna* which was displayed in many local towns and featured a variation on the unique Calabrian approach to giving directions for it is not clear where the *Sagra* is to be held. The only mention of Savelli is in the small logos on the top left. The poster for the *Sagra della Salsiccia e della Patata Silana* (sausage and local potato) at Cutura in the *Sila Piccola* was more specific.

Before long, we too were parked up at the roadside by a small copse and ferreting around on the ground for the chestnuts that others had missed; we always carry a couple of bags in the car for such emergencies.

By the time we got to Savelli it was time for a coffee and it was then that we realised that the chestnut was a big thing locally for there were posters everywhere advertising the following weekend's *Sagra della Castagna*.

A *sagra* is an Italian excuse for a party, it is a festival generally centred on some abundant local food; animal or vegetable: *Sacra del Pollo* (chicken), *Sagra del Cinghiale* (wild boar), *Sagra del Maiale* (pork), *Sagra del Coniglio* (rabbit), *Sagra della Pecora* (sheep), *Sagra della Lepre* (hare), *Sagra della Mucca Podolica* (podolica cow), *Sagra della Trippa* (tripe), *Sagra della Vino* (wine), *Sagra del Funghi Porchini* (mushrooms), *Sagra del Fagiolo* (bean), *Sagra del Ciliegia* (cherry), *Sagra della Polenta* (polenta) ... you name it, there will almost certainly be a *sagra* for it.

Tongue firmly in cheek, I put that theory to the test and searched on the internet to see if there was a *sagra* for *Pasta al Forno*, a Sunday lunchtime favourite for many Calabrian families. Indeed there was.

A Calabrian once suggested to me that I should write a book about all the local Calabrian *sagre* and whilst the idea has merit, it would take at least five years to visit each *sagra*, by which time I would be both exhausted and dreadfully overweight.

Santa Severina has its *Sagra del Arancia,* the Festival of the Orange, but it is a relatively recent and low-key affair and nothing like some of the larger, two-day events in other communities.

Today the *SS107* dissects *La Sila Grande* with two of its most visited towns, San Giovanni in Fiore and Camigliatello Silana, on either side of the road, one at the Crotone end, the other at the Cosenza end.

La Sila Grande is not only dominated by its mountains, and in particular the highest peak, *Monte Botte Donato,* south of Camigliatello, but it is geographically defined by three large lakes: *Il Lago Cecita*, north and east of Camigliatello; *Il Lago Arvo*, on the south-west extremity; and *Il Lago Ampollino* which separates *La Sila Grande* from *La Sila Piccola*. Indeed parts of the latter are in the three different Calabrian provinces: Cosenza, Catanzaro and Crotone. (There is another much smaller lake on the western edge of the *La Sila Piccola* called *Il Lago Passante*)

All are artificial lakes and their construction was being mooted when Douglas (1911) was abroad in the Sila:

"A great project is afoot. As I understand it, a reservoir is being created by damming up the valley of the Ampollina [sic]; the artificial lake thus formed will be enlarged by the additional waters of the Arvo, which are to be led into it by means of a tunnel, about three miles long, passing underneath Monte Nero. The basin, they tell me, will be some ten kilometres in length; the work will cost forty million francs, and will be completed in a couple of years; it will supply the Ionian lowlands with pure water and with power for electric and other industries."

The project was clearly on the drawing board in 1911 but work on Ampollino didn't begin until 1916 and wasn't completed until 1926; work on Arvo began the next year and was completed in 1931 and Cecita became a post-war project that came to fruition in 1951.

Despite their convenient positions either side of the *SS107*, neither San Giovanni in Fiore nor Camigliatello Silana does it for me.

At the risk of yet again upsetting friends from San Giovanni, apart from the small *centro storico*, I find it a sprawling, hotch-potch of a place. And I am not alone; other visitors have found the same and often they were not lucky enough to actually find the best part, the historical centre. At least three small American groups I met independently called their visit there a waste of a day.

Perhaps one of the problems has been this blind spot—to which I have already oft referred—of not providing the visitor with accurate and complete signage. People get frustrated when they think they are heading to their goal (let's say they are following signs to the *centro storico* or to a designated car-

A snowbound junction in the Sila mountains near Camigliatello. Few realise that the Camigliatello area is one of several centres in the Sila with chair lifts and other facilities for those with a passion for sliding in the snow.

park) and then find themselves at a junction with several options and no indication as to which road they should take and with nobody around to ask. Make the right choice and you can revel in whatever the town has to offer; make the wrong choice and you can go round in ever-decreasing circles or, worse still, end up in a rabbit-warren of narrow side streets with no obvious means of escape.

This latter scenario has happened to us several times and most commonly after asking a senior citizen the way and having been given, presumably, accurate directions … but almost certainly by foot which never allows for one-way streets. I sometimes wonder if communities position their oldest residents at every junction just for the purpose of confusing visitors. And while, for me, such inconvenience is no more than a local idiosyncrasy, for others less tolerant of such idiosyncrasies, it can be the last straw. The frustrating thing is that it is unnecessary.

You might conclude that I am overstating this but I am not. It still happens to me frequently though, being almost a native, I am getting better at second-guessing the reasoning of whoever it was who decided that the last few indicators were not required.

With regard to San Giovanni, it was only when I was given a guided tour of the *centro storico* by a friend whose wife was born there, that I saw another side to it. The irony of this was that, on my previous two visits to the town, I had been unable to find the *centro storico*.

While many see San Giovanni in Fiore as the capital of the Sila, and also *La Sila Grande*, I suspect that Camigliatello Silana, one of the Sila's highest towns, may have something to say about that.

Camigliatello is more the sort of place that locals gravitate to for a day out, particularly on a Sunday when there is a popular open-air, local-produce market on the northern outskirts of the town. Camigliatello certainly knows how to woo tourists but all we found was a main street with lots of shops displaying the usual touristy knick-knacks and an abundance of eateries offering indifferent fare at inflated prices with slovenly service as an optional extra. Having already waited twenty minutes to be served at one such establishment, we left and went to another, only to find ourselves in exactly the same situation and when we saw what others were tucking in to, decided to beat a hasty retreat and drive home.

Covered in snow it is certainly picturesque and the surrounding countryside soon transforms itself into a ski resort with Camigliatello at its centre. But for my money it is Camigliatello's location that is the most interesting thing about the town … in fact if you follow signs to Camigliatello and at the last moment turn away from the town you're sure to end up in some of the most glorious parts of *La Sila Grande*.

In recent years there has been a blossoming of interest in the ecology of the area and a resulting increase in the number of nature trails and small reserves such as the *Riserva Naturale i Giganti della Sila* and the *Riserva Statale Golia Corvo*.

The former lies south of Camigliatello in the shadow of Monte Botte Donato and gets its name from its abundant, and gigantic, pine trees that can be up to forty-five metres tall. The latter is north-east of the town, at the far end of *Il Lago Cecità* and gets its name from the ravens which share the reserve with pine martens, wild cats, badgers, polecats and a plethora of school parties.

Riserva Statale Golia Corvo also lies near the slopes of Monte Pettinascura from where you can gaze down upon the valleys of the rivers Lese and Neto as they rush to their union west of Santa Severina.

In between these two reserves, on the outskirts of Camigliatello itself, is a large estate, one of the erstwhile demesnes of the Barracca family and, as I have already mentioned, now the site of the park known as 'Old Calabria'

Cutting down a huge tree in the Sila the hard way ... with axes. No wonder someone decided to have a break and relax inside the front notch or undercut. Some of the pines in the Sila can have a diameter of more than two metres, a girth of nearly eight metres.

inspired by and in honour of Norman Douglas' book of the same name.

As I've noted elsewhere, sometimes it is unclear from Douglas' *Old Calabria* where exactly he visited as there are often references to at least two previous journeys in Calabria:

"I remember, some years ago, that during the last week of August a lump of snow, which a goat-boy produced as his contribution to our luncheon, did not melt in the bright sunshine on the summit of Monte Nero."

Nevertheless, as far as I am aware, Douglas did not venture west of San Giovanni in Fiore so he apparently never visited the part of the Sila where his name is remembered most. That said, on his trek down from Longobucco to San Giovanni he passed round *Monte Pettinascura* and at that point was not far from what is now *Parco Old Calabria*. He does refer to the view from *Monte Pettinascura* but, arguably, this is a second-hand observation:

"... and, with the help of a little imagination here and there, its [the river Neto's] whole course can be traced from eminences like that of Pettinascura."

Before finally leaving San Giovanni in Fiore to head south into *La Sila Piccola*, Douglas took one last parting shot at a town he clearly loved to hate and which, not surprisingly, does not appear to revere his name in the same way as others:

"Were I sultan of San Giovanni, I would certainly begin by a general bombardment. Little in the town is worth preserving from a cataclysm save the women, and perhaps the old convent on the summit of the hill where the French lodged during their brigand-wars ..."

My parting shot regarding San Giovanni will be from the pen of Leslie Gardiner (1966) who observed:

"San Giovanni in Fiore [is] a large, sleepy village which has nothing attractive about it except its name ..."

Heading south, Douglas passed through the area where now lies lake Ampollino, along the southern shores of which *La Sila Grande* becomes *La Sila Piccola*.

At the core of the *La Sila Piccola* is the ancient forest of Gariglione, its peak, the mountain of the same name; it is this part of the Sila we can see from the ramparts of Santa Severina's Norman castle. In January and February the accumulation of snow (or lack thereof) is an indication of how well the local skiing season is going. Rightly so, people generally equate the Calabrian climate with the intense summer heat but in winter it is a different story. Sometimes the highest point of the main highway across the mountains, the *SS107*, is closed to traffic.

It is also to *La Sila Piccola* that many people from the provinces of Crotone and Catanzaro flock in the summer to escape the heat—the summer temperature in the Sila is generally ten degrees less than nearer the coast—and it is here that there are a number of 'holiday villages' for those who like it warm, rather than hot.

Norman Douglas was one of the last travellers to experience the valley of the river Ampollino before construction work began in 1916 on damming the head of the valley and in his mind's eye he looked forward to what he gleaned was to be a brave new world of elaborate and ambitious plans to entice visitors to the area:

"The lake is to revolutionise the Sila; to convert these wildernesses into a fashionable watering-place. Enthusiasts already see towns growing upon its shores—there are visions of gorgeous hotels and flocks of summer visitors in elegant toilettes, villa-residences, funicular railways up all the mountains, sailing regattas, and motor-boat services. In the place of the desert there will arise a "Lucerna di Calabria.""

Douglas was not convinced:

"A Calabrian Lucerne. H'm. ..."

But he was not the first to make the Swiss connection for, in 1905, American Italphile, Mary Berenson, said something not dissimilar:

"... we have come to the most beautiful scenery, like the best of Switzerland."

Up to a point Douglas' scepticism was justified. From the beginning, there

La Piccola Sila mountains as seen from Santa Severina; the distant peak to the left of centre is Monte Gariglione; behind the cloud on the right lies the town of Cotronei.

have been attempts to woo visitors and, particularly around lake Ampollino, lakeside holiday villas and villages did spring up, and even some hotels, but in recent years it has all started to become something of an anachronism.

I recall friends showing us round one of the clusters of chalet-style houses—basically summer retreats—near Trepidò, most of which looked as if they had seen better times. Their own property was indeed looking very sorry for itself; we eventually gained access having negotiated metre-high grass and a reluctant keyhole. Being fond of our creature comforts, we knew that, even for a few days in the summer, this would not have been an inspiring alternative to the more intense heat nearer the coast. I suspected too that our friends' young daughter was of like mind.

In this particular area they knew of only one house where the owners stayed put all the year round.

We moved onwards and upwards to the small hillside community of *Villaggio Baffa*—one of several such communities on the southern shores of lake Ampollino—where our friends spent most of the time pointing out the many imposing houses that were now for sale.

On the same guided tour we walked along a secluded woodland track where, despite the season, the light struggled to penetrate the canopy of trees. The track came to an abrupt end at the side of a long, broad clearing, stripped of vegetation but serving no apparent purpose other than, on one side, as the site of an elaborate go-kart track. There then followed a guessing game as to the reason why anyone might have created such a huge empty space in these mountains?

The solution, eventually revealed, was ingenious though probably not very practical. Somebody thought that what the Sila really needed to attract wealthy tourists was its own airstrip and this was it, *L'Aviosuperficie delle Montagne del Meridion*e, the airstrip in the southern mountains or, as it's known by aviators, *L'Aviosuperficie Franca*.

Needless to say, since its inauguration in 2002 it has not been the busiest airstrip in Italy, nevertheless private planes come and go, often in flurries, and park up by the go-kart track.

The adjacent *Villaggio di Palumbo*, a purpose-built holiday-home village which we first visited in 2009, is beginning to feel run down as is the nearby lakeside hamlet of Trepidò. Younger families generally want to be by the sea; older families may prefer the cooler summer ambience of the mountains but as they get older, the upkeep of such properties, occupied for perhaps only eight weeks a year, becomes more arduous. It soon becomes easier to stay at home, close the shutters and tolerate the heat.

The story is much the same in other parts of the Sila. On the shores of lake Arvo at Lorica we met a couple from England who had bought a villa there only to find that, for all but a few months in the summer, the area was a virtual wasteland—their words, not mine—and, in the depths of winter, often inaccessible to all but vehicles equipped with snow-chains. And now their dream lakeside villa is almost impossible to sell without incurring a massive loss.

While the holiday-village dreams of the Sila in general and *La Sila Piccola* in particular are looking a little tarnished these days, I accidentally discovered

The many faces of the original Villaggio Mancuso, all but Bar Rotonda abandoned and at the mercy of the elements.

that it all started here with unbridled enthusiasm back in the 1920s and not long after Douglas was pooh-poohing the very idea of a 'Calabrian Lucerne'.

Having dropped Kay off at Lamezia Terme Airport, I decided to stop overnight at one of my favourite towns, Tiriolo, and to return to Santa Severina the following day by a more circuitous route that would take me along the serpentine western perimeter of *La Sila Piccola*. The northern, eastern and southern parts of the *La Sila Piccola* were familiar territory, my journey from Tiriolo up to Lake Ampollino and round to Trepidò would complete the circle, fill in the blanks and I would also have the opportunity to visit places with which I already felt some tenuous affinity …

Gimigliano, the town from which Mark Rotella's family emigrated to America and about which he wrote with such emotion, authority and humour in *Stolen Figs*.

Fossato Serralto, the small hilltop town from which the Cubello family emigrated in the 1960s, a family I caught up with in the Bronx (New York) in 2012 when I visited America to research *Thank You Uncle Sam*.

Taverna, Douglas's first overnight stop after leaving San Giovanni and where he fared not much better … 'Taverna belies its name. The only tavern discoverable was a composite hovel, half wine-shop, half hen-house, whose proprietor … stoutly refused to produce anything eatable'.

And finally, as lunchtime beckoned, the highlight when I found myself driving through the curious, eclectic mix of old and new that represents the past and present of the Sila's first holiday village. Inaugurated in the late 1920s, *Il Villaggio Mancuso* was created to service the summertime needs of the good folks of Catanzaro who sought—and could afford—a cooler life.

It was like stepping back in time. On one side of the road only there were old abandoned wooden buildings, many of which were clearly struggling to remain upright, their weather-worn façades jaded and faded, just crying out for a coat of paint … for somebody who cared. And in the middle of it all there was the eccentric, circular, three-storey edifice of the Bar La Rotonda; every bit as quaint inside as it was out.

The original circular bar, with minimalist tables and seating, has a very low ceiling and in one corner (if you can have a corner in a circular space) there is the correspondingly low doorway to the bathroom on which is pinned a yellow notice.

"The following have been in this bathroom—which dates back to 1928—though we know not what they did there: Benito Mussolini, Sofia Loren and Amedeo Nazzari. This is why it has never been renovated."

I'm assuming the first two of these luminaries need no introduction; the third, Amedeo Nazzari, was the Italian Errol Flynn, a prolific and flamboyant Sardinian actor, before and after the war, and famous for, among other things, his romanticised portrayal of the Calabrian 'brigand' Musolino in the 1950 film, *Il Brigante Musolino*.

I had a superb home-made pasta lunch and a glass of red wine in Bar La Rotonda; it cost just 7€. I also used the bathroom (just to get my name on the list) before wandering round what was left of a unique village that time almost forgot. For a few moments I stood in the centre of the road with, on one side the stoical remnants of the original Sila holiday village, and on the other its modern counterpart. One like a bizarre film set, the other featureless, but stable.

In 1957 Eric Whelpton and his wife passed along this same road but, as the 'season' had not yet begun (officially it used to begin on 15 June), *Il Villaggio Mancuso* was completely deserted. Nevertheless they were given an insight into life at Mancuso in its heyday:

"... we stopped for a moment to inspect the gaily painted chalets of different sizes which are let out to entire families or individual guests who can either live *en pension* or feed *à la carte* at the central restaurant where all the meals are served.

"Since there are few distractions up in the Sila, a theatre has been built as well as a bathing pool and a number of tennis courts.

"The village seemed to me just the place for a restful holiday, for the chalets are widely spaced, the air is really invigorating, and the walks through the woods are enchanting."

Eric Whelpton's description had all the hallmarks of someone who had just swallowed the official guide to the village. The Whelptons were experiencing Mancuso in the post-war era and what nobody told them was that some of the grander buildings had been requisitioned as homes for Italian officers during the war years when the area became a centre for military exercises. Later it took on a similar role when Mancuso was under the control of American forces and officers were once again billeted here.

On the south-east edge of *La Sila Piccola* there is the small town of Sersale, a town that none of the travellers who came to Calabria ever visited. Sersale clings to the foothills of the Sila and overlooks the Ionian Sea; indeed it is probably the Sila town closest to any sea; and the vistas are stunning.

And it was here that a chance encounter set me off on the trail that eventually resulted in the book *Thank You Uncle Sam*.

We knew that the area around Sersale was known for its *cascate*, its waterfalls, and these were the goal when we arrived in the town on the last day in March. A mid-morning cup of coffee beckoned followed by a quick walk round the town before setting off into its hinterland in search of *cascate*.

In a small park near where we had our coffee fix, there sat a group of elderly citizens vociferously putting the world to rights. They greeted us with that look that, in a single glance, was really asking, in a friendly way of course, who we were, where we were from and what we doing in Sersale. So we obliged and soon they had all the answers which, as is the way of things, led to more questions.

Out of the blue, one man, older and taller than the others but with a brightness in his eye that belied his years, suddenly started to speak to us in English with a distinct American twang. Originally from Sersale, Nicola had lived most of his life in Indiana and Indianapolis in particular and was surprised to know that we had both been there, and in my case twice. Despite having children and grandchildren in America, Nicola had decided to return to his roots and spend his last years in the town he grew up in. He still visited family in America from time to time and they also came to Sersale but home for Nicola was once again Sersale and he was clearly content to be sitting in this small park sharing life's memories with his boyhood friends.

Nicola went on to tell me about the others who had left Sersale over the years to settle in America and about the many Calabrians from other parts of the region he had met in and around Indianapolis. Until that moment I had been pretty much in the dark about the extent of Calabrian emigration and that brief encounter in Sersale was one of the triggers that eventually took me to the United States to research *Thank You Uncle Sam*. And though I didn't travel to Indiana, the antecedents of one of the families I met elsewhere first settled there when they came to the States in the early 1900s.

Nicola pointed us in the right direction out of town for the *cascate* and also recommended an out-of-the-way *agriturismo* for lunch … he'd not been there himself but knew that people spoke highly of it.

Having lived in America, eating out was not as much a mystery to Nicola as it would have been for some of his Calabrian contemporaries. And, not surprisingly, his directions were pretty accurate; perhaps his years in America had finally purged him of the Calabrian way of doing things.

Having spend a couple of hours exploring the wonderful hinterland of Sersale and the many *cascate* lurking in the deep, river-cut fissures cutting through the foothills of *La Sila Piccola*, we headed for the *Agriturismo Carrozzino* (the name usually refers to a two-wheeled, horse-drawn buggy or trap) and that excellent lunch with which Nicola had whetted our appetite.

We knew it was quite a way out of town in an isolated location near to Zagarise but our route was well signposted and we soon found it.

It was only then that we realised that the one thing that Nicola did not know about the *Agriturismo Carrozzino* was which day of the week it closed.

Crestfallen, we were just about to head back to Sersale when a woman appeared who, when she saw the disappointed look on our faces and despite the fact that it was her day off, insisted on preparing lunch for us. She suggested it would be something basic but such a concept is not part of the Calabrian cook's psyche and so, not surprisingly, we were treated to the sort of Calabrian generosity and hospitality we'd come to expect.

(On a more recent return visit to Sersale we learnt that Nicola passed away in 2014; he had led a rich life both in Sersale and Indiana and had enjoyed his last years with his friends in his home town on the very edge of *La Sila Piccola* overlooking the Ionian Sea.)

The river Crócchio near Sersale tumbles down from the heart of *La Sila Piccola*. To the south of the town, on the river Fegato, is the *Canyon delle Valli Cupe*, a high, narrow, breathtaking gorge.

That day we also visited the *Il Canyon delle Valli Cupe*, also on the outskirts of Sersale though it was not an easy place to get to; it was signposted well but the narrow, sand-covered and pot-holed road itself made us feel we'd taken a wrong turn somewhere. Nevertheless we persevered and finally parked up next to the access point and the interpretation boards which indicated that it was a 1.3 kilometre walk with difficulty level 'T'; on the other hand there was no indication as to what was implied by level of difficulty 'T'. Did it stand for *terribile* or *tranquillo*, *tremendo* or *tortuoso*? Or none of the above?

We started to descend the well-signposted, wooded track until, that was, Kay decided that, bearing in mind we would have to climb back up, her knees could not cope any more. We were at a bend in the track where there was a bench-seat so I was delegated to continue downwards on behalf of us both while she waited and listened to the silence.

I finally reached the bed of the slow-running river, crossed it and followed the signs to the canyon itself and, just before I entered the narrow gorge, acknowledged the only others—three young men—who had made it down that morning. These three had come prepared and were clearly there for the day as they'd already lit a small fire and were making themselves a hot drink. Five minutes later I passed them again on my way back from the canyon and this time we exchanged a few more pleasantries. They asked me if I was alone and when I told them that Kay was having a break further back up the hill, they looked horrified. They explained that it was not a good idea to travel alone in these woods because of the possibility of running into a wild boar, *il cinghiale*. I thanked them for their concern and, as I started my ascent, tried to phone Kay but there was no signal ... she would just have to tough it out if a wild boar turned up.

Reunited with Kay we both wondered whether the 'wild boar' scare was just one of those stories that locals liked to intimidate visitors with as we were pretty sure there hadn't been any 'Beware of the wild boar' signs anywhere in the woods themselves or by the interpretation boards by the road. We checked and there weren't.

I thought back to a similar story when we bumped into a few lads by the river Neto where we were on the look-out for a few angular-shaped stones to use as book-ends. They had just emerged unscathed from the dry river bed but warned us that it was infested with snakes. If it was, we never saw a single one. And a similar warning is always voiced during the wild asparagus season but again, to date, we've never seen or heard a single snake.

Are such warnings, I wonder, just a modern version of the 'beware of the brigands' stories that, for well over a century, Calabrians loved to share with travellers passing through but that few ever experienced?

How things have changed since the general advice for travellers was that the mountains of Calabria in general, and the Sila in particular, were the most inhospitable in Europe and best avoided. And what a pity so many of those who came to Calabria consciously steered clear of the Sila. Many glimpsed the Sila from afar as they skirted round Tiriolo and Catanzaro but only Norman Douglas (1911), the Whelptons (1957) and Leslie Gardiner (1966) ever really experienced and revelled in the primordial majesty of these mountains.

The western edge of La Serra, the canopy of trees on the never-ending road from Laureana di Borrello to Mongiano.

La Serra

My friend Antonio was bemoaning his lot. It was September and he had just heard where he would be teaching for the next year. Not having a contract tied to a specific school, each year he was allocated a post at a different school ... and this year he was going to Serra San Bruno, a place to which he could not commute every day from Santa Severina.

But, for Antonio, despite the inconvenience there was a silver lining ... he was going to be teaching in one of the most beautiful parts of Calabria. As if trying to convince himself—and me—that he had actually been rewarded in some way, he waxed lyrical about La Serra, the more so when he realised I'd never been there, though I knew several travellers who had.

In those few moments Antonio convinced me that my life was the poorer for such an omission and that I should rectify the matter forthwith. Sadly, when I did finally get round to it, my on-the-spot guide had moved on to another posting closer to home and in a less attractive area.

I was returning from the Aspromonte through the heart of southern Calabria and on my itinerary were some of the out-of-the-way places that I'd read about but to which few of my Calabrians friends had ever been. Even the capital of the region, San Serra Bruno itself, is not on many people's radar.

It was the day I had to make a diversion around Plasesano to get to Laureana di Borrello because of the landslide that had blocked the road between the two towns (see chapter *Making Connections*).

Leaving Laureano I found the signs to my destination, Mongiano, confusing and had to ask directions before setting off along one of the most remote roads I'd ever been on. More than once I thought about turning back, convinced that somewhere I must have taken a wrong turn. I was travelling across a monotonous plain before plunging into a bosky netherworld, a canopy of tall trees pierced by occasional shafts of strong sunlight. It was close to half and hour since I'd seen another vehicle so I pulled over and walked along the middle of the road, mesmerised by both the random discipline of the trees and the wanton confusion of the light. It was as a journey into the unknown, a secluded place where I might almost have been the first to have discovered it, the first to have revelled in its stunning viridity.

Still wondering whether or not I was on the right road, I stumbled into Mongiana, a sleepy, unimposing place which belied its history. That said, Richard Keppel-Craven (1818) was none too impressed with the town:

"... a collection of wooden huts, among which are a few larger edifices, dignified with the name of houses ; the whole constituting an establishment called La Mongiana ..."

But Mongiana was not about its huts and houses, it was a community of crucial importance throughout the 19th century to the Bourbon regime based in Naples:

" ... [here] the different branches of iron founding are carried on under the auspices of government, for the purposes of furnishing arms and artillery to the Neapolitan army."

Unlike me, he was given the grand tour:

"The officer who presided over it received me in his house, and I passed the remainder of the day in visiting the various departments confided to his superintendence. The population of La Mongiana amounts to about 300 persons, of which the half consists of workmen or agents employed in the foundery."

Craufurd Tait Ramage (1828) had a 'hands-on' look as well:

"I found the iron-foundry of Mongiana to be of considerable size, but foolishly erected a great distance from the mines. It was intended that the foundry should be surrounded by wood, from which charcoal might be procured, as no mineral coal has yet been discovered in the vicinity."

Ramage had walked from Passano near Stilo where the mines were located; the miners whom he met there had advised him against going on to Mongiana without an escort but he ignored their advice and, just as I had,

Nestling in a quiet glade in the shadow of a picturesque bosky backdrop are the ruins of Mongiana's erstwhile industrial lifeblood, its iron foundry.

found himself in a secluded, almost primordial, place:

"Every step presented new beauties, and opened to the eye fresh objects of admiration. There was a wildness in the scenery, and a gloom in the darkly-wooded mountains, that overpowered the mind. All was silent save the sound of some distant waterfall, or the low moaning of the breeze through the aged forest."

Here Ramage had an unexpected encounter with 'a large body of armed men, reclining under the trees'. His first instinct was that finally he had met up with some of Calabria's notorious brigands:

"I cannot say that I did not begin to repent having allowed my admiration of scenery to lead me into this dangerous rencontre [encounter]. I had sufficient time, before I reached them, to recal [sic] to my recollection all the barbarities that the brigands of the mountains are accused of having committed."

He had of course read it all wrong. He had stumbled upon a group of men who worked for the iron foundry at Mongiana and whose job it was to mark the trees to be cut down for charcoal. They invited Ramage to eat and then, over dinner in the woods, chastised him for having 'acted with great foolishness in advancing into this part of Calabria without a guard'.

Today the ruins of the Mongiana foundry are tucked away in a small vale at the bottom of the town where once several streams created sufficient water-wheel power to serve the foundry's mechanical needs.

Today there is also a museum, *Il Museo delle Reali Ferriere Borboniche*, in the town's erstwhile armoury which houses an impressive collection of prints, photographs and artefacts that details the foundry's importance to the Bourbon regime (and southern Italy) from the early 1770s until 1880.

Work started on the conversion in the late 1970s but it was not inaugurated until 2013. Extraordinary that such a project should have taken so long to see the light of day when the foundry itself was up and running in less that a year and remained a working plant for over a century. Not unnaturally I smelt the hand of the mafia but I was wrong for there is little mafia presence in the area … must just have been a mix of some old-fashioned incompetence and indifference, though I am not sure at what level.

Instead of heading straight for my goal, Serra San Bruno, I couldn't resist a detour to seek out another relic of the Bourbon era, a little-known hamlet that few Calabrians have ever visited, Ferdinandea … no prizes for guessing after which Bourbon king it was named.

I ascended via a heavily wooded road that seemed to be twisting and

Why, I wonder, did it take so long to convert this ... into this?

A gun inscribed with its place of origin ... Mongiana and Italy's first steel suspension bridge, constructed in 1832 using Mongiana steel; the bridge spanned the river Gargliano, once the northern border of the Kingdom of the Two Sicilies.

What remains of the façade *(right)* and the massive foundry at Ferdinandea; it was here that the first cannons were made in the Kingdom of the Two Sicilies using iron forged in nearby Mongiana.

turning to nowhere in particular; only the sign pointing up the hill gave me any confidence that this was indeed the way. Finally the beech- and fir-lined road straightened before opening out into a clearing where a gated driveway led to a large palatial residence, or perhaps erstwhile residence, I was not sure which. To my left, the long, low building covered in rampant, destructive greenery, was what I had come to see. This was what was left of the Ferdinandea Foundry which, like at that at Mongiana, had served the Bourbon regime well.

Long and low the foundry may have appeared but that is only the facade, it extends back a long way and drops the equivalent of at least two stories; it is truly a massive structure. In 1839, Italy's first railway, the Kingdom of the Two Sicilies line linking Naples with Portici (near Herculanium) was completed with rails forged at the Ferdinandea foundry.

The gated, large residence was the administrative centre as well as barracks and stables for those whose kept order locally; it was also to where the king himself came when he needed a break from the pressures of monarchy and wanted to indulge in a spot of hunting.

Within two decades of unification all iron-works in the area were closed. In 1875 the Ferdinandea complex passed into the hands of Achille Fazzari, a friend of Garibaldi, but by 1881 all mining activities had ceased.

Ferdinandea is nearer than Mongiana to the site of the Monte Stella mines near Passano, an area also visited by Edwatd Lear (1847) while staying at Stilo. It was at Passano that Ramage too spent time with the local miners, but Lear was on an altogether different mission to Ramage, *he* was a landscape painter and therefore saw things from a different perspective and made no mention of the area's mining communities:

"The gorge between Stilo and Bassano [sic] is excessively grand, but the villages were not much to tempt me to sketch them; the morning's walk, however, was delightful, if only for the opportunity it offered of observing the universally courteous and urbane manners of the peasantry."

Today it is Lear's view of things that reigns in this corner of the Serra. The erstwhile industrial component is long gone; nature continues to reclaim the places that were once an important part of the economy of the Kingdom of the Two Sicilies and Calabria in particular. As I left Ferdinandea and Mongiana behind and once again plunged into tunnels of tall pines and scattered beeches, it was difficult to imagine the sounds and smells of man's daily toil that once held sway in these mountains.

Serra San Bruno is a tidy place set in glorious countryside; I could see why my teaching friend was so fond of it.

Richard Keppel-Craven (1818) on the other hand was less forthcoming:

"The town of La Serra is composed of straggling, irregular houses, almost all constructed of wood, and not rising above one story: they are generally elevated a few feet above the level of the street, and accessible by a flight of wooden steps."

A decade later Ramage was of like mind but at least he offered an explanation and some encouragement:

"Having reached the small village of Serra, I found it to consist principally of wooded houses of the most miserable description. The frequent earthquakes to which they are subject render it the only material to which they can have recourse with any degree of safety. Serra possesses nothing to interest the stranger, and is only worthy of a visit from the picturesque nature of the scenery with which it is surrounded."

Keppel-Craven took a closer at what made the place tick and, not surprisingly given its location, noticed that a disproportionate number of its 4500 inhabitants seemed to be either blacksmiths or carpenters. But with the demise of the blacksmith, and to a lesser extent the carpenter, Serra San Bruno evolved in much the same way as other Calabrian towns have done and these days fulfils the routine needs of the traveller for rations and repose.

I was nonetheless curious about the town for this was the site of one of my favourite tales about the time when the Napoleonic regime was in power (1806–1815) and preoccupied with silencing local, pro-Bourbon brigands. The story also shows the infamous brigand-catcher, General Manhès, in a different light to that broadcast by some of his critics. Douglas (1911) tells the story best:

"I know nothing of its [Serra San Bruno's] history save that it has the reputation of being one of the most bigoted places in Calabria—a fact of which the sagacious General Manhès availed himself when he devised his original and effective plan of chastising the inhabitants for a piece of atrocious conduct on their part. He caused all the local priests to be arrested and imprisoned; the churches were closed, and the town placed under what might be called an interdict. The natives took it quietly at first, but soon the terror of the situation dawned upon them. No religious marriages, no baptisms, no funerals—the comforts of heaven refused to living and dead alike. The strain grew intolerable and, in a panic of remorse, the populace hunted down their own brigand-relations and handed them over to Manhès, who duly executed them, one and all. Then the interdict was taken off and the priests set at liberty; and a certain writer tells us that the people were so charmed with the General's humane and businesslike methods that they forthwith christened him "Saint Manhès," a name which, he avers, has clung to him ever since."

This was the same General Manhès who showed such cunning when dealing with Don Alfonso Barracco, the wealthy Sila landowner who was turning a blind eye to the activities of the brigands in his sphere of influence.

The 'certain writer' referred to by Douglas was David Hilton who penned a two-volume book on brigandage, published in 1864, in which he maintained that through Manhès' actions 'Serra was thoroughly cured of the brigandage disease'.

Although the Serra and Serra San Bruno are in the province of Vibo Valéntia, the gateway for many to this area is Stilo, a large town nestling in the shadow of Monte Consolino in the Serra's south eastern extremity and in Reggio Calabria. Indeed three of Calabria's five provinces, Catanzaro, Vibo Valéntia and Reggio Calabria meet in the Serra.

My first visit to Stilo was the old-fashioned way, from the coast near the site of Magna Græcia's Caulon, and my first impression was that there seemed to be a disproportionate number of Fiat Stilos in the area. In Italian *stilo* means 'style' and also happens to be the name of this town … little wonder so many of its residents couldn't resist the temptation to buy a Stilo. I suppose I only noticed this curiosity as I too was driving a Stilo.

Just as Gerace was the inland offspring of the Greek Locri Epizephyrii, Stilo has a similar relationship with Caulon, though only recently has it been shown to be so. As I have already mentioned the ruins of the Greek settlement have been found at Punto Stilo on the coast and not, as many expected, at modern Caulónia, far south and inland.

Edward Lear (1847), who had already fallen in love with Gerace, was likewise impressed with Stilo. Even though he arrived there at dusk, enough of what he saw appealed to his landscape painter's eye.

"… there was enough light to perceive that its general aspect was most promisingly picturesque; standing immediately below perpendicular precipices, it is built on a sort of amphitheatrical terrace, the projecting rocks at each extremity crowned with the most picturesque churches and convents.

"There appeared to be more evidence of care and cleanliness in the streets than in other Calabrian places we had passed through, and there was an air of orderly feeling and decent neatness, which struck us as remarkable in a place more remote from the capital than any we had yet visited."

Douglas (1911) gently chastises Lear for revelling in the beauty of the place but neglecting to mention one of its most famous buildings, the Cattolica, a Byzantine church dating from the 9th century. I think Douglas was being a little harsh; true, the Cattolica is a unique building but, as Lear, often reminds his reader, he is a landscape painter who sees the whole rather than the part.

On the other hand Douglas would have approved of Hutton (1912) who spoke of little else on his brief visit to the town. And, as if to placate the ghost of Douglas, likewise Eric Whelpton (1957) and Leslie Gardiner (1966) though the latter does so with an irreverent edge to his language as if he's trying to ensure that Douglas twists and turns in his grave:

" ... one of those tiny ancient doll's houses of churches ... the building so

Not the prescribed photo of the Cattolica at Stilo but one that puts it in its setting ... I think Leslie Gardiner would have approved.

Somewhere twixt Bivongi and Ferdinandea is the Cascata di Marmarico; as the crow flies a few miles from the erstwhile mining centre of Pazzano, now just a quiet corner of Calabria.

tiny you might almost pick it up in your arms."

Like me, Gardiner clearly resents 'doing the rounds' of what other people have deemed to be worth seeing, of religiously following the tourist trails:

"Ritual prescribes that, having done the church, you climb the hillside behind it to a spot where acanthus leaves frame its five little dustbin lids of copulas, the deep green setting off the orange-yellow. There you take your photograph, and then depart ..."

Gardiner continues in like vein as he describes how he was all but frog-marched up to the Cattolica in the first place by half the town; it was as if 'every able-bodied inhabitant must be given a shot at the visitor'. His account of his brief visit to Stilo is one of the funniest pieces of travel writing I have come across ... even if, reluctantly, he started to weaken:

"And yet ... the little church is almost worth it."

Despite being a part of the Apennines, Calabria's contribution to the spine of Italy, the Serra does not have the dramatic elevations of the region's three other mountain ranges. But it is this 'otherness', this homeliness that sets it apart from its loftier neighbours, that is its charm. And somewhere in the middle of it all, somewhere in the mountains between Stilo and Serra San Bruno, there is a waterfall. With a drop of 114 metres, *la Cascata di Marmarico* is the tallest waterfall in southern Italy and from all accounts is an awesome sight ... the problem is that for years it has been almost inaccessible to ordinary folk. Whichever way you go, from Bivongi or from Ferdinandea, it involves a four-hour round trek into the mountains. These days, while still not the most accessible part of the mountains, at least there is an alternative to shank's pony in the form of off-road vehicles from Bivongi that can take the intrepid traveller most of the way.

Despite having emailed in advance, the day I turned up in Bivongi there were no such vehicles to be seen or hired; I had to forget about Marmarico and instead make do with imagining this place, and sleepy Pazzano which I'd just passed through, as grimy hubs of a the 19th-century mining industry where over three hundred beasts of burden plied between here and the foundries at Ferdinandia and Mongiana with coal and charcoal.

Lear (1847), on the other hand, ignoring the area's industrial life-blood, focuses instead on the kindness of the those he met en route from Pazzano to Bivongi:

"There were few who did not offer me pears, and parties of women laden with baskets of figs would stop and select the best for us."

In this respect, nothing has changed in Calabria for centuries.

L'Aspromonte

Before we came to live in Calabaria and would drive south from Lamezia to catch the ferry to Sicily, I became increasingly aware of the range of mountains looming higher to the east. And at the time that was the extent of my knowledge.

Gradually I became more enlightened ...

I discovered it was in there that John Paul Getty III was held captive.
I discovered this was where Garibaldi had been shot in the foot.
I discovered that the roads from one coast to the other are not the best.
I discovered that today many of the towns are considered off limits.
I discovered that only a few early travellers ventured into the mountains.
I discovered that this mountain range is called the Aspromonte.
I discovered that *aspro* means rugged or harsh.

My first tentative foray into the Aspromonte was when I visited Gerace. Not very adventurous, I know, but Gerace being a 'normal' sort of place with no mafia connections and no reputation for mutilating rich American heirs, it was the obvious place to begin. Also, among others, Edward Lear (1847) waxed lyrical about Gerace to such an extent that I could hardly not visit. Later, as I have already described, I crossed from coast to coast, Locri to Gioia Tauro via Gerace, Cittanova and Taurianova.

The northern Aspromonte from the road near Gerace.

But Lear was not the first; nor was Richard Keppel-Craven (1818) despite having crossed the mountains via *il Passo di Mercante* when it was no more than a track and one with a notorious reputation. The first Briton to write about crossing the Aspromonte was the prisoner Philip Elmhirst who, in October 1809 was given no choice in the matter. With, he estimated, around eighty others, Elmhirst crossed the mountains from Gerace to Cittanova (then Casal Nuova) en route to Monte Leone.

Having survived a ferocious thunderstorm a couple of hours into the climb, his efforts were compensated by 'a picture at once awful and sublime':

"All that the mind is capable of inventing of the wild, the grand, and the terrific, was here realized, and presented to the view. The mountains in some places were nearly perpendicular; and, although united below in one vast base, they consisted of detached ridges, which were mostly covered with trees and brushwood to their summits."

Six and a half hours into their journey they reached the highest point of this part of the Aspromonte's spine from where they could see both seas, the Tyrrhenian to the north-west and the Ionian behind them to the east.

Richard Keppel-Craven (1818) travelling in the opposite direction took in the same vista and noted something different about the two seas:

"An observation which I had previously made, with regard to their respective colours, was here corroborated by immediate comparison. The tint of the Ionian is a whitish blue, lighter in shade, but much less clear than the waters of the Tyrrhenian, whose emerald hue and singular transparency add considerable beauty to the shores they bathe."

He doesn't mention where the sun was at the time.

Keppel-Craven had approached Casal Nuovo from the north, from the Serra mountains via Mongiana and found himself at what was the western gateway to the Aspromonte and he paints an idyllic picture of the area and its mountainous backdrop:

"... Casalnovo, from its proximity to the mountains, is noted for the coolness and salubrity of its atmosphere. To these advantages of situation it adds fertility of soil, producing an abundant variety of vegetables and fruits, while the hills, forming its background, afford excellent pasture. From these several brooks descend, and work some overshot mills, which, from their particular mode of construction, are very picturesque objects."

Half a page earlier he was less enthusiastic about the town itself and its housing 'being all low and built of wood' with a 'very mean appearance'. He was describing the aftermath of one of the events that truly shaped—or rather reshaped—the Aspromonte mountains, the earthquakes of 1783. The poor housing he saw were *barrache*, the makeshift wooden shelters hastily constructed thirty-five years earlier to house the survivors; these days they would be tents.

He goes on to give one of the most moving descriptions of how those events reformed the Aspromonte; of how towns, villages and communities were obliterated, of how the aftermath affected the day-to-day lives of the survivors and of how the landscape was completely transformed.

What Keppel-Craven saw around him was the new version of the Aspromonte landscape, a work in progress, its numerous raw scars still healing; I realise I have already quoted some of this in an earlier chapter:

"Thirty-five years have elapsed since the occurrence of this dire calamity, and, during the ten first which succeeded it, the paternal solicitude of the sovereign, and the attention of his government, had united in beneficent efforts to restore prosperity to this afflicted province; but the political vicissitudes to which it afterwards was exposed, have probably retarded the improvements which should have been the result of those measures. As it is, the industry of man, combined with the natural fertility of the soil and mildness of climate, have greatly remedied the evils it has suffered, especially in all parts open to cultivation; but, even without being acquainted with the exact nature of these evils, it is impossible not to perceive, even in a transient examination, that this country has undergone some alterations as tremendous as they are indelible."

The remains of Bruzzano Vecchio, finally abandoned after the 1908 earthquake.

The political point Keppel-Craven was making was that, for some of those thirty-five years (briefly in 1799 and for nine years between 1806 and 1815,) Calabria was under French rule. The Napoleonic Wars ended just three years before he came to Calabria and at the time anything that might point a finger at the French was considered fair comment. That said, the generally accepted view these days is that the infrastructure of Calabria improved considerably under French rule and particularly so under Murat.

When, over a century later, the physical and emotional scars of that time had finally healed, disaster struck again in the shape of the 1905 and 1908 earthquakes, centred on Reggio Calabria and Messina in Sicily. For many communities in the southern Aspromonte it was the last straw; some towns, like what is now called Bruzzano Vecchio, threw in the towel and relocated and many others headed west to Palermo, en route to the United States, Argentina or Brazil.

Another century has passed and once again rampant nature has disguised the evidence and another incarnation of the Aspromonte has evolved, today's living, thriving, majestic inheritance of those scars, finally healed and hidden. Until the next time, that is.

It is the stilted east-west road north of Gerace, the SS281, which follows the river valleys flowing off the watershed of Monte Cappellano that today roughly defines the northern limit of the mountains. From here down to the tiptoe of Calabria, the Aspromonte reigns supreme ... and all within the province of Reggio Calabria.

On the internet you can find a map of Calabrian towns with links to the mafia and in which the leading *'ndrangheta* clans are named ... and hopefully shamed though I suspect that is too much to ask. Overwhelmingly the places highlighted are in the province of Reggio Calabria and, of those, half are located in towns close to or in the Aspromonte. Surely the only National Park with such intimate ties to the mafia?

I am emphasising the mafia connection because, were it not for this, many Calabrians would make greater use of their National Park, as would of course a greater number of tourists. Even a website designed specifically to attract (or discourage) tourists describes the area thus:

"The mountains are probably best known, though, as the home of 'ndrangheta, the Calabrian mafia. Back when the group used to kidnap people for ransom, they would hide their prisoners in the Aspromonte.

Although there is still organized crime in the area, the mountains no longer serve as such a refuge."

It is scandalous that so much of the Asptomonte landscape is blighted by the presence of mafia towns. And though there is absolutely no reason not to visit such areas, generally people don't. As I've already mentioned, when I tell Calabrian friends about some of the places I've visited, stayed even, they are genuinely horrified.

While at Bova, Edward Lear (1847) planned the next day's travels round the eastern fringes of the Aspromonte:

"Tomorrow we start for Staíti, San Angelo di Bianco [Sant'Ágata del Bianco], and San Luca …"

En route he also passed through Bruzanno but there is scarcely a single Calabrian who would make that journey today as all four places have mafia connections. Today, his destination, San Luca, would be considered the worst of a bad lot.

Lear's literary legacy is a description of a delightful journey that most of the modern generation will never experience. First Staíti:

"The setting sun prevented our sketching, but we resolved to return to this most exquisite scenery, from Staíti, which now towered above us on the opposite side of a deep dark gully, filled with wondrous groups of giant ilex

Lear's drawing of the spectacular hilltop town of San Giorgio just north of what was then Casal Nuovo.

[holly]. Here, too, were the first symptoms of local colour in costume, the women wearing bright blue dresses with orange borders, and all we saw gave promise of real unmixed Calabrian characteristics, unspoiled by high roads and the changes of all-assimilating civilization.

Then Bruzzano in the lee of the mountains:

"Many charming views are there round Brazzano, looking through pergolas to the sea and cape, with glittering Brancaleone to the south, and the blue wooded hills towards the north."

Still climbing he approached Sant'Agata del Bianco:

"Smooth walks led us through rich chestnut woods … or along narrow high-banked lanes of red earth, with feathery oak over head, and the eastern sea shining through the branches over the woodland tracts we had last left, and the chalk-white fiumaras [torrents] and golden sandy plain far below."

And returning to San Luca from Santa Maria di Polsi:

"… we enjoyed the magnificent landscape of distant hills [as] we descended to the depths of the torrent bed, and its gay oleander-trees by the ferny glens and ilex ravines …"

It's all still there … only the will to visit, or even just pass through, such places is lacking. And it is not about history repeating itself—'fear of brigands' in the past becoming 'fear of the mafia' today—it's that generally mafia towns are such dreary places. It's not that you feel intimidated (though I suppose some people do), it's just as if the colour has been drained away and what's left is a gloomy-grey monochrome.

Is it too much to expect that the towns dotted in and around such a glorious, untouched landscape, a National Park no less, should reflect their environment and be thriving and welcoming towns, bursting with amenities and smiles?

At the time of writing not one of the towns featured in Lear's walk offers accommodation or proper respite for the hungry traveller. On the other hand, at Morano Calabro in the Pollino mountains—which has a population only moderately greater than that of San Luca—I found five places to stay and ten places to eat. Indeed, if you check an internet site like Booking.com it is easy to find all sorts of accommodation available *within* all the National Parks and Reserves *except* the Aspromonte. Now, either the scenery in those areas is infinitely more spectacular … or there is another reason?

Of course when Lear was travelling from Staíti to San Luca he did so across country, along the tracks which, at the time, linked one community with another. Today all these towns are fed by winding roads from the coast which climb upwards and onwards into the mountains where, in terms of vehicular access, most of them just peter out. Irrespective of the mafia and the lack of amenities, any ideas I may have had of experiencing this 'exquisite scenery' for myself by following in Lear's footsteps, were therefore unrealistic.

Lear's route was along the eastern edge of the Aspromonte and, though the western edge of the mountains also has its fair share of mafia-related communities, their presence seems less invasive and they are therefore more accessible. Perhaps the fact that there is a good, albeit serpentine, north-south road that skirts the western Aspromonte has enabled towns with inclinations towards the 'dark side' to take tentative steps towards normality.

The route from Taurianova to Mélito di Porto Salvo on the southern coast starts and finishes with towns with a mafia presence and there are another couple of such towns in between but the ambience is different. I stayed several nights in Taurianova and got the sense that this was a place striving towards being ordinary, of offering good accommodation and places to eat. Though not in the Aspromonte, I had a similar feeling at Mélito.

The few travellers who came this way talked of two towns in particular, Casal Nuovo and Terranova both close to the junction of the east-west and north-south tracks which more or less defined the north-west corner of the Aspromonte.

On today's maps that function is the role of the aforementioned Taurianova, the largest town in the area; Casal Nuovo appears not to exist and Terranova is a small hamlet to the south of Taurianova. It is all very confusing.

In 1828 Ramage stopped off at Casal Nuovo en route to tackling the perceived dangers of the trans-Aspromonte pass, *Il Passo del Mercante*, en route to Gerace. He noted that, in the aftermath of the 1783 earthquake, the houses were largely made of wood and that the 'greater part of the village had been swallowed up'.

Nearly two decades later Lear (1847) was also in Casal Nuovo and in nearby Terranova and, speaking of the latter, made an almost identical observation:

"The old city is altogether overwhelmed and buried in chasms, and below crags and dells, and its successor is a single straggling street of lowly dwellings of most melancholy appearance."

Earthquakes not only begat structural changes but over the years names, locations and status changed; and sometimes the memories of older names were best forgotten.

Five years after Lear was in Casal Nuovo it had evolved as Cittanova; it is its near neighbour, the larger Taurianova, that is the new kid on the block. Taurianova is a fascist-era (1928) amalgamation of several smaller hamlets which eventually enveloped each other until Taurianova became a *comune* in its own right just after the war. One of Taurianova's satellite communities is Terranova Sappo Minulio which is the original Terranova that Lear described as 'once the largest town of the district'.

Many travellers who came to the Aspromonte spoke of the many *fiumare* or torrents, they had to negotiate. Lear saw them as no more than a stony hindrance to making progress rather than true water courses and had this to say about the river Verde near Sant'Ágata del Bianco:

"… The Fiume Verde, a river in winter, was now reduced to a sham of a stream, containing as many tadpoles as drops of water, and barely admitting the least face-washing refreshment."

There are literally dozens of such torrents that flow off the Aspromonte and into both the Tyrrhenian and Ionian seas, though more so on the Ionian side. For example, depending on the season, in the twenty-seven miles between Marina di Gioisa Ionica and Brancaleone Marina no less than nine *fiumare* trickle or roar into the Ionian Sea.

Leslie Gardiner (1966) wrote passionately about how these *fiumare* effected the local environment and likened their power to devastate and transform to the ravages of foreign invasions and earthquakes. He went on:

"Heading south towards Reggio you enter the real *fiumara* country, the lad of super-torrents. They begin round the edges of Calabria's central plateaux, gashing the rims of the granite masses of the Aspromonte.

"As soon as the winter storms cease, most Italian torrents run dry. Those of Calabria are dry for fully six months. By April the *fiumare* have carried as much snow to the sea as they are likely to for the year. Their serpentine valleys—serpentine because débris blocks them in spate and constantly forces them into fresh channels—are dotted with muddy pools. Their last descents on the sea are steep ladders of dry rubble, tufa and spring flowers."

When I first drove along the coast running parallel to the Aspromonte, I couldn't help but notice the lengthy road bridges spanning what seemed to be nothing but an almost dry river bed. Later, the first time I saw one of these *fiumare* in full, ferocious spate, I remember wondering if the bridge I was driving across was indeed up to such an aggressive assault. It was.

Norman Douglas (1911) was the only traveller to see the Aspromonte up close and personal, only Douglas entered the heart of the mountains and crossed the region via its highest peak, Montalto (also known as Monte Cocuzza); high enough at 6414 feet but in Pollino terms it lacks over 1000 feet. Douglas was on his way from Delianuova to Bova, as the crow flies a mere seventeen miles, nevertheless such an indirect trek across such inhospitable terrain that many would-be guides at Delianuova said it couldn't be done.

Douglas had travelled from Sinapoli with a young guide who was prepared to take him to on to Montalto the next day but Douglas was suspicious of his motives and sought someone else. The landlord of the inn where he was staying accompanied him a-knocking at doors but the general response was the same: 'To Montalto, yes; to Bova, no!'

Finally they arrived at the home of a retired brigand with a reputation for dark deeds in his murky past. Douglas clearly revelled in such encounters:

"We found the patriarch sitting in a simple but tidy chamber, smoking his pipe and playing with a baby; his daughter-in-law rose as we entered, and discreetly moved into an adjoining room. The cheery cut-throat put the baby down to crawl on the floor, and his eyes sparkled when he heard of Bova.

""Ah, one speaks of Bova!" he said. "A fine walk over the mountain!" He much regretted that he was too old for the trip, but so-and-so, he thought, might know something of the country.

"The person he had named was found after some further search. He was a bronzed, clean-shaven type of about fifty, who began by refusing his services point-blank, but soon relented, on hearing the ex-brigand's recommendation of his qualities."

At dawn the following morning they set off to climb Montalto:

"Chestnuts gave way to beeches, but the summit receded ever further from us. And even before reaching the uplands, the so-called Piano di Carmelia, we encountered a bank of bad weather. A glance at the map will show that Montalto must be a cloud-gatherer, drawing to its flanks every wreath of vapour that rises from Ionian and Tyrrhenian; a west wind was blowing that morning, and thick fogs clung to the skirts of the peak. We reached the summit (1956 metres) at last, drenched in an icy bath of rain and sleet, and with fingers so numbed that we could hardly hold our sticks."

In such conditions, a view was there none so they started their decent into kinder conditions:

"Passing through magnificent groves of fir, we descended rapidly into another climate, into realms of golden sunshine. Among these trees I espied what has become quite a rare bird in Italy—the common wood-pigeon. The few that remain have been driven into the most secluded recesses of the mountains; it was different in the days of Theocritus, who sang of this amiable fowl when the climate was colder and the woodlands reached as far as the now barren seashore. To the firs succeeded long stretches of odorous pines interspersed with Mediterranean heath (brayère), which here grows to a height of twelve feet …"

(More on Douglas' climatic observations in a later chapter.)

Douglas summed up his unique Aspromonte experience:
"It is an incredibly harsh agglomeration of hill and dale, and the geology of the district … reveals a perfect chaos of rocks of every age, torn into gullies by earthquakes and other cataclysms of the past … Once the higher ground, the nucleus of the group, is left behind, the wanderer finds himself lost in a maze of contorted ravines, winding about without any apparent system of watershed. Does the liquid flow north or south? Who can tell! The track crawls in and out of valleys, mounts upwards to heights of sun-scorched bracken and cistus, descends once more into dewy glades hemmed in by precipices and overhung by drooping fernery. It crosses streams of crystal clearness, rises afresh in endless gyrations under the pines only to vanish, yet again, into the twilight of deeper abysses, where it skirts the rivulet along precarious ledges, until some new obstruction blocks the way—so it writhes about for long, long hours …"

I knew I wasn't up to emulating Douglas' epic journey and, besides, a Calabrian author, Francesco Bevilacqua, had already done it and written an account of following in Douglas's footsteps, *Sulle Tracce di Norman Douglas*. No, I had to come up with something Douglas never thought of, an adventure that was infinitely more audacious than climbing a mere mountain. So I decided to visit three places in one day, the Aspromonte's most famous waterfall, the Cascata di Maisano (more accessible than Marmarico in the Serra but still a bit of a trek from the nearest road) and Calabria's two most notorious mafia strongholds, Platì, the home town of the two sisters involved in the court case with celebrity chef Nigella Lawson referred to earlier, and San Luca, the birthplace of Calabrian author Corrado Alvaro.

I found accommodation between Santo Stefano (which spawned 'brigand' Musolino) and Gambarie and the plan was to set off early in the morning for the waterfall, then return north via Gambarie to Delianuova to pick up the road that would take me eastwards across the mountains and through Platì to the Ionian coast near Bovalino. After a break at Bovalino I would have a short drive down the coast before turning inland to San Luca. I would then return to Bovalino and stay the night there.

Well, that was the plan.

Despite the predictions of my host at Santo Stefano, the weather was not 'cloudy with some sun'. On the contrary, it was a drizzly, misty morning, as I set off early for the waterfall. I guessed I was on a wild goose chase before I even started out but put my faith in the possibility that there might be a break in the weather by the time I reached the nearest point by road, the Menta Dam.

At the dam the weather had indeed changed ... it was worse; low cloud was hanging over the hills, the drizzle had become more persistent and a bitter wind had picked up. As the crow flies I was only three miles from Montalto and I recalled Douglas' words about it being a cloud-gatherer; every hill and mountain that morning was a cloud-gatherer. Any crow attempting that journey was onto a loser.

Nevertheless, I got out of the car and walked to the closed-off road that crossed the roof of the dam and I knew that the additional hour's walk to the waterfall was not on the cards. Well, at least I had tried. Instead I made do with a photograph of the lake and the dam.

I headed back up to the main road and turned north to Delianuova where I would turn east into the unknown and cross the mountains via Platì to the Ionian coast. But Delianuova was one of those Calabrian places where they had decided to dispense with the convention of directional road signs and, as I had been so sure it would be straightforward to find my way onto the right road, I had not set up the car's GPS, which I tended to only use in large cities. When I realised that the choices I had already made—at two junctions

The Menta Dam and adjoining lake the nearest point by road to the Cascata di Maisano: in the background the closest mountains are already gathering clouds.

where there were no signs—were clearly wrong, I stopped and asked a couple of locals for a bit of guidance.

I said I wanted to go to Bovalino via the Platì road, a route they just discounted immediately and, as if they'd misheard me, started to give me alternatives. I repeated that I wanted to go via Platì and they told me in no uncertain terms that I couldn't go that way, their suggested routes were much better. They didn't say 'safer' but I knew what they meant … or I thought I did. I persisted with my chosen route and told them I had to go via Platì and they wanted to know why. They clearly had never met anyone who wanted to pass through Platì who wasn't actually from there and therefore would know the route.

Eventually they gave in and told me to turn right at the next junction and to keep climbing on the same road. Thus began a road trip I shall never forget.

Even as I left Delianuovo, I was still seeking succour in at least one road-sign that might belatedly confirm I was on the right track. Nothing. I continued to climb as instructed.

At first the road was not unlike that from Gambarie to Delianuova, mostly gloomy, sometimes downright dark, always wet, often misty and partially covered with heaped clusters of fallen, russet pine-needles swept to the verges by the wind.

The weather was closing in and gradually the mist became a fog and a road, already difficult to define, became almost impossible. I saw no other car on the move for perhaps seven miles and then, just ahead, I picked up the tail-lights of a car going in the same direction as me. Abruptly it pulled over on the left so I pulled alongside, eager to confirm that I was indeed on the right road.

I asked the woman passenger if we were on the road to Platì. She looked at me vaguely, shrugged her shoulders and said she didn't know. Her male companion, who had got out of the car, looked just as vague and offer no further insight into where exactly we were.

As I pulled away all I could think of was what they might have been doing out on this road to, from their viewpoint, nowhere. If it was to indulge in a bit of hanky-panky, then why on earth didn't they pull off the road miles back … it would have been just as private, just as dark and just as inclement? And weren't they at all curious about this road? After all there were many places where it was decidedly hard-going, where the surface had been eroded or butchered and never repaired. It was an obstacle course of weaving around or over huge potholes; sometimes there were so many they were impossible to avoid as were the large expanses of black surface water which, it occurred to me, might easily have been fathomless sinkholes.

That may have been the only car on the move but there were lots of goats on the move, taking their morning constitutional, it seemed, along a road where they clearly did not expect to see moving vehicles. Once, after sneaking past about twenty of them in a rare, mist-less moment, I stopped and got out to take a photo ... they all turned and ran back whence they'd just come.

On the other hand, I did pass a dozen or more cars parked up by the side of the road, but never a driver in sight. To keep me sane I started to mentally list the possible reasons for this phenomenon: the cars had been abandoned; the driver had gone for a walk in the woods never to be seen again; people hunting for mushrooms or collecting chestnuts; shepherds looking for their goats; someone having a very long, secret, off-road pee; maybe a couple into things you can only do in a moist, misty forest; a shallow grave being dug; a body being buried. Who knows?

To assuage that niggling doubt about where I might be, I pulled over where there were no parked cars and no wandering goats and set up the GPS. I entered the address of the Bed & Breakfast I was staying at in Bovalino that evening, knowing that, if this was indeed the road to Platì, then the GPS would pick it up as being the shortest route there ... though it did occur to me that there might be no satellite signal in these woods as it was already clear that my cellphone was not picking up anything. Thankfully the screen sprung into life and that soft, purposeful voice I knew so well gave me hope as, with the merest trace of emotion, she confirmed that I was to keep going in the same direction along the same road. I wanted to give her a hug but

Scaredy-cat goats on the run east of Delianuova.

made do with blowing her a kiss. I pressed on.

The mist and the drizzle were lifting as the trees stepped back a little from the road to let the odd shaft of sunlight penetrate. The mist had become a haze and I could see some light at the end of the tunnel and then, suddenly, the first road sign I'd seen since before passing through Delianuova. I was at a sort of staggered crossroads and 'the voice' was giving me precise directions but, despite her reassuring ways, I doubted her on this occasion; my own built-in GPS was saying something different. I had already started to follow her instructions but after only a couple of hundred yards decided to pull over and check it out on a real map. I soon found the configuration of roads that I was seeing on the GPS monitor. It was a revelation.

First of all I was right to have had doubts about 'the voice's' chosen route to Bovalino ... it certainly seemed likely to be a better road but was longer and not via Platì. Also, I discovered that I had reached this point from Delianuova via a different road completely and not the one I thought I was on. Indeed, according to my trusty *Touring Club Italiano* road atlas, my travelling-in-Calabria bible, this secondary road was defined as 'passable with difficulty' and therefore not a recommended route at all. I was sure the worst was over for the next part of the journey to Platì was nine miles on a 'narrow, asphalt regional connecting road', the designated SS112.

The juxtaposition of roads finally implanted in my mind, I turned round and headed back to that junction and turned left to take the more direct route to Platì. Almost immediately I passed a sign that I recognised advising me that the route was 'interrota', a familiar sign on Calabrian roads and one generally ignored by Calabrians. It means that the normal flow of traffic has been interrupted, usually by some sort of natural disruption, a landslide onto the road or part of the road itself having fallen away; or both. There had been an 'interrota' sign between Santa Severina and San Mauro for nearly four years but, as far as locals were concerned, the road never closed. Calabrians normally ignore such signs and carry on. Which is exactly what I did.

There were many times in the next forty-five minutes when I was to regret that decision. Unknown to me at the time I was setting off along a road that resembled a war-zone. My natural instinct for survival continually did battle with my curiosity and my ever-expanding Calabrian gene. I wondered what Norman Douglas would have done? He too would have carried on.

Huge boulders had tumbled down the mountainside onto the road. Where there weren't boulders, what asphalt there was left was strewn with rocks, rubble and earth of all shapes and sizes. It was like a man-made set for some apocalyptic movie that they forgot to clear up afterwards. It was difficult to decide which part or stretch of the road was particularly 'interrota'; defending on your definition it was either all or none. There were stretches where parts of the road had fallen away leaving a ragged asphalt edge and a potential plunge into the abyss; but, with care, even these were passable and soon weaving round the scattered rockfalls and other debris became almost second nature.

The sad irony was that this was not some back-road but the SS112, a highway that dissects a designated National Park. When I had occasion to take my eye off the road and take in the view, I was privy to a glorious, breathtaking landscape, the Aspromonte in full spate.

As I passed another three wandering pigs—all black—I could see, tucked away in the valley below what I knew must be Platì, I stopped a couple of

Rocks, rubble and a pig on the road to Platì.

Like any other Calabrian town in the Aspromonte, from a distance Platì looks no different.

times to take photographs, much as I had done on other roads; only this time I was pretty sure I wasn't going to encounter any other traffic; the odd pig perhaps, but no traffic. I was definitely the only person travelling to Platì that day from the west; probably that week, maybe that month, possibly that year.

From my vantage point in the hills, Platì looked just like any other Calabrian town nestling in the folds of the valley. There was no large finger pointing from above warning the unwary that this was a mafia stronghold. Nor would you have known that underneath the town there is a tunnel network, once kept in good order by the local mafia bosses to facilitate their hasty exit should the long arm of the law come a-knocking.

Any sense of anxiety I may have had before setting out that morning had long dissipated, the rigours of the drive had already seen to that and I was now also being seduced by the splendour of the Aspromonte landscape.

In the last mile or so the serpentine road began to return to some sense of normality as it merged with the random housing that defined the outskirts of Platì. I drove through the town slowly, through streets that were dowdy, featureless and monochromatic, though less so than as I had expected; it was the views from above on the approach to the town, the multifarious terracotta hues of the roof tiles, that gave this town colour.

There were more cars than I expected and I even got snarled up in one of those short-lived Calabrian traffic jams when two cars travelling in opposite directions stop so that their drivers can have a chat. The few people on the streets were mostly young men chatting in groups, their womenfolk—mothers, sisters, girlfriends—were surely attending to the midday pasta.

My pale-green Stilo turned a few curious heads, and I could see that people knew there was a stranger in their midst; once or twice I nodded in confident salutation. Given the direction from which I had come, they probably thought I was lost. I passed what looked like a new road project on the outskirts of the town where a concrete viaduct took a more direct route towards the town centre than the road I was on. Something was not quite right ... it seemed both new and derelict at the same time.

I didn't know what to expect as I left the eastern outskirts of the town to descend to the Ionian coast and a late lunch at Bovalino. But this half of the trans-Aspromonte SS112 was just as surprising for being unexpectedly and boringly ordinary. It was a different world, a good road with what looked like a relatively new section midway. This was Platì's only real link to the outside world now that the way west, my chosen route, had been all but abandoned.

Before continuing my journey to San Luca, I ate at a small restaurant in Bovalino run, as it happened, by two young men who had escaped from Platì, one of whom helped fill me in on some of the details about that viaduct to nowhere; the rest I gleaned from the internet.

The viaduct was (and, in theory, still is) part of a grand project, *La nuova arteria collega molti centri dell'Aspromonte all'A3 Salerno-Reggio Calabria e alla Strada Statale Jonic*a, a new artery linking the A3 *autostrada* in the west with the Ionian coast road which seems to have been started in the middle, on the outskirts of Platì. That in itself was a bad idea and I suspect that the funding somehow evaporated and the project withered on the *'ndrangheta* vine; apart that is for the few hundred yards of pointless viaduct, with neither beginning nor end on the outskirts of Platì. That said, there was a grand opening of sorts in 2012 of a little less than a kilometre (912 metres to be precise) halfway between Platì and the coast. Since then nothing.

But the so-called Bagnara–Bovalino project could explain the apparent abandonment of the road west of Platì for the new road would have replaced this, though with few views of the National Park unless they were to be painted on the walls of the proposed four-mile tunnel through the mountains.

After lunch I headed south on the old coast road before joining the SS106 that runs from Taranto in Puglia down to Reggio Calabria. On the outskirts of Bovalino, sandwiched between road and railway, I passed an apartment block known locally as the Paul Getty block, apparently so-called in recognition of the Getty family's involuntary contribution to financing its construction. A few miles further on I turned inland once again heading for the second notorious *'ndrangheta* stronghold in the area, San Luca.

The Platì viaduct, the road to nowhere, an isolated icon to good intentions that never materialised. Apartments in Bovalino known locally- as the Paul Getty apartments.

As I drove towards the town, which I could see nestling in the comforting arms of the Aspromonte foothills, I was trying to recall conversations with Calabrian friends about which town had the worse reputation, Platì or San Luca; the consensus seemed to be in favour of San Luca. On the other hand, Edward Lear, leaving the town in 1847, reflected on 'San Luca and its kind homely set of inhabitants.' Mind you, his last meal there, and the open generosity he was shown, was still fresh in his mind:

" ... they offered snow and wine, and a clean cloth being spread, maccaroni, eggs, ricotta, honey and pears, soon exhibited proof of their ready hospitality."

Having just eaten, I decided to decline such enticements, were they to be on offer during my short visit to the town. As it happened they weren't, but San Luca was not as I expected. It was early afternoon and therefore I was not surprised that streets were all but empty. The few heads there were out and about turned noticeably when they saw a car that was not local.

What did surprise me was that many of the apartments, drab and devoid of character as most were, had balconies festooned in all sorts of greenery, Whatever else transpired here, people seemed fond of their plants and appeared to take a pride in their upkeep, even if the apartment itself was clearly a work-in-progress—unrendered, unpainted, unfinished. Local writer Corrado Alvaro

Some travellers still pass through the town on their way to a well-know Calabrian landmark in the shadow of Montalto, the sanctuary of Santa Maria di Polsi; others prefer to make the journey there from the west, from near Gambarie, just to avoid San Luca.

Lear came to Maria di Polsi from San Luca when it had a different ambience; for him and his guide it was an arduous trek, climbing and crossing torrents, and it was not until the following day's daylight that he could appreciate the scene which, of course, he later drew:

"Assuredly, Sta Maria di Polsi is one of the most remarkable scenes I ever beheld: the building is picturesque, but of no great antiquity, with no pretensions to architectural taste; it stands on a rising ground above the great torrent, which comes down from the very summit of Aspromonte, the highest point of which—Montalto—is the "roof and crown" of the picture."

These days the annual festival associated with the sanctuary is said to be controlled by the local *'ndrangheta*—if this is indeed the case, it is yet another example of lines between church and mafia becoming blurred, entangled even, with the former seemingly unable or unwilling to disentangle itself with much success.

As I retraced my steps to the coast and my overnight stopover at Bovalino, I reflected on my madcap drive that day and particularly on Platì and San Luca. I knew that when I returned home and told people where I had been, they would look at me with the sort of disbelief associated with a holiday in Baghdad. Calabrians have grown accustomed to labelling these towns—and others—with the stigma of the *'ndrangheta* and by default they gradually evolve into no-go areas and their segregated existence becomes self-perpetuating. Both towns are in glorious settings, they are in an ancient and magnificent mountain range that is now a National Park. Without the 'mafia' tag both would be bursting at the seams with visitors, bed & breakfasts would be overflowing and that great little restaurant run by Ciccio and Franco in Bovalino, would be chuck-full of happy eaters, laughing and over-indulging ... in their home-town of Platì.

Without mentioning the mafia directly, Leslie Gardiner (1966) reflected on what renowned Calabrian writer, Corrado Alvaro (1918-1956), had to say about the 'permanently sick face' of his native San Luca when he called it a face 'on which sorrow finds no place, because sorrow is its natural expression'.

Alvaro also wrote the following:

"The blackest despair that can take hold of society is the fear that living honesty is futile."

One day, in Platì and San Luca and other mafia strongholds, that fear will pass, but only Calabrians can make it happen.

The welcoming gateway to San Luca with special mention of its two twinned towns though, strangely, I could find no reference to San Luca on the website of either Vallerano or Cascia. Edward Lear's depiction of the sanctuary of Santa Maria di Polsi in the shadow of Montalto. Writer Corrado Alvaro, San Luca's most famous son.

Pizzo ... a Calabrian contradiction

"Its [Pizzo's] present inhabitants ... are almost all fishermen and mariners, and are reckoned an industrious but somewhat turbulent race, for I frequently heard at other places on the coast the reproach of being of Pizzo addressed to its natives on the slightest altercation; *Tu sei del Pizzo, e questo basta!*"
Richard Keppel-Craven *A Tour through the Southern Provinces of the Kingdom of Naples*

Pizzo is a popular place.

Many people, Calabrians and visitors alike, head for this picturesque town, its steep streets clinging to the Tyrrhenian shore south of at the southern end of the *Golfo di S. Eufémia*. When we first dropped down off the A3 *autostrada* it was for the same reason as everyone else ... we wanted to try the ice-cream.

Pizzo has established a reputation for a particular type of ice-cream and the two—the town's name and the name of the ice-cream, *tartufo*—have become almost synonymous.

The *tartufo* story dates back only as far as 1952 when a distant relative of unified Italy's first king, Vittorio Emanuelle II, was visiting the town on the occasion of *le nozze*, the post-marriage dinner party of a local aristocratic dignitary. To get over the potential embarrassment resulting from the unfortunate paucity of cup-like receptacles for the planned ice-cream dessert, a local *mastro pasticcere* (pastry chef), created a new-style ice-cream that could be served on a small plate. Out of a we-must-not-offend-the-aristocracy necessity, Don Pippo de Maria invented the *tartufo*.

Understandably the de Maria family (who, at the time ran Bar Dante) became protective of their *tartufo* recipe but others copied the concept and today it is almost impossible to walk around the town centre without being cajoled into taking a seat and indulging in a *tartufo*-style ice-cream.

The difference between the *tartufo* and other ice-creams is that it is normally composed of two or more flavours and has a frozen fruit, such as cherry, raspberry or strawberry, in the centre.

The first time we visited Pizzo we were sitting outside an ice-cream parlour enjoying our *tartufo* when I looked across the road and couldn't resist taking several photos which, for me, summed up everything about Pizzo. I noticed that the waitress who had served us was looking along my line of sight to see what it was I found so interesting. Eventually she gave in and came over to ask me outright what it was I'd found so fascinating.

"Murat and *tartufo*," I explained, expecting her to pick up on the irony.

She looked puzzled.

"People visit Pizzo for two reasons, for *tartufo* and Murat … and there they are next door to each other." I repeated as I pointed across the street.

Looking a little querulous she asked, "What about the sea and the sun?"

"And maybe those too," I added feebly.

But she understood what I was trying to say. Across the road next to a rival *tartufo* ice-cream parlour was the Hotel Murat. For the people of Pizzo both were money-spinners for Joachim Murat, once king of southern Italy, was executed here in the castle and has since become something of a local hero, even though it was the people of Pizzo who ultimately betrayed him.

It is a story told and retold down the years and, like many such stories it has grown legs. Let me explain …

As husband to Caroline Bonaparte, Joachim Murat was the brother-in-law of Napoleon Bonaparte. From 1808 until 1815 he was king of the peninsular half of the Two Sicilies—from Naples to Reggio Calabria and everything in-between. His title was King of Naples.

With the fall of Napoleon in May 1815, he went into exile in Corsica; the Bourbons returned to power in the newly-titled Kingdom of the Two Sicilies under Ferdinand IV.

On 9 October 1815, with a small band of followers, Murat landed at Pizzo on the west coast of Calabria between Lamezia and Tropea expecting to rally support for retaking southern Italy as its king.Instead he encountered hostility which eventually led to his arrest, a brief trial and execution by firing squad at Pizzo Castle on 13 October. He was buried at Pizzo.

Reputedly his last words were directed to his executioners:

"Soldiers! Do your duty! Straight to the heart but spare the face. Fire!"

All in all, much the same story as any tourist will find in Pizzo Castle's small explanatory leaflet ... or even *Wikipedia*.

The first traveller to reference the Murat story was Richard Keppel-Craven who passed through Pizzo in 1818, just three years after the above events.

"Joachim Murat, in the autumn of 1815, landed at il Pizzo with a few followers, and was arrested by its inhabitants, whom he had in vain stimulated to join him, thrown Into a prison, condemned to be shot by a military commission in virtue of a law which he himself had promulgated, and executed four days after his ill-advised arrival.

"When Murat repaired to the public square of II Pizzo, and harangued the astonished multitude, calling upon them to recognize him as their lawful sovereign, and distributing the proclamations to the same effect which he had brought with him, the people listened to him with mute surprise, and slunk away one by one to their habitations, which they cautiously, but without delay, shut up; leaving him and his adherents to ponder on the Inauspicious commencement of their enterprise."

Following this rebuff, Murat decided to lead his followers (around thirty) to Monteleone—today's Vibo Valéntia and a seven-mile climb from Pizzo. Murat it was who had raised Monteleone to the rank of a provincial capital so, not unreasonably, he was expecting more support there than he had received in Pizzo.

I suspect Murat was aware that the Calabria he inherited in 1808 and the Calabria he left seven years later were two different places. During his reign many reforms—including land reform that did not benefit the landed gentry—were brought into place and many infrastructure projects initiated. There were those prepared to forgot his French-ness and looked instead at what he had achieved so, from his point of view, he had reason to believe that people might rally to his cause.

Ramage (1828) takes up the story, thirteen years after the events:

"As no one seemed willing to bring forward the horses for which he called, he inquired for the road to Monteleone, the chief city in the vicinity, and began to mount the hill to the post road.

"In the mean time a person had proceeded to give information to the commanding officer that Murat had landed, and was haranguing the soldiers in the public square. The officer immediately ordered a party of men to hurry forward to the point, where the road from Pizzo joined that to Monteleone, while he himself followed in the direct that Murat had taken. Murat had reached the heights where the two roads meet, when an officer stepped forward, and said, "I arrest you in the name of King Ferdinand as a traitor." Murat's men immediately prepared to resist, and had levelled their guns, when Murat called out to them not to fire, while the officer opposed to him ordered his men to aim at Murat, yet no one shot took effect. It is difficult to account for Murat's indecision at this moment, as no one who has read his history cab doubt that he was brave to a fault, but instead of making any resistance, he fled down a precipitous bank and reached the shore."

Richard Keppel-Craven again:

"In this precipitous retreat be was accompanied by his own little troop, and followed by the townspeople and their leader; but found on his arrival at the beach, that the vessels which had brought him and his party had, through mistake, fear, or treachery, put to sea again. He jumped Into a fishing-boat, and was endeavouring to push it off from the shingles, when his opponents having overtaken him, and a shot from them having wounded one of his companions, he held up a white handkerchief. In token of surrender, and was led, or rather hurried to the little fort, dignified with the name of castle, and forming the citadel of Il Pizzo.

"In his way there he suffered, from the mob which collected, the most injurious treatment; and it is even said that a woman, who conceived herself aggrieved in the loss of one of her sons, executed as a bandit, probably most deservedly, through his orders some years before, tore off one of the whiskers from his cheek, in a fit of revenge upon the presumed author of her misfortune."

Queueing up at Pizzo Castle for a glimpse of where Murat was incarcerated and shot.

These two versions of the story, as recounted by Keppel-Craven and Ramage, differ only in some small details; for example, Ramage has Murat's spurs getting caught in some fishing nets on the shore which delayed his retreat and makes no menton of the white handkerchief. But these are minor inconsistencies. Both also concur on what happened next.

First the more succinct Keppel-Craven:

"He was at first thrust into a wretched cell, where he passed the night, but was removed to a more decent apartment, and furnished with every immediate article of necessity, through the order of the commandant of the division, who arrived from Monteleone early the next morning. A telegraphic despatch communicated the intelligence of his descent to Naples, and the same mode of conveyance brought back the order to proceed immediately on his judgment. He had landed on the 8th of October, and on the 13th, the court having pronounced sentence, he was executed, after having confessed himself, and written to his wife.

"The fortress in which he was shut up is of very small dimensions; on a platform which extends over the first story, two parallel walls form a kind of uncovered corridor of about twelve paces in length, terminating in a parapet towards the sea. He stood with his back against this, and having himself given the signal, received the fire of the soldiers placed at the opposite extremity, and fell with his head against the door of a room in which all the officers who had accompanied him were at the time confined."

Ramage offers a more detailed, and slightly more embellished, account of the actual execution:

"He [Murat] then addressed the officers to the following effect: "Officers, I have commanded in many battles; I should wish to give the word of command for the last time, if you can grant me that request." Permission having been given, he called out, in a clear and firm voice: "Soldiers, form line," when six drew themselves up about ten feet from him. "Prepare arms, present"—and having in his possession a gold repeater [a type of pocket-watch] with his wife's miniature upon it, he drew it from his pocket, and as he raised it to his lips, called out—"Fire!" He fell back against a door, and as he appeared to struggle, three soldiers, who had been placed on a roof above, fired a volley at his head, which put him out of pain."

The curious thing about these two stories is that neither mentions Murat's last words as being: "Soldiers! Do your duty! Straight to the heart but spare the face. Fire!"

In this respect what is particularly interesting is that Ramage was taken on a clandestine tour of the castle by the actual gaoler who had looked after Murat during his few days as a prisoner there thirteen years earlier. This had come about after Ramage had got into a religious argument with a local officer of the law, a lieutenant who, at one point, threatened to arrest Ramage for his apparent heresies. Ramage stood his ground and as part of their ongoing peace process, the lieutenant retracted and granted Ramage's wish of visiting the castle to experience the Murat story at first hand. That said, Ramage was still suspicious of the lieutenant's motives:

"I accepted his offer, though I had no confidence in his honour, and imagined that his kindness might be a pretence to get me within the walls of the prison without exciting the attention of the inhabitants. I showed, however, no appearance of shrinking, though it was an anxious moment when I heard the gate grate behind me. The gaoler was introduced, and his appearance was not prepossessing as to make me wish for a more intimate acquaintance. There was, of course, not longer any necessity for concealment, and as the lieutenant seemed to take no further steps, I became convinced that my suspicions were unjust."

So Ramage's account would seem to be, more or less, straight from the horse's mouth for nobody could have been closer to the truth of these events than the gaoler who was there and witnessed them.

As far as I can discern, the first mention of the 'spare-the-face' story is found in Alexandre Dumas' book *Voyage en Calabre* in which he too visited Pizzo. But Dumas did not visit the area until 1835 and, of course he was known for being a writer of fiction; he was also French and Murat's life and death were wont to be romanticised in his country of birth.

Dumas' account is full of what appears to be detailed, direct speech by and between the key protagonists ... such as might be found in a work of fiction. This is the Dumas version of the denouement:

""Friends", he [Murat] said to the waiting soldiers, "you know that I will give the order to fire; the courtyard is very narrow so that you can aim true: aim for the heart, spare the face.""

Three Dumas paragraphs later, Murat finally gets on with it:

"Then Murat gave the order to fire, coolly, calmly, unhurried, without hesitation, as if it had been a straightforward business. On the word 'fire', there were only three shots, Murat remained on his feet. Of the fearful soldiers, six had not fired, three had fired over his head."

Naturally enough in the Dumas version of events, Murat had to be executed again and this time they hit him.

(Alexandre Dumas went on to write a fanciful biography of Joachim

Murat; simply called *Murat*; it was published in 1840.)

It is more than likely of course that both Keppel-Craven's, three-years-after-the-event version and eye-witness' account reported by Ramage are nearer to the truth of what happened at Pizzo Castle on 13 October 1815.

Just as likely is that Dumas' account is just romanticised, absurd fiction posing as fact which is precisely why it is this version, and in particular the 'spare-the-face' story, that has survived the doubtful test of time. It is—as was Dumas' forte—a rollicking good, spiced-up yarn; there just doesn't appear to be any first-hand evidence to support it.

On its Murat page, *Wikipedia* repeats the same 'spare-the-face' account though credits Caroline Murat with the story in her 1910 book, *My Memoirs*. Caroline was Joachim Murat's grand-daughter and her account of the same events is full of even more unsubstantiated and absurd fantasies than even Dumas could muster, including the notion that all these things came to pass on 13 October because the number thirteen had always been a curse on the family.

For the truth of what happened to Joachim Murat in Pizzo in 1815, my money's on the unimpeachable experiences of Richard Keppel-Craven and Craufurd Tait Ramage, two writers whom no-one has ever considered as pertinent sources in the quest for the truth about Murat's death.

Joachim Murat was a flamboyant and charismatic man and, by all accounts, a courageous and brilliant general on the battlefield. He was a man who, in retrospect, did much for the south of the Italian peninsula during his short reign as King of Naples ... though of course he made enemies of those who didn't benefit from the changes or who lost sway. He had vowed to eradicate the political brigandage which was making life difficult for the French administration; it was Murat who appointed General Manhès to oversee this cleaning-up operation but ultimately it was Murat's policy. The woman who alledgedly tore off one of his whiskers in Pizzo, did so, it was said, because her son had been executed as a bandit.

Leslie Gardiner (1966) summed up the story of Pizzo and Murat in a characteristically thoughtful fashion, imbued with the merest hint of irony:

"The story of Joachim Murat should interest all who travel through Calabria. It was Murat who first opened up the province for the foreign tourist by extending a highway through Italy which had never gone further than Naples. In 1808 he continued it southward to Salerno and Lagonegro [in Campania], then into Calabria to Castrovillari, Cosenza, Catanzaro and

Reggio. (It is the present *Strada Statale* 19.) 'Give me a hundred Neapolitan bravoes,' he used to say, 'and I will conquer Europe'—but he pinned his faith in Calabrian bravoes in the end, and by them, on the sands of Pizzo, in a tragedy of misunderstanding and mistrust, he was escorted to his execution."

Despite the obvious fictions now woven into Murat's final few days, there is one other element about the story—a contradiction—that I find curious: the way in which the town of Pizzo now embraces Murat.

Murat is not just made out to be the hero, but a hero of Pizzo no less, almost as if he were a *pizzitano* born and bred. But it was because he was shunned and abused by the people of Pizzo that he became this 'heroic' figure in the first place. As Gardiner put it, the people of Pizzo did indeed escort him to his execution.

Perhaps there is some sort of collective guilt that has been passed down through the generations regarding what this small community did to a man not generally perceived as a tyrant.

Perhaps the tourist trade in Murat-orabilia has helped assuage this guilt.

The flamboyant and charismatic Joachim Murat, called by some 'the Dandy King'. In the tiny courtyard within the battlements of Pizzo Castle, there is a small plaque with the minimum of information 'the place of execution, 13·10·1815'; it is assumed the visitor will know whose execution. The courtyard is indeed miniscule and the firing squad's muskets must surely have been only a few feet from Murat himself. A target difficult to miss.

The Provincial Capitals

> "By a late decree the divisions of this important province had been augmented to three; the two northern, bearing their ancient denominations of Calabria Citra and Ultra, and the third, with Reggio for its capital, having assumed that of Calabria Ultra Secunda."
> **Richard Keppel-Craven** *A Tour through the Southern Provinces of the Kingdom of Naples*

Keppel-Craven (1818) picked up on the administrative restructure that followed French rule in 1816, even if he did get their designations a little mixed up. The third was indeed Calabria Ultra Seconda but this was centred on Catanzaro and Reggio Calabria was the capital of Calabria Ultra *Prima*. These three eventually evolved into what became the provinces of Cosenza, Catanzaro and Reggio Calabria, with capital cities of the same names.

In 1992 local government reorganisation created two more provinces, Vibo Valéntia and Crotone, both of which were up and running by early 1995. This reorganisation reduced the size of the largest of the three original provinces, Catanzaro. Thus today Calabria has five provincial capitals: Catanzaro, Cosenza, Crotone, Reggio Calabria and Vibo Valéntia.

So here, alphabetically, is some background to these five cities; what made them important and what, if anything, makes them interesting. Conveniently Catanzaro, the provincial capital, is first on the list.

Catanzaro
Richard Keppel-Craven (1818) was wont to listen to gossip:
"I was informed that this city, though containing 12,000 inhabitants, and possessing every advantage requisite to such population, offered little worthy

of notice in point of antiquity of date, beauty of situation, or local interest."

Unlike Keppel-Craven, the first time I saw Catanzaro, I went, "Wow".

At the time he wrote the above, Keppel-Craven was ten miles away from Catanzaro but had passed closer a day earlier when even the view from the coast four miles away did not inspire. Mind you, apart from all the negative points he listed, there were the following extenuating circumstances to consider:

"The house which I inhabited [near Squillace], besides the pleasure afforded by my friend and that of his inmates and family, possessed a charm perfectly novel in Italy for it was removed from all other habitations, and therefore realised the only idea that an Englishman can form of a country residence."

Difficult choice.

Despite the fact that Catanzaro has no obvious Magna Græcia connections, all but a handful of my travelling companions went there (the no-shows were Hill, Lear and Lowe) and admittedly Richard Keppel-Craven only had a peek.

Henry Swinburne (1777) offered a simplistic history of the city:

"Catanzaro was built in 963, by order of the Emperor Nicephrius, as a post of strength against the Saracens. Its situation on an eminence, in the pass between the mountains and the sea, seems judiciously chosen for the purpose of repelling those Infidels, who, from Africa or Sicily, were wont to make good their landing at Reggio. Increase of inhabitants and of size

Santa Maria della Roccelletta as it is today and as depicted following the earthquakes of 1783 by French illustrator Claude Louis Chatelet in Jean-Claude Richard's *Voyage Pittorèsque.*

caused it to be deemed a proper residence for the officers who compose the provincial tribunal; and, in 1593, it arrived at the dignity of capital, formerly the right of Reggio."

Although the current site of the city, 'in the pass between the mountains and the sea', has no Magna Græcia credentials, it is in an area where indeed an offshoot of Greek civilisation was established and flourished. The nearby coastal archæological site of Roccelletta was the Roman Scolacium before which it was Magna Græcia's Skillakion (or Scyllacium as Ramage called it), name giver to today's Squillace.

From wherever you see Catanzaro, the dramatic elevated site clearly says 'fortress', a vista which Keppel-Craven played down when all he saw was 'beauty of situation'. It is little wonder that this was one of the last Calabrian citadels to fall under the sword of the Norman conqueror, Robert Guiscard.

Ramage (1828) approached Catanzaro from Roccelletta where he had been led to believe he would find 'the remains of an ancient temple'. It was not what he as expecting:

"I was a little disappointed to find it a large building of the middle ages, of which it was impossible to determine the use. At all events, it was neither of Roman or Greek construction, and the tradition is that it was destroyed a few centuries ago by the Turks, who used to keep this part of Italy in a constant state of terror."

The building he was referring to was the ruins of a Norman basilica dedicated to Santa Maria della Roccella which was partially destroyed by the last of the five earthquakes in 1783 ... easier to point the finger at the Turks than a so-called act of god. What a pity Ramage didn't investigate further for he was but a stone's throw from the Roman and Greek ruins that he was longing to explore. The remains of Roman Scolacium and Greek Scyllacium—with the latter being under the former—more or less occupy the same site as the Norman basilica.

Ramage also mentions that the adjacent landscape was prolific with mulberry trees, a source of food for the silkworm and a sure sign that this was an area known for its silk. Indeed since Byzantine times Catanzaro was one of the Italian peninsula's principal centres for the production of silk with its heyday in the 16th and 17th centuries when its international trade brought worldwide fame.

Indeed Catanzaro's dependence on silk and its material offshoots was one of the elements that led to the town being dubbed the city of the three Vs. Leslie Gardiner (1966) explains:

"Medieval Italy called the place the city of the three V's—*velluti, venti e Vitaliano*. The last-named was the local saint; *velluti* were the velvets, damasks and brocades which the *catanzaresi* were once so skilful in manufacturing that the French imported native weavers to instruct the ladies of Touraine. As for *venti*, the town is swept day and night by the breeze."

As we shall see in a later chapter, the produce of the lowly silkworm has enjoyed a recent renaissance.

Gissing (1897) also noted the importance of the town's silk industry but had more pressing issues on his mind for, as we shall see later in this chapter, he was anxious to vacate Crotone and get to Catanzaro.

Because of the unfortunate health issues he succumbed to at Crotone, his fervent desire was to get out of that city and bask in what he hoped would be the fresher air of Catanzaro. Eventually he made it and clearly felt the better for it:

"Catanzaro must be one of the healthiest spots in Southern Italy; perhaps it has no rival in this respect among the towns south of Rome. The furious winds, with which my acquaintances threatened me, did not blow during my stay, but there was always more or less breeze, and the kind of breeze

Via Bellavista was once a place to gather and gaze out across the countryside from the heights of Catanzaro; these days such a view is hard to find.

that refreshes. I should like to visit Catanzaro in the summer; probably one would have all the joy of glorious sunshine without oppressive heat, and in the landscape in those glowing days would be indescribably beautiful."

Gissing enjoyed Catanzaro and eventually put behind him his memories of Crotone and what he called its 'malaria-stricken population':

"I rejoiced in the healthy aspect of the mountain folk. Even a deformed beggar, who dragged himself painfully along the pavement, had so ruddy a face that it was hard to feel compassion for him. And the wayside children— it was a pleasure to watch them at their games. Such children in Italy do not, as a rule, seem happy; too often they look ill, cheerless, burdened before their time; at Catanzaro they are as robust and lively as heart could wish, and their voices ring delightfully upon the ear."

That the air is indeed fresh at Catanzaro is beyond debate; its lofty position sandwiched between two river valleys (the Fuimarella and the Musofalo) that merge south of the city to run across a broadening plain towards the sea, sees to that. Edward Hutton was impressed:

"The true delight of Catanzaro is to be found in its extraordinary situation and the amazing views it offers you of the great country in which it lies."

This 'extraordinary situation' has brought with it problems of access. In times past, when people were used to walking (and climbing) long distances and had beasts of burden aplenty, it was less of a problem. But motorised transport, both trains and cars, changed people's expectations and for Catanzaro this ultimately led to two projects that, in Calabria terms, were unique.

With the main station situated at normal ground level below the city's northern escarpment, a funicular-style railway was inaugurated in 1910 that climbed directly up to the city centre. In 1954 a minor accident coincided with the burgeoning post-war age of the motor car and the funicular closed; rejuvenated it reopened in 1998.

Within a decade motor transport itself was causing problems and more direct access to and around the city was guaranteed by the completion in 1962 of the ambitious Bisantis Viaduct which spans the deep gorge of the river Fiumarella.

Only two of my travelling companions might have seen it; only Leslie Gardiner (1966) did:

"A modern wonder of Europe, a lodestar for engineering students of the nations according to the *catanzaresi*, arches over the valley. t is one of the highest single span bridges in the world and it brings traffic into the city from the road they call *Strada dei Due Mare*, the Highway of Two Seas."

Unusually, in the list of Catanzara attractions on the city's *Wikipedia* site the viaduct comes top, before all the churches and other city landmarks ... possibly because, in the early sixties, it was the highest concrete arch bridge in the world; it also had the longest arch span. These days it is the second highest in Europe but nonetheless it remains an impressive sight, particularly at night.

But even as far back as the early part of last century, Edward Hutton (1912) had waxed lyrical about the roads around Catanzaro. He was particularly impressed with the bus service to and from Cosenza:

"... before the coming of the automobile meant a journey of two days, almost impossible in winter and always full of a sort of misery. To-day you may leave Cosenza at half-past seven in the morning and be in Catanzaro by half-past two ..."

Today there are those who are inclined to castigate any expansion of road networks as if it were some sort of malediction or the work of the devil; they forget just how important such developments were for many people. Hutton, still eulogising about the fast road between Cosenza and Catanzaro, observed the ways in which isolated communities were advantaged:

"It is enough to notice the difficulty of obtaining seats to see at once how welcome it is to the people. It is cheaper, and certainly as expeditious as most of the railways here in the South, and quite as comfortable. Moreover, it can go where the railway cannot penetrate; it passes not under but over hills. In

Catanzaro's Bisantis Viaduct crosses the gorge of the Fiumarella. In less dramatic mode, the town's funicular railway plods up and down the hill to and from Piazza Roma in less than two minutes.

all things it is to be praised; and its effect upon the isolated communities of this glorious but neglected and despised Calabria cannot but be good ..."

As I have already observed, people who live on the eastern seaboard of Calabria still bemoan the fact that they appear to have been omitted from the region's transport infrastructure. Catanzaro is the exception. These days the carriageways traversing the Bisantis Viaduct link into the fastest east-west route across Calabria; by car about twenty-five minutes from coast to coast. Via the A3 *autostrada* it is another half hour to Cosenza knocking six hours off what Hutton thought was miracle of modern transportation at the time.

Having made it to the top Eric Whelpton (1957) was not overly impressed with the city itself but, like everyone else before and since, he could not escape the amazing views:

"Though the narrow streets of the centre itself are crowded, there is nothing of interest to be seen except for the astonishing prospects of mountains and valleys that are to be had on every side of the fringes of the city."

A decade later Morton saw those narrow streets in a different light:

"One climbs a steep road to the old city to find oneself in narrow streets of massive stone houses and minute shops in whose tiny windows are sometimes surprisingly displayed the last word in electrical equipment, televisions sets and tape-recorders. It is typical of southern Italy that one should look through medieval windows-frames at radio equipment."

Things have changed somewhat: the city has grown and prospered and with this growth Whelpton's vistas are harder to stumble across—with everything so tightly packed the edges are more difficult to find; nevertheless it's worth the effort to seek them out. Likewise Morton's medieval window-frames displaying electrical goods as, not surprisingly, such things have migrated to the high street or the nearest commercial park.

Returning to the 'wow' factor I experienced when I first set eyes on Catanzaro; I was not alone for, the view *of* the town (rather than the view *from* the town) has been called 'the queen of panoramas'. It is truly stunning and for me the essence of the city.

Many Calabrians, for whom such dramatic vistas are commonplace, see their capital city only from the inside and find it wanting. Of course it is a hotchpotch of the new, the old and the older but isn't every city that struggles to echo the present and reflect the past in a confined space?

Not for the first time, I will let Leslie Gardiner (1966) have the last word. He was being driven back to Catanzaro when his driver, (Princess) Maria

Pignatelli—a Florence-born feminist married to a Calabrian nobleman from Cerchiara—said that the view of the city reminded her 'of a man in an expensive cloak with only a dirty shirt underneath.'

Gardiner thought that a bit harsh:

""That's unfair," I said. "If that silhouette were in Tuscany, everyone would be in raptures over it."

"Certainly. But then it would not be Catanzaro. They would have clothed it decently under the showy cloak.""

Ironically, following her death two years later in a road accident, Maria Pignatelli's collection of some 1500 books was left to a Calabrian library ... *La Biblioteca Provinciale 'Bruno Chimirri' di Catanzaro*. One of those books must surely have been her own *Introduzione alla Calabria*, published the same year she was, for a few weeks, Leslie Gardiner's travelling companion.

Dammit, *I* will have the last word.

I too think Maria Pignatelli *was* being unfair. Catanzaro's perceived dowdiness then was no more than part of the process of an ancient citadel catching up with the rest of Italy, of slowly embracing the twentieth century just as others had done.

Still in its confined space, it has caught up.

A young Maria Pignatelli—full name Marchesa Maria Elia De Seta Pignatelli—who was in her late sixties when she accompanied Leslie Gardiner for some of his Calabrian travels. Catanzaro makes the most of its confined space and today's view from the top invariably takes in the adjacent road network.

Cosenza

Henry Swinburne (1780) knew his history:

"Cosenza was the capital of the Brutian state, and of some consequence during the second Punic war."

Swinburne was the first of my travelling friends to visit the city, an archbishopric no less, and continued his historical summary with an account of the death of Louis of Anjou at Cosenza:

"Lewis the Third of Anjou, adopted by Joan the Second, died here in 1434 ... [he] was a prince of mild unambitious disposition, though not deficient in courage or military abilities ... Calabrians were particularly affected with the loss of so virtuous and benelovent a master, under whose administration their province had enjoyed uncommon happiness."

Louis of Anjou was no more Calabrian than I am; Cosenza was the place he happened to expire for, though his adopted mother, Queen Joanna II of Naples, had given him the title Duke of Calabria, his main seat of power remained Naples. His expiry at Cosenza was due to a 'fever' which was generally a euphemism for malaria. The life of Joanna herself—who adopted Louis for political motives—is an extraordinary tale of intrigues, lovers, conspirators, adopted sons and premature deaths (a few of them from natural causes), the like of which couldn't be made up.

But poor Louis was not the only person to succumb to a 'fever' at Cosenza and Louis' story pales into insignificance when it comes to the first notable expiration at Cosenza over a thousand years earlier. Swinburne was the only traveller to give space to Louis of Anjou; on the other hand almost everyone else, including Swinburne himself, gave reams of space to the events following the death of Alaric the Visigoth at Cosenza ... of a 'fever'.

My first encounter with Cosenza was a little more mundane; Alaric, even if I had I heard of his demise at Cosenza, could not have been further from my mind. My radar was concentrating instead on trying to successfully circumnavigate the untidy outskirts of Cosenza as I tried to find my way from the A3 *autostrada* to our holiday destination on the other side of the Sila mountains. I had no interest in where I was, only in trying to make sense of the confusing, unhelpful and erratic road signs that I was expecting would take me round to the SS107 and the route east without incident. No thanks to the signs of the time, I made it.

A few weeks later I was rewarded with a completely different aspect to the city when I was driven there by our *agriturismo* host Vincenzo and, having recrossed the mountains, descended towards the extensive plain wherein lies the sprawling city. The sprawl is of course modern Cosenza, hanging on to the south-east corner of which, at the confluence of the Crati and Busento rivers, lies the old town, the town that Swinburne visited:

"Cosenza is pleasantly situated, about twelve miles from the Mediterranean sea, at the southern extremity of a spacious plain which, upon a considerable breadth, extends above twenty miles down the course of the river Crati. The city stands upon seven hills ... at the foot of the declivity the Crati, coming from the eastern vallies of the Sila, receives the waters of the Basiento ..."

Swinburne then launches into the story of Alaric and I will do likewise but with the help of most of my travelling companions who came here and couldn't help but retell the bizarre story of the Visigoth king.

After Swinburne came Brian Hill (1791), who stopped off at Cosenza on his way north, but wrote not a word on Alaric; perhaps, unlike others, he has not yet read Edward Gibbon's recently published *The History of the Decline and Fall of the Roman Empire*; perhaps he is just preoccupied with his lodgings:

" ... of all the filthy holes, called inns, we have yet met with, this is the most abominable."

The lower slopes of Cosenza old town as they are today; world-weary apartments that look out over the river Crati, Calabria's longest river. At the top of the hill, just left of centre, are the remains of Cosenza's Norman castle.

"[Cosenza is] the place of sepulture of Alaric, the Arian king of the Visigoths, who, after having plundered Rome, and wasted the whole of Italy, relieved the apprehensions of the timid Honorius, and the fears of Sicily, which he menaced, by his sudden death at Cosenza."

Craufurd Tait Ramage (1828) puts some meat on the bones:
"I was curious to see the burial-place of Alaric, the celebrated King of the Goths, who died here A.D. 410; ... [and who] was afraid, from the cruelties he had committed on the inhabitants, that his dead body would be abused ..."

John Arthur Strutt (1841) can see it all from his window:
"The inn, however, is in a gay situation; commanding a view of the principal street, the ass-market, the river Valsento, the bed of which formed the grave of Alaric, king of the Goths, and the bridge over it."

Edward Lear (1847) never came this far north, but Emily Lowe (1858) did and was, it seems, staying in the same inn as Strutt and teases her readers with an abridged version of the story:
"What do you think, reader, was the prospect in front of the house? The site of the burial-place of Alaric!
"Immediately under the two windows met the Busento and the Crati, the two rivers which were stopped in their course until the Last of the Goths was interred beneath the passage of their returning waters."

George Gissing (1897) devotes a whole chapter to the story of Alaric's and his internment at Cosenza but includes a note of scepticism:
"Now, tradition has it that Alaric was buried close to the confluence of the Busento and the Crati. If so, he lay in full view of the town. But the Goths are said to have slain all their prisoners who took part in the work, to ensure secrecy. Are we to suppose that Consentia was depopulated? On any other supposition the story must be incorrect, and Alaric's tomb would have to be sought at least half a mile away, where the Busento is hidden in its deep valley."

Norman Douglas (1911) who knew everything there was to know about everywhere, opts for saying not a single word on Alaric. It's unusual for him to be so tight-lipped ... in ignoring the king of the Goths' Cosenza burial, I wonder is he making some sort of statement about the story?

Edward Hutrton (1912) on the other hand decides to quote the source that so many others, including Ramage, have used, the author of *The History of the Decline and Fall of the Roman Empire*, Edward Gibbon:

"The ferocious character of the barbarians was displayed in the funeral of a hero, whose valour and fortune they celebrated with mournful applause. By the labour of a captive multitude they forcibly diverted the course of the Busentinus (Buxentius), a small river that washes the walls of Consentia. The royal sepulchre, adorned with the splendid spoils and trophies of Rome, was constructed in the vacant bed; the waters were then restored to the natural channel, and the secret spot where the remains of Alaric had been deposited was for ever concealed by the inhuman massacre of the prisoners, who had been employed to execute the work."

Eric Whelpton (1957) literally takes a leaf out of Hutton's account by also quoting Edward Gibbon verbatim. His only other comment is to restate the obvious:

"... it is possible that immense wealth lies beneath the bed of the Busento, the stream that flows swiftly through the town."

Leslie Gardiner (1966) makes oblique references to the story in a way that suggests he is not totally convinced of its provenance. In search of an old

There are countless depictions of Alaric as a long-haired, decadent, axe-wielding barbarian when in fact he was nothing of the sort; some argue he was more Roman than the Romans. The signet ring seems to be the only authentic image of him while the painting on the right is almost the only subsequent representation that reflects the ring.

railway line in Cosenza, he notes with the merest hint of irony:

"[at a] spot quite near the river bed where Alaric and his treasure are supposed to lie hidden and which, like Alaric's grave, is unsignposted and hard to find."

And later, at the nearby station:

"You look for a booking-clerk at Cosenza, and begin to think that it would be easier to go looking for Alaric.

Finally, Henry Morton (1967) tries to picture the scene, to put the supposed events into some local and seasonal perspective. He and the town's Tourist Bureau chief, Dr Valente, are sitting by the spot where the rivers meet; it also happens to be the right time of year, after Alaric's September visit to Reggio and before the winter set in and the Busento became a raging torrent:

"'I sometimes think,' mused Dr Valente, 'that the whole story may be one of history's picturesque fictions. Yet the ancient authorities tell us that this happened, so what are we to say?'

"'Has anyone tried to find the tomb?' I asked.

"'Yes, every year an archaeological team arrives from Piacenza, Parma and Bologna to dig in the river-bed at various points. So far they have found nothing.'"

As others have already noted, the source for the story of Alaric's death and subsequent bizarre entombment at Cosenza was Edward Gibbon in his *The History of the Decline and Fall of the Roman Empire*. The story appears in Volume Three, published in March 1781, time enough for Swinburne to have digested it before the 1785 publication of his travels in Calabria five years earlier. The two men were also contemporaries and indeed an earlier work by Swinburne is cited in Gibbon's *History*.

Gibbon gives *his* source for the Alaric entombment story as the sixth-century historian Jordanes, the so-called 'ancient authorities' referred to above by Dr Valente. Jordanes' *De Origine Actibusque Getarum* (*The Origin and Deeds of the Getae/Goths*), better known as the *Getica*, was published around 551CE, one hundred and thirty years *after* Alaric's death.

Many of today's scholars interested in this period have cast doubts on a number of Jordanes' accounts in the *Getica*, though not specifically the Alaric story as it is a mere side-show within the greater political and military upheavals of the time.

I checked references to Cosenza in books written by British 'Grand Tour' travellers who visited the town *before* Swinburne and *before* Gibbon's opus and found that neither Sir Thomas Hoby (travelling between 1547 and 1564) nor Richard Pococke (travelling in 1733) nor Sir William Young (travelling in 1772) made any reference to the Alaric story.

Indeed Hoby writes about both rivers and not a word on the ill-fated Alaric, alive or dead:

"The river Crati, called in old time Cratis, has its beginning about six miles above Cosenza on the east side out of a plentiful fountain of water. When it comes to the town it is fair and large, and there enters into it before it comes under the bridge the river called the Busento."

On the other hand Young was more preoccupied with the 'daring Villiany of the lower People; who in this Capital ... look like the most cut-throat Devils I ever beheld'. I suspect his observations were in part influenced by the 'Hospitality of the better sort of Inhabitants' that he enjoyed there.

Like the Loch Ness monster and Bigfoot, the tale of Alaric's entombment at Cosenza is no more than a good yarn ... which is why the countless searches of the area in and around the Busento have come up with zilch. That said, unlike the Loch Ness monster and Bigfoot, Alaric the Goth did exist.

Of course old town Cozenza isn't all just about the life and death of Alaric; had not his planned foray into Sicily been thwarted by the weather he wouldn't have been there in the first place. That he succumbed to 'a fever'

A romanticised mosaic of the historian Jordanes and a more realistic depiction of Edward Gibbon—co-authors of the Alaric-was-buried-under-the-Busento story.

was hardly surprising bearing in mind the proclivities of the low-lying parts of Calabria. Swinburne (1780) was particularly aware of the problem in the plain close to Cosenza:

"The low grounds are fertile in an eminent degree; but from their situation and frequent waterings exhale vapours in summer that constitute a *Mal Aria* very productive of fevers."

Keppel-Craven (1818) was aware of it too but was assured that the higher parts of the town were healthier:

" ... the badness of its air in modern times has greatly contributed to the state of comparative insignificance to which it is now reduced. The vicinity of the above-mentioned rivers [Crati and Busento] seems to afford better foundation for this reproach ... but I was nevertheless assured, that only the lower division of the city, more immediately exposed to the vapours exhaling from the waters, deserves it, while the upper portion is free from insalubrity."

Nor did all the travellers that came here only talk of their experiences in terms of Alaric and the 'badness of the air' for they knew they were in an important and ancient city, the erstwhile capital of the Bruttians and the capital of Hither (or Higher) Calabria. For many, Cosenza was the most important city in Calabria in that it was situated on the main post-road between Naples and Reggio Calabria.

By the time Ramage (1828) dropped by, things seemed to have moved on from Brian Hill's 'of all the filthy holes, called inns, we have yet met with, this is the most abominable' experience:

"Towards evening, I strolled through the capital of Hither Calabria and found more appearance of wealth and comfort than anything I had yet observed since I had left Naples. Not a single beggar annoyed me, though there were many poor people around. The streets are narrow, as all Italian towns are, to protect from the direct rays of the sun, though it must cause the interior of their houses to be stifling from want of ventilation."

Strutt (1841) visited Cosenza only thirteen years after Ramage and yet their impressions of the place were light years apart. There is of course the possibility that one was there on a good day and the other on a bad, but I was curious as to what else might have caused such a marked difference in Strutt's tone:

"The Calabrians of this province have a very bad reputation, and it is no small proof of the correctness of the imputation, that Cosenza, with a population of less than twenty thousand inhabitants, has, at this time, thirteen hundred robbers and murderers in its prisons."

I suspect both these figures are exaggerated, nonetheless Strutt, six years after a devastating earthquake, picked up quite a different ambience to Ramage. I wondered which side of the fence the next traveller would sit?

That next traveller was Emily Lowe (1858) and she did indeed have an opinion:

"Cosenza is a town panting for liberty and advancement, consequently severely repressed; hardly a family is without some of its members in prison, and the young men are never allowed to travel, or exercise their talents in any other place ..."

There are two things to note about the apparent contradictions between Ramage on the one hand and Strutt and Lowe on the other.

Firstly, it is clear from his writing that Ramage was someone who liked to experience things for himself on the ground; Strutt and Lowe, on the other hand, generally experienced things second-hand, through the experiences of others and thus often accepted what people told them without question or a second opinion. In Cosenza, what Ramage wrote is what he experienced and observed; what the other two 'saw' is what they were told.

Secondly, Ramage was in Calabria, just three years after the end of French rule when, as evidenced by his and other accounts, there was a degree of stability and order in the region that had previously been lacking; generally

Following their trial at Cosenza in 1844 the Bandiera brothers and seven of their fellow-revolutionaries were executed at nearby Vallone di Rovito.

things were peaceful. Under the reinstated Bourbon regime some things deteriorated; As Ramage notes, some of what the French had achieved under Murat was cast aside and clearly it did not take long for this to change the ambience of a large town such as Cosenza:

"The French generally conveyed a great benefit on the country by reforming the legal code, which, before their time, exhibited a strange incongruous mass. The Code Napoleon now, however, supersede these multifarious enactments, modified, indeed, immemorial customs of the country, though it was not without a struggle that it maintained its ground on the return of the Bourbons. They made an attempt to re-establish the ancient order of things: the benefit of the change, however, had become so evident, that the most devoted friends of the Bourbons insisted that the organic law of Murat should be continued, and Ferdinand I was obliged to yield."

Ramage goes on to explain how, under the new regime, the good in Murat's law withered on the vine as corruption flourished and how it could be in people's interest 'to lengthen out a trial till doomsday' ... and in so doing keep the prisons full.

Lowe's reference to the town 'panting for liberty' has to be seen in the context of when she was in Calabria. In 1858 the political drive towards unification was in full voice; in less than three years the Kingdom of the Two Sicilies was no more

It was also near old-town Cosenza, not far from Piazza Fratelli Bandiera, that the Bandiera affair came to its inevitable, and bloody, end with the 1844 execution of the two brothers, Emilio and Attilio, and seven of their group. Their inspiration had come from a short-lived, pro-unification uprising at Cosenza earlier that year and though their futile attempt at revolution started near Crotone, it ended here at Vallone de Rovito.

By the time Gissing (1897) was here, the revolution had happened and the Italian peninsula was finally a political entity. It was time to ring the changes and for Gissing there is good and bad:

"The new age declares itself here and there at Cosenza. A squalid railway station, a hideous railway bridge, have brought the town into the European network; and the craze for building, which has disfigured and half ruined Italy, shows itself in an immense new theatre—Teatro Garibaldi—just being finished. The old one, which stands ruinous close by, struck me as, if anything, too large for the town; possibly it had been damaged by an earthquake, the commonest sort of disaster at Cosenza. On the front of the new edifice I found two inscriptions, both exulting over the fall of the papal power; one was interesting enough to copy.

"20 Sept., 1870. This political date marks the end of theocracy in civil life. The day which ends its moral rule will begin the epoch of humanity."

Perhaps by 1909, when the new theatre was completed, the memory of Garibaldi and the legacy of unification in the south had already begun to tarnish for it never bore his name. It became instead the Teatro Comunale A Rendano after the Cosenza-born pianist, Alfonso Rendano. The theatre's elegant façade adorns one side of the Piazza XV Marzo opposite the equally elegant Palazzo del Governo, the administrative headquarters for the province of Cosenza, Calabria's largest province.

Cosenza's old town is a random patchwork of all that time has done to this part of Calabria. Here elegance, disorder and decay share the same space; a space bursting with stories of kings, queens, conquerors and battalions of ordinary folk just hoping to survive the skirmishes and the earthquakes.

It also has a new and larger appendage, a sprawling, modern city, where café culture, shopping and traffic jams rule the roost.

Clockwise from above left:
A corner of Cosenza as it was in 1897 when Gissing was here. The river Busento meanders round the corner close to the church of San Domenico; the confluence with the river Crati is just out of sight to the centre-left.
Today two massive columns support a railway bridge crossing the confluence (Crati right, Busente left); surprising that Alaric's treasure was not found when it was being constructed. Cosenza's Teatro Comunale, now known as *Il Teatro di Tradizione Alfonso Rendano*.

Crotone

Richard Keppel-Craven (1818) was a daydreamer:

"The testimonies of several ancient authors concur in assigning the first rank among the illustrious cities of Magna Graecia to Croton, which, as late as the descent of Pyrrhus [c280BCE], measured 12,000 paces in circuit."

Keppel-Craven must have known that, though Crotone was indeed at the very heart of Magna Græcia, the lone column at Capo Colonna was the only part of Magna Græcia in Calabria that he was ever likely to set eyes on. The remains of the erstwhile Temple of Hera, at what is now called Capo Colonna, represent an important out-of-town sanctuary cloaked in religious symbolism but situated on the Lacinian promontory about seven miles south of the city itself. As described in an earlier chapter, the other forty-seven columns of this once magnificent edifice have succumbed to time, pillaging, earthquakes and recycling … probably mostly the latter.

In modern terms Ktoton (its Greek name) was not very large, the 12000 paces that Keppel-Craven cites represents a circle with a diameter of about three and a half miles. And for the moment that lone, much photographed, iconic column at Capo Colonna remains all there is for the traveller to see. There are of course Greek artefacts at the town's museum by the castle and every so often there is a flurry of excavation here and there but, unlike the other major Greek sites at Sibari, Caulon and Locri, there is a modern city sitting on top of almost everything.

For the moment, and for the foreseeable future, the remains at Capo Colonna *are* Greek Kroton.

Undaunted, Keppel-Craven continued with his eulogy to Crotone:

"The salubrity of its atmosphere was supposed to exert so peculiar an influence on the race which inhabited it, that they seemed superior in corporeal beauty and strength to the rest of mankind: for no country produced so many powerful athletae or beautiful women. The name of Milo, the wrestler, would alone have given it celebrity, even if we had not known that seven combatants who gained the prizes of the Stadium in one of the Olympic games were Crotoniates; …[we] have, moreover, a list of philosophers and eminent physicians, who were natives of this city, and, lastly, Pythagoras himself, though not born here, chose it for his residence, and immortalized its name by founding his school within its walls."

I will return to the 'salubrity of its atmosphere' but focus first on Kroton's other ancient claims to fame mentioned by Keppel-Craven: the legendary Olympian, Milo of Kroton, and the city's association with Pythagoras or, as he is known in Italian, Pitagora.

Milo, who was born and died in Kroton in the 6th century BCE, was a legend in his own lifetime who won Olympic gold as a wrestler. He was a prolific award-winner and not just at the Athens Olympics where he won six times but also at other games in the ancient world: seven times at the Pythian Games at Delphi, ten at the Isthmian Games at Corinth, and nine at the Nemean Games. Of course all such statistics should be consumed with a large pinch of salt, there being no conclusive evidence that he achieved such phenomenal success.

He was a contemporary of the philosopher and mathematician Pythagoras and here there is some confusion regarding their relationship as there was also a contemporary athletic trainer called Pythagoras of Samos who could have been a different Pythagoras or indeed the same Pythagoras. And if Milo did indeed save the life of Pythagoras when a pillar collapsed and he stepped in to support the roof while those below escaped, then which Pythagoras? And if Milo did indeed marry the daughter of Pythagoras ... then which Pythagoras? Or was there just the one Pythagoras ... philosopher, mathematician *and* athletic trainer?

Like many stories from the time, there are too many unanswered and unanswerable questions and where there are answers, usually there are more than a few and often these are contradictory.

Milo of Kroton tying to split a tree and, so the tale goes, when he got his hands trapped in it, was attacked and devoured by wolves. The Obama Bin Laden look-a-like is Pythagoras.

That Milo was an accomplished athlete and that Pythagoras was a mathematician and philosopher is almost the extent of our irrefutable knowledge.

To this day I can still not only recite verbatim Pythagoras' Theorem but I also understand it and can actually prove it to a sceptic; my understanding of this simple formula was one of the things that made me realise that mathematics could be fun. Imagine my surprise therefore when I discovered that Pythagoras (born in Samos, a Greek island off the coast of modern Turkey, c570 BCE; died in Metapontum in today's Basilicata c495 BCE) had actually lived nearby in Crotone, that we were near neighbours in place but not time.

I also recall hearing somewhere that however good a mathematician Pythagoras might have been, he wasn't particularly *simpatico* as a person. It is something that always stuck in my mind and so, now that he was almost in my circle of friends *and* our local airport now bore his name, it seemed worth checking up on him.

You could have knocked me down with a feather when I discovered that he may not have been the first to come across the relationships in a right-angled triangle and that the square of the hypotenuse (the side opposite the right angle) is equal to the sum of the squares of the other two sides. Others had worked it out earlier but, so the story that justifies the appendage of his name to the theorem goes, Pythagoras was the first to demonstrate a proof of the theorem. On today's internet there are literally dozens of diagrams, some animated, that demonstrate and prove the veracity of Pythagoras' Theorem.

The legacy of his theorem is only a small part of the life of Pythagoras at Crotone for he became better known as a philosopher and the leader of a cult, a school, a way of life … people have given it many names. I'll let Swinburne (1777) have the first word on Pythagoras, and Morton (1967) the last. First Swinburne:

"Pythagoras, after his long peregrinations in search of knowledge, fixed his residence in this place [Kroton] … This incomparable sage spent the latter part of his life in training up disciples to the rigid exercise of sublime and moral virtue, and instructing the Crotoniates in the true arts of government, such as alone can insure happiness, glory, and independence."

Now Morton:

"Even if he wrote anything, not a word has survived, though his teaching is well known. He taught serenity and self-discipline; he was a vegetarian, though for some unknown reason he forbade his followers to eat beans; he believed in the therapeutic value of music; he taught that vice is a sickness of the soul and that virtue is rewarded by translation into some higher form of being after death. Though his teaching was not intended to be political, he believed that human affairs should be conducted by a disciplined, élite aristocracy. To be a Pythagorean was rather like membership of an exclusive club, or perhaps it might be compared to mediaeval knighthood or even Freemasonry."

As I relish my baked beans and dislike cults, a Pythagorean I am not.

Kroton's defeat in battle by fellow Greeks, the Locrians, marked the beginning of its decline, a decline made irreversible after Roman occupation and the subsequent changing of hands again and again as its decrease in influence was matched by its reduction in size.

In 1818 Keppel-Craven estimated its population to be about 5000 with a preponderance of 'some ancient and very rich families'. These families will have included the Baracca and Apa families about whom I have already written; both farmed the fine pastures along the Neto valley and both still exist. Generally he was not impressed:

"In its present state, Cotrone, as the reader may observe, offers little or nothing to arrest the attention of the traveller: not only all vestiges of its ancient splendour are erased, but even the local charms which Theocritus so sweetly described have now vanished, if they ever existed."

But it was not all doom and gloom:

"I must, however, observe, that the banks of the Esaro produce in quantity the sweet pea in a wild state, but adorned with a greater variety of colour, and a stronger fragrance than any I ever saw cultivated in our gardens."

Craufurd Tait Ramage (1848) was really looking forward to visiting Crotone for he recalled how Milo's feats of strength were 'among the wonders' of his 'boyish days'. It came as a bit of a shock therefore when the reality did not quite live up to the fantasy as he perused the crowded town square:

"It was in vain that I looked around to discover the athletic forms and brawny muscles of former times. The stare of stolid ignorance, the look of unintelligent curiosity, were the only striking features in the character of the modern inhabitants of Crotone."

Ramage emphasises the city's decline by noting how the city walls that once formed a twelve-mile circle now 'scarcely form a circuit of one mile'.

So this was the city, this ancient Greek city, the home of Milo and Pythagaros and of a rich Hellenic inheritance that most 19th century travellers found. Unlike Sibaris, Caulon and, to some extent, Locri at least

Crotone had survived on more or less the same site as its Greek origins. The problem was that the new incarnation in no way emulated these travellers' expectations.

In 1928, amid the fascist era's scramble to emulate and cultivate an idealistic and classical past, the city finally reverted to the nearest modern equivalent of its old name of Kroton and became Crotone. Thus ended the tongue-twisting variations which, with that misplaced 'r', earlier travellers had to contend with in Cortone and Cotrone.

In the early 20th century, in their respective travelogues, two men, George Gissing (1897) and Norman Douglas (1911), devoted more pages than usual to their time at Crotone, though for very different reasons. And somehow both left their mark on Crotone, in much the same way as Edward Lear (1847) left his on Gerace.

Over the winter of of 2008-09 I read both Gissing's *By the Ionian Sea* and Douglas' *Old Calabria*. Douglas of course knew that Gissing had been in Crotone only a few years earlier and had clearly read Gissing's account of his time there. Talking of Crotone's cemetery and Gissing, Douglas wrote this:

"He expired in February 1901—the year of the publication of the "Ionian Sea," and they showed me his tomb near the right side of the entrance; a poor little grave, with a wooden cross bearing a number, which will soon be removed to make room for another one."

Not unnaturally I was interested to find Gissing's tomb and so, on a bright and crisp spring day, we spent several hours walking up and down the rows of the dead, scouring every headstone in the cemetery, in search of dear George Gissing. I had assumed of course that the number had now been changed for a name and that perhaps he had been given a more prominent position bearing in mind his writings were not unknown locally.

It was an interesting interlude; we enjoyed our day out with the dead even if Gissing didn't seem to be among them. Back home I checked the internet to see if, perhaps, there might be some more information. There was: in 1903, at the age of forty-six, George Gissing died in France where he was buried at Saint-Jean-de-Luz; he had written twenty-three novels in his short life.

For years I thought that Douglas had just got it wrong, I wasn't going to hold it against him that he's sent us on a wild goose chase in Crotone cemetery; not finding Gissing tomb was the only blip in an otherwise good day. I can recommend reading headstones, even in a foreign language.

Five years on and I had nearly finished re-reading *Old Calabria*; I was halfway through the chapter entitled *Memories of Gissing* and was abruptly aware of the respect that Douglas must have had for Gissing; to write about an earlier traveller in such a way was both unusual and deferential. I came to the part about Crotone cemetery:

"And what of Gissing's other friend, the amiable guardian of the cemetery? "His simple good nature and intelligence greatly won upon me. I like to think of him as still quietly happy amid his garden walls, tending flowers that grow over the dead at Cotrone."

"Dead, like those whose graves he tended; like Gissing himself. He expired in February 1901—the year of the publication of the "Ionian Sea," and they showed me his tomb near the right side of the entrance; a poor little grave, with a wooden cross bearing a number, which will soon be removed to make room for another one"

I paused ... I re-read it and knew I was blushing with embarrassment as I became aware of the unspoken injustice I had done Douglas; five years earlier I had completely misread his intent. Douglas was not referring to the death of Gissing at all but to the death of Gissing's friend 'the amiable guardian of the cemetery'. But I was not alone for I later discovered that Eric Whelpton (1957) made the same mistake on reading Douglas and assumed that Gissing had returned to Crotone where he died in 1901.

It was Gissing's experiences at Crotone that led me to wonder how Richard

Crotone cemetery today ... where Gissing is not buried but where the cemetery's 'amiable gardener' was interred in 1901.

Keppel-Craven had come to write about the 'salubrity of its atmosphere'. Gissing would scarcely have agreed for his Crotone sojourn was largely spent in his room at the town's Concordia Hotel under the watchful eye of local physician, Doctor Sculco.

Gissing arrived at Crotone by train from Sibari:

"A wind was rising; at the dim little stations I heard it moan and buffet, and my carriage, where all through the journey I sat alone, seemed the more comfortable. Rain began to fall, and when, about ten o'clock, I alighted at Cotrone, the night was loud with storm."

After a short journey in a 'shabby, creaking, mud-plastered sort of coach' he was unceremoniously deposited outside the Albergo Concordia in the town centre. Without any help from a porter or receptionist he took it upon himself to find a room:

"Happily I did not suffer from my lack of experience; after trying one or two doors in vain, I found a sleeping place which seemed to be unoccupied, and straightway took possession of it."

Over the next two days he visited the town hall, an orange grove and the cemetery—where he met its 'amiable guardian'—before reflecting on what he thought about the town. He didn't seem too impressed:

"The people are all more or less unhealthy; one meets peasants horribly disfigured with life-long malaria. There is an agreeable cordiality in the middle classes; business men from whom I sought casual information, even if we only exchanged a few words in the street, shook hands with me at parting. I found no one who had much good to say of his native place; every one complained of a lack of water. Indeed, Cotrone has as good as no water supply. One or two wells I saw, jealously guarded: the water they yield is not really fit for drinking, and people who can afford it purchase water which comes from a distance in earthenware jars."

Later, having described the eating habits of the locals who ate at the Concordia each evening, he realised he wasn't at his best:

"I dwell upon the question of food because it was on this day that I began to feel a loss of appetite and found myself disgusted with the dishes set before me. In ordinary health I have the happiest qualification of the traveller, an ability to eat and enjoy the familiar dishes of any quasi-civilized country; it was a bad sign when I grew fastidious. After a mere pretence of dinner, I lay down in my room to rest and read. But I could do neither; it grew plain to me that I was feverish. Through a sleepless night, the fever manifestly increasing, I wished that illness had fallen on me anywhere rather than at Cotrone."

Thereafter it was the course of his illness that occupied much of his time at Crotone. The reader is introduced to those who took care of him and in particular Doctor Riccardo Sculco.

Being ill in a foreign language is not easy, I know I have experienced it myself several times and have even had a major operation in a foreign language. With compassion, irony and humour Gissing goes on to describe the course of his illness and the relationships between the main protagonists—the doctor, the female owner, the cook, the waiter and the twelve year-old male 'chambermaid'—in the finespun medical, culinary and boisterous ballet that unfolds in the Albergo Concordia.

After a few days Gissing became more tolerant of the Concordia and its staff and though he yearned to leave—he had not yet been to Capo Colonna—he did as the good Doctor Sculco said and stayed in bed. He also became an object of curiosity:

"Whilst my fever was high, little groups of people often came into the room, to stand and stare at me, exchanging, in a low voice, remarks which they supposed I did not hear, or, hearing, could not understand; as a matter of fact, their dialect was now intelligible enough to me, and I knew that they discussed my chances of surviving. Their natures were not sanguine. A result, doubtless, of the unhealthy climate, every one at Cotrone seemed in a more or less gloomy state of mind."

The twelve year-old 'chambermaid' was the owner's son who dropped in on Gissing every evening:

"At an uncertain hour of the evening he entered (of course, without knocking), doffed his cap in salutation, and began by asking how I found

Gissing's room at the Concordia as it is today; note the washbasin and jug in the alcove.
Dr Riccardo Sculco (1855-1931) who looked after Gissing so well at the Concordia.

myself. The question could not have been more deliberately and thoughtfully put by the Doctor himself. When I replied that I was better, the little man expressed his satisfaction, and went on to make a few remarks about the *pessimo tempo* [bad weather]. Finally, with a gesture of politeness, he inquired whether I would permit him *"di fare un po' di pulizia"*—to clean up a little, and this he proceeded to do with much briskness. Excepting the good Sculco, my chambermaid was altogether the most civilized person I met at Cotrone."

As his health improved, Gissing was keen to leave Crotone for what he hoped would be a more agreeable destination:

"My thoughts turned continually to Catanzaro. It is a city set upon a hill ... and I felt that if I could but escape thither, I should regain health and strength. Here at Cotrone the air oppressed and enfeebled me; the neighbourhood of the sea brought no freshness. From time to time the fever seemed to be overcome, but it lingered still in my blood and made my nights restless. I must away to Catanzaro."

Dr Sculco advised patience but Gissing's mind was made up. He was reconciled to the knowledge that he would never see the remains of the Temple of Hera at Capo Colonna and the good doctor willingly took him on an imaginary visit by describing everything in detail to him.

A few days later, feeble though he still was, he determined to leave:

"To my delight I looked forth next morning on a sunny and calm sky, such as I had not seen during all my stay at Cotrone. I felt better, and decided to leave for Catanzaro by train in the early afternoon. Shaking still, but heartened by the sunshine, I took a short walk, and looked for the last time at the Lacinian promontory."

Crotone left an indelible mark on George Gissing and, unknown to him at the time, his writing about his time there did the same for Crotone

---

Norman Douglas (1911) also stayed in the Concordia (as did French travel-writer François Lenormant in 1882) and, comparing it to the Gissing experience, found it transformed:

"The establishment has vastly improved since those days. The food is good and varied, the charges moderate; the place is spotlessly clean in every part—I could only wish that the hotels in some of our English country towns were up to the standard of the "Concordia" in this respect. It is also enlarged; the old dining-room, whose guests are so humorously described by him, is now my favourite bedroom, while those wretched oil-lamps sputtering on the wall have been replaced by a lavish use of electricity."

All but one of the staff that Gissing described with such lucidity and humour were now dead:

"But the little waiter is alive and now married; and Doctor Sculco still resides in his aristocratic *palazzo* up that winding way in the old town, with the escutcheon of a scorpion—portentous emblem for a doctor—over its entrance. He is a little greyer, no doubt; but the same genial and alert personage as in those days."

Douglas, who had been here before, saw more of the good in Crotone:

"One might do worse than spend a quiet month or two at Cotrone in the spring, for the place grows upon one: it is so reposeful and orderly. But not in winter. Gissing committed the common error of visiting south Italy at that season when, even if the weather will pass, the country and its inhabitants are not true to themselves. You must not come to these parts in winter time. Nor yet in the autumn, for the surrounding district is highly malarious."

If I didn't know Douglas better, I might suspect him of having been paid to eulogise about Crotone for he alone among travellers paints such a picture:

"I usually take a final dip in the sea [in the] evening. After that, it is advisable to absorb an ice or two—they are excellent, at Cotrone—and a glass of Strega liqueur, to ward off the effects of over-work. Next, a brief promenade through the clean, well-lighted streets and now populous streets, or along the boulevard Margherita to view the rank and fashion taking the

The Concordia Hotel as it is today.

air by the murmuring waves, under the cliff-like battlements of Charles the Fifth's castle; and so to dinner."

In 1999 American writer, John Keahey, visited Crotone to research his book about Gissing, *A Sweet and Glorious Land*, and found that the Concordia had changed its name to the Hotel Italia. He will be pleased to hear that it is once again called the Concordia and is full of all kinds of memorabilia relating to its renowned travelling clientele—François Lenormant, George Gissing and Norman Douglas.

It is hard to equate today's Crotone with its past which is why so many travellers were disappointed in what they found. Because of its position on the Ionian seaboard and being the only major deep-water and sheltered port between Taranto (in Puglia) and Reggio Calabria, Crotone has always been vulnerable. It is no accident that major battles were fought here and foreign invaders saw it as a prize. Time and history have been unkind to Crotone.

From the early 16th century the town has been dominated by the castle built by Holy Roman Emperor, Charles V (who was also Charles I of Spain). Crotone Castle still oversees the port and for visitors to the city it has probably been the only constant feature for the last five hundred years. It is still there between the port and the old town though its edifice is less commanding these days as encroaching apartments and shops make it more difficult to appreciate just how gargantuan it is. The area also houses the town's excellent museum and its collection of Greek and Roman artefacts.

In 1995 Crotone became a Province in its own right as a result of local government re-organisation initiated in 1992. Thus it is only relatively recently that Crotone, now a provincial capital, has ceased playing second fiddle to its near neighbour Catanzaro.

It has been a struggle to cast off the legacies of the past, not solely the distant past dominated by changes of regime, malaria and earthquakes but also post-war when the city has suffered from inadequate housing schemes and poorly executed industrial projects. And, of course when such proposals did get off the ground, it was like an open invitation for the mafia to step in and sequester their share of the spoils.

Crotone is my local city; I know it more intimately than others so I make no apology for treating it slightly different to the other provincial capitals.

I first visited to Crotone in 2006 and was not impressed. The city was dirty and untidy and had an air of decay and indifference; there was the sense that nobody cared about anything. When I read Douglas' glowing account I was difficult to believe he was writing about the same Crotone.

Almost a decade on and things are changing, slowly it is true, but nevertheless noticeably improving. Foreign cruise ships now stop off at Crotone and their human cargo is bussed to Le Castella, Santa Severina and

A corner of the Castle of Charles V at Crotone ... these days it is difficult to appreciate just how large it is and it's almost impossible to photograph its entirety except from the air. Also the town has encroached into the walls surrounding the castle with rear windows and balconies from the street above overhanging the castle precincts.

Not in the vacant centre of the square named after him, is a modern sculpture dedicated to Pythagoras and crowned with the visual proof of his theorem on the properties of the right-angled triangle.

The harbour-front statue of Crotone-born Rino Gaetano with his trademark top-hat.

Cirò. Derelict industrial plants are being dismantled; billboards recognising the city's Magna Græcia heritage and plugging the museum are appearing; the airport has re-opened (but at the time of writing that could be a short-lived asset); for good or bad, there's even a McDonalds.

But—there's always a 'but'—the summer of 2015 was blighted by headlines such as this: *'Crotone, no bathing on the beach: bacteriological risks, tourists bewildered'*. Yes, people's holidays were spoilt by sewage flowing into the sea close to the many local beaches; you could lie on the beach and soak up the sun but to enter the water was forbidden during one of the hottest summers in recent years. It's the sort of thing that you might expect to happen in a third-world country, not an ancient city that hosts cruise ships full of American.

So, for me, Crotone continues to be a work in progress though, despite the irritations and frustrations, it is a place with which I feel an affinity. There are so many things I will it to do better but I am not disheartened for I feel sure it will eventually overcome these legacies of the past.

I will let George Gissing have (almost) the last word. Despite—or because of—his illness there, I sense he too had an affinity with Crotone; these were his thoughts the morning he woke to hear music playing in a Crotone street:

"At the moment when this strain broke upon my ear, I was thinking ill of Cotrone and its inhabitants; in the first pause of the music I reproached myself bitterly for narrowness and ingratitude. All the faults of the Italian people are whelmed in forgiveness as soon as their music sounds under the Italian sky. One remembers all they have suffered, all they have achieved in spite of wrong. Brute races have flung themselves, one after another, upon this sweet and glorious land; conquest and slavery, from age to age, have been the people's lot. Tread where one will, the soil has been drenched with blood. An immemorial woe sounds even through the lilting notes of Italian gaiety. It is a country wearied and regretful, looking ever backward to the things of old; trivial in its latter life, and unable to hope sincerely for the future. Moved by these voices singing over the dust of Croton, I asked pardon for all my foolish irritation, my impertinent fault-finding. Why had I come hither, if it was not that I loved land and people? And had I not richly known the recompense of my love?"

Well, almost the last word; that goes to iconic Crotone-born rock star Rino Gaetano—killed in a car accident in 1981—who, though he and his family moved to Rome when he was nine, learnt his music on the streets of Crotone. He later penned a song that has truly become a Calabrian anthem, *Ma il cielo e sempre più blu*, But the sky is always bluer ...

Reggio di Calabria

Emily Lowe (1858) was definitely unimpressed:

"The town of Reggio, which by an extraordinary hallucination once called itself "le petit Paris," totters on its legs like a baby; two-thirds of the buildings were levelled at once by a grand earthquake, and little shocks are constantly adding to the heaps of rubbish."

Lowe is, I assume, alluding to the earthquakes of 1783 when the deep south of Calabria was particularly affected. That said, there were subsequent quakes, tremors and aftershocks throughout the region after 1783.

Part of Reggio has another nickname for the promenade that runs along the seafront and looks across the Straits of Messina to Sicily has been dubbed 'the most beautiful kilometre in Italy'. Many would take issue with that and substitute 'the most' for 'a'; nevertheless it is a delightful promenade and is taken full advantage of by walkers, joggers and cyclists —the latter often seem to have omitted to attach a bell to their handlebars or perhaps have forgotten how to use it.

This 'beautiful kilometre' was created as a direct result of the two earthquakes that hit Reggio (and Messina) in 1905 and 1908. So much damage was done to the city, and particularly the seafront that the rebuilding started from Reggio's own ground zero.

What Emily Lowe observed was bad enough but nothing compared to the later devastation suffered by the people of Reggio.

The most beautiful kilometre in Italy? The busy seafront promenade at Reggio Calabria.

For Lowe and her mother, Reggio Calabria was the beginning of their Calabrian adventure as indeed it was for all those who came across from Sicily; for others it was their last port of call in Calabria before continuing their journey to Sicily or back to Naples.

Like Lowe, few of the other, earlier travellers were impressed with their first impressions of the city. Henry Swinburne (1777) was the first to visit but of course he was the only one to do so *before* the earthquakes:

"Reggio can boast of neither beautiful buildings nor strong fortifications." Brian Hill (1891) came eight years after the earthquakes but, unusually, does not dwell on their aftermath:

"We had at Regio, upon a smaller scale, the same melancholy view as Messina; the mortality was less than in most of the neighbouring towns, as only one hundred and twenty persons were killed, of which seventeen were found dead in one house; several perished upon the seashore, where the waves rose to the height of seventy palms [about sixty feet], and threw the bodies into the air, which rested in falling upon the trees and ruins."

It is true that the interior of Calabria was most severely affected by the 1783 earthquakes but at first Hill's account of casualties at Reggio seemed a little sanitised mainly because there was no mention of the conditions on the ground, particularly the housing. For a clearer picture I reread Sir William Hamilton's first-hand account penned in May 1783 and published that same month in *The British Magazine and Review*:

"I arrived about sun-set at Reggio, which I found less damage than I expected, though not a house in it is habitable or inhabited, and all the people live in barracks [*barrache*, temporary wooden housing] or tents: but, after having been several days in the plain, where every building is levelled to the ground, a house with a roof, or a church with a steeple, was to me a new and refreshing object."

The general feeling that recovery from the earthquakes remained a work in progress was something that every traveller seemed to pick up on when they visited Reggio but by the time George Gissing (1897) there were clear signs that progress was being made:

"[The earthquake] of 1783, which wrought destruction throughout Calabria, laid Reggio in ruins, so that to-day it has the aspect of a newly-built city, curving its regular streets, amphitheatre-wise, upon the slope that rises between shore and mountain.

"The rebuilding of Reggio has made it clean and sweet; its air is blended from that of mountain and sea, ever renewed, delicate and inspiring."

These optimistic words of Gissing were short-lived. Eight years later in

1905 and worse again in 1908, two devastating earthquakes once again took Reggio Calabria back to the drawing board.

Douglas (1911) was there shortly afterwards and wrote the following:

"A young fellow, one of the survivors, attached himself to me in the capacity of guide through the ruins of Reggio. He wore the characteristic

An artist's impression of Reggio Calabria following the 5 February earthquake in 1783.

Chaos on the streets of Reggio Calabria following the 1908 earthquake.

earthquake look, a dazed and bewildered expression of countenance; he spoke in a singularly deliberate manner. Knowing the country, I was soon bending my steps in the direction of the cemetery, chiefly for the sake of the exquisite view from those windswept heights, and to breathe more freely after the dust and desolation of the lower parts. This burial-ground is in the same state as that of Messina, once the pride of its citizens; the insane frolic of nature has not respected the slumber of the dead or their commemorative shrines; it has made a mockery of the place, twisting the solemn monuments into repulsive and irreverential shapes."

Like Crotone, Reggio never really stood a chance; earthquakes apart, its position at the very tip of Calabria and facing Sicily has always made it vulnerable, as easy target for those heading across the Straits of Messina in both directions.

George Gissing summed up the problem:

"By its natural situation Reggio is marked for an unquiet history. It was a gateway of Magna Graecia; it lay straight in the track of conquering Rome when she moved towards Sicily; it offered points of strategic importance to every invader or defender of the peninsula throughout the mediaeval wars. Goth and Saracen, Norman, Teuton and Turk, seized, pillaged, and abandoned, each in turn, this stronghold overlooking the narrow sea."

I have already written at length about the earthquakes of 1905 and 1908, the latter having the unenviable plaudit of being the most destructive earthquake that Europe has ever experienced. Fifteen thousand died at Reggio, believed to be approximately one third of the city's population.

Post-1908, Hutton (1912) mirrored Gissing's thoughts but also reflected on this most recent calamity:

We enter Magna Graecia today through a ruined gate ... Reggio di Calabria has to-day nothing but the spectacle of her latest misery to offer to the traveller. The most unfortunate of Italian cities, she has from her foundation suffered every violation of nature and man; fire, sword, and earthquake have from time immemorial continually laid her in ruins."

By 1957 when Eric Whelpton visited the city, he was disappointed that the opportunity to rebuild on a grander scale had not been grasped by the city fathers:

"Unfortunately the planners and architects lost a fine opportunity of laying out the new town on a magnificent scale, because landowners would not be shifted from their property, and so the present streets are not nearly as wide as they should be. In winter the whole of the life of Reggio is concentrated in the long and narrow Corso Garibaldi which runs parallel to the magnificent avenue on the sea front."

What Whelpton and all other travellers fail to mention is that in Calabria wherever there is civil chaos and disorder, the mafia is not far behind. Whatever decisions were taken about the rebuilding of Reggio will have been taken, to varying degrees, with other considerations in mind. Bottom of the list will have been what might be best for the city and its citizens.

As it was in the post-1908 period, so it is today. Catanzaro may be the capital of Calabria but Reggio Calabria is the *'ndrangheta* capital of the region. But travellers were not inclined to mention this aspect of life in and around Reggio though I suspect some were aware of it.

On the other hand, many did mention a phenomenon for which Reggio is not only famous but the term now used to describe the same phenomena worldwide originates at Reggio—the Fata Morgana. Eric Whelpton (1957) described it almost as if it were tangible as opposed to something illusory:

"From the mainland shore there is an occasional vision of the Fata Morgana, a mirage of a splendid and magical city of palaces, tall buildings, towers and minarets, which rise out of the waters of the straits when the air is absolutely still."

Gardiner (1966) explained the science:

"What happens, it seems, is that the atmospheric peculiarities of the locality—affected perhaps by volcanic dust from Etna or Strómboli—cause a mirror-image of the city of Messina to appear in the strait. There is a vertical magnification which distorts the buildings, making them appear tall as skyscrapers."

Henry Morton (1967) explained the derivation of the name:

"As interesting as the optical delusion is the name, which was given to it by the Normans, 'Fata' in Italian means 'fairy', and the Fairy Morgana was no other than King Arthur's rather difficult sister, Morgan le Fay."

In the Arthurian legend, Morgan le Fay was a sorceress, the sort whose witchcraft could create mirages, such as that seen in the Strait of Messina, where fairy castles in the air might lure unwary sailors to their death.

On my several visits to Reggio Calabria I have never witnessed the Fata Morgana, nor has any of the locals I have met there. That, of course, does not hinder people talking about it, nor of knowing a friend of a friend who has experienced it.

Swinburne (1777) didn't actually know Father Angelucci but he knew what he wrote about *his* first-hand experience of the Fata Morgana on 14 August 1643:

"The sea that washes the Sicilian shore welled up, and became, for ten miles in length, like a chain of dark mountains; while the waters near our Calabrian coast grew quite smooth and in an instant appeared as one clear polished mirror, reclining against the aforesaid ridge. On this glass was depicted, in *chiaro scuro*, a string of several thousand of pilasters, all equal in altitude, distance, and degree of light and shade. In a moment they lost half their height, and bent into arcades, like Roman aqueducts. A long cornice was next formed on the top, and above it rose castles innumerable, all perfectly alike. These soon split into towers, which were shortly after lost in colonnades, then windows, and at last ended in pines, cypresses, and other trees, even and similar. This is the *Fata Morgana*, which, for twenty-six years, I had thought a mere fable."

While my several visits to Reggio did not yield the merest glimpse of the Fata Morgana or any direct links with the mafia, in relation to the latter I was aware that the elected local authority had been dissolved in 2012 because of its alleged mafia links and the city was being run by an appointed Commissioner (*Commissione Straordinaria*). This is the normal procedure in Calabria (and elsewhere in Italy) when the elected council and/or its leader (*sindaco*) have been shown to have direct or indirect links to the mafia. From October that year until October 2014 the city was run by such a Commissioner.

Arguably the fact that local government normality had returned to Reggio Calabria is an indication that the mafia's influence is waning but there are those who remain sceptical. The mafia has many faces and many of those faces are just like the guy sitting next to you in a bar or restaurant or on the train; they don't all wear dark suits and dark glasses. This is the perennial problem: people have voted for what they believed to be a group untainted by the mafia and have only realised later that nothing had changed, that friendships, connivance and collusion are what the mafia excel at.

The word from Reggio is that, with the new, young *sindaco*, things have changed, that the current regime is robustly anti-mafia and will not be seduced and manipulated by it. Time will tell.

Mafia capital or not, generally Reggio Calabria does not exude that down-at-heel feel that other mafia towns do. Tourists and locals walk the streets in safety and in numbers; there are dozens of places to stay and to eat. And, should they get bored with the seafront, the adjacent artworks, the museums, the history, the galleries and the shops along Corso Garibaldi, then there's always that ferry across to Sicily.

Reggio is not the closest place to the Sicilian port of Messina, that's Villa San Giovanni, round the corner and a little bit up the coast, its from here and not Reggio that the main car and train ferry services between Calabria and Sicily operate. The first time I came this far south I didn't realise this; I'd never heard of Villa San Giovanni nor, for that matter, did I really know I was in Calabria, in fact I didn't even have a map. I was vaguely heading for Sicily and just assumed that Reggio was where you caught the ferry ... to which end I had arranged to pick up a hire car at Lamezia airport.

I was travelling alone but, having landed at Lamezia over an hour late, I offered a lift to Jack, next to me on the flight, who had just missed his train. I ended up in Reggio that night because that's where he was going and it was then that things took an unexpected turn as I described in *Stumbling through Italy*. This is a slightly shorter version of that encounter.

I should explain that, from our in-flight chat, I already knew that Jack was gay. I surmised that, like others before him, he had picked up that I was not fazed by his sexual orientation. I had already found a way to indicate that I was straight and so we were both at ease with our differences.

"Jack accepted my offer of a lift to Reggio and called his friend Paolo, a university lecturer in Reggio, to explain the change of plan—he'd now be

Artwork alongside Reggio's promenade and a legacy of Magna Græcia in the museum.

arriving by car and that there would be an extra mouth to feed and a bed to make ready. My accommodation in Reggio Calabria was sorted.

"The welcome from Paolo and his friend Octavia was effusive and genuine; they were both delighted to see their friend Jack and extended their welcome to me, his last-minute, straight companion and chauffeur.

"We ate and drank exceptionally well, though for much of the time my over-active imagination was trying to work out the relationships between everyone. Jack and Paolo were clearly 'warm brothers'; Octavia was married and on holiday from Milan to where she was returning the following day but there seemed more to her relationship with Paolo than met the eye.

"I was enjoying myself and not at all phased when Agnella arrived to say farewell to Octavia ... I was beginning to get the picture, albeit one that didn't fit in with my original alcohol-induced speculation.

"The laughing and the drinking continued as the clock swept past two in the morning and we decided it was time to sleep. We had arranged that, after breakfast, Paolo would take me to the ferry for Messina.

"Breakfast came and went for five weary bodies and was yet another culinary delight made all the more glorious by my first glimpse of Sicily, basking in the mid-morning sun in a limpid green sea. I was impatient to leave, I just wanted to say my 'goodbyes' and head to the ferry but this was Calabria and I went along with the slower pace until Paolo was ready.

"As he cranked up his scooter, his *motorino*, Paolo gave me his number and insisted that I call him from Messina on my way back so that we all could have lunch together."

My first visit to Reggio was definitely a unique experience. As far as I am aware, none of my other travelling companions experienced anything quite like it ... though there is at least one who might well have.

I did meet up with Paolo later on that same trip and again when I returned to Reggio two weeks later. But that was more than fifteen years ago and, still today, every time I go there, I'm always on the lookout for him; one of the problems is that I've no idea what part of Reggio I was in.

Despite the devastation, the terrible loss of life and the mass exodus to pastures new in the wake of 1908, Reggio Calabria grew again from the ashes and today is a thriving city that boasts not only 'the most beautiful kilometre in Italy' but also one of Italy's (and Magna Græcia's) most important treasures, the magnificent Riace Bronzes.

Because of what happened here over a century ago, Reggio Calabria has no *centro storico* like other Calabrian regional capitals; the not-so-broad, and seemingly never-ending, Corso Garibaldi and its feast of modern shopping is the nearest to an historical centre. The rebuilding of the city did not deal kindly with what might now be considered to be its historic architectural heritage. And following another significant earthquake in 1923, some of what remained of Reggio's Norman castle was demolished and today only the 15th century Aragonese part survives—on one side of the aptly-named Piazza Castello.

Given everything that history has thrown at Reggio Calabria, the story of a boy born there in 1946 is quite remarkable.

One of four children, he became interested in Reggio's Greek heritage and studied the classics for a short time at the local Liceo Classico. He later studied architecture while at the same time he was learning the sewing business from his mother who was a professional dressmaker with a shop near the cathedral. At the age of twenty-five he moved to Milan to work in the fashion business. His name was Gianni Versace.

In 1992, this is what Versace had to say about his home town:

"Reggio [is] the place where, little by little, I began to appreciate the *Iliad*, the *Odyssey*, the *Aeneid*, where I began to breathe the art of Magna Græcia."

Gianni Versace was murdered in Miami in 1995.

What remains of Reggio Calabria's castle; originally a Norman stronghold, only the Aragonese towers remain. Reggio's seafront boulevard is linked to the higher Corso Garibaldi by a moving walkway ... ideal for us 'oldies'.

Vibo Valéntia

Edward Hutton (1912) called it one thing:

"… the gloriously situated city of Monteleone, 1500 feet above the sea … still boasts a ruined castle built by Frederick II."

And Eric Whelpton (1957) called it another, albeit with little passion:

"As the attractions of this part of Calabria are scenic rather than architectural, I certainly would be inclined to by-pass Vibo Valéntia …"

In between these two, in 1928, Monteleone reverted to its original name of Vibo Valéntia. Name changes were not uncommon during the fascist era, particularly those which looked back to an earlier classical heritage.

Unaware that there was another to follow, Richard Keppel-Craven (1818) explained the various changes in name:

"The situation of Monteleone is allowed by most antiquarians to be the same with that of Hipponium, a city whose Greek name was changed into the Latin Vibo Valéntia, or Vibona. Strabo attributes its foundation to the Locrians, from whom it was wrested by the Bruttii, who afterwards yielded it to the Romans. Athenaeus extols the magnificence and taste displayed in the habitations of Hipponium, and more particularly the mosaic pavements with which they were adorned."

Unlike some other major Magna Græcia sites—notably Sibari, Caulon and Locri Epizephyrii—the 'antiquaries' got the location of the Greek settlement more or less right for the ruins of Hipponion are indeed under the present city. Like those at Crotone, most are, of course, hidden from view but there are scattered outcrops where, miraculously, more recent building did not encroach. Like many of the Greek settlements near to Calabria's west coast, Hipponion was a secondary settlement in the sense that it was founded by those from an already established community, in this case Locrians. Further south near Rosarno is the Magna Græcia site of Medma which was also founded by Locrians.

For centuries Monteleone—I will call it Monteleone up to references pre-1928—had been an important staging post on the route south between Naples and Reggio Calabria. When Swinburne came here in 1780 he was very impressed:

"[Monteleone is] a considerable town placed upon the brow of a hill facing the south, in a most incomparable situation; from the road I had long enjoyed the view of it, The Baronial castle occupies the highest part, embowered in handsome tufts of deciduous and evergreen trees; the town crowns the rest of the slope in a very happy manner."

Indeed almost everyone who came here would sing its praises to some degree but only Richard Keppel-Craven (1818), the first traveller to write about Calabria following the Napoleonic era, came up with a gem of a story about the two generals who fought each other at the Battle of Máida in 1806, the French Jean Regnier and the British John Stuart. Both generals sojourned—at different times of course—at Monteleone *and* in the same house, though only Regnier left his artistic mark on the town. Keppel-Craven, who was also residing in the same house, was taken on a whistle-stop tour of the town by his host:

"There are a few very good pictures in the churches; among which, one by Baccio di Rosa made me regret that the declining light was insufficient to do justice to its beauties. I was hurried from it to be shown a pictorial performance of certainly less merit, though highly curious, from having been executed by General Regnier; it was in a temporary theatre, which had been

The road sign outside Vibo Valéntia's castle acknowledges the town's erstwhile name.

Side by side at last ... the French general (left) with the artistic bent, Jean Regnier, and his adversary, the British victor at the Battle of Máida, Sir John Stuart. Both stayed at Monteleone in the same *palazzo* as Richard Keppel-Craven.

fitted up by the French army In its leisure from more active employment. It seems that all hands were anxious in contributing to its embellishment, and the commander In chief had condescended to paint the fronts of the boxes. This officer, as well as his opponent, Sir John Stuart, had successively resided In the house where I was received; and It was somewhat curious to hear my host and his family give an account of these distinguished personages with a mixture of praise and censure which did honour to their impartiality. It was Indeed as difficult to decide which of their two characters had excited the highest degree of estimation, as it was easy to discover that which had Impressed the strongest feeling of dread."

This last sentence is meant to convey to Keppel-Craven's readership that the locals feared the French; I wonder, however, had Keppel-Craven been French, whether his host might have conveyed the opposite impression.

In 1995, just like Crotone, Vibo Valéntia became the capital of a new province of the same name, the south-western part of what had been the province of Catanzaro. Its new status put the city on the map and, with its Greek ancestry, it became a place worthy of more than a second glance.

I had already visited the other four provincial capitals many times before my first visit to Vibo Valéntia and was pleasantly surprised. The frenetic quality that the others often display was missing; this was a city where unruffled elegance and charm were the prevailing ambiance.

Craufurd Tait Ramage (1828) got it spot on:

"It is, indeed, a lovely spot."

He elaborated:

"The city is built upon a hill of considerable height, which commands a wide view of the country, extending from the bay of St. Euphemia ... to that of Gioia and the Apennines. A magnificent spectacle strikes the eye all around, and the view is crowned in the distance by the bluish smoke of Etna. A castle, surrounded by fine trees, gives it a commanding appearance; and at a short distance lofty mountains, covered with forests, secure it from the cold winds of the north."

Though at first I thought a glimpse of Etna from here—some ninety miles distant—to be somewhat fanciful, I understand that, in certain conditions, it is indeed possible. Much nearer of course is the volcanic island of Strómboli, one of the Lipari islands off the north coast of Sicily ... indeed uninterrupted views of Strómboli are a feature of the town.

Given its position, Monteleone suffered from the 1783 earthquakes; the epicentres of the last three—Soriano Calabro, Filadelfia and Valleflorita—were all close, the first only eight miles away. Swinburne's visit was before these events, Keppel-Craven's thirty-five years after. Only Brian Hill (1791) had real experience of the aftermath which resulted in a little local difficulty when it came to finding accommodation there; he and his brother took their predicament to a well-dressed young man they saw in the crowd:

"He seemed, indeed, to commiserate our case, but with a too significant shrug of the shoulders, gave us to understand that to procure us a lodging would be extremely difficult, if not impossible, most of the houses and convents having been either thrown down, or so much damaged by the great earthquake, as yet to be uninhabitable, and the people generally living in barracks [wooden, shack-like structures]."

But with the help of their new friend they did find lodgings with an unusual host, a man who was a sailor six days a week and a priest on the seventh. Hill's description of the kindnesses shown to his party by those who themselves had suffered unimaginable hardship is quite touching:

"This hospitable gentleman shewed us his own ruined house, which had certainly been a handsome structure, and much lamented that it was not in his power to receive us in it; but he and his wife now occupied a small barrack, which I verily believe he would have constrained us to accept, whatever inconveniences his own family might have suffered, if he had not

The view up towards the castle from the lower town and the view looking down the same thoroughfare from near the castle.

found us another habitation."

Hill was, I imagine, prepared to sleep anywhere as long as it *wasn't* the local hostelry:

"In what was called the inn it was impossible for a living creature to lie down, without being speedily covered with other *living creatures* innumerable."

What Keppel-Craven (1818) and Ramage (1828) experienced was the new Monteleone risen from the rubble. This was a city used to being at the centre of things but Ramage realised that, despite its erstwhile status, it had already started to lose its tarnish and its importance:

"Monteleone ... was the capital of a province till within the last few years, when the district was divided. Reggio and Catanzaro are now the seats of government, and in consequence the streets of Monteleone have a more deserted and gloomy appearance than you are prepared to accept from the size and respectability of the houses."

Ironic that, following the end of French rule in 1815 and the return of the Bourbon monarchy, the old structure of Calabria was changed and with it the status of Monteleone until, in 1995, that same status was re-established.

It was to Monteleone that the British prisoner Philip Elmhirst was brought in 1810, he was thus one of the first to see how the town, its streets and its housing, was developing post-earthquakes:

"The streets are regular and straight, but they are indifferently paved, and the gutters are in the middle of them. The principal one extends the whole length of the city, from the castle to the northern entrance, about three quarters of a mile; and where it crosses at right angles the other main street, which forms the eastern and western entrances, the market is held."

Elmhirst was likewise impressed with the town's castle:

"At the upper end of the town, on the summit of the mountain, are the ruins of a castle built in the middle ages by an ancestor of the Pignatelli family. A great part of it, from the goodness of the materials and workmanship, remains entire; and it appears to have been a place of considerable strength, having been defended on the east and south sides by a steep precipice, Facing the town, the declivity is at first abrupt, and every for its defence that skill could devise was used on that quarter. The French have repaired the stairs, and made the ascent to the top easy, as they have there erected a telegraph, and they could not for that purpose chosen a situation commanding a greater extent of country."

The 'telegraph' referred to by Elmhirst was a recent invention (1791) by the French brothers Chappe. It was a signalling device that sent visual messages across country from elevated positions in sight of each other and inadvertently gave the same name to countless locations worldwide that remain today. How many towns have a Telegraph Hill?

The principal was simple: a tower with a mechanism that could change the position and alignment of its configuration of pivoting arms, that could be seen by an operator on another hill with a similar tower; the same message could then be passed on to other towers atop other hills.

And, as it happens, on the same site today at Monteleone there is a formidable cluster of communication masts doing more or less the same thing, albeit a little faster and to a greater audience.

As we have seen, it was to Monteleone, his erstwhile capital, that Joachim Murat was heading following his landing at Pizzo in early October 1815, as part of his abortive attempt to win back the south from the Bourbons. He knew the town well and it was clearly strategically important to his ambitions; he was probably aware too that, a few months earlier, the military garrison based there had been relocated to Tropea on the coast. Added to which he would have been keen to exploit the town's loss of prestige, its demotion, that followed the return of the Bourbon monarchy. The 'French'

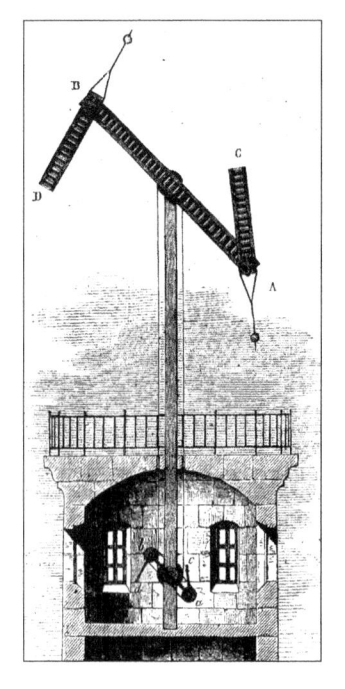

The Chappe 'telegraph', a version of which stood on elevated land by Monteleone Castle, On the same site today, an array of communication masts doing much the same thing, albeit a tad faster.

telegraph was used by Murat's captors at Pizzo to quickly establish the royal wishes in respect of what should happen to him and, as we know, he was condemned to death and executed at Pizzo castle.

At such times people, particularly military personnel, were adept at switching sides as and when it was clearly expedient. For one son of Monteleone, Michele Morelli, it became almost an art-form. Not for him the ignominy that befell other Bourbon officers who, according to Philip Elmhirst, 'were thrown into prison [in Monteleone], because they refused to renounce their allegiance and serve their oppressors'. (For Elmhirst these 'oppressors' were, of course, the common enemy, the French.)

Born into a wealthy Monteleone family in 1792, Michele Morelli chose a short-lived military career in the Bourbon army and soon found himself instead fighting in the French army of Joachim Murat, under whom he participated in the Russian campaign of 1812 when he was promoted to second lieutenant. After the return of the Bourbons, he was still doing military service, this time as a Bourbon second lieutenant stationed in Campania in a unit that specifically targeted local brigands and where, in 1820, he figured prominently in a minor revolt *against* his new masters.

He had become a supporter of the Carbonari, a disparate group of secret societies and in 1821 he and a fellow officer, Neapolitan Giuseppe Silvati, marched their cavalry regiments on Nota to demand change, specifically they wanted the Bourbons to move towards becoming a constitutional monarchy. King Ferdinand appeared to concede that a new constitution and parliament were just around the corner and the revolt petered out. In 1822 both Morelli and Silvati were tried and hanged in Naples for their part in the uprising.

Thus Monteleonean Michele Morelli became, like the Bandiera brothers, what is called an Italian patriot, his status as such consolidated by his untimely demise and immortalised by the town's classically styled statue commemorating his brief life. In Italian terms a patriot is generally one whose aspirations and actions ultimately led to the unification of Italy. A noble goal at the time but, in retrospect, many southerners might wish it had been more of an alliance of equals rather than the rape of the south.

During his time in Monteleone, Midshipman Philip Elmhirst was, in theory at least, a prisoner, though never imprisoned; as a British officer, he had the run of the town and actually visited both of the town's two gaols.

In one, the larger, were incarcerated the usual suspects and was 'constantly crowded with criminals'. But there were three other distinct groups held here:

the lower-ranked mariners under Elmhirst's command whom he visited every day; the 'men of talent, honour and patriotism' who were pro-Bourbon and therefore anti-French and remained married to their principles; and females.

Try as he might he could not gain access to the female part of the prison but he did explain why most of the inmates were there:

"The upper story of the prison was appropriated to females; and most of those now confined had not been convicted of any crime, but were imprisoned because it was supposed they either favoured the brigands, or had conveyed supplies to them. Neither the infirmity of age nor the inexperience of youth, could escape suspicions of that nature; and decrepid women, and little children, frequently on those grounds alone, were consigned to this loathsome receptacle, and found themselves accused of treason, although their very appearance would convince any one of the absurdity of the charge."

Despite having mentioned their 'very appearance' Elmhirst goes on to acknowledge that he 'never could procure admittance into these apartments' but that he had been told that the conditions were worse than those of the men and also more crowded.

Monteleone's second gaol was near the centre of the town and was 'set apart for the reception of brigands of the most daring and unequivocal description'; male brigands, that is.

Elmhirst goes into considerable gruesome detail about the fate of those who were brought here: their time in prison, their trial, their execution and the disposal of their bodies. He summed up as follows:

"Scarcely a day passed during my stay at Monte Leone that was not marked by the execution of two or more of the brigands. From the frequency of the occurrence it became at last almost unnoticed. Even curiosity, which generally delights in such scenes was satiated; and it was seldom that many idle spectators were present on the occasion."

As well as documenting those who were imprisoned for not towing the French line, Elmhirst also wrote about the exploits of one Andreas Orlando, an ex-brigand of 'a bold, artful and enterprising spirit' who did the exact opposite and became adept at locating brigands on behalf of the French.

It's difficult to gauge to what extend his descriptions are just anti-French propaganda and to what extent accurate and disciplined observation.

Following his unfortunate encounter with the Albanians of Caraffa and his forced sojourn at Cortale, Arthur John Strutt (1841) crossed to the Tyrrhenian coast and was hastening south when he passed through Monteleone. But, unlike so many others before and since, he was decidedly unimpressed. Perhaps the 'gloomy appearance' following the town's political demotion that Ramage (1828) alluded to had become worse and was all that Strutt saw:

"We have been walking through the town, which offers, absolutely nothing, interesting or beautiful. We are housed in a tolerable semblance of an inn, and whilst our dinner, or rather supper, is preparing, we have been paying a visit to the Marchese A …"

Strutt seemingly never even cast a glance up the main street to the hard-to-miss castle atop its hill; he was clearly eager to be on his way:

"We left Monteleone this morning, to my great satisfaction; for, I know not why, I disliked the place from the moment I set foot in it."

Had he been travelling at the beginning of the 20th century, Strutt would have been even less impressed with Monteleone for, on 8 September 1905, it was one of several Calabrian towns and villages to be hit by a devastating earthquake. The same earthquake affected both Reggio Calabria in the south and Cosenza to the north with its epicentre somewhere in the Nicastro area.

Only six died in the Forgiari district of Monteleone itself but the nearby community of Zammarò was all but destroyed and seventy of its residents perished; many local villages lost sixty and more people each. Official figures showed that, in Cosenza, Catanzaro and Reggio Calabria provinces, 557 died and 2615 were injured; serious damage was inflicted on 753 disparate Calabrian communities, most of which, like Monteleone, were in the province of Catanzaro where 6186 buildings were either destroyed or seriously damaged.

There may have been only six deaths in Monteleone itself but there was large-scale destruction to the infrastructure of the town; so much so that it was felt serious enough to cast the royal eye over the desolation and desperation—presumably in the hope that those effected might be so grateful for the royal presence that they might forget their on-going predicament.

Five days later King Victor Emmanuel came to Monteleone and was driven round other communities in the area, including the ruins of Zammarò. Courtesy of Associated Press, the story of his visit found its way into, among other newspapers worldwide, the *Los Angeles Herald*:

KING VICTOR EMMANUEL VISITS EARTHQUAKE SCENE
Is 'greeted by Population With Cries of "Help" and Fearlessly Explores the Ruins
MONTELEONE, Sept. 13.—King Victor Emmanuel arrived here to-day and was greeted with cries from the populace of "Help". His majesty visited the ruins despite the danger of falling walls, The remains of the cathedral are threatening to fall momentarily.

The king went into a subterranean fissure whence a child, Maria Antonio Ceccoli, had been taken out alive after being 48 hours under the debris. Her aunt, who was crying beside the ruins, thought she heard the voice of her niece and called some soldiers who, after vigorous efforts, brought up the child almost dead and carried her to the hospital where her condition is critical.
Other stricken village were afterwards visited.

Despite diligent research I could find no record of how this royal visit benefitted the populace, no record as to what extend the cries of 'help' were either heeded or acted upon.

As I have already noted, I was more than a little impressed with modern Vibo Valéntia; perhaps its new status as a provincial capital has given it a renewed sense of purpose.

Overseeing it all—and unperturbed by Strutt's apparent lack of interest—are the impressive remains of the town's Norman castle, built, it is believed, atop the Hipponion acropolis using materials from the nearby Greek temples. Today it houses a museum.

And, as if to thank you for making the effort of walking to the top of the hill, in the lee of the castle there is a splendid café overlooking the town, the Tyrrhenian Sea, Strómboli and, in the distant haze, perhaps even Etna itself.

Perhaps Appian of Alexandria (c. 95CE – c. 165CE)—a Roman historian of Greek origin—should have the last word. Despite all the things that history and nature have pitched at Monteleone and Vibo Valéntia, Appian's description of it as one of the 'most flourishing cities of Italy' is not as far-fetched as it might seem.

The distraught inhabitants of Zammarò make way for the diminutive Italian monarch, Vittorio Emmanule III, as he picks his way through the ruins of their town in the wake of the devastating 1905 earthquake. The castle at the top of the town.

Seeing is believing

"We were enchanted this morning with the costume of the peasants; so much so indeed that we were tempted to stay in order to make a careful sketch of a very pretty girl ..."
Arthur John Strutt *A pedestrian tour in Calabria and Sicily*

It was a beautiful June morning and I was in the same hilltop town as Strutt was in 1841. I was not expecting to come across anyone wearing the traditional peasant costume for which the town remained well-known.

I espied instead two ladies of a certain age sitting and chatting side by side in a wide, sun-facing doorway and made a beeline for them. I was sure these two were from the right generation; they were just what I was looking for and I wanted to show them something. Their ageing faces belied the curiosity still in their eyes and I knew they would be completely unfazed by a stranger clutching a sheet of white paper interrupting their sunny morning routine.

The sheet of paper was a photocopy of a photograph from *Calabria and the Aeolian Island*s by Eric Whelpton (1957); a photo of three young women—taken by Whelpton's wife Barbara—all of whom were wearing the same traditional costume, albeit in black and white, that had clearly enthralled Strutt all those years ago.

We exchanged a few pleasantries about the weather before I explained that I was writing a book about Calabria and was interested to know if they knew any of the women in the photograph and, if so, did any still live locally. They told me to hold on—*aspetta*—as, in concert, both reached down for their handbags and began rummaging around until they located their respective spectacles. Properly equipped for the task ahead, they scrutinising the photo. Slowly they studied, pointed, nodded and muttered before looking up to

The three young women whom Barbara Whelpton Crocker photographed in Tiriolo in 1957. Today Tiriolo still retains the traditions of the colourful costumes once worn by many Calabrian peasants as host to the *Museo del Costume Calabrese*.

confirm that they could name all three. They were pleased with themselves; it was as if I had asked them to participate in a game show and they had successfully completed the first round.

This was more than I could have hoped for but, before I could extract any further details, one volunteered some additional information:

"Of course, they're all dead now," she said, matter-of-factly at first, "all three died very young, just a year or two apart. Such a shame, we were all such good friends."

They rattled off the names of all three as if they'd only been speaking with them the day before yesterday, then paused for breath and looked suitably contrite as if they'd let me down in some way.

For a moment or two they were lost in thoughts and memories that drifted back across half a century or more until one refocused on the here and now and became unexpectedly animated; she started waving her hands in recognition:

"I know who you are," she exclaimed with absolute certainly, "you're that writer, the one from America … the one who was born in … in …"

Still getting over the shock that they might have thought I actually had Calabrian roots, I helped out.

"… in Gimigliano?" I suggested.

"That's the place, Gimigliano … up there in the mountains." Lest I might be disorientated, she flicked her head a little to the left to convey the general whereabouts of Gimigliano.

"Mark Rotella." My response was more of a statement than a question.

"Yes, yes, Rotella … of course, I remember now … the Rotella family from Gimigliano … you're the one from America who writes the books, aren't you?"

I hated to disappoint two of Mark Rotella's devoted fans but I had to admit that I was not he … but that I knew who they meant and had read and enjoyed his book about Calabria, *Stolen Figs: and other Adventures in Calabria*. Indeed I also had to confess that I might never have come here to this town had it not been for *Stolen Figs*.

It was Mark Rotella's description of Tiriolo that, ten years earlier, had put this small hilltop town, not far from Catanzaro, at the top of my must-visit places in Calabria.

Curiously Strutt, the first to visit Tiriolo, does not directly mention the other reason that makes this town special. Perhaps he didn't realise …

"Before leaving Terriolo, however, I should inform you, that it is most picturesquely situated on a very considerable eminence; and at the foot of a crowning peak, which very much tempted us to stay and scale its heights.

The view, however, even from its base, is extremely fine, commanding the whole country as far as the Gulf of Squillace."

If only he'd looked in the opposite direction.

Craufurd Tait Ramage (1828) knew what he was looking for:

"After resting for some hours at Catanzaro I determined to visit Tiriolo, a village nine miles distant, picturesquely situated on a declivity of the Apennines, from which I could look down on the Tuscan and Ionian seas at the same time, and from which the water flows into both seas."

Emily Lowe (1857), working her way up Murat's old post-road from Reggio to Cosenza, didn't pick up on it; she and her mother were too busy with breakfast after a long night in the post-chaise to really take in the view:

"A village rises on the highest point, where sat an amphitheatred town of old. Tiriolo is its name, and two charming Signore de Rosas gave us a breakfast, romantic as the view their pretty eyes gazed upon through the portico."

Norman Douglas (1911) had been here before but didn't quite spell it out ... perhaps he thought everyone had read Ramage:

"Viewed from Catanzaro, one of the hills of Tiriolo looks like a broken volcanic crater. It is a limestone ridge, decked with those characteristic flowers like *Campanula fragilis* which you will vainly seek on the Sila. For Tiriolo lies

An attempt at photographing both seas as a panorama: the Ionian Sea is on the left and the Tyrrhenian on the right. Tiriolo itself lies on the southern foothills of the Sila mountains

on the watershed; there (to quote from a "Person of Quality" [17th century author of *Parthenopoeia*, Scipio Mazzella] "where the Apennine is drawn into so narrow a point, that the rain-water which descendeth from the ridge of some one house, falleth on the left in the Terrene Sea, and on the right into the Adriatick [the Ionian Sea] ..."

Clearly Edward Hutton (1912) had read Ramage and spelt it out in layman's language:

" ... at Tiriolo ... you may look upon both seas, the Ionian and the Tyrrhene, the Gulf of Squillace on the east and the Gulf of S. Eufémia on the west."

Eric Whelpton (1957), whose book it was that contained the photo of the four young girls in traditional costume, also went on to explain the town's position in terms of its strategic importance:

"There are the ruins of the castle at Tiriolo, ageless now, after being rebuilt so many times throughout the centuries, for the Calabrian peninsula narrows down to a neck of perhaps twenty-four miles between Catanzaro and Sant' Eufémia, and so the isthmus has always been of strategic importance."

Like Barbara Whelpton, Leslie Gardiner (1966) managed to photograph some local women in traditional attire; he knew what he was looking for, but it wasn't the best of days:

while in the central distance are the lesser slopes of the Apennines, the spine of Italy, as they continue south to become eventually La Serra and ultimately the Aspromonte range.

"We could see neither Ionian nor Tyrrhenian Sea, because the gale bleared our eyes."

When, eventually, I did get round to visiting Tiriolo I was alone. I had dropped Kay off at Lamezia Airport and had arranged to stay overnight at Tiriolo on my way home. I had two quests: to see if could find any or all of the young women in Barbara Whelpton's photograph and, more importantly, I wanted to gaze down on both the Ionian and Tyrrhenian Seas with no more than the turn of the head.

The first, as I have already described, was not to be; the second I achieved from several parts of the town but most spectacularly from the disjointed ruins of the town's castle.

Both Strutt and Douglas made reference to a second hill alongside the one atop which sits Tiriolo itself: the former described it as 'a crowning peak, which very much tempted us to stay and scale its heights' and the latter as resembling 'a broken volcanic crater'. This second hill rises higher than the town and, I was assured, offers even more staggering views in all directions but, as was clear from my vantage point in the castle, it was much more than a leisurely stroll to get to the top. Today this 'crowning peak' has found its niche as the perfect site for an array of telecommunications masts.

That first evening in Tiriolo, happy with my day's work, I headed for the restaurant nearest to my accommodation in the lower part of town. The door was ajar so I went inside and waited to be seated even though I was clearly the sole customer. I could hear people chattering from what I assumed was the kitchen, but nobody appeared to check for potential customers.

Short of calling out or screaming, I made all the usual discreet noises to attract attention: I coughed, I tapped the top of the bar, I shuffled my feet, I walked up and down, I turned the pages of the menu, I rattled my keys, I whistled a happy tune. Still nobody emerged. I gave up and very audibly exited, opting instead to climb back up towards the old town and the restaurant there, Due Mari, that I already knew had a view to match its name. As it happened this turned out to be a fortuitus change in plan for at Due Mari—which I discovered was also a small hotel—I met a couple who have since become good friends.

Since then, Kay and I have returned to dine and stay in Tiriolo many times; for us it has a similar ambience to that of Santa Severina. But there is a bonus: the amazing panorama across the narrow waist of Calabria and, glistening at its extremes, *i due mari*, the Ionian and Tyrrhenian Seas.

Travellers to tourists

"[Gerace] really is a fantastic site and ... I thought that had it been in north or central Italy it would have been known to everybody and be as famous as San Gimignano."

Henry Morton *A traveller in Southern Italy*

Generally those who came to Calabria before the 1850s were eccentric or adventurous travellers who were pushing the boundaries of the so-called 'Grand Tour' beyond their perceived limits.

In the next hundred years those who ventured this far south lived in a world where the 'tour' was beginning to evolve into 'tour-ism' and increasingly travellers had expectations of the places they visited. They became less reliant on letters of introduction and the hospitality of strangers and more used to staying at inns and hotels and eating at restaurants.

In Calabria these changes came about at a different pace simply because fewer people visited the toe of Italy; there was no need for an inn if nobody wanted to stay overnight.

These days Calabria is no different to other parts of Italy in what it has to offer the traveller: you can stay in a bed & breakfast or a five-star hotel or eat at the local pizzeria or an up-market restaurant. As a resident, I am aware that, in this area, the changes had been incredibly fast; the expectations of Calabrians themselves and visitors to Calabria have accelerated the changes.

What is interesting is to see, through the eyes of other travellers, just how these changes have evolved.

Then, as now, people used Calabria as the inevitable link between the delights of Naples and the perceived exoticism of Sicily. I did so myself for many years; at a time when there were cheap flights to Lamezia Terme but not yet to Catania or Palermo, this was the quickest route to Sicily. I had no idea I was travelling through Calabria and no sense of it as a possible destination in its own right; I had no understanding of its classical heritage, nor as a part of Italy where the Greek civilization once flourished.

Yet as long ago as 1780, classicists like Henry Swinburne (by definition and by education, nearly every traveller at the time was a classicist) knew about Magna Græcia, knew more about Calabria than many do nowadays, even Calabrians. Having travelled in Sicily, Swinburne (1780) was able to make comparisons and was enthusiastic about the landscape as he approached Nicastro:

"These scenes and the environs of Monteleone equal in beauty the most delightful spots of Sicily; and upon the whole, I think that Calabria has greatly the advantage over that island in its general aspect."

He then goes on to question the perceived wisdom regarding the safety of travellers at the time:

"None of the country people or travellers I met on the road from Tropea carried any arms; and yet, if credit is due to the repeated accounts I was stunned with, there is more occasion for them here than in Sicily, where everyone travels armed."

The first two of four pages of useful information provided by Swinburne for the would-be traveller to the Two Sicilies (Sicily and Calabria). The other two pages are overleaf.

In case his travels might inspire others, Swinburne appended some basic and useful information—coinage, weights and measures, principal roads, staging posts, routes accessible by buggy or mules—for those who might feel inclined to follow in his footsteps which suggests that his purpose was not merely to recount his experiences and impressions but to encourage others to go and do likewise. It appears to have worked and Keppel-Craven referenced Swinburne dozens of times while Ramage acknowledged both but distanced himself from them too:

"I believe that I accomplished what had never, so far as I am aware, been attempted before. Swinburne in the years 1777–1780, and Keppel Craven in 1818, had gone pretty nearly over the same ground; but they travelled with all the attendance of high rank, and protected by a constant guard of soldiers. I went alone, often on foot, without a guard, always unarmed, and only once with a guard of armed men across a dangerous pass of the Southern Apennines."

Neither Keppel-Craven nor Ramage seems to have been aware of Brian Hill's travels, nor he of Swinburne's.

Perhaps all of these travellers inspired the authors of *A handbook for travellers in southern Italy: being a guide for the continental portion of the Kingdom of the Two Sicilies*, published in 1855. Though replete with classical references, the fact that such a book existed at all suggests that the face of the travel was changing. Neither Swinburne nor Keppel-Craven, for example, would have needed such a guide ... most of the information they needed was already in their classical heads.

In 1891 Augustus Hare's *Cities of southern Italy and Sicily* was added to the literature and for the first time the information was not riddled with endless classical references. This is the entry for Monteleone:

"The road now enters the land of the orange and myrtle, and reaches *Monteleone*, where there is a tolerable inn, a fine castle built by Frederick II., and a most exquisite view. It occupies the site of the Greek city Hippo, said to have been founded by a colony from Locri in B.C. 388. There was a famous temple of Proserpine here, of which the ruins were destroyed by Count Roger, and its pillars used in building the cathedral of Mileto. Some remains of the ancient walls are still visible."

Hare's Crotone entry named—and shamed—the town's two inns:
"Inns, *Albergo della Concordia*, very miserable; *Minerva*, quite wretched."

The London-based publisher of the aforementioned handbook for travellers in southern Italy, published in 1891, was one John Murray. The style and format of this and other similar handbooks for travellers commissioned and published by Murray became so popular that the genre was copied and improved on by a German publisher, Karl Baedeker, based in Leipzig.

From the 1830s Baedeker—and with respectful acknowledgement to John Murray—published a series of guides that eventually covered all of Europe, North Africa, the Middle East, Asia and North and South America. The Baedeker guides were translated into dozens of languages, and soon became the guide of choice throughout the embryonic tourist industry. The Baedeker guide which included travel information for Calabria, *Southern Italy, Sicily, the Lipari Islands*, was first published in 1867; this was its introduction to the region:

"Calabria is rarely visited by travellers. It abounds in beautiful scenery; but the length of the journey, the indifference of the inns and the insecurity of the roads, which has of late increased, at present deter all but the most enterprising. After the completion of the network of railways projected for S. Italy these inconveniences will cease to exist. The line is now completed as far as Eboli [in Campania, south-east of Salerno], from which the distance to Reggio is 327 M. The journey is performed by the Corriere [stagecoach] in 75 hrs.; fare 63 fr. 75 c. Vetturini [driver of horse-drawn carriage] require

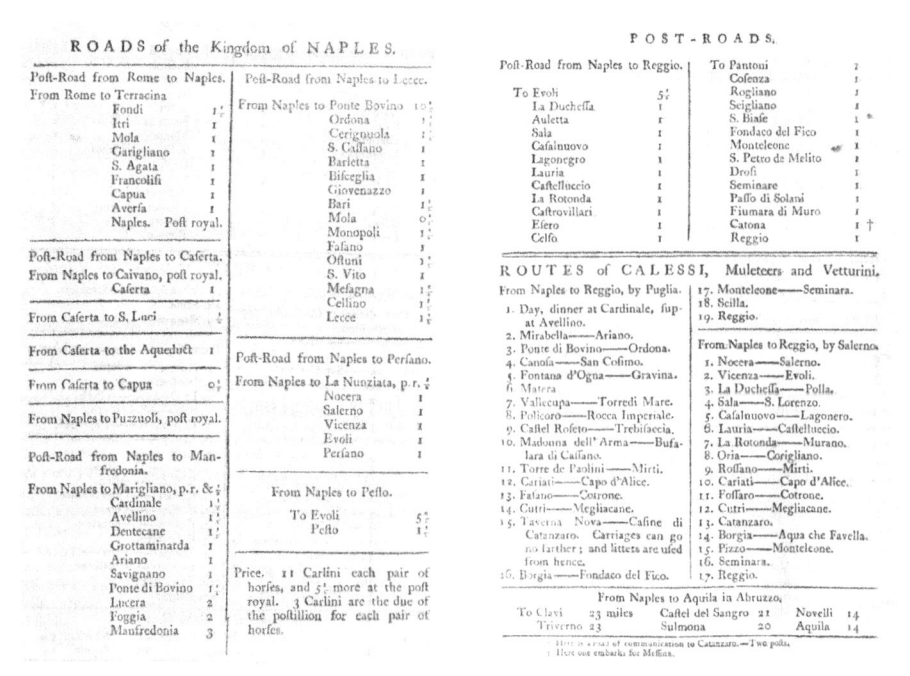

The third and fourth of Swinburne's four pages of useful information; these two focus on details of the roads south from Naples.

8—9 days; hotel-expenses had better be included in the contract."

In the late 19th and early 20th centuries, the Baedeker guides were the universal bible for travellers and at the same time transformed travelling and were surely instrumental in the transition that saw the few travellers become the many tourists.

On *his* travels Norman Douglas (1911) was carrying the German edition of Baedeker's *Southern Italy, Sicily, the Lipari Islands* guide to help him on his way. As we have seen, Douglas had an aversion to using letters of introduction when it came to finding accommodation and places to eat so he was using his trusty Baedeker as he passed through Basilicata on his way to Calabria and made the following observation about an overnight stop at Policoro:

"Exhausted with the morning's walk … I sought refuge, contrary to my usual custom, in the chief hotel, intending to rest awhile and then seek other quarters. The establishment was described as "ganz ordentlich" [pretty good] in Baedeker. But, alas! I found little peace or content. The bed on which I had hoped to repose was already occupied by several other inmates. Prompted by curiosity, I counted up to fifty-two of them; after that, my interest in the matter faded away. It became too monotonous."

According to Morton (1967), a later edition of the same Daedeker guide was less enthusiastic about travelling in Calabria:

"As recently as 1912 Baedeker warned his readers not to go there unless they were provide with introductions to the local gentry who would put them up, since no hotels existed anywhere except in the larger towns, and even those were of the most squalid description."

But like most guides such as Baedeker their destiny is to be out of date almost before the ink has dried on the paper.

On his way south Henry Morton had a minor contretemps with an English tourist who was clutching her Baedeker guide which she clearly saw as an irrefutable source of information. Morton had politely suggested to her that, just because her hotel was selling postcards of local women dressed in traditional costumes, did not mean that she would see anyone so attired. The woman then resorted to the oracle of oracles:

"… she produced, in support of her argument the 1962 edition of Baedeker's *Touring Guide to Italy*, in which we read that 'the women wear a curiously severe costume and sit on the floor in church, in Oriental style'."

A subsequent visit to the local church that Sunday morning confirmed that the Baedeker to be out of date:

"… the church was full of old women in black with coloured head-scarves, all sitting on benches."

Baedeker ceased publishing guides in the 1970s by which time other publishers—most notably America-based Foder (1949) and Frommer (1957)—had joined the market.

Swinburne frequently used the word 'tour' to describe his travels between 1777 and 1780 and it was around this time that the word 'tourist' was first coined. Clearly when Richard Colt Hoare used it in his *Hints to Travellers in Italy* in 1815—'having once more conducted the tourist to the shores of Naples ...'—it had become an accepted term but the first British traveller to Calabria to use it was George Gissing (1891), though not directly about himself. The morning he was so moved by the sound of music from the street below his bedroom window in Crotone, Gissing was in melancholic mood and began to question some of the sentiments he had expressed about the local people and Italy in general:

"Moved by these voices singing over the dust of Croton, I asked pardon for all my foolish irritation, my impertinent fault-finding. Why had I come hither, if it was not that I loved land and people? And had I not richly known the recompense of my love?

"Legitimately enough one may condemn the rulers of Italy, those who take upon themselves to shape her political life, and recklessly load her with burdens insupportable. But among the simple on Italian soil a wandering stranger has no right to nurse national superiorities, to indulge a contemptuous impatience. It is the touch of tourist vulgarity."

While cleansing himself of his irritation in respect of Italy and Italians, he showed a modicum of that same irritation when it came to linking the word

Pioneers in the publication of travel guides, on the left Englishman John Murray and on the right man who made it an art-form, German publisher Karl Baedeker.

'tourist' with 'vulgarity', even though he was referring to himself.

Later Gissing observed a fellow passenger in a railway carriage who didn't fit his visual profile of the stereotypical Calabrian so he indulged in a little speculation:

"He was a man at once plump and muscular, his sturdy limbs well exhibited in a shooting costume. On his face glowed the richest hue of health; his eyes glistened merrily. With him he carried a basket, which, as soon as he was settled, gave forth an abundant meal. The gusto of his eating, the satisfaction with which he eyed his glasses of red wine, excited my appetite. But who was he? Not, I could see, a tourist; yet how account for this health and vigour in a native of the district?"

For some travellers, the tourist clearly was some sort of intolerant sub-species. Douglas (1911) confirmed this when writing about the Arbëreshë 'capital', San Demetrio Corone:

"The adventurous type of Anglo-Saxon probably thinks the country too tame; scholars, too trite; ordinary tourists, too dirty."

I wondered if Douglas had hit on the essential difference between the traveller and the tourist; the former could and would tolerate sub-standard overnight conditions and paucity of places to eat well—or even just to eat—the latter couldn't and wouldn't and certainly thought he shouldn't.

Any tourist experiencing this particular overnight stop between Lamezia and Cosenza, described by Brian Hill (1791), would have blown a gasket; Hill, on the other hand, tried to the make the best of it and then wrote about it:

"The house where we lay last night is erected merely for *accommodation* of travellers, and is such a curious tottering old structure, that the slightest shock of an earthquake would immediately level it to the ground. We preferred *this inn* to one four miles nearer Cosenza, that had two days before been robbed by twelve ruffians ...

"One room where the meat was cooked, the bread baked, and where the fowls roosted, was for the greatest part of the evening, the only place we could find to fit in; and our company—mulemen, soldiers, a Neapolitan fiddler, and two poor young men, who kept the house, doomed to speedy death by the effects of a Malaria fever. As there was a great fire, but no chimney, the walls and roof were black as jet, and curiously adorned with cobwebs, furred by foot in a manner really beautiful. After all the inconveniences we had experienced, we were still too nice to submit to sleep in that apartment, and with that company, and therefore, without ceremony, searched the whole house for another chamber, and we found three, but the floor of one was so full of holes that there was danger of falling through; another was previously engaged by the pigs, one of which, that lay concealed under some dirty straw, jumped up suddenly and gave a great snort, just as my nephew was congratulating himself on the comfortable birth he had found out; the third room was a granary some inches deep in dust; we made choice of the last, swept some of the filth, and sat down to supper, highly pleased with pour discovery."

Of course it was to avoid such experiences that many travellers at the time relied on letters of introduction to the home of a local dignitary—often the town's *sindaco*, its mayor— which generally ensured fine eating and a good night's sleep, uninterrupted by members of the animal kingdom. The sort of conditions that Hill and his group experienced were not confined to Calabria; those who also travelled in Apulia, Basilicata and Sicily, found conditions much the same, and sometimes even worse.

Conditions in the south did not therefore entice the visitor but this was exacerbated by the fact that Italians themselves were wont to put people off from travelling south of Naples. As Hutton (1912) discovered, their reasoning did not necessarily have to have any foundation in fact:

"Kindly and well-meaning people in Naples who had heard by chance of our intention, Italians every one, would have saved us from they knew not what. Not one of them had ever been into the South—they assured us of that; it was unsafe, uncivilized, a country of brigands, hopelessly lost to the modern world, reeking with malaria, and altogether as unattractive in every way as any place could well be.

""What are you going for?" they constantly demanded.

""There is nothing to see, nothing to eat, no inns, no beds, no roads even, and of course no railways; moreover, you will certainly be robbed and very likely murdered ...""

"Let me hasten to say that what we found was something very different from this. To begin with the roads everywhere is the South are good, the trains as a rule punctual if slow, the inns in the larger places fairly clean and comfortable, the food a little rough and monotonous but plentiful."

Those who travelled in Calabria post-war—Eric Whelpton (1957), Leslie Gardiner (1966) and Henry Morton (1967)—were the first to realise that travelling and travellers had evolved and that they were writing for a different audience and, more importantly, a wider, less classical, audience. Modes of travel were changing and host countries for the traveller were increasingly providing facilities more in tune with what the tourist expected ... something pretty much the same as what they had at home.

Calabria was not in the vanguard, nor indeed in the second wave, of such tourist destinations, but individuals and tourist organisations were beginning to catch on. It is clear that Whelpton, Gardiner and Morton all used local tourist facilities and principals to garner information and to visit the sites with the most potential as tourist attractions.

That said, their subsequent writings were a strange mix of what they, as curious travellers, wanted to see and write about, and what their hosts wanted to shown them. Although what all three wrote was clearly on the cusp between the traditional travelogue and the conventional guide, I sense that all struggled with the occasions when they were at risk of becoming the reluctant tool of the local tourist officials.

What changed things was, initially, the internal combustion engine that evolved into public and private transport and, most recently, flying. Whelpton, Gardiner and Morton all made use of the former though it was Edward Hutton (1912) who was the first to see the potential of public transport:

"It is cheaper, and certainly as expeditious as most of the railways here in the South, and quite as comfortable. Moreover, it can go where the railway cannot penetrate; it passes not under but over the hills. In all things it is to be praised …"

Edward Hutton (1912) made a prediction:

"… little by little people will come into the south from central Italy and Calabria will be discovered. When this happens a new playground will be opened for us all, and such a one as we have never dreamed of. For there can indeed be few provinces of Europe lovelier or mire noble that this … But even after two thousand years, let no one despair of the south. With the new communications it will be discovered, and will again lift up its head."

One world war later, and Eric Whelpton (1957) was still looking forward to the same 'new playground' but offered an explanation for its late arrival:

"Most southern Italians do not use inns or hotels, because they can nearly always find acquaintances or friends who will receive them into their homes. Conditions in Calabria are improving rapidly, but many years must elapse before it will be possible to stay in remote regions in any kind of real comfort or hygiene."

Leslie Gardiner (1966) quoted Hutton's vision and added his own thoughts:

"The prophecy has still to be fulfilled, but now is a good time to restate it, when the planners are ruling straight lines for *autostrade* across the map and Italy's domestic airline company is proposing extensions."

It falls on me to contribute a progress report.

Gardiner used the word *autostrade* in the plural, but today's Calabria has only the one *autostrada*—the A3 or, as he called it, the *Autostrada del Sole*, the motorway of the sun. Sadly Gardiner did not allow for the five decades of confusion, conspiracy and corruption as a result of which the road he described so well and with such hope for Calabria remains, at the time of writing, a work-in-progress.

On the brighter side, except for some mafia towns, the level and availability of accommodation and places to eat is generally no different to other parts of the south and of the Italian peninsula and islands; through the universal media, those who provide such services are aware of and motivated by the same experiences and expectations as everyone else.

Where Calabria does fall short—apart from the fact that there is still only the one motorway—is in the realm of its transport infrastructure. North-south the western coast has a fast train service and the nearby A3 *autostrada*; on the other hand, the eastern side has a poor (though slowly improving) road network and a train service that might have been considered adequate a century ago.

But these days what people increasingly seek and expect is good flight connections, preferably low-cost. And, sadly, Calabria is wanting in this area too. It is not the number of airports that is the problem—there are three, at Lamezia Terme, Crotone and Reggio Calabria which is, arguably, one too many for the region—but rather the number of flights.

Lamezia Terme is by far the largest of these and can claim to be 'international'; currently there are up to five flights daily to and from Reggio and three to and from Crotone, all with destinations within Italy. Once again it is the eastern seaboard that lacks adequate connections with the rest of the region and beyond. If you land at Lamezia, and want to visit anywhere near the east coast by car, then you have to cross the mountains and from Lamezia itself the road to the Ionian coast is excellent. But, that's where it ends … travel north or south along the Ionian coast is less accommodating.

The region has exceptional historical and natural resources but unfortunately not all of these are exploited to the full because of where they are. In Calabrian terms 'where they are' has two downsides: being on the eastern seaboard, where the transport infrastructure is wanting, and having mafia connections. Some places suffer from both and it's inevitable that, for example, some people who would like to visit the Magna Græcia site of Locri Epizephyrii are going to be put off from doing so by the reputation of Locri the mafia town.

On two consecutive summers, when I was in my mid-twenties I travelled to what was then Yugoslavia, to the part today known as Croatia. It was the cusp of the seventies, at a time when many unthinking British holidaymakers headed for Franco's Spain and even the more adventurous seldom travelled much further afield. One of the things that soon became apparent was that the Germans had already discovered the delights of Yugoslavia and the locals responded accordingly by advertising all their wares—chiefly accommodation, restaurants and food—in their native Serbo-Croat and German, but rarely in English.

A little over a decade earlier Eric Whelpton (1957) had had a similar experience in Calabria; he was at an overcrowded station where he and his wife Barbara were crammed into a single carriage alongside local people, including a number boys and girls returning home from school:

"Within a few minutes of starting, two courteous young men offered us their seats, and we were soon the centre of an animated group of people who plied us with questions of all kinds.

"The animation became even greater when we revealed the fact that we were English and not German as they expected, for German tourists are so numerous that they have little news value in southern Italy."

Throughout the seventies, eighties and nineties it was German—and to a lesser extent Dutch—tourists who came to Calabria ... which makes it all the more inexplicable as to why the schools at the time generally taught French as their second language.

One German in particular, Herr Müller-Toscano, saw the potential of Calabria and in the mid-sixties created the holiday village of Bagamoyo close to Sibari. Strange that a place known as one of the centres of Greek civilization should host the area's first such establishment, stranger still that it should bear a name of a Swahili seaport near Dar-es-Salaam.

Leslie Gardiner (1966) visited the site, then still a work in progress, where its visionary owner explained the reasoning:

"[Bagamoyo] was once the embarkation point for slaves to the Orient, as Freetown was for America. It was a place of lamentation. The name means 'Where I left my heart'."

Gardiner explained Herr Müller-Toscano's concept for Bagamoyo:

"His grand scheme was a hotel-theatre-lido complex, to recreate for the tourist of the nineteen-sixties gracious living in the style ancient Sybaris was accustomed to."

When Gardiner was there Bagamoyo was still a work in progress and things were not going according to plan:

"His main project, the split-level jigsaw of hotel bedrooms among the mimosas, remains unfulfilled, lacking essential services. The ditch which straggles through the property, fore-runner of a scenic motor-boat waterway for taking guests between patio and beach cabin, has partly filled up again with sand. The geraniums and gladioli, prematurely planted round a rudimentary *plage*, hang their heads in despair. Every day Herr Müller-Toscano entertains parties of journalists or officials: The staff must keep its hand in."

Despite the despair of the geraniums and the gladioli, Herr Müller-Toscano steadfast doggedness did finally win through and Bagamoyo is still there today. Year in, year out, from May to September, Italian families still wander down to the Ionian shore to cool off or just sit round the pool, glass in hand. It *is* a lovely spot ... but nevertheless it remains my idea of holiday hell.

In 2009 the Calabrian tourist industry sponsored a publicity campaign in the UK where a thousand London cabs were emblazed with the image of the Aragonese castle at Le Castella, a well-known Italian footballer with hand on heart, Corigliano Calabro-born Rino Gattuso, and the slogan *Come to Calabria. The sunny heart of Italy*. At the time, the final choice of castle for this campaign was between Santa Severina and Le Castella; rightly they chose the latter, the Aragonese castle in the sea.

Had we not already discovered Calabria, this is the sort of campaign that might have appealed to Kay and I. For independent travellers—which is, after all, what Swinburne *et al* were—Calabria remains the perfect destination with the right balance of modern 'tourist' facilities and attractions and that raw, off-the-beaten-track element that I for one, find so appealing.

The Dutch and Germans continue to come to Calabria and are, by far, the mainstay of the foreign tourist industry. But, increasingly, the British are discovering that there is more to southern Italy than just Sicily and there are now package holidays flying into Lamezia, usually transporting their clients to resorts on the nearby Tyrrhenian coast. The romantic-sounding Tropea is a favourite destination ... ironic therefore that for most Calabrians Tropea is famous for its rugby-ball shaped red onions.

Americans too are beginning to include Calabria in their European itineraries, particularly those who have an ulterior motive and want to get a sense of where their ancestors came from. Helping such people with their quests has itself become an offshoot of the tourist industry.

A handful of times each holiday season, cruise liners tie up at Crotone and their stir-crazy human cargo is taken on a whistle-stop tour of the nearest places of interest which usually include the castles at Le Castella and Santa Severina and the most accessible remnant of Magna Græcia locally, Capa Colonna.

Henry Morton's (1967) comment about Gerace quoted at the beginning of this chapter is probably true; if Gerace had been in north or central Italy it would have been as famous as the likes of San Gimignano in Tuscany. Indeed I suspect it would have been more famous and that the same could also be said about Santa Severina.

Calabria is a relative newcomer to the tourist game and sometimes it can be its own worst enemy; it will get so much right and then cast a careless spanner in the works by getting something simple, completely wrong … like the abandoned Coca-Cola refrigerator at the Locri amphitheatre. Unfortunately tourists remember the irritations and deficiencies and forget the overall picture and the good things; and today it is so easy to leave a comment on the internet … and such comments live forever.

One example immediately springs to mind.

An American woman, Eileen Rifkin, came to live in Crotone, stayed a year and, for personal reasons, returned to the States. Back in California, she wrote a blog about her time in Calabria and mostly it was positive but there were two negatives.

One concerned the afternoon siesta with which she had difficulty though in reality this is no more than the difference between cultures and just something you can either adapt to or not; it's not compulsory.

The other was something that most people do not associate with modern society except perhaps in third-world countries. This extract from Eileen's blog explains:

"Also, in Calabria, you won't find toilets seats in public places, even some of the best restaurants! You have to squat!!!"

This is often true but would have been truer had she inserted the word 'always' between 'won't' and 'find' and, for the record, I don't like it any more than she did. But what I think is more pertinent is that it would cost so little to put it right; it is such a simple thing to sort out. But, to date, I really don't think anyone has ever thought of doing so; there are those who would wonder what all the fuss was about.

How difficult would it be for local authorities, aided and abetted by tourist organisations, to insist that it were so? How difficult would it be to enforce? How difficult would it be make sure every bar, café or restaurant had a working toilet seat in every toilet? The threat of closure for not complying would probably do the trick.

It's as straightforward as excommunicating those who were clearly seen on video to facilitate the bowing of the Madonna outside the Oppido home of the local mafia boss or removing the out-of-keeping Coca-Cola fridge from Locri's Greek amphitheatre. None of it is exactly rocket science, is it?

I wonder how many people have not returned to Calabria (or indeed other parts of the south) because such a basic facility did not meet their expectations? How might those who disembarked from their state-of-the-art, toilet-seated cruise ship at Crotone have felt, had they had to use some of the seat-less shore-based facilities? Pretty pissed off, I suspect.

Those whose job it is to promote Calabria should take note of what seems a small consideration, for it is an unfortunate fact of life that people who read the above-mentioned blog will probably *not* be visiting Calabria in the foreseeable future.

And that would be their loss.

A London cab enticing people to visit Calabria with castle, footballer and open invitation.

Leaving Calabria

"The people are generally in wretched poverty, and [it seems] that it is increasing. They live chiefly on bread from chestnuts, which are gathered in the extensive forests of La Sila, and in winter they migrate to Sicily in search of food, though I could not make out how they could procure it there more easily than in Calabria."
Craufurd Tait Ramage *The Nooks and by-ways of Italy: Wanderings in search of its ancient remains and modern superstitions*

Ramage's (1828) thoughts about the poverty-induced migrating instincts of the people of Rogliano (a small town midway between Lamezia and Cosenza) is the first mention by any of the early travellers of what ultimately became a flood of emigration in the late 19th and early 20th centuries. Moving to Sicily was hardly emigrating in the conventional sense, nevertheless it was no less of decision borne on necessity than the choice made by many others later in the century. Ramage did go on suggest another reason for that seasonal move to Sicily for he was told that many Calabrian men had a second family there.

In *Thank you Uncle Sam*, I wrote extensively about this phenomenon (and in particular those—the majority—who chose to go to the United States) and the reasons for it; how it was that desperate people made life-changing decisions in the hope of bettering themselves and, more importantly, how and if their dreams were realised. While researching the book I was told a story that reminded me of Ramage's tale about people migrating for reasons other than economic: in 1906 Bruno Cortese's decision to leave Calabria was prompted by pressure to marry that came from the family of a young woman with whom he had become romantically involved.

Every individual, every family, who left their Calabrian homeland did so for a myriad of reasons though above all the economic reality of remaining was an overriding factor. The endemic malaria didn't help either.

For those born and bred in southern Calabria the earthquake of 1905 was bad enough but when, three years later, another, more devastating quake struck the same area, that was the last straw. In the south, particularly in the province of Reggio Calabria, scarcely a community was spared; it is little wonder therefore that many people voted with their feet and headed either north to Naples or across the Straits of Messina to Palermo clutching a one-way ticket to anywhere.

After the Irish, Italian emigrants were the second largest ethnic group to cross the Atlantic in search of a new life. In smallish numbers at first, this exodus began in the last decade of the 19th century and gained momentum in the first two decades of the new century. Though people emigrated from every corner of the Italian peninsula, by far the majority who did so were from southern Italy and Sicily.

Because he travelled in Calabria in 1911, Norman Douglas was the sole traveller to observe at first hand the repercussions of emigration and he wrote extensively and authoritatively about its impact on many of the communities he visited:

"The men of Morano emigrate to America; two-thirds of the adult and adolescent male population are at this moment on the other side of the Atlantic."

In the Ellis Island archive I had found a similar picture in other Calabrian towns. For example, on 1 May 1910 the *Batavia* docked in New York. On board were forty-six people from Petilia Policastro, a small Calabrian village

When the *Batavia* arrived in New York in May 1910 it carried forty-three men from a single Calabrian village, Petilia Policastro.

in the foothills of the Sila mountains; all but three of them were men. Two days later another eight arrived on another ship and the following week a further thirteen. Even with this degree of emigration, in the twenty years between 1881 and 1901, Petilia Policastro's population rose slightly (17.5%) while, in the same period—as observed by Douglas—the population of Morano Calabro dropped drastically, by nearly 34%.

For obvious reasons families and friends from places like Morano Calabro and Petilia Policastro emigrated in groups and they retained their group mentality once they arrived in the United States. Calabrians tended to congregate in Brooklyn while Sicilians found *paesani* (people from their home town or surrounding area) in what became known as Little Italy in Lower Manhattan. Many Calabrians ended up in the Park Street area of Brooklyn and often initially in Skillman Street where, it would seem, there were several tenements that served as clearing houses for newly-arrived Calabrians.

That people tended to gravitate to areas where their *paesani* lived is not surprising. From tenement blocks in half a dozen Brooklyn streets to a largish community in Kenosha, Wisconsin, there was safety, familiarity and cooperation in numbers.

Because there were—and to some extent still are—clusters of Calabrians in particular American towns and cities it is possible that Calabrian immigrants were more Calabrian and less Italian than others. The question is, was this a self-inflicted segregation or was it a reflection of how other Italians perceived Calabrians? It remains the case today that there are many Italians who view Calabria as a backward region of their country, inhabited by lazy individuals who don't pay taxes. Perhaps all the hard-working Calabrians emigrated?

For example, generally speaking Boston Italian immigrants lived in what was known as the city's North End but, according to Stephen Puleo in his book *The Boston Italians*, Calabrians tended to mix instead with other non-Italian immigrants and peopled Boston's South End.

Similarly, while there must surely have been some Calabrians who gravitated to the area of New York around Mulberry Street and Mott Street (Little Italy), in researching *Thank you Uncle Sam*, I never came across a single one.

Then again, perhaps this is not surprising for, at the time, Mott Street in particular was home mostly to Sicilian families, many of whom—rightly or wrongly—had a reputation for being 'connected'. It was here that one of New York's notorious gangsters, Ignazio Lupo, opened the largest of several wholesale grocery stores through which he preyed on other Italians.

In Acri Douglas found a picture similar to the one he found in Morano.

"Acri is a large place, and its air of prosperity contrasts with the slumberous decay of San Demetrio; there is silk-rearing, and so much emigration into America that nearly every man I addressed replied in English."

Here Douglas hit upon a peculiarly Italian phenomenon, that of the *ritornati*, those who emigrated and returned, sometimes to emigrate a second or third time. Once again, I came across many *ritornati* while writing *Thank you Uncle Sam*: one man actually emigrated four times to America, and even did so twice in the same year. Given the hardships of the Atlantic crossing this was indeed no mean undertaking. What was also strange about the story of Enrico Marchese was that his illegitimate Calabrian son, Giuseppe Bonocore, never knew that his father was a serial emigrator even when, in his twenties, he himself emigrated to the same city, Chicago.

Douglas commented too on the social aspects of emigration and the Calabrian psyche:

"All over the Sila there is a large preponderance of women over men, nearly the whole male section of the community, save the quite young and the decrepit, being in America. This emigration brings much money into the country and many new ideas; but the inhabitants have yet to learn the proper use of their wealth, and to acquire a modern standard of comfort. Together with the Sardinians, these Calabrians are the hardiest of native races, and this is what makes them prefer the strenuous but lucrative life in North American mines to the easier career in Argentina, which Neapolitans favour. There they learn English. They remember their families and the village that gave them birth, but their patriotism towards Casa Savoia [the House of Savoy, the ruling monarchy in Italy at the time] is of the slenderest. How could it be otherwise? I have spoken to numbers of them, and this is what they say:

"This country has done nothing for us; why should we fight its battles? Not long ago we were almost devouring each other in our hunger; what did they do to help us? If we have emerged from misery, it is due to our own initiative and the work of our own hands; if we have decent clothes and decent houses, it is because they drove us from our old homes with their infamous misgovernment to seek work abroad.

"Perfectly true! They have redeemed themselves, though the new regime has hardly had a fair trial. And the drawbacks of emigration (such as a slight increase of tuberculosis and alcoholism) are nothing compared with the unprecedented material prosperity and enlightenment. There has also been—in these parts, at all events—a marked diminution of crime.

"No wonder, seeing that three-quarters of the most energetic and turbulent elements are at present in America, where they recruit the Black Hand. That the Bruttian is not yet ripe for town life, that his virtues are pastoral rather than civic, might have been expected; but the Arab domination of much of his territory, one suspects, may have infused fiercer strains into his character and helped to deserve for him that epithet of *sanguinario* by which he is proud to be known."

As I observed in an earlier chapter, Douglas' reference to the Black Hand, basically an extortion racket, the *modus operandi* of mafia organisations (though the word 'mafia' was little used at the time), is the only reference, albeit an oblique one, that any traveller ever made to organised crime.

Lunching with a citizen of Stróngoli, Douglas was given an insight into why so many Stróngolese had emigrated:

"You were speaking about the emptiness of our streets ... And yet, up to a short time ago, there was no emigration from this place. Then a change came about: I'll tell you how it was. There was a *guardia di finanze* here—a miserable octroi [taxation] official. To keep up the name of his family, he married an heiress; not for the sake of having progeny, but—well! He began buying up all the land round about—slowly, systematically, cautiously—till, by dint of threats and intrigues, he absorbed nearly all the surrounding country. Inch by inch, he ate it up; with his wife's money. That was his idea of perpetuating his memory. All the small proprietors were driven from their domains and fled to America to escape starvation; immense tracts of well-cultivated land are now almost desert. Look at the country! But some day he will get his reward; under the ribs, you know."

Whether or not Douglas' host's prediction came to pass I have no way of knowing ... perhaps he survived and one of his descendants became the Baron Berlingiere, the landowner who, in 1949, was the focus of the agrarian protests locally which led to what was known as the Melissa Massacre (see pages 96)?

When in America, I was aware that there were many who had left Stróngoli and I met several of their descendants. There was, for example, a significant community of Stróngolese in North Adams, Massachusetts, who, in the wake of the construction of the Hoosac Rail Tunnel in 1875 by mainly Irish immigrants, found work in one the many fabric printing works for which the area subsequently became well-known.

Pat Scida, an eighty-something resident of Lynbrook, Long Island, told me the story of his father, Pasquale, who left Stróngoli in 1912, the same year as the *Titanic* went down. Having done two stints in the army, Pasquale was more literate than most of his fellow Stróngolese and so did well for himself in North Adams before moving to Brooklyn where he got a job as a garbage collector—a job for life and a job with a pension.

Pat, his son and *first generation* American, retired as a Senior Vice-President of Morgan Stanley Bank in Manhattan.

Douglas, ever adept at attracting the intrigue of strangers, also had an interesting encounter with a young lad who herded goats:

"A goat-boy, a sad little fellow, sprang out of the earth as I dutifully wandered about here. He volunteered to show me not only Stróngoli, but all Calabria; in fact, his heart's desire was soon manifest: to escape from home and find his way to America under my passport and protection.

"Here was his chance—a foreigner (American) returning sooner or later to his own country! He pressed the matter with naif forcefulness. Vainly I told him that there were other lands on earth; that I was not going to America. He shook his head and sagely remarked:

""I have understood. You think my journey would cost too much. But you, also, must understand. Once I get work there, I will repay you every farthing."

"As a consolation, I offered him some cigarettes. He accepted one; pensive, unresigned."

While in the Pollino mountains he observed the following:

"True Italians will soon be rare as the dodo in these parts. These *americani* cast off their ancient animistic traits and patriarchal disposition with the ease of a serpent; a new creature emerges, of a wholly different character—sophisticated, extortionate at times, often practical and in so far useful;

Inside the Arnold Print Works in North Adams where many Stróngolese worked.

scorner of every tradition, infernally wideawake and curiously deficient in what the Germans call "Gemuet" (one of those words which we sadly need in our own language). Instead of being regaled with tales of Saint Venus and fairies and the Evil Eye, I learnt a good deal about the price of food in the Brazilian highlands."

But, as a male of the species, Douglas saw also an upside to mass emigration:
"It will not take you long to discover that the chief objects of interest in San Giovanni are the women. Many Calabrian villages still possess their distinctive costume—Marcellinara and Cimigliano are celebrated in this respect—but it would be difficult to find anywhere an equal number of handsome women on such a restricted space. In olden days it was dangerous to approach these attractive and mirthful creatures; they were jealously guarded by brothers and husbands. But the brothers and husbands, thank God, are now in America, and you may be as friendly with them as ever you please, provided you confine your serious attentions to not more than two or three. Secrecy in such matters is out of the question, as with the Arabs; there is too much gossip, and too little coyness about what is natural; your friendships are openly recognized, and tacitly approved. The priests do not interfere; their hands are full."

It is ironic that the reason many travellers came to Calabria was to experience the remnants of a culture and people that emigrated from their native Greece over two thousand years ago.
In addition many of those who emigrated from Calabria at the beginning of the 20th century were descendents of Albanian immigrants—they came, they largely clung on to their Arbëreshë language and culture, and they lost it only when they moved on again to the Americas or Australia. Emigration and immigration have always been part of Calabria's history.

At the time of writing, immigration to western Europe from some middle-eastern countries in turmoil is a political hot potato. Many of those in host countries, such as Italy, have family in America, Canada, Brazil, Argentine or Australia—ancestors who emigrated from *their* homeland through the same economic necessity that now brings others to their doorstep.
These ancestors will have suffered the same emotional turmoil about leaving their homeland, their families, their culture and their language as is written on the faces of today's immigrants. And like today's immigrants, those on the move over a century ago will have become resigned to and endured the same deprivations and indignities on their voyage to their new

life. For those who chose America this was indeed a terrible voyage across the Atlantic that could last up to two weeks, sometimes longer. And, then as now, not everyone made it; many fell by the wayside en route.

How easy it is to forget.

This historical amnesia was brought home to me when I met up with two American friends in Rome. Both had the right to call themselves Americans because their grandparents had emigrated to America and, like millions of others, were once new immigrants in a strange land. One in particular seemed to have forgotten her roots.

They had been in Rome less than a day and the first impression of the amnesiac was that it was 'full of immigrants'. It was clear from her tone that she didn't remotely see these immigrants as a good thing; nor, from the perspective of her white, middle-class American background, did she have any empathy with such people. It probably did not help that the immigrants she was referring to were not white themselves, more Middle Eastern in appearance, a bit like how Christ would have looked.

A descendent of another Calabrian immigrant, mindful of the contradiction in being seen to be anti-immigration, later espoused a new rationale to explain away his distaste for the new wave of immigrants in his cosy corner of America:

"It's the fact that they're *not* European ... that's the problem."

What he was really saying was that they were not white; they were in fact from Honduras which made me wonder whether or not he would consider the Italian-born Guatamalan wife of my Calabrian friend to be an acceptable immigrant? After all, despite being Italian, she does not look European.

Would-be emigrants arriving at the Emigration Office in Naples prior to departure. For nearly all Calabrians the last view of their native land was of the Bay of Naples.

I wonder if a first-generation amnesiac of Irish immigrant stock in New York or New Jersey around the 1900s might well have made a similar comment about the wave of swarthy, southern Italians arriving daily at Ellis Island.

Many Calabrians who emigrated to America in the early 20th century (and remained to become American citizens) did not share with their children and grandchildren the details of their journey nor any real sense of the hardship they endured both before leaving Calabria and during their first months and years in their new home. From those that did, in *Thank you Uncle Sam* I pieced together the following pictures of the reality of emigration for Calabrians.

First the language:

"I wondered … whether the fact that so few passed on their experience of coming to America—the journey to Naples, the two-week crossing to New York, their Ellis Island experience and finding their way to their first American home—was because they experienced it all in their native language or dialect. All the anticipation, the fear, the degradation, the pain … all these emotions were coped with and locked away in another language, a language that would soon become part of their past, a language their children would probably never speak."

And secondly those first weeks and months in America:

"As if the journey were not bad enough, for many the conditions they experienced in America were not much better than in Calabria, Basilicata or Apulia. In lower Manhattan and Brooklyn the tenements were often squalid, infested and dark and the streets noisy, frenetic and chaotic. The chances of seeing the open sky, fields as far as the eye could see or folding mountains was slim … the other side of the coin was that, if you worked hard, you could almost certainly better your lot in life. In Calabria there were friends and family, sky, fields and mountains but the prognosis was the same—a meagre, disease-ridden existence, punctuated with natural disasters, as far as the mind could wander."

Finally, through the eyes of the Piro family who left Roccabernarda in the 1960s, it is clear that, though things had clearly improved—for example air transport had replaced the arduous sea crossing—life stateside for the post-war Calabrian immigrant was not always the anticipated bed of roses:

"Ippolito looked back on their first six years in America with little enthusiasm.

"They were", he said, "hell".

"We left heaven for hell", he repeated, as if to emphasise the point."

CAMPANIA
BASILICATA
Rocca Imperiale
Montegiordano
Roseto
Amendolara
Tórtora Marina
Práia a Mare
Papasídero
Mormanno
Trebisacce
Scalea
La Pollino
Il Mar Ionio
Sibari
Diamante
Mirti
Belvedere
Corigliano Calabro
Rossano
CALABRIA
Cariati
Punto Alici
Cirò
Cirò Marina
Páola
Marina di Stróngoli
COSENZA
La Sila
Santa Severina
Amantea
CROTONE
Cámpora San Giovanni
Cutro
San Mango
Lacinian Promotory
Roccabernarda Station
Il Mar Tirreno
Lamezia Terme
Botricello
Gizzeria Lido
CATANZARO
Le Castella
Máida Marina
Lido di Catanzaro
Stalleti
'Fondaco del Fico'
Pizzo
Il Mar Ionio
Soverato
Tropea
VIBO VALÉNTIA
Capo Vaticano
Nicótera
Rosarno
Gióia Tauro
Riace Marina
Palmi
Punto del Faro
Rocella Jonica
Gerace
Bagnara
Marina di Gioiosa Jonica
Lo Stretto di Messina
L'Aspromonte
Locri
Scilla
Villa San Giovanni
Bovalino
SICILIA
REGGIO DI CALABRIA
Bianco
Capo Bruzzano
Capo dell'Armi
Mélito di Porto Salvo
Capo Spartivento

Coasting along

"At Monte Giordano we entered Upper or Hither Calabria. The inn wearing the face of dirt and poverty, I rode four miles further to Roseto, where my guide assured me he had an acquaintance who would be happy to accommodate me with a room."

Henry Swinburne *Travels in the Two Sicilies*

Some of the earlier travellers did indeed cross Calabria from coast to coast but, because of the mountains and the perceived threat of brigands, many more travelled in a generally north-south direction and followed the coast, if not the coastline.

Unlike today, when tourism drives the infrastructure to a degree, these older routes followed the line of the coast but from a respectable distance inland. They did so because the tracks (and later the roads) linked the places where people lived which was generally the higher ground and not the malarial land between hills and sea. The exceptions were of course those places where the higher land came down to the coast.

Therefore this chapter—the nearest this book gets to resembling a guide—is a short imaginary jaunt from coast to coast but, instead of traversing the region, it will follow the Calabrian coastline—after Apulia, the second longest in Italy—from Basilicata in the north-east, down the Ionian coast (today's SS106) to Reggio Calabria and then back up to the north-west alongside the Tyrrhenian Sea (the SS18). Places like Sibari, Crotone, Locri, Reggio Calabria, Pizzo and Lamezia Terme that I have already referred to in some detail are not included except, literally, in passing.

Before Henry Swinburne (1777) entered Calabria at Monte Giordano (written Montegiordano today) he had already passed by the town of Rocca Imperiale, likewise Keppel-Craven (1818):

"Monte Giordano, the next town I saw, and the first in Calabria, presented the same aspect as Rocca Imperiale, which may also be said of Roseto; and I afterwards found that almost every small town in Calabria, particularly on the eastern coast, was constructed after the same model."

But boundaries have shifted and today it is Rocca Imperiale that is the first Calabrian town on the eastern seaboard after leaving Basilicata.

Not unexpectedly, most of the towns mentioned by the earlier travellers—Rocca Imperiale, Montegiordano, Roseto and Amendolara—are not actually on the sea at all, but some miles inland though of course today all have their shoreline offshoots, originally links to the passing seaborne trade in passengers and produce but today more often holiday destinations. As the higher land comes closest to the coast at Roseto, the town itself is only a short distance inland and its impressive castle is right on the shoreline.

For Richard Keppel-Craven, Amendolara was the lengthy, blunt and brutal blueprint for the Calabrian town of the time—and its inhabitants.

First the place:

"This small town afforded me the first and most perfect specimen of all those which I afterwards visited in this province. Its position, on an insulated cone, surrounded on all sides but one by a precipice of frightful depth and steepness, renders it almost inaccessible; and its inhabitants experienced the advantages of such a situation in the year 1806, when they successfully defended it against 200 brigands, who retired from the siege they had begun, after having sacked and burnt part of the house where I was received, and which is just outside of its ramparts: these are formed by the close junction

Road, castle, sea at Roseto.

of the exterior houses with one another, or portions of thick wall, where an interval breaks the connexion. A population, somewhat under the number of 1000, inhabit it, and the interior aspect is as wretched as its outward appearance is singular: the streets, narrow and unpaved, were composed of low huts, blackened with smoke; they were full of dung, and shreds of black cloth or serge, forming mattrasses and blankets for a race of pigs, apparently as numerous, and hardly more prolific than their possessors: the male proportion of the last was almost all assembled in evening conversation just without the walls, leaving their interior and the female inhabitants to the company above mentioned."

Then the people:

"The women were mostly of large stature, attired in a body and petticoat of coarse scarlet cloth: the latter appendage was composed of plaits so innumerable as to stick out at a considerable distance from the hips, and being mostly threadbare and faded, formed no ornamental addition to forms as uncouth as they were unfeminine, and countenances impressed with a ferocious scowl, which I fain would have interpreted as the stare of curiosity. The shift, of which the full sleeves are seen, is drawn in round the throat, reminding one of many antique statues; and on their head they wear a coarse cloth, folded flat like a napkin, as in the Terra di Lavoro [literally 'land of work' and geographically, southern Lazio and northern Campania], and some parts of the pontifical states.

"The men were usually clad in short jackets and close hose, of no very particular shape, but almost all invariably of black cloth, which accounted for the quantity of cuttings of that material I had observed in the streets on my entrance. They mostly had leather gaiters, or coarse stockings, with a shoe of undrest skin, tied on by thongs of the same, half way up the leg, forming complete sandals. Their hats had scarcely any brims, and the crown, which is high, terminates in a sharp point. Their demeanour was civil, but perfectly different from that of the natives of the other provinces I had seen. A look of independence, but not unmixed with melancholy and distrust, was observable in their countenances, bearing, in other respects, an expression far from unpleasing."

Such places were also refuges, for centres of habitation inland and on high land had an additional advantage in that they were less vulnerable to those who came by sea to plunder, most notably Turkish corsairs (a corsair was a pirate usually associated with the coast of North Africa, the Barbary coast, and by default also Saracens and the Ottoman Empire) who frequently took people as slaves. At Trebisacce, the largest town in the area and another place where the higher land descends to the sea, Ramage (1828) came across such a local man who had been captured by the Turks:

"I met a coast-guard at the village of Trebisacce, where I stopped a few hours during the heat of the day, who had been taken prisoner about thirty years ago and carried to Algiers. I was amused to find that he rather regretted his release from slavery, as he acknowledged that he used to receive plenty of excellent mutton, to which in his days of freedom he is now an entire stranger."

From Ramage's viewpoint Roseto had moved on from Keppel-Craven's blueprint and he found it to be 'picturesquely situated amidst broken ravines'. By the time Hutton (1912) was in the area, it seems the transformation was complete:

"There is nothing more picturesque upon all this coast than Trebisaccie, Amendolara upon its isolated rock, and Roseto in its ravine, or Rocca Imperiale."

Ramage who was travelling northwards from Trebisacce and heading for Taranto in Apulia, was keen to try and keep to the coast but he was told that this was not a practical idea:

"I was warned by my friends at Roseto that little intercourse was kept up with the eastern part of Italy except by sea, and that I would find the coast for the last fifty miles in approaching Taranto so barren and ill-furnished with water that it would be no easy task to accomplish the enterprise.

Ramage had no time for the notion of 'impossibility' and decided to defy his advisors and press on:

"Onward I was resolved to go, till I knocked my head against an impenetrable wall, and you will be amused to see how gradually one difficulty after another disappeared."

Thus, unlike other travellers, he saw these same small towns from afar:

"Since I left Roseto, I have only seen in the distance one or two small villages, perched picturesquely on conical-shaped hills at some distance from the sea, and have not encountered a single human being."

In this part of Calabria, the town I know best is Trebisacce which I find an enchanting place, particularly the old town on the gentle slopes between the sea and the elevated new road.

There, many years ago, I met an elderly Trebisaccesa; then in her nineties and always dressed in black, Maria was the grandmother of a friend. She didn't say much but she had the most amazing, all-telling eyes and a wicked sense of humour that, from the moment we met, we shared in silence and furtive glances.

At the time, I was wont to make slightly tongue-in-cheek remarks about my friend's father, Maria's son-in-law, that sometimes carried a comic double meaning. Maria didn't say much but she was the only one to see this other side to what I had said and she would bow her head slightly, move her hand across her face and, from behind her arthritic fingers, focus those bright, knowing eyes directly at me as she tried desperately to conceal a laugh. Sadly Maria no longer graces the streets of Trebisacce but for me her clandestine chuckle is the thing I remember most each time I pass above the town on that modern highway.

Beyond Trebisacce it is Sibari, its ruins, its museum and the mouth of the Crati that dominate the road south to Corigliano Calabro and Rossano. Like most of the other towns, these two are inland citadels, but they are unique in that, it seems to me, both were designed for locals only. Both demonstrate a total disregard for anyone who might be a stranger through the total absence of helpful road signs. It's almost as if they are trying to keep people out; worse still, once inside there appears to be no means of escape except by tailgating other cars or navigating by the sun. For a while I opted for the former until, that is, I ended up in the car-park of Lidl the supermarket; in the end navigating by the sun proved more reliable.

I spent a very frustrating hour or two in and around both towns and in the end, I just gave up and headed back to the main coast road.

Not surprisingly, Henry Swinburne (1777) had no such problems and clearly took to Corigliano (full name Corigliano Calabro to distinguish it from the delightful Corigliano d'Otranto in Apulia) but mainly because its then size and the fact that the local land-owning family was perceived as being more 'humane' to those who worked their land than their counterparts elsewhere in Calabria:

"The little town of Corigliano rises boldly on the peak of the richly clothed knoll, like the watch-tower and safeguard of all these natural treasures. It is a duchy belonging to the Saluzzi, a Genoese family … their lord has the reputation of being one of the most humane, as well as opulent, feudatories in the province."

Today, as you might expect, there are three Coriglianos, the original castle-crested, sign-lacking, town, its less elevated neighbour, Corigliano Scalo, and the port of Corigliano. In Swinburne's day this was no more than a jetty on the seashore rather than a port of any strategic significance:

"... whole droves of mules and asses laden with oranges just plucked ... were carrying them to the sea-shore, to be embarked in small boats for Taranto and Gallipoli [in Apulia]."

Today's port, formerly known as the Porto di Sibari, is a modern, elaborate affair, the Ionian coast's version—albeit on a smaller scale—of the Tyrrhenian's Gioia Tauro. At the time of writing it is largely devoid of maritime traffic but there is local optimism that this will soon change as carriers increasingly see the benefits of having a modern docking facility on the Suez Canal-facing side of the Italian peninsula. One of the problems is something I have mentioned before—the lack of a good transport infrastructure on the eastern seaboard. Painfully, slowly and in random, short stretches, the SS106 is being upgraded, none of which, again at the time of writing, is anywhere close to Corigliano. The only way the port can efficiently disperse its containers is to cross Calabria to the A3 *autostrada* and a road to facilitate this has been upgraded though it is no motorway.

Beyond Rossano —famous for the Amarelli family and their *Museo della Liquiricia*—is Mirto close to where the river Trionto enters the sea. It is over this river that the new *Sila-Mare* road (see page 343) strides, though of course it will be many years before it lives up to its name and actually links the Greek Sila with the sea.

Henry Swinburne (1777), hoping to make Cariati before nightfall, stayed instead at Mirto overnight:

The new port at Corigliano ... white elephant or ahead of its time?

"We rode all the afternoon in a most beautiful vale, cultivated with great neatness, and abounding with pulse and vegetables of various forts. We passed several rivulets that water and fertilize these fields. The Trionto alone deserves the name of river, though not a navigable one, as some geographers style it. One of our horses falling lame, we were obliged to take up our abode for the night at Mirti, a single house, or Fondaco. This inn was better than I expected, and the host very civil."

Yet another 'fondaco' though, as few travellers followed the coastline hereabouts this is the only mention of such a staging-post similar to the *Fondaco del Fico* on the other coast between Pizzo and Lamezia. One of the others that did so, Richard Keppel-Craven (1818), does mention a remarkably similar place but does not use the word 'fondaco' to describe it:

"… the modern Trionto … throws itself into the Ionian at a point called from it, three or four miles to the north-east of the Hylias [a nearby river, possibly today's Colognati, which may have been the border between Magna Græcia's Sybaris and Kroton], and where I stopped to bait [eat and rest] at a farm-house situated at a short distance from the sea. I here obtained some bread and wine, and the surrounding sheaves of ripe grain just cut afforded ample store of refreshment for our horses."

(An Italian dictionary defines 'fondaco' thus: 'in the Middle Ages and the following centuries it was a building for use by foreign merchants as accommodation, storage of goods and a place of collective bargaining'.)

On today's road, Cariati is a bit of a bottleneck. For Keppel-Craven (1818) it was 'a wretched place'; ten years later for Ramage 'a wretched village'. Ramage explained why:

"It has been plundered by Turkish corsairs, has suffered from the hordes of brigands, and was nearly destroyed by the French in 1806."

But as if that wasn't bad enough:

"I rested at Cariati for a short time, till the insects became so annoying that I was fairly driven out, and I determined to push on …"

Nearly a decade later Edward Hutton (1912) just called it 'miserable'.

For me Cariati means that I am nearly home; travelling south it is the gateway to Calabria's most well-know wine-producing area, the Cirò. The town itself is up in the hills and it has its coast-side spin-off in the shape of Cirò Marina but between the two and indeed the whole surrounding area is bursting with vineyards and *cantine* where you can buy by the bottle or just turn up with a few empty five-litre demijohns.

Close to Cirò Marina is Punta Alice, that marks the southern point of the massive Golfo di Taranto (the northern point being Punta Ristola in Apulia) and where, according to Swinburne (1777) there used also to be a Greek temple:

"It was famous for a temple of Apollo Halyus, of which I could not discover the smallest vestige; the waves of the sea having covered, or the hand of man removed, every stone of it. During supper, the keeper of the neighbouring watch-tower came to pay me a visit. A glass or two of wine restored that liberty to his tongue which respect had retrained; and, after endeavouring to impress me with a high idea or his courage, and the havoc he would make with his single gun in an army of Algerines [a name related to those from Algeria but used to encompasses all Arab invaders], he entertained me with several anecdotes or his brother-warders."

Though Swinburne seemed to be enjoying the local wine, a couple of paragraphs earlier he was giving it the thumbs down:

"The territory produces also very fine oil and corn, execrable wine, but good water."

When we first came to this part of Calabria, we sampled the wine from many of the local *cantine* until we found the one that had the perfect balance of rich, fresh taste ... and price. It was a couple of years into our quest before someone suggested we try a small *cantina* at Marina di Stróngoli and we've been buying our wine there ever since. Of course most people with a patch of land in and around most Calabria towns produce wine for the family and it is this that is normally available by the jug at most local restaurants and pizzerias. That said, the more people who try our wine from Marina di Stróngoli, the more we get asked to pick up a demijohn or two for them next time we're there.

Also, tucked away on the inland side of the road, in the shadow of Stróngoli itself, is Calabria's first *agriturismo* (farmhouse accommodation offering local produce), the Dattilo. In addition to the apartments and restaurant, there is also a small, award-winning *cantina* that produces some of the finest wines in Calabria and beyond.

Ironically Richard Keppel-Craven (1818), atop the hill that is Stróngoli itself—Petelia that was, back in Spartacus' day—was looking south-west and made the following observation:

"Mount Clibanus is seen rising more inland, between the towns of Cutro and Santa Severina. This last is the ancient Siberena, extolled by Pliny for the excellence of its wines."

Today there are few *cantine* close to Santa Severina; on the other hand the wines the wines of Cirò have won recognition, not just within Italy but also at an international level.

Hugging the coast, more or less the whole way from Basilicata to Reggio Calabria, is the railway. It is a single track affair and to catch sight of an actual train from the adjacent SS106 is a rare event indeed.

South of Crotone both it and the road leave the coast to take quite different routes around the western side of the 'island', a large, sparsely-inhabited, low-lying promontory, known as the Lacinian Promontory, that juts out into the Ionian Sea. It is here that the lone Greek column of the Temple of Hera at Capo Colonna stands; here too is the down-at-heel town of Isola di Capo Rizzuto where lurk a number of mafia families and their entourages surrounded by countless windmills from which they made obscene amounts of money.

Alongside the road at Sant'Anna is a large camp for processing and housing immigrants and opposite is the tiny Crotone Airport which, at its height, serves no more than three flights each way a day; further evidence of the extent to which the transport infrastructure on the east is lacking.

Road and sea reunite close to one of the jewels of Calabria, the small coastal town of Le Castella.

It is the castle at Le Castella that steals the show. Spanish Aragonese in origin, it sits in the sea, joined to the mainland by a short neck of land; truly a stunning sight. But a sight that Swinburne (1777) appears not have experienced for, unusually, he approached Le Castella by sea and came into the harbour which is literally round the point from the castle and neither one is visible from the other:

"The sky was overcast, and threatened rain, which made us keep close to the more. We rowed round the little harbour of Casstelle, probably the place formerly called Castra Hannibalis, from which that able, but ill-seconded general [Hannibal], embarked for Carthage."

On his short passage from Crotone, and not to be stunned by the famous castle, Swinburne picked up on another story for which the town is well-known, albeit a story which has been embellished over the years:

"As we sailed along, the man at the helm pointed out to me several inland towns of little note, but beautiful objects from the sea. Cutro was one, remarkable for having given birth to Galeni, a renegade, who, in the sixteenth century, rose to great honour at the Ottoman Porte, and, by the name of Ulucciali Baffá, commanded the Turkish fleet, was Viceroy of Algiers and Tunis, and became one of the greatest scourges of Christendom. In the height of his prosperity, he was desirous of bestowing a part of his wealth upon his aged mother, who lived in poverty at Cutro; but that spirited old woman refused to accept of the smallest token from a son, who had forsaken the religion of his fathers, and professed himself the sworn enemy of Christianity."

If you have to be born somewhere in that general area then, by any standard, Le Castella wins hands down over Cutro ... it's on the sea, has a stunning castle and doesn't have the mafia connotations associated with Cutro. Also the Ucciali story has all the elements of romantic intrigue: local lad gets carried off by Arab 'baddies' ... converts and becomes the golden boy of Arab corsairs ... rises up through the ranks to become a respected commander ... decides to return home to visit mum ... mum rejects her non-Christian son.

It could even be a musical ... well, actually it has been, created by my dear friends and musicians extraordinary, Domenico Stumpo and his wife Francesca Loria. Stumpo (he is the only Calabrian I call by his surname, I just like saying the word) will, I suspect, not approve of me casting some doubts on the story of Ucciali and in particular the latter's special relationship with Le Castella which now boasts two statues of him in full Ottoman regalia.

To Google him (itself problematic as his name is spelt in many different ways: Occhialì, Lucciali, Ulucciali, Ucciali and Uluç Ali Pascià) is to find

The stunning Aragonese castle-in-the-sea at Le Castella and the two representations of Ucciali that adorn the town and unquestioningly cement his special relationship with it.

that his place of birth is often omitted completely or given as Le Castella *or* Cutro. Nowhere could I find a primary source that credited Le Castella for spawning the baby Uccialì (né Galeni). *Wikipedia*, which normally cites and annotates its sources, does not mention where he was born other than in Calabria; furthermore the returning-to-Calabria-to-meet-mum story is mentioned only in terms of being a legend.

It has even been suggested by those really who want him to have hailed from Le Castella that the town was once part of a greater Cutro—and this despite the fact that they are fifteen kilometres apart as the crow flies and probably had fewer than a couple of thousand inhabitants between them at the time. Documents relating to the mid-16th century do not suggest that the towns were other than two separate entities; you were born in Cutro or you were born in what was then called Castelle.

Personally, I would put more trust in the Galeni lad's origins as told to Swinburne by his helmsman and which Swinburne himself did not seem to doubt. The man at the helm was not only a local man but was clearly relating a story that had been passed down the generations by those who lived there. And, of course, he made no mention of Uccialì having returned to Calabria.

Furthermore, the entry for Castelle in Rampoldi's authoritative *Corografia dell'Italia*, published in 1832, makes no mention of Uccialì's connection with the town ... nor with Cutro, it has to be said.

There being no actual evidence that he ever returned to Calabria to see his mother, it is more likely that this story has its roots in ecclesiastical propaganda, not unknown at the time, to illustrate how the low-born Christian woman rejected the rich and powerful Muslim, even if he was her son. It would appear that Christian motherly love did not go as far as sanctioning having a Muslim son.

What *is* well-documented is the story of Uluç Ali Pascià (his Arab name) and how he rose through the ranks from captured galley slave in 1536 to Beylerbey (Chief Governor) of Alexandria in 1565. Two years later, Sultan Selim II appointed him as the Pasha and Beylerbey of Algiers, the most powerful of the Ottoman regions in North Africa. Three years later he left North Africa to take command of one flank of Ali Pasha's fleet in the Battle of Lepanto. For the Ottoman fleet this was a disastrous battle though not so for Uluç Ali who not only captured the flagship of the Maltese Knights but also was able to extricate his ships from the mayhem and get back to Istanbul with eighty-seven vessels. His reward from the Sultan was his appointment, in 1571, as Kapudan Pasha (Grand Admiral) and Beylerbey of the Isles.

Over the following fifteen years, until his death in 1587, Uluç Ali was involved in numerous battles, skirmishes and raids in every corner of the Mediterranean and the Black Sea which only served to add to his prestige as a man of immense military and naval acumen.

One of these raids was indeed into Calabria in 1576 and perhaps it is this that spawned the story about his rejection by his mother. Pushing eighty (and therefore lucky still to be alive some might say), maybe she just didn't recognise him in all his finery. On the other hand, the raid in question was at the gates of Trebisacce, over a hundred miles away from Castelle by sea. In reality nowhere in his busy, and well-documented, schedule of battles, skirmishes and raids does he seem to have taken time off for a family visit.

His story is reminiscent of the tale Ramage (1828) was told in Trebisacce (see a few pages back) of how, in the late 18th century, Turkish corsairs were still pestering the people of that town and how one Trebisaccese taken prisoner had returned to his home town only to discover that there was something to be said for life as a captive on the Barbary coast.

The Ucciali story is an example of how a few known events can be hijacked, manipulated, embellished and romanticised without any reference to the historical record or conditions at the time. Take, for example, the 'revisiting mum' element and how it has evolved into something almost as mundane as catching the overnight ferry from Istanbul to Calabria to drop in on the folks back home for the first time in forty years. The reality is that, had Uluç Ali Pascià tried to land at Castelle, his Turkish fleet would have been perceived as the enemy and he would have received the same welcome he got at Trebisacce when the locals staved off the incursion for three days before help arrived. Sticking his hand in the air and protesting that he was on a home-visit would probably not have cut it.

With due respect to my good friend Stumpo and the good burghers of Le Castella, this is, I believe, a more authentic version of the Ucciali story ... albeit a tad abbreviated but nevertheless, even if I say so myself, it still has that romantic edge that could make it into a good musical:

"A Calabrian man, born in the hills somewhere between Cutro and Le Castella in the early 16th century, was captured by Turkish corsairs, became one himself and died in Istanbul having become a very powerful and respected servant of the Ottoman Empire."

※

Several coastal hamlets later, road and railway reunite near Steccato di Cutro and the infamous Roccabernarda Station before a string of seaside hamlets—

Botricello, Cropani Marina, Sellia Marin, Simeri Mare—that for the summer driver are a nightmare. They are an unavoidable part of the journey from the Crotone area to Lamezia Airport and the least attractive part of it. Bottricello is three kilometres long and has over thirty pedestrian crossings though, this being Calabria, most people cross anywhere but the crossings.

Another such bottleneck is Catanzaro Lido, the gateway to Catanzaro itself on the one hand and on the other to never-ending string of coastal offshoots of erstwhile hilltop towns that all now have their 'Marina', 'Lido' or 'Scala' appendage. Far too many also have 'mafia' written all over them for the local *'ndrangheta* clans were not backward in coming forward to control something they thought might be lucrative … tourism. I was told once that, a couple of decades ago, when well-meaning entrepreneurs wanted to open restaurants and hotels along the coast to foster tourism, they found that the local mafia controlled the water supply and that, unless they paid up, they dried up. I suspect that in some of these towns, nothing has changed; even though they cater for tourists, a few still retain that dowdy, mafia-town, complexion.

It was not by accident that few of the earlier travellers came along this coast; for a start there was no road and, besides, it was easier to use the hillside tracks that linked towns and villages where there was at least a chance of accommodation and a place to eat. Also, such towns were generally malaria-free and, being on the higher ground, the numerous *fiumare* that fell from La Serra and the Aspromonte mountains were easier to cross inland.

For these travellers there were four places of interest, three of which were inland—Squillace, Castelvetere [today's Caulónia] and Gerace—the other, Locri, the coastal offshoot of Gerace, was worth the effort because of its Magna Græcia connections. Squillace and Castelvetere were also only of interest because of their Magna Græcia connections but the assumptions of the time regarding the precise location of these Greek communities were incorrect and all are now known to have been on the coast.

Henry Swinburne (1777) made rapid progress between Staletti (near Squillace) and Monasterace, having seemingly covered the thirty miles over hills and down dales in less than a day:

"We passed below Stellati, a town of one thousand two hundred souls, on a hill composed of pebbles and mineral particles, glued together by a viscous earth. As we advanced southward, the country fell off in beauty, and the foil in richness, from a mellow loam to a poor blue clay. The cotton fields have not the wholesome appearance of those farther north. We slept at Monasterace, a poor village on an eminence. The road to it was good, except near the torrents, which, in great numbers, roll down from the mountains, and tear the plain to pieces."

The next day he headed on down to Castelvetere where he thought he might find some evidence of Greek Caulon ... he did not know it at the time but his overnight stop at Monasterace was only a couple of miles from where the ruins of Caulon were later found at Punto Stilo, right on the sea.

By the time that Gissing (1897) and Douglas (1911) were abroad things were different with both the road and railway hugging the coast the whole way down to the south and round the corner to Reggio Calabria. Douglas had been in Serra San Bruno and was heading for Crotone when he took a detour, as it happens to one of my favourite places on this coast, Soverato:

"Finding little else of interest in Serra, and hungering for the flesh-pots of Cotrone, I descended by the postal diligence to Soverato, nearly a day's journey. Old Soverato is in ruins, but the new town seems to thrive in spite of being surrounded by deserts of malaria. While waiting for supper and the train to Cotrone, I strolled along the beach, and soon found myself sitting beside the bleached anatomy of some stranded leviathan, and gazing at the mountains of Squillace that glowed in the soft lights of sunset. The shore was deserted save for myself and a portly dogana-official [customs official] who was playing with his little son—trying to amuse him by elephantine gambols on the sand, regardless of his uniform and manly dignity. Notwithstanding his rotundity, he was an active and resourceful parent, and enjoyed himself vastly; the boy pretending, as polite children sometimes do, to enter into the fun of the game."

Leslie Gardner (1966) approached the town with high hopes:

The inauguration of the line from the station at Gioiosa Jonica Superiore in 1932.

"Soverato, thirteen miles from Catanzaro Lido, going south, is the one coastal town of the Ionian shore which looks, until you look closely, like the palm-embowered, flower-festooned riviera sun-trap every seaside place in Calabria ought to be."

His guide, the incomparable Princess Maria Pignatelli, explained how the town had secured major international investors and was on the cusp of becoming an 'international tourist city … [the] new Taormina'. Gardiner was not convinced and tempered his observations with a touch of realism:

"There are three Soveratos in ascending order, going inland: Soverato Marina, Soverato Superiore and Soverato Vecchio. Marina, compressed between hill and strand, is the place in touch with the world, with railway and coast road. Much remains to be done before this place becomes a new Taormina [Sicilian town where DH Lawrence and Truman Capote used to live]: olive woods to be turned into amusement parks, cactus plantations to be uprooted for minigolf and paddling pools, the acres of clover and sand to be parcelled out for bathing establishments or open-air ballrooms."

Despite the fact that Soverato is a pleasant and popular seaside destination, thankfully the tongue-in-cheek, how-to-spoil-a-coastal-town picture that Gardner painted did not happen. Yes, like most coastal towns, Soverato has succumbed to the tourist season but it also has managed to retain its dignity.

I am fond of Soverato for several reasons: it only a ninety-minute drive from Santa Severina; it is the home of Ulderico Nisticò; it has an excellent out-of-season hotel right in the centre; and it has a top-notch restaurant. When we got to know the proprietors of the latter, Dora and Francesco, and that they used to live and work in New York, we finally understood their particular twist on Italian cuisine that, for us, was the main attraction.

Between Monasterace and Locri lies the sleepy coastal community of Riace Marina, the town bearing the same name is on the hill a few miles inland. None of the travellers ever mentioned either town, though a few passed through Riace Marina by road or on the train without comment. Lear (1847) stayed on the village on the neighbouring hill, Stignano, but clearly was not interested in Riace; his sights were set on Stilo.

All that changed in 1972 when Rome chemist, Stefano Mariottini, was snorkeling two hundred metres offshore from Riace and noticed an arm sticking up from the sand. He had stumbled upon the first of what came to be known as the Riace Bronzes.

Of course, though the bronzes bear the name of the town nearest to which they were found, scarcely anything has changed … Riace Marina is still one of those places along the Ionian shore which only springs to live for a few summer months each year.

The long-winded Marina di Gioiosa Ionica has no such claim to fame but it well illustrates the relationship between the *superiore* town in the hills, the *inferiore* part of the same town and its more modern maritime offshoot. This is Leslie Gardiner's (1966) view of it:

"Gioiosa looks like a small metropolis of the hills, but the upper town is all high walls and barred windows, without provision for a stranger. In the lower part you find a general store and buy ice-cream, which you seated on a barrel of figs, while a cross-section of the population in and dumbly stares. The Calabro-Lucane line maintains an infrequent service down the valley to the *marina*—or you may walk, it is an easy journey—where the inns welcome foreign tourists and their travel cheques."

These days, of course, if you haven't a car, walking is the only option and all the travel cheques have expired.

Beyond Locri, and almost the whole way to Reggio Calabria, from time to time there is more of a sense of having entered bandit country; a look at Google's *'ndrangheta* map will explain why.

But it is not all gloom and doom for this is Calabria's Jasmine Coast, the name the brainchild of some long-dead tourist official which conjures up the beautiful fragrance of *gelsomino* and the clean, serene waters of the Ionian Sea sparkling under an unrelenting sun.

Edward Lear (1847) spent a lot of time in this part of Calabria but mainly in the hinterland though he did touch the shore at Bovalino:

"Our route was a weary one, as it was ever descending straight to the sea in the midst of the stony oleander-dotted water-course hot and tedious; near the coast we came to sandy roads for two hours, with our old friends cactus and aloe bordering cultivated grounds to the water's edge, from which our halt was hardly a mile distant.

"It was late when we arrived below Bovalino, sparkling on its chalky height in the last sunbeams, and as we found that to go on to Ardore would have been too far and fatiguing, we turned through olive grounds from the sea, and began the long ascent to the town, which we reached at dusk. Bovalino is a place of considerable size, and we were charmed by its strongly defined Calabrese character, as we ascended the winding pathways full of homeward-bound peasants, the costume of the women being prettier here than any we had yet seen."

Lear was heading for Ardore and, unusually, chose to travel along the shore but, having been delayed at San Luca, he realised he wasn't going to make Ardore before nightfall and cut back inland to stay overnight at Bovalino instead. This was 1847 and Bovalino was Bovalino; now the same town 'sparkling on its chalky height' is called Bovalino *Superiore* as the 'new' Bovalino, Bovalino Marina, is by the sea. This now is the 'place of considerable size' and one of the most pleasant towns on the Jasmine Coast.

Lear was made most welcome by his host, Count Garrolo, and his description of his short stay with the excessively garrulous Garrolo is one of the most entertaining in the book. This was his parting shot:

"Addio, Conte Garrolo! a merry obliging little man you are as ever lived, and the funniest of created counts all over the world."

Eric Whelpton (1957) also took to Bovalino:
"Bovalino Marina on the coastal road, six miles from Bianco, is a cheerful town which appears to be really prosperous, and the inhabitants look happy and well fed. The innkeeper, who had spent some years in Australia, proudly showed us the improvements he was making to his house, which included modern plumbing, running water in every room, and several bathrooms.

"This inn is quite unpretentious, but is the first suitable place for a stay or a meal on the road from Reggio to Catanzaro."

I too was more than a little impressed with Bovalino; I found the same uncomplicated generosity as Lear had—albeit less vociferous and on the coast—and also managed to find an unassuming little restaurant which, on the first evening I ate there, was packed to the gunwales and so I thought it prudent to book for the following evening, a Saturday. When I arrived promptly at eight, I had the whole place to myself: when I left at two in the morning, I was still the only paying customer in the building.

I really did try to leave several times before Saturday became Sunday; I was feeling guilty that I was taking up a table for two on a busy evening when groups who hadn't booked were being turned away.

I got up several times and indicated that there were people waiting to be seated but each time I was told to sit and not to worry:

"*Non ti preoccupare,*" my genial hosts, Franco and Ciccio, would say as they kept me topped up with a gorgeous house red wine and explained that those waiting were all groups of four or more and that my table in the corner only seated one comfortably and two at a pinch.

Then, somehow, I got talking to my neighbours, a large eccentric, birthday-celebrating family which seemed to possess a degree of fluidity; not only did they keep changing places but even the people changed, some disappeared, others occupied the vacant chair. They were amused to have an English-speaking, token Calabrian at the next table and made sure my glass was always full as all the inter-familial relationships were explained to me ... they clearly thought I still had the capacity to remember them.

As they got up to leave, I tagged along behind and almost got as far as the cash-desk but, being the last in the line, I got chatting to a family of latecomers just finishing their meal. This foursome, two adults—he Calabrian, she Brazilian and living in Rome—and their super-intelligent children, one girl, one boy, were all keen to practise their English and invited me to join them for a *liquore* ... or two, or maybe it was three. After all, we were all emigrants and immigrants of one kind or another and had lots of stories to share.

It was now well past midnight and when my international friends got up to leave, I followed suit. Out of the corner of my eye I could see that the staff, glad finally to see the back of us, had already started to prepare a long table for their after-work feast.

This time I did actually manage to get as far as the cash-desk and settle my account. The hard and dangerous sorted, I was denied those final few steps into the outside world by Ciccio (or maybe it was Franco) and escorted instead back into the restaurant where a place had been laid for me at the staff's table where a piping hot seafood spaghetti and a carafe or two of red wine awaited. I didn't have the mental capacity to argue and, besides, it was getting on for five hours since I had eaten.

It was gone two-thirty when I eventually crawled into bed, very much the worse for wear and desperately trying to cling on to fond memories of my several memorable meals in Bovalino.

At Bianco, Swinburne (1777) had clearly had enough of the typical Calabrian hillside village:

"It is called Bianco, from the chalky hill it stands upon, and consists of houses built of stone and mud, covered with tufted boughs. The appearance of every thing about it was so dreary, the looks of the villagers so squallid, and the evening so stormy, that I was glad to remain in my smoky crib and comfort myself with some white wine of a strong body and flavour, though rather too great a decree of roughness."

In need of a break, he headed for the coast:

"We descended the mountain at the hazard of our lives, by a miry narrow road, buttressed up with posts, over which are laid wooden bridges that quiver with the pressure even of a foot traveller. As it had rained very hard all night, our leader prudently preferred a longer way by the sands, to a short cut through the mountains. We crossed the isthmus of Cape Bruzzano, where the Locrians first landed, and remained four years before they moved northward. The low grounds are extremely rich in herbage, and produce spontaneously thick crops of sainfoin [a forage crop], which are not turned to proper account; half the grass is suffered to rot on the ground for want of cattle to consume it.

"I dined at Brancaleone, a small village; and afterwards rode to examine Cape Spartivento, the most southerly point of Italy. It is surrounded by small islands, and numerous rocky shelves, on which the waves break with great fury as they are driven down the streights. From this angle we struck into the mountains …"

As did Edward Hutton (1912):
"Capo Spartivento is the south-eastern headland of this vast promontory or peninsula of the Bruttii; passing it one looks eastward towards Greece over the Ionian Sea. At Capo Spartivento, very weary and disheartened because of all the desolation of the coast here at the foot of the Aspromonte, the scarcity of the villages, the barbaric Greek of their few inhabitants, the darkness of the heights, the wilderness that here lines the classic sea, we took train for Gerace, for the road beyond the Marina di Brancaleone is steep and difficult, leaving the desolate shore for the more desolate hills, while the line clings to the sea, the only friendly thing in all this country."

Clearly Hutton was not over-impressed, particularly with the 'barbaric' Greek still spoken in the area; this was not ancient Greek, not Albanian Greek, but Greco-Calabro, the Greek left over from the Byzantine era.

While scrutinising Capo Spartivento, neither Swinburne nor Hutton made mention of Mongibello, an increasingly dominant visual interloper in these parts from just across the water.

Edward Lear (1847) who, more than any other traveller, explored this corner of Calabria, explains:

"Mongibello, the Saracenic name of Mount Etna, is generally in use among the Sicilians and the Calabresi."

Heading towards Reggio by train, Leslie Gardiner (1966) saw Etna for the first time:

"It was curious to see travellers, who must have been so familiar with the sight, dropping what they were doing and gazing on Etna's white dome against the red sky of a spring evening, when it appeared through the compartment window. "Mongibello" I heard reverently murmured. There is something mystical about the mountain for Calabrians, although it does not belong to them. Perhaps my fellow passengers were not all that familiar with the sight, after all. Perhaps we saw Etna in conditions of rare clarity. In ten days at Reggio I did not set eyes on it again, for mist."

Having also made that same journey by train for Mélito, I understand what Gardiner means. Mongibello seems to play tricks with the light. One minute it is clear and majestic, the next ill-defined and you're not sure if it is a mountain at all.

Another British traveller sailed these waters in 1819, just four years after hostilities with the French had ceased. Betsey Fremantle—who kept a diary of her travels—was aboard *HMS Rochfort* with her husband, Captain Thomas Fremantle, who had been appointed Commander-in-Chief of the British Mediterranean Fleet in 1818. *HMS Rochfort* was a 'third-rate ship of the line' which meant it carried 74 guns and was faster than other so-called first- and second-rate vessels. They sailed through the Straits of Messina twice, the first time, on May 26, they made slow progress in the waters around southern Calabria:

"The wind died away towards eveng. & we were becalmed off Etna, which is covered with snow, & has not thrown up any fire since 1812."

On the return trip a month later wind-wise they did not fare much better; Etna on the other hand was making more of a fuss:

"We had to beat all day against a foul wind, but had Etna in sight, & really it is the most magnificent sight just now. The black smoke which comes out of the crater is very thick, & is carried a considerable way like a black cloud. The scenery all day was quite beautiful as we sail'd close in shore from the Calabrian coast to that of Sicily, & I was looking out almost all day. We remain'd off Reggio, tacking backwards & forwards, between that place & Messina, not wishing to risk the straits at night with the wind against us."

To witness an eruption of Mongibello is, they say, both a magnificent and fearful sight; I imagine it depends on how close you are. I have been atop Mongibello four times and been close to it many, many times without ever having seen so much as a spark.

As she passed along the Calabrian coast, Betsey Fremantle will have seen a number of hilltop towns set back from the shore for none of their modern offshoots between Capo Spartivento and Mélito di Porto Salvo—Palizzi Marina, Bova Marina, Codulfuri Marina, Marina di San Lorenzo—existed at the time except as occasional jetties for loading and unloading produce.

Beyond Mélito di Porto Salvo—where Garibaldi landed twice from Sicily en route to first glory and then ignominy—the line of the coast turns northwest at Capo dell'Armi, then northwards at Punta di Pellaro towards Reggio Calabria. Punta di Pellaro is not only the extreme southwestern point of mainland Italy but also is generally regarded as the last point in the Apennine chain. It is from between these two headlands that the views of Mongibello are, in Lear's words, 'increasing in magnificence'.

Between San Gregório and Archi, a distance of about eleven kilometres, which includes the city of Reggio Calabria, the line of the coast is accompanied by a flurry of train stations, no less than ten that bear the city's name—from Reggio Calabria San Gregório to Reggio Calabria Archi.

Although there is a ferry terminal at Reggio Calabria which serves Messina, the main ferry port is Villa San Giovanni about nine miles to the north where the Straits of Messina are at their narrowest. Under sail in Strutt's day (1841) the journey took about the same time as it does today:

"This is the general place of embarkation; with a fair wind, one may run over in about twenty minutes."

The journey between Reggio and Villa San Giovanni was something that many travellers made on foot and I once toyed with the idea of following suit but checked it out by car first. I was glad I did.

Reggio Calabria's northward sprawl as far as Archi is punctuated by a hotch-potch of sprawling satellite conurbations each seemingly intent on outdoing the others for the accolade of having the dowdiest apartments and down-at-heel shops; the overriding impression was of an urban no man's land, struggling to keep its head above water. Even in the car, I felt uncomfortable and, aware that Reggio was the unofficial capital of the *'ndrangheta*, decided that to walk the route was not one of my better ideas. Next time, I thought, I'll use the *autostrada* as I usually do.

I wondered later whether I was judging the area solely on a visual impression, albeit one that tied in with my experience of other mafia strongholds. So I checked out each coastal cluster up to Villa San Giovanni—Pentimele, Archi, Gallico, Catona, Concessa—and found several reports of *'ndrangheta* activity—from murders to arrests—over the last decade. But I also found reports of another activity, of ordinary people in these same areas confronting the mafia by demonstrating against their malignance and demanding the right to live a normal life. Also I discovered that Gallico, Catona and Concessa had thriving tourist industries just as predicted by a brochure that Leslie Gardiner (1966) came across:

"It offers you Villa San Giovanni, where the train ferry from Messina comes in; Marina di Gallico, much frequented by campers and caravanners from the overnight parking lots beneath olive and oleander; Catona, a more elegant resort with night life which is expensive by southern standards."

There is also a well-documented mafia presence at Villa San Giovanni but it appears more muted perhaps because the town's more obvious function is as the main port to and from Sicily. In the past, during what was called the Second 'Ndrangheta War (1985–1991), the local clans fought it out with their Reggio Calabria-based rivals; in half a dozen years over seven hundred *'ndrine* died.

A container ship passing through the Straits of Messina between Scilla and Punta del Faro. It was via the pylon on Sicily that electricity came to the island from mainland Calabria.

Scilla Castle from the town's beach to the south and from the rocky shore of Chianalea on the northern side.

All of which is a far cry from the experience of Keppel-Craven (1818):

"Just beyond ... is the beautiful village of Villa S. Giovanni, where I was induced to stop for the night by the lateness of the hour, excluding all hope of reaching Reggio by day-light, and the want of repose, but too severely experienced by our whole cavalcade. I rested at the house of one of the richest inhabitants of this place, who has established a very extensive and successful silk manufactory."

Likewise Edward Lear (1847):

"At Villa San Giovanni, which is the centre of a knot of scattered villages covering that part of the Calabrian coast opposite to the Faro [Punta del Faro, the north-east tip of Sicily], we found a good locanda, and halted for midday rest, as well as for maccaroni, occhiali, which are a very good fish, molignani, as good a vegetable, and Lipari wine."

Villa San Giovanni and Scilla are equidistant from the Punta del Faro; in terms of ambience, however, they are light years distant. Scilla is undoubtedly the gem of the so-called Costa Viola.

My first three visits to the town were all unintentional and told me nothing about Scilla. The first two were in the company of people I had met in Reggio who insisted that I follow them there and enjoy the beach ... which is what happened the first time but not the second as I was unable to find a parking space and instead beat a hasty retreat to Lamezia and the flight home. The third time it was pitch black when, returning from Sicily around two in the morning, I was forced to follow a diversion off the *autostrada* which took me through Scilla. Nevertheless I knew enough about Scilla to realise it was a place where I'd like to get to know better which is why one Christmas, with Kay in England, I spent a week there.

There are three elements to Scilla: there is the focal point, Scilla Castle, jutting out to sea on a headland that protects the *centro storico* behind it and keeps the other two elements apart; below and to the south of the castle is the short beach with its adjacent touristy paraphernalia while to the north is the old fishing quarter known as Chianalea. It was in the narrow, cobbled streets of Chianalea that I spent Christmas.

Most of the travellers who came here were preoccupied with a single mythical story but, being steeped in their classical upbringing, almost all presumed that their readers were conversant with the story of Scylla and Charybdis; only Eric Whelpton (1957) did not make this assumption:

"According to Homer, the monstrous Scylla dwelt in a cave "in the dark rock whose peak reached to the wide heaven, and is encompassed by a dark cloud".

"She had twelve feet and six heads, with triple rows of teeth, and swooped down on sailors in the ships that passed by, so that none could escape her.

"Beyond lurked another peril just as great—the dread whirlpool of Charybdis, which sucked down men and boats into her dark and swirling depths.

"Warned by Circe, Ulysses lashed himself to the helm, and bandaged the eyes of his crew and plugged their ears with wax, to escape the lure of the sirens. Then having passed them, he was to steer "close to the rocks and away from the wave", to avoid the still greater menace of Scylla and Charybdis.

"Then as we learned in our youth, the monster snatched six of his best sailors, dragged them to the mouth of her cave, and devoured them before the horror-struck eyes of their comrades.

"The ship sailed through to calmer waters, and the bold Ulysses survived to return to Penelope after his protracted adventures and wanderings.

"The whirlpool Charybdis is still there, so slight that it endangers no one."

This then is the origin of the myth that has grown up around the dangers in navigating the Straits of Messina between Calabria, specifically that part between Scilla and Punta del Faro on Sicily. Today, as Whelpton stated, the dangers are minimal for hundreds of years of earthquakes have transformed the depths of both the land and the sea; and while there remains a natural whirlpool in the Straits, the monster seems to have moved on, at some point reinventing itself as the *'ndrangheta*.

Of course the story of Scylla and Charybdis is also a metaphor for being 'between the devil and the deep blue sea' or 'between a rock and a hard place' or 'on the horns of a dilemma' and even 'out of the frying pan into the fire'.

From the little harbour below the castle and the whole way along Chianelea

A *luntro* and her crew in search of swordfish off Scilla in the 1960s.
The modern *feluca* has a very high 'crow's nest' and a long extended prow for the harpoonist.

there are still fishing boats that go out to sea on a daily basis and every day the many local restaurants offer fresh fish. Along with other neighbouring Calabrian and Sicilian towns, the traditional fishing boat for catching swordfish was the *luntro* with its unique 'crow's nest' for the lookout. The *feluca* is a larger version which also incorporates a long extended prow for the harpoonist which keeps him well ahead of any movement the boat might make and the fish might sense. These days it is all much more sophisticated and there are state-of-the-art, all-steel *feluche* that ply these waters in search of swordfish.

Further up the coast, Bagnara Calabra has the same fishing history, and the same hills coming down to the sea, but without the myth and without the idyllic setting; nevertheless many travellers found it a pleasing place ... even after the earthquake of 1783. Brian Hill (1791) passed through while rebuilding was still on-going:

"Bagnara, situated on the side of a steep mountain, was entirely overthrown, and 4350 persons killed. It is rebuilding in a manner truly astonishing, when it is considered, that the ground on which it stands is subject to frequent agitations. As it was only ten o'clock when we arrived at Bagnara ..."

As a footnote to this description, Hill detailed the idiosyncrasies of how Calabrians kept time:

"I have all along set down the hours according to the English method of calculation, but, throughout Sicily and Calabria, they regulate the time according to the setting of the sun, by counting the twenty-fours hours round. Thus the first hour after sun set is always one o'clock, the second two o'clock, and so on to twenty-four. It has an odd sound to strangers, to hear the people talk of fourteen, fifteen, o'clock, &c. and, till one is a little used to it, often causes much confusion; for instance, if in the month of February, you wanted to set off from any place about six or seven o'clock, according to the English way of reckoning time, and were not to accommodate your orders to the usage of the country, your beasts and litiga [litter] would be ready for you about midnight; and if you wished to have your dinner at two or three o'clock, you would have it about seven or eight at night."

When I first read this I wondered whether the element of fluidity that often accompanies today's Calabrian time-keeping had its roots in this antiquated system. If, for example, a concert were to be scheduled to start at nine in the evening in Santa Severina's *piazza*, it would be a rare occasion indeed if it were to actually begin much before ten. And if it's not going to begin until ten, why put nine on the poster? Indeed, when I am involved in any arrangement that involves a specific time, I automatically clarify whether we are talking normal time of Calabrian time. A query that is usually met with a nervous laugh and a knowing nod of the head.

At Bagnara, Richard Keppel-Craven (1818) didn't notice the post-earthquake improvements for he had eyes only for one bewitching woman:

"On crossing the streams of Bagnara a young woman of the most extraordinary beauty arrested my attention. The steepness of the road, and its difficulty just at that spot, where the loose stones in the torrent rendered the footing very insecure, made it impossible to stop; and the transient glance to which I was compelled to limit my admiration, probably heightened the effect of the apparition which called it forth; but I can with truth aver, that nothing in human shape ever approached so nearly to all the ideas we are wont to form to ourselves of a supernatural being. Regularity of feature was combined with brilliancy of complexion, expression of countenance, and exquisite symmetry as well as gracefulness of form; her dark blue eyes glowed in softened radiance beneath straight black eyebrows, and her smooth low forehead was shaded by a profusion of light brown hair. Her teeth were no less perfect than the smile of goodness which disclosed them; while her cheeks bloomed in all the freshness of the most brilliant health."

Edward Lear (1817), approaching from the sea, had his landscape painter brain in gear:

"Bagnara rises from the water's edge in an amphitheatre of buildings, crowned by a high rock which is joined to the mountain above by a castle and aqueduct, and is assuredly one of the most imposing and stately towns in appearance which we have yet seen."

Survivors of the December 1908 earthquake at Palmi with Monte Elia in the background.

Calabrian poet Lorenzo Calogero, born near Palmi.

My experience was more akin to that of Leslie Gardner (1966):
"Bagnara's promenade, lined with low terraced fishermen's cottages and cobbled alleyways to the main road behind, might be a Devon village."

The wide, gently-curving bay that encapsulates both Scilla and Bagnara, ends at Palmi, one of the largest cities on the Tyrrhenian coast.

For centuries because of its position, Palmi had suffered sporadic earthquake damage but the 1908 quake that centred on Reggio Calabria and Messina was, for Palmi, catastrophic.

I have already noted how Douglas' *Old Calabria* seems to be a fusion of more than one Calabrian journey. His account of being at Palmi throws up another example for he talks only of the town's oil industry with no mention of the 1908 earthquake at all. This would suggest Douglas was there *before* it happened. On the other hand, Edward Hutton (1912), *was* travelling in the area at the time he said he was:

"Of Palmi amid its gardens, its orange groves, and wonderful olive-yard, really only the glorious view of the island [Sicily] are left to us. It is best to leave it, to forget, and to climb thence through the olive gardens, the great hill of Monte Elia upon whose slopes it lies in ruin, to gaze upon Etna and Sicily."

For Emily Lowe (1858), it could not have been more different:

"... Palma ... taking its name from the palms which love to grow around it; and as the bay beneath is that of La Gioja or "Joy," the trees show a charming discrimination: reciprocating their friendliness, the inhabitants have erected a monument to their honour,—the waters of the fountain on the marketplace, dropping from the leaves of a lofty white marble palm."

Today Palmi, rebuilt and rejuvenated, has become something of a cultural centre. The *Casa della Cultura Leonida Rèpaci* was inaugurated in 1982 — named after local writer and political activist Leonida Rèpaci (1898–1985)— hosts conferences, debates, concerts, exhibitions and a variety of other cultural events. As well as Rèpaci, the renowned Italian opera composer, Francesco Cilea (1866-1950), was born here and poet Lorenzo Calogero (1910–1961) came from nearby Melicuccà.

Emily Lowe's (1858) journey through Calabria was of the whistle-stop variety. She travelled along the post-road built by Murat, what is now called the SS19. From Reggio Calabria the road—in places now superseded by the SS18—initially followed the coast almost as far as Lamezia before cutting inland to Tiriolo thence to continue its tortuous way up to Cosenza and beyond; other than local traffic, this more serpentine northern section is and now seldom used.

Lowe and her mother literally travelled with the carriage that carried the post, *la dilagenza postale*:

"Most people have an idea that this principality, which gives its name to the king's eldest son [Francesco's official title was Duke of Calabria], commences close to Naples, instead of being divided from it by several provinces, and consisting of three parts—Principato Ultra Prima, capital Reggio; Ultra Seconda, capital Catanzaro; and Citeriore, chief town Cosenza, our destination.

"The Posta traverses them three times a week, continuing for five days and nights, through Basilicata and Bari [Eboli—Bari is on the opposite coast in Apulia] to Naples. At nine o'clock in the morning it left Reggio."

Apart from breaks to eat, freshen up, and change horses, the *dilagenza postale* was the Lowes' home-from-home, day and night; they passed through some parts of Calabria and never saw a thing. Here they were preparing to leave Palmi where the climbed aboard a different *dilagenza*:

"The carriage had been changed for one more solid, as the hilly district as commencing; we had the front coupé with a cupboard opening into the boot; and the Corriere [driver-cum-courier] the back one to himself. Lofty ground was rising in front; we took a long look at the disappearing coast, saw the last angle of Trinacria [another name for Sicily that reflects its triangular shape] like a tiny foot in the sea, and could but send the isle a few salutations in its own national way, thus—by placing a kiss on the fingers of the left hand, laying it on the palm of the right, and blowing it off affectionately towards any land one wishes well to. The road then sunk between the mountains, and darkness covered all."

Beyond Palmi, the post-road continued to Gioia Tauro after which it gradually left the coast as it headed north-east towards Rosarno, Vibo Valéntia and Pizzo; it was around here that Emily Lowe caught her last glimpse of Sicily. The road strode across the inland base of the large promontory that juts out into the Tyrrhenian Sea like some huge carbuncle of the Calabrian foot of Italy. We, on the other hand, will stick to the coast.

But first a post-related diversion. As the infrastructure Calabria improved throughout the 19th century and into the 20th, new and better roads, the railway and mechanised public transport cut down travelling times … albeit at the expense of the coastal services such as those operated by the Peirano Danovaro Company. Norman Douglas (1911) put it all in perspective:

"Not long ago it was a considerable undertaking to reach this little place [Tiriolo on the aforementioned post-road], but nowadays a public motor-car whirls you up and down the ravines at an alarming pace and will deposit you, within a few hours, at remote Cosenza, once an enormous drive. It is the same all over modern Calabria. The diligence service, for instance, that used to take fourteen hours from San Giovanni to Cosenza has been replaced by motors that cover the distance in four or five. One is glad to save time, but this new element of mechanical hurry has produced a corresponding kind of traveller--a machine-made creature, devoid of the humanity of the old; it has done away with the personal note of conviviality that reigned in the post-carriages. What jocund friendships were made, what songs and tales applauded, during those interminable hours in the lumbering chaise!"

His postal reflections continued, though it is not clear whether he is talking about Calabria or England:

"A postman whom I knew delivered the letters only once every three days, alleging, as unanswerable argument in his defence, that his brother's wife had fifteen children."

But this story does have parallels in today's Calabria as for years the region has had a bad reputation when it comes to the non-Calabrian public's perception of its postal services. That said, I have found little evidence of it; yes, odd letters have gone astray but no more than anywhere else. I suspect this reputation emanates from the uncanny power of unproven hearsay.

On the other hand, for years the residents of one particular Calabrian town were unsure why it was they did not seem to receive the same amount of mail as their friends and family in neighbouring communities. And, like Douglas' story, it was rare for them to receive more than a couple of deliveries a week, and *never* on consecutive days.

As Calabria stumbled into the digital age, many turned to the internet and ordered what they needed online which would then arrive via a courier and, occasionally, by post.

Marco, a resident of the town, ordered some cables through Amazon and, a few days later, received an email from the third-party seller inviting him to comment on their service ... he replied that he would do so when the package arrived. The next morning Marco received a call from the seller querying his reply as he had evidence—in the form of a signature—from the local postal services that the goods had indeed been delivered.

"Ah", Marco explained, "our *postino* sometimes does that if we're not in and he has to leave it somewhere else."

"But ..." asserted the seller, " ... that is not legal ... a *postino* cannot sign for people's mail."

Reluctantly the seller agreed to send a replacement but said he would investigate the matter further. The next day an agitated *postino* turned up on Marco's doorstep with the original package which had clearly been opened. He wanted to know why Marco had complained to his superiors at the local post distribution centre and was told that *he* hadn't complained but that clearly the seller had.

It was this sequence of events that led to a story that made headlines throughout the region: the story of a *postino* who only delivered some of the mail, who hoarded what he didn't deliver and who, from time to time, opened and kept things of value in other people's mail. Several van-loads of undelivered mail were taken from his premises, sorted and finally delivered by five postmen brought in to clear up the mess. For weeks people were receiving mail which they had been expecting for up to seven years.

The town has a new *postino*.

With Emily Lowe disappearing into the inland distance we keep to the carbuncle's coastline and head for Nicótera. Lowe was not the only one to take the short cut for only Hutton (1912) went the whole way round the coast of the promontory, though Swinburne did start his second (1780) Calabrian journey halfway along at the region's best-known resort, Tropea.

But first Nicótera. Hutton passed by without a mention but Nicótera had the last laugh for, fifty years later, the town was at the centre of a scientific study that, arguably, influenced or changed eating habits worldwide.

Between 1957 and 1969 the hillside community of Nicótera—as opposed to its coastal offshoot—was chosen as one of seven communties whose

A sketch of Strómboli by Johann Wolfgang von Goethe which, some say, could only have been made from Tropea even though there is no evidence that he ever set foot in Calabria.

diet would be scrutinised as part of a worldwide study ... the others were in Finland, Greece, Holland, Japan, the United States and Yugoslavia. This was the brainchild of American professor Ancel Keys who, aware that southern Italy, and Calabria in particular, had the highest concentration of centenarians in the world, initiated his study to examine the links between longevity, health (and in particular cardio-vascular disease) and diet.

It was as a result of this 'Seven Countries Study' that the so-called 'Mediterranean diet' came into prominence. Although the detail of some of Keys' conclusions are now being questioned, he was a pioneer in raising awareness of the effect of different dietary fatty acids on serum cholesterol levels. Ancel Keys lived to be a centenarian himself; he died in 2004.

The head of the carbuncle looms in the form of Capo di Vaticano, the southern limit of the Golfo di S. Eufémia and a popular tourist destination because of its dramatic cliffs, many beaches that look out on the clear waters of the Tyrrhenian Sea. It is also close to Tropea, famous for its elongated, sweet, red onions and probably Calabria's number one tourist destination. Swinburne (1880) disembarked here having visited the Lipardi Islands, though it was not his destination of choice:

"... but [the wind] soon veered about to the N. W. and baffled all our attempts to make Cape Suvero [the northern extremity of the Golfo di S. Eufémia]. The steersman observing the gale from that quarter was increasing, and the difficulties of proceeding insurmountable, turned the helm about, and ran for the piaggia [beach] of Tropea, where we moored under the shelter of a rock. In about an hour, as the weather was prodigiously clear, and the situation of our anchoring place closely defended from the wind, I was led to hope we might continue our voyage at least by coasting round the gulf instead of striking across it. But no sooner had we sallied from our well-covered creek, than we found our boat tossed about by an impetuous contrary wind, which it was out of our power to resist; it therefore behoved us to return to Tropea; our bark was drawn ashore, and lodgings procured for me at a solitary convent of Minims [order of friars], on a hill above the road, and some distance from the city."

Having ended up here by accident, he was glad he did:

"The streets of Tropea are narrow, the houses high and built of stone, with great solidity. Two gates give admittance, one to persons coming up the hill from the bay, the other to such as approach along the high plain, on which there is a pleasant walk near two miles long. This level is half a mile broad between the sea and a chain of mountains so steep and rugged, that they seem to cut off all communication by land with the rest of Calabria. The whole flat, and the sides of the hills, yield abundance of grapes, mulberries, olives, pulse, vegetables and garden fruit: copious streams rush from the mountain; and after watering the orchard are collected into one body, and turn a great number of mills."

I have been to Tropea twice, just to satisfy my curiosity. I cannot deny that it is indeed an enchanting town with an abundance of steep and interesting cobbled alleyways running down to the sea with the volcanic island of Strómboli ever-present in the background. Idyllic some might say. It's just that, as soon as I enter a tourist trap, I have an impelling urge to escape and, sadly, like many such places, Tropea suffers from out-of-season blues. Maybe I'm just getting old.

Just before the coast road catches up with the more direct routes north-south, the SS18 and the A3 *autostrada*, there are Bivona and Vibo Valéntia Marina, both coastal offshoots of the province's capital atop the hill. And round the corner Pizzo where the unfortunate Joachim Murat met his end.

Between here and Nicastro, the prevalence of malaria ensured that the plain of Sant'Eufémia and its coastline perimeter were not an option; besides, the inland route offered a tried and tested inn, the *Fondaco del Fico*.

Today, with malaria no longer a factor, the many beaches are an attraction for those who disperse from the nearby Lamezia Airport, though as yet there are few coastal communities. Here you go down to the sea from the main road, there is no coastal road as such and, around the airport, the main road goes even further inland before teaming up with the coast again at Gizzera Lido.

It is in this area that the original site of Sant'Eufémia used to be before the terrible earthquake and tsunami that devastated the area in 1638 and which Swinburne (1780) detailed by quoting the eye-witness account of Athanasius Kircher (see page 162). Just inland from Gizzera Lido is all that now remains in the form of Sant'Eufémia Vetere.

The route for many of the early travellers from the Lamezia area took them inland straight to Cosenza via Rogliano, much as today's A3 *autostrada* does. Only Eric Whelpton (1957) ventured along the coast between Lamezia and Páola, it was as if it were a no-go area but in reality it was no more than the usual dichotomy between inland hilltop towns and the malarial plain ... added to which talk of bandits was but a mere irritant; though how bandits seemed always to be immune to malaria is not known.

Ramage (1828) did get close when he passed through San Mango, a small town on the river Savuto, the same Savuto where the foolhardy Henry, son of Frederick II (1194 – 1250), met his untimely end. The Savuto is a mighty torrent, especially in winter, and was a major obstacle to travellers, there being no crossing point until well inland on the road to Rogliano. Indeed this still remains the case except for the modern coast road and even the A3 *autostrada* bides its time before straddling the Savuto.

Because his guide was concerned about possible brigand activity in the area, reluctantly Ramage agreed to cross the Savuto for the second time:

"It was no easy task to climb the bank, which was covered in short brushwood, and I was alarmed by observing the number of vipers and serpents what we disturbed by basking in the sun.

"After some time we again left the river and struck across the country, arriving at last at a few houses, which I found to be San Mango. It was not, therefore without a feeling of pleasure that I entered the miserable village of San Mango, which assumed in my eyes the delight of a city of refuge."

It is surprising that, despite such travellers' preoccupation with Magna Græcia, nobody tried to locate the site of Greek Temesa. This ancient colony, an ally of Sibari, was known to have been situated near to the mouth of the Savuto. For centuries its exact whereabouts were no less of a puzzle that the remains of Sibari and Caulon but have only recently been pinpointed near the coast to the south of modern Cámpora San Giovanni.

When Whelpton (1957) travelled up towards Páola, he did little more than list the towns en route, though he did verbally linger awhile at Amantea to relate the part the town played in the resistance against the French in 1806 and 1807. These days the sporadic remains of the town's castle look down on a typical Calabria coastal resort; attempts to make the castle ruins as much a draw as the crystal-clear waters of the Tyrrhenian Sea are, alas, unlikely to be cost-effective.

Many Calabrians think that the road that goes east-west through and across the Sila mountains (the SS107) links the provincial capitals of Crotone and Cosenza, And indeed it does ... but it actually links Crotone with Páola on the opposite coast, over twenty-five miles beyond Cosenza.

When I told friends that I had just spent a weekend in Páola they assumed I had been making a pilgrimage to *Il Santuario di San Francesco*, a large, and well-known sanctuary on the outskirts of the town named after the patron saint of Calabria. I had to explain that actually, though I had seen the sanctuary from the road, I was more interested in getting a feel for the town to where Craufurd Tait Ramage had come by sea from Scalea in 1828, from where Emily Lowe left Calabria in 1858 and where George Gissing first set foot in Calabria in 1897.

Páola was one of the places where passing boat traffic came ashore. It was important because it was more of a coastal community than other towns, a place where the high land comes almost to the shore and one which did not suffer from the seasonal, malarial woes in the same way as other Calabrian coastal communities. Páola expanded and prospered, the more so when it became a major station on the rail service from Naples to Sicily.

Swinburne (1780) came here from Cosenza with the aim of picking up a *feluca* to take him to Naples but, because at the time the coastal service was more of a hit and miss affair, he had to return to Cosenza and travel overland to Campo Tenese, thence into Basilicata.

While Swinburne's day out in Páola was centred chiefly around reflections on the name giver of *Il Santuario di San Francesco*, Francesco di Páola (1416 – 1507), my weekend there coincided with a massive fair, at the time the largest such event I'd ever experienced. The main event, on the Saturday evening, was an open-air concert in the square by, of all people, the so-called Italian Bee-Gees, a local tribute band complete with squeaky high voices. It was the last thing I expected and it left me wondering what Ramage, Lowe and Gissing did not expect to encounter here.

Ramage (1828), being of Scottish Protestant stock, was particularly intrigued that parts of the town's hinterland had been peopled by French Protestants as far back as the mid-16th century. He even met one, a woman, whose attire gave her away and whose antecedents had clearly survived the ferocious extermination process unleashed by the incumbent church.

Looking down on Páola from the old road across the mountains to Cosenza.

For Emily Lowe (1858) Páola was her last port of call in Calabria but it wasn't as easy to get away as she was expecting:

"Mamma began to think we had been long enough in the country, and had better float away by the next steamer; this was daily expected, should the weather be fine, as Paolo [sic] has no port, but a tolerably sheltered beach and several steamers stop for merchandise on their way to and from Naples."

Their steamer, or *Vapore*, did not materialise.

"The next day the weather was fine, and we had been assured the Vapore would arrive, yet the hours wore away without it appearing; at length our *entourage* confessed it never came on Sundays, the custom-house and public offices being closed everywhere. This incident painfully displayed their proneness to deviate in trivial matters from strict veracity."

Before he even left Naples, George Gissing (1897) had an image of Páola;

"It is now more than a twelvemonth since I began to think of Paola, and an image of the place has grown in my mind. I picture a little marina; a yellowish little town just above; and behind, rising grandly, the long range of mountains which guard the shore of Calabria. Paola has no special interest that I know of, but it is the nearest point on the coast to Cosenza, which has interest in abundance; by landing here I make a modestly adventurous beginning of my ramble in the South."

Having arrived by sea, he did not plan on staying long until, that is, he discovered that, contrary to what he'd been led to believe, the *corriere* to Cosenza had long gone; he finally negotiated alternative transport:

"For an hour I rambled about the town's one street, very picturesque and rich in colour, with rushing fountains where women drew fair water in jugs and jars of antique beauty. Whilst I was thus loitering in the sunshine, two well-dressed men approached me, and with somewhat excessive courtesy began conversation. They understood that I was about to drive to Cosenza. A delightful day, and a magnificent country! They too thought of journeying to Cosenza, and, in short, would I allow them to share my carriage? Now this was annoying; I much preferred to be alone with my thoughts; but it seemed ungracious to refuse. After a glance at their smiling faces, I answered that whatever room remained in the vehicle was at their service—on the natural understanding that they shared the expense; and to this, with the best grace in the world, they at once agreed. We took momentary leave of each other, with much bowing and flourishing of hats, and the amusing thing was that I never beheld those gentlemen again."

When *I* finally left Páola, I chose to take the old road and cross the mountains by the same route that Gissing took to Cosenza. Apart from a few itinerant goats, I was, or thought I was, the only living creature on this tortuous back-road. As I rounded yet another bend, I saw the sunlight bounce off the side of another vehicle half-concealed on the right-hand verge. It was only when I saw the red 'Stop' baton shoot out before me at the end of an extended and uniformed arm that I realised I'd woken up two *Carabiniere*, hitherto enjoying a siesta and clearly not expecting to see another vehicle on this deserted road.

I pulled over to have my documents checked and, the formalities completed, the ambience became more relaxed as my new best friends queried how I'd come to be on this road at all and not its newer, more direct, incarnation. My natural instinct was to ask them the same but I thought better of it and launched into a tongue-in-cheek version of the truth.

One day they will probably tell their grandchildren about the day they pulled over the grandson of the famous English writer, George Gissing.

Basilicata beckoned; I was back in Páola with a view to heading straight up the coast and into Basilicata. I had been told I must visit Diamante, it was, after all only twenty minutes away. I thought I had also been told it was a picturesque resort town with seafront houses, their walls painted in a range of bold colours. But I got that completely wrong, my understanding of

Diamante: picturesque coastal community, not least because of its surfeit of murals.

Italian at the time was half based on what I actually understood and half on whatever seemed to make sense to fill in the blanks.

En route I stopped off at Belvedere to have lunch and take a photo of its castle but came away with only the latter. Diamante was now my lunchtime destination, I was sure I'd find somewhere in among those wonderful, multi-coloured waterside houses. As I approached the town I stopped to check that it was actually Diamante for there appeared to be nothing special about the houses overlooking the small bay and harbour.

It being just on the cusp of the tourist season I got parked easily and started off in search of these colourful homes that had been tucked away in my mind's eye for almost three years. Overlooking the sea there was nothing that remotely fitted that snapshot in my mind so, stomach rumbling, I headed for the *centro storico*, in search of food.

Almost immediately I came across a house with a painting on its wall, a mural; I stood in front of it, admiring the artist's skill, took a photo and thought what an interesting idea. Round the corner there was another; and next to it, another. The more I found—and there were lots more—the more I tried to recall that three-year-old conversation that brought me here in the first place. Two words filtered through: 'walls' and 'colourful'; I had clearly missed the difference between *mura*, meaning 'wall', and *murale*, meaning 'mural'. Diamante is the town of murals.

And, for the record, it might be twenty Calabrian minutes from Páola, but in the real world it is over twice that.

I was the only traveller to visit Diamante; some passed through by train and even Ramage (1828), at sea between Scalea and Páola, made no mention of it though he did espy Belvedere and considered landing there. He was impressed with the respect shown to him by the ship's crew and was sure he knew why they looked after him so well:

"The civility of these people may be partly explained from the circumstance of a considerable traffic in raisins being at one time carried on with England, though it has ceased, chiefly, I believe, from the Ionian Islands having come into our possession, from which we derive a large proportion of that article. Wherever there is intercourse with England, you are sure to be treated with respect, though they may try to overcharge and plunder you."

Just before Scalea, the last major town in the north-west, there is the estuary of the river Lao, which rises in the Pollino mountains of Basilicata where it is known as the Mercure. It was from Scalea that Ramage opted to travel south by *feluca* rather than risk the overland trip. (At the time, being at the start of his journey, he still believed the stories he had been told about brigands lurking behind every tree. Later his actual experiences of Calabria led him to query this.)

Like most of the towns along this Tyrrhenian coastline, for a few months each year Scalea gets taken over by seasonal visitors seeking no more than sun, sand and seafood. The old town itself towers over this transitory seaside landscape like some aloof, disapproving parent.

The wind being capricious, Ramage was having difficulty in getting under way:

"I proceeded to the shore to see if they were making any preparations for our departure. The wind continued unfavourable, and they gave no hope of our starting before evening. In a short time the beach exhibited an animated scene, from the inhabitants crowding to make their bargains with the fishermen, who had returned with a considerable load of fish. They were several kinds, of which two were familiar enough to me, the palamji [a kind of mackerel] and the sarde [sardine]; of these I bought for twopence as much as I though would make a tolerable breakfast."

There follows reams and reams of diversionary tales before he finally got underway and he had to remind his readers of his location seven pages earlier:

"You have heard that I was detained at Scalea yesterday by the unfavourable state of the weather. Towards evening there seemed some prospects of a change, and it was agreed that I should be called by one of the boatmen, if they determined to start. I merely threw myself on top of the bed, ready to move at a moment's notice. Accordingly, a little after midnight I was roused, and proceeded at once to the house of the captain of the guard, under whose command, as the boat was carrying government despatches, it was placed. The house as in sad confusion. However, I was received with civility, and waited with patience till everything was got ready, It was evident that the wife of the captain and his family though his departure for a few days a sad event, and attended by great dangers. His wife was in tears, and clung to his neck in unfeigned grief. I was not sorry when the last sounds of her voice rung in my ear, bearing *buono viaggio*, repeated for the fiftieth time."

With Ramage heading south to being his amazing Calabrian adventure, I do what I usually do when in the Scalea area and head further north towards Práia a Mare and Tórtora Marina, the last (or first) coastal outposts on Calabria's western coast. Having satisfied myself that they are still there, I turn back towards Scalea and veer off into the hills towards the valley of the Lao and Papasidero and on to Mormanno to the Chiarelli family for dinner.

But apart from the *'ndrangheta* ...?

"The old man told me, that vipers and martens were remarkably fond of manna. He had himself frequently seen the little quadruped at the tree; but never the reptile, though many of his acquaintance had."
Henry Swinburne *Travels in the Two Sicilies*

Several travellers to Calabria mention 'manna' as being something particular to the region. But, apart from manna—and of course the *'ndrangheta*—there were and are several other Calabrian specialities that few outside Calabria are aware of. This chapter therefore aims to increase that awareness.

Henry Swinburne (1777) explained about manna which he first encountered in the north-east of Calabria between Roseto and Trebisacce:

"The lower parts of the mountains abound with the Ornus, or small-leaved flowering manna ash which grows spontaneously and without any culture, except that the woodmen cut down all the strong stems that grow above the thickness of a man's leg.'

Swinburne went on to explain how the manna, a whitish, glutinous liquid that soon hardened in the sun, was extracted from the tree by making horizontal incisions in the bark. The manna was said to have medicinal properties, particularly in relation to digestive problems, but it did not help those whose job it was to harvest it.

Swinburne also explained the monarchy's manna monopoly:

"All manna belongs to the King, who gives it in farm to a set of contractors. To gather it, a certain number of countrymen are furnished by the feudatory ... During the season, which continues about a month, these fellows are not allowed to absent themselves a single day, or undertake the least work of any other kind, however indispensable for the preservation of their own little private harvest. The peasants are punished with the utmost severity. if detected in burning, destroying, or damaging any of these trees, that cause to them so much vexation; and are sent to prison, if the smallest quantity of the juice is found in their house."

There was an upside in that they could eat as much as they wanted while harvesting but as they were paid for the amount harvested this was not necessarily a good idea.

Manna was pushed as a cure-all. In addition to the monarchy, its unproven powers and benefits were also hustled by the Church, the monarchy's age-old ally in maintaining the *status quo*. This caused the skeptical Craufurd Tait Ramage's hackles to rise:

"They contrive by some means, I dare say not remarkable for ingenuity, to cause a statue of our Saviour to perspire manna ... I have already, however, seen enough of these mummeries at Naples and its immediate vicinity. The manna is, of course, a cure for all sorts of diseases, and brings a considerable sum into the treasury of the monastery. If one happens to recover, after he has employed this manna, the monks take care that it should be announced in all parts of the country; and, in cases of failure, they have it always in their power to say that it arises from a doubt in the mind of the patient as to the efficacy of the remedy."

Proof, if proof were needed, that little changes.

The ornus, the small-leaved flowering manna ash and its harvest of white manna oozing from a cut in the bark.

CALABRIA

Though Douglas (1911) mentioned the 'stuff', he did not pursue the manna matter with his usual diligence, perhaps because it was clearly a product on the decline:

"The manna ash used to be cultivated in these parts. I cannot tell whether its purgative secretion is still in favour. The confusion between this stuff and the biblical manna gave rise to the legends about Calabria where "manna droppeth as dew from Heaven.""

Nevertheless, in 1966 Henry Morton still found evidence of manna harvesting in Calabria:

"... I came to an orchard in which a man was taking some substance from the trunks of trees. He told me he was gathering manna."

Like Douglas he explained away the biblical references and continued:

"In Italy manna does not fall from heaven ... It is a sugary resin – it tastes sweet – that oozes from the punctured trunks and stems of the ash tree (*fraximus ornus*), which is indigenous to the southern Mediterranean."

Morton climbed over a wall for a closer look at the manna gatherer:

"Cuts are made in the trees and after some hours, when the sap or juice which oozes out has dried, it is gathered. The farmer told me that though the ash tree is common in Calabria, as far as he knew it was cultivated commercially only in Sicily."

Morton also noted that the gathering of manna was a self-defeating exercise unless trees were replaced:

"In Calabria the trees gradually bleed to death. Beginning at the bottom of the trunk, the farmer cuts the tree all the way up, then starts on another side until eventually the tree is covered with gashes and had to be cut down."

Morton's manna-gathering friend was correct, these days it is commercially produced only in Sicily. And, not surprisingly, these days too it has joined the ranks of those cure-alls that rely on nothing more than tradition and unsubstantiated hearsay to 'legitimise' their efficacy rather than evidence. Were a pharmaceutical company to make similar claims without supporting research and evidence would it not be hounded out of existence by a hostile media?

I talked to the local pharmacist in Santa Severina about manna and he showed me a packet of small manna 'sticks' that people sometimes used as a 'natural' laxative. He also shared another use for manna that he was aware of in some of Italy's larger cities where heroin users would grate the manna sticks into a fine powder to combine with heroin to make the latter go further.

For some it clearly continues to be manna from heaven.

Swinburne, Douglas and Morton all stumbled across manna in roughly the same part of Calabria, close to the eastern (Ionian) seaboard of Cosenza province. Here too there was—and still is—another product that, though not exclusive to Calabria, has strong associations with the region. So much so that, at the time of writing, there is only one Liquorice Museum in the world—at Rossano in Calabria.

Richard Keppel-Craven (1818) was the first to notice the flowers:

"In the course of this day (June the 1st) I traversed alternately large tracts of liquorice in bloom, which seems a plant indigenous to the soil, and considerable portions of corn-land, the produce of which was falling under the reaper's sickle."

At the time he was between Cosenza and Acri but he came across it again on the eastern seaboard where its cultivation was more purposeful:

"But the principal branch of revenue [at Policoro] proceeds from the oil and liquorice; for the last article a large manufactory is established very near the house. The proximity of the sea, which allows of vessels being loaded with these objects within a mile of the seat of their growth, groves of no small assistance towards the gains derived from them."

Liquorice production, it seemed, was often suspended by local difficulties still blamed at the time on the *mal aria* associated with stagnant waters:

"I was assured here, though not for the first time, that all land which

Three faces of Amarelli: the works as they are today and (*inset right*) the original warehouse, the *concio*, now houses the company's famous *Museo della Liquiricia*; the more modern add-on to the left of which is the Amarelli shop where you can buy liquorice (*inset left*).

spontaneously produced the liquorice root in abundance was afflicted with this scourge."

At Corigliano Calabro, a few miles from Rossano, Ramage (1828) noted the town' importance as a centre for trade in three commodities:

"Corigliano is the principal depôt for the timber felled in the province, and also for the manna trade and liquorice factories."

By the time Gissing (1897) was travelling in Calabria the liquorice trade was using the port of Crotone to export its wares:

"The goods warehoused here are chiefly wine and oil, oranges and liquorice. (A great deal of liquorice grows around the southern gulf.) At certain moments, indicated by the markets at home or abroad, these stores are conveyed to the harbour, and shipped away."

Almost certainly the observations of both Ramage and Gissing were related to the productions of liquorice products by the Amarelli family from Rossano. Indeed, it is likely that the warehouses they were referring to would have been predominantly stocked by Amarelli.

As far back as the early 16th century, the Amarelli family of Rossano was harvesting and selling liquorice roots—initially believing that it would invigorate those such as soldiers on the march and labourers involved in heavy work—but it wasn't until the 18th century that they first extracted the juice from the root and preserved it as a commercial product.

In 1731, a great warehouse, known as the *concio*, was constructed specifically for this purpose and it is the renovated structure that is now the family's famous *Museo della Liquiricia*, a unique museum which tells the story of the Amarelli family itself as well as everything you'd want to know about liquorice from root to shop. And of course the Amarelli shop is next door, lest you leave without liquorice.

On the same site—albeit on the other side of the SS106 for the site is now dissected by this busy highway—are the works where the company still produces its extensive range of liquorice products, now as well known in America as they are in Calabria.

In 2014, an award was presented to a co-operative of young Calabrians in recognition of what they had achieved in re-establishing a traditional industry, once prolific throughout the region, the manufacture of silk.

Il Nido di Seta (literally the silk nest) is based at San Floro south-east of Catanzaro, the same small town which Arthur John Strutt (1841) and his friends visited with their host and saviour, Don Domenico Cefaly, following their unfortunate encounter with ne'er do wells near Caraffa. Coincidentally, Don Domenico was also involved in the silk industry.

The manufacture of silk was once a major activity throughout the Kingdom of the Two Sicilies and Calabria, and its mulberry trees—the leaves of which are the staple diet of the silkworm—played no small part in that.

Richard Keppel-Craven (1818) recorded its importance to the economy of Cosenza, though it seemed to be even more important further south:

"The fabrication, of silk, and the exports arising from the culture of oranges and lemons, form the principal commercial resources of Reggio."

Likewise Edward Lear (1847) was aware of the silk industry around Reggio though his abiding memory seems to have been of the smell as he talked of 'oderiferous factories'.

Craufurd Tait Ramage (1828) first encountered it at Nocera, just north of Lamezia:

"I left Nocera at an early hour this morning with my friendly host, and proceeded down the banks of the Savuto, passing groves of mulberries, which were growing in abundance. Nocera had at one time been the seat of a considerable manufacture of silk; like everything else in the kingdom it was dwindling to nothing."

On the other hand, he found the opposite was the case near Gerace, where, as we have seen, he also came up against some typical Calabrian superstition:

"We passed also a few mulberry-trees, which supply food for the silkworm, and I find that the manufacture of silk is pursued with considerable success.

Sorting silkworm cocoons at Cosenza.

I expressed a wish to see the cocoons (bacche di seta) but I observed from their answer that they were averse to the proposal and I afterwards found the cause of the refusal to be not particularly flattering to me. They are afraid to expose the silkworm to the gaze of a stranger lest an ill-omened look should destroy them."

After he left Cortale, Strutt (1841) headed south-west, passing through Curinga on his way to the coast; here he found the locals actively involved in what would seem to have been a cottage industry:

"The people of Conga [Curinga] were very busy winding the silk off their cocoons; the apparatus being generally situated under a trellis work of vine, in front of their houses. Silkworms are reared in considerable quantities both here and at Cortale. Don Domenico had two very large rooms of them."

In the province of Reggio Calabria, Emily Lowe (1858), the only female traveller and clearly interested in the manufacture of silk, explained how people's homes were taken over by the humble silkworm:

"The silkworms, in winter tied up in bags like small shot, have their season in the summer, and reside entirely with the peasants. Rows of canes are fastened across the rooms, about a foot from the ceiling; upon them are laid mats, and on these dwell the little spinners for their whole existence, from the mulberry-leaf to the cocoon age. In very small cottages there seemed hardly space to crawl into the beds beneath these awnings, while in others there was room to sling a tiny hammock from them for the baby. Skeins of glossy golden silk, like Helen's hair, were plaited and bound into large bundles, and placed in a deserted residence near the sea, ready for embarkation to countries possessing the appurtenances for weaving them into rustling flounces."

Later Lowe visited the Cosenza silk manufactory of the husband of her hostess whom she called 'Donna Bella'. With this name Lowe was bestowing a degree of anonymity on her hostess for, at the time, Donna Bella's husband was spending a few months behind bars for his revolutionary activities. His original sentence had been twenty-five years but silk-merchant-class strings had been obviously pulled and his release was imminent.

Here at Cosenza she experienced the next stage in the process, what happened to the 'plaited and bound large bundles' that were the product of the cottage industry she experienced further south:

"She fixed the next day for us to visit the silk manufactory. It contained about a hundred looms, constructed at Naples by English artisans, and worked by hydraulic pressure in the season, which was then over. For many years, their superintendent had been an Englishman, whom they spoke of as "Povero Tom Vilkins" [Poor Tom Wilkins]. He was drowned in the Mediterranean at the wreck of the Ercolano [1854]."

Of the six Calabria-based companies plying their silk products at London's Great Exhibition of 1862, one was from Villa San Giovanni, two from Reggio Calabria and three from Cosenza; one of the three from Cosenza was called Mirabelli. Given Emily Lowe's choice of name for her hostess and guide, it is not unreasonable to assume that it was the Mirabelli manufactory she visited.

And, given the year, nor is it unreasonable to assume that the revolutionary husband in question was one of those advocating Italian unification which, within two years of Lowe's Calabrian adventure, was to become a reality. Ironic, therefore, that it was following—some would say because of—unification that the silk industry in Calabria began its irreversible decline. In the end Donna Bella's man, whether Signor Mirabelli or not, was perhaps no more than akin to the proverbial turkey voting for Christmas.

Today, at nearby Mendicino, there is a museum dedicated to the history of Calabria's silk heritage, *Il Museo della Seta*. In the 19th century the small town was one of the most important centres for the production of raw silk; the surrounding countryside was literally covered with mulberry trees and every household bred silkworms.

In 1857, around the time when Emily Lowe was in nearby Cosenza, there

Catanzaro was not only the centre of Calabria's silk industry but at one time had such prestige internationally that silk weavers shared their expertise with the French.

were forty mills in which, for about four months of the year, thirty men and 320 women (of whom 120 were girls) worked twelve hours a day. It goes without saying that they were not paid very much even with the small additional handout on the town's saint day.

By 1878, following a worldwide downturn in the demand for silk, there were only two small factories left in Mendicino; both were automated and employed no more than a couple of dozen workers each for about two months every year.

Catanzaro was once the unofficial capital of Calabria's silk industry and had an reputation that went far beyond the city, the Kingdom of the Two Sicilies and even the Italian peninsula. In the fifteenth century it was silk weavers form Catanzaro who, under the auspices of the French king Louis XI, brought their skills to Tours in France to help establish that city's silk industry. Indeed it was a weaver from Catanzaro named Giovanni working in Tours who invented an innovative loom that could be worked by only one weaver and, as such, can be considered as a progenitor of later mechanised looms such as those that Emily Lowe saw in Cosenza.

In 1862, however, not a single representative of Catanzaro's silk industry turned up in London to promote their wares at the Great Exhibition. This was of course just two years after unification, just two years after many of the south's assets had coincidentally found a new home in the north.

Nevertheless, when George Gissing (1897) visited Catanzaro, silk production was still struggling on in the present tense: 'the town has certain industries, especially the manufacture of silk'. By the time Norman Douglas (1911) and Edward Hutton (1912) passed through it had seemingly drifted into the past tense for, unusually for both, neither mentioned it.

It is fitting therefore that it is close to Catanzaro, at San Floro, that *Il Nido di Seta* has rekindled interest in Calabria's silk industry by both manufacturing silk and welcoming visitors, especially schools, to share in the experience.

But the last word on Calabria and its silkworms has to go to Edward Lear (1847) and his description of an evening with a eccentric family in Staíti in the Aspromonte foothills. Lear was looking forward to visiting the 'hanging woods and crags' of nearby Pietrapennata the following day and had already become a trifle disenchanted with some of his hosts' rooms which he described as 'so full of silkworms as to be beyond measure disgusting'.

He was no less enamoured with Staíti itself:

"To the cultivation of this domestic creature all Staíti is devoted; yellow cocoons in immense heaps are piled up in every possible place, and the atmosphere may be conceived rather than described; for there is no more sickening odour than that of many thousand caterpillars confined in the closest chambers. Almost did we repent of ever having come into these Calabrian lands!"

And that was all *before* sitting down to dine with the Musitani family:

"Nor did the annoyances of a tribe of spoiled children and barking dogs add charms to the family dinner. But the "vermi di seta" were our chief horror; and so completely did silkworms seem the life and air, end and material, of all Staíti, that we felt more than half sure, on contemplating three or four suspicious-looking dishes, that those interesting lepidoptera farmed a great part of the groundwork of our banquet—silkworms plain boiled, stewed chrysalis, and moth tarts.

"Glad we were to rush out, to sit and draw among the rocks …"

I had known Attilio Pugliese for about five years; he was Santa Severinese who had spent most of his working life in the Lazio area south of Rome. Now, having just retired, he was spending more time in his home town.

We were having an *aperitivo* in one of the bars in the piazza when he put his hand into his pocket and took out a pipe; not to smoke, but to show me. The pipe was all his own handiwork for Attilio was carrying on a Calabrian tradition, the making of briar pipes.

Ramage (1818), heading towards Squillace from the northern slopes of La Serra, was the first to remark on Calabrian briar:

Erica in the wild and the finished pipe, hand-made by Attilio Pugliese.

"There were magnificent chestnuts and oaks, while the hedges were formed of the holly, the sweet-briar, and woodbine."

But it was Douglas who explained how an English diplomat exploited the humble briar:

"To the firs succeeded long stretches of odorous pines interspersed with Mediterranean heath (brayère), which here grows to a height of twelve feet; one thinks of the number of briar pipes that could be cut out of its knotty roots. A British Vice-Consul at Reggio, Mr. Kerrich, started this industry about the year 1899; he collected the roots, which were sawn into blocks and then sent to France and America to be made into pipes. This Calabrian briar was considered superior to the French kind, and Mr. Kerrich had large sales on both sides of the Atlantic; his chief difficulty was want of labour owing to emigration."

Two years earlier, before getting in on the act himself, Vice-Consul Kerrich had reported on the quality of the Calabrian briar:

"A fact worth knowing is the existence in this province of the finest briar-wood yet known. A French firm and an Italian have established factories for the trimming of the briar, and are doing an enormous business. The roughly-shaped pipes are principally exported to France and the United States of America."

What began as the exporting of briar soon became a cottage industry which has since flourished in Calabria and these days there are several renowned pipe-makers in the region and many well-known brands internationally now source their briar here in Calabria.

In 1966 Henry Morton was shown round a small factory on the coast near Reggio Calabria.

"I stepped, it seemed, into the nineteenth century when Mr Kerrich first sawed up his briar roots. The little factory with its flapping belts and its unprotected saws and wheels would give an English factory inspector a fit, yet everybody seemed to have the correct number of fingers and to be in the best of spirits. On the ground floor were sacks full of giant briar roots which had been collected by peasants in the Aspromonte. Eight men sawed them into neat blocks about five inches square, setting aside the best for export to England."

What Morton witnessed was a highly automated process:

"The actual manufacture of a pipe seemed to me a rapid and simple process. A block of briar was held in a machine for a few moments and withdrawn as a pipe bowl and stem. In a matter of minutes forty or fifty of these had accumulated on a wooden tray which was carried up a latter to an upper room where a number of young girls fitted the vulcanite mouthpieces, polished the bowls and dyed them."

Today, with all forms of smoking on the decline, the hand-made pipe is more sought after by *aficionados* and the Calabria pipe-industry (as opposed to the supply of briar) has reverted to a small number of individual craftsmen scattered throughout the region.

For my friend Attilio, however, it is no more than an occasional hobby; each pipe he makes is a labour of love and can take up to a month from being no more than a lump of briar root to be a shining, hand-crafted masterpiece.

Calabrian schoolchildren are taught that at five every afternoon, the English stop what they are doing to partake of a cup of tea. In our household we do indeed often stop for an afternoon cuppa, but usually around four to four-thirty. And sometimes that cup of tea is Earl Grey.

I mention this as, what has made Earl Grey tea, Earl Grey Tea, since the mid-19th century is the addition of one particular ingredient: bergamot. And bergamot comes, of course, from Calabria—exclusively from the province of Reggio Calabria—and is surely the region's most famous product and export.

For Henry Swinburne (1777) the bergamot was more than just another fruit that grew in the south:

"Oranges, and their kindred fruits, arrive at great perfection in these plains, which are said to be the first spot in Italy where their culture was

Everything used to be done by hand and for those whose job it was to literally have hands-on contact with the bergamot there was a downside as their skin would soon start to become a distinctive yellow-orange colour.

attempted, and from which it was extended over the country. The Rheggians carry on a lucrative traffic with the French and Genoese in essence of citron, orange, and bergamot. The spirit is extracted by paring off the rhind of the fruit with a broad knife, pressing the peel between wooden pincers against a spunge; and, as soon as the spunge is saturated, the volatile liquor is squeezed into a phial, and sold at fifteen carlines an ounce."

Seventy years later, when Edward Lear (1847) was in the south, he observed how the bergamot and other *agrumi* (citrus fruits) were in abundance:

"... their thick verdure stretched from hill to shore as far as the eye can reach on either side, and only divided by the broad white lines of occasional torrent courses."

He singled out the bergamot as having special importance:

"The bergamot orange, from the peel of which the well-know perfume is extracted, is cultivated to a great extent round Reggio, and the fruit forms a considerable article of commerce."

It was from around the 1820s that bergamot extract first came to be used in Britain as a tea flavouring but it was not for another decade that the name of Earl Grey came to be associated with it. However, there is no single, precise and irrefutable connection to Earl Grey, the British Prime Minister and architect of the Reform Bill of 1832, the only certainty is that it was the humble bergamot that made this tea distinctive.

The bergamot has been variously described as the being like an orange, like a lemon and a cross between an orange and a lime; I would describe it thus: it has the form of an orange, is the size of a lemon, with a colour nearer lime than lemon and a more uneven texture than any of the others.

Emily Lowe (1858) saw it as lemon-like and went on to describe its harvest:

"Peasants in the national dress of the province ... were throwing them into baskets, held by graceful girls in many colours, who bore them to the cottages, where a quantity at once were put into a round pressing machine, with brass divisions; this revolved forty times, then a bell rang, and the fruit were lifted out whole, but their spirit had passed into a vessel beneath; eight or ten thousand making twelve ponds of perfume of exquisite quality, exported for adulteration in England."

Not for the first time, Leslie Gardiner (1966) explained everything there was to know about something; firstly the climate where grows the bergamot:

"Of all the wonders of the south, the bergamot orange must be the most wonderful. It is Reggio's possession and pride: no other spot on earth can produce it. The fruit demands a clay-chalk alluvial soil, frequent irrigation, strong sunlight and so on. It will not survive outside a 39- to 114-degree Fahrenheit range [4°C – 45°C], or where temperatures fluctuate appreciably between day and night. Satisfy all those requirements and still the plant takes ill and dies —everywhere in the world but along one south-facing terrace between Reggio and Mélito on the very tip of Italy's toe."

Then what it is ... and isn't:

"The fruit is of mysterious origin and I suspect genealogy, a hybrid (something like an orange crossed with lime to the layman's eye) which came from nowhere and whose parentage can never be determined; a mongrel intruder which grew wild in this one charmed spot (where peasants at first treated it as a weed and threw it out) not earlier than the sixteen-sixties. (Citrons were known to the Romans, the lemon appeared in Italy in the seventh century, the bitter orange in the tenth and the sweet orange in the fourteenth.)"

Then its properties:

"The powerful odour of bergamot rind attracted perfumiers' notice. In the eighteenth century *aqua admirabilis* was all the rage—a toilet water which, marketed under the name eau-de-cologne from the city of its manufacture, vanquished all European competition. Its inventor had taken bergamot essence for his base, For the chemists of the Pompadour and du Barry era it had the magical property of combining smoothly with other essential oils, of—as a Parisian experimenter put it—'bringing out the best in them and imparting to them indefinable sweetness and exquisite freshness.'"

Finally its production:

"Farmers of Reggio, under the stimulus of international demand, began replacing some of their orange and lemon groves with orchards of bergamot, The industry has been expanding ever since, in the cautious fashion of all Mezzogiorno industries, but it remains small, quaint and untidy."

Things have changed and through the expertise of the *Stazione Sperimentale per l'Industria delle Essenze e dei Derivivate Agrumari* (which dates from 1929 and which Gardiner visited) the bergamot industry has performed well on the world stage. Small it remains, but no longer is it quaint and tidy.

Nowadays its cultivation and harvesting is big business and, as is the way of things these days, the Calabrian suppliers of bergamot have appended claims about its medicinal qualities—most notably in reducing those 'bad' cholesterol levels that plague many of us. Now the bergamot may well have medicinal benefits and uses but unfortunately the evidence for this remains limited and is therefore inconclusive ... though, as ever, the tabloid press does not make the same distinctions when it subtly gives the impression that something is beyond dispute.

Matters of life and death

"It is a proverb much in use in the neighbouring provinces, *Che una serva Calabrese piu ama far un figlio ehe un bucato* i.e. "A Calabrian maidservant prefers the labour of childbirth to that of a wash.""
Henry Swinburne *Travels in the Two Sicilies*

The above proverb is of course the product of rivalry between neighbouring provinces and no doubt Calabrians had something similar to say about people from Basilicata or Campania. But the truth that lies therein is that in the 18th century childbirth was a more routine affair for the ordinary Calabrian but, unlike today, an infant's chances of survival were not necessarily great. And while this was not confined to Calabria, or even Italy, it does appear that the things taken for granted in Europe regarding childbirth (and the expected survival of mother and child) generally touched the south of Italy later than other places.

Even within living memory there are stories of Calabrian women who went off into the woods or the countryside to do some chore and returned carrying a newborn baby.

Ramage (1828) had heard the same stories and put it down to the inherent nature of the Calabrian woman:

"The women are endowed by nature with sufficient fecundity, and bring forth their offspring almost without a groan. It is a common thing for a woman, far gone with child, to go up to the forest for fuel, and to be there surprised with the pains of childbirth, perhaps battened by her toil: She is nowise dismayed at the solitude all around her, or the distance from home, but delivers herself of the infant, which she folds up in her apron, and, after a little rest, carries to her cottage."

While at Catanzaro, George Gissing (1897) observed the next stage of bringing up baby:

"Each of the women had a baby hanging at her back, together with miscellaneous goods which she had purchased in the town: though so heavily burdened, they walked erect, and with the free step of mountaineers."

Of course these days there are different expectations for the modern Calabrian family. It too is touched by the glossy magazines and the internet and, through them, the modern crazes and pressures that are a constant bombardment to the senses and the pocket.

That said, as yet the Calabria woman does not seem to have fallen for it all hook, line and sinker. A greater degree of common sense seems to have prevailed, possibly because the experiences of parents and grandparents are fresher in the mind and the sense of family generally remains a strong force. Also, until recently, not everyone had the wherewithal to indulge in fashionable fads; and, perhaps, not having been able to afford the latest 'must-have' aid to parenthood bliss, has highlighted their lack of real value.

For whatever reasons, today's Calabrian way of birth and bringing up baby seems to me, a mere male, infinitely more civilised and practical than it seems to be elsewhere; and, above all, it appears to be less fraught.

Despite the fact that the hierarchy of the Catholic church teaches against

A class of twenty-two boys at Santa Severina in the late forties; today in the same class of boys *and* girls, there would be even fewer children. Over the same period the town's population has declined by 30%, the school population by more than 60%.

contraception, Italy's birthrate is falling fast; either people have forgotten how to do it or they are making a conscious decision to ignore the church.

In the past large families were the norm and a family of a dozen or more children was not infrequent, Also, it is only relatively recently that Calabrian families have had the luxury of expecting their pregnancy to result in a live birth or that the new-botn infant would survive into adulthood.

One elderly woman showed me a small square along a Santa Severina side-street which, when she was young in the sixties, was the playground, she reckoned, for around eighty children, including her and her three siblings. Today the space where these boisterous voices learnt to play lies silent; it is home instead for half a dozen parked cars and a handful of cats.

In 1858 Emily Lowe was in Páola when the weather took a turn for the worse:

"I am sorry to say snow had begun very improperly to fall, the town of Paolo [sic] requiring no addition to its shaken wretchedness; the flakes falling on a bier then passing, made the habit of bearing about the uncovered dead appear most uncomfortably ghastly. The line of tottering houses called a street, was filled by the funeral procession in pointed masks with holes in their eyes, and as they were following an infant corpse, were also robed in white trimmed with blue; over which, on account of the weather, they had grotesquely placed projecting wide-awake hats and "policemen" capes."

Like most notable events in Calabrian culture, death and its aftermath have always been essentially ritualistic. Swinburne's (1777) exposition would have been repeated in like fashion in most Calabrian communities:

"The virtues as well as vices of a deceased father of a family are recapitulated by the oldest person in company. The widow repeats his words, adds comments of her own, then roars out loudly, and plucks off handfuls of her hair, which she throws over the bier, Daughters tear their locks, and beat their breasts, but remain silent. More distant relations repeat the oration coolly, and commit no outrage upon their persons. When the kinsman of a baron or rich citizen dies, a number of old women are hired to perform all these ceremonies for the family."

Keppel-Craven (1818) was dining with a well-to-do family in Corigliano when a funeral procession passed by:

"I was called up from dinner with this interesting family to look from their windows at a funeral, which had halted under them. This was an observance their acquaintance with the deceased made it incumbent they should attend to. The corpse, uncovered as usual, was that of a stout, swarthy man, of about fifty, who having during life been much addicted to the sports of the field, was carried to the grave attired in the dress suited to those pursuits. The bier was set down under the window, as a mark of attention to my host, while the priests round it continued their dismal chants. A long train of neighbours and friends followed in silence; and after them, a group of females, mostly weeping, led the widow, whose face presented the paleness and immobility of a statue ; but at regular intervals, she plucked two or three hairs from the dishevelled black tresses, which reached from her forehead to her knees, an operation as regularly interrupted by her assistant supporters, who replaced her hands by her sides, where they remained inactive only until the next impulse. The blacksmiths, cobblers, carpenters, and fruitsellers, who were all exercising their different trades in the open street as usual, suspended their noisy occupations for a while, during which the beating of the linen at the neighbouring fountain was also hushed. All these were resumed with redoubled energy when the procession moved onwards, and left no impression upon my friends sufficiently strong to delay our immediate return to the dinner table."

News of a death travels fast. The first sign is the sonorous peel of bells, the *campana a lutto*, the meaning of which everyone recognises. Even while the bells are still ringing, people will gather in small groups until word gets round and soon the deceased's name, cause of death and location (home, hospital, care home, Santa Severina or Santa Severinese living elsewhere) is common knowledge; this usually takes less than five minutes.

Within hours the notices go up at all the information boards throughout the town; this will include the basic details about the deceased, age, time and place of death and the funeral time, usually the following afternoon.

Calabrians are normally buried within thirty-six hours of death. Funeral homes are only for cities and even these are a recent addition to the ritual. The body is laid out in its coffin in the home literally within a few hours of death. If it was the deceased's wish, those born in Santa Severina who die elsewhere, will be back in their hometown just in time for their own funeral.

Unfortunately I have been to too many funerals in Santa Severina but I never find them morbid affairs. People dress normally; black is not *de rigueur* and I was very much overdressed at the first one I attended. As it should be, being there is more important than how you look. There is also an element that is more akin to the actions of Keppel-Craven's host who went straight back to dinner afterwards; generally when it's over, it's over. Though of course for the family it is different.

In a modern setting, the rituals have evolved; they're still there, but the wailing mourners are a thing of the past. That said, I have noticed that when the (closed) bier passes through the narrow streets it is sometimes accompanied by a wailing from older women who watch its passing from inside their homes.

There is an element to the funeral service itself that I find slightly comical. As the service progresses inside the church, groups of men start to gather and hover outside waiting for the right moment (when the service is drawing to a conclusion) to make a beeline for the door. Having slipped in at the back, they sign the book of condolences before joining the rest of the congregation already queueing up to shake hands with the family of the deceased. This in itself has clearly become a ritual.

A death used to trigger a year of mourning which could be quite strict in what was allowed and what was not. Families now interpret this in different ways and, increasingly, in a less rigid way. Some families will not participate in any festive event for one year; for others life goes on as before. Some women will wear black for a year; others dress as seems appropriate.

Our friend Carlo was to marry in September 2009 when, six months earlier, his bride-to-be's brother-in-law died. For a while the wedding was in doubt until both families agreed that it could go ahead. Then, a few month's later, Carlo's mother died. The wedding only went ahead because his mother (who had been ill for a short time) had told the priest that, in the event of her death, the wedding should not be postponed.

Everything surrounding a death has deep religious significance and is centred on and organised around the church. Even those whom I know to be rabid nonbelievers seem to have accepted that, in death, they will no longer call the shots. The system will take over and, like it or not, they will play the lead in the church's ritualistic send-off even though it might have been something they will have regaled against most of their life. There really is no other choice ... though perhaps that will change. And perhaps I might play a small part in that change.

Before I came to Calabria I was looking at two scenarios regarding what might happen to my defunct body assuming I popped my clogs in the UK. I had decided to either leave my body to science, to a medical school, or have it cremated. The former was my preferred option as both my uncle Billy and my cousin Betty had done the same and I admired them for that; unfortunately their gestures were at a time (the 1950s and the 1960s respectively) when the idea of harvesting organs was not yet in vogue.

When I first came to Calabria to live, I had to revisit these options. I researched both many years ago and found that it was indeed possible to donate one's body to medical research but only in the north of Italy. Likewise cremation, not a problem north of Naples but a bit hit and miss further south. That said, over the years, the provision of crematoriums has been working its way slowly southwards.

By 2015, the only Italian region *without* a crematorium was—you've guessed it—Calabria. But that has now changed and, finally, there is a state-of-the-art crematorium between Lamezia and Cosenza. Not unusually, Calabria is the last corner of Italy to wriggle its way into the 21st century but, by leaving it so long, it has ended up with one of the most up-to-date facilities in Italy.

I know, I have been there and booked my oven.

A climate of change

"Passing through magnificent groves of fir, we descended rapidly into another climate, into realms of golden sunshine. Among these trees I espied what has become quite a rare bird in Italy—the common wood-pigeon. The few that remain have been driven into the most secluded recesses of the mountains; it was different in the days of Theocritus [3rd century BCE], who sang of this amiable fowl when the climate was colder and the woodlands reached as far as the now barren seashore."

Norman Douglas *Old Calabria*

Like almost everyone else in the known universe, today's Calabrians like to talk about the weather. Like everyone else too, more often than not they forget what it was like last week, last month or last year.

If it's very hot or cold or rainy or windy, they shake their collective heads and grumble, forgetting that last month they did the same, and for exactly the same reason. And last year too.

If, in December, someone were to mention that it felt like spring, most would agree in a way that suggests it's a unique weather phenomenon … until, that is, a spoilsport like me chips in to remind them that it was more or less the same last December, and the December before. To which of course they also agree. When, during a warm spell in April, someone says it's just like August, I make a mental note to drop into the August chit-chat that the hot weather is just like April; which, of course, it will not be.

And, it goes without saying, on no day of the year is the Calabrian weather ever perfect, let alone 'normal'. There is always something wrong with it; it's either too this or too that or, if it is actually an all-too-rare 'perfect' day, it's almost certain to be abnormal for the time of year.

I suspect the Calabrians are not unique in this.

Talking about the current weather is generally no more than just a means of making conversation, of communicating with friends and neighbours and a means of indulging in *vapid* or *non-confrontational* conversation. How many times have you heard people talk about the weather (as opposed to the climate) and *disagree*? If it's hot, it's hot; if it's windy, it's windy; what's not to agree about?

These days, in a region that is essentially rural in character, other than for the few caught up in the infrequent extreme events, the weather impacts less on everyday lives and, in general, people have very short-term weather memories, unless jogged by a scurrilous media.

Because I have had to adjust to an altogether different climate and weather cycle, I generally recall Calabrian weather events better than most of my fellow Calabrians. For example when someone talks of a bad storm in terms of it being the worst they can remember, I am able to remind them of 25 September 2009 and how the ramp to the road bridge over the river Neto was swept away. I remember the dates of such events by linking them to other events or occasions ... in this case it was easy as it happened the day before our friend Carlo's wedding, a day on which the terrible storms impacted greatly on the festivities. In fact the weather was so bad that it was impossible for Carlo and Anna-Maria to take the wedding photographs they had planned

An extreme Calabrian weather event memorable only because it was a friend's wedding day.

… so, after the honeymoon, they donned their wedding gear once again and had the photos taken on a bright mid-October day.

When people talk of the summer of 2015's exceptionally high temperatures, I can remind them about June 2007 when, though I was not in Calabria at the time, a friend emailed me to congratulate me on having departed at just the right moment … he claimed the temperature was then in the high forties. Very high it certainly was but Roberto was hyping it up a bit … officially the highest temperature at the time at the Crotone weather station was on 25 June when it reached 42°C. Of course it may have been higher (or lower) at other locations in the area.

The highest temperature in 2015 was a full 5°C lower when, on 20 and 21 July, it was a paltry 37°C. Eight years on and people had already forgotten 2007, instead they were coping with—and talking about—the heat of the moment. It just seemed hotter because it lasted over a longer period.

For Calabrian families in the past whose livelihood used to be based more on what they could eke out of the land, their reading of the weather was more than important, it was crucial. That said, people accepted the weather for what they believed it to be—God-sent. They did not linger on its vicissitudes for two reasons: they had to get on with life and work through it or starve; nor were they being continually bombarded with media accounts of their misfortune in finding themselves right in the path of the deluge, the drought or the drama.

Norman Douglas (1911) gave voice to their simple logic:

"On occasions of drought or flood there is not a word of complaint. I have known these field-faring men and women for thirty years, and have yet to hear a single one of them grumble at the weather. It is not indifference; it is true philosophy—acquiescence in the inevitable.

"They have the same forgiveness for the shortcomings of nature as for a wayward child. And no wonder they are distrustful. Ages of oppression and misrule have passed over their heads; sun and rain, with all their caprice, have been kinder friends to them than their earthly masters."

Also, memories of serious or prolonged weather events paled into insignificance when compared to the havoc wreaked by earthquakes, seaquakes and tsunamis. Such events in Calabria (most notably those of 1638, 1783 and 1908) resulted in dramatic, almost instantaneous, changes in the landscape—particularly in mountainous areas—and, to some extent, the local weather conditions. Earthquakes radically transformed huge tracts of the mountains and changed the course and impact of rivers and thus the route that rainfall and melted snows took to reach the sea.

Richard Keppel-Craven (1818) witnessed the aftermath of one of the 1783 quakes at Terranova:

'The luxuriance of vegetation peculiar to all the rents and chasms produced by this extraordinary convulsion, is not the least remarkable circumstance attending it; and the changes which were perceptible in the course of the neighbouring streams, their total failure in some places, and their unexpected appearance in others, may perhaps rank amongst its more immediate causes.

Not having been primed or influenced by a capricious and torpid media, it is enlightening to view things through the eyes of earlier travellers who had no climate agenda, save just noting their observations and conversations. Such diarists knew about changing climate but hadn't heard of climate change; they just listened to and recorded what people thought was important at the time. They may not have heard of climate change but most had a deep understanding of history and historical perspectives which told them that the climate was always in a state of flux.

Elsewhere in this book I have quoted travellers' experiences in Calabria only but, because the vagaries of the climate have no respect for man-made borders, I have included some of their observations from their travels in nearby regions, notably Apulia and Sicily.

Brian Hill (1791) experienced, second-hand, the last throes of the Little Ice Age while across the Straits of Messina in south-east Sicily:

"The last of these gentlemen, who, in other respects, seemed to be a man of sense and veracity, informed us, that the ice had been strong enough this winter to *bear an ox*, and was *a foot in thickness*. But such severity of weather is, without doubt, unknown in thirty-seven degrees of north latitude; certain I am, that in latitude thirty-eight, and that at Palermo [in Sicily], the ice in the severest part of winter was never thicker than half a crown, and even that was reckoned very extraordinary, ice in Palermo being as wonderful as an horse in Venice."

Ten days later in Calabria, on 14 March, at Monteleone (today's Vibo Valéntia) Hill was still preoccupied with the unseasonably cold weather:

"A sharp frost and ice last night."

He went on to record first-hand how, the further south he travelled from Britain, the *colder* it became which, of course, was not what he and his group were expecting:

"Uncommonly mild as all accounts from England state the winter to have been, so severe a season through all parts of the continent, where we have been, was scarcely ever felt. While we were in Germany, particularly when travelling through the Tyrol, the cold was intense, all the way from Venice to Rome, we found the weather very little warmer. And all the time we were in Sicily and Calabria, we had several raw bleak days with snow and frost occasionally; so that my brother ... heartily wished himself by a good Shropshire coal-fire, being fully persuaded, that there was no country whatever where all winter comforts were to be found more than at home."

As Hill's brother had been advised by his British physician to spend the winter in a warm climate, the winter of 1790-91 in southern Europe was not going according to plan.

Richard Keppel-Craven (1818) considered the weather before and after the 1783 series of terrible earthquakes in February and March:

"The summer of the preceding year had been remarkably hot, and followed by violent and continued rains till the month of January. The winter was rather more severe than usual, as may be inferred from the frost on the night of the 5th and 6th of February. It has been observed that this month and the following have in these regions been marked by the recurrence of four several earthquakes of more than ordinary violence.

"A thick fog succeeded the spring, and seemed suspended over all Calabria for some months, obscuring its shores from navigators, and only indicating their proximity by its existence, so unusual in these latitudes. It is difficult to imagine a more extraordinary picture than the appearance of this portion of Italy, during the first few months which followed this awful visitation, by which an extent of territory, exceeding 140 miles, was more or less laid waste, and which can only be assimilated to the dissolution of the human energies and frame under the activity of operation of a violent poison. Here the finest works of nature, and the improvements they had received from the industry of man, were swept away by the same terrible agency which hurled mountains from their bases, and checked rivers in their speed. The convulsion extended from sea to sea, and the wreck throughout was universal."

Travelling in the south, Craufurd Tait Ramage (1828) also pondered on the changes in climate since Roman times and considered another possible factor—volcanic activity—though he doesn't seem entirely convinced:

"However picturesque all this coast may be, and interesting from its connexion with world-known recollections, there is a feeling of loneliness and desolation from a want of human beings. It must have been in later Roman times a healthy climate, as the aristocracy had their summer residences along the coast; and yet, at the present moment, to live here during the hot season is considered fatal. Why it should be so if is difficult to say, unless the numerous eruptions have changed the character of the climate."

Ramage's fatalistic reference is of course about the prevalence of malaria in low-lying coastal areas, at a time when the connection between malaria and the mosquito had not been made. Like others before and since, Ramage saw no reason not to go along with the observations of Vitruvius on the subject. The 1st century CE Roman writer accounted for the unhealthy climate that brought much suffering to so many people as *mal aria*, bad air, caught in the morning breezes which, mingled with the mist of the marshes, caused 'the poisonous breath of creatures of the marshes' to be 'wafted into the bodies of the inhabitants'.

On his long, arduous trek across the summit of Montalto, the highest peak in the Aspromonte mountains, Norman Douglas (1911) reflected upon the paucity of wood-pigeons compared with Roman times. His conclusion (quoted at the beginning of this chapter) was based on what he, and his contemporaries, knew about the climate 2300 years earlier when it was known to have been cooler than it was in the early 20th century; indeed cold enough for Rome's river Tiber to freeze. He also knew that, between the two, the European climate was to get warmer before the onset of another cooler period during the Dark Ages, then rise again during the Medieval Warming Period and fall again as the Little Ice Age heralded another cool period.

What Douglas was inadvertently demonstrating to his readers (now as then) was an example of the real climatic peaks and troughs—an understanding of which was second nature to him and his classically-educated contemporaries—that somehow were omitted from the smooth-shafted hockey-stick graph that influenced so many towards the end of the 20th century.

When Douglas talked of how 'woodlands reached as far as the now barren seashore', he was merely illustrating how nature adapted—and will always adapt—to a changing climate: when the climate subsequently warmed up, the woodlands receded as part of a natural cycle. In concert with the trees, other wildlife—not solely the wood-pigeon—will have come and gone, found new habitats, adapted, migrated, evolved; this is what has always happened and will continue to happen; the humble wood-pigeons worked it out to their advantage and did so by themselves without any input from the panicking tendencies of mankind.

Just as the wood-pigeon adapted when its habitat and food sources changed, any Calabrian communities relying on the wood-pigeon for the evening meal would also have adapted and even migrated towards the shore and into areas previously uninhabitable because of malaria.

The fact that some areas were at times malarial and at times not is no more than the cycle of a changing climate which in turn sometimes went hand in hand with how—and if—the land was cultivated.

When Douglas (1911) was in Calabria the relationship between mosquito and malaria had been established but the disease was still endemic in many areas and sometimes its spread could be aggravated by artificial irrigation. Referring to this practice, Douglas related the then need to water the land at all to changes in the climate:

"It is doubtful whether the custom goes back into remote antiquity, for the climate used to be moister and could dispense with these practices. Certain products, once grown in Calabria, no longer thrive there, on account of the increased dryness and lack of rainfall."

Travelling in southern Italy around the same time as Douglas, Edward Hutton (1912) mulled over how things had changed in nearby Apulia:

"Whether of old it was covered in its high places with forests now destroyed or whether the climate has changed from other causes, Apulia to-day is no longer the fruitful land of which we read of old: it suffers everywhere from an aridity and a lack of rain that often threaten to make it utterly desolate."

Travellers such as Hill, Keppel-Craven, Ramage, Douglas and Hutton did not need computer models to tell them that the climate was changing for they knew it had always been so. They were brought up on a diet of classical history and literature and knew all there was to know about the ancient and medieval worlds and, with it, the vagaries and consequences of the prevailing climate. What's more, their experience of their own contemporary time told them that nothing had changed, the same old cycles were still being played out; the natural world, man included, had and always would *respond* to the prevailing climatic changes and played no discernible part in their *cause*.

Not surprisingly, it was Norman Douglas (1911) who succinctly put everything in its historical perspective; and to him the last word. Well, almost:

"These Calabrian conditions are only part of a general change of climate which seems to have taken place all over Italy; a change to which Columella [Roman writer on agriculture, 4–c70CE] refers when, quoting Saserna [Hostilius Saserna, agricultural writer, 1st century BCE], he says that formerly the vine and olive could not prosper "by reason of the severe winter" in certain places where they have since become abundant, "thanks to a milder temperature." We never hear of the frozen Tiber nowadays, and many remarks of the ancients as to the moist and cold climate seem strange to us. Pliny praises the chestnuts [presumably horse chestnuts] of Tarentum; I question whether the tree could survive the hot climate of to-day. Nobody could induce "splendid beeches" to grow in the lowlands of Latium, yet Theophrastus, a botanist, says that they were drawn from this region for shipbuilding purposes. This gradual desiccation has probably gone on for long ages; so Signor Cavara [Italian botanist Fridiano Cavara, 1857–1929] has discovered old trunks of white fir in districts of the Apennines where such a plant could not possibly grow to-day."

As I have observed more than once, from birth these travellers were immersed in everything that was written about the Italian peninsula. The literature of the Mediterranean—from philosophical treatises to grand tomes about great wars and charismatic leaders—is full of clues to the prevailing climate and how it has changed since man put pen to paper; and before.

As we have already seen with regard to, for example, the stories of Alaric, Ucciali, Joachim Murat and *il Fondaco del Fico*, travellers' observations and experiences are also an important contemporary source that ought not to be ignored. Their understanding of what, climate-wise, had happened, and what was happening, is a resource that surely must call into question some of the hysteria currently prevalent around a changing climate; hysteria that gives the impression it is all something new, something mankind has created as opposed to something that has always occurred and has been documented many times over.

If a handful of British travellers in a small part of southern Italy can illustrate that climate change has been, and is, an on-going process, then it is probable that the diaries of other travellers in Europe and elsewhere will confirm the same message. The historical record that they clarify says that highs and lows, hot and cold, peaks and troughs, have always been the way of things, long-term and short-term; it says that flora and fauna, including man, have of necessity learnt to adapt; it says it will happen again … and again.

It says that no Calabrian, no Briton, no American, can do anything to avoid or circumvent this. It says that climate changes are as uncompromising as they are inevitable and will not succumb to ineffectual tinkering.

It reminds us that, in Britain, King Canute was the last to try

Calabrian women

"The inhabitants of Tiriolo are a race of sturdy mountaineers, and its women were particularly striking for their Amazonian figures. Their dress adds to their masculine appearance, and I confess that I felt no inclination to do anything to excite their indignation. I met several who were carrying water on their head, and I could not but admire the magnificence of their form."
Craufurd Tait Ramage *The Nooks and by-ways of Italy: Wanderings in search of its ancient remains and modern superstitions*

Until recently, most travellers called a spade a spade. Generally they were neither restrained or embarrassed by what we would now call political correctness. And of course they saw things in terms of their own experiences back home and frequently assumed that how they did things there was the prescribed way for all mankind.

In this respect, attitudes to, and the role of, women can be quite enlightening so here, without comment, are some of my fellow-travellers' observations of, and encounters with, Calabrian women; most first-hand, a few second. My own contribution will, I hope, bring things up to date

Henry Swinburne (1777); at Gerace:
"In the evening I joined a crowd that was dragging a woman to church, in order to have the devil driven out of her by exorcisms. She was a middle-aged person, and seemed to be in very strong convulsions, which every body present firmly believed to proceed from a demoniacal possession. The priest refusing to come, some of the assistants grew impatient, and pulled the woman so very roughly, that Belzebub thought better to decamp. The patient rose up, and though confused and panting for breath, very soon recovered her

senses, and ran away full speed to her own house. From these circumstances I inferred, there was more roguery in her case than real disorder.

"All convulsions of the kind are attributed to assaults of malignant spirit. Near fifteen hundred women, pretending to be tormented by these imps, go up annually to Soriano [Calabro], to be cured of the possession by looking at a portrait of St. Dominick, sent down as a present from the celestial gallery. By these pretexts, they obtain from their tyrannical spouses leave to make this pleasant pilgrimage, and a pair of holiday shoes, without which it would be highly disrespectful to present themselves before the holy picture. A priest of that convent told me a story of a demoniac, who, after going through the usual course of cure, was sent to confess her sins to him. As he was perfectly well acquainted with all the tricks, he ordered her to give him the true reason of her acting that farce, and threatened her, in case of obstinacy, with a visit from a real devil, who would torment her in good earnest. The poor woman, terrified to death at the menace, frankly acknowledged, that having been married by her parents against her inclinations to a goatherd, who stank intolerably of his goats and cheeses, she abhorred his approach, and feigned, possession to avoid cohabiting with him. Having this wormed the secret out of her, the priest, in hopes of alleviating her misfortune, sent for her husband, and as he knew it would be in vain to attempt to argue him out of a belief of the devil's being in his wife, he planned a different mode of attack, and informed the simple

Only the façade of San Domenico at Soriano Calabro survived the 1783 earthquake; here, said Swinburne, some 1500 women annually were 'cured' of there demoniacal possession.

fellow, that he had discovered what particular kind of spirit it was; that this demon was remarkable for an outrageous antipathy to goatherds, and that no exorcisms could prevent him from plaguing them. The poor man, whose first profession had been gardening, and whose success in the other line of business had not been very great, readily consented to return to his old way of labour, if that would keep Satan out of his house. The friar procured a garden for him, and a chapman for his flock, and soon had the happiness of seeing the married couple well settled, and perfectly satisfied with each other."

Henry Swinburne (1780); on his way to Nicastro:
"At this passage of the Amato we met a company of Greeks [Arbëreshë] of both sexes belonging to a neighbouring village: their dress was remarkably tawdry, with a great deal of red and yellow; the women were much handsomer than the generality of Calabrian females."

Brian Hill (1791); on road construction following the 1783 earthquake:
"We saw not less than two hundred people at work with barrows, spades, picks, baskets, &c. the latter of which were chiefly carried by women and children, which are so numerous throughout Calabria, that it is no uncommon sight to see from fifteen to twenty in one house, or about the door. And indeed when we consider that the women marry at twelve or thirteen years of age, and continue to breed as long as those in more northern climate, we cannot wonder at the great population we see in every part of this country nor that it should so soon recover from the desolations made by earthquakes."

Richard Keppel-Craven (1818); his first impressions of Calabria:
"The women were mostly of large stature, attired in a body and petticoat of coarse scarlet cloth: the latter appendage was composed of plaits so innumerable as to stick out at a considerable distance from the hips, and being mostly thread-bare and faded, formed no ornamental addition to forms as uncouth as they were unfeminine, and countenances impressed with a ferocious scowl, which I fain would have interpreted as the stare of curiosity."

Craufurd Tait Ramage (1828) at Cirò:
"The oaken gates of Ciro were now open, and a few of its inhabitants were idling with some girls washing linen at the fountain outside the walls. I have in general been disappointed with the appearance of the women, as they lose at an early age whatever personal beauty they may have possessed by the laborious and toilsome life to which they are exposed. I have been particularly struck by the number of women I have observed in field labour; and on calling

the attention of one of the natives to the circumstance, he acknowledged that the women were more industrious, and performed more labour, than their husbands. The education of women of the lower ranks is entirely neglected, and I believe that, even in the higher classes, it is not uncommon to find that they are unable to write. Their manners, however, are pleasing from their simplicity, and I was often astonished to observe with what perfect nonchalance they talked on subjects which are not normally introduced by us in presence of ladies, and I felt at times rather out of countenance, while they evidently were not aware that they were doing anything of which they need feel ashamed. You will understand how matters are in respect to marriage, when I tell you the law enjoins no marriage to take place before the bridegroom is fourteen and the bride twelve years of age, The ceremony must be contracted in the sight of the Church, if it is to have civil validity either for the parties themselves or for the children. There is, however, a civil act (atto civile), for the execution of which civil officers are appointed, but its limits its provisions concerning marriage to the civil and political effects, leaving all the duties that religion imposes untouched and unchanged. Separation may be obtained, but there can be no complete divorce. The husband may prefer a complaint for adultery, and the guilty wife is confined for three months to two years in a

Calabrian *brigantessa* Maria Oliviero was born near Cosenza. She was Pietro Monaco's wife and a member of his brigand gang opposed to unification and supportive of the Bourbon monarchy. Monaco was killed in 1863 and Maria subsequently imprisoned.

The power of the camera *(right)*: a more romantized brigand image of the impeccably turned-out *brigantessa* Michelina di Cesare from Caserta near Naples, who also fought against unification. The 1868 photo of her stripped body in brutal death is less romantic. The stories told to Strutt and Lowe are altogether different tales. Given the dates—long after French rule and pre-unification—these bands were probably no more than common bandits.

house of correction. The adulterer is fined from fifty to five hundred ducats."

Arthur John Strutt (1841); at Caraffa:
"The last of the trio [three women from Caraffa] was Petronilla Jaccia, notorious as having been the wife of a brigand, whose expeditions she had frequently accompanied, and whose infamous exploits she had vigorously seconded and shared. Petronilla is exactly what romantic young ladies would imagine a bandit's bride to be; tall, dark, with regular features, black eyes, and no inconsiderable portion of sullen beauty; it is, indeed, shrewdly reported, at Caraffa, that she has been eminently indebted to her personal attractions for delivery from more than one well deserved judicial chastisement. Once, in particular, when under actual sentence of death, it would have gone hard with her, had not a private interview with the judge softened his obdurate sense of duty ; and induced him to exert himself in procuring her a reprieve. Now, however, the bold husband, who led her into such dangers, is no more ; he was murdered by some of his men, a few years ago; and Petronilla, collecting the spoil his valour and her own had won, retired to her native village, where she at present resides, one of the richest and most consequential of its inhabitants. This little knowledge of her history, communicated to us, *sans façon* [informally] in her presence, despite of her dark looks, made us pay particular attention to the heroine, whose erect position, and dignified indifference, challenged our pencils. Over her cap, a long black veil, hanging down her back, showed that she was in mourning for her deceased lord; the large sleeves of her *camiscia* [blouse] embroidered like the others, hung so low as entirely to conceal her hands; the rich scarlet and yellow body of her dress was partially hidden by a singular ornament, having the appearance of a breastplate and back-piece, covered with sparkling silver and gilt work ; the rest of her attire resembled that of the other two."

Edward Lear (1847) at Condufóri in the foothills of the Aspromonte.
"Condufóri, a little village, wedged in a nook between two hills, the torrent at its feet, and the mountain mass of high Apennine threateningly above it, was at length reached, and the house of Don Giuseppe Tropæano discovered. Alas! the master was away at the Marina, or Scala, and our appearance threw his old sister into such a state of alarm, that we speedily perceived all hope of lodging and dining was at an end. We stood humbly on the steps of the old lady's house, and entreated her only to read the letter we had brought—but not she! she would say nothing to us. "Sono femmina," "Sono femmina," she constantly declared—a fact we had never ventured to doubt, in spite of her immoderate size and ugliness—"Sono femmina, e non so niente." [I am

a woman and don't know anything.] No persuasions could soften her, so we were actually forced to turn away in hunger and disgust."

Emily Lowe (1858); at Páola shortly before returning by sea to Naples.
"After dinner he gave us, as dessert, brigand stories: the most remarkable was of the woman-captain of the band then encamping above the town.

"She was the wife of a peasant, and during his absence received frequent visits from a neighbour.

"Her little girl of ten years old was unwittingly present at one of these interviews, and said, 'I shall tell papa, when he comes back, how kind that forester is to you, dear mamma.'

"The pair exchanged glances.

"'Go my darling,' she said, 'and hat the large stove to bake some bread ready for papa.'

"'I have.'

"'Go again, and make it hotter, that papa's bread may be brown,'

"'Oh! mamma, it's red-hot now.'

"'Come down, then, and help me to bake.'

"She seized her daughter by the heels, and threw her in!

"After some hours, the peasant-husband returned.

"'I smell something burning,' said he.

"''Tis but the meat preparing for your supper,'

An early 20th-century view of Crotone's *Albergo Concordia*, the building on the right with the street-level canopy. Both George Gissing and Norman Douglas stayed here; for a modern view of the Hotel Concordia, see page 434.

"'Meat, flesh—it appears to me like human flesh—WHERE IS NINA?'
"A shot through his head was her reply.
"His wife had seized the gun and fired; then donning his clothes, she joined the brigand band with the forester. This occurred last July"'

George Gissing (1897); holed up ill at the *Albergo Concordia* in Crotone:
"He [Doctor Sculco] arrived about half-past nine, and was agreeably surprised to find me no worse. But the way in which his directions had been carried out did not altogether please him. He called the landlady, and soundly rated her. This scene was interesting, it had a fine flavour of the Middle Ages. The Doctor addressed mine hostess of the *Concordia* as "thou," and with magnificent disdain refused to hear her excuses; she, the stout, noisy woman, who ruled her own underlings with contemptuous rigour, was all subservience before this social superior, and whined to him for pardon. "What water is this?" asked Dr. Sculco, sternly, taking up the corked jar that stood on the floor. The hostess replied that it was drinking water, purchased with good money. Thereupon he poured out a little, held it up to the light, and remarked in a matter-of-fact tone, "I don't believe you."

"I had some fear that my hostess might visit upon me her resentment of the Doctor's reproaches; but nothing of the kind. When we were alone, she sat down by me, and asked what I should really like to eat. If I did not care for a beefsteak of veal, could I eat a beefsteak of mutton? It was not the first time that such a choice had been offered me, for, in the South, *bistecca* commonly means a slice of meat done on the grill or in the oven. Never have I sat down to a *bistecca* which was fit for man's consumption, and, of course, at the *Concordia* it would be rather worse than anywhere else. I persuaded the good woman to supply me with a little broth.

"Another time my hostess fell foul of the waiter, because he had brought me goat's milk which was very sour. There ensued the most comical scene. In an access of fury the stout woman raged and stormed; the waiter, a lank young fellow, with a simple, good-natured face, after trying to explain that he had committed the fault by inadvertence, suddenly raised his hand, like one about to exhort a congregation, and exclaimed in a tone of injured remonstrance, "un po' di calma! Un po' di calma!" [A little calm!] My explosion of laughter at this inimitable utterance put an end to the strife. The youth laughed with me; his mistress bustled him out of the room, and then began to inform me that he was weak in his head. Ah! she exclaimed, her life with these people! what it cost her to keep them in anything like order! When she retired, I heard her expectorating violently in the corridor; a habit with every inmate of this genial hostelry."

Norman Douglas (1911); seeking somewhere to rest in Spezzano Albanese:
"Despairing, I entered a small shop wherein I had observed the only signs of life so far—an Albanian woman spinning in patriarchal fashion. It was a low-ceilinged room, stocked with candles, seeds, and other commodities which a humble householder might desire to purchase, including certain of those water-gugglets of Corigliano ware in whose shapely contours something of the artistic dreamings of old Sybaris still seems to linger. The proprietress, clothed in gaudily picturesque costume, greeted me with a smile and the easy familiarity which I have since discovered to be natural to all these women. She had a room, she said, where I could rest; there was also food, such as it was, cheese, and wine, and—

"Fruit?" I queried.

"Ah, you like fruit? Well, we may not so much as speak about it just now—the cholera, the doctors, the policeman, the prison! I was going to say *salami*"

"Salami? I thanked her. I know Calabrian pigs and what they feed on, though it would be hard to describe in the language of polite society.

"Despite the heat and the swarms of flies in that chamber, I felt little desire for repose after her simple repast; the dame was so affable and entertaining that we soon became great friends. I caused her some amusement by my efforts to understand and pronounce her language—these folk speak Albanian and Italian with equal facility—which seemed to my unpractised ears as hopeless as Finnish. Very patiently, she gave me a long lesson during which I thought to pick up a few words and phrases, but the upshot of it all was:

""You'll never learn it. You have begun a hundred years too late."

"I tried her with modern Greek, but among such fragments as remained on my tongue after a lapse of over twenty years, only hit upon one word that she could understand.

""Quite right!" she said encouragingly. "Why don't you always speak properly? And now, let me hear a little of your own language."

"I gave utterance to a few verses of Shakespeare, which caused considerable merriment.

""Do you mean to tell me," she asked, "that people really talk like that?"
""Of course they do."
""And pretend to understand what it means?"
""Why, naturally"
""Maybe they do," she agreed. "But only when they want to be thought funny by their friends.""

Edward Hutton (1912); at Tiriolo:
"For the traveller the delight of Tiriolo is the costumes of the women, which

are most beautiful and picturesque. With the coming of the automobile it is to be feared these will disappear, but they have not gone yet. Almost every girl in the place wears the old-fashioned dress of the commune and is, and not only on this account, a delight to the eyes."

Eric Whelpton (1957); on the train heading north from Reggio Calabria:
"As we flashed through Bagnara, the land of stay-at-home husbands, we caught a glimpse of happy card-players sitting outside their one-storeyed houses deeply engrossed in their games.

"Since everyone appears to be satisfied, I do not know why anyone should criticize their way of arranging matrimonial affairs.

"In countries which are developed commercially and financially, doctors are preoccupied by suburban neurosis, the disease which besets many women who are forced to stay alone all day whilst their husbands go out to work. Now that there are so many labour-saving devices some of these wives have not enough to do.

"Clearly the ladies of Bagnara must lead such full lives that they do not suffer from suburban neurosis, if indeed they have a moment to reflect and indulge in any form of hysteria."

Leslie Gardiner (1966); at an unnamed Arbëreshë town south of Lungro:
"Mrs Varibob had been a beauty in her day, one of the sultry, mysterious, violet-eyed girls who bloom in the harsh soil of the primitive south. She told us, after some coaxing, how she danced before Mussolini and Hitler in the thirties, at the grand folk festival to which two champions from every Italian district were summoned. She had forgotten her partner's name, forgotten how she travelled, forgotten what sights she saw or how long she stayed, forgotten even where the spectacle took place until we mentioned Villa Borghese. But she remembered every detail of her costume.

"She must in those days have looked very much like her daughter, who sat listening and refilling our cups, resolute but shy, smoothing her hips and pulling at the hem of her red cardigan whenever her hands were unoccupied. How can two intelligent and attractive women spend their days in an unlit room with drawn curtains, crouched over a niggardly fire, listening to a cheap alarm clock ticking the years away, as these two apparently did? As women of the rural south are supposed to do from an early youth until a late age, from all I have seen. For how many millions in Spain, Italy, the Balkans and the East, is life half dull manual labour and the other half long hours in a darkened room?"

Henry Morton (1967); driving from Cosenza to Nicastro:
"There are few places left in the world where the appearance of a motor-car stampedes mules and goats, but this is one of them. The mules are ridden by old women in black who wear scarves almost like yashmaks. They sit sideways and have little control if the mule suddenly decides to mount a bank.

"Here I saw for the first time women in regional costume riding mules or donkeys or striding along the road balancing jars or boxes upon their heads. They wore black bodices and black skirts looped back into a kind of bustle, revealing scarlet petticoats. They walked like queens. Those who carried burdens did so upon turban-like head-pads."

It has been argued that a society and its culture can be judged by examining the role played by its women both in terms of what is expected of them and their own expectations.

Although there have always been individual Calabrian women who have broken the mould—by being brigands, for example—Calabrian women generally have clung on to the expectations of the society in which they lived. And, generally, the changing role of women in society has been at a slower pace in the south as compared to other parts of Italy.

In the past, the fact that one part of a country developed at a different pace

La vendemmia (grape-harvest, usually in September) near Tiriolo in the 1950s when the womenfolk were still used to balancing baskets of grapes on their heads.
Though an uncommon sight these days, In 2013, in the Sila, I did see a woman attired completed in black, walking alongside a main road balancing a basket on her head. I did have a camera with me but felt it may have been an intrusion to stop and photograph her.

to another has not been unusual but after Italian unification the difference between north and south, and particularly Calabria, became increasingly marked.

Clearly what follows will take me into the land of generalisations where lurk the exceptions to the rule. Also, my generalisations will use Santa Severina as their benchmark; in the respect it has many things in its favour. First and foremost I live there and for a decade have observed and got to know many of its people, both women and men.

Also, as suggested elsewhere, Santa Severina is arguably a microcosm of Calabria; it is neither remote nor an appendage to a large city; it is half an hour away from the nearest city, Crotone; it is a mix of old, established families, professional classes, artisans and labourers; because of its castle, it has a modest tourist industry which means people are accustomed to seeing strangers; it has a *liceo*, an academic secondary-level school to which students from other towns and villages come; many men still work the land part-time and many retired working-men still do so full-time; it still has daily door-to-door vendors who sell fresh bread, cheese, fruit and vegetables, fish and cold meats, pots and pans, clothes, household wares; it has a dwindling population; it has almost no public transport; there is no obvious *'ndrangheta* presence.

As I have already mentioned, by almost every measure the Kingdom of the Two Sicilies was the richest part of the Italian peninsula before unification. The fact that this wealth was swiftly transferred north and the seat of the new government (initially Turin in Piedmont), and thereafter the south was all but ignored, soon became a bone of contention. The tables were turned: the richer south soon became the poorest part of the new nation with an economy based largely on agriculture while the north became the focus of industrial development and growth.

In the early 20th century, and to a lesser extent in the 1960s, millions of southerners emigrated with the result that many communities, depopulated and disillusioned, all but disappeared. Many of those who stayed migrated instead to northern Italian cities to find work; after the war this became a flood as people went beyond Italy to find employment in Germany's burgeoning car and engineering industries.

This still happens; in the short time we have lived in Calabria we know of many young people who have left Santa Severina to find work in the north and beyond. Some return; most don't except to visit family.

With many menfolk living away from home, and with many of those who remained working on the land, the role of Calabrian women did not change at the same pace as elsewhere in Italy, still less when compared with other parts of Europe. (My generalisations mostly relate to Calabrian *rural* communities, of which there are thousands; I realise that life in the region's major cities has progressed at a different rate.)

Generally, the cultural and sexual revolutions of the sixties, seventies and eighties passed Calabrian women by. That said, the young women who went to university at this time experienced a different world for a few years and, if they returned to their home town or village, they did so with different expectations. But also at that time, fewer girls left their home towns for university than is the case now. It has to be remembered that, in Calabria itself, there was no university until the early seventies; now there are three: the University of Calabria at Cosenza (1972); the University of Mediterranean Studies at Reggio Calabria (1982); and the University of Magna Græcia at Catanzaro (1998).

It used to be unusual to see a woman behind the wheel of a car, so much so that peoplecan often recall who the first woman was in their town to have had a driving licence. In Santa Severina that accolade goes to Filomena Schipani who, in the early 1960s, not only got her driving licence but did so to run a taxi service to and from Crotone.

Apart from the likes of Filomena, there remains a generation of Calabria women whose life experiences have centred around their home town and family communities in ways that are different from their contemporaries in other European countries, particularly northern Europe. This generation's life experiences have focussed on two things: having children and maintaining the home in terms of raising children, cooking, washing and cleaning. Some would of course argue—and with some justification—that the sense of family still prevalent in Calabrian society is to be envied in this day and age.

I see these women every day on our morning walk around the town. They stand in the doorway to greet us, ask how many circuits we have done or how many we still have to do; they rarely leave the house except for occasional visits to the doctor, the pharmacy, the post office, the church or very near family; many have children and grandchildren living in nearby cities or 'up north'; they rely on street vendors for their basic needs and friends and family with cars to visit the larger supermarkets nearer Crotone; they watch a lot of television; they are invariably cheerful; many are widows.

But things are changing.

These days even elderly Calabrian women experience, albeit second-hand, the ways in which women's roles are changing in the wider world—at least all those with a television in their home. It may be too late for some but they are aware that many things have moved on and especially around the aspirations of women. They are aware, as never before, how life for their daughters and grand-daughters has changed beyond recognition within a very short timescale. Their daughters and grand-daughters themselves have expectations of living a different life but this can only truly comes about when their menfolk go along with it; in Calabrian society, the 'new' woman is only as emancipated as her Calabrian man.

Leslie Gardiner (1966) was privy to a unique female perspective on the Calabrian man when a woman, part of a group walking near Tiriolo, fell:

"It is so embarrassing for a woman in Calabria. One does not want gallantry, that is boring, but expects consideration. To the Calabrians, women are nothing, just a nuisance. Unless they are their own women, their own property."

In *Stumbling through Italy* I described Santa Severina's early evening *passeggiata,* summer's leisurely, repetitive stroll within a small space, often a *piazza*. It was June 2006, we were on holiday, and every evening about six we went up to the town (from the out-of-town *agriturismo* where we were staying) for an *aperitivo* at Carlo's bar. Santa Severina's *passeggiata* would be in full swing and we could watch its progress from our *piazza*-side table.

"... the oval shape of the *piazza* made for a more ordered and predictable route from church to castle and back again. Every so often people sitting at the bars would get up and filter in; just as often some of those walking would slope off and bag an empty table.

"The 'regulars' in rural communities such as Santa Severina, were mainly men; generally any women were either one half of a young couple showing their togetherness to the world or perhaps part of a small group, most often in their thirties or forties, who had probably grown up and gone to university in a world very different to that of their mothers. And of course there were the inevitable exceptions."

(I went on to describe many of the people I observed; all now have names though of course at the time they were all strangers.)

"With the clock approaching half-seven, the *passeggiata* started to wind down. Slowly, almost imperceptibly, the square would begin to empty as, first, the 'independent' women headed home to prepare dinner, leaving the more senior (male) citizens to do a few more circuits before they too wandered off home to see what delicacy their womenfolk had prepared."

The 'independent' women I referred to were those who could walk, socialise *and* cook; most of the town's other womenfolk were already at home preparing dinner for the family. The exception to this is early evening on Sunday when, with the main family meal of the week (Sunday lunch) out of the way, more women venture up into the square with their menfolk.

What I did not realise back in 2006 was that generally when people started to filter back into the square *after* dinner, there are generally more women than before; while most settled for a night in, some joined their menfolk for a lap or two of the square and a chance to catch up with the gossip.

On hot summer evenings, when it is almost too hot to be indoors, small groups of women (men too sometimes) come together outside their houses and talk the night away. Should we be returning home on such an evening, we run the gauntlet of our female neighbours doing exactly this and our 'foreign' take on things offers the group a few moments of congenial distraction.

Nevertheless, even with a decade of hindsight, my description of the *passeggiata* would remain generally unchanged except that, were I to write it again, I would have to include those younger fathers pushing baby buggies, often without their wives or partners. Also, even ten years ago, almost every family unit was based on a husband and a wife; today, though that is still the case for most, there are more couple cohabiting and some also have children.

This inevitably leads on to another aspect of life in Calabria: the influence of organised religion—and specifically the Catholic church—on communities and in particular its impact on women. It has been well-documented by

In 2016, apart from younger women, life in Santa Severina's square remains mostly a male affair; here a group of men are playing cards, keenly observed by even more men. On the right is Gino Sculco on his annual two-month visit to his birthplace from New Jersey. In reality, during the hot summer months the stay-at-home women could well be out enjoying a late-evening, impromptu doorstep gathering of friends and neighbours.

specialist researchers in this field of study that women are generally drawn more to religion, both organised and otherwise, than are men. (Curiously, research has also indicated that this also applies to politically aware women who seem to reject towing the line in one area but tolerate it in another.)

The church's historic influence over how people act—from contraception to abortion, from divorce to same-sex relationships—remains stronger in the south than in other parts of Italy which, of course, the church would say is a good thing ... though that fails to explain the mafia. What it does explain is how the expectations of Calabrian women are different to those further north.

In Santa Severina, for example, it is clear that by far the majority of regular churchgoers are women, often elderly women and frequently widows. Every May there is also a daily service in the small Byzantine church of Santa Filomena ... the congregation is entirely women.

At the same time—as I observed in *Scratching the toe of Italy*—the town boasts more non-believers than one might expect for such a small community and, unusually, some of these are women. That said, most of the wives of the men I know to be non-believers, themselves go to church regularly; perhaps they are praying for their lapsed menfolk?

There is also a class dimension to how the role of women is changing ... which will not come as any surprise.

It is my experience that class differences in Santa Severina are more blurred than, for example, in the UK; they may have been more defined fifty years ago but there has definitely been a levelling with people of different socioeconomic groups communicating with each other in an easy manner. Private social friendships and liaisons might be more closely based on class and professional paths but these lines are definitely blurred.

That said, generally the women who are from the professional classes are less likely to conform to the traditional role of the Calabrian woman, mainly because many, if not most, went to university and/or travelled more widely than others in the seventies, eighties and nineties.

Sina Audia was born in Santa Severina. She and her husband Gino Sculco emigrated to America in the sixties; I ate with them and their extended family in their New Jersey home while researching *Thank You Uncle Sam*.

Every couple of years Sina and Gino return to their home town for up to two months, normally most of July and August. During this time it is rare to see Sina out and about in the town; neither she nor Gino drive, they rely instead on friends and family for transport when they need it. During her time in Santa Severina, Sina reverts to being a typical Calabrian housewife of a certain age though, unlike others, she and Gino often come up to the square in the late evening when it's cooler for a chat with old friends.

In New Jersey, to see Sina's diminutive form behind the wheel of a large, black SUV was a culture shock. If her Santa Severina friends and neighbours were to see the other Sina, the one who speaks English, lives in America and drives a huge car, they would scarcely recognise her.

When I put this to Sina, she just smiled an unassuming smile; unlike all her childhood friends in Santa Severina she has been exposed to two cultures, two infinitely different ways of life ... and she can 'do' both.

But Sina is unique; back in the sixties, difficult as it was for her, she seized an opportunity to change her life. Had she not done so, she would probably be one of the Santa Severina women that we meet on our morning walk. Not that this is a bad thing; they seem genuinely happy with the life choices they made by just assimilating and repeating the traditions they grew up with.

There will, I believe, be just one more generation—albeit a much smaller generation—like this before the majority of Santa Severina's women, and those in other similar Calabrian communities, are truly more like their northern European counterparts.

Of course this begs the question of whether or not it will be a good thing, of whether or not Calabrian women have something to offer the women of other, seemingly more sophisticated, communities?

There is of course one area of Calabrian society where, in recent years, the role of Calabrian women has been crucial—in standing up to the *'ndrangheta*. Women like Elisabetta Tripodi, Maria Carmela Lanzetta and Lea Garofolo have taken stands against organised crime; in the case of Lea Garofolo this meant confronting head-on her husband's way of life. She paid with her life.

Since I first wrote about Elisabetta Tripodi, the elected mayor of Rosarno, and her struggle to wrest the town from the *'ndrangheta*, things have moved on. Her struggle ultimately—some might say inevitably—came to an end when eleven members of the council resigned in May 2015.

Interviewed in *ilfattoquotidiano.it* by Eva Catizone, herself an ex-mayor of Cosenza, this is what Elisabetta Tripodi had to say:

"A weight has been lifted from my shoulders for the town council had become like Vietnam; I did not resign sooner out of respect for the office I hold. What I have done I did it for my city, I put myself forward, not for political motives, and I would do so again. I can hold up my head and say that the foundations have been laid for change, I only hope that the clock is not turned back."

Santa Severina

"In the valley of the Neto is the little archiepiscopal city of S. Severina, anciently Siberina, where Pope S. Zacharias (741) was born, the son of a man who bore the Greek name of Polychronius."
Augustus Hare *Cities of Southern Italy and Sicily*

It would seem inappropriate not to finish this book without focusing for a few pages on Santa Severina, even though, apart from myself, most of the travellers who came to Calabria in the last two hundred years never actually visited the town. That said, some, like Keppel-Craven (1818) and Eric Whelpton (1957), mentioned it in passing, both figuratively and literally.

Keppel-Craven looked across the valley of the river Neto from Stróngoli and described what he saw:

"The view from a platform near this church is more extensive than beautiful. The high range of the Apennines, called, from the forests that cover them, La Sila, forms the bounding line on one side, and below them the eye follows the naked waste beyond Cotrone, to the Lacinian promontory, near Capo delle Colonne. Mount Clibanus is seen rising more inland, between the towns of Cutro and Santa Severina. This last is the ancient Siberena, extolled by Pliny for the excellence of its wines."

I too have taken in the same vista from Stróngoli and Keppel-Craven's description has changed little across nearly two centuries. However, Mount Clibanus has undergone a name change and, although it looks like it sits somewhere between Santa Severina and Cutro, that is more than a trick of perspective for Montefuscaldo, as it is now known, is less than a mile from the outskirts of Santa Severina, but over seven from Cutro as the crow flies.

Eric and Barbara Whelpton, approaching the town from the opposite direction, from San Giovanni in Fiore, looked but probably didn't touch:

"Descending further into the an amphitheatre of hill, the road passes through Santa Severina, a town of ancient origin with a population of Greek and Albanian descent."

In respect of the ancient origin he is spot on and indeed strong Byzantine Greek influences remain in the town but Santa Severina was never an 'Albanian' settlement in the same way as other towns in the hills across the valley of the Neto. In the 15th century a small Albanian community settled in the town to escape Turkish persecution.

As I have noted elsewhere, the context of Whelpton's descriptions are sometimes ambiguous as occasionally there is the sense that he is just passing on what he has been told rather than describing what he has experienced. It's as if he being fed information by someone trying to 'sell' Calabria and therefore on the cusp of becoming a guide-book rather than a travelogue. With regard to Santa Severina, he goes on to describe the town in some detail and, despite having read and re-read his description, I cannot make up mind as to whether or not he ever set foot in it the town. That said, he clearly had a much closer encounter than Keppel-Craven.

The tiny Byzantine church of Santa Filomena; they say that there were once nine churches in the town's *centro storico*.

"This place was reconquered by the Byzantines in the tenth century and then captured by the Normans after a long and difficult siege.

"In the present day [1957], despite conquests and severe earthquakes there are still no less than three Byzantine churches in Santa Severina besides a baptistry of the same period which has been carefully restored.

"The roof of the Byzantine church of Santa Filomena is supported by sixteen columns decorated with oriental designs. Two porches were added to this building by the Normans who were also responsible for the construction of the Cathedral, now so much restored that only a few twelfth-century arches remain.

"The immense castle was built by the great conqueror, Robert Guiscard, on the foundations of a Byzantine fortress which he caused to be demolished."

Anyone trying to write a description of Santa Severina for the tourist market would be hard-pressed to better Whelpton's effort.

In his *Heel to Toe*, Charles Lister did actually make it to Santa Severina. He was travelling from Apulia first on a bicycle and then on a capricious moped, which he called AB, which was long past its sell-by-date. He had almost got as far as the *bivio* (junction) at the bottom of the hill which, through four hairpin bends ascends to the town's *centro storico*, over 1000 feet above sea level. It is this junction which in effect separates the town's two distinct zones, the lower town from the *centro storico*, the older stone-built houses from the more modern brick-built ones.

Lister made it to the top eventually ... but AB didn't. These are the bare bones of what happened:

"It [the journey from Crotone] was fun. Till the climb started. AB took one look at what was above, gave a whimper of horror and collapsed. That produced a quandary; leave it in the ditch and get it nicked, or a reversal of roles and I'd do the work for a change. So I pushed and it wasn't funny.

"My legs ached, I puffed, I cursed, I gulped for oxygen, sweat went everywhere it shouldn't and ended up on my shoes ... I did five yards at a time, hating every car that rattled down and every silly little house that I began to pass ... My knees became agony, as if the bones were rubbing together and all the flesh had gone, the backs of my thighs were painful jelly starting to go solid.

"I was resting and heard a donkey clip-clopping up, so I got out the camera, but he rattled on past, shouting 'that'll be five thousand lire' before I could release the shutter. All I got was the donkey's bottom.

"Somewhere up the hill a woman came out to watch me, so I asked her where the castle was and she came out with the meaningless Italian distance of *'due passi'* or two paces, which can mean anything between 500 yards and three miles …

"When I asked her in breathless gulps if I could leave AB with her, she nodded and gave me a glass of wine as black as squid's ink, and I sat on a wall feeling like a punctured tyre and waiting for my knees to re-joint as I drank it.

"I felt slightly less encumbered after that, almost springy, going round a spaghetti of corners until I was right at the foot of the castle walls, and they stretched up yards and yards and yards into somewhere above, into the sky even, almost sloping, so the people at the top could just laugh at the no-hopers at the bottom …

"I trudged round it looking for a way up and in, under arches and along corridors, till I found some steps. I ended up right in the middle of Robert's [Robert Guiscard] castle, which was as big as a full-sized cricket field with the towers at the corners. It was like a little village, with shops at one end selling groceries, sweets and drinks. There was a post office (God help the postman!), the town hall, a bar, more offices, a schoolroom full of noisy children, a playground, several gateways leading to houses further up the hill, and a small car park."

When I first read this (several years before I ever came to Santa Severina), I tried to imagine the scene and wondered whether the story about the temporary demise of AB was perhaps a little exaggerated. The problem was that I could find no date to hang it on. There is the publication date of the book (2002) but no indication within the text as to when Lister actually was in Calabria. I got the impression that it was quite some time before the publication date, perhaps a decade or more. I know most of the houses up the hill to the town as I had often walked it and I also suspected that the woman involved almost certainly had passed away and that most of the houses were now probably occupied by younger families.

Eventually I caught up with Charles Lister himself and at first he too was vague about exactly when he travelled … at the time his notes were in out-of-the-way places and his recollections of the trip were no more precise than 'the nineties'. I felt it would be ungallant to push him. From the things he did remember and his generous description of arriving at Santa Severina, I began to piece together my version of the story from my knowledge of the town. For example, from our conversation I realised that he had approached the town from Crotone on the old road, now a long-abandoned route, though still just about driveable by those with masochistic tendencies and good posterior suspension.

Then, out of the blue, he sent me a detailed extract from his notes which not only confirmed my instincts about when he actually was here, but was even more precise than I could have expected. Charles Lister, in his own words 'a panting paralytic', climbed the hill to Santa Severina's Norman castle on 27 April, 1992 and on the same day managed to exert grievous bodily harm on one of the town's sacred artefacts.

But first a slight diversion to try to give a flavour of what life is like atop this hill in what is a fairly typical Calabrian town, at least in terms of the services and amenities on offer; nor is Santa Severina untypical in terms of its size and population. In the province of Crotone, as in every Calabrian province, life goes on in hundreds of towns such as Santa Severina; it is generally the newer, coastal communities that experience seasonal upheavals.

Every morning, before showering, before breakfast, we walk the waking streets of Santa Severina and, depending on the precise time of day, these are some of our daily experiences.

It is a short climb from the front door to the main road that runs along the eastern side of the town. Via Grecia is our main thoroughfare but it warrants the term 'main' only in the sense that it is the road that gives access to this part of the town. Vehicular access to where we live is restricted and only facilitates the smallest of cars and two going in opposite directions have no chance of passing. This, then, is an imaginary morning walk, up to ninety percent of which could occur on any given day.

As we turn on to Via Grecia, we greet some of the children making their way towards the Middle School, a space being shared of late by pupils from the Elementary School while their school is being made earthquake-proof. Most take the opportunity to practice their English and a few get beyond the mere 'Good Morning' and venture to ask how we are. As we approach the school itself we get ready to brave the many greetings in English from those early birds already in the school's elevated playground.

Sometimes we pass as one of the yellow school buses turns in and discharges its shipment of kids, laden with bulging rucksacks, outside the school. If Raffaele, the nine-year-old nephew of one of the local car mechanics, sees us he always pauses to shake my hand. For Raffaele we are almost family as we first met him not long after he had learnt to walk; we were in his grandmother's house next to the garage where his uncle Enzo was nursing our car back to health. Raffaele's mature take on meeting and greeting adults is by no means unique; it has been our experience that boys and girls of all ages are taught to respect this simple social convention with maturity and sincerity. And they never cease to surprise us.

The last house on the left, before the climb up to the main road, a proper main road that runs up towards the town square, was once the town's prison. The high walls are topped with even taller netted iron stanchions, their short elbows themselves crowned with barbed wire, remain as a reminder of days long gone. We used to be neighbours to the late Antonietta whose job in her younger days was to cook for the inmates, some of whom came from other surrounding villages; most of the crimes, she recalled, were drink-related.

Beyond the erstwhile prison, the railings to the left offer a leaning post from which to drink in the spectacular views across the valley towards Scandale and Crotone beyond; we pause for a while to take in the panorama that stretches from Stróngoli in the north to San Mauro and Cutro in the south and to reflect on how fortunate we are to have such an amazing vista on our daily doorstep.

Looking directly down stirs different emotions for this is where there should be a dynamic and well-signed park with interpretation boards for the ruined and derelict buildings, including, I am told, a synagogue and the town's erstwhile east gate. It is said that this part of Santa Severina, the 'Greek' quarter, fell down into the valley during the 1783 earthquake though, as I

The unfinished park and the ruins of some of Santa Severina's history; sadly the ornate lighting by the well-defined paths did not feel the surge of electricity for almost a decade. A little further one of the bakeries that provides fresh bread to Santa Severina.

have already indicated, I suspect the real culprit was the later 1832 quake, the epicentre of which was just a few miles away somewhere between San Mauro and Cutro.

The aforementioned park project was started under the tutelage of the town's ex-mayor, Bruno Cortese—who had to relinquish the post after ten years in office—and it was never completed by his successor. Bruno's strength was that he was always looking for ways to bring people to Santa Severina while at the same time providing something that would benefits the local people, his constituents. This was such a project but alas, at the time of writing, just one of several of Bruno's projects that the new administration deemed not worthy of completion.

As we approach the main road, where we will turn right up towards the square, the air is full of the intoxicating aroma of freshly-baked bread; we are approaching one of the town's two bakeries right on the corner. Until recently we used to give the baker, Gino, a wave as he loaded his small three-wheeled Ape van for his first run of the day round the town's narrow streets. Gino has now retired but his work carries on under new ownership who, like Gino, will have been kneading since five in the morning having first lit the wood-burning ovens. Now on their second baking of the day, the temptation to linger awhile and to become enveloped in the tantalising smells emanating from his tiny stone-built kingdom is difficult to resist ... but onward and upward.

Today, it being an imaginary Wednesday, there is no queue forming outside one of the town's two doctors' surgeries opposite which are the newly renovated premises of *Figaro*, the domain of Giancarlo and one of the town's hairdressing salons. Every so often, if we see that he's not too busy, we'll pop in for a quick trim.

We pass the territory of Billy the dog who quietly oversees everything without making a fuss from the safety of the outer gate of his house; if he's not there then we will probably bump into him later on out walk.

A little further up the gentle incline we pass the workshop of one of the town's several carpenters. Mastro Alfredo is the master who taught many of the others and he often beckons us to cross to his workshop so that he can show off his latest commission. Our wonderment at such skill and craftsmanship in such elderly, work-worn hands is genuine though, at a more practical level, if I ever want a piece of wood cut to size, this is where I come.

On the right, opposite the entrance to the car park beneath the castle, we pass the small Byzantine church of Santa Filomena, about which Eric Whelpton wrote, just beyond which a road branches off to the right and descends to the Middle School which, were we not so intent on clocking up our walking miles, would be a more direct route to and from home.

Still climbing, we once again admire the views across the valley of the river Neto. At the bend, which is truly the gateway to the *centro storico*, we pause to greet and exchange weather forecasts with the usual suspects, a small group of elderly men who generally flit between leaning on the roadside railings to take in the view and reposing on a wooden bench in front of what we call the 'dead board'. The 'dead board' is where notices are posted to announce a death, including those born in Santa Severina but who may have died elsewhere. No new notices this morning, nevertheless I check with the ever-smiling Salvatore that he is indeed still alive; he squeezes my hand with affection to confirm that there is still a pulse.

Instead of turning left up to the square, we swing right past the closed-up home of our friend Luigi Apa. Every year Luigi and his wife over-winter with their son in Rome and they will not return for another few weeks. Below Luigi's house is another of the *centro storico*'s fifteen-and-a-half businesses, run by Mario, the brother of our dear friend Carlo who himself runs one of the square's four café-bars. Mario is the local newsagent and sells almost everything else imaginable; from batteries to books, from trinkets to toys, from purses to pens, from watches to watercolours. At Mario's you can buy and top up your phone, make a photocopy and have your passport photograph taken. In this veritable 'Aladdin's Cave' it is rare to not to find what you want.

Opposite Mario's is one of the town's two hairdressers, the recently refurbished salon of Antonio Bruno, from which his daughters also run a Catholic charity that offers social service assistance to those in need. Antonio is always at his post early and his white-coated form is generally standing in the doorway in search of custom. On one occasion he asked us to wait a moment while he fetched something from inside … he returned with a small pair of scissors with which he unceremoniously clipped a wayward hair from my earlobe.

Above Antonio's is the home of Raffaele Faragò, an eccentric character who proudly displays the flag of international communism on every national holiday and sometimes plays the *Internationale*; on such occasions visitors to the town cast his balcony a disbelieving glance. Despite being near neighbours and of a similar age, politically Raffaele and Luigi Apa are poles apart as the latter was born into an old, established Calabrian family, the sort of people Raffaele would, in theory, have nothing to do with. But this is Santa Severina and life is too short to harbour such out-of-date rivalries.

We head down Corsa de Riso, past one of the *centro storico*'s two small *alimentari*, a grocery shop—provisions store is what they were once called before the advent of the supermarket—where most of the basics are always available. As the road kinks to the right there is another shop that sells fancy goods, gifts and some clothes. This is the province of Yola who is also a teacher and so opening hours have a flexible nature, a reflection of her teaching duties.

After the redundant façade of the town's old Post Office, replaced by smaller premises by the advent of new technologies, the road begins to drop down to the short northern edge of the hill, where Corso de Riso becomes Corso Aristipo and where two roads join from the left, Via dei Bizantini and Via Miseria. The former runs directly up to the square and is home to another *alimentari*, the owner of which is also the town's funeral director and the man responsible for keeping the 'dead boards' up to date; halfway along Via Miseria is the town's well-known Dance School and at the far end is the newer Post Office and the *centro storico*'s only restaurant, *La Locando del Re*.

It is on the short northern side that there have been a number of landslides in recent years. Being north-facing it is generally more susceptible to the elements and when it rains, the lack of sun means that it doesn't dry out as quickly as the rest; hence the landslides. Over the past few years strenuous efforts have been made to underpin the rock face to prevent further loss. So far, so good.

We veer left again and are now walking down the western edge, always the coldest side of the hill. Teachers at the local schools maintain that they can tell where their students live just by the clothes they wear to school in the winter … those from the western side are always well wrapped up, even though it's less than five minutes walk away.

For the next few hundred yards we have to keep our eyes firmly fixed on where we walk as, despite a theoretical clamp down by the *comune*, it can be a minefield of dog-shit. As I have already said, here, as in other communities in other countries, there are those who don't really 'get' the social considerations and responsibilities that come with dog ownership. The problem is exacerbated in towns like Santa Severina as the streets are narrow and there are few open spaces … except those spaces that seem to lie between the ears of certain dog owners.

On our right we pass the narrow entrance to the *Quartiere San Domenico*, a cluster of houses hanging on to the western edge of *lo scoglio*. Here an old, refurbished path that once clung to the very edge now comes to an abrupt end thanks to a recent landslide. This path was once another way down to the lower town by foot or by mule but in the last few decades it has just got shorter and shorter and now goes nowhere in particular.

Occasional gaps between the houses along Corso Aristipo reveal breathtaking views of the foothills of the Sila mountains as, on the 'inland' side, we pass the home of our friend Franco Severini and his wife Renata. Franco, a retired director of the local high school, the *liceo*, is also the author of several books, most notably the definitive work on Norman and Swabian castles in Calabria. From time to time a cup of coffee with friends such as Franco and Renata and others diverts us from our morning walking routine.

A few yards on is the tiny house where we lived for six weeks when we first came to Santa Severina. It is in a small square called Largo Borelli, named after Diodato Borelli (1838–1881), a physician, writer and humanitarian who was born in the town. The *liceo* also bears his name.

Between Largo Borelli and the western edge of *lo scoglio* there is a purpose-built open area with seating, a place from which to enjoy the setting sun and look out over the lower town and towards the Sila mountains. For us, when we lived nearby, it was the *only* place to get some late summer sun.

The road begins to gently climb again and, amid a flurry of *vicoli* on both sides (*vicoli* are narrow, car-less, but not necessarily *Ape*-less, alleyways), we pause to greet some of our erstwhile neighbours: the genial, sophisticated and gritty Sofia, Antonio whose two sisters, Franca and Elvira, both emigrated to America and *'professore'* Giovanni (a nickname that reflects his accumulated knowledge and not any academic title he may have acquired at university). Giovanni frequently greets us from the balcony where he is enjoying his first cigarette of the day; I often try to woo him with my Juliet impression but to no avail.

They, and others, have given up asking us where we are going and instead ask us which lap we are on for they know this is our daily routine and that we always do at least three circuits of the town. Were we dressed differently and at another time of day then we would be running the gauntlet of more pointed questions: "Where are you going?" "What's in the bag?" "When do you next go to visit family?". Such inquisitiveness is not meant to be impertinent; there is no ulterior motive other than passing the time of day and exchanging a few pleasantries.

It is along this stretch that we often pass the town's refuse collectors who, every morning six days a week, gather up all the bags left out for them, different colours for everything recyclable: paper & card, plastic & tin, glass, organic and, one day a week, anything that isn't recyclable. For each bag they pick up, they leave another of the same colour; it's a simple and efficient system. Today they are nowhere to be seen.

The climb becomes a little steeper as the road continues on towards the car park below and around three sides of the castle. The arch of the old west gate crosses, just beyond which, on the left, is the veranda of the *La Locando del Re* and, as Corso Aristipo merges with the car park there is the flight of steps up to the square that also passes the entrances to both the restaurant and the ever-queueing world of the Post Office

On the right is the town's 'half' business, the now vacant premises of the *La BCC del Crotonese Credito Cooperativo* that retains only its 'hole-in-the-wall, its cash machine or ATM facility. Round the corner to the right is a steep, serpentine road that goes down to the south gate and offers an alternative route out of town but only for those on foot or on three-wheels.

At this 'junction' we turn sharp left, past the town's other doctor's surgery—both surgeries are rarely open at the same time—where we are greeted by the queue of prescription seekers. All look well enough and the word 'queue' is only a convenient description for there is no ordered line in the conventional sense. Some of those outside are indulging in a last cigarette before it's their turn to go in and swear they've given up. As each new 'patient' arrives he or she asks, "*Chi è l'ultimo?*" The last person to join the 'queue' owns up and the order of entry is established.

As I have explained elsewhere, by an accident of geography we attended neither of the town's surgeries but went instead to a doctor in nearby Roccabernarda. But we soon realised the downside of this when, one summer, I had a severe allergic reaction and needed a more immediate and frequent service and preferably not one eight miles away. So we hastily made the change to this particular Santa Severina surgery.

We are now in the car park below the impressive battlements of Santa Severina's Norman castle. We pass under the high arches that carry the access walkway from the front gates of the castle into the square before turning right to continue alongside the high, east-facing walls, their spring outcrops of wild flowers continuing to defy all horticultural logic. We are heading towards the small square and open-air theatre at the rear of the castle, where the ASL, the *Azienda Sanitaria Provinciale*, the local health centre, is located.

But instead we turn sharp left past the *Scuola Elementare* and the drop-in centre for young adults with learning difficulties and along an elevated road that runs parallel to and above the road we walked along earlier between Gino's bakery and the Byzantine church of *Santa Filomena*. We have almost come full circle and it is here that we run often run into Billy, out for his morning walk with his owner. Unusually Ciccio *does* clean up after Billy but then he did live and work in Switzerland for a number of years and has clearly imported some of its standards to the town of his birth.

As we pass the home of the town's pharmacist, Salvatore, we resist the temptation to turn up one of the two short roads into the town's square and press on past the offices of the Pro Loco—a sort of information centre for the town's residents that sponsors publications, research and cultural events—and, next to it, the social club for the town's senior citizens, the town's senior *male* citizens, that is, for I have never seen a woman grace it.

Mario's 'Aladdin's Cave' is in sight and here we start on another circuit though this time, when we return to Salvatore's house, we *do* turn up left and into the square to seek out our first cup of coffee of the day, most often at the bar of our friend Carlo.

It being Wednesday, when we enter the large, open, oval space between the church and the castle that is home to the Town Hall, the pharmacy and four bars, it is market day. Today Santa Severina's pride and joy, its delightful square, is also home to the market which alternates each week between the *centro storico*'s square and another square in the lower town ... one week up

Santa Severina's Norman castle and, around it, the town's main car park.

the top, the next down the bottom.

As Calabrian local town markets go, it is a moderate affair, mostly stalls selling clothes, shoes and household goods; there is usually only one produce stall, selling cooked meats and cheeses; other produce, such as fruit and vegetables, fish and bread, are already catered for by street-by-street, door-to-door vendors. Naturally on market days these vendors too pause a little longer than usual in the square.

Above all else, however, it is a social occasion, an opportunity for people to catch up on all the news and gossip.

As we cross towards Carlo's bar, *La Rosa dei Venti*, we pass the group of senior citizens who, most mornings, sit outside his cousin Pino's bar, *Bar Millennium*, putting the world to rights; today they have to put up with less space than usual, but they persevere … it is only one day every two weeks, after all. At Carlo's we have our first coffee of the day as women who, clutching clothes they hope will transform them into La Loren, make a beeline for the bar's bathroom facilities, now an impromptu changing room.

Sated, we do a tour of the market and spend the next half hour talking to people we haven't seen for at least two weeks. We walk as far as where Via dei Bizantini leaves the square between the church and Alessio's *La Piazza* bar. Here the local postman, Enzo, is handing out post to those who have spotted his van outside the church; they are like bees round a honey pot but Enzo doesn't mind and when our eyes meet he acknowledges with a shake of his head … no post for us this day. Enzo lives in Crotone and from time to time we go out for a pizza with him and his American wife, Wendy.

We rarely buy anything in the market, the exception being when Kay, a passionate knitter, spots some wool at the haberdasher's stall and we get side-tracked. Next to this stall is the main vehicular entrance and exit to the square for vehicles and here we start our descent once again, past the *Jolly Bar*, the domain of another Pino.

Though the prices in the *centro storico*'s four bars are all the same, they differ in their clientele and their ambience. *La Piazza* is definitely the one that the younger element favour, possibly because Alessio himself is younger than the others; but smokers, young and old, frequent it too for it is also the upper town's only *tabaccheria*.

The *Jolly Bar*, on the other hand, is definitely a man's bar and just round the corner from the senior citizens' social club. It's the place for the beer drinkers and the card players though, of course everyone is welcome … except if your weakness is red wine.

The *Bar Millennium* and *La Rosa dei Venti* share a similar clientele and who is sitting where at any given time will often depend on where the sun is.

We, on the other hand, will frequent Carlo's bar almost every day of the year (except Tuesdays when he is closed) for we have known Carlo since before we came to live here. We were at the funeral of his mother, we endured the terrible weather on the day he married Anna-Maria and have been to every birthday party of their daughter Giovanna. To us Carlo is more than a bar owner, he is a dear friend ... one of the last people we say goodbye to when we leave, and one of the first we greet on our return.

So we leave the square behind and descend once more past Mario's 'Aladdin's Cave', past *Santa Filomina*, past Mastro Alfredo's workshop, past *Figaro*, past Gino's bakery and down Via Grecia, past the now-quiet Middle School, in search of a shower and breakfast.

In the lower town much the same sorts of facilities are available. There are probably a few more shops and it is here too that the town's largest supermarket is located. It's easier to smoke yourself to death down below as there are two *tabaccherie*; it's also easier to insure your car as there are also two insurance brokers; no pharmacist but, among others, an ironmongers, a

Market day in Santa Severina as seen from the castle battlements. At the far end is the 'Cathedral'; the towered building on the left is the Town Hall.

florist, a butchers, a *pasticceria* and of course several bars and, at the time of writing, one restaurant.

The town's petrol station is on road out of town to Crotone; it is also a *tabaccherie* and there is an adjoining restaurant, *La Grigleria del Borgo*.

It is time to return to Charles Lister whom I left several pages back having just made it up to the *centro storico*, exhausted after having pushed this ageing and capricious moped to the lower outskirts of Santa Severina where he temporarily abandoned it.

In the square he encountered some schoolchildren who acknowledged his 'Englishness' by barracking him with the only two words in English they knew: 'Manchester United'. He would not have known it at the time, but the only foreign language taught in local schools until relatively recently was French. He continues:

"For some reason the lady of the wine, who was supposed to be guarding AB, had followed me up and wanted me to see the cathedral, which she obviously considered more significant than a Norman castle. It was lower down the slope and I was surprised to find a large wooden model of a dragon inside the entrance. It must have been quite old because when I patted it the entire tail fell off, followed by a shower of woodworm dust. I managed to replace it eventually by commandeering some notices about forthcoming services, which I stuffed into the dragon's open fundament followed by the tail."

When Charles Lister retold me the story he mentioned how aggrieved his shadow—the woman who was supposed to be looking after the capricious AB—was when he appeared to be destroying one of her church's prize artefacts. Nevertheless, her sense of conviviality got the better of her and when he returned to the lower town to retrieve AB, she invited him in and he was shown typical Calabrian hospitality. Fed and watered and clutching a bottle of the family's blood-red wine, a happier Charles Lister returned to Crotone.

I knew I couldn't leave it there. In much the same way as I felt compelled to locate the *Fondaco del Fico* and find out what really happened to Joachim Murat at Pizzo Castle, Charles' exploits in Santa Severina left me with two, possibly three, loose ends: I wanted to find the woman and the family who helped him, to hear their side of the same story and to locate the dragon he had inadvertently mutilated in the church. But which church for he himself was not sure?

There were two clues to the latter in his description of it being 'lower down the slope' which seemed to suggest it was *not* the church in the square but perhaps the aforementioned Santa Filomena; on the other hand he called it a 'cathedral' which was indeed often appended to the town's main church located at one end of the square, even if that church wasn't lower down any slope ... or so I thought at the time.

I sent him photos of both and while he was deliberating I went off to see if any of the other churches in and around the town's *centro storico* might fit the bill; they say there were once eight or nine. I knew that most of the artefacts of those no longer active (which was all but two) were now housed in the Diocesan Museum next to the 'cathedral'.

Charles got back to me with some additional information which in turn sent me up to the square with a mission.

The dragon 'model' had indeed been a feature of the square's main church, the 'cathedral', until it too was moved to the Diocesan Museum. For repair?

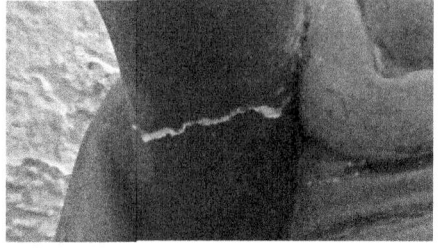

The tale of the dragon's tail resolved ... though it was actually Satan's tail. Left is the complete statue; top right the part of the tail that most visitors will remember and below it the part I will remember ... the tell-tale break at the root of the story.

These days the short walk the castle to the square involves crossing a narrow walkway on a slight incline atop a high, arched bridge that spans the castle car park. This walkway was, I discovered, once a steeper incline before the castle and the square were given a face-lift in recent decades which in turn made access from one to the other more user-friendly. I understood now why Charles Lister described it as being 'lower down the slope'.

In the Diocesan Museum it didn't take me long to find the statue of the Archangel Michael slaying Satan. Though Charles Lister refers to it being a dragon in his book, in his notes he uses the phrase 'serpent Devil' and, in some depictions of the same myth, Satan is represented by a dragon or a dragon-cum-devil. And here it was, before my very eyes and, it appeared, with its tail in one piece.

Starting at the tail's forked extremity I started running my hand down its smooth form until I reached the point where it might have appeared to the innocent bystander that I was taking an unhealthy interest in Satan's anatomy. And it was at that point I felt something, a definite break in the hitherto smooth surface. I bent down to take a closer look and there was no mistaking it, there had been some sort of breakage and, though everything had been put back together again and, possibly because it was in a place to all intents and purposes unseen by only the most curious of visitors, the break had never been 'tidied up'. Not even a lick of paint to disguise where there were definite rough white edges and a slight, uneven gap that clearly defined some previous mishap. I could not be sure whether or not Charles' makeshift repair was still *in situ*, whether or not the two halves of Satan's tail were still held together by 'notices about forthcoming services' for 1992. With uncharacteristic resolve I resisted the temptation to investigate further.

And only I, and perhaps a family I had yet to find, knew the full sordid story of the tail-breaking English traveller. Naturally the first person I shared the evidence with was Charles Lister himself.

There remained therefore one final quest, the mystery of that family and in particular the woman who helped him that day. Charles, who at first was perplexed as to why I should even be interested in his tale of the tail, had been seduced by the thrill of the chase and was now as keen as I was that I should find the family. And besides he wanted me to pass on his heartfelt thanks once again.

A few local enquiries led me to believe that they probably lived in a strange triangular-shaped house on the corner where the old and new roads meet. Unfortunately the family had moved to Milan and for most of the year the house lay empty. Occasionally however they returned to Santa Severina to meet up with old friends and to give the house an airing. I was told they drove a red car so I just had to keep an eye out for a such a vehicle parked outside the house and perhaps an open shutter or two … and pounce. I also hoped my Italian was good enough to get across enough of the story to confirm that they were the indeed right family.

I was also aware that, this being Calabria, if it were not the family I was looking for, then word would soon get out and about and others would do the legwork for me and eventually someone might just turn up on my doorstep one day. Nor would I have been surprised if more than one family were to lay claim to the story.

I was completely wrong about the family from the house on the corner. I knew it the moment they opened the door for there was no way I could imagine the woman of this house being the warm-hearted woman who helped Charles Lister all those years ago. They made it clear they knew nothing about these events and, unusually, were not in any way helpful regarding who, if any, of their erstwhile neighbours it could be. Perhaps they had lived in the north too long; perhaps they didn't like foreigners.

By this time I'd had another clue to work with from the recesses of Charles' memory … he recalled that the family had a daughter, 'a seventeen year-old flame-haired beauty' who talked to him about performing in the Greek tragedy, *Andromeda* (*Andromaca* in Italian), the following month in the castle. For me this meant that I was now looking for a family who, in 1992, had a daughter finishing off her education at the *liceo*, the local high school which also serves other towns and villages in the area.

As I suspected, word had already got out and about and super-sleuth Gino Bubba it was who was the first to come up with a theory. Gino, a retired *vigile* (local copper), accosted me in the square one Sunday morning. Retired or not, Gino was nevertheless as adept as any youngster at flashing though the map App on his smart-phone to share his thoughts with me based on the age of the unnamed girl at the time. He showed me the house where the D'Alfonso family used to live. It was in the right part of the lower town, on the old road but close to the junction with the newer road; *and* they had three daughters, at least two of whom could have been, he reckoned, about the right age to still have been at school at the time.

That was the good news; the bad news was that the family had long since left Santa Severina and the mother, now widowed, lived with one of her daughters 'up north'. She did return occasionally but not very often and, frustratingly, I had missed her most recent visit by a few weeks.

Another way of checking whether or not this might be the right family was to try and find a copy of the cast list for the May 1992 performance of *Andromaca* and so I set this in motion through my teacher friend, neighbour and super-super sleuth, Silvana Gerardi; Silvana said she would speak to a colleague at the *liceo*. I also ran Gino's 'd'Alfonso' theory past her and she immediately knocked it on the head … she agreed that the children were the right age but was sure they had *not* gone to the *liceo* and therefore would not have been in *Andromaca*.

Two hours later Silvana sent me an email with an attachment; it was a copy of the poster for the 1992 performance of *Andromaca*. Her accompanying note was brief and to the point:

"*Sicuramente era Elisa Tigano.*" (It was definitely Elisa Tigano.)

Elisa had the part of Corifea, the leader of the chorus, in *Andromaca* in the castle on 23 and 24 May 1992 and that year she was the sole member of the named cast who came from Santa Severina. Later in the afternoon Silvana and I studied a map of the town on my iPad and we soon located Elisa's house; like the other two possibilities, the location satisfied all the criteria. Even better, the family, Francesco Tigano and Maria Ierardi, were still living in the same house though their daughter Elisa had moved to Naples. I could scarcely wait to talk to them and to hear what they remembered about the day the English traveller dropped by.

The next day therefore another itinerant English-speaking stranger dropped by to see if they really were the family that had helped Charles Lister.

With a broad smile, the ebullient Maria confirmed that, though she could not recall the details of the story, she and her husband had often helped strangers in need … after all, for years that had also run a small bar nearby where they sometimes came across travellers who were in need of more than just a glass of wine or a bottle of beer. She told me the story of a Californian family who had run out of petrol on a Sunday and hadn't enough to return to their base in the Sila mountains. The owner of Santa Severina's petrol station was out of town so Maria's husband Francesco went with the family to nearby San Mauro where he asked his friend, the owner of the local station, to open up for a few moments and fill up the car. A few months later Maria and Francesco received a package from America with gifts for all the family.

Maria laughed and knowingly nodded her head when I told herb how Charles Lister had called her 'the lady of the wine', *la donna del vino*; I could see that she found the nickname quite appealing. Francesco confirmed that the wine they would have shared with Charles was their own home-made vintage and they were both more than a little pleased when I told them that he described it as being 'as black as squid's ink'. I asked her about her daughter having been to England which Charles mentioned in his book, but she said he was mistaken, though perhaps they had talked about her desire to travel.

Despite the fact that Maria was vague when it came to the part about following Charles up to the square and how he had come to break off the devil's tail, I was sure my quest was complete and later emailed Charles and sent him a photo of Maria and Francesco which I had taken that day.

The next day Charles, clearly inspired by what I was up to in Santa Severina, told me he had come across some 'slides' of his visit to the town but added that, due to his lack of technological know-how, getting them to me might prove somewhat problematic or, as he put it, 'If I know how to get two or three S. Sev attached to a pigeon you might be amused.'

The pigeon was not required for the next day I received an email with four colour photos attached. There were three of the castle and, posing outside their home, one of the family who had helped him: father, mother and daughter. I printed off a copy to give to them next time I was passing.

I also showed the photo to Silvana who took one look at it and told me it wasn't the Tigano family but another whose name she had forgotten; nor could she recall where they lived. Frankly, I thought she'd got it wrong.

I had all but forgotten the wise words of Silvana when, almost a week later, I dropped in to see Maria and showed her the photo; she took one look at

The poster for Euripede's *Andromaca* in May 1992 detailing the part played by Elisa Tigano (the leader of the Chorus, Corefea) which led me to the Tigano family.
Having tracked down Elisa's parents, Francesco Tigano and Maria Ierardi, I was convinced I'd found the family who helped an exhausted Charles Lister back in 1992.

it and said, "That's the Verzino family; they live round the corner, the last house out of town on the old road."

To say that I was gobsmacked doesn't quite cover it. I thanked Maria for this new information and beat a hasty retreat, still trying to figure out how it was that not only had I been so sure I had found the right family but *the family itself* also seemed pretty sure. I guessed something has got lost in translation.

I thought back to that tongue-in-cheek notion I'd had a few weeks (and a few pages) earlier when I suggested that it wasn't beyond the realms of possibility that I might find more than one claimant to the accolade of having given succour to the flagging Charles Lister … ?

Moments later and, as confused as a dog chasing its own tail, I rang the bell of the last house as you exit Santa Severina on the old road to Crotone.

A few moments later a woman appeared on a first floor balcony; I asked her if this is where the Verzino family lived. She nodded and somehow with that same nod she asked me what I wanted … I was definitely getting better at deciphering Calabrian hand and head gestures. I held up the photo like some hopeful Romeo and asked my Juliet if this was her family. She leaned out over the balcony to take a closer look but I could see she wasn't sure though clearly my gestures were saying 'trust me' for she asked me to wait a moment and she'd come down.

Maria Salerno—whom I had already recognised as a more likely older incarnation of the woman in the photo than her namesake up the road—was scrutinising said photo as I told her how I'd come by it. For the umpteenth time I repeated the story of the weary English traveller who came this way twenty-three years earlier, the man who took the photo, the man who left his moped at her house, the man who drank her wine.

"Yes, yes", she said, her gaze still riveted on the photo as the memories flowed back across the years, "I remember him, his *motorino* had broken down. He left it here and went up to the town, he wanted to see the castle."

She handed me back the photo though I could see its image was still clearly fixed in her mind's eye.

"My daughter is thinner now," she said as if I was some itinerant suitor.

I returned the photo to her and told her it was hers to keep.

As we were talking a pick-up truck pulled into the short driveway and the man who got out, clearly Maria's husband, was just as clearly the same man in Charles's photo; in twenty-three years he had scarcely changed.

Upstairs in the kitchen Maria, Vincenzo and I went over the story again and this time, I let them fill in the gaps, I let them elaborate on the detail ... I wanted to be absolutely sure that this time I was with the right family.

Within minutes, as I was downing a refreshing beer Calabrian-style straight from the bottle, I knew I had found them. This time there was no doubt and I was experiencing first-hand the kind of hospitality Charles had encountered in the same house; mind you I had already experienced the same at the home of Francesco and Maria in pursuit of the same mission.

Both Maria and Vincenzo beamed when I told them how Charles had described their wine, 'as black as squid's ink'; better still Vincenzo sprang into action and produced a five-litre demijohn as if he'd been waiting for just such an occasion to show it off. As he poured me a small glass, he explained that he wasn't being mean but that this brew was just as potent as the one back in 1992. But, he explained as he filled a plastic two-litre bottle, if I liked, I could take some home with me.

I was about to say, in Italian of course, "Is the Pope Catholic?", the response that most of my Italian friends would expect of me to something as obvious as being asked if I wanted to take home some red wine. On this occasion I thought better of it ... it was too early in our relationship to have to explain such a concept.

Vincenzo and Maria have three children, two of whom are married and live away. Only the girl in the photo, their daughter Anna Maria, still lives at home though that day she was at work as a teacher in nearby Petilia

The photo Charles Lister sent me of the family who looked after his decrepit AB and plied him with wine 'as black as squid's ink'.

Policastro. As it was nearing lunchtime, and I could see that Maria's gaze was increasingly focussing on whatever was bubbling away on the stove, I suggested we reconvene early one evening when Anna Maria was at home. I said I would bring Charles book with me and try to translate the relevant pages … I had yet to tell Maria that he called her the 'lady of the wine'.

Clutching my bottle of as-black-as-squid's-ink red wine and a bag of fresh eggs, I headed home satisfied that finally I had found the family who had helped Charles Lister. In my mind there remained just a couple of loose ends but I was sure that when we met again, Anna-Maria would help resolve those.

A few days later Kay and I popped in on the Verzino household and finally met Anna-Maria who, fortunately, was able to recall some of the detail of the day Charles dropped by. I particularly wanted to know how it was that she was in *Andromaca* but her name was missing from the poster; I was also eager to clear up who it was Charles saw up in the square and who witnessed his mutilation of the statue as, the first time we met, Maria did not recall having done so and suggested it may have been her daughter.

Meeting Anna Maria Verzino was a revelation. Kay and I found ourselves in the company of a sharp, erudite and engaging young woman who remembered the details of Charles Lister's visit to her home as if it were yesterday and together we cleared up the question of the poster for *Andromaca*.

Anna Maria was definitely part of the play's chorus *and* she had the photos to prove it, several of which I had already seen both at the *liceo* and at Elisa Tigano's home. At first she wasn't sure how it was that her name had been omitted on the poster until, that is, I put on my graphic designer's hat.

In 1992, when the poster was created, I was a graphic designer and I imagine that the technology for adjusting type to fit into a given space was probably in its infancy in Italy, given that it was only a few years older in the UK and America. Thus, whoever was responsible for creating the *Andromaca* poster was using the basic typographic technology of the time and decided it was easier to omit the name of the last member of the chorus as it would have created an extra, and very short, line of text.

Alphabetically that last name would have been 'Verzino Anna Maria'. But someone deemed the name expendable in much the same way as another participant had his surname truncated to a single letter on the same poster.

When we talked about the woman who apparently witnessed Charles' act of vandalism on the devil in the church, neither Anna Maria nor her mother remembered seeing him do the deed though Anna Maria did follow him up to the square.

Before we left, I revealed to Maria that Charles had called her 'the lady of the wine', a nickname she seemed to relish every bit as much as the other Maria. The mention of the red nectar prompted Vincenzo to spring into action and he disappeared momentarily and returned clutching yet another bottle of the very same, yet another bag of eggs and a bag of fresh broad beans. All bounty from the land around the Verzino home and, just as in 1992, shared with others.

Since meeting the Verzino family, we have become good friends and Anna Maria has rekindled a friendship with Charles Lister who was more than a little surprised to have this young woman, whom he described to me as a 'flame-haired beauty', back in his life.

Until very recently Kay and I were the only residents of Santa Severina to have read this brief account of what occurred that day in April 1992. And of course I realise that in the grand scheme of things my pursuit of it was no more than an engaging and obsessive diversion, a story that was, as Charles Lister himself suggested when I first spoke to him about it, not all that relevant to anything or anyone.

This is true, but it was a tale, in the pursuance of which, I learnt more about the town in which I live and inadvertently contributed a little something to its story. I met people I'd never met before and made new friends; I set

The Verzino family, Vincenzo, Anna Maria and Maria, outside their home in 2015.

others thinking about who lived where in the early nineties; I got to know the curator of the Diocesan Museum who subsequently learnt something she didn't know about one of the Museum's exhibits; I got to know some of the teaching and non-teaching staff at the *liceo*; and I made more than a few people laugh.

Santa Severina is where I live; it is also, as I've said more than a few times, a microcosm of Calabria itself. Like the rest of Calabria it has been touched by most of the foreign incursions and political and social upheavals of the last three thousand years. Its customs, traditions and people are generally no different to those of other Calabrians and their communities that I, and many others, have encountered in our travels. It has been my experience that, with few exceptions, people throughout Calabria, throughout southern Italy, are just as open and hospitable as they are here in Santa Severina.

The obvious exceptions are the towns that have a strong *'ndrangheta* presence, places where many of the inhabitants would dearly love to be able to snap their fingers and transform their home town into an 'ordinary' community such as Santa Severina.

Increasingly, people's aspirations for themselves and their families are no different to other places; generally no different to people in Petilia Policastro, in Crotone, in Rome, in Milan, in Paris, in London or in New York; the universal media has seen to that. People, even the elderly, in Santa Severina—and places even smaller and more remote—have computers, tablets and smart-phones and have therefore the same access to the news, the latest in hair fashions and shopping online as everyone else.

In such Calabrian communities it will be the fortitude and courage of such people that will finally isolate those whose aim is the mayhem of manipulation, misappropriation and murder. Of course I realise it won't happen overnight but, I believe, it will happen. It is a slow and perilous process but one that will inevitably gather momentum until mafia-infested communities finally rid themselves of those elements that hitherto have thrived on their acquiescence and sometimes their complicity.

The more people get a taste of life 'outside' and the angrier they become about what is happening to their town, the more they will realise what they can achieve for themselves and their communities.

Despite the fact that few travellers came to Santa Severina, in the age of the tourist (as opposed to the traveller) they certainly do now. Drawn by its

Byzantine relics, its impressive Norman castle, its delightful square and its reputation as a tidy, well-appointed town, it is definitely a place on the radar of tour companies and independent travellers who venture south to Calabria.

Were it not so, then we might never have done so ourselves … and this book would never have been written.

Changing Calabria?

"After we have goone a good while from hense [Laino in Basilicata] we cum at lengthe to descende from the hilles throwgh a strait, sharpe roode and stonie waye, which a man wolde judge to have been cutt owt of the rocke by force of hand, for it is on both sides as yf a man shulde enter into a gate. When we were doone these hilles we cum into a faire plaine, and on the right hand there is open the hille's side the town of Murano."
Sir Thomas Hoby *The Travels and Life of Sir Thomas Hoby, Knight of Bisham Abbey, Written by himself 1547–1564*

This book has taken a little longer to write than anticipated, almost two years longer. I am steering it towards a conclusion now because I realise that it will never truly be finished as making connections between my experiences and those of other travellers will always be on-going.

The above quotation is the first description of Calabria written in English that I could find. In it, Sir Thomas Holby describes the same journey that many others later made to enter Calabria from the north by passing through the narrow Pass of Campo Tenese in the Pollino mountains. Unlike, for example, Brian Hill (1791), the notion that it might be 'the most dangerous pass in all Calabria' had not yet become the maxim for would-be travellers. Holby saw only its natural attributes.

This notion that Hill hawked—that Calabria was a region better avoided—is one that seems to have evolved sometime between the mid-16th century and when John Dryden Junior travelled there a century and a half later. Dryden, however, seems to relate supposed barbarity to the squalor in which the people lived and gives no evidence to support his choice of words:

"We never lay ashore in any place, but always in our felucca, and, indeed, we found nothing but bare walls wherever we put in: and those people of Calabria are so barbarous as well as poor, that, when we only came into their bare rooms, where was not to be found so much as a chair to sit on, to sup there as well as we cou'd, they wou'd have exacted above a carlin a head of us, besides the reck'ning, for our chambering, as they termed it, for they cou'd not give it the name of a night's lodging, for we went down to lye in our felucca."

Before Dryden's account was published posthumously in 1776, Richard Pococke (1734) had also travelled through the region and made not a single mention of its 'barbarous' inhabitants.

Nevertheless by the time Henry Swinburne (1777) was travelling, the accepted notion was that to travel into Calabria was to set foot in the 'badlands'. While still at Naples, Swinburne was brought up to speed on what to expect:

"It would require a prudent, inflexible, and long exertion of impartial criminal justice, to reduce to order the fierce untractable assassin of the mountainous regions of Calabria, who being driven by the oppression of the barons and officers of the revenue to penury and despair, sets little value upon his life, and braves danger to the last drop of his blood."

It may be that some people travelled in Calabria *because* there was a perceived element of danger in doing so ... it is not beyond the realms of possibility that I myself felt impelled to visit the mafia towns with the worst reputations for the same motives ... though in my case I was confident that I would re-emerge unscathed.

The reason I am going over such old ground is that, even in the 21st century, in some quarters Calabria still has almost the same reputation as it had two hundred and fifty years ago. And it is a reputation that seems to be peddled by other Italians as much as by those outside the Italian peninsula.

In *Scratching the Toe of Italy* I recounted the story of how, in September 2008 on the train from Dusseldorf to Verona, en route to our new home in Calabria and with our little Renault Clio tagging along behind, we shared our forthcoming adventure with a German couple on the first leg of their three-week holiday in Italy:

" ... the only part ... they found difficult to grasp was why we were going to Calabria. They had been to many parts of Italy but had clearly avoided the deep south; they had, I guessed, succumbed to the oft-broadcast notion that the south was the pits, the arsehole of Italy, the unsophisticated and uninviting rump of a fragile nation.

"We were not unaware of this reputation, this stereotypical view of a part of Italy that has had such a chequered and uncompromising history, home to ruffians, kidnappers, brigands, and their modern incarnation the *'ndrangheta*, that even some Italians would think twice about setting foot in it.

"I'm not sure we convinced our German friends that we wouldn't be on the same train as them in three week's time; they heading back home to Bonn, we scurrying post-haste back to England. Or perhaps they saw us as another couple of ruffians that would fit in just fine in Calabrian society."

Little wonder that, when one Calabrian asked me to tell him one thing I would change about Calabria, my response was simple … its name. He laughed awkwardly, then seemed to understand that I was not just being funny, that perhaps I was making a serious point.

The name 'Calabria' has baggage, so much so that Calabrians themselves are not immune to it; I would be rich beyond the dreams of avarice were I to have been given one euro by every *Calabrian* who has ever asked me, "Why? Why have you come to live in Calabria?"

Lacking in the above written version of their question, is the incredulity in their voices when they ask it … and the accompanying hand gestures.

I have a stock answer which usually includes the same four elements:

"The climate, the food … the wine … and the people."

After the second I pause momentarily and then they laugh and nod in agreement when I tag on 'the wine' almost as an afterthought; the second afterthought, 'the people', therefore often takes them by surprise, until they realise that, to me, it is by far the most important.

In hindsight, I think that the question I was asked about what, if anything, I would change about Calabria, is deserving of a better response than just saying, 'its name'.

I wouldn't want Calabria to change too much … just a handful of tweaks here and there, and in no particular order, the sorts of things that, from my perspective, would just make life better for everybody. And most Calabrians would agree with all that follows. But I do realise too that, in spelling these out, I am also bringing to the table things from other cultures where I have lived and worked. In doing so, I also understand that I have no business criticising other travellers for doing the same.

—⚹—

The first 'tweak' relates to the role of animals and I suspect Craufurd Tait Ramage (1828) might have agreed:

"I am lodged in the house [at Scalea] of a policeman, dirty and uncomfortable, yet I contrived to sleep soundly for many hours, till I was awoke at daybreak by a fearful uproar that took place in my room. I had entered the house after sunset, and the dimness of a small lamp was scarcely sufficient to enable me to examine into what sort of bed I was ushered. On awaking, I found it was the sleeping apartment of a very heterogeneous collection of animals. Above me had roosted a number of chickens, while ducks and pigs had spent the night amicably together on the floor. It was the pugnacious or playful propensities of two young pigs that had created all the tumult, as they had upset the pole upon which the chickens sat, and they naturally took refuge on my bed."

This grey area between the role and place of animals in and around the home that Ramage experienced in 1828 has remained grey in Calabria; perhaps less grey than it was but nonetheless it needs addressing.

For most Calabrians living in a rural or semi-rural environment, animals generally served no purpose other than as part of the food cycle; until recently the idea of animals as domestic pets was seldom on the radar. The only animal with a semi-domestic role was the dog and many travellers encountered dog-owners, particularly in the more important houses, the sorts of well-appointed places where they were accustomed to staying overnight.

This was Edward Lear's experience in Stignano in 1847:

"At dinner, also, there was a most confused assemblage of large dogs under the table who fought for casual crumbs and bones, and when they did not accidentally bite one's extremities, rushed, wildly barking, all about the little room."

Having just set foot in Calabria, Norman Douglas (1911) treated his readers to one of his many fine-crafted and astute observations about life in the south; this one, of course, just happens to be about animals:

"We are in the south. One sees it in sundry small ways—in the behaviour of the cats, for instance ...

"The Tarentines [people from Taranto in Apulia], they say, imported the cat into Europe. If those of south Italy still resemble their old Nubian ancestors, the beast would assuredly not have been worth the trouble of acclimatizing. On entering these regions, one of the first things that strikes me is the difference between the appearance of cats and dogs hereabouts, and in England or any northern country; and the difference in their temperaments. Our dogs are alert in their movements and of wideawake features; here they are drowsy and degraded mongrels, with expressionless eyes. Our cats are sleek and slumberous; here they prowl about haggard, shifty and careworn, their fur in patches and their ears a-tremble from nervous anxiety. That domestic animals such as these should be fed at home does not commend itself to the common people; they must forage for their food abroad. Dogs eat offal, while the others hunt for lizards in the fields. A lizard diet is supposed to reduce their weight (it would certainly reduce mine); but I suspect that southern cats are emaciated not only from this cause, but from systematic starvation. Many a kitten is born that never tastes a drop of cow's milk from the cradle to the grave, and little enough of its own mother's.

"To say that our English *zoophilomania*—our cult of lap-dog—smacks of degeneracy does not mean that I sympathize with the ill-treatment of beasts which annoys many visitors to these parts and has been attributed to "Saracenic" influences. Wrongly, of course; one might as well attribute it to the old Greeks. Poor Saracens! They are a sort of whipping-boy, all over the country. The chief sinner in this respect is the Vatican, which has authorized cruelty to animals by its official teaching. When Lord Odo Russell [a British diplomat] enquired of the Pope regarding the foundation of a society for the prevention of cruelty to animals in Italy, the papal answer was: "Such an association *could not be sanctioned* by the Holy See, being founded on a theological error, to wit, that Christians owed any duties to animals." This language has the inestimable and rather unusual merit of being perspicuous."

In today's Calabria, in films and on television, people are exposed to cats and dogs portrayed in a benign household environment and some are persuaded their life will be the poorer if they fail to become pet owners; Supermarkets too have cashed in on the pet culture and only recently have aisles of cat and dog food appeared.

But, it seems to me, for whatever historical and cultural reasons, being a pet owner is not something most Calabrians do naturally and therefore they do not always think of the consequences. In particular, many of these embryonic dog-owners do not make any allowances for the fact that what goes in one end has to come out the other. Quite simply, it is not something anyone considered in the past when animals were accommodated in many houses and outbuildings, most often in a separate 'room' on the ground floor in what these days would be the *magazzino* for wine and preserves.

Every morning on our walk around the town Kay and I would have to negotiate the residue of such a narrow and unsociable attitude. The 'pick-it-up-and-bag-it' philosophy has only just started to reach the south and even a large conurbation like Crotone has not dealt adequately with the problem.

Things are definitely improving in Santa Severina, thanks in part to a couple of pioneers with something in common ... they both used to live in Switzerland.

Tweak number two is related to this but focuses on residue of a different kind, the sort of litter that these days is seen less often on the streets of other parts of European towns and cities. Once again there are historical and cultural explanations—some might say excuses—that are to do with education and the hardships of life ... and people's priorities. Nevertheless, to a man, people who smoke manage to observe the law when it comes to not smoking in bars and restaurants but many ignore that other law which states that you shouldn't just throw the empty packet out the car window or drop it on the street.

It is of course a question of education and getting across the importance of taking pride in, and having respect for, the local environment. Santa Severina has a sophisticated system for the daily collection of household rubbish which is second to none and yet it also has a litter problem, albeit one that is less severe than other towns of a similar size and certainly less of a problem than a decade ago.

Tweak number three also has its origins in the past and in some way puts the other two into a kind of context. It is also multi-layered and complex.

Many Calabrians have grown up with the notion that others regard them as almost an inferior species and, to some extent, some Calabrians have contributed to making this notion a self-fulfilling prophecy. Great injustices were inflicted on the south and on Calabria in particular in the wake of Italian unification and, as recent historical research has illustrated, there is justified resentment about this. But, armed with this new understanding of what really happened to the south, there are some Calabrians who are fixed in the mind-set that it's all somebody else's fault and that it's up to others to 'fix' it, to somehow turn back the clock.

Certainly a recognition by others that there were indeed gross injustices and the south has justifiable grievances would be a step in the right direction but Calabrians must also play their part. Calabrians need to hold their heads up and embrace all of their past as far back as Magna Græcia and beyond; they must not, as a few do, simply wallow in the unfortunate legacies and brutalities of unification and think that all they have to do is point a finger at this single root cause and it will all go away.

By taking their eye off the ball Calabrians have allowed parasites like the *'ndrangheta* to call the tune; they have allowed fellow Calabrians to line their pockets and then give *them* the bad name.

We were eating out with some friends, Gianluca and Rosaria, he Calabrian and she from Piedmont; unfortunately for some Calabrians, hung up on the unification issue, the *piemontesi* are akin to Hitler's storm-troopers. Rosaria is not a typical *piemontesi*, after all her husband is Calabrian, her home is in Calabria and, furthermore, she is politically realistic about what had happened in the south, post-unification. Nevertheless, what started out as a bit of friendly banter about her place of birth, escalated to the point where Rosaria was verbally attacked by the adults from another table. It was as if she personally had committed some of the atrocities that, ironically, she herself would admit did take place in the south at the hands of the *piemontesi* ... albeit one hundred and fifty years earlier!

Picking up that I was not Calabrian, one woman started to lecture me about the history of unification and Calabria itself until, that is, she realised that I knew as much about it, if not more, than she did.

For Rosario and Gianluca it was both an unwarrantable and embarrassing encounter when all they expected from their day out was to enjoy Sunday lunch in the warm Calabrian sun with some friends.

So my third tweak would be for people to acknowledge the wrongs inflicted on the south, post-unification, but also to understand that the clock cannot be put back and that a more pressing issue is how to reclaim the region from the *'ndrangheta* which is, by far, the greatest challenge that faces Calabria and Calabrians.

In this latter respect the role of Calabrian women is important for, as we have seen, it is women like Elisabetta Tripodi, Maria Carmela Lanzetta and the late Lea Garofolo, have been at the forefront of the fight against those whose business it seems to be to further incapacitate Calabria and Calabrians. Historically mafia members have had the disingenuous gall to label themselves 'men of respect' but in Calabria, as elsewhere, they demonstrate zero respect for their region and its people.

Tweak number four is straightforward and relates to eating out. I yearn for the choice I have in other places, the choice to eat Chinese, Thai, Indian, Mexican or Greek cuisine. It's not that I have a problem with Italian or Calabrian food, it's just that Calabrians are generally conservative about what they eat so there is little or no choice other than Italian, though that is starting to change in some of the provincial capitals, albeit at a snail's pace.

It is for this reason that, when I am abroad, I rarely eat either pizza or pasta. On one occasion, having booked into a bed & breakfast in Belfast, my kindly host emailed me a list of all the Italian restaurants in the area; I emailed back, thanked him for his thoughtfulness, and asked him to send me that other list, the list of all the non-Italian restaurants in the area.

Tweak number five concerns the rule of law. For some reason there appears to be a strata of Calabrian society that does not believe that other Italian and European laws or conventions apply to them. The perfect example is the story, probably apocryphal, of the small Calabrian town where, seemingly, nobody owned a television ... or rather, nobody paid for a television licence.

In Santa Severina, the road leading up to the square is supposed to be a clearway; the signs are there—presumably the community paid to have them made and erected—yet few take any notice. There is a one-way system to and from the Middle School; many ignore it. Vehicles, except those making deliveries, are not supposed to park in the square; but they do.

The problem is enforcement. It seems to me that the *comune* is not prepared to enact the local statutes and make someone pay by actually fining them for, in such a small community, the perpetrator is likely to be a friend, a family member, an employee of the *comune* or even a councillor.

When someone dies as a result of a fire engine or an ambulance being unable to get to its destination quickly enough because of illegally-parked cars, then, as is the way of things, there will be much finger-pointing and the

If creative parking were an Olympic sports, Calabrians would excel.
Why take up one bay at the supermarket when you can have four all to yourself?
Park where you can ... even if it's on a pedestrian crossing *and* half on the pavement.

local by-laws will instantly be enforced. Just a pity a tragedy has to happen first.

That said, Leslie Gardiner (1966), on the train to Catanzaro, observed that, even back then, such an attitude was nothing new:

"Sometimes an arrogant young farmer boards the train. He is not to be cowed by city airs, nor demoralised by city gadgets: He comes in by the door marked 'Entrance Forbidden', stands on the platform labelled 'No standing on this platform' or sits in the corner seat 'Reserved for War Invalids' and lights up his black cheroot under the sign 'No Smoking'. No one remonstrates."

And as for the parking ... well that little hot potato would be a chapter on its own. Don't get me started ...

And one last little tweak. Calabrians—and, it has to be said, many other Italians—complain about local and national bureaucracy. It is certainly a problem and one that does seem to be endemic. As it happens, the very day I am writing this, I have been experiencing a new incarnation of it.

Because of our age and level of income, my wife and I are entitled to a 'Ticket' which means we don't have to pay for medical prescriptions. Though there is, in theory at least, an income-related element to this, the cut-off point is so high that almost everybody over sixty-five in a town like Santa Severina will qualify. (Other 'Tickets' relate to specific medical conditions.)

My wife and I have had this 'Ticket' for a year and have never been means-tested ... in fact I know of nobody who qualifies for this 'Ticket' who has ever been means-tested. In reality the only qualification is age.

So why is it that, bearing in mind it is not possible for us to get younger and unlikely that we will win the lottery, we should have to renew it every year? What exactly is the point of having to queue up on a designated day for up to an hour to be issued with another piece of paper that says exactly the same as the one we already have except for the date?

By definition, we and others will *always* qualify for this particular 'Ticket' on age grounds ... so why hasn't somebody thought of giving us a break and maybe check up on us every five years?

There are many other examples of this sort of bureaucracy-almost-for-the-sake-of-it and much of it is Italian while some of it is, I suspect, peculiar to Calabria.

In post-unification Italian terms, at almost every level Calabria has seemed to be playing catch-up. Although the gap has been narrowing, the deep south has invariably been the last to benefit from innovation and though that generally remains the case, thankfully things are improving.

When I first heard about Italy's new smart-card Identity Card that would replace the old, inconveniently-sized and easily-damaged paper version, I bounced along to the local town hall, new mug-shots in hand, to avail myself of the new technology. But it wasn't to be; there was—and remains so at the time of writing—no specific date for its inauguration in Calabria; 2018 has been mooted but in reality it is anyone's guess. Generally the northern regions of Italy will benefit first from such innovations … sometimes I wonder if the powers-that-be, seeking guinea-pigs to test a new and potentially dangerous drug, would, for the first time, choose Calabria.

In reality I know I can make do with my paper Identity Card, even though it doesn't wash well nor fit comfortably in a wallet. I've had it for eight years now and the only time I use it is as a photocopy for things like the prescription 'Ticket' or renewing my driving licence.

I can step around the dog-shit for as long as it takes for owners to own-up to their anti-social behaviour.

I can pick up the discarded cigarette packet or plastic bottle and put it in one of the many waste-bins in and around the town.

I can order oriental ingredients online and cook my own Chow Mein.

I can try to demonstrate my understanding of Calabria's past without getting my friends—or myself—into a slanging match.

I can park responsibly and drive around those who don't.

And of course, apart from my craving for alternative cuisines, the majority of Calabrians would agree with every one of my little gripes.

When I am outside Calabria I yearn to return here. I have no idea why it is so, I just know that for me Calabria is a very important place; it has become, after all, my home.

Nevertheless I continue to struggle with the language as, throughout Calabria, many still talk in their own local dialect and, if you're lucky, also in Italian. Most of those who travelled here, had the same problem: they could converse in Italian with their guides and their overnight hosts but couldn't get their heads—or their tongues—around the many dialects they encountered en route.

On the other hand, most had a distinct advantage over my experience in that, because the northern provinces were an important Grand Tour destination, they were generally conversant with Italian from an early age. That said, as Ramage (1828) discovered, even Italian was not always sufficient:

"I am sorry to say that I find it impossible to understand the language of the Calabrese peasant, and my Italian is equally unintelligible to him. The Calabrese dialect is peculiar; I am not, however, sufficiently versed in it to decide whether it may not be the pronunciation rather than the roots of the language, in which it differs from the pure Italian."

In this respect we have been a little more fortunate for, although as a matter of course many still communicate in dialect, most Calabrians now understand Italian; without Italian they couldn't watch television, pay bills or talk to their doctor. Because it's what their parents speak, some of the current generation come to school speaking mostly dialect and, to varying degrees, have to be taught Italian. Essentially most Calabrians are bilingual.

When we came to live in Calabria our Italian was of the 'eat, meet and greet' variety and, though we have made progress, the extant dialects and our own advancing years have made it difficult to assimilate a new and complicated language, particularly as we speak English at home. Grudgingly, we have accepted that we will never be fluent, nor remotely so.

Living in the toe of Italy is therefore a daily challenge but nonetheless a rewarding, and often humbling, experience. I acknowledge that, even if I were to have greater language proficiency, I can never truly experience what it feels like to be Calabrian but, thanks in part to my thirteen fellow-travellers, I am having a better shot at it that many other *stranieri* who have come this way.

Which brings me back to that stock answer to the 'why-have-you-come-to-live-in-Calabria question … the climate, the food, the wine and the people. In reality, as I have said, the latter is by far the most important. It did not bring us here but it's why we stayed.

Despite all the things that have been thrown at the toe of Italy since time immemorial, today's Calabrians exude a generous, uncomplicated and open disposition that is as overwhelming as it is instinctive, as straightforward as it is genuine. What's more, they inhabit a region that is stunningly replete both in its historical legacy and its rich and diverse landscapes.

That then was my last word on Calabria and Calabrians; it is only fitting therefore that I should give each of my fellow traveller's *their* lasts words too and thank them all for coming all this way in circumstances which, for most, were a lot more difficult than anything I have experienced.

Herewith, their final thoughts, reflections and observations about their diverse Calabrian journeys.

Henry Swinburne (1780): "Though Calabria is in bad repute as to safety for travellers, the people seem perfectly honest towards one another; for their houses have no bolts or bars to the door; and, during the owner's absence, are left to the mercy of every passenger."

Brian Hill (1797): "We have now taken our leave of the two Calabria's, so famous for their desperate banditti, and surely the most savage country in Europe."

Richard Keppel-Craven (1818): "Here I own that I experienced a sensation of unqualified regret at quitting Calabria. Its varied beauties had gained a kind of magic ascendency over my mind, which I felt would be lasting; and it seemed as if it was impossible that any other tract I might visit in future could produce impressions so pleasing, or so indelible."

Craufurd Tait Ramage (1828): "They were interested ... in one who showed such a desire to make himself acquainted with their manners and customs, as I never attempted to throw ridicule on what might appear silly and absurd, but always acknowledged that every nation has a right to its own peculiar views in the affairs of life and in religion. Superstitious no doubt the lower classes are, but pious to a degree to which I am afraid we must grant that we have no pretensions. They are impulsive, like children, ready to use the stiletto on the slightest provocation; yet with all this there is a kindness of manner and a lovableness that throw a veil over many imperfections."

John Arthur Strutt (1841): "We went, this morning, to walk about the town [Reggio Calabria], which wore a very gay aspect; not so much, however, on the quay, as in a long, handsome street running parallel to it, which seems to be here what the Toledo is at Naples. The shops are all open, in spite of it being Sunday morning; and the number of fruit-stalls, with their oranges, three for a grano [at the time a little less than a halfpenny], their apricots and plums, the gaudy booths of lemonade sellers, the blue striped tent cloths over the shops, the unpaved streets, the white flat-roofed houses, and the deep blue sky, all reminded us that we were in a town of the south."

Edward Lear (1847): "I leave the shores of Calabria with a grating feeling I cannot describe. The uncertainty of the fate of many kind and agreeable families ... is not pleasant to reflect on. Gloom, gloom, overshadows the memory of a tour so agreeably begun, and which should have extended yet through two provinces. The bright morning route of the traveller overcast with cloud and storm [the short-lived revolt of 1847 in Reggio Calabria] before mid-day."

Emily Lowe (1859): "… but in the little every-day passages of life, partly from volubility, and partly from a good-natured wish to say what is pleasing, they [Sicilians and Calabrians] are liable to slips of the tongue which would degrade and English gentleman. Still, as we had not a single disagreeable dispute in the whole of Sicily and Calabria, I cannot be severe on their morals; and on the following day, when the Sorrento [a steamer] really came, and the whole place seemed to have assembled to launch the boat which was to bear us away, we felt a strong pull at our hearts. Farewell Calabria, coast and mountains!"

George Gissing (1897): "Alone and quiet, I heard the washing of the waves; I saw the evening fall on cloud-wreathed Etna, the twinkling lights come forth on Scylla and Charybdis; and, as I looked my last towards the Ionian Sea, I wished it were mine to wander endlessly amid the silence of the ancient world, to-day and all its sounds forgotten."

Norman Douglas (1911): "Calabria is not a land to traverse alone. It is too wistful and stricken; too deficient in those externals that conduce to comfort. Its charms do not appeal to the eye of romance, and the man who would perambulate Magna Græcia as he does the Alps would soon regret his choice. The joys of Calabria are not to be bought, like those of Switzerland, for gold."

Edward Hutton (1912): "There is nothing more picturesque upon all this coast than Trebisaccie, Amendolara upon its isolated rock, and Roseto in its ravine, or Rocca Imperiale."

Eric Whelpton (1957): "Strangely enough, we both felt very sad. Calabria is a harsh, stern country, still lacking in urbanity, and with few fine monuments or works of art. The inhabitants do not open their hearts readily to newcomers, but when they do, their welcome is as unforgettable as the rugged landscape of the wooded Sila, the golden shores of the Ionian Coast and the distant views of Etna across the blue waters of the Straits of Messina."

Leslie Gardiner (1966): "I boarded the train for Naples, and we idled the day away, taking on and discharging our cargoes of flowers, Albanian women, baskets of beans, more Albanian women. The rear half of the train was a medley of dishevelled hair, torn lace coloured silks and muscular hairy legs. The man next to me, a plump fellow in a flashy blue chalk-striped suit, shook his head. "Calabria," he said with deep contempt. The aged, dessicated passenger opposite, a large noble head on a thin little body, echoed "Calabria" with a sigh, as he tried to get himself to sleep again."

Henry Morton (1967): "In the morning, with no breath of wind stirring, the sky as blue as the sea, I went on south past the little marinas grouped round the Gulf of Squillace. The mountains rose inland where every hill lifted its ancient town into the sunlight; romantic to look at from a distance, but I knew how many were moribund, inhabited by women and old men."

It goes without saying that the many other snippets I have quoted throughout this book from the travels and of my thirteen fellow travellers and others are exactly that, no more than mere 'snippets', mere glimpses. The experiences they recorded are rich with so much more than I have been able to fit into these pages.

And of course the interpretation of their experiences and the opinions expressed are mine and mine alone.

And finally, from time to time I have been asked if I have a favourite among these fellow travellers, a question which is frequently followed up by the response expected of me by my interrogator. "Norman Douglas?"

My actual response has always been, "I've never really thought about it … I'll have to think about that." Though, much as I enjoyed it, I suspected it was unlikely to be Norman Douglas' *Old Calabria*.

In giving it some thought, I decided on an arbitrary sub-division into travellers who came to Calabria before unification and those who came after (there being almost an equal number of each) and select one from each half.

So, in my mind I decided on two, only to discover later that they had something in common that hadn't occurred to me at the time …

Travellers' Biographies

Henry Swinburne (Bristol 1743–Trinidad 1803)
Travels in the Two Sicilies; Volume 1 and Volume 4
Educated in Yorkshire and lived much of his adult life in Europe where he travelled widely. Published four volumes on travels in the Kingdom of the Two Sicilies as well as books on Spain. Died of sunstroke.

Rev. Brian Hill (1756–1831 Wem, Salop)
Observations and Remarks in a Journey through Sicily and Calabria in the year 1791
Educated at Oxford and became a cleric. Uncle to Sir Rowland Hill who reformed Britain's postal service with the introduction of the Penny Post. Brian Hill also wrote another book, *Henry and Acasto*, a moral, poetical tale.

Richard Hill
brother and
travelling companion

The Honourable Richard Keppel-Craven (1779–Naples 1851)
A Tour through the Southern Provinces of the Kingdom of Naples
Educated at Oxford; raised in France and eventually settled in Italy. Also wrote about Abruzzi and northern provinces of Naples and later a book of sketches. One of triumvirate (others were Sir William Drummond and Sir Willlian Gell) of British *literati* and scholarly gentlemen who lived in Naples at the time.

Craufurd Tait Ramage (Newhaven 1803–Dumfriesshire 1878)
The Nooks and by-ways of Italy: Wanderings in search of its ancient remains and modern superstitions
Educated at Edinburgh: became tutor to the Lushington family in Naples before touring Italy. Returned to Scotland and continued as tutor to several notable families; became vice-master at Wallace Hall Academy. Wrote four anthologies entitled *Beautiful Thoughts* of Greek, Latin, French & Italian and German & Spanish authors.

Arthur John Strutt (Chelmsford 1819–1888 Rome)
A pedestrian Tour in Calabria and Sicily
English painter, engraver, writer, traveller and archaeologist; son of the landscape painter Jacob George Strutt and writer and traveller Elizabeth Strutt. Lived most of his live in Rome where he and his father shared a studio. Described as 'a very clever painter of landscapes and Roman costumes'.

Edward Lear (Holloway, London 1812–1888 San Remo)
Journals of a Landscape Painter in Southern Calabria
Youngest survivor of 22 children; was brought up by his sister, 21 years his senior. Had artistic bent and specialised in ornithological field; later achieved recognition in several related fields: as artist, illustrator, musician, author and poet. Famous for his Nonsense Songs such as *The Owl and the Pussy-Cat* and, my favourite, *The Dong with the Luminous Nose*.

Emily Lowe (born Exeter; died Torquay 1882)
Unprotected Females in Sicily, Calabria, and on the Top of Mount Aetna
Before marrying Sir Robert Clifford, she and her mother, Helen, had already travelled to Norway, Sicily & Calabria and written about both adventures. An accomplished sailor and the first Englishwoman to command her own yacht. A no-nonsense woman whose maxim was 'If you want a thing done, do it yourself'.

George Gissing (Wakefield, Yorkshire 1857–1903 France)
By the Ionian Sea
Essentially a novelist rather than travel writer. His brilliant academic career in Manchester was interrupted when he was found guilty of stealing to help out a woman-friend, Nell. Spent a year working in America in late 1870s; returned to Britain and later married Nell. Had several other important relationships in later life. Some novels published posthumously.

Norman Douglas (Thüringen 1868–1952 Capri)
Old Calabria
Born in Austria, educated in Scotland and settled in Capri. Left diplomatic service in St Petersburg following sex scandal and later married his cousin. Moved in literary circles in Italy but had to leave before war because of another scandal. Lived in France and London before returning to Capri. Reputed dying words: 'Get those fucking nuns away from me'.

Edward Hutton (Hampstead 1875–1969 London)
Naples and Southern Italy
Italophile and prolific travel writer, much more so than his contemporary and friend Norman Douglas. Lived much of life near Florence which he considered his spiritual home. In 1905 published the first of series of nine illustrated books on different regions of Italy. In 1917 Hutton was honoured by the Italian government for his services to the country.

Eric Whelpton (Abingdon 1894–1981)
Calabria and the Aeolian Islands
Educated at Oxford; prolific travel writer; first book published in genre was about Dublin. Friend of Dorothy Sayers and, according to his largely autobiographical, *The Making of an Englishman*, he may have been her inspiration for the eccentric character of Lord Peter Wimsey. During the war was BBC news correspondent in France and reportedly on a Gestapo blacklist.

Leslie Gardiner (Scotland 1921–1997)
South to Calabria
Seventeen years in the navy gave Gardiner a taste for travel which later became a way of life as a travel writer and broadcaster. Published books on travelling in many European countries but had special relationship with Italy and Italians from whom he received awards for his work. Apart from which the man is a complete mystery.

Henry Morton (Ashton-under-Lyne 1892–1979 Cape Town)
A Traveller in Southern Italy
A prolific travel writer. Started out as journalist and in 1923, working for the *Daily Express*, he outmanoeuvred the *Times* correspondent at the opening of the Tomb of Tutankhamun. First travel book, *The Heart of London*, was published in 1925. A biography published in 2004 created controversy when it alleged that he may once have been a Nazi sympathiser.

Niall Allsop (Belfast 1944–)
Calabria: Travels in the toe of Italy
Began his working life as a primary school teacher in London and in 1971 took up his first headship. Left teaching in the early 1980s to become a freelance photo-journalist specialising in the UK's inland waterways and wrote extensively in this field. Was a graphic designer for twenty years before moving to Calabria, since when he has written a number of books, including several with southern Italian themes.

Selected Bibliography

OP indicates the year of the Original Publication; web addresses are given for books sourced online.

Thirteen Fellow Travellers

Henry Swinburne: *Travels in the Two Sicilies; Volume 1 and Volume 4* (OP 1783, www.archive.org)

Brian Hill: *Observations and Remarks in a Journey through Sicily and Calabria in the year 1791* (OP 1792, www.babel.hathitrust.com)

Richard Keppel-Craven: *A Tour through the Southern Provinces of the Kingdom of Naples* (OP 1821, www.archive.org)

Craufurd Tait Ramage: *The Nooks and by-ways of Italy: Wanderings in search of its ancient remains and modern superstitions* (OP 1868, www.babel.hathitrust.com)

Arthur John Strutt: *A pedestrian Tour in Calabria and Sicily* (OP 1842, www.archive.org)

Edward Lear: *Journals of a Landscape Painter in Southern Calabria* (OP 1852, Forgotten Books, 2012)

Emily Lowe: *Unprotected Females in Sicily, Calabria, and on the Top of Mount Aetna* (OP 1859, www.books.google.it)

George Gissing: *By the Ionian Sea* (OP 1901, Valde Books, 2009)

Norman Douglas: *Old Calabria* (OP 1915, Cosimo Classics, 2008)

Edward Hutton: *Naples and Southern Italy* (OP 1915, www.archive.org)

Eric and Barbara Whelpton: *Calabria and the Aeolian Islands* (Robert Hale Limited, 1957)

Leslie Gardiner: *South to Calabria* (William Blackwood, 1968)

Henry Morton: *A Traveller in Southern Italy* (Methuen, 1969)

Books and Publications in English

Carmine Abate: *Between Two Seas*, translated by Antony Shugaar (European Editions, 2007)

Pino Aprile: *Terroni: All that has been done to ensure that the Italians of the South became 'southerners'*, translated by Ilaria Marra Rosiglioni (Bordighere Press, 2011)

Jeremy Black: *The Grand Tour in the Eighteenth Century* (Sutton Publishing, 2003)

Patrick Brydone: *A Tour through Sicily and Malta* (OP 1813, www.books.google.it)

Peter Chiarella: *Calabrian Tales: A Memoir of 19th Century Southern Italy* (Regent Press 2002)

Peter Chiarella: *Out of Calabria:* (Trafford Publishing 2007)

John A. Davis: *Naples and Napoleon: Southern Italy and the European Revolutions, 1780-1860* (Oxford University Press, 2006)

John Dickie: *Cosa Nostra: A History of the Sicilian Mafia* (Hodder & Stoughton, 2004)

John Dickie: *Mafia Republic: Italy's Criminal Curse: Cosa Nostra, Camorra and 'ndrangheta from 1946 to the present* (Hodder & Stoughton, 2013)

John Dryden Junior: *A Voyage to Sicily and Malta* (OP 1776, www.babel.hathitrust.com)

Christopher Duggan: *The Force of Destiny: A History of Italy since 1796* (Allen Lane / Penguin Books, 2007)

Philip J Elmhirst: *Occurrences during a six month's residence in the province of Calabria Ulteriore in 1809-10, etc.* (OP 1819, British Library 2014)

Matthew Fort: *Eating up Italy: Voyages on a Vespa* (Harper Perennial, 2005)

Alexander Campbell Fraser: *Life and Letters of George Berkeley* (OP 1771, www.forgottenbooks.com)

Betsey Freemantle: *Travels in the Two Sicilies 1817-1820*, edited by Nigel Foxell (Mailer Press, 2007)

Johann Wolfgang von Goethe: *Italian Journey*, translated by W H Auden and Elizabeth Mayer (Penguin Books, 1970)

Karen Haid: *Calabria: The other Italy* (Mill City Press, 2015)

Sir William Hamilton: *An account of the earthquakes in Calabria, Sicily, &c. As communicated to the Royal Society* in *The British Magazine and Review* (OP 1783, www.books.google.it)

Augustus Hare: *Cities of Southern Italy and Sicily* (OP 1891, www.archive.org)

Annie Hawes: *Journey to the South* (Penguin Books, 2005)
Christopher Hibbert: *The Grand Tour* (GP Putman's Sons, 1969)
David Hilton: *Brigandage in South Italy* (OP 1864, www.archive.org)
Sir Thomas Hoby: *The Travels and Life of Sir Thomas Hoby, Knight of Bisham Abbey, Written by himself 1547–1564* (OP 1902, www.archive.org)
Mrs (Anna) Jameson: *Memoirs of Celebrated Female Sovereigns* (OP 1869, www.books.google.it)
RM Johnston: *The Napoleonic Empire in Southern Italy and the Rise of the Secret Societies* (OP 1904, www.archive.org)
John Keahey: *A Sweet and Glorious Land: Revisiting the Ionian Sea* (Thomas Dunne Books, 2000)
DH Lawrence: *Sea and Sardinia* (various editions, 1921 to 1997)
Charles Lister: *Heel to Toe: Encounters in the South of Italy* (Secker & Warburg, 2002)
Elpis Melena: *Calabria and the Liparian Islands in the year 1858* (OP 1862, www.archive.org)
William J. C. Moens, Anne Warlters Moens: *English Travellers and Italian Brigands: A Narrative of Capture and Captivity* (OP 1866, www.archive.org)
Thomas Nugent: *The grand tour. Containing an exact description of most of the cities, towns, and remarkable places of Europe. Together with a distinct account of the post-roads and stages, with their respective distances ... Likewise directions relating to the manner and expence of travelling ...* (OP 1749, www.babel.hathitrust.com)
Richard Pococke: *A description of the East and some other Countries; Volume 2, Part 1* (OP 1745, www.archive.org)
Stephen Puleo: *Boston Italians* (Beacon Press, 2007)
Benjamin Rand: *The Correspondence of George Berkeley and Sir John Percival* (OP 1914, www.archive.org)
Mark Rotella: *Stolen Figs: And other Adventures in Calabria* (North Point Press, 2003)
Duret de Tavel: *Calabria During a Military Residence of Three Years: In a Series of Letters* (OP 1832, www.books.google.it)
Thomas Watkins: *Travels Through Swisserland, Italy, Sicily, the Greek Islands, to Constantinople, Through Part of Greece, Ragusa and the Dalmatian Isles* (OP 1792, www.books.google.it)
Sir William Young: *A Journal of a Summer's Excursion by the Road of Montecasino to Naples. And from thence over all the Southern Parts of Italy, Sicily, and Malta in the year 1772* (OP c1773, www.books.google.it)

Books in Italian

Giuseppe Antonelli (l'Editore): *Nuovo dizionario geografico universale statistico-storico-commerciale, Volumes 1–4* (OP 1827–1833, www.babel.hathitrust.com)

Francesco Bavilacqua: *Sulle Tracce di Norman Douglas: Avventure fra le montagne della Vecchia Calabria* (Rubbettino, 2012)

Bernard e Mary Berenson: *In Calabria* (Rubbettino, 2008)

Charles Didier: *Viaggio in Calabria* (Rubbettino, 2008)

Alexandre Dumas: *Viaggio in Calabria* (Ilisso / Rubbettino, 2006)

Giovanni Fiore: *Della Calabria illustrata opera varia istorica, Volume 1* (OP 1691, www.books.google.it)

Franco Severini Giordano: *I Castelli Norman-Svevi di Calabria nelle fonti scritte* (Calabria Letteraria Editrice, 2014)

Lorenza Giustiniani: *Dizionario geografico-ragionato del Regno di Napoli, Volumes 1–10* (OP 1797–1805, www.books.google.it)

Emily Lowe: *Donne Indifese in Calabria* (Rubbettino, 2012)

Francesco de Luca: *Santa Severina: La Nave di Pietra* (Pro Loco 'siberene' di Santa Severina, 1986)

Giuseppe Marino: *Il terremoto del 1832 nel Marchesato Crotonese: I danni e la ricostruzione di Caccuri* (Editoriale Progetto 2000, 2012)

Ulderico Nisticò: *Contrastoria delle Calabrie* (Rubbettino 2009)

Ulderico Nisticò: *Storia delle Italie dal 1734 al 1870* (Città del Sole, 2012)

Antonio Piromalli: *La Letteratura Calabrese, 3° Edizione in due volumi* (Pellegrini Editore, 1996)

Páola Praticò: *Malandrini* (Città del Sole, 2013)

Giovanni B. Rampoldi: *Corografia dell'Italia, Volume 1* (OP 1832, www.books.google.it)

Giovanni B. Rampoldi: *Corografia dell'Italia, Volume 2* (OP 1833, www.books.google.it)

Giovanni B. Rampoldi: *Corografia dell'Italia, Volume 3* (OP 1834, www.books.google.it)

Fernanda Rossi: *Itinerari e viaggiatori inglesi nella Calabria del '700 e '800* (Rubbettino, 2001)

D de Sterlich: *Cronica delle due Sicilie* (OP 1841, www.archive.org)

Franco Taverniti: *Visioni di Calabria nei Disegni di Teodoro Brenson* (Silvana Editoriale, 1992)

Other Sources and Maps

Atlante Stradale d'Italia: Sud (Touring Club Italiano, 2004)
Encyclopedia Britannica (www.britannica.com)
La mappa della ndrangheta in Calabria (www.google.com)
Maps.App, Version 2.0 (1738.4.23) (Apple Inc 2012–2014)
Wikipedia (www.en.wikipedia.org / www.it.wikipedia.org)

Other related titles by Niall Allsop

Keeping up with DH Lawrence: On the trail of David and Frieda Lawrence in Sicily, Sea and Sardinia (Inscritto, 2010)

Stumbling through Italy: Tales of Tuscany, Sicily, Sardinia, Apulia, Calabria and places in-between (Inscritto, 2011)

Scratching the toe of Italy: Expecting the unexpected in Calabria (Inscritto, 2012)

Thank you Uncle Sam: From Calabria to America; Family stories of Emigration (Inscritto, 2013; Italian edition 2016)

Printed in Great Britain
by Amazon